POLITICAL THINKING, POLITICAL THEORY, AND CIVIL SOCIETY

Second Edition

Steven M. DeLue

Miami University

New York   San Francisco   Boston
London   Toronto   Sydney   Tokyo   Singapore   Madrid
Mexico City   Munich   Paris   Cape Town   Hong Kong   Montreal

Publisher: Priscilla McGeehon
Senior Editor: Eric Stano
Associate Editor: Anita Castro
Marketing Manager: Megan Galvin-Fak
Production Manager: Donna DeBenedictis
Project Coordination, Text Design, and Electronic Page Makeup: Elm Street Publishing
    Services, Inc.
Cover Designer/Manager: Nancy Danahy
Manufacturing Buyer: Al Dorsey
Printer and Binder: Hamilton Printing
Cover Printer: Phoenix Color Corp.

For permission to use copyrighted material, grateful acknowledgment is made to the copyright holders on p. 375, which are hereby made part of this copyright page.

Library of Congress Cataloging-in-Publication Data

DeLue, Steven M.
    Political thinking, political theory, and civil society / by Steven M. DeLue.—2nd ed.
        p. cm.
    Includes bibliographical references and index.
    ISBN 0-321-08559-0
      1. Civil society. 2. Political science—Philosophy. I. Title

JC337 .D45 2001
320'.01—dc21
                                                              00-067838

Please visit our website at http://www.ablongman.com

ISBN 0-321-08559-0

1 2 3 4 5 6 7 8 9 10—HT—04 03 02 01

CONTENTS

Part II   Modern and Contemporary Approaches to Civil Society

PART III *Critiques of Civil Society*

PREFACE

As in the first edition, the new edition of this book remains committed, first and foremost, to helping students engage in political thinking. The book is designed to help students, as they take part in discussions of enduring questions such as the nature of justice or the good life, to compare and contrast their own views and arguments with those provided by others. Toward this end, I have continued in this edition to employ several strategies to achieve this purpose.

First, I hope the organization of the book will help students learn to compare and contrast the various arguments swirling around the main theme of the book, the idea of a civil society. To this end, the major writers discussed in this book are read not only with an interest in understanding their views but also with an interest in understanding their relationship to the idea of a civil society. Further, the critiques of civil society thinking in the last part of the book are designed to help students compare different approaches to civil society and to critique its place in the modern world.

Second, I hope to further students' engagement in political thinking by showing them the importance of understanding, as they study political ideas, the historical contexts and issues that provide the background setting for the writers, and the ideas discussed here. Understanding the context that is the grounding for a thinker's ideas helps students to see important relationships between major issues and the way thinkers are limited in addressing these issues by the circumstances within which they write and think.

The third strategy used to encourage political thinking is through the "Response and Rejoinder" sections at the conclusion of the chapters in the last two-thirds of the book. Here, I have tried to develop the ways the different thinkers would have viewed each other's ideas and arguments. I hope these sections will encourage students to imagine themselves engaged in a dialogue with the various thinkers discussed throughout this book.

Another major objective is to discuss the idea of a civil society. My position is that a civil society is essential for individuals seeking personal freedom while at the same time recognizing the importance of civic engagement. We live in a world where freedom seems to be given priority over civic engagement, but it is also true that without a strong sense of civic commitment, we cannot maintain the environment that protects and furthers freedom. I have expanded the treatment of civil society in this edition with a concluding chapter that examines many of the controversies now given centrality of place in the vast literature on civil society, as well as in the ongoing public discussion of civil society.

The final purpose of this book is to explain the works of major writers in political theory. A textbook cannot be a substitute for primary sources, but it is also the case that a good textbook can help students appreciate and understand primary sources. I hope this book will be useful to those like myself who wish to encourage students to read the enduring works of political philosophy. In writing the book, then, I have often tried to explicate the main ideas in major primary texts that instructors teaching political theory are likely to assign students. I have expanded this aspect of the book by including a chapter in the first part of the book on non-Christian medieval thinkers, including prominent writers from the Jewish and the Islamic traditions. Also, I have added a section on Cicero in Chapter 4.

There are several ways to use this book, depending on the intentions of the instructor. For those wishing to provide students with background to help them understand many of the ideas in the history of political ideas, the book can be read in sequential fashion, starting from Chapter 1 on civil society and then moving on to discuss the other thinkers. The book, when read in this fashion, allows students to discuss various writers not just in terms of their historical contexts but in terms of the lead idea. This permits students to compare and contrast the different approaches to political thinking to the idea of a civil society.

However, instructors need not be bound by the idea of civil society if they prefer not to be. Other ideas can be used as the basis for comparing different political visions found in political thinking. Thus, those who want to employ alternative integrating themes can make use of this book as well. To give a partial list of the themes that could be used, I point to the following: the nature of a just or good society, the place of rights in society, the role and importance of public reason and deliberation, the character of civic virtue in the different views of political thinking, the political significance of ideas such as toleration and mutual respect, the role and structure of the state, the basis for constitutional government and the way to conceptualize the idea of legitimate authority, the different faces of democracy, and the relationship among pre-modern, modern, and post-modern views of the nature of society and politics.

For those who wish to use this book in a course on political thinking, it is possible to emphasize the idea of civil society and make it the grounds for comparing and contrasting different arguments with respect to this central theme. In this case, the instructor might only want students to read the Introduction and the two chapters on civil society, Chapters 1 and 18, and move directly to the second and third parts, which together, address modern, contemporary, and critical approaches to civil society. Those who want to integrate into this endeavor classical, Christian, and non-Christian views may do that as well by using, selectively, material from the first part. The option also remains open for faculty who would like to use alternative integrating themes as the basis for a political thinking class, themes such as those mentioned in the preceding paragraph.

I am grateful to the people at Longman, most importantly Anita Castro, for providing me with an opportunity to prepare a second edition of this book. Doing so has allowed me a chance to incorporate some of the insights from those who have used the book in the first edition, as well as some of what I have learned from using it in my own classes. I value all the useful advice provided by the various readers of the manuscript. In particular, I would like to thank David L. Cingranelli, Binghamton University; Clarke Cochran, Texas Tech University; and John R. Pottenger, University of Alabama in Huntsville. I have made use of reviewer and student comments to punch up the quality of the writing and to make the book as error free and as comprehensive as possible. The errors that remain are my responsibility.

Finally, I wish to thank my wife, Karen, whose patience and helpful suggestions make clear to me why civil society is so important—it helps to preserve the sanctity of special partnerships of love and mutual respect.

Steven M. DeLue
Oxford, Ohio

INTRODUCTION

I. Political Thinking and Political Theory

Individuals engage in political thinking when they seek to determine which political ideas offer more promise, which political solutions best respond to particular challenges, and which political regimes best meet the needs of people. The challenge of this book is to familiarize people with the nature of political thinking in the hope that readers will be encouraged to engage in this activity themselves. Because we will be discussing different political theories throughout the book, it is well, before proceeding, to say a few words concerning what political theory is and how we should understand political thinking in relation to it.

I will use the term *political theory* interchangeably with the term *political philosophy*.[1] A political theory is constructed as a response to enduring questions that hold the attention of the political theorist. What are some of the questions I have in mind? Plato asked how justice and its important contributions to human life are possible in the face of a society that treats the idea of justice with skepticism. Hobbes wanted to know why society can become mired in a state of war, and he asked how (or even if) it is possible to overcome this prospect and achieve peace and freedom. Rawls asked how to construct a society in which people with conflicting but equally reasonable moral perspectives can accord respect to each other's basic rights.

Political theorists are concerned with many other questions as well, and here I will list only a few of them. For instance, they seek to demonstrate the nature of the common good and the kind of politics that can best approximate it. Others will discuss the definition of the public realm, distinguishing the functions of the public realm from the private realm. Still others want to know what constitutes our obligations and duties as citizens, and how obligations and duties are distinct from rights. Throughout political thinking there is a concern with the role of the family, with religion, and with various structures of government in securing what is commonly referred to as the rule of law. Further, we are treated to many discussions of various types of regimes, including of course the nature of democracy and how it is distinguished from other types of political forms. And finally, as we discuss in this book, others will emphasize a quest to preserve civil society in the face of circumstances that threaten its existence.

To address questions such as these, political theorists construct scenarios that are designed to demonstrate the major obstacles that must be faced on behalf of the key objectives that are sought. Thus, if we wish to create a world in which each person is provided the same rights, we must first ask what stands in the way of our doing so. Then we must ask how best to remove these obstacles so that an equal rights doctrine can be made a central part of society. As we go about this undertaking, we construct a picture of the world that explains why the society impedes rights, but, in addition, the picture of the world should explain what factors could help society promote them.

From this enterprise, a political theorist may develop a full-blown theory that explains the relationships among all the significant dimensions of a given issue. To take the example of rights for instance, a theory would explain what rights are, how they are established and developed in society, and what major obstacles must be overcome in order to achieve the full attainment of rights. As the theorist engages in this activity, he or she will discuss many factors and their relationship to each other, including the role of government, the place of education, the nature of the social and cultural realities that must be in place, and so on.

Now, political theorists can never comprehend all the factors that need to be considered in order to address the questions at hand. This circumstance arises from the fact that political theorists view the world from a limited and partial point of view. After all, political theorists have their own biases and tendencies to favor one viewpoint over another, and this fact necessarily prevents political theorists from seeing all that must be known about an issue. As a result, all a political theorist can provide is a "vision," to use Sheldon Wolin's term, that describes the possible relationships among the key elements of society, including people and institutions, in order to address a given question.[2] But "possible" understandings are not the same as perfect knowledge of social and political events. In consequence, in developing a vision that explains the obstacles that must be confronted in order to achieve key objectives or answer enduring questions, political theorists inevitably operate from incomplete understandings.

Given that political theorists approach the development of their theories from their own particular experiences and points of view, it is possible that theorists will develop competing theories with respect to the same question. Thus, one theorist may provide a theory that emphasizes certain conceptions of the state that another theorist will reject; a second theorist may define certain cultural conditions that a third theorist would not think are relevant, and so on.[3] In any event, what becomes clear is that any particular theory, when seen from the standpoint of another theory, can be said, in some sense, to lack completeness and comprehensiveness with respect to the question that is asked. As a result, the activity of political philosophy necessarily involves political theorists in arguments with each other over whose theories best explain the world and best help to resolve a particular question.

II. THE LINK BETWEEN POLITICAL THEORY AND POLITICAL THINKING

What is the relationship between political thinking and political theory? Both are linked by a common need to address significant and enduring political and social questions. During the course of addressing these questions, political thinking is always drawn back to political theory. For in answering key questions, a person engaged in political thinking often makes use of different visions of political life provided by various political theorists. In doing so, political thinking challenges those who uphold these visions to provide worthy answers to the questions that are being asked.

Political thinking is always fertile ground from which to launch a challenge to a particular vision described in a political theory, because, as we just saw, no vision is ever complete and all visions necessarily include some important elements of reality, while downplaying the importance of others. A person engaged in political thinking often highlights this shortcoming by arguing that a particular political vision is just not complete enough to help one understand as fully as necessary a particular social or political reality.

When one vision of the political world does not appear to afford a good basis for addressing a particular question, then a person engaged in political thinking may turn to another theory, with the intention of determining whether the alternative theory does a better job in addressing a given question. During the course of pondering vexing questions, a person may explore as well as compare and contrast many different political theories. For instance, perhaps in addressing the question of justice, we start off with Plato, move on to Aristotle, and conclude with Hegel. In each case, we are comparing different accounts, defending one account against another account, shoring up perhaps one vision and demonstrating the weakness of another. Ultimately, we hope to arrive at a conception of justice that we can defend against our critics. During the process, we may reject all known visions of political philosophy on the subject at hand and create a new one instead. As we do, we may occasion an entirely new political theory to address an important problem raised by political thinking.

Political thinking draws upon political theory. Without the latter, the former cannot take place. Once the process of political thinking begins, though, a person involved in this activity is committed to testing various visions that are articulated in different political theories. And, in doing so, a person engaged in political thinking searches for an all-embracing vision of political life that demonstrates in a way never before possible a definitive answer to the question being raised. Of course, we may never reach this point, and thus people who engage in political thinking are often left to ponder the usefulness of different political theories.

III. SOCRATES OF THE APOLOGY AND THE CRITO[4]

Because the classic defense of political thinking is found in Plato's account of Socrates in the *Apology* and the *Crito,* it behooves us to discuss the main themes of these dialogues. This exercise will also prepare the reader for the treatment of Plato's *Republic* in Chapter 2.

Before discussing these dialogues, it is important to provide some background about Socrates (470–399 B.C.E.*), the individual whom Plato admired and whom he made, as we see in Chapter 2, his main protagonist in the *Republic*. Socrates lived in Athens during a period when efforts to maintain democracy were displaced by oligarchic and tyrannical rule. After the defeat of Athens in 404 B.C.E. in the Peloponnesian War with Sparta, Spartan forces occupied Athens. At this time, an oligarchic party in Athens, with the help of the Spartans, took this opportunity to undermine Athenian democracy by establishing the rule of what has become known in history as the control of the "Thirty Tyrants." These people were to have established a new democratic constitution, but in fact they refused to do so. Instead, they executed not only well-known democrats, but also other oligarchs who stood for the rule of law.[5] Eventually 3000 citizens deposed the oligarchy, and over a period of several months democracy was restored in 403 B.C.E.[6]

Socrates was not popular with the new democratic regime. He taught that politics required a special kind of expertise that ordinary people skilled in other crafts do not necessarily possess. To the average Athenian, Socrates's views seemed to have a great affinity with the positions held by the oligarchs. Thus, the Athenians, who at the time harbored the memories of oligarchic terror, wanted nothing more to do with oligarchy. And in consequence, the Athenians rejected Socrates as a threat to democracy. Socrates was then put on trial and ultimately condemned to death.[7] Plato in the *Crito* and in the *Apology* as well as in the *Republic* memorializes both Socrates's commitment to truth-seeking and to the view that political regimes should be run by experts who understand how to use power for moral purposes.

In what follows, we provide an interpretation of the *Apology* and the *Crito* that demonstrates the importance of political thinking.

In the *Apology,* Socrates was accused of not believing in Athenian gods, of "making the weaker argument appear stronger," and of corrupting the youth. Socrates believed himself innocent, and, despite long and convincing defenses of his conduct, a legitimate Athenian court found him guilty and sentenced him to death. Socrates with the mildest of urgings allowed us, the readers, to conclude that he is guilty merely of engaging in political thinking.

Why did the Athenians find Socrates's use of political thinking so objectionable? To answer this question, it must be clear what Socrates hoped to accomplish with political thinking. He sought to use political thinking to address key, enduring questions pertaining to the best forms of moral and political life. For instance, he asked questions such as what is justice, what is piety, what is the nature of law, and what is the common good? To answer these questions, Socrates engaged in the process called *dialectical* argument.

How does this process proceed? A question is stated, for example, what is justice, and various conceptions of justice are presented. From among those conceptions of justice considered, the objective is to find the one conception that is true. To this end, people are asked to provide their own views on each conception, including the reasons that explain why particular conceptions should not be accepted. These reasons are then carefully examined. As telling reasons emerge to deny the validity of certain conceptions, these con-

---

* B.C.E. is the term currently in use to refer to the time Before the Common Era.

ceptions are no longer considered, and the list of possible conceptions of justice is narrowed. Ultimately, as one goes through the list, one hopes to find a conception of justice that is comprehensive enough to withstand any further challenge. The remaining conception becomes the basis for answering the initial question, namely, what is justice? Indeed, Plato's *Republic* will be modeled along these lines, as we will see in Chapter 2.

To engage in political thinking, then, requires a discourse involving others who are willing to have their views tested in public. And this is the approach to political thinking that Socrates took throughout his whole life. In the *Apology,* Socrates said, "I still go about testing and examining every man whom I think wise, whether he is a citizen or a stranger."[8] But it is precisely this activity, Socrates believes, that has gotten him into trouble. He tells us that "persons who are cross-examined get angry with me instead of with themselves, and say that Socrates is an abomination and corrupts the youth."[9]

But why did the Athenians get angry with Socrates? Is it that the people associated him with oligarchy or are there other reasons? We can only speculate, of course, about what the reasons for their anger might be. But the speculation is useful because it will demonstrate a general problem that the process of political thinking poses for many even today.

One reason for Athenian skepticism of Socrates's efforts might be that, for them to engage in dialectical argument, individuals had to accept that existing views and opinions might be wrong and thus subject to revision or elimination. But that outcome could have very adverse consequences for people. Sometimes maintaining the status quo view of substantial ideas of justice or piety, for instance, is important for protecting what constitutes one's existing way of life.

Another reason for skepticism of Socrates's endeavors might have to do with the fact that his approach requires people to consider their own views in a context of contesting opinions. In this case, for those committed to finding common definitions of key concepts, political thinking suggests a risk much different from the risks presented to those who fear that political thinking will disrupt the status quo. In considering diverse views and in accepting the challenge they represent to one's own opinions, one confronts the possibility that no shared understanding will ever be reached. In this case, the search for the answer to important political questions will be ongoing and perpetual, as it becomes clear that good arguments constantly appear to counter reasonable views. Here, what is troubling is discovering that social reality is not necessarily a solidified condition based on acknowledged truth but that it is a condition requiring continuing acceptance of diverse views and opinions, many of which cannot be reconciled or easily combined.

Socrates hoped to avoid this possible outcome of political thinking and to find the comprehensive definitions of key concepts that could ground social reality in truth. He always seemed confident that he would. But, still, in approaching the search for truth through the process of dialectical argument, he risked falling into a myriad of unsolvable problems and a world of irresolution.

Socrates was willing to assume these risks. But it appears, however, that the Athenians were not. In consequence, Socrates was sentenced to death, and his sentence symbolizes the Athenians' refusal to engage in political thinking and to tolerate its liabilities. So committed was Socrates to this enterprise that, in the *Crito,* when Crito enters the prison to convince Socrates to accept his, Crito's, offer of escape, Socrates argued that he would not leave unless he could be convinced that leaving was the just thing to do.

Socrates said, "If we ought never to act unjustly at all, ought we to repay injustice with injustice, as the multitude thinks we may?"[10]

In raising this question, Socrates took the moment with Crito to dramatize the importance of political thinking. All major issues must be subject to the analysis pursued in the dialectical form of argument, which undergirds political thinking. This objective is achieved in the *Crito* during the course of the famous imagined discussion with the laws of the society. Here, Socrates engages in a discussion with the laws as if the laws were wise people whom Socrates is cross-examining. A major contention that is implicit in the argument presented by the laws is that, by fleeing, Socrates would be violating the laws of Athens. Why is this the case? A legitimate court has convicted him, and the laws require that people who are convicted accept their sentence.

But why, Socrates seems to ask, is it wrong to violate the laws and as in this case flea Athens after conviction by a legitimate proceeding? The laws answer that it is wrong to violate *just* laws, and in fact the laws of Athens are on the whole just. Why are the laws just, Socrates seems to ask? In the main, the laws are just because they have provided benefits of critical importance to the moral maturation and intellectual development of individuals in the society. In making their case to Socrates, the laws indicate that they have provided Socrates with an education that has prepared him for life, including a life of political thinking. In fact, the laws demonstrate that they have not prevented him from engaging in political thinking. The laws have permitted him to debate the state's policies and, if and when he disagrees with them, to try to convince the state to change its positions. The laws permit him to leave without penalty if the policies that the state adopts are not ones that he concurs with.[11]

The implication of the arguments made by the laws is now clear. Socrates's complaint should not be against the laws, because they are just. His complaint should be launched against the people of Athens who have acted unjustly toward him. Furthermore, because the laws are just, Socrates owes them his undying allegiance. He must do nothing to harm them. If he were to disobey just laws, he would in fact be acting in ways that were harmful to the laws and, by doing so, compounding the injustice already committed against him. Given these views, Socrates decides that the just thing to do is to accept his execution.

Furthermore, by supporting just laws, Socrates upholds what is one of their central purposes, which as we saw, was to protect political thinking. The search for truth demands nothing less. Socrates, were he alive today, would no doubt reinforce this point. Campaign managers and media experts who have little concern for political thinking now conduct contemporary politics. Their objective is not to encourage the dialectical approach to examining ideas demanded by political thinking, but to incur from the populace the desired, as defined by the campaign managers, response to various cues that they hope can be used to marshal mass support for particular candidates or issues. Campaign strategists see political thinking as a threat to those like themselves who hope to turn societies into large crowds, where the crowd mind imputes opinions to citizens. As a result, individuals are no longer able to forge their own judgments through the process of comparing and contrasting ideas, a process that is integral to the dialectical mode of thought. Many now are aware that this goes on, and many resent it. But pointing out the problem is not enough. Restoring to the culture an understanding of the art of political thinking is fundamental to securing a democratic politics capable of securing the rights of each citizen. I hope this book makes a contribution to this effort.

IV. THE REST OF THE BOOK

My approach in this book is to provide examples of political thinking, examples that I hope will encourage the reader to engage in political thinking him or herself. This means writing in the spirit of Socrates's dialectical approach so that readers become practiced in comparing and contrasting political visions and arguments. To this end, I plan to discuss how one thinker would defend his or her vision of society against other thinkers. In the process of this undertaking, my intention is to ask readers to question my interpretation of the "possible" arguments that I suggest the respective thinkers would use in responding to other thinkers.

In order to facilitate this endeavor, I will develop the nature and the importance of a civil society as a major theme. As I discuss the different visions emanating from the different approaches to political thinking addressed in this book, I will discuss how these different visions bear on this central theme. For instance, interwoven throughout the discussions will be questions such as, would Plato support a civil society? How would Aristotle have responded to the question of civil society? Why is Locke's theory likely to support a civil society? But why is Rousseau's vision less likely?

My effort to encourage political thinking is carried out as well by the addition in the book's second and third parts of a "response and rejoinder" section, normally at the end of each chapter. In this section, I try to imagine how the various thinkers would have responded to one another. In particular, I ask how thinkers who come before others would respond to the people who come after them, and, in addition, I try to demonstrate the way later thinkers would respond to critiques by earlier ones. In all cases, my concern is with how certain thinkers would respond to each other on a variety of issues touched on in each chapter. Whereas the civil society question is the central theme, the response and rejoinder sections are designed to develop a discussion across a variety of questions found in the different visions described throughout the book.

In the remaining part of this section, I will provide a brief overview of the thinkers I cover. The first chapter is a discussion of civil society. Here, I will develop the main conception of a civil society that will be referred to throughout this book as I discuss the various visions found in the political theories that I address.

In Part I, there is a discussion of classical Greek, Christian, and some non-Christian visions of political philosophy. Regarding the classical Greek dimension, there are chapters on Plato and Aristotle. I address Christian thought with a chapter that includes medieval and Reformation Christian thinkers. I also include a chapter on non-Christian medieval thinkers, including Maimonides, and important Islamic thinkers such as Averroes, Alfarabi, and Avicenna. These chapters are designed to demonstrate how civic virtue in the classical Greek, Christian, and non-Christian worlds differ from the view of civic virtue found in modern conceptions of civil society. I have written these chapters to demonstrate that, whereas classical Greek, Christian, and non-Christian thinkers are not principally responsible for developing the notion of a civil society, there are still important elements in these writers' views that are made a part of civil society thinking. Readers should keep in mind that Chapter 5 in Part I, the chapter on Machiavelli, provides the transition to the modern conception of civil society and civic virtue, developed in the second part.

I turn in Part II to liberal and conservative views of civil society. Liberal views of civil society seek to secure the broadest possible individual freedom by protecting citizens' basic rights. The classical Greek, Christian, and non-Christian traditions envision individuals as part of a society that is subject to the overarching conception of the common purpose that dictates the nature of one's place and one's role in society. In contrast, a liberal view of civil society asserts that individuals should define their own moral purposes, and that political equality, secured by rights, allows them to do so. Included in the liberal category are writers such as Thomas Hobbes, John Locke, Immanuel Kant, G. W. F. Hegel, John Stuart Mill, and John Rawls. The chapter on Jean Jacques Rousseau should be viewed as a critique of the liberal views of civil society found in Hobbes and Locke.

Conservative writers, while accepting the fundamental importance of human freedom, worry that the emphasis on rights may go so far that the norms and traditions that underscore community life, also necessary for securing freedom, are neglected. In the process of making this mistake the importance of orienting people to understand the types of social relationships and the basic values needed to secure a rich and full life are denied a place of prominence. Included among writers in this tradition are Edmund Burke, Alexis de Tocqueville, and Michael Oakeshott. Conservatives, not unlike writers in the classical Greek, Christian, and non-Christian traditions, seek to maintain an integrated social order in which each person's identity is part of the larger context of traditions and common ways of experiencing life. For the conservative, when individuals are cut off from such attachments, they are robbed of the real sources of identity, the aspects of experience that give meaning and significance to one's life.

Part III contains critiques of the modern views of civil society. Here, we discuss feminist and Marxist critiques as well as the views put forward by Friedrich Nietzsche and Michel Foucault. Why have these people been selected? Their accounts are of great importance because each, from a different perspective, seeks to demonstrate that civil society is merely a mask to hide or to give cover to, in the name of important ideals such as rights and civic virtue, repressive relationships. Each of these ways of thinking discussed here, then, raises the question about whether the idea of a civil society represents a worthy enterprise.

The Nietzschean and Marxist arguments, for different reasons, would answer this question with a loud and resounding no. For Marx, a civil society is nothing more than a way to disguise the brute power of the capitalist class. Thus to achieve worker liberation, it is necessary to have a revolution that overthrows the owner class along with the civil society that supports the owners. For Nietzsche and those who follow him, a civil society blunts the imagination and destroys the creative power of individuals so that, in the long run, individuals are unable to achieve the liberation that civil society promises. Nietzsche would thus hark back to a different social arrangement, one in which society is, in the main, under the dominant power of an aristocratic class that is able to set a new and more liberatory course for society. Michel Foucault will pursue a Nietzschean unmasking of the oppressive dimensions of civil society, also. However, he will update his critique to fit modern organizational life and development, and he will demand a politics that supports those techniques, peculiar to his own brand of political theory, that permit individuals to overcome modern repression. Feminists, however, for the most part do retain an essential faith in civil society. Feminists take this view so long as major reforms are provided that help to make civil society not just a place where males flourish at the cost of females, but where all can flourish in a setting conducive to full human freedom.

In Chapter 18, I conclude the book by providing an overview of the state of civil society in today's world. Here, I discuss many of the major challenges that writers seeking to preserve civil society must face. I also address many of the reasons why civil society is in eclipse today as well as describe some of the efforts to restore it to health.

Endnotes

1. In taking this position I follow Sheldon Wolin. See Sheldon S. Wolin, *Politics and Vision, Continuity and Innovation in Western Political Thought,* (Boston: Little, Brown, and Co., 1960), p. 21. For a different view, one that distinguishes political theory from political philosophy, see Nannerl O. Keohane, "Philosophy, Theory, Ideology," *Political Theory,* 4:1, February, 1976, pp. 81–82.

2. Wolin, *Politics and Vision,* pp. 18–19.

3. Ibid., p. 19.

4. My account is based on my interpretation of Plato's Apology and the Crito in Plato, Euthyphro, Apology and Crito, trans. F. J. Church, (Indianapolis: Bobbs-Merrill Company, 1956), pp. 21–67.

5. Irving M. Zeitlin, *Plato's Vision, The Classical Origins of Social and Political Thought,* (Englewood Cliffs, N. J.: Prentice Hall, 1993), pp. 47–48.

6. Mulford Q. Sibley, *Political Ideas and Ideologies: A History of Political Thought,* (New York: Harper and Row, 1970), p. 44.

7. Zeitlin, *Plato's Vision,* p. 59.

8. *Apology,* Church Edition, p. 28.

9. Ibid., p. 28.

10. *Crito,* Church edition, p. 59.

11. Ibid., pp. 60–61.

Partial Bibliography and Further Reading

Keohane, Nannerl O. "Philosophy, Theory, Ideology," *Political Theory, 4:1,* February, 1976, pp. 81–82.

Wolin, Sheldon S. *Politics and Vision, Continuity and Innovation in Western Political Thought.* Boston: Little, Brown, and Co., 1960.

Zeitlin, Irving M. *Plato's Vision: The Classical Origins of Social and Political Thought.* Englewood Cliffs, N. J.: Prentice Hall, 1993.

The Importance of a Civil Society

I. Civil Society: The Problem Faced

In this section, I develop the basic dimensions of a civil society. Those readers who are desirous of receiving a more thorough treatment of the subject may wish to read Chapter 18 next. Chapter 18 also discusses the threats that are posed to civil society in contemporary society as well as many related issues such as the relationship of civil society to multiculturalism, to religion, to globalization, to civility, and to civic renewal projects. I have saved these matters for the conclusion because I think that they are best addressed after having completed a journey through political theory.

The term *civil society* has several uses. In one use a "civil society" refers to a regime committed to secure the rule of law on behalf of the common good. In contemporary society the common good refers to a variety of possible items, including but not limited to the provision of basic rights, public safety, education, systems of communication and roads, national parks, and so on. But the term *civil society* has another use as well, and it is this second use that will be given a predominant place in this book. The second use of the term refers to a space that exists between the national government and the individual. In that space, there are a variety of different groups and associations, each of which is dedicated to uphold certain values and to achieve particular ends.

As contemporary writer Jean Bethke Elshtain says, a civil society refers to many different forms of associations, often called voluntary groups or secondary institutions, such as families, religious organizations, trade unions, self-help groups, charitable associations, neighborhood organizations, private clubs and organizations, and so on. These organizations, which exist outside the formal structures of government power, point to a separate sphere. In that sphere individuals are free to pursue a variety of life experiences made possible by the different associations people may join.[1] An important aspect of a civil society is that, as a separate sphere, civil society acts as a buffer against the power of the central government, and, in this role, encourages an atmosphere that allows various groups to follow their own courses without fear of central government intrusions.

Moreover, these groups are also independent of large corporate, business organizations whose power to dominate markets and to influence governments is vast and decisive. Corporations such as Microsoft or General Motors have the power to dictate many of the terms of their workers' lives. A civil society counters this tendency by acting as a buffer against large corporate power just as it acts as a buffer against the power of the central government. As a buffer, a civil society permits individuals to determine through the associations they make with others what they do with their free time, what religious beliefs, if any, they hold, what friends and life-long partners they choose, what kinds of civic activities they will pursue, and so on.

But as Nancy Rosenblum says, American political theorists tend to focus less upon the separate sphere as a buffer against the central government and more upon the moral education obtained in the groups that make up the separate sphere.[2] I think that there is less focus as well on civil society as a buffer against corporate power than there is on the need to see civil society as a basis for moral education. On this view, then, people enter the separate sphere, participate in groups, and receive from this experience an important moral dimension to their lives. Here, the connections people forge in the various groups of a civil society help them maintain a sense of civic responsibility for the welfare of many others, including one's neighbors, friends, and society. Owing to this important experience in civil society, out-of-control, unlimited egoism is subordinated to the norms of civic conduct.[3] Consequently, a civil society, as it stresses the separate sphere of groups and voluntary associations, points to important civic values that the society as a whole expects its members to embrace.

Because civic values are important in discussions of civil society, it is necessary to describe the nature of the moral environment that a civil society as a separate sphere promotes. What is the nature of this moral environment? A civil society is associated with an environment in which individuals are accorded political equality and thus guaranteed the same rights, while at the same time maintaining among themselves a commitment to uphold *civic virtue*. Civic virtue refers to the respect citizens have for the common standards and conception of the common good integral to the life of a community. So on the one hand, individuals are to be accorded full dignity and respect by being provided the same package of rights that guarantee among other things freedom of association, speech, conscience, due process of law, and ownership of private property. With these rights, individuals gain not only the ability to influence the political decisions of the government, but they achieve the capability to pursue reasonable, self-defined life objectives. On the other hand, a civil society encourages people to endorse the common standards deemed necessary to maintain a decent and "civic" life. In upholding the common norms, individuals manifest respect for civic virtue and, in consequence, maintain a commitment to the common good.[4]

This conception of civil society suggests two different approaches to the way we come to understand ourselves as individuals. First, when individuals see themselves as equals, they are likely to think of themselves as independent and self-standing persons whose way of life predominately derives from their own reflections and choices and not from impositions emanating from outside their lives. However, the civic virtue dimension of civil society proposes that there are common standards that all members of the society are expected to support. Specifically, this means one must manifest allegiance to all the norms associated with good citizenship.

Now, there are many values allied with the civic virtue dimension of civil society. Here, I will give a few examples, but it must be clear that the list I provide is neither determinative nor exhaustive, but rather this list is an illustration of what is meant, generally, when the civic virtue side of civil society is discussed. For instance, there are what William Galston refers to as "general virtues" including both respect for the laws and the basic political principles and institutions of the society.[5] Further, there are the basic civic virtues of *tolerance and mutual respect,* to which we give special emphasis in Section VI.

In addition, as Galston indicates, citizen or civic virtues also include concerns for how people should approach participation in the economic life of the society.[6] Each individual must have a work ethic or an ability to do one's job well during the course of supporting oneself. Furthermore, the work environment requires that individuals learn to adapt to the changing circumstances of economic life by acquiring new skills or updating existing ones. Also, as we discuss in our review of Adam Smith's concept of the modern market economy in Section VII, individuals must be able, in the name of longer-term self-interests, to save certain amounts of their incomes, even when doing so requires sacrifice of immediate short-term desires.

A civil society, at its heart, can be characterized by a tension between an individualist viewpoint that is guaranteed by the provision of basic rights and the communal dimension of society that reflects a need to respect the civic virtue requirements. The goal of a civil society is to permit people to pursue their own concepts of life, while at the same time respecting civic virtue obligations and constraints. In general, there are several approaches to this objective, and each approach establishes baseline values for the society as a whole to adopt and for the various groups that make up a civil society to uphold. Here, following Rosenblum, I discuss three different approaches, one suggesting a *democratic* civil society, another suggesting a civil society of *mediating* groups, and a third suggesting a *liberal* view of civil society.[7]

II. THE DEMOCRATIC CIVIL SOCIETY

In this section, we discuss the democratic approach to achieving a setting in which the individualist and the communal perspectives are bridged.[8] A society of this sort expects all citizens to take part in defining the rules and norms by which each will be governed. In a democratic setting, people enter the public deliberation as individuals, with their own interests and needs. But during the course of the deliberation, each person articulates his or her interests in a way that helps create a common, shared policy orientation. For instance, in discussing the best approach to cleaning up the environment, I may enter the political arena with my own particular commitment to protect as many green spaces as possible. Others may seek to clear some of these spaces for building new work places. As a result of the deliberation, a way is discovered to achieve a fair accommodation between the opposing views.

Thus, as Rosenblum points out, advocates of a democratic civil society suggest that democratic participation in major institutions—including trade unions, churches, or the professions—would help people develop a capacity for deliberating with others on behalf of determining the common good.[9] In consequence, people would learn to think of themselves as citizens as well as private individuals. And when the two roles were in conflict with each other, the citizen role would always take precedence.

In a democratic civil society, then, individuals, through their trade unions and work associations, should be able to have important influence in shaping their work environment even to the point of helping determine the nature and purpose of the work they do. At the same time, in the other associations, such as religious groups or charitable organizations, the members should help shape the policies there as well. Furthermore, the experience of democratic life in various group settings orients people to be attuned to the needs of the larger society. Here, as a result of democratic experience in civil society associations, when groups participate in the society's national politics they will be more capable of considering a broad array of interests on behalf of searching for the common good.

Thus, those who support democratic approaches to civil society seek to make the norms of democratic life a part of all forms of group life. Otherwise, the ability of individuals to learn how to embrace and to consider other views and to make them a part of the deliberation with others would not be possible. For instance, families can conform to democratic norms when there is shared responsibility for parenting and when there is a fair division of labor within the family setting.[10] Similarly, labor unions should not be dominated by an elite few but should be open to full participation by all members in making key policies.

Alternatively, the democratic approach suggests that groups not presently democratic should be made so. The democratic approach recognizes that some associations have excluded in the past individuals merely owing to their status as women and minorities. Under the democratic approach, associations should ensure that in the future individuals previously excluded merely on the grounds of gender or race are included in the "rational democratic discourse" that should take place in groups.[11]

But the problem with the democratic view is that it superimposes onto all persons a democratic culture, and not all persons even when they are democrats want to spend so large a portion of their lives making collective decisions. To have to spend most of one's time preparing to take part in fashioning the policy of one's group or of one's government, for instance, would take time away from other kinds of activities that individuals might find just as important, if not more so. Included here might be activities such as taking part in relationships with friends, or taking part in religious engagements, and so on.[12] As long as citizens believe that the government can and will protect their basic rights, as well as offer them opportunities for participation during "critical moments" such as national elections, the need for participation may become minimized for many.

III. Civil Society of Mediating Groups

The mediating view of civil society suggests that individuals create their own organizations to provide important services, such as education or care for the elderly. Moreover, individuals in these groups manifest a civic commitment to care for the needs of each other, and through this experience individuals create among themselves a sense of belonging, within an integrated and well-ordered community. Here, as voluntary groups assume many of the functions of government, individuals act in ways that are in keeping with respect for the common good of others.

The problem with this view is that in diminishing the need for government, the basic legal institutions that are necessary for maintaining a civil society may lose their fundamental importance to many people. For instance, as we will discuss in Chapter 18, some individuals today advocate the use of community organizations to dispense basic welfare benefits to people, such as job training. But do mediating groups that engage in this activity have sufficient resources to provide these services on the massive scales that are necessary? Given that they may not, government's role becomes all the more necessary.

There is thus a need to recognize the importance of the larger environment in which a civil society exists. This environment includes those political and legal institutions that maintain essential services, which, for instance, secure basic rights, provide protection from criminals, and so on. Without government services of this sort, and in particular without the prospect of maintaining the rule of law, a civil society could not be sustained over the long run.[13]

IV. CIVIL SOCIETY: THE LIBERAL SOLUTION

In the liberal view of civil society, the main objective is to promote respect for the diversity of values and ways of life in society.[14] This goal is made possible only in a society that is designed to permit a person the opportunity to move in and out of the different group settings and affiliations in order to afford a person the chance to discover and then live a way of life that a person would find most suitable. Indeed, as people are free to enter and to leave groups, they find ways to compensate for the lack of opportunities found in one group with the enhanced opportunities discovered in another.

Thus, if it were the case that I have a need for religious experience, I should be free to enter those groups that would facilitate this need. However, as a result of a subsequent decision that another way of life might be best for me, I should be able to leave the religious group and enter groups that I believed most suited my needs. People should have the right to enter and to leave groups, always, of course, on terms that the groups themselves determine are acceptable. Still, groups, in establishing their internal norms, must always be supportive of the need to not deny any members their basic rights as citizens.

Moreover, the liberal conception of civil society requires a spirit of openness that permits individuals to create new groups and organizations when individuals find it necessary to do so. Existing groups must not stand in the way of new group formations, and new groups must not trample upon the prerogatives of existing groups. In upholding these requirements, opportunities would be provided for those who want to form groups that secure a democratic or participatory experience. Or, alternately, it would be possible for individuals to create and join groups performing an important mediating or service role in society.

Finally, the provision of rights should not be based upon whether individuals are members of groups. Instead, each individual must be guaranteed the same basic rights, regardless of which groups he or she might be members of, and each person, regardless of his or her group memberships, must acknowledge the rights of others.[15]

Now, one might ask, how is the liberal view of society likely to promote the idea of civic virtue? Is not the liberal view merely one dimensional, emphasizing for the most part the side that fosters individual choice and excluding for the most part the civic virtue side?

V. LIBERAL CIVIL SOCIETY: THE JUSTIFICATION

A liberal civil society, which permits individuals the freedom to enter different groups as the basis for pursuing self-determined ways of life, can survive only when there is respect for shared civic norms. Why is this depiction of reality in a civil society accurate? I will answer this question with an example. If I wish to pursue a legal career, I must adhere to the standards of conduct that define the path for success in this arena. Now, to be sure, the norms I uphold in this case are not necessarily all civic norms. Following the protocol required to write a legal brief refers to standards established by the legal profession solely. The legal profession, just as any other organization whether it is a religious group, a trade union, or a charitable group, has its own standards that members must uphold. But these professional or group norms point to the importance of civic norms. To uphold the standards of the legal profession, I will have to practice many important civic norms. For instance, I will have to display a good work ethic, respect for the laws of the society, acceptance of basic citizen duties, such as paying taxes and performing needed volunteer work, a concern for the larger good of society, and so on.

So civic norms abound in a liberal civil society. In supporting these civic norms, I not only enhance my own opportunities, but at the same time I recognize the need to modify my own personal goals when they conflict with civic standards. At other times, in order to practice civic norms, it may be necessary for me to question the basic fairness of an association of which I am a member. On these occasions, it is right for others or me to evaluate existing group norms in light of the opportunities they provide or fail to provide. For instance, if a private club excludes certain categories of people because of their race or their gender, and if, as a result, these individuals are denied full rights and opportunities accorded all others in society, then it is necessary to work for reform of these practices. Thus, if a private country club is a setting in which important real estate transactions are made, and if this club denies women realtors entrance, then women, for reasons of gender alone, are denied opportunities provided to men. In this case, advocating reform is an understandable practice.

Because a liberal civil society provides many different kinds of groups, there will be different prospects for people to pursue. In this way, a liberal civil society helps to sustain a diversity of ways of life. But, in doing so, it is inevitable that there will be people with different and competing interests, often in conflict with each other. We witness this fact of life all the time. Lawyers and doctors each have professional associations that advocate different policies with respect to standards pertaining to situations in which patients can sue doctors. Religious groups compete with each other for converts. Neighborhood organizations compete with each other for federal dollars. Charitable organizations compete with each other for the private donor's money. Trade unions fight against business-group-backed laws limiting the conditions of union membership. The list describing the different kinds of competition is long. Furthermore, intense competition may engender attitudes of conniving and cunning. Demeanors of this sort can cause individuals to have little regard for the rights of others.

This situation represents an important danger for people in a liberal civil society whose main concern is to protect the basic rights of individuals. Now, the function of the state in a liberal civil society is to secure rights by affording protection to individuals from those in society who would take away their rights. But, in addition to the state's efforts in this regard, respect for rights is maintained in two other important ways, and each of these ways introduces additional and important conceptions of civic virtue.

Critical to maintaining a civil society is the need to manifest either toleration or mutual respect. Each of these outlooks signifies a demeanor of a different sort, but, as I will argue, mutual respect is more desirable than toleration as a civic virtue. Still, toleration can become the basis for achieving mutual respect, and, because of this fact, toleration is a civic virtue of high importance, also.

VI. THE CIVIC VIRTUES OF TOLERATION AND MUTUAL RESPECT

The norm associated with toleration is that individuals agree to live-and-let-live by creating separate places in society where people with various lifestyles can practice their beliefs and ways of life. In classical liberalism, as we shall see in discussing Locke, religious toleration suggests that in tolerating other religious views, one is not required to understand, to come to grips with, or to even test out another's views on oneself. One is asked, instead, just not to interfere with another's religious practices. As a result of toleration, the right to not be hindered in one's religious beliefs is protected for all.

The conduct we maintain during the course of just tolerating others may lead us to never know about or understand the values of the others whom we tolerate. The doctrine of toleration encourages us to create walls around others and ourselves, and these walls often make the people we tolerate seem even more alien and strange as time goes on. The problem with this attitude is that it may orient us to believe that people who are different from us and whom we tolerate really do not deserve to be accorded those basic rights that a civil society is committed to provide all citizens. Often this attitude has led to situations in which the rights accorded the "tolerated" may not have the same worth as the rights accorded other members of the society. This means that, even though all have the same rights, owing to a difference in the worth of rights some can do far more with their rights than others can.

Many examples of the consequences of this kind of situation abound. In this country, after official segregation of African Americans ended, a doctrine of live-and-let-live toleration, embodied in the idea of integration, was maintained toward African Americans who were now free to participate in society on the same terms as whites. But because of continuing racist attitudes, various barriers remain in place, and these obstacles unfairly limit the opportunities for African Americans. In consequence, they have not enjoyed the full measure of rights granted whites. For Native Americans, the live-and-let-live approach has meant for some confinement to reservations. The latter came to symbolize policies that on the whole did not work to secure the same worth to their rights as provided to mainstream

Americans. For women, historically, the household setting has often been the place where women are subordinated to the needs of men and kept from larger participation in the society, including its workplaces and its public, political structure. Reforms of these practices have led to the passage of laws that deny discrimination in various workplace and educational environments. The impact of these laws has been to require men to live-and-let-live with women in the public settings of work, education, and politics. But still, many barriers exist that stifle the full advancement of women in many settings. These barriers include subtle forms of discrimination predicated upon attitudes that establish an implicit agreement among men that women should not be permitted to advance to the higher echelon of many work places. This is what many call the "glass ceiling."

Here, the "tolerated" may find themselves marginalized, as in the cases of many women, African Americans, and Native Americans. In consequence, these individuals may suffer a loss of opportunities, especially when compared to those members of society who are advantaged, owing to their gender, race, or ethnic background. The best way to overcome this situation is to advance beyond toleration by teaching the importance of people's learning to understand, to respect, and to consider the views of others that are different from them. To move in this direction is to embrace the civic virtue of mutual respect.

The mode of interaction required for maintaining mutual respect requires that individuals who share a basic commitment to respect the rights of others, however different others may be in status or outlook, seek to understand each other's interests and perspectives. Here, as I interact with people with different values from my own, my intention should be to learn about and accord respect for the different ideas, points of views, and attitudes that these individuals may hold on issues of common importance to each of us. In discussing political questions, I should be willing to engage not only the people who are in my own professional or religious affiliations, but I should also engage those who are in professional and religious groups different from my own. I should try to find out why others who live in contexts different from mine hold the views they profess, and I should seek to determine the reasons used by them to justify their positions. During the course of doing so, I help to make room for other views differing from mine, and I remove the walls that might separate me from others. In this new setting, others are not alien to me, and I would have no trouble according them, in the full measure possible, the rights due to them.

To be sure, we cannot accord to all people in society an effort to understand their views, their aspirations, and their ways of life. There are just too many people for that. But we can accord respect in the sense just defined to those with whom we come into contact. As we manifest this kind of respect for others, and indeed, as the bulk of the members of society do so as well, then, mutual respect would become a widely held civic virtue.

Still, despite the importance of mutual respect, it may be the case that toleration is the best we can do. Indeed, in some circumstances toleration may be a first step in the long journey to achieving what is clearly the higher-order condition of mutual respect. At first, in order for society to have social peace, toleration may be the only practical and appropriate doctrine. Take for instance a society that has experienced many years of turmoil between several groups. Here, owing to a long period of hateful conflict, it might be too much to expect that individuals would come to engage in relationships of mutual understanding. Still, at least in learning to live-and-let-live, the violence between groups would be ended, and the way would be set for a future in which mutually respectful discourses might begin to occur between groups who were former enemies. In the Middle East, for instance, the doctrine of toleration, if established today, might lead tomorrow to a new commitment to a form of civic virtue that could cause people, who previously manifested mutual distaste or even hatred, to engage each other in a dialogue of mutual recognition and understanding.

Toleration is important for another reason. Where the state must force people to respect the rights of all members, then the state may use policies designed to intimidate people, such as illegal force or constant surveillance, and these policies would place both the separate sphere and basic rights in jeopardy. This condition is avoided when individuals, through a commitment to toleration, voluntarily respect the rights of others. Here, the state could protect rights and the rule of law through approaches that are not intimidating but that enhance the opportunities for all citizens in the various domains of life, such as work, education, art, or the enjoyment of nature.

Still, a civil society as a separate sphere of groups and associations, when it is at its best, embodies both the civic virtues of toleration and mutual respect. In this circumstance, a civil society can be a setting with many diverse groups, each of which contains members from across the social and political spectrum of society. Here, even though a group is dedicated to a central purpose, such as providing public service or enabling people to come together to discuss great books, a group nonetheless includes people from different racial or religious or class backgrounds or from different political and social philosophies. And thus disagreements within as well as among groups are always likely. Where the civic virtue of toleration is complemented by the civic virtue of mutual respect, however, individuals become practiced in the art of a give-and-take discourse that is designed to find a common ground among competing views within groups, as well as within the society at large. As a result, the quest for inclusion becomes a primary focus of groups in civil society, and this search makes rights-respecting conduct more likely, thus helping to secure a state and society dedicated to protecting the rights of all its citizens.

VII. The Market Dimension of Civil Society: Adam Smith's Dilemma

What I have highlighted in the last several sections is an environment with a multitude of voluntary groups, each of which exists to facilitate a wide diversity of life choices. Allowing people the freedom to choose their own ways of life and permitting group contexts for realizing the ways of life people may choose is a vision of society modeled along the lines of a free market. As in a free market, each person is to have the freedom to choose the way of life he or she determines best. But, for some, the idea of the free market as it pertains to economic activities represents severe problems for a civil society and, in particular, for its need to sustain civic virtues such as toleration and mutual respect.

In discussing the implications of the free market for civil society there is no person more important than the eighteenth-century Scottish economist and moral philosopher, Adam Smith (1723–1790). Smith's *The Wealth of Nations* is, as Max Lerner points out, "the foundation-work of modern economic thought."[16] Smith's view of market relationships suggests a market setting in civil society in which an individual "neither intends to promote the public interest, nor knows how much he is promoting it." Indeed, the individual is concerned only to promote his own "security," but, in the process of doing so, he "is led by an invisible hand to promote an end which was no part of his intention."[17] And that end is the common good.

For Smith, the "invisible hand" refers to those free market rules that indicate the ways of life individuals must adopt as a condition for successful attainment of one's interests. So individuals, in seeking their own interests within the free market setting, not only recognize the existence of constraints, but these constraints permit the natural unfolding in society of those activities that realize over the long term the best interest of all members of the society.

Why and on what basis is this outcome possible? Answering this question revolves around what Smith saw was the main question he sought to answer in writing *The Wealth of Nations.* Smith argued that, in "savage nations of hunters and fishers," all who are able work in useful endeavors, but the total amount of goods produced is not enough to meet the needs of the people. Such nations are so poor that they are forced at times to abandon their young, their old people, and their sick to hunger or "to be devoured by wild beasts."[18] In contrast, in a modern, civilized, manufacturing society not all people perform productive work, but the product from those who do productive work is large enough to supply even the poorest worker who "is frugal and industrious" with a "greater share of the necessaries and conveniencies [sic] of life than it is possible for any savage to acquire."[19] So the answer to our question about how the collective good is realized when individuals act only for their own interest revolves around demonstrating how, in a manufacturing society operating by free market values, it is the case that there still redounds to society a surplus of wealth sufficient to provide all with a decent life even when not all perform productive labor. How is this end possible?

Smith answered this question by demonstrating how the productive power of workers has been increased in manufacturing societies. The principal way by which this outcome has been achieved is through the introduction of a division of labor. This method of organizing work allows for the introduction of machinery, it improves the skills and dexterity of workers, and it introduces many efficiencies into the work process.[20] Overall, these factors contribute to the enhanced production of each worker, such that a given worker is able to produce not just enough for himself of a given good, but enough units of that good for many others as well. To be sure, as a result of these advances in the productive process, the average working individual did not find himself at the same level as the wealthy classes in Europe.[21] Still, the working person, although not at the level of the rich in his own country, exceeded the level of the wealthiest people in the poorest countries during Smith's time.[22]

What prompts a new, more productive division of labor to arise in the first place? The division of labor evolves from the tendency people possess to exchange one "thing for another."[23] Self-interest considerations push us to engage in such exchanges with others. Some people have an interest in producing certain goods, and others have an interest in producing other goods. Moreover, in each case, each person has an interest in possessing or acquiring the goods that others produce. But to be in a position to acquire the goods of others, a person must produce a surplus of goods, so that he has enough goods both to supply himself and to sell to others. With the money he receives from selling his surplus goods to others, he can then purchase the different items he has an interest in acquiring.[24]

Thus, over time, each person finds that one's interest is best served by specializing in producing one type of good and in finding the best way to produce a surplus of that product.

But to succeed in this endeavor, individuals must accept the values of thrift and parsimony. That is, individuals must learn to practice moderation with respect to personal spending habits as a condition for success in the market setting. Why is this the case? As we have just indicated, it is in our self-interest to produce a surplus of goods. Now, one use to which the surplus is put is for personal consumption. Here, I exchange my surplus for money that enables me to purchase other goods that I want and need. But if I want to continue to build up my surplus, I must take some of it and invest it by purchasing those goods that allow me to engage in more efficient forms of production, thus yielding me more profit.[25]

At the heart of the manufacturing society stands an individual both willing and ready to acquire more goods, but at the same time this individual is enlightened enough to know that he must practice the virtues of frugality and saving money to be successful.[26] This ethos, when made a standard part of society, helps to make clear the origin of "capital." A person who has sufficient wealth to maintain himself and yet still has enough left over may invest this surplus wealth with the intention of creating additional wealth. In doing so, the person creates capital. Here, capital represents the surplus wealth a person uses to improve land or to further invest in such goods as machines, for the purpose of realizing additional profits.[27] For Smith, self-interest, when placed in the market setting of the manufacturing economy, produces the basis for capital growth in society, a form of growth that helps to supply everyone with the basis for a decent life.

Smith's argument thus explains the way the common good is achieved in an environment in which self-interest-oriented behavior is encouraged. The natural question in this circumstance is whether the civic virtues we have discussed, in particular toleration and mutual respect, would have any place in Smith's civil society. Smith would certainly contend that these civic virtues are to be a part of his view of society. Indeed, Smith, in *The Theory of Moral Sentiments,* argued that individuals are not simply oriented to their own ends and needs, but, in addition, there is a propensity in persons to sympathize with others.[28] To make his point, Smith said that human beings are conscious of the fact that it is always necessary to view themselves from the standpoint of the way all others would view them, what Smith refers to as the *impartial spectator* point of view. From this standpoint, as "he [a person] views himself in the light in which he is conscious that others will view him," a person understands that he is not to consider himself better than any other person among the multitude of people making up society.[29] Naturally, individuals will always "prefer themselves to the rest of mankind," but that mentality must be balanced against the spectator perspective that exhorts us to "view ourselves not so much according to that light in which we may naturally appear to ourselves, as according to that in which we naturally appear to others."[30] Given this moral point of view, we understand that we are to "humble the arrogance of . . . self-love, and bring it down to something which other men can go along with."[31] Thus, as we pursue our fortunes in life, we must always attempt to interact with others in ways that all consider to be fair. Smith said, "in the race for wealth, and honours, and preferments, he may run as hard as he can and strain every nerve and every muscle, in order to outstrip all his competitors. But if he should jostle, or throw down any of them, the indulgence of the spectators is entirely at an end."[32] Here, the natural sympathy Smith described would make the liberal commitment to the civic virtues of mutual respect and toleration matters of great importance.

Finally, as another way to maintain regard for rights, it should be clear that Smith provided, as all civil society theorists do, an important role to the state. Smith did support the presence and importance of civil government. Indeed, for Smith, "the first duty of the sovereign" is defending the society from foreign attack.[33] Furthermore, government has a prime role in protecting each member of the society from "injustice or oppression" inflicted by other members.[34] Here, a major concern is "to prevent the members of a society from incroaching [*sic*] on one another's property, or seizing what is not their own."[35] The government must provide justice to all citizens by protecting what each has a "right to and could justly demand from others."[36] To this end, the civil government must maintain a system that is designed to administer justice. Thus, Smith's commitment to the invisible hand never denied the need for a government that could provide for the essential needs of society. What Smith did disapprove of is the need for government regulation of domestic market activities. For when governments regulate domestic industry through various policies, including placing tariffs on goods from foreign manufacturers, the result is to discourage the development of capital growth in a society.[37] So Smith hoped to restore "freedom of trade," but he thought that private interests as well as public prejudice in Britain opposed this objective, and, owing to these elements, free trade would never be fully revived.[38]

Given Smith's views of civil government and the place of sympathy in his theory, the self-interest orientation of Smith's free market setting, which is highlighted in *The Wealth of Nations,* would not undermine civic virtue commitments. Still, some would argue that the free market setting and the cultural attitudes that grow up around it undermine the prospect of achieving Smith's depiction of civil society, a depiction that is no doubt compatible with the civic virtues of both mutual respect and toleration described in the previous section. Indeed, the concern that the market will have a corrosive moral influence on civil society is a major theme throughout this book. This theme is manifested in the work of a wide range of thinkers we will discuss in the second and third parts, including Jean-Jacques Rousseau, G. W. F. Hegel, John Stuart Mill, Alexis de Tocqueville, Michael Oakeshott, John Rawls, and, of course, Karl Marx. A major worry of these writers is that the market may turn civil society into an environment in which individuals pursue their interests, selfishly, with little regard for the needs of others and with no concern to maintain the commitment to the virtues of civic life. Here, the hope of sustaining the larger moral environment that promotes both individualist goals alongside a respect for civic virtues that define our citizenship responsibilities is all but lost.

A final problem is that, in a context in which the market dominates, the only important values are materialist or utilitarian ones, and other values that are critical to full human flourishing are denied a place. But values that have to do with the spiritual or the aesthetic or the intellectual or the moral sides of persons, as well as values that provide a sense of belonging and community, are critically important, too. A civil society must protect these values as well. But where the market dominates, materialist values push other values to the sidelines. Critics as well as supporters of civil society will make these issues central, as we will demonstrate throughout this book.

VIII. THE IMPORTANCE OF CIVIL SOCIETY

Civil society is an important subject because it is only in a civil society that individuals develop the moral capacity and awareness that helps to protect the basic freedom that people in modern society value. In general, outside of a civil society environment, citizens have no regard for the standards of citizenship, including toleration and mutual respect, and then, instead of a setting that secures rights and freedom, a society emerges that may well be hostile to them. And without freedom, individuals lack an ability to find lives for themselves that each person considers meaningful, significant, and of enduring value.

Obviously, few would wish to experience this fate for themselves. Yet, today many either do not think that civil society is in danger or, if they recognize that it is, they are not willing to be part of a campaign to save it. Standing by and watching civil society dissolve, a consequence of not having a strong political will to defend it, can lead only to the worst possible outcome in which the goods of civil society, including individual freedom and the norms of civic life, disappear. The result of this tragedy is a life that loses its energy for many, and, instead of the happiness associated with a free and meaningful life, individuals must accept the loneliness of their insignificance.

Endnotes

1. Jean Bethke Elshtain, *Democracy on Trial,* (New York: Basic Books: 1995), pp. 5–6.

2. The view of civil society that I use here is modeled upon Nancy L. Rosenblum's in "The Moral Uses of Civil Society: Three Views," *The Newsletter of PEGS: The Committee on the Political Economy of the Good Society,* Supplement to 3:2, Summer, 1993, p. 3, now called *The Good Society.*

3. Elshtain, *Democracy on Trial,* pp. 6–7,13,19.

4. Nancy L. Rosenblum, "The Moral Uses of Civil Society," p. 3.

5. William A. Galston, *Liberal Purposes, Goods, Virtues and Diversity in the Liberal State,* (Cambridge: Cambridge University Press, 1991). See his chapter on liberal virtues, especially pp. 221, 223–25. Also, Nancy L. Rosenblum, "The Moral Uses of Civil Society," p. 3.

6. Galston, *Liberal Purposes,* pp. 223–24. Also, Nancy L. Rosenblum, "The Moral Uses of Civil Society," p. 3.

7. Nancy L. Rosenblum, "The Moral Uses of Civil Society," p. 4.

8. Ibid., p. 4. My view follows Rosenblum's understanding of democratic civil society. Also, see Benjamin R. Barber, *Strong Democracy, Participatory Politics for a Democratic Age,* (Berkeley: University of California Press, 1984), Ch. 6, especially pp. 117–33.

9. Nancy L. Rosenblum, "The Moral Uses of Civil Society," p. 4.

10. Ibid., p. 4.

11. Ibid., p. 4.

12. Ibid., p. 4.

13. Ibid., p. 4.

14. Ibid., p. 4.

15. Ibid., p. 4.

16. Max Lerner, "Introduction," to *An Inquiry into the Nature and Causes of The Wealth of Nations,* edited by Edwin Cannan, (New York: Modern Library: 1937), p. v. From here on I refer to this volume as *The Wealth of Nations.* In addition to page numbers, I refer to part, chapter, and paragraph in the numbers next to the page.

17. Smith, *The Wealth of Nations,* p. 423, IV:II: 9.

18. Ibid., p. lviii, Introduction, 4.

19. Ibid., p. lviii, Introduction, 4.

20. Ibid., pp. 3–12, especially, p. 7, I:I.

21. Ibid., p. 12, I:I:11.

22. Ibid., p. 12, I:I:11.

23. Ibid., p. 13, I:II:1.

24. Ibid., p. 15, I:II:3.

25. Ibid., pp. 262–63, II:I:2–4.

26. Ibid., p. 322, II:III:20.

27. Ibid., pp. 262–63, II:I:2–4.

28. Adam Smith, *The Theory of Moral Sentiments,* (Indianapolis: Liberty Classics, 1976), p. 51 sect I. Ch. 1. para. 11; also, pp. 54, Sect. I. Ch. 2, para. 1.

29. Ibid., p. 162, Sect II. Ch. 2. para. 1.

30. Ibid., pp. 161–62, Sect II. Ch. 2. para. 1.

31. Ibid., p. 162, Sect II. Ch. 2. para. 1.

32. Ibid., p. 162, Sect II. Ch. 2. para. 1.

33. Smith, *The Wealth of Nations,* p. 668, V:I:42.
34. Ibid., p. 669, V:I:45.
35. Adam Smith, *Lectures on Jurisprudence,* edited by R.L. Meek, D.D. Raphael, and P.G. Stein, (Indianapolis: Liberty Classics, 1978), p. 5.
36. Ibid., p. 7.
37. Smith, *The Wealth of Nations,* p. 425, IV:II:13.
38. Ibid., pp. 437–38, IV:II:43.

Partial Bibliography and Further Reading

Barber, Benjamin R. *Strong Democracy, Participatory Politics for a Democratic Age.* Berkeley: University of California Press, 1984.

Becker, Marvin. *The Emergence of Civil Society in the 18th Century.* Bloomington, Indiana: Indiana University Press, 1994.

Cohen, Jean L. *Civil Society and Political Theory.* Cambridge, Mass: M.I.T Press, 1992.

Elshtain, Jean Bethke. New York: *Democracy on Trial,* Basic Books, 1995.

Galston, William A. *Liberal Purposes, Goods, Virtues and Diversity in the Liberal State.* Cambridge: Cambridge University Press, 1991.

Ignatieff, Michael. *The Needs of Strangers.* London: Penguin Books, 1984.

Rosenblum, Nancy L. "The Moral Uses of Civil Society: Three Views." *The Newsletter of PEGS: The Committee on the Political Economy of the Good Society.* Supplement to 3:2, Summer, 1993, now called *The Good Society.*

Seligman, Adam, B. *The Idea of Civil Society.* Toronto: Free Press, 1992.

Smith, Adam. *An Inquiry into the Nature and Causes of The Wealth of Nations.* Edited by Edwin Cannan. New York: Modern Library, 1937.

2

Plato: Civic Virtue and the Just Society

I. Introduction

Plato's (428–348 B.C.E.) principal concern in the *Republic* is to define the nature of a just society. Plato's political thinking as with Aristotle's, (whom we discuss in the next chapter) addresses the problems of the chief political unit each knew, the city-state. Plato's Athens, like all city-states, was a small political community of about 300,000 people. In Athens, there were three main groups: slaves, resident aliens, and citizens. Slaves, who represented about a third of the Athenian population, had no role in government. Resident aliens, like the slaves, were not permitted any role in the political life of Athens but were free men, not subject to social subordination as were slaves. Citizenship was granted to about 100,000 individuals whose parents had been citizens. Citizens, including native tradesmen, artisans, and farmers, as well as the wealthy landowners, could participate in public affairs. The extent of their participation depended on the nature of the regime in power at the time. In some Athenian regimes, citizens (and here we are speaking only of males) were eligible for many different public offices, ranging from participation in the courts, to representative bodies, and to executive councils, but, in other regimes, limitations were placed on the public offices a person could hold. Still, in general and regardless of the regime, all male citizens could take part in the Assembly, which operated as a town meeting for all citizens who came together to discuss and to debate matters of public concern. The Assembly, which met about ten times a year, was not a mechanism for direct democracy; rather, policy was devised and carried out by representative bodies who were responsible to the Assembly. The representative bodies were a cross section of the citizens, and to ensure as equal a chance for participation as possible members to the representative bodies were chosen by lot.[1]

In Athens, and especially during the leadership of Pericles (495–429 B.C.E.), the animating spirit was that citizens should be able to take part in public affairs. Indeed, as George Sabine said, "This ideal of a common life in which all might actively share presupposed an optimistic estimate of the natural political capacity of the average man."[2]

Moreover, general participation was designed to encourage individuals to think of themselves as part of the larger community whose interest each individual served.

But this ideal was never fully realized in practice because persistent and severe conflict between citizens who represented different economic interests remained strong.[3] Those citizens with aristocratic backgrounds, who came from old families born to wealth, predicated their economic and social position upon their landholdings. Those citizens promoting democracy, mainly consisting of people who could profit from trade, sought to expand Athenian participation in trade by making Athens a major naval power. The aristocratic group maintained strong opposition to this approach, since it would require taxing their property to support a large naval force.[4]

Plato saw these realities and the turmoil associated with them as proof that democracy could not achieve a stable society. His solution was to emphasize the central place of rational intelligence and the wise ruler in predicating stability upon a moral conception of a just society. On this view, Plato did not think that all people were equally capable of holding public office, nor did he think that the experience of participation in public affairs would by itself teach people to work with each other to achieve the common good. In contrast, the basis for moral unity rested with knowledge of what constitutes the just "form" or model of society.[5]

What is the just form of society for Plato? At this point, it is worth providing an overview of Plato's argument, as a way to prepare the reader for the general themes in this chapter.

Plato's "Just Society"

For Plato, justice is a condition in which the various parts of human personality (or what he also refers to as the *soul*) are properly arranged and ordered. Individuals are characterized by a rational element, which is the seat of the search for truth. In addition, the soul is motivated by appetite to attain wealth or pursue sexual desire. The third part of the soul is the spirited part, which is concerned with displaying the courage necessary to act for the common welfare and win honor from others for doing so. Finding the proper arrangement among these parts of the soul is critical to achieving justice not only in the personalities of each citizen, but in the society at large. Here, for Plato, the rational part of the soul should rule the other two parts. If the other parts of the soul were to dominate reason, then the soul would be out of balance and the individual would neither deliberate nor act in the best interests of either himself or of society. Indeed, in this circumstance, the appetite and the spirited part might even be in conflict with each other, a situation that would ensure not only personal unhappiness, but also an inability to perform well the various tasks and functions that secure important basic needs for society.

One caveat must be made before proceeding. In developing Plato's views, it must be clear that Plato admired Socrates's dialectical approach to the search for truth and knowledge. What approach did Socrates use? For Socrates, truth-revealing inquiry begins, as we saw in the Introduction, from the standpoint of a reasoned discourse among individuals whose only objective is truth. The *Republic* is a dialogue between Socrates and his compatriots.[6] To avoid confusion, it should be clear that when Socrates is referred to in the *Republic,* as well as in this chapter, it is really Plato who is talking and who speaks through Socrates. It must also be clear that Plato sees himself as emulating Socrates's dialectical method. The basic purpose of Plato's approach, then, is to demonstrate that the main avenue to truth is testing propositions against other propositions to determine which ones have truth and which ones lack truth.

This discourse leads to the development of rational concepts, or what otherwise are referred to as the *forms,* or *ideas of good order.* These forms should be used as guides in developing the main roles and institutions of society as well as the various parts of the souls of individuals, so that each member of society is able to contribute to the common good. In contributing to the common good, which in Plato's case means citizens acting to help maintain the form of a just society, citizens manifest civic virtue.

II. PLATO'S REPUBLIC: WHAT JUSTICE IS NOT: CEPHALUS AND POLEMARCHUS

Plato began the *Republic* by demonstrating in his various dialogues how far his own society was from holding a valid understanding of the nature of justice. Indeed, as he discussed the views of justice current during his times, Plato always seemed to have in the back of his mind a more authentic version of justice than he believed his contemporaries held. To make his view more clear, he had to first demonstrate to his colleagues why their views were wrong. In doing so, he examined conventional views of justice that, during his times, were taken to be valid and demonstrated why, upon analysis, these views were deficient. To this end, he engaged the arguments of Cephalus and Polemarchus and, in doing so, like Socrates, he challenged those who held those conventional views to defend them against his, that is Plato's, own arguments.

Cephalus is a "money maker" or a man engaged in business that by Plato's own account does not seem to "love money too much." Socrates asked Cephalus to explain the "greatest good" he has received from being wealthy.[7] Cephalus responds that men of wealth like him seek a clear conscience; they do not want to cheat or deceive anyone, lest after death they may suffer terrible punishments. Socrates summarized Cephalus's response to what the latter thinks by describing justice as following the principle that the just person is one who always seeks to tell the truth and one who tries to pay his debts. In other words, one must always keep one's agreements with others. But Socrates responded by saying that this principle could not be upheld on all occasions. Socrates asked if one should return a weapon lent to one by a friend when the friend, after going mad, asked for it back. Clearly in this case, it is necessary to violate an agreement, and Cephalus agreed.[8]

Keeping one's agreements with other individuals, although an important virtue, is not *the* virtue that should be made the basis of all social interactions in the society. More important, by implication, is that one should uphold one's obligations and duties to the larger society. And when one focuses solely on obligations owed to other individuals, it might well be that one overlooks the obligations owed to the larger society. That is what the example of keeping an agreement with a madman shows. Although the madman, in asking for the return of the weapon, may pose no harm to the person who lent it to him, he does pose harm to the society. Thus, owing to the obligation we have to protect society from murder and mayhem, we have no duty to return a weapon to a madman. In a similar fashion, wealthy businessmen such as Cephalus should ponder whether their keeping agreements with each other, in order to make possible greater wealth for themselves, causes harm to the larger society. Clearly, Plato thought it might.

Next, as a definition of justice, Polemarchus suggested the idea that "it is just to give each person what is owed to him."[9] Socrates, after a series of comments and rejoinders with Polemarchus, concluded that justice as described by Polemarchus involved treating "friends well and enemies badly."[10] Socrates flatly rejected this principle for defining justice. For Socrates, justice is clearly a major virtue, and virtues cannot be used to do harm to others. To put this point differently, for Socrates, to use one's skills and abilities to harm another is to use them in a manner that contradicts their purpose. If we are teachers of music we should use our skills to make people musical, not unmusical.[11] To do otherwise would suggest a form of society in which people turned virtue into a license that permitted them to use their best abilities and skills to impair human flourishing. But in a just society, people should use their skills to enhance and to enrich the lives of others.

III. WHAT JUSTICE IS NOT: THRASYMACHUS

But why can it not be argued that helping friends and keeping agreements are important virtues for people to follow? Indeed, are these values not essential to any conception of civic virtue? Plato might certainly answer this question in the affirmative. But his point seems to be that civic virtue is not the same thing as justice, and it is wrong to define the latter in terms of the former. Perhaps, as we will see later, civic virtue contributes to a just society, but, in doing so, it contributes to a value of singular importance, one that signals the overall basic good to which all members of society should be oriented. Here, the value of the highest importance toward which all other values must contribute is justice.

Thus, in criticizing certain approaches to civic virtue, Plato did not intend to deny its importance. This fact is best seen in his treatment of Thrasymachus whose view of justice, as we shall see, would completely deny any respect for civic virtue. Thrasymachus argued that what is just is what the strongest and the most powerful say is just. On this view, there is little room for civic virtue. For civic virtue presumes that people will make sacrifices for the larger good. Thrasymachus's position manifests the arrogance of those who owing to their extraordinary power need never contemplate making sacrifices for the larger good. Rather, people who hold Thrasymachus's view just define the larger good to suit their own interests, thus putting themselves in a position where they never have to manifest civic virtue. The following account of Socrates's discussion with Thrasymachus elaborates on this point.

Thrasymachus's Arguments

Thrasymachus said that each regime has a ruling group, and the ruling party makes laws in its own interest. Furthermore, the ruling party claims that whatever is in its own interest is also in the interest of the whole society. Socrates responded by saying that the ruling powers are fallible and at times they make mistakes and thus put into place policies that are not to their advantage.[12] On this view, it is not always the case, then, that what is in the interest of the stronger is either in their own interest or in the interest of the society. With these arguments, Thrasymachus is now forced to qualify his view of justice, and he no longer can hold that justice is "what the stronger believes to be to his advantage, whether it is in fact to his advantage or not."[13]

Thrasymachus's approach to recoup his position is to qualify what he meant by saying that justice is the interest of the stronger. In particular, Thrasymachus shows that the ruler is stronger because he is much like any other kind of expert—say doctors—in that, like them, owing to expertise, a ruler is not likely to make a mistake.[14] The reason for this view is that, in each case, whether we are talking of a ruler or a doctor, each operates by the knowledge that makes one capable of performing with excellence. Given this view, the ruler is stronger because unlike ordinary citizens the rulers are less likely to make mistakes in ruling, including mistakes that would harm the ruler's interest.

This response prompts a discussion of the nature of a craft, such as medicine. Socrates said that a craft suggests an activity in which a person uses his skills to attain only the purposes of the craft.[15] This means for Socrates that a doctor uses his skills not to advance his own interests, such as making money, but to advance the interests of his patients. In the same way, a ruler, by analogy to other crafts, should use his knowledge to advance the interests of the citizens.[16]

In arguing this view, Socrates suggested that rulers must put aside their own interests and make the interests of the community primary. This commitment is the essence of what constitutes a life of civic virtue. Indeed, for Plato, rulers, like doctors, must exercise their skills so that they are in keeping with a commitment to serve the needs of their community. And thus rulers must not seek "anything other than what is best for the things it rules and cares for, and this is true both of public and private kinds of rule."[17] In consequence, a person concerned with the interests of the citizens does not enter politics to provide for his own advantage or to attain goods such as money and honor, but he enters politics to help those who are weaker than himself.[18] In fact, what draws many lesser people to politics is not what draws the good individual to politics. What attracts the good person to politics is fear of those who see politics as a way to promote their own interest at the cost of the society's interest. Good people fear being ruled by "someone worse than [themselves]." This fear "makes decent people rule when they do."[19]

No reasonable person wants to be ruled by someone whose main purpose in ruling is advancing only his own interests. But that is what Thrasymachus advocated. For Thrasymachus, those who commit acts of injustice are "clever and good." Indeed, for Thrasymachus, those who "are completely unjust" can "bring cities and whole communities under their power."[20] There is great profit in injustice, then.

Socrates attacked this position, arguing that the desire to act unjustly is a defect in the character of people. And the contention that injustice is a defect is easy to prove. Any society that was designed to act for unjust purposes will never succeed because the society will become riddled through and through with hatred and quarreling, thus making it impossible for people to work together as a unified community.[21] This point is very important because the major purpose of any society is to serve the basic needs of its citizens, and a society that is unable to act in a unified fashion cannot possibly achieve this objective. Only people committed to the larger good of the community, those who manifest civic virtue and a concomitant commitment to justice, should be rulers, because it is only these people who can create the conditions that make possible the just, well-ordered society that Plato hoped to achieve.

Another important proof that injustice is an undesirable defect arises from the contention that no person would ever be personally happy were he or she to live one's life outside of a commitment to justice. Why is this? No person wants merely to live, said Socrates, but to live well and living well means being able to perform well one's functions in society. But one cannot perform one's functions well if one's soul has been deprived of the "peculiar virtue" that allows one to execute one's tasks at the level of excellence required for the good performance of a task. The virtue of the soul that enables one to perform well one's function is justice, and thus it follows that "a just soul and a just man will live well." Moreover, this state is desirable for people because one who lives well leads a "blessed and happy" life.[22]

IV. THE NEXT QUESTION: WHAT IS JUSTICE?

Socrates has now demonstrated not only what justice is not, but he has demonstrated, also, that it is far better or advantageous to lead a just life than to lead an unjust one. But Socrates suggested that in making these points he has raised another important question. In particular, he has yet to tell us exactly what justice is. And, since a just life is to be a happy life, if it is not possible to demonstrate the nature of justice and how justice as a virtue contributes to our well being, it will not be possible to demonstrate the basis for a happy life.[23]

Socrates thus felt compelled to demonstrate to Glaucon the definition of justice, intending to show him not only that justice is a good, but that it is "one of the greatest goods."[24] As one of the greatest goods, what kind of good is justice? Justice is a good that not only provides an important result for its holder, but it is important for its own sake as well. Goods that are good for their own sake do not include money, for instance, but they do include "seeing, hearing, knowing, being healthy and all other goods that are fruitful by their own nature and not simply because of reputation."[25] A good that is good for its own sake, then, is one that is so essential to life that it would be impossible to imagine a worthwhile life in the absence of that good. Such is the case with knowing, seeing, and hearing as well as justice. It is for this reason that justice is the basis for a life "blessed with happiness."[26]

But whereas it is intuitively clear to all what knowing, seeing, hearing, and good health are, it is not intuitively clear what justice is. To make a careful representation of justice, it is necessary to turn to sound, rational argument as opposed to intuition.

So what is a just society? What arguments defend the conception of justice Plato supports? In the next sections we will begin to address these questions.

V. THE BASIC DIMENSIONS OF SOCIETY

The early part of the *Republic,* which is a discourse between Socrates and the various individuals we have mentioned, now turns more to a conversation dominated by Socrates. Socrates's intent in this conversation, which involves Glaucon, is to provide a basic lecture on the fundamentals of social organization, and, once he has done that, to build from these fundamentals to develop his conception of justice.

The starting point, then, for describing justice is that, in any society, it is clear that people have basic physical needs and thus they desire those material goods that satisfy these needs. Moreover, people by themselves cannot provide for these needs. So societies are formed for this purpose. In particular, we are told that, to secure the basic requirements of the citizens for food, shelter, and clothing, society needs a class of working people including farmers, builders, and weavers.[27] There also must be a marketplace where citizens can purchase the various goods that the different groups produce. Money is invented to facilitate exchanges. In the market setting, there are many merchants and retailers or shopkeepers trading their goods for money. These are people "whose bodies are the weakest and who aren't fit to do any other kind of work."[28]

In this setting, all the basic needs that people have are cared for, and people live a long, peaceful, and healthy life in a just society, which they bequeath to their children. But Glaucon suggests to Socrates that Socrates's city is not satisfactory because people will want luxuries as well as having their basic needs satisfied.[29] Socrates thought that the city built on serving basic needs is the "true and healthy city." But he conceded the need to include in his discussion of a model for a just city what presumably some people want: namely, in addition to providing for basic needs a city must provide luxuries, as well. Socrates called this city the city with a "fever." Here, Socrates described a city in which some people will seek to have fine clothes and good food. In addition, some people seek to have comfortable and decorated furniture, as well as prostitutes for sexual pleasure. Also, there will be people to provide art, music, and dance, as well as goods such as jewelry.[30] In order to enjoy these goods, people will have to have leisure time, and this dimension is secured by providing them with a class of servants, including tutors and cooks who take care of the day-to-day necessities of life.[31] Finally, and most tragically, the quest for luxuries becomes the main motive for war as people, in the search for the "endless acquisition of money" for the sake of luxuries, seek to take each other's resources.[32]

In accepting that the pursuit of wealth and money is the essential motivation in society, Plato certainly accepted the notion of private ownership. Being able to have exclusive ownership to property provides one with an incentive to perform the necessary work that produces both basic goods and luxuries. Still, Plato did not intend to make a conception of society that emphasized the pursuit of wealth and luxury the basis for defining a just order. As we can see from his view of the origin of war, which emanates from the constant pursuit of wealth, Plato clearly feared making appetite the main motivating and dominant force in society. To avoid this circumstance, appetite—in this case the quest for luxuries and wealth embodied in private property ownership—must be limited by the constraints of reason. Here, property ownership need not symbolize the unlimited pursuit of appetite, but a willingness to use one's property in ways that support the common good. To achieve a society with this possibility, Plato discussed the role of the guardians.

VI. THE GUARDIANS AND THE THREE PARTS OF THE SOUL

As we have mentioned, Plato distinguished three parts to the soul. In addition to the rational part that deliberates with the intention to determine truth, there is the part referred to as appetite and the spirited part. The appetite, says Socrates, "is the largest part in each person's soul and is by nature most insatiable for money." Moreover the appetite is motivated by the "pleasures of the body."[33] Still, the appetite can be made subject to the commands of reason. One basis for this contention is the presence of the spirited part. Socrates views the spirited part as the "helper of the rational part," or as the dimension of the soul committed to see that the rational conception of good order is realized.[34] Socrates says, "I don't think you can say that you've ever seen spirit, either in yourself or anyone else, ally itself with an appetite to do what reason has decided must not be done."[35] In resisting appetite but in promoting the goals of reason, the spirited part manifests courage because, in holding steadfast to the "declarations of reason about what is to be feared and what isn't," the spirited part enables individuals to endure the pain of promoting the reasonable course.[36] Here, the spirited part signifies a desire to win honor from others for upholding the common good.

Moreover, for Socrates, the spirited part must be "rightly nurtured," lest instead of courage it manifests itself as "hard and harsh."[37] In this case, as opposed to working for the goals of reason, it might work against them. This view suggests that the spirited element is a fierce sort of passion or emotion that, if improperly developed, harms instead of helps the quest to realize the common good.

There are several other important implications to be gleaned here as well. First, Plato is not saying that the appetite can or should be completely suppressed. Still, however, the appetite must be constrained by reason and the spirited part, lest appetite lead to a situation in which individuals are prone, as Socrates says, to seek to "enslave and rule over the classes it isn't fit to rule, thereby overturning everyone's whole life."[38] Here, those who are motivated by their appetite to acquire wealth and luxuries, for instance, must accept the regimen of a society that requires them to conduct their lives in keeping with the norms established by reason.

The problem, then, for Plato, and this is the second important implication of his three-part view of the soul, is to harness both the appetite and the spirited part so that each serves the goals posited by reason. To this end, Plato emphasized the importance of a special class of citizens, whom he called *guardians*.

Now, there are different types of guardians, and furthermore, guardians have two major functions, ruling and guarding the city. The "best of the guardians," as Socrates referred to them, are rulers.[39] Those guardians, who have acted as both rulers and as protectors of the city, presumably through military exploits, are referred to as "complete guardians." Younger people, who show promise of being guardians in the future, but who have as yet not proved themselves capable of being "complete guardians," are called *auxiliaries* who act as assistants to the guardians.[40] The auxiliaries assist the guardians by supporting their objectives and helping to carry them out.[41] The auxiliaries would certainly help the guardians fulfill their military duties. In the latter role, guardians would manifest courage and a desire for honor, as well as the various skills associated with soldiering. For Plato, it is a mistake to believe that people, who have expertise in other areas of life, say as farmers or craftsmen will also have the knowledge and skill needed to be good warriors. In all cases, the "complete guardians" act from an unstinting commitment to protect the society from "external enemies and internal friends."[42]

Moreover, guardians must be properly educated so that they are able to perform their functions well. Here, Plato's key point is that, without a proper system of training, individuals will not attain the appropriate degree of civic virtue that will enable them to act in the best interests of society. Speaking specifically of the auxiliaries, for instance, who possess military prowess, it is important to make certain that they do not use that power against the best interests of the people they are supposed to protect.[43] Indeed, we are told that guardians will "be gentle to their own people and harsh to the enemy."[44] That is why to the question, Who will guard the guardians?, Plato would certainly answer, no one will have to, because the guardians, owing to proper education, are the model of rational self-command.

Plato, in discussing the guardians, had in mind people who could be trusted with great power and authority, and yet ordinary citizens would never fear that they would harm society. The guardians, as rulers or as soldiers, are the moral saviors of the society because they act always and only for the common good. Finding them will be a society's greatest challenge. Children will have to be watched and monitored to determine whether they demonstrate guardian traits, to be either rulers or auxiliaries.[45] This view suggests that, when proper candidates for a guardian life are found, they must be separated from the rest of the society. This will be necessary in order to raise these people independently from the ordinary influences that, if not properly controlled, would tend to deny the proper training that makes both the appetite and the spirit subject to reason.

Thus, guardians, unlike ordinary people, own no private property, accumulate no luxury, live in common with other guardians, and are not allowed to have their own families. Within guardian communities, each parent is the parent of all the children. No parent claims a child as his or her own, nor does any parent claim a special status for children he or she helped to conceive.[46] Were people to do so, guardians would identify too closely with "their" own children. And this would cause guardians to define their objectives in a narrower way than would be healthy for society. Guardians are not to place the needs of their own children above those of others and certainly not above the needs of the whole community. The words *mine* and *not mine* for Socrates must have reference only to what the community as a whole defines as *mine* and *not mine*. When these words refer to any particular individual's preferences, then that person's ability to support the common good will be very weak.[47]

Each person who is a guardian must orient oneself to support the good of the community. Such individuals will not be limited to men, but will include consideration of women as guardians, also. In support of this position, Plato even suggested that the relationship between the sexes should be different for guardians from what this relationship entails for ordinary citizens. Male guardians should be willing to accept the view that some women have the ability to perform all essential guardian functions and those women who have this ability should be given the same opportunity as men to be guardians.[48] Now, Socrates's position in comparing men and women is to accept the general prejudice of his age and to say that on the whole men are superior to women. He says in discussing various life activities that "in all of them women are weaker than men" or, in other terms, women perform them less well than men. However, there will be some women who have guardian natures, and these women, even if weaker than men, are "adequate for the task" and should be allowed to be guardians.[49]

Why, if Plato had such a patronizing view toward women, did he grant them the opportunity to be guardians? Perhaps, Plato's actual intention in according women a place in society as guardians was to reduce their sexual importance to men. Here, as men look upon women as partners in a common enterprise, possibly they will not seek to conquer women sexually. In this case, Plato's commitment to sexual equality for guardians was merely a way to check male sexual aggressiveness, which, if unleashed, would make the appetite the primary factor and deny respect for reason. Plato argued on behalf of women's being allowed to be guardians for reasons of securing a society committed to the common good and not because he was principally a proponent of gender equality.

The commitment to the common good and the need to create a special class of people able to bring about this great goal make it necessary for the introduction of manipulative techniques regarding marriage and childbearing. Marriages among guardians will be regulated in order to match people with the best combination of qualities to each other. To make this outcome possible, there will be lotteries in which people choose their mates, but these lotteries will be rigged so that the best people are matched together. And further, even though the number of children will be regulated by the rulers, those men who are successful in war will be able to have sex more frequently so that they can father as many children as possible. This will ensure a larger and better stock of children.[50] For others, full sexual freedom is regained after they have passed the childbearing age. In this case, people can have sex with anyone they chose to have sex with, but if they should conceive a child by accident, their offspring would be killed.[51]

VII. THE PHILOSOPHER AS KING

For Socrates (or Plato, who, as we have said, speaks through Socrates), the "best of the guardians" must be rulers, and, to this end, must train for the life of philosophy, which will be a major part of a ruler's life. Socrates argued that "future rulers" must, in childhood, be offered basic training in geometry and mathematical calculation as well as all other topics needed to prepare them to engage in dialectical thinking.[52]

Not everyone will be permitted to complete the course that leads to elevation to philosopher/ruler. Indeed, Socrates sought individuals who could use dialectical thinking to construct a unified and true picture of the reality under study, or, as in *The Republic,* of a just society. Those individuals with this ability will be screened from the rest and when they reach the age of 30 they will undergo training in the techniques of dialectical argument. Socrates did not want to have those who are capable of philosophy trained in dialectical argument younger than age 30 because he feared that when people are exposed to the techniques of argument as young persons they will employ these techniques merely to demonstrate an ability to refute other arguments. Such people merely seek to best others in argument as opposed to using argument to find truth.[53] But Socrates said that "an older person won't want to take part in such madness. He'll imitate someone who is willing to engage in discussion in order to look for the truth, rather than someone who plays at contradiction for sport."[54]

Again, those who are capable of dialectical thinking will be selected for training in the dialectic at the age of 30. After five years of training in this endeavor, in which they learn how to find truth, the future ruler will be sent into the "cave," a term for ordinary society, to live with average people. In the cave, future rulers take part in military matters "and occupy the other offices suitable for young people, so that they won't be inferior to the others in experience. But in these, too, they must be tested to see whether they'll remain steadfast when they're pulled this way or that or shift their ground."[55] A person will undergo this experience for 15 years and then at the age of 50 these individuals will be permitted to spend most of their time with philosophy, but, as Socrates said, "when his turn comes, he must labor in politics and rule for the city's sake."[56] These individuals, both men and women alike, will be given the task of putting "the city, its citizens, and themselves in order."[57]

Socrates said that, until "philosophers rule as kings" or until kings act as philosophers, it will be impossible to marry power to philosophy and thus create cities bent upon avoiding evil and achieving good.[58] Why are philosophers especially suited for linking power and morality? The answer lies in their character. Philosophers are gentle people, they are not cowardly or slavish, they are lovers of knowledge, they are not desirous of money or luxuries, and they learn quickly and with ease.[59] When power is placed into the hands of people with these characteristics, we can be assured that it will not be used to advance a quest for personal wealth. But instead power will be used to support, in a steadfast and courageous way, a desire to make sure that the goods defined by reason are made the main objective of society.

VIII. Justice, Civic Virtue, and the Noble Lie

To make possible a society in which an ethical order based on reason can be achieved, the guardians need to provide a basic education that teaches children civic virtue.[60] In particular, children must be taught the importance of law-abiding behavior if they are to mature into law-abiding people. To this end, children must take part in games that teach the importance of respect for law, and music and poetry must be designed for the same reason. Respect for lawfulness is also taught by learning to accept the authority of one's elders and by being taught to care for one's parents.[61] When people are filled with good habits such as these, they are likely, from their own volition, to maintain conduct that contributes to the basic good of the society. Furthermore, these people will know what is best for the city and, in consequence, what laws need to be legislated. Indeed, for Socrates, when right conduct is not a part of the ingrained civic outlook of people, efforts to achieve good ends for the city through legislation will always fall short of the mark. The reason for this is that people who lack the habits of civic virtue are like "sick people" who are prone to the extremes of appetite, and thus they are not likely to listen to those who warn against the harmful effects of lechery, drunkenness, and overeating.[62]

Once a basic commitment to civic virtue or a general respect for the common good of the society is in place, then the city has been properly established and a basis exists for the flourishing of other critical virtues in the city: wisdom, courage, moderation, and justice.[63] It is clear that these basic virtues are linked so that justice, the highest and most important of the four, cannot exist unless the others do. To explain this point, I will describe each virtue in turn.

Wisdom, Courage, Moderation, and Justice

First take *wisdom.* In discussing wisdom, Socrates distinguished between the knowledge possessed by particular craftsmen and the kind of knowledge needed to govern a state. Those who possess the latter kind of knowledge, the philosophers, have the knowledge necessary to understand what is needed to secure a well-ordered city, including how to create good relations internally as well as between the city and other cities.[64] *Courage* is a capacity that enables people to maintain a steadfast commitment to uphold the basic values given to society by those who make the laws. Here, the laws embody fundamental beliefs that society is to protect, and individuals who manifest courage uphold these values, regardless of any particular difficulties or pains such actions may entail.[65] *Moderation* is a third important virtue, and it suggests "self-control" or the ability to constrain our desires so that they do not rule our lives. Possessing moderation, individuals are not given to extreme modes of behavior, and in consequence the different parts of the society are more able to co-exist together in harmonious and cooperative relationships.[66] A city that possesses moderation "makes the weakest, the strongest, and those in between—whether in regard to reason, physical strength, numbers, wealth, or anything else—all sing the same song together."[67] Where moderation is the norm, each is able to contribute to the common needs of the society, and the quest for luxury or any other desire is not allowed to defeat this objective.

These values create the setting that is conducive to *justice,* the fourth essential virtue. Justice is mentioned last after the first three virtues because it is clear that the first three prepare the ground for justice. Indeed, Socrates said that justice would be what was "left over in the city when moderation, courage, and wisdom have been found."[68] Given this view of the relationship among the basic virtues, how would this relationship be rendered into concrete, practical terms to define the vision of a just society? A city with moderation, courage, and wisdom is just because each person has a role for which he or she is best qualified and, in performing that role well, each contributes in essential ways to the community's common good. Socrates's view was that "everyone must practice one of the occupations . . . for which he is naturally best suited."[69] This state of affairs represents the condition of a just society. As Socrates said, "this doing one's own work . . . is justice."[70] Indeed, a just society is one in which "each does his own work and doesn't meddle with what is other people's" and this value, the value of doing one's own work, "rivals wisdom, moderation and courage in its contribution to the virtue of the city."[71]

A society in which each person makes a contribution to the good of the whole, in keeping with one's basic abilities and skills, is a society that manifests what might be called *external justice.* Clearly, for Plato such a state is predicated upon a *meritocratic principle* of each person's being assigned to those tasks for which one is, as Socrates says, "best suited." Here, the workers should carry out the particular skills of their respective crafts, the auxiliaries should perform well their warrior role, and the philosophers should be good rulers.

The problem with maintaining this principle is how best to persuade people of its truth. After all, as a consequence of adhering to the norms of Plato's just society, some will be given more important tasks than will others, so how will those on the bottom of society accept this outcome? Socrates's answer was to invoke a lie in the name of securing justice. Here, it would seem that, in addition to learning the habits of basic civic virtue as a way to encourage people to contribute to the common good, a citizen must be made to believe a falsehood about the reason that justice is a worthy value. Obviously, then, the habits of civic virtue, such as law-abiding behavior, are by themselves not sufficient to secure support for the ways of life of a just society.

Thus, Socrates referred to a "noble falsehood" that could be used to persuade the rulers and the people in the city of the importance of all people's accepting the role in society for which they are most naturally suited. According to the falsehood that Socrates would teach, even though "all in the city are brothers," the god who created people placed a different metal in each person. He put gold into those who would be rulers; silver into those who would be auxiliaries; and iron and bronze into those who would be farmers and craftsmen (workers). Moreover, god engineered people so that they would, for the most part, produce children like themselves. Still, it is possible that children with silver or bronze metal will be born from a gold parent or vice versa. When this event occurs it is god's intention that people be placed into positions in society appropriate to their abilities and coincident with the particular metal of their souls. For instance, if it is the case that the children of rulers are found to have a soul with bronze, then these people should be placed into the farmer or worker class. On the other hand, if the offspring of the worker class have gold in their souls, they should be given training to become rulers.[72]

A lie can be noble and thus worthy if it is used for a good reason. And Plato would no doubt envision several good reasons for his noble lie. The first good reason, as just indicated, is that the lie maintains support for the external justice of a meritocracy. Another good reason for the lie is that it encourages what underlies external justice, namely, the proper ordering or the arranging of the key elements of the soul: reason, appetite, and spirit. I call this condition of the soul *internal justice,* and it represents a condition of mind that is the highest-order possibility of human life, a condition that the just city secures.

What is internal justice or the justice of the soul, and why is it such a valuable condition? Each of the parts of the soul has its own objectives and, in achieving these objectives, one is able to attain the pleasure associated with that part. Thus, in realizing the objectives of the spirited part, one receives the pleasures associated with manifesting the courage to uphold the common good; in realizing the objectives of the appetite one realizes pleasures associated with receiving money. But for Socrates when one's focus is entirely upon either of these dimensions to the exclusion of the direction provided by one's reason, or what Socrates refers to as "those pleasures that reason approves" of, then one does not "attain the truest possible pleasures" associated with the appetite and the spirited part of the soul.[73] For instance, take a situation where either the spirited part or the appetite is made so central in one's life that the importance of reason is downplayed. Here, a person pursuing the objectives of the spirited part of the soul, outside the direction of reason, may become so desirous of success in battle that he becomes overly violent and loses the ability to make decisions that would bring about the victory he seeks. Or, a person whose only quest in life is to accumulate money may end up having no regard for the goods that reason stipulates, and, in consequence, such a person may destroy all relationships with others who love him.

Moreover, when a person allows himself to become maniacally dedicated to the objectives of the spirited part and the appetite at the same time, he may set in motion two powerful desires, each warring with the other. For instance, a person desirous of both showing courage and having money may find that to have the former he may have to sacrifice the quest for money. But the appetite may demand that one's quest to demonstrate courage and dedication to the common good take a back seat to money. In this case, the quest to serve society is always at war with the urge for money. In contrast, when a person allows his reason or philosophical part to have the upper hand, this tragedy is avoided. For Socrates, "therefore, when the entire soul follows the philosophic part, and there is no civil war in it, each part of it does its own work exclusively and is just, and in particular it enjoys its own pleasures, the best and truest pleasures possible for it."[74]

Now a well-ordered and balanced soul brings happiness to the individual, but, in addition, such a soul is able to make an important contribution to maintaining the well-ordered character of society. Here, owing to the fact that the appetite and the spirited part are under the direction of the philosophic part, it follows that individuals maintain an internal balance to their personalities that would permit them to be able to perform well the various tasks for which they are best suited. The internal justice of the soul is linked to and supports the external justice of a meritocratic life.

Given this account of internal justice, for Socrates it is now understandable why it is best for "everyone to be ruled by divine reason, preferably within himself and his own, otherwise imposed from without, so that as far as possible all will be alike and friends, governed by the same thing."[75] It must be clear that, to attain this objective, the real city is not so much the external city in which people live their daily lives, although it is of course that, too. But the real city is the properly arranged soul, and unless this state of mind is possible, there will be no happiness or external justice. As Socrates said, "it's also our aim in ruling our children, we don't allow them to be free until we establish a constitution in them, just as in a city, and by—fostering their best part with our own—equip them with a guardian and ruler similar to our own to take our place. Then, and only then, we set them free."[76] When the city reaches this stage, the habits of civic virtue—which contribute to each citizen's ability to support the common good by upholding basic virtues such as moderation, courage, wisdom, and justice—as well as Plato's noble falsehood have both paved the way not only for a good constitution in the state, but an equally good one in the soul of each individual.

IX. DEMOCRACY AND INJUSTICE

The hope for the good city must be contrasted with the reality of the bad ones. For Plato, timocracy, oligarchy, and democracy are corrupted regimes that propel society in the direction of tyranny. The implications for people are severe and tragic. In what follows, I provide a brief summary of Plato's argument. To understand Plato's account, it is important to recognize that regimes are distinguished by the fact that different characteristics of the soul come to dominate them. In the best city, the Republic, the faculty of reason is preeminent. But in the lesser regimes, either the spirited part of the soul or the appetite dominates.[77]

In a *timocracy,* the spirited part dominates and thus the regime is dedicated to make honor, courage, and the love of military victory the main objective.[78] This situation results from the dueling tendencies in a timocracy. On the one hand, there are those who seek to acquire wealth, and on the other there are those who manifest aristocratic tendencies and who want to govern by virtue. A civil war breaks out between the two groups, but it ends with a compromise that permits private property in land and the enslavement of peasants to work the land. In addition, war-related activities become a main aspect of life. The individuals appointed as rulers will be "spirited and simpler" people who will spend their time engaging in war as a means for gaining honor from others. Further, they will satisfy their own appetites with other people's money, while saving their own. Still, of the two passions—that for money and honor—the latter dominates, and thus there is continual quest for military victory. In this setting, there is no interest in making philosophy and the rational dimension of the soul count for much in society.[79]

The next regime is *oligarchy,* a regime in which "victory-loving and honor-loving people become lovers of making money, or money lovers."[80] Here, the appetite takes over as money is valued more than virtue, and the wealthy people are admired and made the rulers. Indeed, the political system is designed so that only people with property may hold office and the poor have no opportunity to rule, even if a poor person could do a better job.[81] A major characteristic of this kind of society is that money is not used to support a life of luxury so much as it is used to satisfy necessary needs or appetites, and the rest of the money one accumulates from the profits of one's enterprises is hoarded.[82] Also, in this kind of society in which money is worshipped and virtue is lost sight of many people avoid responsibility for their own lives. In consequence, some sell all they own to others, and by doing so many people no longer have the means or are willing to perform essential functions as workers and craftsmen, and, instead, they become poor people without the means to make a living. These people become "drones," who must live off the labor of others. Some do so as beggars and others do so as "evildoers" who commit crimes and become thieves and pickpockets.[83]

Naturally the poor become resentful of the rich, and the poor see the rich as undeserving of their station. When the poor overthrow the rich, they establish a *democracy.* Here, each person is given a chance to take part in ruling the city.[84] Democracies quickly become societies in which the appetite, in this case not just for basic or necessary needs, but for unnecessary goods (or goods such as luxuries that people could live without), is allowed unlimited freedom. In an atmosphere of "general permissiveness," individuals lack sufficient self-control and all pleasures are declared to be of equal value. Indeed, the democrat cannot distinguish between "fine and good desires" and those that are "evil." The democrat pursues whatever desire is at hand, and there is no basis for establishing a rational order to life. But the democrat calls this way of life free and happy, when in fact this way of life is a passport to "extreme slavery" or tyranny.[85]

Finally, there is *tyranny.* The latter evolves from democracy, and it is associated with a form of appetite that is "lawless," because it promotes desires that, in addition to being unnecessary, will not accept the discipline of reason.[86] The setting that culminates in the rule of the appetite not subject to the discipline of reason is characterized by an "insatiable desire for freedom."[87] Indeed, Socrates blames an extreme desire for freedom for the emergence of tyranny.[88] In this setting, the ruling class consists of people who can make no useful contributions to society, the "drones" who were part of oligarchic life. The ruling drones seek to maintain power by currying favor with the common people. To this end, the ruling class postures as the champion of the people against the rich, and thus the ruling class promises to take money from the rich and give it to the people. However, the ruling drones keep for themselves the largest part of the money that they take from the rich.[89] The rich complain before the common people while the ruling drones accuse the rich of plotting to hurt the ordinary people. The rich, in turn, fearing that the ordinary people will side with the ruling drones, react by becoming like oligarchs and demand rule by the rich. All of this feuding culminates in both the rich and the drones being charged with crimes and being put on trial.[90] In the midst of this general disorder, the people decide to set up one person as their champion. The latter becomes a tyrant when he dominates the "docile mob" and resorts to violent and coercive tactics, including inciting a civil war against the rich.[91] Ultimately, the people realize they have created a monster, and they thus order him to leave the city, but he refuses and he uses violence to retain control.[92]

The story just described demonstrates that when civic virtue is eroded and, in consequence, the great virtues such as justice, moderation, courage, and wisdom are no longer a part of the life of the city, appetite in its various forms and with its harmful effects rules a city. In the context of what Plato described, it is best for cities to follow a just course.

However, the good consequences of justice and the terrible ones following injustice exist not only for cities, but they exist for individuals as well. Socrates concluded the

Republic by making clear the nature of the personal advantages of leading a just life and the disadvantages for individuals of leading an unjust life. Thus, Socrates argued that the gods will always help a just person in need "either during his lifetime or afterwards," because the gods "never neglect anyone who eagerly wishes to become just."[93] Socrates asked whether it is not true that just people "enjoy a good reputation and collect the prizes from other human beings?"[94] In contrast, Socrates said the unjust person will become "wretched," and he will be "ridiculed." Indeed, the unjust will be "beaten with whips, and made to suffer those punishments, such as racking and burning, which you rightly described as crude."[95]

This fate awaits the unjust person in the life to come, as well. In his discussion of the Myth of Er, Socrates gave an account of the terror and pain that await unjust individuals in the afterlife. He cautioned Glaucon to practice justice and to act in accordance with reason in every way, so that he will be able to receive the rewards from the gods while on earth and after his death. In this case, Socrates concluded, "we'll do well and be happy."[96]

The account Socrates provided here suggests that, if people cannot be persuaded to act justly through a reasoned discourse as he had provided throughout the *Republic,* then perhaps a picture of the terrible pains they will suffer for acting unjustly will frighten people into a life of justice. Fear, then, may achieve what reason cannot.

X. Plato and Civil Society

Plato's political theory is an account of justice both in the society and in the individual. This struggle for justice does not have to include, as it later will, the need to integrate into society the idea of people as free and equal moral persons, subject to rules that all accept as a condition for their common equality. Instead, justice must culminate in a city that encourages the proper arrangement of the essential parts of the soul. Here, individuals will not have equal rights as in the modern world. Still, there is a commitment to give to each person something of great import, a life whose essential elements are in concord with each other. When the souls of persons are properly constituted, they can contribute in essential and necessary ways to society, making possible a just order. For Plato, only when there is justice in the individual can there be justice in society.

What are the implications of this view for civil society? At first glance, the answer to this question might suggest a pessimistic answer. If by a civil society we mean a setting that contains both a separate sphere of voluntary associations, as well as an overarching commitment to shared norms such as respect for both the freedom and rights of individuals, then Plato's republic would certainly find these arrangements unacceptable. After all, a separate sphere of voluntary groups, acting independently of the ruler, in this case philosopher king, would make it difficult for the state to have a central role in coordinating the activities of the different classes, so that overall the common good could be achieved. Indeed, Plato's guardians, who raise children in common and whose marriages are arranged by an elite group of rulers, would find the civil society setting intolerable. Similar rejection of civil society would be manifested by Plato's guardian/rulers, who had no difficulty resorting to the manipulative techniques associated with Plato's "noble falsehood."

On the other hand, there is a sense in which Plato's arguments, at least indirectly, suggest the need for a civil society. For the fact is that Plato's philosopher king establishes the role of an independent spokesperson for truth. Clearly, the philosopher class, especially as manifested by the actions of Socrates and by Plato's depiction of the truth-seeking individual, can function well only if it has the freedom that permits it independence from all external shaping influences and forces. Truth seeking thrives in an environment free from unruly emotions, as well as external efforts by tyrants to coerce thought. Plato's philosopher king could flourish only in a society that provides a separate sphere, operating within a larger moral environment that is dedicated to securing individual rights and those civic virtues that make such rights possible. Thus, whereas Plato's philosopher king might not advocate a civil society, it is hard to imagine how he could survive without one.

Of course to the last argument, it could be claimed that the philosopher king would not be able to achieve his or her objectives except in the special setting of Plato's Republic. Only in a setting in which society is organized to make certain that political rule is reserved for those with the highest wisdom will the philosophers ever feel capable of engaging in philosophy. Outside of this type of society, no philosopher would be secure enough to practice philosophy. What reasons support this position? First, truth seeking threatens existing norms, and often when contemporary opinions are challenged, those who do so are considered liabilities to the society, and in this circumstance made subject to forms of intolerance and social exclusion. Thus, only in Plato's Republic, where society is designed to protect the philosopher, could the philosopher be free to practice his or her art. Second, it is only in Plato's Republic where the system of education can be designed to develop the philosophical acumen of individuals. In societies where matters other than philosophy are emphasized, matters such as the pursuit of money or pleasure or even rights, for instance, a person with philosophical ability will never be able to develop one's basic philosophical talent. But Plato's Republic will ensure a place where the training for philosophy will always supplant in importance all other activities and interests.

The civil society proponent would respond by arguing that a civil society can protect philosophers from mob intolerance, and it can also provide the training people must have to become philosophers. To say otherwise is to place philosophy in jeopardy by having to associate it with a form of elite life that menaces the basic freedoms a civil society protects and that the life of philosophy surely needs.

Endnotes

1. George H. Sabine, *A History of Political Theory*, (New York: Holt, Rinehart, and Winston, 1963), pp. 4–9, 15. Also, Sibley, *Political Ideas and Ideologies*, p. 44.

2. Sabine, *A History of Political Theory*, p. 14.

3. Ibid., p. 15.

4. Ibid., p. 23.

5. Ibid., pp. 33–34, 15.

6. In discussing Plato's views in the *Republic* I will, in referring to Plato's views, use Socrates's name at times because the latter is the main figure in the *Republic* and, indeed, Socrates can be viewed as reflecting Plato's views in the *Republic*. Also, the translation I am using is that by

G.M.A. Grube, *Plato's Republic*, 2nd edition revised by C.D.C. Reeve, (Indianapolis: Hackett Publishing Co., 1992). References are to the standard numbers used in all texts.

7. Ibid., pp. 4–5, 330b–d.

8. Ibid., pp. 5–6, 331c–331d.

9. Ibid., p. 6, 331e.

10. Ibid., p. 7, 332e.

11. Ibid., pp. 10–11, 335a–e.

12. Ibid., pp. 14–15, 338c–339c.

13. Ibid., p. 16, 340c.

14. Ibid., pp. 16–17, 340e–341a.

15. Ibid., p. 18, 342b–c.
16. Ibid., pp. 18–19, 342c–e.
17. Ibid., p. 21, 345d.
18. Ibid., p. 22, 346e; p. 23, 347b.
19. Ibid., p. 23, 347c.
20. Ibid., p. 24, 348d; p. 27, 350c.
21. Ibid., p. 28, 351d–352a.
22. Ibid., p. 31, 353e, 354a.
23. Ibid., p. 31, 354b–c.
24. Ibid., p. 42, 367d; p. 33, 357a–c, p. 34, 358a.
25. Ibid., p. 42, 367d.
26. Ibid., p. 34, 358a.
27. Ibid., p. 44, 369d.
28. Ibid., p. 46, 371b–d.
29. Ibid., pp. 47–48, 372d–e.
30. Ibid., p. 48, 373a–c.
31. Ibid., p. 48., 373c.
32. Ibid., p. 48, 373d–e.
33. Ibid., p. 118, 442b. See "Introduction" to Grube edition of *The Republic,* p. xv.
34. *Republic,* p. 116, 441a.
35. Ibid., p. 116, 440b.
36. Ibid., p. 118, 442c; p. 50, 375b.
37. Ibid., p. 87, 410d.
38. Ibid., p. 118, 442b.
39. Ibid., p. 89, 412c.
40. Ibid., pp. 90–91, 414a–c.
41. Ibid., p. 90, 414b.
42. Ibid., pp. 49–50, 374c–375a, p. 90, 414b.
43. Ibid., p. 92, 416a–c.
44. Ibid., p. 50, 375b–c.
45. Ibid., p. 90, 414a.
46. Ibid., pp. 92–93, 416b–c, p. 136, 461d–e, pp. 138–39, 464a–e.
47. Ibid., pp. 136–37, 462c–d.
48. Ibid., p. 130, 456b.
49. Ibid., p. 129, 455c–e, p. 130, 456a–b.
50. Ibid., p. 134, 459e–460c.
51. Ibid., p. 135, 461c. There are other limitations. A man is not to have sex with his daughter, mother, his daughter's children, or his mother's relatives, and a woman is not to have sex with her son or any of his children or her father and his relatives.
52. Ibid., pp. 208–09, 536d–537d.
53. Ibid., p. 209, 537c–d, p. 211, 539b–d.
54. Ibid., p. 211, 539c–d.
55. Ibid., p. 211, 539d–e, also, p. 209, 537d.
56. Ibid., p. 212, 540b.
57. Ibid., p. 212, 540b.
58. Ibid., p. 148, 473d.
59. Ibid., pp. 158–60, 485a, 485e, 486b–d.
60. Ibid., p. 99, 424a. My interpretation of civic virtue follows Grube's view, p. 94.
61. Ibid., p. 100, 424d–425b.
62. Ibid., pp. 100–01, 425d–426b.
63. Ibid., p. 102, 427d.
64. Ibid., pp. 103–04, 428b–429a.
65. Ibid., p. 104, 429b–d.
66. Ibid., pp. 106–07, 430e–432a.
67. Ibid., p. 107, 432a.
68. Ibid., p. 108, 433b.
69. Ibid., p. 108, 433a.
70. Ibid., p. 108, 433b, p. 109, 433e.
71. Ibid., p. 108, 433c–e.
72. Ibid., pp. 91–92, 414c–415d.
73. Ibid., pp. 257–58, 586d, also 586c.
74. Ibid., p. 258, 586e.
75. Ibid., p. 262, 590d.
76. Ibid., p. 262, 590d–591a.
77. Ibid., p. 214, 544d.
78. Ibid., p. 215, 545b, p. 218, 548d.
79. Ibid., pp. 217–18, 547b–548d.
80. Ibid., p. 221, 551a.
81. Ibid., p. 221, 551b–c.
82. Ibid., p. 224, 554a.
83. Ibid., p. 223, 552d–e; p. 222, 552a–c.
84. Ibid., p. 227, 556d, 557a.
85. Ibid., pp. 231–32, 561b–d; also, p. 234, 563e–564a.
86. Ibid., p. 232, 562a, pp. 241–42, 571b–c.
87. Ibid., pp. 232–33, 562c.
88. Ibid., p. 234, 563e–564a.
89. Ibid., pp. 235–36, 564d–565b.
90. Ibid., p. 236, 565b–c.
91. Ibid., p. 236, 565d–566a.
92. Ibid., p. 240, 569a–b.
93. Ibid., p. 284, 613a.
94. Ibid., p. 284, 613c.
95. Ibid., p. 285, 613d.
96. Ibid., p. 292, 621d, p. 287, 615d–616a.

Partial Bibliography and Further Reading

Barker, Ernest, Sir. *The Political Thought of Plato and Aristotle.* New York: Russell & Russell, 1959.

Buchan, Morag. *Women in Plato's Political Theory.* New York: Routledge, 1999.

Euben, J. Peter. *The Tragedy of Political Theory: The Road Not Taken.* Princeton, N.J.: Princeton University Press, 1990.

Gulley, Norman. *Plato's Theory of Knowledge.* London, Methuen; New York, Barnes & Noble Books, 1973.

Lycos, Kimon. *Plato on Justice and Power: Reading Book*

I of Plato's Republic. Albany, New York: State University of New York Press, 1987.

Mara, Gerald M. *Socrates' Discursive Democracy: Logos and Ergon in Platonic Political Philosophy.* Albany: State University of New York Press, 1997.

Melling, David J. *Understanding Plato.* Oxford; New York: Oxford University Press, 1987.

Nehamas, Alexander. *Virtues of Authenticity: Essays on Plato and Socrates.* Princeton, N.J.: Princeton University Press, 1999.

Reeve, C.D.C. *Philosopher-Kings: The Argument of Plato's Republic,* Princeton, N.J.: Princeton University Press, 1988.

Seung, T. K. Plato *Rediscovered: Human Value and Social Order.* Lanham, Md.: Rowman & Littlefield Publishers, 1996.

Strauss, Leo. *Studies in Platonic Political Philosophy.* with an introduction by Thomas L. Pangle. Chicago: University of Chicago Press, 1983.

Wood, Ellen Meiksins, and Wood, Neal. *Class Ideology and Ancient Political Theory: Socrates, Plato, and Aristotle in Social Context.* Oxford: B. Blackwell, 1978.

Zeitlin, Irving M. *The Classical Origins of Social and Political Thought.* New Jersey: Prentice Hall, 1993.

3

Aristotle's Response to Plato:
The Importance of Friendship

I. Introduction

Aristotle (384–322 B.C.E.) became Plato's student in 367 B.C.E. and for twenty years continued an association with Plato. During this time, Aristotle's thought was heavily shaped by Plato's views, and, as John Morrall says, Aristotle "never entirely renounced" Plato's influence.[1] Thus, Aristotle no less than Plato divided the soul into two parts, the rational and the nonrational. The former is the higher part because it is grounded in reason, and the other part, which includes the world of appetite and desire, is nonetheless capable of obeying the requirements of reason.[2] Owing to this basic, shared assumption, both argued that the state must educate its citizens to understand as well as to act in keeping with a view of society that embodies the best achievements of the rational part of life. Indeed, civic virtue, the commitment to the common good, pertains to those habits that enable one to uphold the qualities of a rational life.

Still, over his career, Aristotle did take steps to revise some of the main elements of Plato's political vision. Aristotle's departures from Plato had to do with Aristotle's intention to draw a more comprehensive picture of the rational way of life than he thought Plato had done. Aristotle thus hoped to enlarge Plato's vision of society, so that it included what Aristotle thought Plato had omitted.

To provide an overview as to how Aristotle approached this objective, it is necessary to review an essential element of Plato's Republic. Plato's Republic, in establishing the reign of reason in a just society including of course the just soul, envisioned a society in which workers, guardians, and philosophers would each have separate but important functions in achieving the overall good of the society. To sustain people's commitment to their roles, Plato advocated ruler manipulation of people through such tactics as regulating the marriages of the guardians or the teaching of a "noble falsehood" that suggests that the god of creation wants all people to be placed in roles that are appropriate to their native abilities. Thus, when the habits of civic virtue are insufficient to secure citizens' acceptance of their roles, modes of subtle force become necessary.

In contrast, Aristotle's approach to ensuring that people perform well the functions for which they are best suited is to emphasize the central place in people's lives of community. For Aristotle, it is precisely this experience that must be at the center of all social and political life if the society is to facilitate all citizens' contributions to the common good. Aristotle thus saw the *civic virtue of friendship* as having a powerful role to play in society, for when people are friends they are bound together by common moral values. This experience enables people to collaborate to achieve communal goals by manifesting the individual excellence needed to perform well the various functions in society. Indeed, as Morrall says, for Aristotle the basis of society is a "communal solidarity springing from an affective friendship towards one's fellow-citizens," and the Greek word for this experience is *koinonia*.[3]

In this chapter, the importance of friendship in Aristotle's thought will orient my discussion of his view of politics and of his possible approach to civil society. Before developing his view of friendship, it is necessary to distinguish his approach to studying politics from the approach taken by Plato.

II. SCIENTIFIC KNOWLEDGE AND PRACTICAL INTELLIGENCE

For Aristotle, two major forms of knowledge are scientific knowledge and practical intelligence.[4]

Scientific knowledge indicates the possession of "eternal things," which are "indestructible."[5] The latter suggests principles that are considered true on their face, and for which no further justification is needed. From these principles, it is possible to construct a deductive system of thought, called a *theory,* which enables us to make predictions about future events pertaining to matters under study in a particular area or domain of investigation.[6] For instance, given a theory that explains the origin of a certain illness, we can be certain that when we apply a treatment sanctioned by the theory the patient will recover his health.[7]

Whereas scientific knowledge is able to provide universal, precise, and unvarying understanding about what it studies, practical intelligence is unable to provide similar certitude in discussing its field of concern. The difference between what each type of thinking is able to achieve has to do with the different realities each studies. Science studies nature, and practical intelligence is concerned with those actions in the realm of experience that are good, in this case morally and rationally good, for human beings.[8] The world of nature investigated by science is a world in which invariant relationships exist among the various components of a field of knowledge, such as the human body. But constancy among the factors that make up human experience—and in particular the world of ethics and politics—does not exist to the same degree as it does in nature. Aristotle said in his *Ethics* that "what is fine and what is just, the topics of inquiry in political science differ and vary so much that they seem to rest on convention only, not on nature."[9] Consequently, in discussing politics, the concern is to help define the "good" or the basis for a rational life for both the individual and the society, but the method used in finding the rational way of life in society will never have the exactitude found in scientific thinking. For Aristotle, then, we "should not seek the same degree of exactness in all sorts of arguments alike."[10] We will be able to understand the realm of politics and ethics "roughly and in outline" form, only.[11]

As Martha Nussbaum says, practical intelligence manifests an ability to "understand and grasp the salient features, the practical meaning, of concrete particulars."[12] Thus, practical intelligence requires that we remain concerned with the particular facts of ongoing circumstances in which decisions must be made. Focusing upon these particulars, instead of theories that consist of well-developed deductively based systems of rules to explain the ever-recurring structure of nature, practical intelligence can describe only patterns and tendencies that provide general guidelines for how to understand as well as to act in the world. Here, recognition must be given to the fact that the world of experience is subject to unpredictable changes. In consequence, practical intelligence must be able to accept the flux of circumstances and be flexible enough to improvise and change strategies and plans in the face of the unexpected.[13]

Given the importance of focusing on particulars as well as the flux they signify, the person of practical intelligence understands that often theories, which derive from deductive systems of reasoning, will prove useless, and they may be a hindrance to understanding and action. There is a good reason for this conclusion. A general theory will simplify the world too much, and in consequence a theory will allow us to see only certain elements of reality; therefore, it may deny us access to crucial elements we should see. For instance, before the fall of the Berlin Wall in 1989 almost no one in the United States government, including the intelligence community, predicted this event. Why was this? Almost certainly the answer is that ever since the end of World War II, Americans tended to see communism as a monolithic ideology that united the Eastern bloc countries, including the former Soviet Union, against the West. Thus, even if eastern bloc nations did have their differences, their ideological solidarity was such that it was not even thinkable that their union would dissolve. Here, the commitment to view the Eastern bloc in a way that reconfirmed a particular theory about communism prevented American policymakers from seeing the other realities—including the persistent unhappiness with Soviet rule and a desire to pursue a course similar to the West—that ultimately had the greatest impact in affecting events.

Finally, how does one come to possess practical intelligence? It emerges as a result of much experience in life in which an individual works, over many years, at understanding the meaning of events for developing courses of action that are useful in achieving particular goals.[14] Young people can become accomplished in deductive systems of thinking such as geometry because learning these systems is merely a matter of learning how to apply the rules given in a theory. But the young cannot be taught the art of practical intelligence, because this ability requires years of experience engaged in the study of human events. The intention of such study is to develop an ability to grasp the significance of particular events for devising guidelines that are useful in directing action.[15]

III. ARISTOTLE ON PLATO'S FORMS AND THE SEARCH FOR HAPPINESS

For Aristotle, a person with practical intelligence seeks the "best good for a human being that is achievable in action."[16] On this view, one should pursue only the best goals that are worthy of human life and that are capable of being realized in practice. Aristotle, in *The Politics,* believed that Plato's theory of the forms violated this requirement. Aristotle argued that Plato's forms do not enable a person either to understand what is possible in particular circumstances or how to act in these circumstances to achieve moral objectives. For Aristotle, then, Plato's forms, as projecting a "total unity" onto society, signify a comprehensive theory about how society should be organized to achieve particular goals. When one approaches society in this way, one may lose sight of the crucial realities that are critical to making important social reforms, as we saw in the last section.

To take Aristotle's own example, in considering Plato's exclusion of private property for the guardians, one must not just consider, as Plato did, the evils that would be eliminated by this proposal. Aristotle believed that it was necessary to consider the benefits that would be denied people as a result of this proposal as well. Plato's quest for "total unity," or a comprehensive theory for establishing a just society, caused him to consider only the first issue and not the second one.[17]

The major danger of Plato's approach is especially important for someone such as Plato who sought to create a system of education that would succeed in orienting people to respect moral values. To educate people properly, it is necessary to put into place those social factors that properly shape people's understanding so that they can act in ways that uphold moral norms. But if one does not consider the benefits and disadvantages of proposals for the development of these social factors, one is unlikely to provide a proper environment within which to educate people to the civic virtues they should maintain. Thus, Aristotle found it "surprising" that Plato, whose Republic is predicated on a system of political and moral education, failed to investigate the impact of his reforms on the actual factors that help to shape human character, factors such as the "social customs," the "mental culture," and the laws.[18]

Moreover, one must keep in mind, as one changes existing habits, laws, or traditions, what the overriding benefit of any such change should be. For Aristotle the overriding purpose of the *polis* (Greek word for city-state) is to achieve happiness. Happiness is an end unlike any other end we may seek in life. People may pursue many ends, such as wealth or flute playing, but these ends have as their goal a larger and more complete end, which is happiness. Thus, happiness represents life's highest possibility because it symbolizes for Aristotle a way of life "more than anything else [that] seems unconditionally complete."[19]

What is the happy life for Aristotle? There are many different functions in society, and each function embodies the rational element when it is performed well or excellently. And this state of affairs takes place only when a function is carried out in conjunction with the virtues or standards appropriate to the excellent performance of the function in question. For instance, to use Aristotle's example, a good harp player will play the harp with excellence because he will embody in his playing the "proper virtue." Here, it is not good enough just to play the harp, but it is necessary to play the harp well by exhibiting in one's performance the appropriate standards of excellence. In carrying out, with excellence, the standards associated with harp playing, one's life manifests virtue.[20]

Now for Aristotle, there are many different activities for people to participate in. In addition to being a harp player, I can be a farmer, a father, and so on. In each case, there are particular standards appropriate to the activity in question. Clearly, the activity of being a harp player does not require adherence to the same standards as being a father. But in each case, the objective of my life should be to perform a given function in a way that exhibits virtue. Here, I am not just a father, but a good father, not just a harp player, but a good harp player, and so on. The good life then is a life that expresses "the best and most complete virtue. Moreover, it [the good life] will be in a complete life." And a person who lives in this fashion throughout his life is "blessed and happy."[21] Happiness emerges for a person who, throughout his whole life, attempts to master the various standards of performance associated with the excellent achievement of the different activities that he engages in.

For Aristotle, human beings are "good" and thus happy when they perform well their functions in society, and people can perform them well only when they uphold the virtues or standards of excellence associated with these functions.[22] How does Plato compare with Aristotle on this issue? Plato's just society has many things in common with Aristotle's to be sure. For instance, for Plato, each person must perform his function in keeping with the standards associated with the good performance of that task. Guardians, workers, and philosophers each operate in terms of the values allied with the tasks they are to perform. And because the good performance of one's various functions is so critical to acting justly and because performing these functions well requires that one adhere to the standards associated with good performance, it would seem that Plato and Aristotle differ very little on what constitutes the primary activity of people in society. For both Plato and Aristotle, individuals must, if they are to lead happy lives, perform well their functions by doing all that is necessary to uphold the standards associated with these functions.

But could Plato have as full and as complete an understanding of what constitutes our functions, or the larger environment in which they occur, as would Aristotle? Aristotle would answer this question in the negative. And the reason once again is that Plato conceptualized the nature of a just society from the standpoint of a comprehensive theory, and, by doing so, he was bound to miss important factors that he should consider. From the standpoint of practical intelligence used by Aristotle, however, we are in a better position to mine human experience for a fuller understanding of its rational character.

As an example of this last point, it is well to mention Aristotle's discussion of moral virtue. For Aristotle, not unlike Plato, moral character is forged by habituation to proper forms of conduct. People, starting as children, learn virtue through practice and not through reasoning and argument about the nature of virtue. But what does habituation to virtue teach? For Aristotle, moral education habituates people to avoid either excess or deficiency, while pursuing the middle ground between both. For instance, to be brave one should neither be afraid all the time nor become rash from the absence of fear. To manifest the virtue of temperance one should neither be a glutton who seeks pleasure all the time nor a complete ascetic who avoids all pleasure. And to practice the virtue of truth-telling one should neither be a braggart who "overstates" issues nor should one be "self-deprecating" by understating the truth.[23] In each case there is a proper middle ground, and knowledge of that dimension allows one to be courageous, temperate, and truth seeking. It would seem that without these general moral virtues one would not be able to be good workers, good family members, or good citizens.

Knowledge of these general moral virtues, which are not apparent in Plato, arises from learning the important lessons of experience, lessons that speak to how a person achieves a virtue in any number of activities throughout life. Implicit in Aristotle's view, then, is that existing ways of life already contain or embody rational characteristics. He worried that, if changes were made in these practices without due consideration to this fact, then some of the rational dimensions of existing practices might be annihilated. As we will see in Section VIII with Aristotle's defense of private property and the family, Aristotle believed that there were rational reasons for maintaining these practices. And he believed that Plato, owing to his theory of justice, was unable to understand how these practices contributed to the overall rational structure of society and thus to people's happiness. Aristotle, along these lines, will also discuss friendship as a basis for communal solidarity as well as his conceptions of the good constitution and public deliberation.

Thus, whereas Plato starts from an ideal of justice and constructs a theory of a rational society based on this ideal, Aristotle starts from existing ways of life and finds the bases for a rational order to life contained in the ongoing practices of society. Armed with this understanding, Aristotle seeks to build upon the rational characteristics that are already a part of existing experience. To describe Aristotle's political vision, then, we start at the ground level and discuss his view of society contained in his concept of the polis.

IV. THE NATURE OF THE POLIS

The polis is made up of a number of associations—most important are families and villages—and its purpose is to make possible the "good life." The polis arises from the fact that individuals could not by themselves create the bases for happiness, for what is necessary are not only those goods that contribute to the material well-being of people, but goods that contribute to people's moral development as well. And only the polis is able to provide all the goods associated with material and moral well-being. Because of this, the polis is called "self-sufficient."[24]

For Aristotle, then, it is clear why human beings are social and political animals. Human beings, unlike animals, are provided by nature with a moral capacity, but, at the same time, they also are born with proclivities to shun the obligations associated with their moral natures.[25] In the polis, individuals are taught how to live morally, and thus the polis is arranged so that humankind is freed from the domination of "lust and gluttony."[26] Aristotle said that "man, when perfected, is the best of animals, but if he is isolated from law and justice he is the worst of all."[27] And individuals are only perfected when they shed any tendency toward isolation and join into political association with others. Here, relationships with others teach important moral values that orient individuals to uphold the common good. Outside of political association with others, there would be no recognition of values such as courage, moderation, generosity, and justice.[28]

The distinctive character of the polis, then, is that it is organized so that the rational or moral dimension always dominates the nonrational element. Indeed, Aristotle argued that there is a natural course of events taking place that ensures the priority of the rational. First, male and female unite from a "natural impulse" and not from a "deliberate intention" to reproduce human life. Next, there must be forms of association that permit the rational element. The latter makes possible the capacity of "forethought," to rule over other elements in society, which lack a capacity for rationality.[29] The family, which provides for "satisfaction of recurrent daily needs,"[30] is arranged so that the male, the ruling or the rational element, rules the female, the children, and the slaves.[31] Now, the male rules his wife "like a statesman over fellow subjects"; his children like a king, and a slave like a master.[32] This means that the male can make decisions for his slaves and his children without consulting them, but in making decisions that affect his wife and the family, he should consult her.

The statesman model also suggests a difference in status between those who rule and those who are ruled. The latter should manifest both high regard and respect for those who have ruling authority. In a similar way, the wife is to maintain respect for the authority of her husband. This is the case because only the male in the household, like the statesman who possesses practical intelligence, has full rational capacities that permit him to deliberate intelligently about important matters. "The slave is entirely without the faculty of deliberation; the female indeed possesses it, but in a form which remains inconclusive; and if children also possess it, it is only in an immature form."[33] This statement suggests that women, although having some dimension of the rational capacity, do not have as fully developed a rational capacity as men do. Women, like others who are of lesser stature than the husband in the household (slaves and children), have only that amount of rational capacity that permits them to perform their functions in the family. Thus, whereas women may have sufficient rational quality to help run the family, they do not have the full rational quality evidenced in men and that men use in making judgments about important issues, either in the public setting or in the family. Aristotle quotes with approval Sophocles who said that "a modest silence is a woman's crown."[34]

As Susan Moller Okin argues in *Women in Western Political Thought,* central to Aristotle's account of society is the view that women are merely to be caretakers of the household and the "bearers" of new citizens, but women can never be citizens themselves. Only the male is allowed to perform the active citizen role, and the household provides the support for him to take part in this role by removing from his shoulders responsibility for the family and placing it upon women.[35] The clear implication of this view is that women must remain in the home because they are inferior to men, or, as Aristotle said, because they lack full deliberative powers. Obviously, this view of women becomes the basis for excluding any consideration of the unjustness of preventing women from participating with men in the public arena where decisions about laws are made.

After the family, the next form of association is the village, and it provides for "more than daily recurrent needs."[36] The village is a grouping of different families into a unit that facilitates exchanges among various families of necessary goods, goods that each family might not be able to provide by themselves. The first method for exchanging goods in the village was through a straight barter of goods for goods. The barter system was too cumbersome for exchanges that involved transactions between people in different villages, and so money was instituted and made the basis for exchanges.[37] With the introduction of money, severe problems emerge that threaten the moral environment of society. Money makes possible retail trade, which, because it is conducted for profit, permits some individuals to acquire large fortunes. Indeed, in the retail atmosphere, individuals may become so preoccupied with money that they use all their abilities and capacities to secure for themselves ever-larger fortunes. Such individuals hold the view that there is no limit to the amount of wealth they can be permitted to acquire. Thus, for Aristotle, the retail experience is unhealthy for society because, instead of orienting people to the morality of the good life, it orients individuals to think that money is "the one aim and everything else must contribute to that aim."[38]

Aristotle's view of the polis, as in Plato's view of society, is that it is organized to provide basic needs. Furthermore, like Plato, Aristotle worried that the mentality of the endless acquisition of money would overwhelm citizens and thus undermine the commitment to make reason the basis for society. But the approach to avoiding this outcome was not through a civic virtue orientation as well as a noble lie that would enable a guardian class of auxiliaries and wise rulers to protect the common good, as Plato had done, but through an effort to create the grounds for community.

V. CITIZENSHIP AND FRIENDSHIP

For Aristotle, friendship is a virtue "most necessary for our life." Without friendship, life would be missing a major dimension and in consequence our lives would lack real significance. Moreover, as a virtue, friendship is only possible among people who practice the moral virtues discussed earlier, such as courage, truthfulness, and temperance.[39] People who practice virtues like these make the search for the middle ground a common feature of their lives. This trait is more likely to enable people to find ways to accommodate each other's needs and thus to become friends. Most importantly by pursuing the middle ground people maintain friendships because together they find ways to achieve shared objectives.

Friendship is thus a source of community because it suggests a basis for people to collaborate for common purposes. Indeed, the experience of friendship for Aristotle contributes to concord among people with respect to the major questions facing society. For Aristotle, then, "concord," a "feature of friendship," is a condition in which the citizens in a city "agree about what is advantageous, make the same decisions, and act on their common resolution."[40] Concord suggests agreement not just on "anything," but on what Aristotle referred to as "large questions" or when, as a result of the agreement, the members of the society all "get what they want" on issues of critical importance to the society.[41] Here, Aristotle, in talking about "large questions," referred to issues such as whether to make alliances with other city-states or whether to make all offices elective. In our society, an important question about which there must be concord if there is to be a sense of community would include the need to secure the same rights to each member of society, so that each member can determine his or her own purposes in life.

What makes possible agreement or concord on large questions of this sort is that, underlying these agreements, are shared moral values. For instance, underlying our contemporary commitment to provide rights to all is the moral commitment to respect equally the full dignity and worth of each individual. Without this shared moral value, we could not agree that providing rights to all is an important good, and society would be filled with extreme conflict between those who advocated rights for all and those who did not. But because our society presumably supports respect for the dignity of each person as a shared moral value, the people in society can agree that a policy to accord rights to everyone is a good policy. Indeed, such a policy, when it has been developed, would confirm in an even stronger sense the place of the shared moral value of equal regard for the dignity of others, and, in doing so, would make an even stronger basis for maintaining friendship and a concomitant sense of community.

Because there exists shared moral values, there can be agreement on important questions so that the society is not torn apart by differences over major issues. It is for this reason that "political friendship," that "is concerned with advantage and with what affects life [as a whole]," is possible.[42] Moreover, people who are friends politically speaking contribute to securing the society's continuing stability. The existence of political friendship helps us understand why Aristotle could say as he did that friendship "would seem to hold cities together, and legislators would seem to be more concerned about it than about justice."[43] As friends, people avoid all forms of "civil conflict" that are associated with "enmity," and the members of the society are able to work together to achieve common ends.[44] Indeed, in this setting people "have no need for justice" or in other terms, no need for a system of laws or rules that impose a just order because, in maintaining the ties of friendship, people act as they should to each other without external prompting of any sort.[45]

But maintaining friendship, especially the type that holds together a community, is possible only among "decent people." Who are decent people? They have an enduring commitment to "what is just and advantageous, and also to seek it in common."[46] Decent people, then, are individuals who are committed to maintain those common moral values that are critical to making possible a rational way of life in society. Such people make the search for the middle ground a common characteristic of their lives. Thus, decent people "are in concord with themselves and with each other, since they are practically of the same mind; for their wishes are stable, not flowing back and forth like a tidal strait."[47]

It follows from the preceding account that "base" people cannot find concord with others except in minor ways because "base" people are those who seek only their own gain and have no regard for the common good, including the search for the middle ground. Now, "base" people understand what constitutes the common moral values, and thus these individuals know what a life of justice entails. Yet, "base" people want others to live such a life, even though they themselves do not want to have to do so. Thus, "base" people are always engaged in conflict with the rest of the society.[48] Obviously, these people represent a threat both to friendship and to the ability of a society to maintain community.

To overcome the threat that this situation poses to society, Aristotle pointed out the importance of institutions that are part of the encompassing social and political environment such as "marriage, kin-groups, religious gatherings, and social pastimes." These practices help produce a basis for a "common social life" by reinforcing through the socialization process the importance of common moral values, and, when these shared moral values are in place, a basis for maintaining friendship among the members of the society exists. Aristotle said that "institutions [such as marriage and religious associations] are the business of friendship. . . . It is friendship . . . which consists in the pursuit of a common social life."[49] In this atmosphere, people maintain a fundamental decency and civility and, as a consequence of this demeanor, they are more likely to perform their respective functions in ways that contribute to the common good of the society.

Friendship, as the ground of community, would permit different people who perform different functions to continue to maintain their commitment to the common good. On this view, then, an important defect of Plato's argument was his failure to make friendship a central civic virtue in the development of a just city and in providing the foundation for other virtues Plato identified, such as moderation, wisdom, and courage.

VI. SLAVERY AND FRIENDSHIP

One consequence of citizenship is that, in order to support its practice, there will have to be a class of noncitizens who perform all the drudge labor so that the citizens, freed from such labor, can perform, fully, their citizenship duties. Aristotle allowed men time for citizenship duties by transferring to women and slaves the job of raising families and maintaining the household. Ordinarily, this situation might create enmity and rebellion on the part of the subordinate class toward the superior class. But, friendship, which can occur among those who are not equals, or citizens and noncitizen members of society (women, children, and slaves), enables individuals who are unequal in status to share a sense of community with those who are citizens and thus of higher stature. Characteristic of friendship among those who are not equal in status is that each party in the relationship has a different function to perform with respect to the other party. And in performing that function each person receives something he or she needs through co-operation with others, and this experience is the basis for different kinds of "love" be-tween people.[50] Again, even among people with unequal status there can be shared moral values, and these values help to justify the inequality in status. It is on this basis that there can be friendship between master and slave.

Aristotle's discussion of slavery indicates what slaves do, how people are justifiably made into slaves, and what he considers to be the moral justification of slavery. For Aristotle, a slave is a person who does not produce goods, but who serves the needs of the household. Slaves are needed to perform many of the activities associated with household life, and, in performing them, presumably, individuals (in this case, the adult male mem-bers of the household) are provided with the leisure time needed to take part in political af-fairs and public activities.[51]

There are two justifications for slavery, conventional or natural, and only the latter form is acceptable to Aristotle. In making people slaves by convention or legality, the powerful subjugate the less powerful to their control, as for instance, when one nation in-vades another and makes the citizens of the invaded nation into slaves. Aristotle believed that conventional slavery is unjust. There are several reasons for his position. First, a war in which one nation invades another and takes the invaded nation's citizens as slaves may, in fact, not be conducted on just grounds. In this case, enslaving others would be unjust. Second, it is possible that people enslaved even in just wars may not deserve to be en-slaved at all. Aristotle condemns the practice of enslaving people as a result of a war, be-cause one may be enslaving persons with a capacity for reason.[52]

From this account, it is clear who can be enslaved and who should not be. Enslaving an-other is legitimate only under a condition in which there is a *natural* relation between master and slave, a relationship in which the slave, lacking in deliberative qualities, is ruled by the person who possesses those qualities.[53] It would not be appropriate to place into slavery a person who possessed deliberative qualities; such a person would be held back from making full use of his powers, and clearly this could not be good for the slave or for the society. Still, slaves have a degree of rationality, however small, that permits them to follow the com-mands of those who have full rational powers and who by virtue of this fact are properly placed in authority over slaves. Those who naturally lack a *full* rational dimension benefit from slavery; such people are provided with necessary goods to ensure their survival and, further, they are able to take part in work that is beneficial to society. And the master benefits because slavery allows him the leisure to contribute to public affairs. Here, slavery is a natural or a moral relationship because it provides mutual benefits to the master and to the slave. Thus, for Aristotle, "there is a community of interest, and a relation of friendship, between master and slave, when both of them naturally merit the position in which they stand."[54]

Slavery is justified in order to make possible the rule of those who have rational capacities and who are in a position to make good use of practical intelligence. Slavery is a means to a higher end; it is itself not an indication of an unjust and immoral state of affairs. The reason it cannot be for Aristotle is that he had no conception of individual rights, which, itself, requires that all individuals be accorded the same dignity. Notwithstanding Aristotle's efforts to reform slavery by denying a right to enslave people with deliberative skills who may have been captured in war, the fact is that his acceptance of slavery remains abhorrent to the modern proponent of civil society.[55]

VII. CITIZENSHIP AND DIFFERENTIALS IN CONTRIBUTION

A polis is a form of society in which the chief goal is "true felicity and goodness."[56] Individuals find in the polis the common goods all share, the means for physical security as well as the basis for a moral and virtuous life. However, the common ends of polis life can only be obtained so long as all accept that different citizens contribute disproportionately to the ends of polis life, and those citizens who contribute more should be honored more. In particular, some citizens, owing to their superior "civic excellence," do more than other citizens to achieve the "good" life for all members of the society. Because of this fact, these individuals are to be accorded "a greater share in the polis."[57] Here, even if citizens are equal in social status or wealth, a person who contributes more to the well-being of the society should receive greater recognition for his contributions to society. Similarly, among people unequal in social status and wealth, it is the person who contributes the most to "civic excellence" who should be rewarded the most.[58]

Disproportionate awards, based on meritorious contributions, although necessary to maintain the polis, may have harmful effects, also. Citizens who are accorded such high regard might engender among other less highly respected citizens envy and contempt. Were this to happen, the concord so necessary for good order would be undermined. But this grim prospect would be averted by the existence of political friendship, which suggests a shared commitment to common moral values. This commitment is the basis for a community in which each citizen learns to respect the accomplishments and contributions of other citizens and to see these contributions as essential to the well-being of the society. Thus, friendship is an important civic virtue because it permits citizens to accept, without rancor, differences in recognition resulting from differences in contributions to the welfare of the society.

VIII. FAMILY AND PRIVATE PROPERTY

Aristotle's account of citizenship and friendship would contribute to limiting the damage from envy, but so would his conception of the family and private property. Both of these institutions are needed in order to enable individuals to feel that their lives have value, and both are necessary dimensions of a well-organized polis that secures a sense of communal solidarity among diverse people, citizens and noncitizens, women and men.

For Aristotle, Plato's guardian community is a "watery sort of fraternity."[59] Aristotle particularly rejected the idea of common families, where the children are the children of all. Aristotle said that

> *men pay most attention to what is their own: they care less for what is common; or, at any rate, they care for it only to the extent to which each is individually concerned. . . . The scheme of Plato means that each citizen will have a thousand sons: they will not be the sons of each citizen individually: and every son will be equally the son of any and every father; and the result will be that every son will be equally neglected by every father.*[60]

Plato's scheme would dilute family bonds so much that no father would have any strong feeling to treat all the other "sons" in the guardian community with very much care and concern. Similarly, in Plato's commune, no son would ever feel any filial relationship to the father figures.[61] This unfortunate outcome would surely contribute to a sense of resentment among many parents toward the community.

Regarding private property, Aristotle said that when people have their own "separate sphere of interest" they are more likely to avoid quarrels and disagreements with each other. Moreover, it is likely that people's interest and intensity in their activities will be increased where private property is permitted "because each will feel that he is applying himself to what is his own."[62] Furthermore, for Aristotle, there is no reason why private property cannot be used to support common communal purposes, as he thinks Plato implied it couldn't do. People can make use of what they own in ways that benefit the society in general. For Aristotle "the better system [than Plato's] is that under which property is privately owned but is put to common use; and the function proper to the legislator is to make men so disposed that they will treat their property in this way."[63]

At first glance, owing to the fact that private property accords people with a separate sphere, it might seem that Aristotle was laying the ground for a civil society. But Aristotle, in linking people to the need to make common use of one's property, insures that the separate sphere of a civil society would not emerge. What Aristotle really means by a separate sphere is just a place that property holders can call their own. But it is not a place that allows individuals autonomy and a wide range of private choices, as would be the case in a civil society, especially a liberal one, described in Chapter 1.

Furthermore, given Aristotle's view of Plato, it might appear that Aristotle tended to think that Plato advocated a scheme of collective ownership of property for all people in society and not just for the guardians. But in fact, that was not the case. As we saw, Plato would have accepted private property for many people outside the guardian category. Further, Plato accepted, as did Aristotle, the idea that appetite could be properly harnessed and controlled by moral training. In this case, as Aristotle said, "moral goodness . . . will ensure that the property of each is made to serve the use of all, in the spirit of the proverb which says 'Friends' goods are goods in common.'"[64] For Aristotle, then, no less than for

Plato, in fact, the concept, "this is mine," should be seen as contributing to the understanding that one is permitted to have personal wealth on the condition that one use it to promote community goals.

IX. CONSTITUTIONS: JUST AND UNJUST

The constitution of a polis pertains to several important characteristics of the political community. A constitution is organized into offices, each of which has certain powers in relation to the common ends and values of the community.[65] A constitution, then, is "an organization of offices in a state, by which the method of their distribution is fixed, the sovereign authority is determined, and the nature of the end to be pursued by the association and all its members is prescribed."[66] Moreover, any constitution is to a large extent influenced in its character by the social and economic classes that dominate the society.[67] Thus, because different classes will predominate, there will be different constitutions. Further, given the variety of constitutions, it is natural to ask what makes a constitution worthy. Aristotle is clear that only those constitutions that promote the common interest can be considered "right constitutions." All others that promote the personal interests of the ruling classes are "perversions."[68]

Aristotle used both the categories of class and of respect for the common interest as a basis for evaluation and description of various constitutions. The three good kinds of constitutions, those based on respect for the common interest, are kingships, aristocracies, and polities. The predominant class in the first is the king, in the second it is the few who are meritorious, and, in the third, it is the many, later referred to as the *middle class*. The perversions of these forms are tyrannies, oligarchies, and democracies. Tyranny is rule by a corrupt single ruler, oligarchy is rule by the wealthy who define the public good in a way that benefits only themselves, and democracy is rule by the many, which in this case is the poor.[69] We will discuss each form of constitution in turn as we distinguish the good from the bad.

The "most nearly divine" of the right kind of constitution is kingship.[70] A kingship is closer in nature to an aristocracy because it is the rule of the "better classes" and, thus, as in an aristocracy, merit is the basis for ruling others. Further, a kingship protects the wealth of property owners from "unjust treatment" arising from those who might otherwise take their property. At the same time, the king protects the rest of society from "arrogance and oppression."[71] Aristotle also said that it is best for kings to accept, as the basis of their regime, the rule of law. "The rule of law is therefore preferable . . . to that of a single citizen." Aristotle went on to say that the "law . . . trains the holders of office expressly in its own spirit," and thus the rule of law enables rulers to settle issues justly.[72] In a society governed by the rule of law, "God and reason rule." But where men alone rule, society falls under the authority of the "beast."[73] When men rule without regard for the rule of law, appetite and out-of-control emotions, and not reason, are the main political forces in society.

The perverted form of kingship is tyranny. The tyrant makes the pursuit of his own interest primary, and he has no concern for the public interest. The tyrant, like the oligarch, amasses great wealth, so that the tyrant is in a position to provide himself with an army as well as with luxuries. The tyrant does not trust the masses of people, and he makes every effort to deny them weapons.[74] He can try to stay in power either by sowing distrust among the people, so there is no united opposition to him, or he can take a higher road and become more like a king. In the latter case, he dedicates himself to uphold the public interest, and through displays of moderation, he is able to win the favor of the mass of people as well as of the aristocrats.[75]

An aristocracy, as already indicated, is rule by the meritorious few.[76] A perverted aristocracy is an oligarchy, a way of life in which the wealthy rule the rest of the society on behalf of their, the wealthy class's, own interest and without respect for the rule of law principle. An oligarchy is distinguished from a democracy by the fact that, in the former case, the rich rule, and in a democracy the poor are in control.[77] Aristotle argued that oligarchies, if they want to continue, should reform themselves. This, they can do by allowing all property holders a chance to hold political office. Further, oligarchs should be willing to occupy the most important public offices without pay, so that it appears to the rest of the citizens, who are excluded from office, that the public officials are concerned with making the public good a priority.[78]

Next, Aristotle turned to a discussion of the polity, "the best constitution and way of life for the *majority* of states and men."[79] In a polity, there is a middle ground between competing forces in society, in this case, between contrasting class perspectives.[80] Thus, in a polity, the middle class acts as a moderating force between two divergent classes in competition with each other, one representing the interests of an oligarchy and the other of a democracy. Generally, some polities show greater tendencies to be like democracies, while others incline in the direction of being like oligarchies.[81]

In any case, a polity is considered the basis for a moderate form of politics. Aristotle said that individuals who are favorable to leading a moderate life are "most ready to listen to reason."[82] Such people manifest the quest to avoid extremes and instead base life on the middle ground, the heart and soul of a virtuous life. Indeed, this moderate way of life is mirrored in the society through the fact that the polity is predicated upon a middle class, a class midway between the rich and the poor. People, who are either in camp, rich or poor, are fanatical with respect to promoting their respective causes and neither can follow the rule of reason. The rich tend to be more violent and are likely to engage in "serious crime," and the poor are given to "roguery and petty offenses."[83]

Obviously in both these settings, citizens would not be ruled by just laws. The rich, because they have too many advantages, never acquire the discipline needed to respect and to uphold just laws. The poor, who lack all advantages, become resentful and mean in spirit, and thus they too would not be able to establish just laws. Where these two classes predominate, the state becomes nothing more than the poor constantly fighting with the rich, a setting "only of slaves and masters: a state of envy on the one side and on the other contempt." Aristotle went on to say that "nothing could be further removed from the spirit of friendship or the temper of political community. Community depends upon friendship; and when there is enmity instead of friendship, men will not even share the same path."[84]

On the other hand, the members of the middle class "suffer least from ambition," and thus they are most capable of ruling in a setting that promotes the common good and a basis for good laws that should be sovereign throughout society. The middle class would seem most able, then, to establish common moral values that could be the basis for friendship and community among the different classes in society.

The common moral values that a polity, through the middle class, promotes are clear as well. "A state aims at being . . . a society composed of equals and peers [who, as such, can be friends and associates]; and the middle class, more than any other, has this sort of composition. It follows that a state which is based on the middle class is bound to be the best constituted."[85] A polity strives toward equality by the way it distributes property. Indeed, a major reason for the success of the polity is that it is based upon a "moderate and adequate [distribution of] property."[86] In a society in which property is distributed unfairly and some have most of it and the rest have nothing, there will be little chance for community. Instead, society will either turn into an oligarchy (the rule by small segments of society who own most of the property) or it will become an "extreme democracy" (the rule of the poor over the rest). Moreover, a reaction against either of these forms of unjust regimes may end up turning the society into a tyranny.[87]

Unfortunately, polities are generally rare because one of the two tendencies, oligarchic or democratic, ultimately comes to dominate. This happens in large part either because the middle class is too small or because there is intense animosity between the mass of people and the rich.[88]

X. DEMOCRACY AND PUBLIC DELIBERATION

Whereas tyranny is the most perverse of the unjust regimes and whereas oligarchy is next to tyranny among the worst regimes, democracy is the "most moderate" among the worst regimes and thus the "least bad" among those considered to be the unjust regimes.[89] Democracy is a form of government based upon the rule of the poor and the "free-born," the vast bulk of the people.[90]

Further, a democracy highlights two views of liberty. The first conception is that individuals should share in being ruled and in ruling.[91] This means that the citizens should each have an opportunity to take part in public office. Furthermore, the collective view of the citizens should prevail on issues such as the nature of law. Here, unlike Plato who argued in the *Republic* that only philosophers should rule, Aristotle thought it quite possible that citizens deliberating together might make the best decisions. Aristotle believed that even if it were the case that an individual by himself will not be a better judge than an expert, still when individuals meet together and make judgments as a result of deliberation, their judgments are better or at least no worse than those of the so-called experts. Aristotle said that "each individual may, indeed, be a worse judge than the experts; but all, when they meet together, are either better than experts or at any rate no worse."[92]

Furthermore, there are many areas of interest in which the experts on particular subjects are not better judges than nonexperts or what could be called *average citizens*. Aristotle said that "a house . . . is something which can be understood by others besides the builder."[93] Extending this analogy to politics, it is likewise possible that ordinary citizens who deliberate together are just as good, if not better, in making judgments about domestic or foreign policy matters as the experts in these respective fields. Perhaps, one reason for this view stems from Aristotle's treatment of practical intelligence. As the reader will remember, practical intelligence is not concerned with providing a theory, with a well-developed system of rules to explain events, but, rather, practical intelligence describes patterns and tendencies that provide guidelines for how to formulate and to think about the law or other public questions. Now, defining these tendencies is a very imprecise science, to be sure. Because events are fluid, it is often difficult to determine the pattern in a series of events. But when people share this endeavor together, they are able to compare and contrast views, and, in the process, they are more likely to create a more accurate picture of events as the basis for the laws they ultimately accept. Thus, when Aristotle said that in a democracy the majority must determine the outcome and that their view is "the expression of justice," it should be understood that the majority decision is to emerge from a process of public deliberation. The latter is to inform the views of people so that their resulting judgment is based on an intelligent assessment of the issues, as opposed to an emotional reaction.[94]

Moreover, this approach to ruling is more likely to avoid political instability. For Aristotle, Plato's approach to ruling, which makes one group of citizens the state's perpetual rulers, denies opportunities for all citizens to take part in holding office. And this situation would "breed discontent and dissension even among the elements which have no particular standing, and, all the more, therefore, among the high-spirited and martial elements."[95] For Aristotle, Plato would thus be unable to maintain among citizens the shared moral values that could bridge the different interests in society and create the bonds of community and friendship Aristotle believed were necessary for a healthy and just political society.

Aristotle's view of common deliberation is certainly made possible by a moral perspective that highlights the search for the middle ground as a critical feature of public and of community life. Further, this approach to common deliberation anticipates civil society thinking discussed in Part II of this book. In particular, when we discuss the prospect of public reason in our chapters on Rousseau, Hegel, Kant, and Rawls, we will be discussing a form of reasoning in which individuals learn to consult the views of others as the basis for developing both their own views and the consensus of the society on a given issue. This experience is fundamental to promoting what we have called in the first chapter *mutual respect,* or the ability of people to understand the views and opinions of those who differ from them.

The second conception of liberty in a democracy is that individuals should have the freedom to "live as they like." "Such a life, the democrats argue, is the function of the free man, just as the function of slaves is *not* to live as they like."[96] Under this form, individuals are to be free from interference from the government. Moreover, this view contributes to a system of liberty that incorporates equality, in which freedom if made possible for one person must be made possible for all persons. It would seem that living as one liked, however, would always conflict with the first view of liberty that emphasizes that individuals should partake in public deliberation of issues. To accomplish this objective, people must accept the fact that at times they must forgo living as they might want to live, in order to help make possible a consensus on important public issues. Only then would it be possible to maintain those shared moral values that are the basis for continuing the bonds of friendship.

Aristotle provided advice on how to improve democracy and move it in the direction of a good, stable regime. He argued that it is necessary to ensure a permanent level of prosperity for the lower classes. "Poverty is the cause of the defects of democracy." Prosperity could be achieved by distributing surpluses in the form of "block grants to the poor."[97] In taking this view, Aristotle would hope to make democracy more like a polity, because this setting would be likely to maintain friendship and thus preserve the community experience that is so essential to securing a good society. Indeed, in this setting, it would be possible to imagine a sufficient degree of trust to permit the kind of public deliberation that democracy demands of its citizens.

Aristotle's discussion of public deliberation in making the law reinforces the view, manifested in his discussion of kingships, that government in a society should be based upon the rule of law and not upon the personal authority of particular rulers. Personal authority, whether exercised by a single person or a body of people, should be used only where, owing to the difficulty in framing general rules that cover all contingencies, there exists no laws to cover a particular matter. In making a strong case for the rule of law over the rule of particular individuals, Aristotle demonstrated his conviction that "the final sovereign" should be the rule of what he called "rightly constituted laws." What are rightly constituted laws? That is a difficult question because, given that different constitutions rest upon particular social classes, laws may be biased in the direction of one class or another. Still, to answer this question, Aristotle suggested the importance of good constitutions to producing good laws. Indeed, he said that just laws are laws that must be "in accordance with right constitutions."[98]

It would seem, given Aristotle's emphasis on allowing experts to be replaced with ordinary citizens in the processes of public deliberation, that one important criterion, among others, for defining just constitutions would be a provision that permits the laws to emanate from the common deliberation of the citizens. And thus Aristotle, in promoting the idea of the rule of law, advocated the rule of citizen deliberation as one important basis for a just polity. In doing so, he demonstrated once again a vision of political life that enlarges upon the one found in Plato.

XI. ARISTOTLE AND CIVIL SOCIETY

Still, despite the emphasis on common deliberation among citizens, it should be clear that Aristotle's view of society excluded a great many from full participation in public life as we saw already with respect to women and slaves. In addition, Aristotle said that "mechanics" and "shopkeepers" engaged in activities that were "ignoble and inimical to goodness," and, in "a state with an ideal constitution," these individuals cannot be citizens taking full part in the government. Work tasks of this sort, just as farming, must be performed by a separate class of people so that others, those who are permitted to be citizens, have the full leisure necessary to participate in government. "Leisure is a necessity, both for growth in goodness and for the pursuit of political activities."[99]

For Aristotle, those people who perform the necessary work of society will not be able to be given access to the type of opportunities that lead to the development of their rational faculties. And thus even in the best city the most that human life has to offer will not be open to all. These views suggest that Aristotle believed that in order for society to achieve its collective purposes there will be some people denied the same justice afforded to others. Now, ironically, there is a virtue to be gained from defining social circumstances in this way. Indeed, such an approach permits Aristotle to define clearly the limits placed on human action, and, with these limitations in mind, the legislator knows the kinds of limitations he must work against in order to bring about a more just society.[100]

What would give Aristotle cause to challenge the limitations of his views of society? It would seem that his commitment to friendship would encourage him to rethink his view of class hierarchy. As we have seen, without friendship there is no basis for community. Now, friendship for Aristotle is predicated upon shared moral values among the different members of the society. But where the moral values in question are ones that cause serious and deep strains and conflicts in society, one could ask whether these values really have moral and rational validity. For how can values that divide people along lines that suggest a lack of fairness be considered morally worthy? Moreover, if one were to conclude that the values in question have no moral validity, then society would lack both shared moral values and the friendship that these values make possible. Aristotle, who wished to make friendship the basis for society, would have no choice, then, but to reform the moral values of society, so that just values could be provided. If he were successful in this endeavor, both friendship and community could be restored.

Moreover, Aristotle's conception of deliberation in a democracy would seem to push him to rethink his acceptance of a class hierarchy that denies citizenship to many categories of people. As we saw, Aristotle's view of deliberation would have people with different views meet together to form their own agenda and their own laws. They are to do so, because their collective wisdom is superior to that of experts. But for a common deliberation to take place, it would be necessary that the factors, such as class hierarchy and privilege that divide people and create mistrust, be minimized. Otherwise, individuals will be unable to deliberate together.

What are the implications of these views for civil society? Now, to be sure, Aristotle did not think that friendship would, of necessity, lead to the development of civil society as a separate sphere discussed in Chapter 1. For Aristotle, all phases of life in the family and the village were to support the priorities of the polis. And thus it would be unlikely that Aristotle would support a separate sphere of groups existing alongside the state as is necessary for a civil society.

Still, if friendship is to be sustained, then one important consequence of sharing moral values must be admitted: namely, that friends are friends to each other because they contribute to each other's sense of self-respect. But how can this outcome take place if as a result of friendship one party is made subordinate to another, for reasons that cannot be rationally justified? Friendship as the basis for society ultimately must come to incorporate, if it is to remain a basis for society, the civic virtue of mutual respect discussed in Chapter 1. This virtue, especially when buttressed by Aristotle's view of public deliberation, would encourage people to find ways to listen to and to understand and to make room for others. But as relationships of this sort are established in the name of maintaining friendship, then a civil society, complete with a separate sphere of groups and a larger moral environment encompassing respect for rights, would emerge as well.

These views suggest that, even if Aristotle did not advocate or embrace the view of civil society argued for here, he still would be closer to understanding and embracing it than would his mentor, Plato.

Endnotes

1. John B. Morrall, *Aristotle,* (London: George Allen and Unwin, 1977), p. 43.

2. Aristotle, *The Politics of Aristotle,* edited and tran. by Ernest Barker, (New York: Oxford University Press, 1965), p. 317, Bk. VII, ch. XIV, para 9. From hereon, in citing from the *Politics,* I will cite the numbers using colons for separation. Thus, the quote just cited would be VII:XIV:9.

3. Morrall, *Aristotle,* p. 100.

4. *Politics,* p. 317; VII:XIV:9, and Barker's commentary on page 320.

5. Aristotle, *Nicomachean Ethics,* translated by Terence Irwin (Indianapolis: Hackett Publishing Co., 1985), p. 151, (1139b23–25).

6. Ibid., p. 156, (1140b30–1141a). "Scientific knowledge is supposition about universals." Also, p. 152 (1139b33–35).

7. This example comes from Martha C. Nussbaum, *The Fragility of Goodness,* (New York: Cambridge University Press, 1986), pp. 94–97. In this example I follow Nussbaum who uses the word *theory* in the way I use it here.

8. Aristotle *Ethics,* p. 154, (1140b5).

9. Ibid., p. 3, (1094a15-18). Here, political science is equated with practical intelligence and both are distinguished from scientific knowledge, *Ethics,* p. 157, (1141aa20–30).

10. Ibid., p. 3, (1094b13).

11. Ibid., p. 4, (1094b21).

12. Martha C. Nussbaum, *The Fragility of Goodness,* p. 305; *Ethics,* p. 158, (1141b15–18).

13. Martha C. Nussbaum, *The Fragility of Goodness,* pp. 302–05.

14. Ibid., p. 305.

15. *Ethics,* pp. 160–61, (1142a14–20).

16. Ibid., p. 158, (1141b13–15).

17. Aristotle, *The Politics,* p. 51, II:5:13–14.

18. Ibid., p. 51, II:5:15.

19. *Ethics,* pp. 13–14, (1097a27–1097b5).

20. Ibid., p. 17, (1098a10–15).

21. Ibid., p. 17, (1098a20).

22. Ibid., p. 42, (1106a15–25).

23. Ibid., p. 33 (1103a15-20); p. 36 (1104a20-25), p. 44 (1107a35-40), p. 48 (1108a20-25).

24. Aristotle, *Politics,* p. 5, I:II:8.

25. Ibid., pp. 5–6, I:II:10–14.

26. Ibid., p. 7, I:II:16.

27. Ibid., p. 7. I:II:15.

28. Nussbaum, *The Fragility of Goodness,* pp. 344–46, 352.

29. *Politics,* p. 3, I:II:2.

30. Ibid., p. 4, I:II:5.

31. Ibid., p. 13, I:V:6, also p. 32, I:XII:1–2.

32. Ibid., p. 32, I:XII:1.

33. Ibid., pp. 32–33, I:XII:2 and p. 35, I:XIII:7.

34. Ibid., p. 36, I:XIII:11.

35. Susan Moller Okin, *Women in Western Political Thought,* (Princeton: Princeton University Press, 1979), pp. 90–92.

36. *Politics,* p. 4, I:II:5.

37. Ibid., pp. 23–24, I:IX:5–9.

38. Ibid., pp. 24–27, I:IX:9, 12–18.

39. *Ethics,* p. 207, (1155a); Nussbaum, *The Fragility of Goodness,* p. 306.

40. *Ethics,* p. 249, (1167a25).

41. Ibid., p. 249, (1167a30–33).

42. Ibid., p. 250, (1167b).

43. Ibid., p. 208, (1155a23–25).

44. Ibid., p. 208, (1155a25).

45. Ibid., p. 208, (1155a25–28).

46. Ibid., p. 250, (1167a 38–40 and 1167b5). See Nussbaum, *The Fragility of Goodness,* pp. 354–56.

47. *Ethics,* p. 250, (1167b5–10).

48. Ibid., p. 250, (1167b10–15).

49. Aristotle, *Politics,* p. 120, III:IX:13.

50. Aristotle, *Ethics,* p. 220, (1158b15–20). Here, Aristotle talked about friendship between a man and a woman, between a son and a father, and between any kind of ruler and those whom he rules, and this clearly includes the master and the slave.

51. Aristotle, *Politics,* p. 10, I:IV:4–5. Also see Barker commentary on page 11.

52. Ibid., pp. 15–16, I:VI:5–9. Also, Nussbaum, *The Fragility of Goodness,* p. 348.

53. Aristotle, *Politics,* p. 16, I:VI:9–10.

54. Ibid., p. 17, I:VI:9–10. Also p. 35, I:XIII:7 and Barker footnote 3.

55. On this point, see Nussbaum, *The Fragility of Goodness,* p. 348.

56. *Politics,* p. 120, III:IX:14.

57. Ibid., p. 120, III:IX:15.

58. Ibid., p. 120, III:IX:15.

59. Ibid., p. 47, II:IV:7.

60. Ibid., p. 44, II:III:4–5.

61. Ibid., p. 47, II:IV:7. "A father would be very little disposed to say 'mine' of a son, and a son would be as little disposed to say 'mine' of a father."

62. Ibid., p. 49, II:V:6.

63. Ibid., p. 50, II:V:8.

64. Ibid., p. 49, II:V:6.

65. Ibid., pp. 110–11, III:VI:1–6.
66. Ibid., p. 156, IV:I:10.
67. Ibid., pp. 108–09, III:V:5–7.
68. Ibid., p. 114, III:VII:2.
69. Ibid., pp. 114–15: III:VII:3–5.
70. Ibid., p. 158, IV:II:2.
71. Ibid., p. 236, V:X:9.
72. Ibid., p. 146, III:XVI:3–5.
73. Ibid., p. 146, III:XVI:3–5.
74. Ibid., pp. 236–37, V:X:9–11.
75. Ibid., p. 246, V:XI:16–17, also, p. 249, V:XI:33.
76. Ibid., pp. 175–76, IV:VIII:7.
77. Ibid., pp.115–16, III:VIII:4.
78. Ibid., pp. 272–73, VI:VII:4–5.
79. Ibid., p. 180, IV:XI:1. Italics in text.
80. Ibid., pp. 180–81, IV:XI:4–8.
81. Ibid., p. 175, IV:VIII:3.
82. Ibid., p. 181, IV:XI:5.
83. Ibid., p. 181, IV:XI:5.
84. Ibid., p. 181, IV:XI:7; also, IV:XI:6.
85. Ibid., p. 181, IV:XI:8.
86. Ibid., p. 182, IV:XI:11.
87. Ibid., p. 182, IV:XI:11.
88. Ibid., p. 183, IV:XI:16–17.
89. Ibid., p. 158, IV:II:2.
90. Ibid., p. 164, IV:IV:6.
91. Ibid., p. 258, VI:II:1–2.
92. Ibid., p. 126, III:XI:14.
93. Ibid., p. 126, III:XI:14.
94. Ibid., p. 258, VI:II:2.
95. Ibid., p. 54, II:V:25.
96. Ibid., p. 258, VI:II:3. Italics in text.
97. Ibid., pp. 268–69, VI:V:8.
98. Ibid., p. 127, III:XI:19–21.
99. Ibid., p. 301, VII:IX:3–4.
100. On this point, see Nussbaum, *The Fragility of Goodness,* p. 347.

Partial Bibliography and Further Reading

Broadie, Sarah. *Ethics with Aristotle.* Oxford: Oxford University Press, 1991.

Cooper, John M. *Reason and Human Good in Aristotle.* Cambridge: Harvard University Press, 1975.

Hardie, William Francis Ross. *Aristotle's Ethical Theory.* Oxford: Oxford University Press, 1980.

Lord, Carnes, and O'Connor, David. Edited. *Essays on the Foundations of Aristotelian Political Science.* Berkeley: University of California Press, 1991.

Morrall, John B. *Aristotle.* London: G. Allen & Unwin, 1977.

Nichols, Mary P. *Citizens and Statesmen: A Study of Aristotle's Politics.* Landham, Md.: Rowman & Littlefield, 1992.

Nussbaum, Martha Craven. *The Fragility of Goodness: Luck and Ethics in Greek Tragedy and Philosophy.* Cambridge: Cambridge University Press, 1986.

Price, A. W. *Love and Friendship in Plato and Aristotle.* Oxford: Oxford University Press, 1989.

Robinson, Timothy. *Aristotle in Outline.* Indianapolis: Hackett, 1995.

Salkever, Stephen G. *Finding the Mean: Theory and Practice in Aristotelian Political Philosophy.* Princeton: Princeton University Press, 1990.

Swanson, Judith A. *The Public and the Private in Aristotle's Political Philosophy.* Ithaca: Cornell University Press, 1992.

White, Stephen A. *Sovereign Virtue: Aristotle on the Relation Between Happiness and Prosperity.* Stanford: Stanford University Press, 1992.

Yack, Bernard. *The Problems of a Political Animal: Community, Justice, and Conflict in Aristotelian Political Thought.* Berkeley: University of California Press, 1993.

4

CHRISTIAN CONCEPTIONS OF CIVIC VIRTUE

I. INTRODUCTION

In this chapter, I survey different Christian perspectives on civic virtue, starting with Saint Augustine (354–430 A.D.) and then moving to late medieval thinker, St. Thomas Aquinas (1225–1274). I conclude the chapter with a discussion of Reformation Christianity, including Martin Luther (1483–1546) and John Calvin (1509–1564). Common to all views of Christianity discussed here is acceptance of the importance of Christian religious institutions to the welfare of individuals in society. In this chapter I discuss the different views of Christianity provided here as I develop the respective conceptions of civic virtue, as well as the implications of these different approaches to Christianity for civil society.

II. INTRODUCTION TO AUGUSTINE: CICERO

The Roman Emperor, Constantine, in 313 A.D. established by edict the toleration of Christianity. By the end of the fourth century, the Empire had moved to support Christianity by destroying its competitors.[1] In particular, Constantine's period marked the beginning of the effort by the Empire to destroy what had been the official Roman religion, paganism. The latter, which included worship of many gods, was subjected throughout the fourth century to various decrees of condemnation, all designed to deny paganism a place in the Empire. This endeavor was strongly resisted by some of the supporters of paganism.[2]

In this context, Augustine wrote the *City of God* to defend the Christian religion against the pagan accusation that Christianity deserved the blame for the decline of the Roman Empire and, in particular, for the "sack" of Rome itself by the Goths in 410 A.D.[3] Augustine defended Christianity by arguing that the actual cause of the misfortunes which the Romans experienced was not Christianity, but the absence of moral restraint on the part of the citizens and leadership of the Empire. "The lust that burned in their [Roman] hearts was more deadly than the flame which consumed their dwellings."[4] Moreover, Augustine said that pagan gods did nothing to "prevent the degeneration of traditional morality."[5] Augustine challenged Roman critics of Christianity "to quote injunctions against luxury and greed, given by their gods to the Roman people."[6] In contrast to pagan teachings, Christian holy books were filled with "those uniquely impressive warnings against greed and self-indulgence, given everywhere to the people assembled to hear them, in thunder of oracles from the clouds of God."[7]

In further support of his case that Christianity was not the cause of the downfall of the Roman Empire, Augustine referred to the writings of Cicero (106 B.C.E.–43 B.C.E.). Cicero's account of the Roman state, in *On the Commonwealth,* was written during the time of Julius Caesar, 60 B.C.E. to 52 B.C.E.[8] Cicero wrote from his experiences as a prominent lawyer and elected public official, who also lived during the political upheaval and power struggles recurrent during the time of Caesar.[9] In the *City of God,* Augustine showed that Cicero's *On the Commonwealth* argued that the Roman commonwealth was predicated upon "a common sense of right and a community of interest."[10] But Cicero's view of the Empire referred to an image of its past greatness, and Cicero lamented that during his time Roman life did not meet the standards set by the past. Augustine demonstrated that Cicero felt that owing to the moral degradation of Roman life, the magnificence of the past might no longer be obtainable in the present. Augustine noted that Cicero made this argument before Christ appeared, and during a time when pagan gods showed "no concern to prevent the ruin and loss of that commonwealth."[11]

The Roman Empire that Cicero hoped to restore embodied the vision of an ancient morality based on long-standing traditions that had been the basis for uniting the diverse cultures and territories of the Empire.[12] Indeed, the ancient standards, if restored and made a part of current practice, would permit a commonwealth based on the rule of law whose origin is universal reason and whose objective is liberty. Liberty, for Cicero, meant the absence of external impediments that keep people from doing as they choose. But this state of affairs is only possible when individuals voluntarily subject themselves to the limitations of law and moral principle. People upheld these standards of civic virtue, then, because doing so was advantageous to securing their freedom. Freedom meant more than just individual choice, however. In addition, freedom permitted citizens to take part in the political affairs of the regime, and in this realm, too, individuals are to display respect for the norms of civic virtue. Cicero's view of freedom, then, is occasioned by his concept of justice. Justice is a way of life that directs us to manifest consideration for the interests of all others, and further, Cicero expects the state to translate this concern into laws that are fair and that are applied impartially. And good laws, when implemented evenly, extend liberty to all.[13]

Lest one think Cicero is the founder of modern, liberal conceptions of civil society, it must be made clear that Cicero's vision of freedom and justice never was used to critique the rigid class hierarchy which favored the aristocratic few against the rest of society. The Roman Empire was based on an agricultural economy with most of the wealth derived from the arduous labor of a large peasant class. Peasant generated wealth was transferred to the aristocracy who used it to maintain a life of privilege, leisure, and control of a vast Empire. In addition, there was a large class of urban workers who performed various jobs in Rome. Some of these people were citizens, others were freedmen who had been released from slavery, and still others were freeborn. Freeborn males, often peasants forced from their homes, provided the necessary labor for building, for hulling materials, and for working on the docks and the nearby farms. Some of the freedmen were skilled craftsmen, tradesmen, teachers, doctors, or artists, and a few were well-educated men of letters. Many freedmen served as household superintendents and civil servants, while some were confidential secretaries. Urban workers lived in impoverished conditions and were subject to the power and needs of the ruling class. The lowest class consisted of slaves, many of whom performed the same functions as urban workers. There was no powerful middle class of prosperous businessmen or professionals.[14]

Cicero's discussion of justice was never designed to provide reforms which would have addressed the misery and injustice inflicted upon peasants and urban workers by the class structure that dominated Roman life. Indeed, Cicero was part of an aristocratic class who took for granted the benefits of life the other classes made possible. By appealing for a restoration of traditional values he sought to secure what he understood to be a civilized life, which in his case meant the preservation of the socially and politically better-off class.[15] He did so despite the fact that in the abstract, at least, his concepts of justice and liberty, if applied to those on the bottom rungs of society, would have suggested social reforms to bring about a more fair and more just circumstance for all people.

Augustine did not take Cicero to task for failing to question the existing class structure and asking how it supported Cicero's ideal of a just commonwealth. Instead, Augustine took issue with Cicero's view that there was a time, a golden age, when Roman life embodied Cicero's conception of civic virtue.[16] Augustine argued that the Roman commonwealth of Cicero's description never in fact existed. He said that "there never was real justice in the [ancient Roman] community."[17] Augustine did not deny that Rome was better ruled by the "Romans of antiquity than by their later successors."[18] Moreover, Augustine could accept that the Roman republic was a commonwealth in the sense that the citizens of Rome were united by a common agreement on behalf of shared objectives. But for Augustine, the moral character of a commonwealth depends upon the objectives of its common efforts. "The better the objects of this agreement, the better the people."[19] But the objects of Roman commonwealth never included a love and respect for God, and in consequence of this fact, there was never in place a commitment to maintain the canons of a virtuous life. "Because God does not rule there [in Rome], the general characteristic of that city is that it is devoid of true justice."[20]

That condition awaits humankind in the world to come, the kingdom beyond this world, the Kingdom of God. True justice is a condition in which every one receives their due when each acts in accordance with the rational or "just order of nature." Whereas Augustine could accept that such an order exists, he argued that true justice is an objective that is not possible in the human world. And this is because individuals, owing to human frailty, are incapable of conduct in keeping with a rational order that requires people to subordinate themselves, body and soul, to God. Augustine asked, "does not justice demonstrate . . . that she is still laboring at her task, rather than resting after reaching its completion?"[21] As Herbert Deane says "only in that city 'whose founder and ruler is Christ' is mutual love the ruling principle, so that there is no need for coercion, punishment, or repression. In that city alone can men realize the noble aims proclaimed by the philosophers of Greece and Rome—complete and unbroken peace, perfect concord and harmony, true self-realization, and perpetual happiness."[22] Augustine's position suggests that while he retained the Platonic ideal of a just society, he did not accept that justice could ever be attained in the earthly condition. Rome is not alone in failing to achieve true justice; this outcome is common to humankind.

What, then, should we hope for in this world? What kind of commonwealth is within our grasp? For Augustine, we can only expect a society that makes possible sufficient order to ensure peace.[23] But why is this the case, or in other terms, why is the hope of Plato deemed impossible by Augustine? Moreover, what are the implications for civic virtue of Augustine's political realism?

III. THE PROBLEM OF SIN

For Augustine, the fall of man, which occurred in the Garden of Eden, is the basis for the inability of society to achieve true justice. When the first man and woman disobeyed God, sin was introduced into the world, and all humankind for the rest of time was punished. The most significant consequence of this event is that we have lost an ability to conduct our lives in keeping with the rule of a rational will, which originally, before the fall, was able to make appetite follow a moral course. Sexual desire is perhaps the most important example of this circumstance. Before the fall, for Augustine Adam and Eve possessed, as Anne Pagels says, "mental mastery over the procreative process: the sexual members, like the other parts of the body, enacted the work of procreation by a deliberate act of will."[24] But after the fall, we lack the ability to control and guide our sexual urges and to subject them to the moral authority of our rational will.

Thus, Augustine said that "had there been no lust," our "sexual organs could have been the obedient servants of mankind, at the bidding of the will."[25] The special casualty of lust is happiness between men and women and love within the family. For instance, owing to the presence of sin, marriage cannot bring about genuine happiness, but instead marriage is suffused with conflict. Had it not been for sin, "marriage would have been worthy of the happiness of paradise, and would have given birth to children to be loved, and yet would not have given rise to any lust to be ashamed of."[26]

This condition seems to imply that even though we may know what constitutes rational conduct, we are forever hampered in our ability to do what is right. Needless to say, this condition would produce for humankind a continuing sense of frustration and unhappiness. Indeed, as Pagels says, "the commonest experiences of frustration—mental agitation, bodily pain, aging, suffering, and death—continually prove to us our incapacity to implement the rule of our will."[27]

What hope, then, are we left with? For Augustine, God can release us from the pain of sin through His granting of grace.[28] Heaven and eternal happiness await those accorded grace. Not all will be granted grace, however. God has predestined only a few to receive this gift. As Deane points out, for Augustine "this minority, the elect, were chosen to receive the gift of faith and, as a consequence, salvation and exemption from the just punishment of sin, without any regard to their future merits or good works." For Augustine, God has condemned the whole human race, now and into the future, to be denied salvation as a result of the fall, but it is through His mercy that a few will be saved.[29]

Putting aside the theological implications of this doctrine, the social and political ones are clear enough. People who lack the knowledge of their ultimate fate will live with a great degree of fear and inner turmoil. And this fact will have favorable consequences to those who wish to rule them. How is this possible? People in Augustine's world lived with the great anxiety and frustration associated with uncertainty. The uncertainty is caused not only by the absence of true justice in society, but also by the fact that one has no certain knowledge that one has been accorded God's grace. The uncertainty can become paralyzing to such an extent that a person, lacking all hope, can never have a moment of happiness or release from the ever-present painfulness of doubt. The only solution is to refuse to let uncertainty take hold in one's life. And having faith in God is one way by which to achieve this objective. But for faith to work to this end, it must be total. Consequently, the quest for faith means one must place oneself into the hands of those who articulate the articles of faith, as well as those who maintain the order of society in which the faithful are protected. In each case, there are institutions of major importance placed in charge of people's lives. In one instance the institution of importance is the church and in the other it is the state.

IV. THE TWO CITIES: THE EARTHLY CITY AND THE HEAVENLY CITY

For Augustine, there are two cities, each based on a different kind of love. "The earthly city was created by self-love reaching to the point of contempt for God, the Heavenly City by the love of God carried as far as contempt of self."[30] In the earthly city, the major objective is to glorify the acts of man, but in the heavenly city, the objective is to live for the glory of God. In the earthly city, those who rule have a "lust for domination" that is manifested in the love of strength and power. In the heavenly city, all look for guidance from God, who manifests the strength of goodness and conscience.[31] Our focus for the rest of this section is the earthly city.

Given the prevalence of sin in the world, the best that any state can achieve is, as we indicated, peace and order. This means that, whereas it is possible to achieve concord among the citizens, a concord that makes peace, stability, and order possible, it is never possible to achieve true justice, a situation in which each person is given one's due.[32] Eternal peace and justice are to be found only in the heavenly city.[33] As mentioned already, true justice awaits us only in the world to come.

If peace is all that we can hope for in this world, what kinds of social arrangements are prescribed to achieve peace? Peaceful relationships begin with the "ordered harmony" among those who live in the same house. Here, a wife obeys her husband, children obey their parents, and servants obey their masters. Those who give commands must manifest concern for the welfare of those whom they give them to.[34] Ultimately, there is a ruler who provides commands to citizens. Moreover, the ruler's main means of maintaining order, fear of punishment, is not used, as Deane says, to "make men good or virtuous, but only less harmful to their fellows."[35]

Indeed, so committed must the state be to maintaining its ability to punish, the fact of the matter is that to achieve this end it must on many occasions punish innocent people. A review of Augustine's descriptions of the plight of citizens in the court system will help make this point clear. Judges, because they cannot see "into the consciences of those on whom they [must] pronounce [guilt or innocence]," are often "compelled to seek the truth by torturing innocent witnesses in a case which is no concern of theirs."[36] But the innocent witness is not the only victim of a trial. In addition, in order to get at the truth, it may be necessary for a judge to torture the accused, too. In doing so, Augustine indicated that the judge acts with a good intention; in particular, he is, after all, seeking the truth so his verdict can be just. He would not want to execute an innocent man. Yet, ironically, the judge may end up killing an innocent victim anyway, during the course of torturing him, to determine the accused person's guilt or innocence. "Consequently, he [the judge] has tortured an innocent man to get to the truth and has killed him while still in ignorance [as to his guilt or innocence]."[37]

Would intelligent, thinking people take their seat on the bench, given that outcomes of this sort are always inevitable? Augustine said that a "wise man" would take his seat as judge; it would be "unthinkable to him that he should shirk [his duty]."[38] To refuse to participate in the legal system as a judge demonstrates a failure to confront and to accept the "wretchedness of man's situation" that causes this dilemma in the first place.[39] In this instance, it must be accepted that people commit crimes and that proving beyond any doubt that they have is often difficult. Sometimes witnesses will not tell the truth, and at other times, defendants will refuse to confess, even after being tortured. Moreover, the accusers may not be able to prove their charges. Yet, judges must make a decision of a defendant's guilt or innocence, even in the absence of the kind of perfect knowledge judges need to prove either one. That is their job. To do that job, at times he "through unavoidable ignorance [on the judge's part of the defendant's guilt or innocence] and the unavoidable duty of judging . . . tortures the innocent." No judge likes to be put into this situation, because no judge wants to cause harm to the innocent. Still, no judge can turn away from the fact that taking part in judging is a "necessity," which arises from our "human wretchedness."[40]

Augustine's discussion suggests that participation in the legal system as a judge is an unhappy obligation, needed to maintain order. Without institutions in place to mete out punishment to people, there would be complete and total chaos. What holds down the chaos is the existence of a state that strikes terror into the hearts of people. And what strikes more terror than the thought of a system that uses irrational means (torture) to achieve rational results (proof of innocence)? If innocent people are tortured, then others who are prone to commit crimes might not do so on the assumption that for certain they will be caught and tortured, too. The legal system that Augustine discussed was the opposite of ours. While we bend over backwards to protect the rights of the accused, thus allowing some guilty people to go free and unpunished, the legal system in Augustine's time moves to the other extreme, demonstrating a readiness to punish the innocent as well as the guilty. In a world in which most people are ruled by sin, heavy punishment applied indiscriminately both to the guilty and to the innocent is the only means to maintain order.

V. IMPLICATIONS OF AUGUSTINE'S VIEW FOR CIVIC VIRTUE AND CIVIL SOCIETY

Augustine's depiction of the earthly city demonstrates that civic virtue does not have the same significance for him that it had for Plato. As we saw in Plato, civic virtue refers to the habits, such as respect for the law, that orient people to uphold the common good.

These habits are the basis for enabling individuals to develop within themselves the proper arrangement of the different parts of the soul, so that overall, each is able to contribute to the needs of the society. Here, civic virtue suggests a basis for perfecting our souls by making our lives conform to the rational order of a just life. In this context, reason rules the appetite and subjects it to the demands of a rational life.

However, Augustine rejected this view entirely. In Augustine, even a person committed to make reason the controlling element over appetite would fall short of achieving a virtuous life. And the basis for this view is that a rational faculty that is not dedicated to serving God is a rational faculty that can never bring people freedom from vice.[41] Moreover, even when people have a belief in God, the peace that faith brings only secures "solace for our wretchedness rather than the joy of blessedness."[42] In this situation, people may hope to receive only forgiveness for their sins but never perfection in the development of their virtues, as Plato had hoped for. In the earthly city, even for the faithful, it will always be the case that no matter how hard people try to subdue sin and appetite with their reason, sin will reappear and undo their best efforts. We can never attain "perfect peace," because, even for the Christian, a life dedicated to the rule of reason always runs afoul of the weaknesses that permit sin to gain the upper hand. Real happiness and true justice await entrance into the heavenly city after we pass from this life. The "ultimate peace," a life in which people are finally "healed" or cured of sin so that they can live as Plato had hoped, in keeping with their reason, awaits us in the life to come, when we have achieved "immortality."[43]

This position should not be construed to exclude the prospect of good rulers. The latter not only benefit those whom they rule by providing some degree of justice, but they benefit themselves because, unlike the wicked, they do not destroy their souls.[44] Thus, as with Plato, there is the hope that the good will rule, but given Augustine's view of the depraved quality of human nature, it is likely that there will be few people who can make justice the main objective of their lives. In this event, true justice, where everyone receives one's due in a rationally ordered society, is a value that would seem for Augustine to be beyond the reach of all states or what he called kingdoms. This outcome is terribly unfortunate, for where justice does not exist, a state is nothing more than a criminal organization. Augustine said,

> *Remove justice, and what are kingdoms but gangs of criminals on a large scale? What are criminal gangs but petty kingdoms? A gang is a group of men under the command of a leader, bound by a compact of association, in which the plunder is divided according to an agreed convention.*[45]

But even in the absence of true justice, the earthly city, by maintaining peace, can still at least avoid the chaos just described, and this possibility is very important for Christians, who in Augustine's period lived among cultures and traditions that often had no appreciation for Christian teaching. A Christian in this setting is often like a "pilgrim in a foreign land."[46] The earthly city, although not based on love of God, can protect peace and, by doing so, permit diverse cultures to coexist in a way that does not interfere with Christians' being able to practice their religion. Christians, as members of the heavenly city during their sojourn on earth, have every interest in working for peaceful coexistence with alien cultures. Indeed, it is peace that enables Christianity to survive and to teach that the real peace "of the perfectly ordered and completely harmonious fellowship in enjoyment of God," awaits the faithful. Christians, then, are engaged in a "pilgrimage," which manifests a deep faith in God's message that the perfect peace and justice of "rational creation" and eternal life can and will ultimately prevail.[47]

Here, Christian civic virtue symbolizes the ability of people to sustain belief in a possible, happy future in a time marked by a personal struggle with sin as well as by societal conflict. The pilgrimage to the better world is merely the experience of a person who must undergo great tests to his or her faith. In addition, civic virtue suggests that, during the pilgrimage to the better world, individuals will work to maintain peace and order. Of course, order is not true justice, which can be realized only in the next world. But as long as there is peace there is some resistance to sin, and thus there remains the hope that Christianity will remain a strong force in the world.

Augustine's world would not accommodate the civil society experience described in Chapter 1. Augustine's faithful live in fear of sin, and thus they are likely to be frightened of their own freedom; indeed, they would tend to see their own freedom as a manifestation of sinfulness. It is not likely, then, that a separate sphere of associations could emerge in Augustine's society, within a larger moral environment committed to those civic virtues, like toleration and mutual respect, that are the basis for people's securing the rights of all individuals. For this situation to emerge, individuals must be first freed from the terrors described by Augustine in the earthly city. Aquinas seems to move in this direction.

VI. St. Thomas Aquinas: Justice Restored

For Augustine, faith and not reason offered a truer picture of our possibilities. For Aquinas (1225–1274) reason is restored as an important resource for understanding the nature of the world. Why is this? During Aquinas's time, largely as a result of Muslim thinkers, Aristotle's writings were rediscovered and they inspired debate and discussion among philosophers and theologians.[48] At first, the Roman Catholic Church resisted Aristotle, even banning his work at the University of Paris. But later, the Church accepted those such as Aquinas who attempted to create a reconciliation between Christianity and Aristotle. In the new synthesis, both reason and faith are co-partners in understanding the just or rational structure of society.

Aquinas accepted Aristotle's view that there is a rational order to society. The farmer contributes food, the religious leaders make possible chances for spiritual awareness, and the rulers provide necessary leadership. Embodied in this view is the notion that God establishes the foundation of a rational order, and the ruler of society must contribute to maintaining the rational order of society and thus help to uphold the common good.[49] Aquinas, unlike Augustine, held a concept of Christianity open to the view that a just, or rationally ordered, society is feasible. In taking this position, Aquinas's view of society provided the hope that a rational unity undergirds society and makes possible Aristotle's communal solidarity. But, unlike Aristotle, he believed that central to this endeavor was acceptance of God as the source of the laws that grounds both the community and the authority that rulers hold over the community.

It should be noted, before proceeding to a discussion of Aquinas's view of law, that his commitment to replicating Aristotle's approach to political community in the Middle Ages provided justification for sustaining medieval Christian societies as well. Medieval societies were smaller units than what had been the experience in the Roman Empire and what would be the experience with the nation-state in modern times. These small units were centered on a king who, as the only landowner, granted his barons rights to land in exchange for their services. The barons in turn had under them serfs, upon whose toil the entire system was based. The serfs worked the land in exchange for food and a place to live.[50] The revenues, which arose from the tenants, barons and serfs alike, were used to maintain an army as well as to secure order within the kingdom. In these communities the kings were owed obedience by barons and serfs. The king was obligated to provide the barons and serfs with protection and to uphold those local customs that defined their rights and prerogatives.[51]

Obviously, then, wide differences in status existed between the king and those who worked for him. Does this mean that these communities lacked common values? Not at all. Feudal societies were Christian, and, furthermore, these societies believed that there were to two authorities, one that was temporal to maintain social order and the other that was spiritual, to teach the lessons of faith. Neither was to interfere with the work of the other, but each was to support the other in keeping with the laws of God and reason.[52]

Aquinas upheld these common standards as well, and he sought to strengthen them and the medieval society that embodied them. To this end, he argued that the political unit was a community making possible collaborative efforts that contributed to the common good and the moral unity of society, much as Aristotle had done. Central to the success of this endeavor was the existence of civil law, whose actual foundation rested with God. Thus, the basis for community was not merely rational laws and common moral values that such laws embody, as Aristotle had argued, but also the realization that the basis for this law, as taught by the Church, was God. Without respect for the Church that teaches God's truth, a community among people would not be possible on earth.

In taking this position, the two realms of king and church should be viewed as complementing each other, and people, by upholding the law and fulfilling their civic virtue obligations, act not only as good citizens but as good Christians, too. This combination is the basis for sustaining community even in a society in which there are wide differences in entitlements and privileges.

We turn now to a discussion of Aquinas's view of law.

VII. THE NATURAL LAW IN AQUINAS

Aquinas said that there are four forms of law. Each form represents a different dimension of reason, and yet all forms of reason are integrated under the divine plan of God. The four forms of law are eternal, natural, divine, and human. *Eternal law* refers to the unchanging, timeless relationships created by God among all things in the universe.[53] The eternal law—when manifested as natural, divine, and human law—guides human beings and the working of society. For instance, *natural law,* which is known through reason, is concerned with defining the standards of good and evil, just and unjust, by which all individuals in the society are to act.[54] *Divine law* arises from revelation, not from reason, and the content of this revelation is the morality described in Scripture.[55] Divine law's importance derives from the fact that natural law, while stating the nature of good and evil, does not by itself make clear the true end to which God directs people. By contrast, divine law makes clear that the true end of life is "eternal happiness." And further, divine law indicates that to achieve this end it is necessary not only to do as the natural law requires but it is also necessary to act according to the "divine" laws given by God's command.[56]

Further, Aquinas's view of divine law is very important in achieving Aristotle's communal setting. Community, as we saw in Aristotle, depends upon the possibility of forms of friendship in which there is a basic understanding among individuals as to what constitutes the common moral values that are vital to the well-being of all members. These values enable people to formulate common opinions about what is best for society with respect to the way people should conduct their lives. Without a conception of the common moral values that ground the community, there might be many contradictory views as to what constitutes proper conduct, and in the face of this situation it would be impossible to clarify the laws all should uphold. Thus, for Aquinas, "different people form different judgments on human acts," and, owing to this fact, "different and contrary laws result."[57] As a result, society would find itself torn by conflict, and in consequence this situation would be antithetical to maintaining community.

To avoid this situation it is necessary to approach matters involving human judgment from the standpoint of the shared understanding of morality found in God's words, and then each person will be able to "know without any doubt what he ought to do and what he ought to avoid."[58] Here, because the laws given by God "cannot err," the ambiguities associated with differences in judgment are fully overcome. In transcending these differences and in defining the common norms of conduct all share, individuals are able, as for Aristotle, to maintain a basis for the affective ties of community.

Finally, divine law suggests that, when people act virtuously, they do so not from the presence of external force alone, but from right motives and choice. Here, the presence of human laws by themselves will not engineer virtuous conduct; individuals must from their own volition deny the influence of evil. Those who make divine law a primary basis for their lives, will, from choice and not from external force, act against evil and in keeping with what natural law requires. This is an important element of Aquinas's argument. If we had to rely upon external human laws threatening force as the basis for conformity with all natural law principles, then the law would become so all-pervasive that it would end up threatening "many good things" and thus hindering the "advance of the common good." For Aquinas, when people do not uphold the canons of moral right from their own volition, then creating a basis for community becomes very difficult. But community, based on recognition of the common good, is necessary, said Aquinas, for "human intercourse."[59] Again, as for Aristotle, the basis for community requires that there be shared moral values. In the case of Aquinas, the shared moral values include not only natural law, but divine law, or that law given to us directly from God through the Scripture. Together, these moral values form the basis for the affective ties of community.

The *human law* embodies the principles of right conduct, or natural law, in rules that govern daily life. Indeed, Aquinas said that "every human law has just so much of the nature of law as it is derived from the law of nature."[60] Since natural law provides the principled foundations of human law, it is well to discuss natural law in some detail.

The main or primary natural law principle is that the *"good is that which all things seek after."* Hence, *"good is to be done and ensued, and evil is to be avoided."* For Aquinas, all other precepts of the natural law stem from this primary principle. This means that we are to do what is good and to avoid doing what is evil.[61] What are the good things we should do, and, just as important, how do we distinguish the good from the bad? For Aquinas, there are natural inclinations that our reason interprets as good, and, in following these inclinations, we do what is morally permissible. Alternatively, we should avoid pursuing ends that are contrary to our natural inclinations, for these ends are evil.

So what are the good things we have natural inclinations to do? First, each of us wants to preserve his or her own life, and by virtue of this inclination, "whatever is a means of preserving human life and of warding off its obstacles belongs to the natural law." Secondly, there is an inclination to do those things that nature ingrains in all animals including human ones; in particular, we have an inclination to engage "in sexual intercourse, education of offspring, and so on." These activities, too, fall under the natural law. Third, there is a natural inclination in human beings to pursue their natures as rational persons, and this inclination exhorts us to "know the truth about God and to live in society." What pertains to this inclination falls under natural law, and this includes an obligation to "shun ignorance, to avoid offending those among whom one has to live, and other such things regarding the above inclination."[62]

Now, the primary natural law principle of always seeking to do good and the precepts that follow from it, such as those just mentioned, I will, following Aquinas, refer to as "common natural law principles" that are used as guides when determining the basis for conduct. Here, it is necessary for people to search for a correct application of these principles, and Aquinas refers to the resulting norms as *secondary principles.* When differences arise over how to interpret the common natural law principles, what is the best way to resolve them? Aquinas believed that "as to certain proper or derived norms, which are, as it were, conclusions of these common [natural law] principles, they are valid and so recognized by all men only in the majority of cases."[63] Because people would be approaching such matters from the perspective of divine law, finding acceptable and valid applications of common natural law principles should not be difficult. Once again, as for Aristotle, having common moral values in the community is the basis for establishing concord among the citizens on important questions, such as in Aquinas's case, providing interpretations of common natural law principles. The only hindrance to achieving acceptable secondary principles emerges during those times when people's reason has been "distorted by passion."[64]

But how useful is Aquinas's natural law doctrine? Those who argue that natural law is not very helpful might point out that too often natural law principles are so vague that they can provide little guidance to us as we try to determine the best route of conduct. For instance, take the natural law principle that requires us to do good and to avoid evil by preserving human life and removing whatever might injure life. What does this principle suggest for how one should determine one's position on abortion? The answer to this question depends largely upon factors other than the principle itself. After all, both those for and against abortion might use this principle to justify their respective positions, but, in the end, each party's decision would be based on other considerations, such as one's view of privacy, of the status of the fetus, and so on. One might use this case to make the claim that natural law principles are not really useful guides in resolving key moral dilemmas such as the dilemma of abortion.

On the other hand, some proponents of natural law might argue that authentic natural law principles provide in a very clear and definitive way the moral course we should take on various key issues. If natural law fails in this regard, it is not so much the fault of natural law, but it is the fault of the natural law theorist who has failed to compose the natural law in a way that makes it useful. Indeed, the proponent of natural law can argue that great progress has been made in the modern world to draw up principles that, in unambiguous ways, prescribe the course of proper conduct. For instance, the contemporary principle that says that individuals should respect the rights of others is very clear as to what kinds of actions are entailed by this principle. From this principle, we know that we should eliminate all slavery as well as remove from society all obstacles that stand in the way of equal rights and fair opportunities for all people, regardless of race, gender, sexual preference, and so on. In this case, natural law is a great help to achieving not only a just society, but also a society that seeks to balance the quest for freedom with the need to secure the basic needs of people.

VIII. HUMAN LAW AND CIVIC VIRTUE

Given these competing views of natural law, which one, it might be asked, does Aquinas subscribe to? Clearly, it was his hope that natural law should represent the precise moral framework for the members of a community. But how can this state of affairs be achieved? Of course, one way would be to teach people the importance of divine law. But another important approach to this objective is to emphasize civic virtue. For Aquinas, people who lack a commitment to make the community's good their own will naturally interpret the natural law in any way they wish, and they will not likely see natural law as providing the precise moral boundaries of life. It is for this reason, for instance, that Aquinas worried that, whereas primary natural law principles cannot be "blotted out from men's hearts," the power of reason to understand the precise significance of these principles for particular actions is compromised by the presence of lust and appetite. In this case, the general principle to be followed is known, but reason is "hindered from applying the general principle to a particular point of practice, on account of concupiscence or some other passion."[65] Moreover, knowledge of the correct secondary principles that individuals should follow can be "blotted out from the human heart by evil persuasions."[66]

Human law is an important instrument in overcoming both of these problems and in giving natural law its recurring importance as a precise set of moral boundaries for determining the nature of conduct. Human law, which embodies natural law principles, must teach virtue and accustom individuals to uphold the teachings of natural law. Through the shaping influence of "training" and in particular the "fear of punishment," individuals learn the "discipline of laws" and are reminded that they must accommodate their lives to the proper course of conduct laid out by both primary and secondary natural law principles.[67] A major function of the community is to teach the important civic virtues that orient people away from tendencies to selfishness and a lack of regard for the common good. In this regard, as in Plato's and Aristotle's views of a rational society, human law helps to clarify the particular roles in the society and what the expected contributions of people to each of those roles should be. For instance, soldiers should defend the nation, priests should provide spiritual knowledge, and rulers should govern justly.[68]

But Aquinas warned us to adopt a practical set of expectations pertaining to what we can hope to achieve through human law. It must be clear that, since the majority of people do not manifest moral perfection, it is impossible to create human laws that will be able to eradicate all vice. The best the human law can do, then, is to eliminate the grosser vices, those actions that, if permitted, would undermine human society, and for this reason there must be laws against murder, theft, and so on.[69]

This point of view suggests, as well, that it would be wrong to try to create human laws that eradicated all vice. Were such an objective to be embodied into human law, there would have to be morals police on every corner questioning each person about the moral nature of their intentions, and each of us would have to check with these police to see whether our proposed activities were morally sanctioned. This situation would hardly be a place receptive to building the affective ties of community. In this spirit, for instance, Aquinas says at times "it is right for those who are in authority to tolerate some evils so as not to prevent other goods or to avoid some worse evil from occurring."[70] Following this line of argument, Aquinas cites with approval Augustine who said, "suppress prostitution and the world will be torn apart by lust." Further, unbelievers may be tolerated for Aquinas, "because a greater good may come of it or some evil may be avoided."[71]

IX. AQUINAS ON THE QUESTION OF CIVIC VIRTUE AND CIVIL SOCIETY

Nonetheless, the major purpose of Aquinas's view of human law would be to teach people the habits of civic virtue, which enable people to uphold the common good. But unlike Aristotle, Aquinas believed that the habits of civic virtue, which teach respect for the moral boundaries embodied in the natural law, could only be sustained over the long run when individuals shared a belief in the Catholic Church's teachings of the nature of divine law. Here, when individuals understand that they are part of a common world ordained by God, they not only understand the origin of morality and natural law, but they also experience as the source of morality the same religious inspiration that helps to bind people together communally. Certainly, Aristotle hoped for a political community predicated upon friendship and communal solidarity, but Aquinas would argue that that hope is best realized when the members of society hold in common a commitment to divine law and faith in the teachings of the Catholic Church.

But from the standpoint of modern civil society thinkers, a significant problem with Aquinas's view of civic virtue would remain. For Aquinas, individuals must make the teachings of the Catholic Church the centerpiece of their lives. Aquinas, in discussing heresy, said that "if it is just for counterfeiters or other criminals to be executed immediately by secular rulers, it is all the more just for heretics once they are convicted of heresy not only to be excommunicated but to be put to death."[72] He qualified this harsh statement by saying that the Church hopes for conversion of "those who are in error." Here, there is no question that Aquinas was protecting society from all those who might undermine belief and with it the benefits of community. Still in taking this view, Aquinas demonstrated that a single institution, the Church, must have a powerful role to play in the moral and intellectual lives of each citizen. Given this fact, individuals, in reasoning about what is best for society, are not to question the Church's authority in matters of truth.

Now as we have seen, a civil society suggests the need for a separate sphere in which individuals can move among different groups and from this experience determine that way of life that is best for themselves. But for Aquinas, this view of society might pose a threat to the autonomy of the Church and in particular to its ability to determine the nature of moral order in the society. We now turn to Reformation thinking to discuss the approach to Christianity found there.

X. LUTHER AND CALVIN: AN INTRODUCTION

For Martin Luther (1483–1546) and John Calvin (1509–1564), the central target is the authority of the Roman Catholic Church. Luther argued, as Sheldon Wolin points out, that "religious experience was located around an intensely personal communication between the individual and God."[73] Individuals must have a direct relationship with God, which is built upon faith. Faith cleanses the soul and allows us to love God. By virtue of faith, our souls desire that "all things" and (most important) our bodies will become morally pure so that we will be able to love God. As a result of faith, then, a person comes to obey the commandments of the Scripture and to repress "lasciviousness and lust." For Luther, "faith alone and the Word of God rule in the soul. Just as the heated iron glows like fire because of the union of fire with it, so the Word imparts its qualities to the soul."[74]

Given this view, Luther sought to remove as much as possible the various structures of established Church authority. These structures only served to impede the direct relationship that individuals must have with God.[75] Moreover, in removing these structures, Luther hoped to accord people greater spiritual freedom. Luther said that an individual is to be "responsible for his own faith, and he must see to it for himself that he believes rightly."[76] In Luther's community of believers, faith is a matter to be left to each individual, and no one is to force another to believe doctrines that individuals do not embrace from their own volition and conscience. "Faith is a free work, to which no one can be forced."[77]

In contrast, as Wolin says, Calvin did not accept that the religious community could exist as a freely subscribed-to setting, governed by persuasion and not force, but that it could exist only if there were maintained a strong structure of authority to secure the "coherence and solidarity of the group." The church community, without restoring a pope, should be governed by a strong leadership group.[78] Thus, Calvin believed that a church, in this case, his church, must establish a regimen of discipline to limit and constrain all people so that they are capable of accepting the teachings of God. Without the discipline the church can provide, human beings will stray from the teachings of the church, and this consequence would "promote the entire dissolution of the Church."[79] Here, the church was right to lay down rules pertaining to people's sex lives, their leisure, and their relationships within families.[80]

Ironically, as individuals are weaned away from the authority of the Roman Catholic Church, they are placed under a new church authority whose purpose, as Wolin argues, is to "mould the members to a common outlook and instruct them in the lessons of the common good."[81] For Calvin, the impact of the new church on individuals would be to make people subject to the requirements of order and discipline or to the norms of civic virtue. And the consequences of this policy would be to insure that each person would be a good contributing member to society, while at the same time a strong and committed believer.[82]

XI. LUTHER AND CALVIN: MORALITY AND CIVIC VIRTUE

Both Luther and Calvin required citizens to have allegiance to the state and to respect its efforts to maintain order. For Luther, were all people to be motivated by God's word, there would be no need for a state to impose order and maintain constraints. Luther said that Christ acknowledged a sword, but he did not need to use it in His Kingdom. But Luther believed that those who live by the word of God, Christians, are in the minority, and thus most people will not be motivated by Christian piety.[83] There is a need for the state, therefore, to use its force to ensure compliance with the law and thus to maintain order sufficient to protect the lives and property of individuals.[84]

Given that Christians' piety makes the use of force as the basis for good conduct unnecessary for them, should Christians submit to a state that uses force to secure compliance with the laws? Luther answered in the affirmative. A true Christian subordinates himself to the state and does all he can "to further government, that it may be sustained and held in honor and fear."[85] In the secular world, the Christian must manifest civic virtue by upholding two contradictory moral systems. His Christian morality requires that he be concerned to labor "on earth not for himself" but for others. Christian morality "impels him to do even that which he need not do." Thus, the Christian helps the sick, and does what is "necessary for his neighbor."[86] But, in addition, the good Christian must contribute his share to the order-keeping dimension of society, and this means that at times he may have to kill for the state. "Therefore, should you see that there is a lack of hangmen, beadles [macebearers], judges, lords or princes, and find that you are qualified, you should offer your services."[87]

Calvin held a similar view of the moral responsibilities of citizenship. He indicated that, in the political world, a major concern of government is with the ongoing needs of physical existence, including the provision of food and clothing as well as enacting laws for the purpose of regulating society by the "rules of holiness, integrity, and sobriety."[88] Thus, it is necessary to recognize the importance of a civil government that supports the worship of God, to preserve "pure" religious doctrines, "to defend the constitution of the Church," and to maintain among men peace and civil justice.[89] To accomplish these purposes, it will be necessary for the state to use methods of severe punishment so that the innocent can be protected from the activities of the "wicked." In doing so, however, the state is not acting in a way that is at "variance" with the reign of Christ. For the truth is that there are some men so wicked and evil that without the authority of the state to crush them there would be no basis for a civil, Christian life.[90] Here, it will be necessary, as in

Luther, for those who are asked to carry out the state's commitment to civil order, to resort to practices that appear to be contrary to Christian morality, such as killing. Indeed, unless evil is resisted by the state, there is no way to provide a sphere that can preserve Christian teaching. Thus, in acting as the state requests, even if this means killing others in the name of resisting evil, one is sustaining the basis for a Christian state, and, actually, then, maintaining a commitment to Christian principles.

Still, for Calvin Christians are warned not to adopt the ways of those from whom the state must protect them. "God not only enjoins the preservation of the mind chaste and pure from every libidinous desire, but prohibits all obscenity of language and external lasciviousness."[91] Also, for Calvin as for Luther, living a life at peace with God requires that we demonstrate charity and service to our neighbors.[92] In living day-to-day life, Christians must manifest civic virtue by being able to "bear injuries and reproaches," and to "do good to them from whom they experience injuries."[93] At the same time, as part of what it means to maintain civic virtue, Christians must obey the state and carry out those policies that promote order and civility.

XII. THE STATE AND INTELLECTUAL FREEDOM IN LUTHER AND CALVIN

In discussing the role of the state, neither Luther nor Calvin saw the state as a protector of intellectual or moral freedom. Initially, it might appear otherwise for Luther who said that the state must not use its authority to interfere with the church teachings and "prescribe laws for the soul."[94] In taking this position, Luther made clear that citizens were not to be bullied by a state seeking to maintain Catholic doctrines. Thus, he said that "if then your prince or temporal lord commands you to hold with the pope, to believe this or that, or commands you to give up certain books, you should say, it does not befit Lucifer to sit by the side of God."[95] The view that the state must not impose Catholic doctrines is in keeping with the previously stated position held by Luther that individuals should derive their faith from their own conscience and volition.[96]

Luther was concerned not only with protecting people from the Catholic Church, but also with securing political order. Wolin says that Luther believed that, in the face of the many evils facing society, the political order is very fragile. To prevent the destruction of the fabric of society, the state was given a divine mission to uphold order, and if successful the state would then help to secure the prospects of the newly reformed church Luther advocated.[97] In taking this direction, Luther believed that the state must protect the doctrines of the reformed church, and thus he contended that the government can deny a right to a person to question the main ideas of the Christian creed. Luther's view would not support ways of life and basic rights for individuals whose conduct was in conflict with church teachings.[98] Ironically, then, Luther, who in the spiritual realm argued for intellectual freedom, must in the political realm argue against it. As Wolin says, "the divine element in political authority was inevitably transformed from a sustaining principle into a repressive, coercive one."[99]

Calvin suggests a repressive state, with respect to freedom of beliefs, too. Quoting scripture, Calvin said that "Rulers are ministers of God, revengers to execute wrath upon him that doeth evil."[100] Christian civil magistrates are the "vicegerents" [deputies] of God, and as such they must always defend God's "honor."[101] Thus, the state must not only protect people's property, maintain peace and secure justice, but it must also make sure that the "law of God be not violated and polluted by public blasphemies."[102] The state held power to promote religious purposes and doctrine. Moreover, both the church and the state were to be partners in maintaining sufficient control and power over individuals to insure that they maintained civil conduct as well as respect for the religious creed. As Wolin says, "in both worlds Calvin conceived man to be a creature of order, subject to restraints and controlled by power."[103] In holding this view, Calvin did not accept that individuals could be permitted to challenge the moral premises upon which his view of the state and church rested, and thus Calvin would deny intellectual freedom in the same way Luther did.[104]

Because Luther's church was to be a community of believers, not subject to repressive church structures, it would seem that Luther more than Calvin would promote the goals of a civil society. But given that Luther's state is as repressive as Calvin's, Luther no more than Calvin could support a separate sphere, independent of the power of the state. Nor would it be the case that Luther any more than Calvin could make possible a moral environment that made a full doctrine of rights a mainstay.

XIII. THE IMPLICATIONS FOR CIVIC VIRTUE AND CIVIL SOCIETY

The doctrine of Christian civic virtue for Luther and Calvin requires individuals to support the state in its effort to thwart sin and protect, as we just demonstrated, the integrity of Christianity, especially against its detractors. Thus, in upholding the habits of civic virtue, citizens make their contributions to the state, maintaining even those functions that might appear to be opposed to Christian beliefs, such as killing. This view of civic virtue, which suggests that citizens must support the state's efforts to maintain peace and civil justice, accepts Augustine's realism that most people will not live lives that minimize the need for the state to use force to ensure the peace. Given that there will be those who always threaten good order, it would be difficult to imagine how, for Luther and Calvin, Aquinas's communal solidarity based upon a rationally organized and structured society would be possible. On this score, Luther and Calvin seem to share with Augustine the same perspective on society.

Still, an important civil society aspect might be said to emerge from the Reformation effort of Luther and Calvin. The Reformation's call for autonomy from external institutions, such as a government-sponsored Catholic Church, points in the direction of a civil society with a separate sphere, as discussed in Chapter 1, in which people can exercise their freedom of conscience and determine their own religious commitments. Of course, the Reformation thinkers discussed here did not demand this kind of environment, and indeed admittedly each of them would have rejected it. Nonetheless, the thrust of the Reformation in arguing that the individual should be governed by his or her faith and not by external, controlling institutions laid the basis for establishing an independent sphere of life, not subject to state interference.

Thus, in uniting the need for autonomy from the Catholic Church with charity and with a concern for others, as Luther and Calvin both did, a basis is created to move in the direction of a civil society. All that is needed to complete the project is to replace the repressive form of state advocated by both Luther and Calvin (as well as the repressive religious community advocated by Calvin) with a state whose foundation is a moral environment that protects rights. Now, some might argue that the writings of Hobbes, Locke, and Kant, whom we discuss in the next part of the book, move in this direction by taking the central Christian ideas of autonomy and charity and rendering them in secular form. If this is the case, then in an indirect way Christian thinking has helped to make possible the experience of a civil society.

XIV. Transition to Machiavelli

Before moving on to discuss these writers in the next section and Machiavelli in the next chapter, it is well to keep in mind the changes taking place during this period with respect to the nature and scope of government. As George Sabine points out, during the fifteenth and sixteenth centuries in Western Europe, political authority for the most part was concentrated in the hands of powerful monarchs, and, as their power grew, the power and influence of other classes, such as the nobility and clergy, were weakened. In this situation, the king became the main figure symbolizing national unity.[105] Moreover, the state was forced to take on a new role in relation to changes in the economic lives of European societies. These changes reflected the fact that trading practices were becoming oriented to larger markets than what had been in existence in medieval Europe. In the medieval community, trade was controlled by producers' guilds, which operated within the confines of local markets or cities. During this period, however, a new bourgeoisie, or middle class, of merchants and businessmen emerged to exploit markets wherever they could find them, and thus no longer was trade confined to local markets found in cities. These people had investment funds to start new businesses, and they sought large returns on their investments. Furthermore, as these merchants created new markets, they were able to exercise control over the production of goods, as well. No longer beholden to the guilds, the new merchant class accumulated enough wealth to challenge the status and position even of the traditional nobility.[106]

In this changing context, there was a need for a central government that could assist the new commercial classes by creating an environment hospitable to their activities. In particular, there needed to be regulations pertaining to prices, to employment conditions, and to the quality of goods.[107] To this end, a more centralized state, under the authority of a powerful king, was deemed desirable by the new business class. This state was larger in size and in reach than the traditional medieval community. Now, instead of one government's controlling a small feudal community, one large, national government held sovereign power over what had been small, independent feudal communities.

The new bourgeoisie, representing new wealth based upon an enterprising mentality, viewed the king, who headed the new centralized state, as a natural ally. For this new class, the king, in administering justice and in maintaining control of the military, was able to make possible the type of stable government that was so necessary for the business activity of the new commercial class. Indeed, the king accorded the security to the new commercial class that the traditional feudal nobility would not have provided. At this time, the commercial class was not willing to create representative institutions that had more stature than the king, because commercial groups could not control parliaments still dominated by the nobility.[108] Later, as we will see in our discussion of Locke, the commercial class did make the parliament the central agency for securing their position in society. But until that time arrived, the king was given that task, as we will see when we discuss Hobbes's thought.

Thus, in this new environment, a new class of merchants calling for independence from traditional medieval ways of life became a powerful new political force in society. But what approach to civic virtue should the new society take? How will these new forms differ from the older forms, just discussed? Machiavelli will begin to answer these questions.

Endnotes

1. Mulford Q. Sibley, *Political Ideas and Ideologies: A History of Political Thought,* (New York: Harper and Row, 1970), p. 170.

2. "Introduction," by John O'Meara in St. Augustine, *City of God,* translated by Henry Bettenson, (London: Penguin Books, 1972), p. x.

3. St. Augustine, *City of God,* translated by Henry Bettenson, (London: Penguin Books, 1972), p. 49, Bk. II, ch. 2. Sabine, *A History of Political Theory,* p. 189.

4. St. Augustine, *City of God,* p. 49, Bk. II, ch. 2; also, p. 50, Bk. II, ch. 3.

5. Ibid., p. 51, Bk. II, ch. 4.

6. Ibid., p. 70, Bk. II, ch. 19.

7. Ibid., p. 70, Bk. II, ch. 19, also pp. 75–76, Bk. II, ch. 22.

8. George H. Sabine and Stanley B. Smith, "Introduction" to Cicero's *On the Commonwealth,* translated with an introduction by George H. Sabine and Stanley B. Smith, (Indianapolis: Bobbs-Merrill:, 1929), pp. 44–45.

9. Ibid., p. 2.

10. Augustine, *City of God,* p. 73, ch. 21.

11. Ibid., p. 74. Bk. II. ch. 21.

12. Neal Wood, *Cicero's Social and Political Thought,* (Berkeley: University of California, 1988), pp. 206–7.

13. George H. Sabine and Stanley B. Smith, "Introduction" to Cicero's *On the Commonwealth,* p. 49, 55–56.

14. Neal Wood, *Cicero's Social and Political Thought,* pp. 16–21.

15. Ibid., pp. 207, 211.

16. George H. Sabine and Stanley B. Smith, "Introduction" to Cicero's *On the Commonwealth,* p. 47.

17. Augustine, *City of God,* p. 75, Bk. II, ch. 21.

18. Ibid., p. 75, Bk.II, ch. 21.

19. Ibid., p. 890, Bk. XIX, ch. 24.

20. Ibid., p. 891, Bk. XIX, ch. 24.

21. Ibid., p. 854, Bk. 19, Ch. 4.

22. Herbert A. Deane, *The Political and Social Ideas of St. Augustine,* (New York: Columbia University Press, 1963). p. 11.

23. Augustine, *City of God,* p. 872, Bk. XIX, ch. 14.

24. Elaine Pagels, *Adam, Eve, and The Serpent,* (New York: Random House, 1988), p. 111; also, pp. 108, 109, and 110.

25. Augustine, *City of God,* p. 585, Bk. 14, ch. 23.

26. Ibid., p. 585, Bk. XIV, ch. 23.

27. Elaine Pagels, *Adam, Eve, and The Serpent,* p. 110, also, p. 108.

28. Augustine, *City of God,* p. 513, Bk. XIII, ch 3.

29. Deane, *The Political And Social Ideas of St. Augustine,* p. 19.

30. Augustine, *City of God,* p. 593, Bk. XIV, ch. 28.

31. Ibid., pp. 593–94, Bk. XIV, ch. 28.

32. Deane, *The Political And Social Ideas of St. Augustine,* pp. 125–26.

33. Augustine, *City of God,* p. 872, Bk. XIX, ch. 14.

34. Ibid., pp. 873–74, Bk. XIX, ch. 14.

35. Deane, *The Political And Social Ideas of St. Augustine,* p. 134; also, pp. 117, 125.

36. Augustine, *City of God,* p. 859, Bk. XIX, ch. 6.

37. Ibid., p. 860, Bk. XIX, ch. 6.

38. Ibid., p. 860, Bk. XIX, ch. 6.

39. Ibid., p. 860, Bk. XIX, ch. 6.

40. Ibid., pp. 860–61, Bk. XIX, ch. 6.

41. Ibid., p. 891, Bk. XIX, ch. 25.

42. Ibid., p. 892, Bk. XIX, ch. 27.

43. Ibid., p. 893, Bk. XIX, ch. 27.

44. Ibid., pp. 138–39, Bk. IV, ch. 3.

45. Ibid., p. 139, Bk. IV, ch. 4.

46. Ibid., pp. 877–78, Bk. XIX, ch. 17.

47. Ibid., pp. 878–79, Bk. XIX, ch. 17.

48. Sabine, *A History of Political Theory,* pp. 247–48, and Paul E. Sigmund, "Introduction," in *St. Thomas Aquinas: On Politics and Ethics,* (New York: Norton, 1988), pp. xvi–xix.

49. Sabine, *A History of Political Theory,* p. 249.

50. Ibid., pp. 214–15.

51. Ibid., p. 216.

52. Ibid., p. 225.

53. St. Thomas Aquinas, *The Summa Theologica,* ed. by Dino Bigongiari, in *The Political Ideas of St. Thomas Aquinas,* (New York: Hafner, 1965), p. 12.

54. Ibid., pp. 13–14.

55. Sabine, *A History of Political Theory,* p. 253.

56. St. Thomas Aquinas, *The Summa Theologica,* ed. by Dino Bigongiari, p. 17.

57. Ibid., p. 17.

58. Ibid., p. 17.

59. Ibid., pp. 17–18.

60. Ibid., p. 58.

61. Ibid., p. 45. Italics in text.

62. Ibid., pp. 45–46.

63. Ibid., pp. 50, 52.

64. Ibid., p. 50.

65. Ibid., p. 54.

66. Ibid., p. 54.

67. Ibid., p. 56.

68. Ibid., p. 63.

69. Ibid., p. 68.

70. Aquinas, *The Summa of Theology,* in *St. Thomas Aquinas: On Politics and Ethics,* edited by Paul E. Sigmund, (New York: Norton and Company, 1988), p. 62.

71. Ibid., p. 62.

72. Ibid., p. 63.

73. Sheldon S. Wolin, *Politics and Vision,* (Boston: Little Brown and Company, l960), p. 149.

74. Luther, "On Christian Liberty," in *Three Treatises: Martin Luther,* (Philadelphia: Fortress Press, 1960), p. 284; also, pp. 282–83, 294–96.

75. Wolin, *Politics and Vision,* p. 152.

76. Martin Luther, "Secular Authority: To What Extent Should It Be Obeyed," in William Ebenstein and Alan O. Ebenstein, *Great Political Thinkers: Plato to the Present* (Chicago: Holt, Rinehart and Winston, 1991), p. 351.

77. Ibid., p. 351.

78. Wolin, *Politics and Vision,* pp. 167–68.

79. John Calvin, "Institutes of the Christian Religion," in Ebenstein, p. 357.

80. Sibley, *Political Ideas and Ideologies,* p. 322.

81. Sheldon S. Wolin, *Politics and Vision,* p. 179.

82. Ibid., pp. 190, 172, 182.

83. Martin Luther, "Secular Authority: To What Extent Should It Be Obeyed?" in Ebenstein, p. 347.

84. Ibid., p. 350.

85. Ibid., p. 348.

86. Ibid., p. 348.

87. Ibid., p. 349.

88. John Calvin, "On Christian Liberty," in *On God and Political Duty,* (Indianapolis: Bobbs-Merrill, 1950), p. 41.

89. John Calvin "Institutes of the Christian Religion," in Ebenstein, pp. 359, 361.

90. Ibid., pp. 359, 361.

91. John Calvin, "On Christian Liberty," in *On God and Political Duty,* p. 43.

92. Ibid., p. 37.

93. John Calvin, "On Civil Government," in *On God and Political Duty,* p. 69.

94. Martin Luther, "Secular Authority: To What Extent Should It Be Obeyed?" p. 350.

95. Ibid., p. 353.

96. Ibid., p. 351.

97. Wolin, *Politics and Vision,* pp. 156–57.

98. Sibley, *Political Ideas and Ideologies,* pp. 318–19.

99. Wolin, *Politics and Vision,* pp. 157–58.

100. John Calvin, "On Civil Government," in *On God and Political Duty,* p. 49.

101. John Calvin, "Institutes of the Christian Religion," in Ebenstein, p. 360.

102. Ibid., p. 360.

103. Wolin, *Politics and Vision,* p. 173.

104. Sibley, *Political Ideas and Ideologies,* p. 323.

105. Sabine, *A History of Political Theory,* pp. 331–32.

106. Ibid., p. 332.

107. Ibid., p. 332.

108. Ibid., p. 333.

Partial Bibliography and Further Reading

Althaus, Paul. *The Ethics of Martin Luther.* Philadelphia: Fortress Press, 1972.

Bainton, Roland Herbert. *Here I Stand: A Life of Martin Luther.* New York: New American Library, 1977.

Brookes, Edgar Harry. *The City of God and The Politics of Crisis.* Oxford: Oxford University Press, 1960.

Brown, Peter Robert Lamont. *Augustine of Hippo: a Biography.* Berkeley, University of California Press, 1967.

Clark, Mary T. *Augustine.* Washington, D.C.: Georgetown University Press, 1994.

Coles, Romand. *Self, Power, Other: Political Theory and Dialogical Ethics.* Ithaca: Cornell University Press, 1992.

Connolly, William E. *The Augustinian Imperative: A Reflection on the Politics of Morality.* Newbury Park, Calif.: Sage Publications, 1993.

Deane, Herbert Andrew. *The Political and Social Ideas of St. Augustine.* New York: Columbia University Press, 1963.

Douglass, E. Jane Dempsey. *Women, Freedom, and Calvin.* Philadelphia: Westminster Press, 1985.

Fife, Robert Herndon. *The Revolt of Martin Luther.* New York, Columbia University Press, 1957.

Harkness, Georgia Elma. *John Calvin: The Man and His Ethics.* New York: Abingdon Press, 1958.

Jenkins, John I. *Knowledge and Faith in Thomas Aquinas.* Cambridge: Cambridge University Press, 1997.

Lage, Dietmar. *Martin Luther's Christology and Ethics.* New York: Mellen Press, 1990.

Luther, Martin. *Three Treatises.* Philadelphia: Fortress Press, 1960.

————. *Reformation Writings.* Translated by Bertram Lee Woolf. New York: Philosophical Library, 1953.

McInerny, Ralph M. *Aquinas on Human Action: A Theory of Practice.* Washington, D.C.: Catholic University of America Press, 1992.

Pagels, Elaine. *Adam, Eve, and The Serpent.* New York: Random House, 1988.

Parker, T. H. L. *John Calvin, a Biography.* London: Dent, 1975.

Sabine, George H. *A History of Political Theory.* New York: Holt, Rinehart, and Winston, 1961.

Walzer, Michael. *The Revolution of the Saints: A Study in the Origins of Radical Politics.* Cambridge: Harvard University Press, 1965.

Wetzel, James. *Augustine and The Limits of Virtue.* Cambridge: Cambridge University Press, 1992.

Wolin, Sheldon S. *Politics and Vision: Continuity and Innovation in Western Political Thought.* Boston: Little, Brown, 1960.

5

NICCOLÒ MACHIAVELLI:
CIVIC VIRTUE AND CIVIL SOCIETY

I. HISTORICAL SETTING AND INTRODUCTION

Niccolò Machiavelli (1469–1526) was, unlike those discussed thus far who approached politics from philosophical, moral, or religious perspectives, a political realist. As such, his main concern was learning how to get and to keep power.[1] Still, it would be wrong to conclude that "Machiavellianism" is a doctrine radically divorced from morality, and thus from a conception of civic virtue. Even though his arguments reflected the view that political authority could no longer be justified on the basis of ecclesiastical or religious grounds, he still understood the importance of maintaining among the members of the society a commitment to the common good. Without the habits of civic virtue, which include respect for the rule of law and which exhort people to promote the common good, societies might be undermined by the natural selfishness found in humankind. As one writer said, for Machiavelli, "men are apt to behave toward one another worse than most savage beasts."[2]

Prior to discussing Machiavelli's doctrines, it is necessary to provide some historical background. Throughout the fifteenth century, a single family, the Medicis, had run Machiavelli's Florence. They had governed Florence as a ruling elite, while making it appear that they were maintaining a republic as opposed to a monarchy. A republic is different from a monarchy in the sense that the latter is governed by a king whose authority derives from family background. A republic on the other hand is a political regime united around promoting a conception of the common good, but it is also presumed that the authority of the government in a republic rests upon citizen participation in determining the common good and the laws that enshrine it.

In 1494 the Medici's dominance came to an end, and there followed a series of republican and Medicean regimes until the Medici family was fully restored in 1512. During this period, Machiavelli assumed various roles, including advisor, bureaucrat, and diplomat. But after 1512, Machiavelli, who had always been committed to republican rule and who had always been anti-Medici, lost all chances for political office, and he was accused of treason, arrested, and even tortured. Eventually, he was cleared of all wrongdoing, and he went to live on a Florentine suburban farm. During this time he wrote *The Prince* and *The Discourses on the First Ten Books of Titus Livius,* both of which we will discuss in this chapter. The former work was written to provide advice and to win back favor from the Medicis, and it is thus dedicated to one of the Medici sons.[3]

Central to Machiavelli's analysis of politics was the revolution in circumstances taking place during his life. Machiavelli wrote during the fifteenth century when Italy was divided into five large states—Florence, Milan, Venice, Naples, and the papal state.[4] During this time, opportunities for economic and cultural growth were abundant. Owing to new trade opportunities, to the breakup of the feudal system, and to the establishment of new crafts, the Italian states became a part of the world economy, participating in international trade and business. But at the same time, the political structures of the Italian states could not accommodate themselves to the challenges presented by the new trading opportunities. These states were constantly involved in various conflicts, and they could not unite to form a single Italian state.[5] Machiavelli believed that the states of the Italian peninsula needed to overcome these conflicts and to form unified states like Spain, France, and England. He also believed that the pope was both too weak to unite Italy and too strong to prevent others from doing so. Machiavelli, who lived during a time that was at the earliest stages of the present-day Western nation-state system, hoped for a form of Italian government that could provide a basis for economic expansion and for eliminating divisiveness.[6]

For Machiavelli, Italy was marked, then, to cite George Sabine, by "arrested political development."[7] To move the Italian states into the modern world, there needed to be a new kind of political ruler who could create political structures that met the challenges of the changing social and economic conditions. Machiavelli's prince would have the responsibility of recasting society and creating a government with sufficient power to achieve prosperity in the new-world setting. The new ruler would help create a republic, backed by the people and institutions that secure some form of citizen participation. And the shared goal of the republic would be to advance the material progress and power of Italy as a whole.

For our purposes, Machiavelli is especially important because, in discussing the agenda for the new ruler, Machiavelli helped to pave the way for a civil society that works to secure the rule of law on behalf of protecting basic individual freedoms. As my discussion of *The Prince, The Discourses on the First Ten Books of Titus Livius,* and *Mandragola* in the rest of this chapter will demonstrate, Machiavelli is a transitional figure in this book. For even as he accepted an old-world commitment to promote the traditions of civic virtue that secured respect for the common good, he, at the same time, realized that the civic virtue orientation had to be made compatible with the quest, found in the new world, for individual liberty. Now, Machiavelli did not engage in writing the political theory of civil society, demonstrating how to define constraints that at the same time secured liberty. That task awaited those who followed him, such as Thomas Hobbes and John Locke. Still, Machiavelli set the stage for those whom we discuss in the next section of the book.

One final point. Machiavelli approached his subject from the standpoint of two types of regimes, monarchies and republics. In *The Prince,* he was concerned with discussing monarchies, especially new ones, and in the *Discourses* he was concerned with republics.[8]

In discussing new monarchies, Machiavelli demonstrated how to use power to create a new political regime within a newly conquered territory. In *The Discourses,* republics are referred to as a form of mixed government, or a government based upon established traditions that include monarchical, aristocratic, and democratic elements. His hope was that these three elements, when allowed to share power together, would help to sustain a commitment to the common good among citizens. Such a regime would permit citizen input on behalf of defining the common good and on behalf of making possible a society dedicated to the rule of law. Owing to the inherent corruptibility of humankind, however, Machiavelli worried that respect for the traditions of civic virtue, including respect for law, would be hard to maintain. This pessimism emanated from his view that human nature, as indicated earlier, is in large part characterized by selfishness and greed, and these tendencies are likely to be exacerbated in a world that more and more emphasized individual freedom. The portrait he painted of human nature in the modern world can be found in his play, *Mandragola,* which I discuss at the end of this chapter.

II. THE PRINCE

A. Monarchy

The Prince is a treatise on how to get and to keep power, and in this work he addressed how these objectives could be achieved in monarchies. In discussing monarchies in *The Prince,* Machiavelli did not dwell on hereditary ones because these states can be sustained merely by retaining allegiance to "ancestral usages."[9] For Machiavelli, "the difficulty of maintaining hereditary states accustomed to a reigning family is far less than in new monarchies."[10] The monarchies that require special attention, then, are those in which a prince is trying to establish sovereignty over a new territory or, in effect, to place himself in control of a regime previously ruled by another. "It is in the new monarchy that difficulties really exist."[11] Securing a prince's power in this situation is fraught with difficulty because there are always still present in society partisans of the old regime who resent the new order.[12] Machiavelli said that

> *it must be considered that there is nothing more difficult to carry out, nor more doubtful of success, nor more dangerous to handle, than to initiate a new order of things. For the reformer has enemies in all those who profit by the old order, and only lukewarm defenders in all those who would profit by the new order, this lukewarmness arising partly from fear of their adversaries, who have the laws in their favour; and partly from the incredulity of mankind, who do not truly believe in anything new until they have had actual experience of it.*[13]

Every prince must face the uncertainties associated with *fortune.* No one can know in advance of a proposed action what the consequences of an intended action might be. For a prince who takes over a previously governed regime, this problem is exacerbated by the hostile environment he faces. There are those who want to restore the old order, as well as so many others who expect the new prince to deliver on all his promises. There are external enemies who will seize upon any weakness they see to invade and overthrow the new regime. For these reasons, it is foolish for a prince to think that he can ever master fortune completely. Still, a prince should be able to master fortune at least partially. Machiavelli said that "fortune is the ruler of half our actions." But nonetheless, fortune allows "the other half or thereabouts to be governed by us."[14]

Thus, despite the obstacles it presented, Machiavelli thought that fortune could be mastered, but only certain people were capable of doing so: in particular, those who are both bold and sagacious. Machiavelli said that "fortune is a woman, and it is necessary, if you wish to master her, to conquer her by force; and it can be seen that she lets herself be overcome by the bold rather than by those who proceed coldly."[15] Indeed, for skilled political leaders, fortune merely represents an opportunity to show how capable they are at mastering events. Machiavelli said that great leaders "owed nothing to fortune but the opportunity which gave them matter to be shaped into what form they thought fit."[16]

Leader virtue, or what Machiavelli called *virtù,* refers to the ability of the prince to carve from the disorder and uncertainty of fortune a political order that incurs people's continuing support for the prince's regime. To this end, the prince manifests *virtù* when he satisfies the yearning of people for the security of their material interests, including such things as people's property and families. Machiavelli held up for high praise leaders who were successful in the effort to secure for people their possessions, in the face of those potential enemies who would take them away.[17] Such leaders became heroes to their people, and they deserve to be accorded glory and fame. In this regard, Machiavelli approved of leaders such as Moses who helped the people of Israel escape from slavery in Egypt.[18] At the same time, Machiavelli attacked leaders who used their abilities to gain power at great cost to their fellow citizens. Leaders in this category were people such as Agathocles, who betrayed his friends and killed his fellow citizens, and these actions cannot be called virtuous. People such as Agathocles, to paraphrase Machiavelli, "gain power, they do not gain glory."[19]

Still, to master circumstances in a manner that wins the people's support, a prince who demonstrates *virtù* may show little regard for traditional moral ideas such as keeping agreements. These conventional moral norms may be essential in conducting relationships within the family or among friends, but they often have no place in a public setting that calls for a prince to manifest the boldness and daring needed to control public events on behalf of creating lasting benefits for people.

The prince, then, must destroy at times in order to make available important goods for his people, and thus it is not always possible or likely that the prince can sustain moral values traditionally considered essential in normal day-to-day settings. Indeed, the science of politics for Machiavelli is derived neither from studies in moral philosophy, nor from theoretical inquiries into natural law, nor from an understanding of theology. Rather, the science of politics evolves from a study of people whose main objective is to acquire power and to use it to create orderly societies that serve people's vital interests.

Moreover, Machiavellian approaches to the discussion of the science of politics always presume that there are only certain people who should become a prince. These people must face the uncertainty of fortune, never knowing in advance the consequences of their actions. To weather the storms associated with this reality, princes must be capable of doing whatever is necessary to survive, including committing violence against their enemies. Those who wish to lead more normal lives, in accordance with traditional moral categories, need not apply. On the other hand, those willing to use whatever means are needed to create regimes that serve people's lasting needs are ideal candidates. What is a prince's reward? Of course, there is the attainment of power that attracts would-be princes. But in addition, people who succeed in creating regimes that protect people's vital interests are remembered favorably for generations to come. In effect, the prince's greatest reward is to be remembered fondly by his nation for his willingness to be bold, daring, and ruthless in the face of great danger. Such people stand against a people's archenemies and survive, and their victory is the nation's triumph.

B. *Innovation through Violence*

To provide an understanding of how a ruler with *virtù* might behave, it is well to give an example of a Machiavellian role model, Cesare Borgia. Initially, fortune smiled on Borgia who gained control of Romagna, a former province in the papal state, with the help of his father, Pope Alexander. Yet, the same fortune that gave him power will later take it away, when his father dies. Machiavelli said that Borgia "acquired the state by the influence of his father and lost it when that influence failed."[20] Still, during the time that Borgia ruled, he demonstrated a masterful control of events. For instance, once he had gained power, Borgia sought to consolidate his grip over Romagna by various means that Machiavelli found praiseworthy. Borgia made friends with those aristocrats who had formerly supported other political elites by giving them new offices and privileges in exchange for their support. Those people whose loyalty could not be bought were forcibly crushed with the help of French troops. Finally, before Borgia gained power, Romagna was ruled by weak people who could not protect the citizens from "every kind of disorder." But once in power, Borgia gained the support of the citizens by giving them "good government" and by bringing peace and ending instability.[21]

To end disorder, it was at times necessary to rely upon extreme cruelty. For this reason, Borgia appointed Remirro de Orco, "a cruel and able man, to whom he gave the fullest authority."[22] Once de Orco had succeeded in bringing order and stability, Borgia, fearing that the citizens would begin to despise him as a result of de Orco's cruelty, removed him from power and established a civil court "under an excellent president, to which each city appointed its own advocate."[23] Now, order would be maintained through public legality as opposed to official violence. Still, Borgia feared that de Orco's actions might arouse toward him hatred from the citizens. In order to avoid this possibility, Borgia sought to distance himself from de Orco. Thus, Borgia murdered de Orco in a way that would draw public approval as well as dissociate Borgia from de Orco's cruelty in the public's mind. So Borgia in a solemn and sanctimonious moment had de Orco "cut in half and placed one morning in the public square . . . with a piece of wood and blood-stained knife by his side. The ferocity of this spectacle caused the people both satisfaction and amazement."[24] The people saw Borgia as their protector, once again, this time against his own hired murderer.

Ultimately, fortune finally triumphed over Borgia and caused his downfall. Upon the death of his father, Borgia was unable to install as pope the person Borgia wanted, but he at least prevented a person whom he did not want. Thus, Julius II, while not Borgia's choice for pope, was still a person Borgia thought he could live with. Still, despite the appointment of Julius II, Borgia was unable to maintain power. Borgia blamed fortune for this outcome. Machiavelli reports that Borgia told him that he had a good plan to keep his power, but owing to his ill health he was not able to execute it. From Borgia's perspective, then, as Machiavelli described the situation, had Borgia been well himself at the time of his father's death, "everything would have been easy." But Borgia told Machiavelli that, at the time of his father's death, he, Borgia, was dying, too.[25] And this fact supposedly ended his hope for continued rule.

However, as Machiavelli knew, Borgia lived another three years, and ultimately he lost his life in a war.[26] So what is the real reason for Borgia's downfall? Machiavelli believed that Borgia made some tactical errors regarding his father's successor. In particular, Borgia, in allowing the elevation of Julius II to pope, "made a bad choice."[27] If Borgia could not have the person as pope whom he wanted, he should have prevented "any one individual being made pope, and he ought never to have permitted any of those cardinals to be raised to the papacy whom he had injured, or who when pope would stand in fear of him. For men commit injuries either through fear or through hate."[28]

Still, on the whole, Machiavelli viewed Borgia as a person who used "force and fraud, to make himself beloved and feared by the people."[29] Whoever wants to destroy one's enemies, introduce innovations, and in general use deception and violence to manipulate circumstances for achieving power "can find no better example than the actions of this man."[30] Well-used power and toughness, just like well-designed deception, are acceptable means for securing power. These tactics are acceptable especially when they are used to establish a political order that is based upon public legality.

C. Techniques of Power: Maintaining Appearances

The Borgia case study in addressing fortune is supplemented by Machiavelli's advice to princes on how to regard their subjects. Here, his interest is in demonstrating to a prince how, once he has gained power, he should act to keep it.[31] Machiavelli's advice is clearly designed to emphasize that the appearance and the style of a prince are critical to his winning the confidence of the citizens. Now, this means that he must often appear to be what he, in fact, is not. He must appear to be "faithful, humane, sincere, religious, and also to be so; but you must have the mind so disposed that when it is needful to be otherwise you may be able to change to the opposite qualities."[32] The prince must be careful, then, when portraying himself, to depict himself in public in ways that make him appealing to the citizens. He must "take great care that nothing goes out of his mouth" that makes it appear that he is not wedded to the qualities just listed, and this point is especially true with respect to religion.[33] People are swayed by the image projected by a prince, and most people do not care to look beyond that image to the real person.

Besides the characteristics just mentioned, there are other qualities that the prince should display, also. A prince should be considered "liberal" as opposed to "miserly," generous as opposed to "rapacious," "trustworthy" as opposed to a man unable to keep his promises, courageous as opposed to cowardly, "serious" as opposed to "frivolous," and "humane" as opposed to "haughty." Now, no prince can embrace all these good qualities and at the same time avoid all the bad ones, but he should avoid any particular vices that "would lose him the state." Yet, when it is necessary for him to manifest particular vices for the sake of preserving his power, he should do so.[34]

Machiavelli's emphasis on a prince's maintaining proper appearances is a point certainly by now well taken by most people who manage modern campaigns and who use television to project the images that entice citizens' support for candidates. Clearly, Machiavelli, like today's campaign manager, had a cynical view of the body politic and its tastes. Thus, Machiavelli said,

> *Let the prince therefore aim at conquering and maintaining the state, and the means will be judged honourable and praised by every one, for the vulgar is always taken by appearances . . . and the world consists only of the vulgar, and the few who are not vulgar are isolated when the many have a rallying point in the prince.*[35]

The emphasis on maintaining a proper appearance before the people suggests that, if one approach to resisting the slings and arrows of fortune is unsuccessful, the prince must be flexible enough to change directions. He cannot be an ideologue who is dedicated to one and only one course of action. Moreover, if, in modifying a previous policy direction, a prince finds it necessary to break a promise, then he should do so. "A prudent ruler ought not to keep faith when, by so doing, it would be against his interest."[36] To be sure, while it is best to appear morally good and upright, the circumstances may dictate that one be like Borgia, ruthless and bold. That is why a prince must "learn how not to be good, and to use this knowledge and not use it, according to the necessity of the case."[37] Maintaining the right appearance, then, is in large part a function of a prince's making the right choices pertaining to how he should act in a given circumstance. If he is humble when he should be bold, he will appear to be unable to carry the mantle of power. He will then appear bumbling and incompetent, and, in consequence, he will open himself up to numerous attacks from his enemies and will be overtaken by fortune.

Still, even when the prince makes the right decisions and maintains an aura of control and competence, this fact by itself will not secure a prince's position. Indeed, if maintaining good appearances were all that were needed, then all a prince would have to do would be that which would win for him the love of all his citizens. Now, certainly all princes do best when they can maintain the faith and love of their people. For Machiavelli, "the best fortress [to protect one's power] is to be found in the love of the people."[38] But Machiavelli made clear that a prince must accept that, for the most part, people will always find fault with him, even when he appears in control of circumstances and maintains the right appearances. Why is this? For Machiavelli, all princes are faced with the age-old question citizens ask politicians: "Yes, you did well by me yesterday, but what have you done for me lately?" Although Machiavelli was not the originator of this question, he might have been. Machiavelli was well aware, then, that most citizens are "ungrateful"; they are "dissemblers"; they are "covetous of gain"; and they are not reliable; in short, "as long as you benefit them, they are entirely yours; they offer you their blood, their goods, their life, and their children . . . but when [any unfortunate circumstance that disadvantages them] approaches, they revolt."[39]

So how is the prince to maintain his power in the face of this type of problem? Machiavelli is clear that, at times, if a prince cannot be loved, then it is best for him to be feared.[40] People must be acquainted with the prince's toughness and with the knowledge that he can use the same force against them that he uses against the enemies of the society or against his own enemies. Still, the prince must recognize his limits to making the general population fear him. He cannot go so far that he invokes the people's hatred.[41] To avoid incurring people's hatred, a prince must not be "rapacious, and [usurp] the property and women of his subjects . . . [nor may he] attack the property or honour of the generality of men."[42] Here, Machiavelli made clear that the prince must recognize that he can survive only as long as he serves well the vital interests of the citizens. If people did not fear conditions that threaten those interests, they would not need a protector, and thus if the prince is perceived as a part of the conditions they fear, they do not need the prince. It is clear that a vital interest for people is security for those things people find most dear, and, in consequence, people expect the prince to create a society that protects their families and properties.

Now, Machiavelli lists different ways by which the prince can protect the vital interests of people. What are these ways? One way is to engage in "great enterprises." Examples of great enterprises include successful military campaigns, which "astonish" the public and which in consequence would presumably engender in the public a sense of national pride. A prince may also engage in domestic actions that serve the public's interest in important ways. Here, a prince seeks "fame for being great and excellent."[43] In each case, a prince's doing good for the society brings admiration from the people, who are grateful to him for the benefits he has bestowed on the society.

Perhaps the most important way to promote people's vital interests is to create a society in which individuals are able to receive those things from life that make their lives pleasing and satisfactory. The prince must work for conditions that ensure the material prosperity of his citizens, and these conditions must permit individuals to take part in ways of life of their own choice. Machiavelli said,

> *Moreover, he must encourage his citizens to follow their callings quietly, whether in commerce, or agriculture, or any other trade that men follow, so that this one shall not refrain from improving his possessions through fear that they may be taken from him, and that one from starting a trade for fear of taxes; but he should offer rewards to whoever does these things, and to whoever seeks in any way to improve his city or state.*[44]

Machiavelli's prince realizes that people will never be free if they live in fear that the fruits of their best efforts will be taken from them. This means that people will only be free to promote a way of life of their own choice when they are convinced that others will not rob them of their gains. It would seem, then, that the prince must put in place a system of laws that protect people's basic interests. Furthermore, for Machiavelli, it is not enough that people be protected from the loss of those goods they acquire from pursuing their own ways of life, but, in addition, people must understand a corresponding responsibility to pursue ways of life that enhance the society as well. So Machiavelli's prince realizes that people, as they follow their own interests, must become wedded to the need to contribute to the larger good of society, and thus the importance of civic virtue remains. To this end,

Machiavelli's prince will provide people with rewards for acting in ways that benefit not just themselves, but the entire society. Machiavelli will build upon this idea in his discussion of republics, as we see in the next section.

III. THE DISCOURSES AND REPUBLICAN FORMS

In *The Prince,* the leader with *virtù* creates an order that is the basis for people's support for his regime. In *The Discourses,* a leader displays *virtù* when he creates lasting institutions that transcend his own reign and that secure people's vital needs for generations to come. Here, the basis for assessing a leader's contributions was not, as in *The Prince,* how a leader such as Borgia had mastered fortune to maintain a regime in his own lifetime, but whether a leader's regime continues to exist long after he has died.[45] For Machiavelli, "the welfare, then, of a republic or a kingdom does not consist in having a prince who governs it wisely during his lifetime, but in having one who will give it such laws that it will maintain itself even after his death."[46]

But creating an enduring political system, in this case a *republic,* which is the topic of *The Discourses,* is difficult because governments, while initiated for reasons of securing justice, are constantly undermined by corruption. Indeed, for Machiavelli the rise and fall of governments are attuned to a cycle in which just governments, owing to corruption, are turned into unjust ones, and then citizens rebel on behalf of restoring justice, but then, corruption once again returns. This cycle is ongoing throughout history. To explain this recurring cycle, Machiavelli discussed six different types of governments. First, there are the three "good" or just types of regimes: monarchy, the rule of the single best man; aristocracy, the rule of the few best men; and democracy, the rule of all. Each of these has a corresponding perverted or unjust form. The corrupt form of monarchy is tyranny, the rule of the single unjust man; the corrupt form of aristocracy is oligarchy, the rule of the few unjust men; and the corrupt form of democracy is anarchy, the rule of the mob.[47]

In the discussion below, I outline the parade of government types that appear throughout the "just to unjust cycle" in order to demonstrate Machiavelli's affinity for mixed governments, or a republic. The latter, which orients people to the common good, contains elements of each of the just kinds of government. The republic is Machiavelli's model regime, which he believed existed in ancient Rome.[48]

The cycle of regime types starts with a discussion of the first governments. Before there were many people, there was no need for government. But as the number of people increased, people found it necessary to unite for the purpose of securing the common welfare. In order to attain their common objectives, the people chose the best and the strongest to lead them. At the same time, people began to distinguish between those among them who were honest and those who were "bad and vicious." The latter were selfish people who could not be trusted with power. These sentiments led to establishing laws to ensure punishment for those who committed wrongful acts against others. "Such was the origin of justice," said Machiavelli. Further, "this caused them [the people], when they had afterwards to choose a prince, neither to look to the strongest nor the bravest, but to the wisest and most just."[49] Thus, the first governments, or monarchies, were founded by great and wise men who symbolized government by the single best person.

When power was transmitted to the next generation, nonelective, hereditary approaches were used. But with the transition, problems arose, and these problems made maintaining a just regime difficult. The children of the first good leaders were spoiled by a life of ease, and in consequence they lacked all recognition of the importance of excelling through displays of virtue and believed, instead, that they should be accorded every possible luxury. "The prince consequently soon drew upon himself the general hatred."[50] And because the people's hatred frightened the prince, the prince decided to protect himself by turning into a tyrant who subdued the people in order to maintain his own rule over them.

The people rebelled against these conditions and those who led the rebellion became known as "liberators."[51] The latter constituted a government with a new ruling class of the nobility and thus created an aristocratic government. Here, the government of the few best men remembered the terrors of tyranny and hoped not to reinstitute them. Consequently, the nobility promoted laws that had as their main objective the public interest. But their children, who succeeded them, were ignorant of what their fathers had tried to accomplish, never having "experienced its [tyranny's] reverses" and, not content "with this civil equality, they in turn gave themselves up to cupidity, ambition, libertinage, and violence and soon caused the aristocratic government to degenerate into an oligarchic tyranny, regardless [or heedless] of all civil rights."[52]

Thus, the oligarchs created the same tyranny that the people had experienced under the first tyrant. The people revolted against this situation and sought the protection of a new prince. But the latter's reign was also tyrannous. So the people, remembering the failures of both the prince who had replaced the oligarchy and of the aristocracy, decided to set up a democracy with the intention that "the authority should not again fall into the hands of a prince or a small number of nobles."[53] But the new form of government remained in place only as long as those who helped found that government lived. When the new generation came into power, it lacked a good memory of the past, and, as in the past, it fell into all the bad habits that brought about oppression. "Each individual only consulted his own passions, and a thousand acts of injustice were daily committed." Democracy turned into anarchy, necessitating the restoration of the prince, the single leader, who could restore order. But once again, the same cycle was repeated, and the society fell into anarchy.[54]

Throughout, it would appear that the enemy of all regimes, especially good regimes, is corruption. Thus, "a legislator who gives to a state which he founds, either of these three [good] forms of government, constitutes it but for a brief time; for no precautions can prevent either one of the three that are reputed good, from degeneration into its opposite kind."[55] However, this pessimism is somewhat chastened by Machiavelli's choice of a mixed regime, which is more likely to withstand the cancer of corruption than the ones just mentioned. In a mixed regime, the three elements, the king, the nobility, and the people, share power. Lycurgus, the great lawgiver of Sparta, suggested this approach for Sparta, and Sparta lasted more than 800 years in general tranquillity. Rome did not have a great leader like Lycurgus, but it did have Romulus and other kings who gave it laws "suited to a free people." Initially, Roman leadership had as its objective a monarchy and not a republic, but, after many years, the monarchy was transformed into a republic when "royal authority" came to share power with the aristocratic elements of society, as well as with the people. This combination "rendered the constitution perfect."[56]

In a mixed government, or republic, the three classes share power, and each will watch and check the other, preventing any single class from dominating the rest. But even in a mixed regime, the responsibility for protecting liberty must be placed, predominately, into the hands of one class. And for Machiavelli, liberty is best protected when it is placed into the hands of the common people. Why is this? Whereas the nobility has a great desire to dominate, the ordinary people only want to be free from domination. Thus, the ordinary people have a greater desire than anyone else to "live in the enjoyment of liberty; so that when the people are entrusted with the care of any privilege or liberty, being less disposed to encroach upon it, they will of necessity take better care of it; and being unable to take it away themselves, will prevent others from doing so."[57]

Given the importance of the people to maintaining liberty, it is critical that the people not become corrupt themselves. "When corruption has taken possession of the whole people, then it cannot preserve its free condition even for the shortest possible time."[58] Indeed, the importance of avoiding corruption among the people is critical to preserving the integrity of the law-making process. Referring to the Roman republic, Machiavelli said that, as long as people were not corrupt, the law-making process was a setting in which citizens proposed what they thought was in the public interest. Here, all citizens were allowed to express their opinions on the proposals, and citizens made their judgments about what was best only after having heard all sides. But when the people became corrupt, the entire process was destroyed. Machiavelli said that "when the citizens had become corrupt, this system [for law making] became the worst possible, for then only the most powerful proposed laws, not for the common good and [for] the liberty of all, but [for] the increase of their own power, and fear restrained all others from speaking against such laws."[59]

Protecting liberty is very difficult, if not impossible, once this course of events takes place, and the only hope of doing so rests with the emergence of a political strong man, such as Machiavelli discussed in *The Prince*. Here, the state must be reduced to "a monarchical, rather than a republican form of government." Machiavelli said that "for men whose turbulence could not be controlled by the simple force of law can be controlled in a measure only by an almost regal power. And the attempt to restore men to good conduct by any other means would be either a most cruel or an impossible undertaking."[60]

But this remedy is not necessary in a society in which there is strong commitment to the canons of civic virtue. For in this context, people do not become corrupted, but instead they develop the habits associated with what is of central importance in Machiavelli's republic, respect for the law. Here, citizens are willing to put aside the temptations to follow their own self-interests, in order to secure the place of the law in the society. But for citizens to follow this path, it is necessary that the laws in the society be good or just. Otherwise, people will not develop the habits necessary to uphold them.

Thus, Machiavelli thought that to maintain support for laws, people must develop those habits that make such a commitment possible. However, in the absence of good laws, these habits will not emerge. Machiavelli said, "for as good habits of the people require good laws to support them [good habits], so laws, to be observed need good habits on the part of the people."[61]

Now, in stressing good laws, what Machiavelli had in mind was the central importance of the rule of law. Good laws have as their objective the common good, but that good cannot be achieved if there are some people who think they are above the law and thus, owing to their higher social status, not subject to it. Machiavelli said that a "well ordered republic" should never "cancel the crimes of its citizens by their merits; but having established rewards for good actions and penalties for evil ones and having rewarded a citizen for good conduct who afterwards commits a wrong, he should be chastised for that without regard to his previous merits. And a state that properly observes this principle will long enjoy its liberty; but if otherwise, it will speedily come to ruin."[62]

Thus, Machiavelli had contempt for those who were not likely to think of themselves as subject to the same law as everyone else. In particular he had in mind a situation in which a corrupt ruling group dominates, as the old traditional, feudal landowning classes were accustomed to doing. These individuals lived off their inherited wealth and did no useful work, and yet they sought to maintain relationships of command toward the rest of the society. Their interest was not the public good, but only their own good. "Such men are pernicious to any country or republic."[63] These men have no respect for the rule of law, because the ordinary people's interest is of a lesser concern than their own. Governed by a corrupt aristocracy, the ordinary people would always fear for their liberty, because neither their property nor their lives nor the lives of their families would be safe.

In contrast, Machiavelli held up for praise the new aristocracy who earned their wealth from "commerce and movable property, and moreover none of them have castles or jurisdiction over subjects."[64] Presumably, these individuals respect ordinary people and work to make possible the rule of good laws that work for the common interest. Indeed, in Venice, where this class is prominent, the ordinary citizens, who are excluded from various offices and honors reserved for the new aristocracy, still are able to find with them a basis for social stability and concord. This situation suggests that the new aristocracy of commerce and business poses no threat to the liberty of ordinary people, but, instead, through their industry and commerce, this new class provides a basis for greater opportunities for all.[65] In such situations, society thrives, there is happiness and prosperity, and the republic is secured.

Other elements than goods laws can contribute to maintaining those good habits of civic virtue that act as a deterrent to the corruption of the citizens. In particular, religious practices and institutions can engender a sense of respect for the traditions of civic virtue that help maintain a commitment to the common good. Thus, Machiavelli said that "as the observance of divine institutions is the cause of greatness of republics, so the disregard of them produces their ruin." And later Machiavelli said that "there is no greater indication of the ruin of a country than to see religion contemned."[66] But Machiavelli did not seem to believe that religious institutions could be the main source of civic virtue any longer, owing to, what he believed was the corruption of the Catholic Church. The Church has "destroyed all piety and religion in Italy."[67] More important, the church cannot be a force for helping to unify the nation and for teaching citizenship on a nationwide basis. For Machiavelli, the Church is a source of "our ruin" because it "has kept and still keeps our country divided."[68]

Finally, for Machiavelli, in great cities or republics, there is a "great affection for liberty,"[69] an affection that grows from the fact that people understand that prosperity and wealth only emerge for a city in which there is liberty. But prosperity alone does not make a city great. In addition, there must be a commitment to the common good by the citizens. Rome's greatness, in fact, was a product of this understanding. Machiavelli said that "the cause of this [Rome's greatness] is manifest, for it is not individual prosperity, but the general good, that makes cities [or republics] great; and certainly the general good is regarded nowhere but in republics, because whatever they do is for the common benefit."[70]

A republic at its best would possess important characteristics of a civil society. There would be a chance for individuals to pursue their own conceptions of what is best but in a setting governed by an overarching conception of the common good. The latter would manifest itself in the form of good laws that secure a basis for equal treatment to all citizens, no matter what class they might come from. But Machiavelli feared that even this way of life would be continually threatened. His fear emanated from the real reason why Machiavelli believed that the habits of civic virtue and good law are needed in the first place. The problem that threatened republican life for Machiavelli was the inherent selfishness of human beings. We turn now to a discussion of this dimension in his play, *Mandragola.*[71]

IV. MANDRAGOLA

Machiavelli's *Mandragola* has a very simple plot. A young man, Callimaco, is smitten by a young, married woman, Lucrezia. She is a very devout Catholic, desirous of pleasing her husband, Nicia. Nicia is a much older man who wants to have children, but he is impotent. Now, Nicia will not admit to his impotence and will not accept responsibility for his wife's inability to become pregnant. He assumes that there is something wrong with her. Using this information, Callimaco constructs, with the help of his servant, a plot to get into Lucrezia's bed. The idea is to convince Nicia that the only way for Lucrezia to become pregnant is if she drinks a medicine called mandragola. Nicia is told that the first man who has intercourse with her after she has drunk the potion dies within a week. Naturally, Nicia does not like this idea, but Callimaco has a way to address his fears. Callimaco suggests that after Lucrezia has had the potion she sleep with a low life, whom Callimaco has kidnapped and placed in her bed.[72] Naturally, the low life will be a disguised Callimaco.

Nicia is easily convinced by Callimaco to take part in the scheme. Deceiving his wife is of no importance to Nicia, since his first goal is to manifest his manhood by having children. (When asked if he is impotent he says, "Me? Impotent? Oh, you'll make me laugh. I don't think there's a man more vigorous and virile to be found in all Florence."[73]) He is too simple-minded to realize that he is being inveigled by Callimaco into allowing his wife to sleep with another man.

But convincing Lucrezia is a more difficult task, since, after all, she is a religious woman and does not believe in adultery. She says at one point:

> *But of all the things that have ever been tried, I think this is the strangest—that I should have to submit my body to this outrage, and to be the cause of a man's death for outraging me. For I couldn't believe it, even if I were the last woman left in the world, and the whole human race had to start all over again from me— that I would be expected to do such a thing.*[74]

To change her mind, her priest, Friar Timoteo, is asked to be a part of the plot and agrees to participate for money. The good Friar tells Lucrezia that sleeping with a strange man for the sake of conceiving a child would not be a sin. After all, there is a positive good that would come from it; namely, creating another "soul for our Good Lord."[75] And this good far outweighs the fear of committing two evils, in this case the possible death of another and adultery. In regard to the first evil, the Friar says that it is not certain that the man who gives Lucrezia the mandragola will die, since not all men who engage in this activity, in fact, die. Regarding adultery, the Friar says that it would be sinful for Lucrezia to displease her husband by not doing as he asks. Moreover, since she takes no pleasure in sleeping with another man, there is no sin in what she is about to do. The Friar tells her that only the "will sins, not the body."[76] Indeed, there is Biblical precedent for her actions. She is acting like the daughters of Lot, who "believing themselves to be the sole surviving women in the world, mated with their father, and because their intention was good, they did not sin."[77]

So Lucrezia accedes to the wishes of the Friar. After all, the Friar is the religious authority, and she is only a fearful woman, whose main objectives in life are to please her husband and to ensure her salvation. The Friar has no problem lying to her because he thinks little of women (they are all "short on brains," he says[78]) and because he wants the money.

In the end everyone appears to get what each wants. Callimaco gets in bed with Lucrezia, and the two conceive a child. Nicia gets his child, a son, without having to think of himself as impotent. The Friar gets his money. And Lucrezia remains in good standing with her husband. Moreover, while in bed with Lucrezia, Callimaco confesses his love to her, and she in turn indicates her belief that the whole event had been "heaven's will," and so she asks Callimaco to stay on and become her "protector" and her "father." Indeed, she decides to maintain the relationship to Callimaco by making him the godfather, and allowing him free access to the house and to her. Nicia even gives Callimaco a key to the house so he can enter whenever he wishes.[79]

V. THE MORAL OF MANDRAGOLA AND CIVIL SOCIETY

Machiavelli in this play demonstrated that modern society, without the tradition of moral restraints that civic virtue requires, can become nothing more than a place for people to victimize each other. The Catholic Church, for Machiavelli, no longer had much of a role in teaching people to treat one another with basic decency. Instead, people approach one another, as they do in the free-market setting, from the standpoint of the need to promote their own naked self-interests. From this perspective, people pursue to the fullest extent possible, regardless of the standards of traditional virtue, whatever pleases them. So if money pleases, one should find a way to gain the sufficient power to obtain money. And similarly with women. For Callimaco, then, if a woman provides pleasure why not find a way to buy her, just as one would buy anything else that gives one pleasure?

The play suggests that a new kind of society is needed, one which permits people to pursue objectives that give them pleasure in life, but without endangering or injuring others. People can advocate their own interests without denying to others basic dignity and self-respect, as was the case for Lucrezia. *The Prince* and *The Discourses* promised precisely this possibility. From the accounts provided in these works, individuals would be permitted to pursue their own happiness in an environment that protected the liberty of all citizens. To accomplish these ends, there must be regard for the habits of civic virtue, which promote respect for the common good and the rule of law. Where these standards are not preserved, society will become an environment in which the laws protect the interests of a few. This situation would give license to a favored group to exploit the rest of the members of society, as Callimaco had Lucrezia. Lost in this setting are the habits of the civic virtue that promote the common good and the standards of basic human decency and civility.

In promoting these views, Machiavelli advanced the idea of civil society, but, in doing so, he did not identify the formal doctrines that undergird such a society. Later thinkers will devise theories that demonstrate the kind of relationship that must occur in order to secure a civil society. Thus, even if Machiavelli did not write the political theory of the new civil society, he helped to define the vision upon which that theory is constructed. In arguing for a regime that seeks to secure the happiness of citizens within the context of respect for civic constraints, he moved society into the modern world, and he opened the door to the type of civil society theorizing that we discuss in Part II.

Endnotes

1. In the rest of this chapter, references to *The Prince* and *The Discourses on the First Ten Books of Titus Livius* are from *The Prince and The Discourses,* introduction by Max Lerner, (New York: Modern Library, 1950).

2. Henry Paolucci, Introduction to *Mandragola,* translated by Anne and Henry Paolucci, (Indianapolis: Bobbs-Merrill, 1957), p. xiii.

3. Max Lerner, Introduction, in *The Prince and The Discourses,* pp. xxv–xxviii. Also, see J. G. A Pocock, *The Machiavellian Moment: Florentine Political Thought and the Atlantic Republican Tradition,* (Princeton: Princeton University Press, 1975), p. 86; Mulford Q. Sibley, *Political Ideas and Ideologies: A History of Political Thought,* (New York: Harper and Row, 1970), pp. 296–97. See Machiavelli, *The Prince,* pp. 3–4 for his dedication of this book to a Medici son.

4. George S. Sabine, *A History of Political Theory,* p. 336.

5. Lerner, Introduction, in *The Prince and The Discourses,* p. xxxiii.

6. Ibid., pp. xxxiii–xxxiv. Also, Sabine, *A History of Political Theory,* p. 337.

7. Sabine, *A History of Political Theory,* p. 336.

8. Machiavelli, *The Prince,* pp. 5–6, chs. 2–3.

9. Ibid., p. 5, ch. 2.

10. Ibid., p. 5, ch. 2.

11. Ibid., p. 6, ch. 3; also see pp. 18–21, chs. 5–6.

12. Ibid., p. 6, ch. 3. "Thus you find enemies in all those whom you have injured by occupying that dominion, and you cannot maintain the friendship of those who have helped you to obtain this possession, as you will not be able to fulfill their expectations. . . ."

13. Ibid., p. 21, ch. 6.

14. Ibid., p. 91, ch. 25.

15. Ibid., p. 94, ch. 25.

16. Ibid., p. 20, ch. 6.

17. See Sheldon S. Wolin, *Politics and Vision,* p. 230.

18. Machiavelli, *The Prince,* p. 21, ch. 6.

19. Ibid., p. 32, ch. 8.

20. Ibid., p. 25, ch. 7.

21. Ibid., pp. 26–27, ch.7.

22. Ibid., p. 27, ch. 7.

23. Ibid., p. 27, ch. 7.

24. Ibid., p. 27, ch. 7.

25. Ibid., p. 29, ch. 7.

26. John T. Scott and Vicki B. Sullivan, "Patricide and the Plot of *The Prince:* Cesare Borgia and Machiavelli's Italy," *American Political Science Review,* 88:4, Dec. 1994, p. 896.

27. Machiavelli, *The Prince,* p. 30, ch. 7.

28. Ibid., p. 30, ch. 7.

29. Ibid., p. 30, ch. 7.

30. Ibid., p. 30, ch. 7.

31. Ibid., p. 56, ch. 15.

32. Ibid., p. 65, ch.18.

33. Ibid., p. 65, ch. 18.

34. Ibid., pp. 56–57, ch. 15.

35. Ibid., p. 66, ch. 18.

36. Ibid., p. 64, ch. 18.

37. Ibid., p. 56, ch. 15.

38. Ibid., p. 81, ch. 20.

39. Ibid., p. 61, ch. 17.

40. Ibid., p. 61, ch. 17.

41. Ibid., pp. 61–62, ch. 17.

42. Ibid., p. 66, ch. 19. Also, see p. 62, ch. 17.
43. Ibid., pp. 81–82, ch. 21.
44. Ibid., p. 85, ch. 21.
45. Wolin, *Politics and Vision,* p. 231.
46. Machiavelli, *The Discourses,* p. 148, Bk. I, ch. 11.
47. Ibid., pp. 111–12, Bk. I, ch. 2.
48. Ibid., p. 111, Bk. I, ch 2.
49. Ibid. p. 112, Bk. I, ch. 2.
50. Ibid., p. 113, Bk. I, ch. 2.
51. Ibid., p. 113, Bk. I, ch. 2.
52. Ibid., p. 113, Bk. I, ch. 2.
53. Ibid., pp. 113–14, Bk. I, ch. 2.
54. Ibid., p. 114, Bk. I, ch. 2.
55. Ibid., p. 112, Bk. I, ch. 2.
56. Ibid., pp. 115–17, Bk. I, ch. 2.
57. Ibid., p. 122, Bk. I, ch. 5.
58. Ibid., p. 161, Bk. I, ch. 16.
59. Ibid., p. 170, Bk. I, ch. 18.
60. Ibid., p. 171, Bk. I, ch. 18.
61. Ibid., p. 168, Bk. I, ch. 18.
62. Ibid., p. 181, Bk. I, ch. 24.
63. Ibid., p. 255, Bk. I, ch. 55.
64. Ibid., p. 257, Bk. I, ch. 56.
65. Ibid., pp. 256–57, Bk. I, ch. 55.
66. Ibid., p. 148, Bk. I, ch. 11; p. 149, Bk. I, ch. 12.
67. Ibid., p. 151, Bk. I, ch. 12.
68. Ibid., p. 151, Bk. I, ch. 12.
69. Ibid., p. 282, Bk. II, ch. 2.
70. Ibid., p. 282, Bk. II, ch. 2.
71. Niccolò Machiavelli, *Mandragola,* translated by Anne and Henry Paolucci, (Indianapolis: Bobbs-Merrill, 1957).
72. Ibid., pp. 22–23.
73. Ibid., p. 18.
74. Ibid., p. 35.
75. Ibid., p. 36.
76. Ibid., p. 36.
77. Ibid., p. 36.
78. Ibid., p. 34.
79. Ibid., pp. 56–59.

Partial Bibliography and Further Reading

Butterfield, Herbert Sir. *The Statecraft of Machiavelli.* New York: Macmillan, 1956.

De Grazia, Sebastian. *Machiavelli in Hell.* Princeton: Princeton University Press, 1988.

Fischer, Markus, *Well-Ordered License: On the Unity of Machiavelli's Thought.* Lanham, Md.: Lexington Books, 2000.

Gilbert, Felix. *History: Choice and Commitment.* Cambridge: Harvard University Press, 1977.

Hexter, J. H. *The Vision of Politics on the Eve of the Reformation: More, Machiavelli, and Seyssel.* New York: Basic Books, 1973.

Pitkin, Hanna Fenichel. *Fortune Is a Woman: Gender and Politics in the Thought of Niccolo Machiavelli.* Berkeley: University of California Press, 1984.

Pocock, J. G. A. *The Machiavellian Moment: Florentine Political Thought and the Atlantic Republican Tradition.* Princeton: Princeton University Press, 1975.

Scott, John T., and Sullivan, Vicki B. "Patricide and the Plot of *The Prince:* Cesare Borgia and Machiavelli's Italy." *American Political Science Review,* 88:4, Dec. 1994.

Sibley, Mulford Q. *Political Ideas and Ideologies: A History of Political Thought.* New York: Harper and Row, 1970.

Smith, Bruce James. *Politics and Remembrance: Republican Themes in Machiavelli, Burke, and Tocqueville.* Princeton: Princeton University Press, 1985.

Strauss, Leo. *Thoughts on Machiavelli.* Chicago: University of Chicago Press, 1984.

6

ELEMENTS OF ISLAMIC AND JEWISH MEDIEVAL POLITICAL THOUGHT

I. INTRODUCTION: ALFARABI'S LEGACY

Aristotle remained outside of philosophical and religious discourse during most of the medieval period in the West, until, as we saw earlier in Chapter 4, in Aquinas's time Aristotle was rediscovered. How did Aristotle and classical Greek thought, including Plato, once again become central to Western thought after so long an absence? The rediscovery of Plato and Aristotle in the Western medieval world was made possible by Islamic culture. As early as the ninth century, the study of Greek contributions in science and philosophy were brought into Islamic society through the monetary support of several Islamic political authorities.[1] And as Islamic society made its way through North Africa and Spain it brought along its intellectual and religious culture, including Greek philosophy.

However, within the Islamic medieval world itself, philosophy did face difficulties surviving. Philosophy, with its origins in Greek culture, often was viewed as a foreign intrusion into Islamic societies and thus resented by religious leaders in the Muslim world. Many Islamic religious leaders thought that Islamic approaches to discovering truth should be followed on all occasions. Those who held this view argued that Islamic sources could best provide an understanding of the structure of nature as well as how to construct a good society based on interpretations of Islamic law in local circumstances.[2]

Of course, in classical Greek philosophy issues such as the structure of nature and the way to achieve a good society were approached from the perspective of reason, and religious arguments had little place. But in Islamic societies, the Koran, the Muslim holy book, as well as the sayings of the Prophet Muhammad and his followers, gave clear answers to vexing questions. As Oliver Leaman says, from the standpoint of Islamic religious leaders, the information from these sources provided "unambiguous answers to the important questions concerning how people ought to live, how the world was created, what sort of state should be constructed, which types of behaviour are valid and which wicked, and so on."[3]

Further, Islam was buttressed by a history of mysticism, which permitted particular individuals with special qualities to claim a direct understanding of God. In the face of this prospect, it is natural that many Islamic religious leaders thought that philosophy was unnecessary. Islamic philosophers disagreed, and to support their arguments they invoked the name of Aristotle. For Islamic religious leaders, however, if Aristotle, a non-Muslim, could evoke truth without Islam, what then would be the value of Islam?[4] And thus Islamic religious leaders often argued against philosophy's methods, suggesting not only that these methods produce flawed reasoning, but also wrong-headed conclusions. In contrast, Islamic philosophers persisted in believing that their methods were the best path to truth.[5]

Despite these complaints from Islamic religious leaders, Greek philosophy had a strong foothold in Islamic societies. The Islamic philosopher who played a substantial role in furthering the study of Greek philosophy in Islamic culture was Alfarabi (870–950).[6] Charles Butterworth says that, "it is now generally conceded that Alfarabi deserves to be recognized as the one who first introduced political philosophy into Islamic culture and that Avicenna . . . and Averroes all take their bearings from him as much as from Plato and Aristotle."[7]

Of Turkish descent, Alfarabi became known in Baghdad as a principal authority on philosophy and logic.[8] He lived during a time of political and social instability. Yet, despite this circumstance, strong support continued during Alfarabi's time for studying Greek philosophy. Indeed, Miriam Galston says that he was part of a period that could be called the "renaissance of Islam." Baghdad had a rich cultural life punctuated by public debates among opposing schools of thought on such subjects as logic and grammar. There were also vigorous discussions as to whether religious writings should be understood literally or were to be interpreted by the methods of philosophy. In addition, Baghdad was a center for philosophers who worked to translate and to comment on the writings of Aristotle, as well as other Greek thinkers. In this setting Alfarabi had a productive career, during which he wrote on Aristotle's ethics, physics, and metaphysics. He also wrote a commentary on Plato's *Laws,* and he prepared summaries of both Aristotle's and Plato's political thought.[9]

Alfarabi, as Miriam Galston says, thought that "religion is an imitation of philosophy."[10] Alfarabi believed that religion and philosophy both seek to know answers to similar questions, but that philosophy provides a superior account of knowledge than does religion.[11] Nonetheless, religion must not be discounted in importance. For Alfarabi, the truths of philosophy are well beyond the grasp of ordinary people to comprehend. But these truths can still be conveyed through religious concepts and symbolism.[12]

A central concern in this chapter is to explain the place of political philosophy in medieval Islamic and Jewish thought. To do so, it is necessary to discuss what I mean by reasoning, the chief function of philosophy. Reasoning is composed of two essential activities. In the first place, reasoning requires us to define the basic assumptions and definitions that are the starting points and building blocks of an argument. Further, once these assumptions are determined, the next question pertains to their accuracy. Indeed, a large part of philosophical analysis involves questioning the validity of basic assumptions by determining if evidence can support them.

Secondly, there is the question of the argument's form. In this regard, it is essential to see if the conclusions of an argument follow logically from the argument's basic assumptions and definitions. The form of the argument thus starts with assumptions "x" and "y," and then moves from them logically to conclusion "z." For instance, often, in religious arguments the basic starting point is the assumption that God exists. The conclusions are what follow logically from that assumption. Once one posits a definition of God and describes God's characteristics, such as for instance (as we will see in Maimonides) the rational ends God makes necessary, then logic is used to construct a fuller, more comprehensive vision of the world that is built from these assumptions.

Political philosophers embrace the techniques of philosophy throughout discussions of political, religious, or ethical matters. Overall, political philosophy, employing well-grounded assumptions and flawless logic, seeks to construct visions that define approaches to enhancing the best prospects of human life. A dominant vision in the works discussed in this chapter embraces the enterprises of classical Greek thinkers such as Plato and Aristotle. In this regard, a main concern of political philosophy is to build communities that satisfy humankind's need for a happy and contented life through a society that teaches moral virtue to its citizens. Moral virtue orients individuals to restrain desires in ways that make possible respect for the common good, as embodied in the laws of a community.

Further, the different writers discussed in this chapter use political philosophy to define the proper relationship between faith and reason. In this regard, the Islamic and Jewish traditions highlighted in this chapter did for Islamic and Jewish thought what Aquinas did for the Christian tradition, as we discussed in Chapter 4. And in doing so, it is necessary to create a secure place for philosophy in society. Moreover, from the standpoint of the main theme of this book, creating a place in society for philosophy helps to pave the way for civil society in future generations. For, to sustain philosophy—and the intellectual inquiry it demands—a space that makes possible toleration and mutual respect for diverse ideas and ways of life is necessary. And that space is called a civil society.

II. AVICENNA: THE PHILOSOPHER AND THE LAWGIVER

Avicenna (980–1037) lived in the Eastern Middle East in Persia or the area that is known now as Iran. His world, like each of the Islamic thinkers discussed here, was feudal, and as such it was filled with diverse power centers, governed by local monarchs, each of whom was grounded in Muslim law and tradition. Avicenna served several of these rulers, first as a physician, but later and for the bulk of his career as a high administrative official in government. As a person of great skill, he could be counted on by local rulers to help manage the state effectively.[13] He performed this role in a context characterized by a tendency of Muslim monarchs to bring to their courts a thriving intellectual culture. As Peter Heath says, "rulers [during Avicenna's times] were perfectly aware that the attendance of eminent poets, noted scholars, and learned theologians at their courts added an aura of cultural glory that reinforced their shaky claims to legitimacy."[14]

Thus, rulers needed philosophers. And the rulers' need for philosophers was matched by the philosophers' need for patrons. Without a patron, a philosopher lacked the financial means needed to continue philosophy. In fact, during the last 15 years of his life, Avicenna found a benefactor who permitted him to devote himself to philosophy.[15] His efforts in this regard yielded very important results. Peter Heath says that Avicenna's main contribution was to forge Aristotle's work into a cohesive and insightful whole for future generations in both Islamic and Western societies.[16]

Avicenna, in addressing major issues, sought to accommodate the truth made available through reason with the worldview that is central to Islamic religious thought. To this end, he began with the view that the elements constituting life—whether in nature or in the human world—need to be explained in terms of cause-and-effect relationships.[17] Avicenna depicted the cosmos as a unified whole, governed by a first principle, also referred to as a first cause, which is known as God. Using the first cause as the main starting point in any argument, all events can be logically understood in terms of a chain of cause-and-effect relationships. As Shlomo Pines says, "in fact, Avicenna's system is strictly deterministic. And this determinism extends to God and His activity."[18] Given this viewpoint, he could conceptualize a unified system that included all elements of the universe, including all things in nature, the solar system, and human life. Reason, when used in this manner, helps to explain the cosmos as well as some of its essential components, including human society.[19]

How did Avicenna conceptualize society? Avicenna believed that individuals are, as Aristotle said, social by nature, and because of this fact people need to be part of a political community if they are to have happy, contented lives. In this community, individuals learn, in keeping with the directive of moral virtue, to discipline their own desires in order to support the common welfare. Ironically, ordinary people are not by themselves capable of forging a political community that achieves this end. Why is this the case? For Avicenna, because each person seeks to make his or her interests primary, people are hostile to each other and moral virtue seems beyond the grasp of most people. As a result, people only accept laws that benefit themselves while harming others. This approach to life guarantees that ordinary people are incapable of forming a political community based on laws that embody the needs of all people.[20]

How can political community, which is so necessary for a decent human life, be formed if ordinary people are incapable of forming it? Avicenna believed that special people or great leaders—called lawgivers or legislators—form political community. Lawgivers are political leaders with special abilities to shape a community, subject to a law common to all. Lawgivers accomplish this purpose even among people who, because of their self-serving demeanors, manifest extreme hostility to each other.[21] In achieving community among people who are so much at odds, lawgivers are similar to prophets. As Pines says in speaking of Avicenna's views on lawgivers, "only a prophet, i.e., a man endowed with certain faculties not found in the common run of people, can create a social bond between them and thus preserve them from the calamities and the destruction that wait upon the solitary."[22]

What produces lawgivers in a situation that seems so hostile to them? After all, if ordinary people are incapable of creating political community, why would special leaders, with the ability to construct political community based on respect for the common good, emerge among them? Avicenna's answer is that such leaders and their successes in obtaining common laws and political community are an inevitable development of nature.[23] The lawgiver is thus a natural product of a world designed to achieve rational ends, such as political community, despite the proclivities of individuals to act otherwise.

An equally important question pertains to what role the philosopher would have in a situation where political community depends for its existence upon the prophetic-like quality of a special leader. Avicenna suggests that true prophets must have the qualities of philosophers.[24] In fact, philosophers naturally inherit the mantle of prophets. As James Morris says, for Avicenna, "the true 'knowers' and rightful 'heirs of the prophets' are the accomplished philosophers."[25] Now, since lawgivers manifest the character of prophets, then the special, political leaders that make possible political community would also be expected to demonstrate the highest qualities of philosophers. Indeed, true leaders are not only the heirs of prophets, but these leaders also embody the best contributions of philosophers. In consequence, to establish political community, there must be political leaders/philosophers who are capable of helping people realize the moral qualities of their social nature, even when ordinary people are not capable of doing so themselves.

In providing such a prominent place for philosophy, Avicenna puts a premium on what philosophy must have to be useful—a place of respect in society. This circumstance helps to set the stage for a civil society, if not in his own times, at least in subsequent generations.

III. AVERROES: THE IMPORTANCE OF DEMOCRACY

Averroes (1126–1198) of Cordoba (in Muslim Spain and Muslim North Africa) maintained his intellectual independence in settings not always receptive to his philosophical activities. Indeed, at the end of his career at the age of seventy, he was banished from Cordoba along with his followers by the Muslim ruler and forbidden, along with everyone else, from engaging in philosophy. Moreover, after his death a year later, a ban on philosophy by the ruling authority remained in place.[26]

A distrust of philosophy characterizes Averroes' circumstances. Muslim Spain and North Africa were the frontiers of Islamic advances into the West, and unlike the eastern Muslim world, which was more settled, Spain and North Africa had to confront traditions hostile to Islam. In the face of this reality, Islamic authorities exhorted people to accept literal teachings, or the exact meaning of the words, of religious texts.[27] Averroes rejected this approach, and according to Fred Bratton held the view that "the philosopher could view it [the Koran] in the light of reason and make his own interpretations."[28] Philosophers, as well as philosophy, survived in many local settings of Muslim Spain and North Africa because the state lacked the total control necessary to prevent philosophy.[29] Thus, in this context, Averroes produced important commentaries on Aristotle and on Plato's *Republic,* the main work discussed in this section.[30]

Averroes, while arguing for the importance of reason as the Greeks had done, still accepted the notion of revealed religion. He held the view that even though philosophy and religion teach the same truth, because reason is fallible, religion, which emanates from an infallible God, must be allowed to set the limits as to what constitutes the acceptable topics for philosophical inquiry.[31] In this regard, Averroes was a precursor of Aquinas, because like Aquinas Averroes sought to establish the appropriate relationship between faith and reason.[32] What is the basis for reconciling the two?

Philosophy, through the use of reason, seeks to know the purposes of life, and to attain this goal it is necessary to have an understanding of the intentions of the world's creator, or God. Religion seeks the same information, not through reason, but through direct knowledge from God. Further, both religion and philosophy in focusing on the same questions also seek to know, in light of the knowledge pertaining to God's intentions in creating the world, how God expects people to conduct their lives.[33] Here, both religion and philosophy can be reconciled on the basis that each seeks knowledge of the good life.

How does Averroes define the vision of the good life that both religion and philosophy should embrace as the preeminent guide for society? As Oliver Leaman says, Averroes maintained, like Aristotle, that people are social animals by nature and as such need political community to satisfy not just basic physical needs, but to live in keeping with moral virtue, or those moral rules that enable people to live justly.[34] Life is only worth living so long as people can be part of communities that contribute to these purposes and that enable people to embody them into their lives.

This view of society is found in Averroes' treatment of Plato's *Republic.* Averroes' commentary on the *Republic* is a summary of Plato's views of politics, which includes his visions of the just society and of the Ideal State.[35] The essence of the just society is that individuals are taught moral virtues appropriate to their place in society, with the intention of making possible a just society. Indeed, Averroes reminds us, as we learned in Chapter 2, that Plato's just society embodies four central moral virtues, including wisdom, courage, temperance (or moderation), and justice. For Plato, justice is the main virtue, and it is manifested in a just society, where individuals perform well the function for which they are best suited by nature.[36] And central to the notion of the just society is the prominent role of the philosopher. Indeed, the best or Ideal State is one in which the philosopher is the "prince and ruler."[37] What are the qualifications of the philosopher who is also, upon possessing these qualities, referred to as a king?[38] The philosopher/king studies all domains of science, loves truth, has no desire for wealth, is not ruled by sensual pleasures, manifests courage, seeks the good for society—which includes justice—and is capable of being a good speaker in matters having to do with philosophy.[39]

After the Ideal State, Averroes discusses the other types of states that Plato notes, and which we described in Chapter 2. Averroes recounts Plato's descriptions of timocracy, a state based on honor. Then, there is oligarchy, where a few with wealth are rulers. Finally, there is democracy, followed by tyranny. Averroes also adds to Plato's list of different states the notion of a state formed from necessity, which I will address later in my treatment of Averroes' view of Plato's discussion of democracy.[40]

In general, for Leaman, Averroes in his commentary on Plato is merely describing elements of Plato's *Republic,* and allowing the reader to determine if Plato's ideas are a good statement of "the just society and the just citizen."[41] However, in my view, Averroes is doing more than just describing Plato's ideas with the intention of allowing readers to determine the validity of Plato's notion of justice as it pertains to the society and to the individual citizen. Averroes is also defending one of Plato's key ideas and criticizing another. In one case—that of enlarging the role for women in society—he makes a strong defense of Plato's ideas on this subject. In the second case, Averroes defends democracy against Plato's own tendency to associate it with the evolution of tyranny. In each case, whether he is defending or criticizing Plato, what Averroes seems to be doing is advocating positions that would not be supported by the leading traditions of his own times. And if my interpretation is valid, then Averroes could be construed, through his commentary on Plato's *Republic,* as seeking to reform his society.

I now explain this argument further by first discussing Averroes' defense of Plato's effort to enlarge the role of women in the *Republic.* And then I will discuss Averroes' critique of Plato's view of democracy.

Averroes, in his discussion of Plato's guardian class, interrupts his description of this dimension and says he wants to investigate if women and men have different natures.[42] Averroes says that men are better at most activities, though women might be better at some others. For instance, men are better at creating music whereas women are better at performing it.[43] Or, women are said to be better at crafts such as weaving and sewing.[44]

The tendency to ascribe different talents and thus roles to men and women should not blind people to the fact that there are women who have the same capacities that men have, as Plato said, to be philosophers, rulers, and guardians.[45] (Guardians are people who are rulers or protectors of the community, and they must manifest military prowess, as discussed in Chapter 2.) Yet, it is clearly the case that the possibility of women assuming roles as rulers, philosophers, or guardians would be overlooked in many societies, according to Averroes. Here, Averroes seems to be suggesting that the understanding of women's possibilities are unnecessarily limited by a tendency to reinforce traditional role divisions between the sexes. Indeed, this perspective when carried out in full tends to limit women to male-dominated households, where they are consigned to tasks such as procreation, rearing children, breast-feeding, and serving their husbands.[46] Here, women are not allowed to contribute fully to all aspects of society. As a result, women appear to be nothing more than "plants."[47]

Identifying women as plants means that they are passive, nonassertive people, incapable of fighting like men on behalf of protecting the state from its enemies. Were this description true, then women could never be guardians. And if women can't be guardians, as explained in Chapter 2, they are denied a chance to be philosophers and rulers too, since people must prove themselves to be among the best of the guardians before they can become rulers and philosophers.

But Averroes says emphatically that women can be guardians just like men. He indicates that a look at animal behavior demonstrates that in many cases both males and females have a capacity to fight enemies. By extension to the human species, it follows that women—just like men—are capable of protecting a state from its enemies.[48] It is a mistake to relegate women to a passive role, one in which they are subordinated to men, based on the idea that women cannot fight and protect the state like men, because they can!

Moreover, when women are placed only in inferior positions to men, great damage is inflicted on to society as a whole. Why is this the case? Averroes refers to societies in which women, who vastly outnumber men, are forced to stay at home in a male-dominated setting, producing and caring for children. As a result, women are not taught many of the basic tasks, as well as the requisite virtues, that allow women to contribute fully to the economic base of society. And, because men alone cannot in these societies provide what is needed to satisfy basic goods—such as shelter, food, and so on—society is thrown into poverty. Averroes says, "that they [women] are a burden upon the men in these States [where they are not taught many basic tasks and requisite virtues] is one of the reasons for the poverty of these States. They [women] are found there in twice the number of men, while at the same time they do not, through training, support any of the necessary activities, except for the few which they undertake mostly at a time when they are obliged to make up their want of funds, like spinning and weaving. *All this is self-evident.*"[49]

In his description of Plato's view of women, then, Averroes, says that the problems raised for society by the limited role allowed to women, as well as the obvious need to enlarge women's role in society, are "self-evident." In saying that Plato's views are self-evident, especially as they pertain to actual settings, Averroes is suggesting that the truth of Plato's views is contained in their mere assertion, and thus further evidence to substantiate them is unnecessary. Averroes, by taking this position, has interspersed in his description of Plato's views his own favorable opinions about the benefits of Plato's advocacy of an expanded role for women. Given this to be the case, it seems acceptable to take these views as Averroes' critique of his society and of those societies with which he is familiar.

I turn now to what I take to be Averroes' defense of democracy. Averroes' embrace of democracy rings clearest when he refused to associate democracy with a necessary slide into tyranny, as Plato had done. Averroes tells us people want democracy, because they wish to be free. He says of democracy: "Thus most of those States existing today are democratic . . . This is the State which the great mass of the people think is the ruling one; since everyone is of the opinion at first thought that he deserves to be a free man."[50] Yet, for Plato, as we saw in Chapter 2, the longing for freedom as the motivation for democracy did pose a threat to a just arrangement of the Ideal State. In Plato's view, freedom led to an excess of desire, and this circumstance, by undermining the rule of reason, spawned the social instability that could be overcome only through the imposition of order from a powerful ruler. This ruler for Plato, after he has established himself, would manipulate the population into allowing him to have total power, and he would thus become a tyrant.[51]

Now, Averroes uses first-hand experience to substantiate Plato's point that at times democracy can lead directly to tyranny. Averroes tells us that his native Cordoba turned to tyranny after having been almost exclusively democratic.[52] Still, as I begin to explain in the next paragraph, for Averroes, democracy need not always turn into tyranny. Indeed, democracy can be an important first step to the Ideal State.

Averroes relates in his commentary on Plato's *Republic* that democratic societies are places where people are free from restraint to do whatever they desire and where each can move in any direction that a person's "soul leads him."[53] Further, in a democratic society, the existence of freedom permits all the qualities that are peculiar to Plato's other types of states. Thus, in a democracy uniformity of outlook is replaced with a variety of ways of life, each of which embodies different values and perspectives. There are some people that love honor, others that love owning property, and still others that love tyranny. Also in a democracy, there are those who possess as well as act from a commitment to the various moral virtues.[54] Owing to these many differences that exist in a democracy, there are bound to be a broad flourishing of "all arts" and ways of life.[55] In consequence of this prospect, Averroes says that it is possible for an Ideal State, run by philosophers, to emerge from democracies.[56]

Why would democracy help to spawn an Ideal State? Averroes seems to answer this question by saying that a democracy is like a multi-colored "garment." And just as many youth and women find a multi-colored garment good for its array of different colors, many people find democracy admirable for its hodgepodge of different ways of life.[57] But why would the fact of democracy containing many differences be a source of attractiveness to people? Here, I can only speculate. But it would seem that a democracy—just like a multi-colored garment that blends many colors into a useful fabric—manifests the possibility of integrating various ways of life into a working whole. And this situation in a democracy could support a rich intellectual life in which a host of perspectives would be assessed during the course of finding the best arguments on any issue under discussion. This setting could contribute well to a culture that supports an interest in philosophy and an appreciation for the Ideal State.

Still, there is a downside to a democratic state containing many differences, and the principal problem is that these differences might produce destructive fragmentation of society. For Averroes, experience with democracies in his own time as well in earlier periods demonstrates that, unless there is a commitment to moral virtue, there will not be sufficient self-restraint to unite the different elements into a community or association, built upon respect for the needs of the whole society. And then, democracy—like a multi-colored garment whose main threads have been ripped—will lose its common fiber and soon perish.[58] In this event, tyranny, or any of the other states that fall short of an ideal society run by philosophers, might well result from democracy. Indeed, Averroes says that because of the diverse tendencies that are allowed expression in a democracy, all the different types of states—including timocracy, oligarchy, and tyranny—are "destined" to arise from democracy.[59]

Here, I focus only on the question of whether democracy is the precursor to tyranny. Plato thinks that this connection is inevitable, because democracy is associated with the pursuit of excess freedom. This circumstance opens the door to seeking freedom in larger and larger amounts, all in the name of securing unlimited desire, a situation in which one desire leads to people having many others, seemingly without end.[60] Indeed, for Averroes, political leaders in a democracy cater to this tendency by providing citizens with what they most desire, as part of what is meant by securing people's freedom.[61] What are the objects of people's desires? Averroes tells us that in democracies—especially newly founded ones—the thirst for acquiring property grows.[62] Plato would no doubt say that this situation encourages people to give a higher place of importance to their desires than to the collective needs of society. And then, to stop the chaos that follows, a single, powerful strong man may be called upon to rule over the society.

As this scenario demonstrates, freedom pursued to excess turns to its opposite, which is tyranny.[63] Here, democracy will fail to survive unless people are able to constrain desire (or what, to use modern terms, I will call self-interest) as a result of their possessing a strong enough sense of moral virtue.[64] Now, Plato had argued that the acquisition of these moral qualities as the basis for stability in his just or Ideal State arises from the fact that people "agree by conviction to keep that which the laws demand."[65] To act from this conviction means that a person would not have a longing for what a person "does not possess."[66] Plato's Ideal State avoids this situation, and thus is able to teach moral virtue, because it focuses people's attention not on pursuing their self-interest, but on doing the jobs for which they are best suited, and thus serving society's interest.[67]

But Averroes seeks to demonstrate that the pursuit of self-interest does not necessarily cause society to slide from democracy to tyranny. He says that in a democracy people may recognize that it is in their self-interest to protect freedom by accepting moral constraints on desire. In this case, for the sake of securing freedom, people will accept a democratic form of authority that is designed to uphold limits on how far people can promote self-interest. This argument anticipates liberal conceptions of the state, discussed in the next section of this book, where freedom is made possible only when individuals accept moral constraints on the pursuit of their interests. What is Averroes's basis for making this claim?

Governments have authority in a democracy only when the governed accept that authority.[68] But in a democracy, a government's authority will not last very long if people, because of their lack of self-constraint, always place their own interests ahead of the interests of society. This understanding is at the core of Averroes' view of democracy. Evidence for this contention arises from Averroes' statement that "in view of the character of this [democratic] State [which provides freedom for each citizen to pursue his or her interests]," it is considered improper "that everything should be permitted to everybody" in a democracy.[69] Indeed, Averroes says that in a democracy people must understand that they cannot have all they desire, or otherwise "a point would be reached when they would murder and plunder one another."[70] Here, people in a democracy could have an interest in a form of authority that makes possible, for the sake of freedom, the moral constraints necessary to avoid the chaos arising from unrestrained self-interest.

Democratic societies in which people have an interest in freedom—as the occasion for moral constraint—may arise from a series of circumstances, beginning with what Averroes refers to as states of "necessity." Indeed, for Averroes the first states to come into existence emanate "naturally" from necessity, a type of state not discussed by Plato.[71] This means that states initially come into existence as a result of people *naturally* joining together to satisfy basic, necessary needs—such as food, shelter, and so on. Further, for Averroes democracy is the first type of state to emerge from states that originate from necessity: for once people have their necessary needs taken care of, they are likely to seek a variety of desires well beyond basic needs, and the new desires are for things such as property and wealth.[72] In this setting, democracies are formed for the sake of providing people with the personal freedom they need to obtain what they desire.

But, as we have seen, a democracy will take a turn toward chaos unless it can be an association with a government whose authority binds people to upholding moral restraints on their desires. Now for Averroes, an association of people that limits desire is a result, not of design, but of "chance."[73] Indeed, in a democracy, a governing authority that necessitates moral constraints on desire is merely "accidental."[74] Why is this the case? As we saw earlier, democratic states in which people seek freedom are filled with diverse people, some supporting honor, some property, and others moral virtue or even tyranny. It is possible that, owing to chance, the makeup of the state will emphasize every other tendency but moral virtue. If this outcome were to take place, then democracies would be unable to maintain a commitment to self-restraint and in consequence democracies could turn toward tyranny. But if by chance, there are enough people who recognize the need for moral virtue, then a democratic government's authority can be predicated on people's acceptance of the need to limit desire for the sake of freedom. In this case, people would be more likely to understand that it is in their self-interest to place limits on their desires, lest society become a place in which overzealous commitment to desire destroys all freedom.

Moreover, the tendency to support democracies from self-interest is strengthened in the face of the need to combat tyranny. Averroes says that Muslim kings of his time become tyrants when they plunder the property of the common people. Indeed, at times a king may tax people and distribute property gained in this manner inequitably. In doing so, a king may display this property before the bulk of the population as a symbol of his power, and this circumstance angers most people. In response, the mass of people hopes to free themselves from these kings. And kings react by attempting to impose a tyranny on ordinary people.[75] In seeking their freedom from corrupt kings as well as in pursuing protection from tyranny, the masses of ordinary people would necessarily share a collective interest in democracy. "Therefore this [democratic] State is in utmost opposition to the tyrannical State."[76] For Averroes, democracy is humankind's ultimate protection against tyranny. And this lesson has strong personal meaning for Averroes who laments tyranny that takes place "in our own time and in our own State."[77]

Further, Averroes warned that in tyrannies, the "priestly part"—or in other terms, religious authority—becomes tyrannical,[78] and when this happens, great "disrepute" accrues to the priestly class. Averroes says that this circumstance, which contradicts the expectation that the priestly parts of society should advance moral excellence,[79] is commonly found in his own time.[80] Thus, insofar as democracy opposes tyranny, democracy helps to ensure a religious authority that promotes, as it should, an Ideal State in which the best—those with philosophical and moral excellence—rule. Certainly, Averroes understood that reason was fallible and that it must work within an Islamic framework, which emanates from an infallible God.[81] But he knew that this outcome could never be realized where tyranny prevailed. And thus democracy has an important role to play in securing the proper relationship between religion and philosophy.

Averroes' commentary on Plato's *Republic* is an important statement of social reform for his own times. Of course, from the way Averroes was treated at the end of his life, as mentioned in the beginning of this section, it is also clear that the ruling, including the religious, authorities of his time rejected his views for reforming society. Still, his thought contributes in important ways to the modern world, because it helped to set the stage for civil society in our own times.

IV. Maimonides: The Limits of Reason and Religion

Moses Maimonides (1135–1204)—a medieval Jewish philosopher, physician, and rabbi—was born in Cordoba. Maimonides and his family had to leave Cordoba in order to escape the intolerance of orthodox Islamic believers who sought to force Jewish and Christian conversion to Islam.[82] Maimonides traveled to Morocco, where intellectual openness did exist. There, he met Islamic scholars who introduced him to Arabic translations of Aristotle. He went from Morocco to Alexandria and settled in Cairo, another city that tolerated intellectual vitality.[83]

Liberal climates tolerating intellectual inquiry, like what existed in Cairo, were in part made possible by the great Muslim leader Saladin, who took back Jerusalem in 1187 C.E. from the Christian Crusaders who had previously taken it from the Muslims. When the Christian Crusaders conquered Jerusalem in 1097 C.E., they slaughtered Jews and Muslims alike. Jews were burned to death in their synagogues where they had sought protection, and Muslims were beheaded with impunity.[84] After retaking Jerusalem, Saladin refused to take revenge for Christian cruelties. He allowed Christians and Jews to leave the city without harm, and Christian priests were permitted to conduct religious services in Jerusalem, Nazareth, and Bethlehem. And later, he opened Jerusalem to Jews, ensuring them complete freedom to rebuild their synagogues and schools. When he became the sultan of Egypt, he supported practices that respected people from other religious faiths, and this circumstance contributed to Cairo becoming a city that welcomed intellectual flourishing.[85]

Studying Maimonides is helpful in addressing one of the central questions that emanated from the experience of the Jewish Diaspora, which took place after the Babylonian captivity during the sixth century B.C.E. As a result, Jews were scattered to countries outside of Palestine.[86] (The word *Palestine* refers here to the ancient country of biblical times or to what is now often called the Holy Land.)[87] In the face of the Diaspora experience and its continuing impact on Jewish life at the time of Maimonides, how did Jews manage to survive as a people, even as they were dispersed across different cultures?

Maimonides maintained that the Jewish people, also referred to in biblical texts as the nation of Israel,[88] survived as a unified community despite being scattered across other nations because of the continuation of a strong presence of what Jews considered to be God's law. Adherence to God's law helped to bind Jews to the core values contained in that law, as well as to the Jewish community that revered it. The law is found principally in the Pentateuch, the first five books of the Old Testament, which are contained in the Torah. In Jewish tradition, the Torah was handed down from God to the Jewish people through Moses, the great liberator of Jews from slavery in Egypt.[89]

For Maimonides, Jewish tradition divides God's law into two essential parts. The Torah contains the written law that Jews are to follow. But the written law has always been supplemented in Jewish tradition by oral commentary designed to demonstrate how that law should be interpreted. In Maimonides' view, Moses, "our master, wrote down the entire *torah* before he died . . . and gave a scroll to each tribe [of Israel]."[90] In addition, for Maimonides, Moses provided an explanation of the written Torah, which he did not write down but which he told the elders in the Jewish community, as well as all of Israel, to follow. And Maimonides calls this verbal explanation the "Oral Torah."[91]

The most important adherents as well as implementers of the Oral Torah were the members of the Jewish Sanhedrin of Jerusalem, the supreme council of the Jews. The Sanhedrin, which existed from the fifth century B.C.E. to the fall of the Second Temple in 70 C.E., acted as a supreme legislature and as the highest court of justice for the Jewish people.[92] The Jewish people, even as they lived under the rule of others, had their own courts to resolve disputes. Each court would seek to settle disputes in keeping with their particular traditions. Matters that could not be resolved went to the Sanhedrin for resolution.[93] To perform this job, the Sanhedrin used the oral tradition to apply the written Torah law in resolving disputes. Maimonides said, "The Great Sanhedrin of Jerusalem is the root of the Oral Law. The members thereof are the pillars of instruction; out of them go forth statutes and judgments to all Israel."[94] Indeed, through their authority, Jews were given a common source of law and identity.

But the Sanhedrin came to an end in 70 C.E. when the Romans destroyed the Second Temple and dispersed Jews from Jerusalem. After this event, there was no longer in place an authoritative source for interpreting the law to all Jews and for ruling over their affairs. And so an alternative source of authority emerged to provide a basis for continuity among the dispersed Jewish people. The new authority emphasized the Torah and its laws as central elements in a covenant between the Jewish people and God. A special group of legal scholars, called either sages or rabbis, was trained in rabbinic academies to interpret the Torah and to explain and to determine what the law meant, not just literally but when applied to actual circumstances during the Jewish people's dispersal throughout various cultures.[95]

These legal scholars—once again called sages or, as I will call them here, rabbis—were different from prophets. Prophets, and of course the great lawgiver Moses, were viewed as possessing wisdom and authority owing in part to their direct relationship to God.[96] But in Jewish tradition, God does not talk through rabbis to the people as God did through Moses. Instead, rabbis, as learned men with wisdom, were to make applications of God's law to particular circumstances, and thereby instruct Jews on how to uphold God's law and in the process maintain the covenant with God.[97]

Maimonides builds upon this tradition when he says that rabbis could make interpretations of divine law in the Torah, so long as they did not change it.[98] Rabbis had similar roles to judges in the United States court system. Judges, in making rulings, must uphold the sacred principles of the United States Constitution. Similarly, rabbis must apply the law without violating the Torah. And, both rabbis and judges must often defend themselves against the charge that their interpretations violate the basic law—the Constitution in the case of judges, the Torah in the case of rabbis.[99] Further, rabbis, like contemporary judges in United States courts, create over time an accumulated body of knowledge that helps to give authority to their interpretations. This knowledge, as opposed to divine revelation, is the basis for subsequent decisions by rabbis. Here, "specialists," the rabbis, as opposed to ordinary individuals make the law that gives continuity to the Jewish community.[100]

Rabbis, while never attempting to supersede the Torah law, sought to apply it to practical circumstances with compassion.[101] When there were disagreements on how best to do so, decisions were often made by a majority vote among the rabbis.[102] Prior to reaching a decision, however, discussions were marked by an intense respect for all views, including ones that dissented from majority positions. Indeed, dissenting positions were given as much legitimacy as accepted ones.[103] Speaking of the rabbinic dynasty that emerged from the followers of first-century C.E. Hillel the Elder, David Shatz says that members of this group emphasized tolerance and patience toward those who disagreed with them. Indeed, for the followers of Hillel, often, as David Shatz says, "a rejected view may reflect greater legal acumen and cogency than the accepted one!"[104]

The work in Jewish tradition that contains rabbinic interpretations of the law is the Talmud. Dating in it origins from 375 C.E., it was written by sages and rabbis across Jewish history. It is a collection of Jewish laws and, as such, contains the oral laws as well as commentaries on them.[105] Maimonides says that the bulk of legal rulings since the days of Moses are contained in the Talmud.[106] Often, a reading of the Talmud provides a full rendering of the various points of view that should be considered in interpreting a particular issue of law, but less clarity in specifying the nature of the law itself. Indeed, as one writer said, "a bright student, they say, could give forty-nine reasons for deciding a point of law one way and forty-nine reasons for deciding it the opposite way—and this sort of thing was never seen within the Jewish tradition as mere sophistry. God's word really was open-textured, available for study, discussion, disagreement, even a kind of intellectual play."[107] Further, if there were no dire need to make a decision on a matter, Talmudic arguments would avoid reaching a conclusion, so that subsequent generations could take up the matter later without being bound to earlier decisions.[108]

From the foregoing account, it is clear that the rabbinic tradition contains two radically different approaches to understanding the Torah. On the one hand, the Torah embodies the eternal laws of God that could not be changed. As we saw, Maimonides said that rabbis could interpret the law but should not change its basic essence. Yet, in interpreting the law the Torah can be perceived as a document that could be adapted to new circumstances. Seen in this light, the Torah is an ever-changing document, as opposed to being a symbol of eternal and absolute laws.[109]

Maimonides, often referred to as the most prominent of the medieval rabbis, hoped to overcome this dualism by writing a legal code that sought to end all the arguments—as found in the Talmud—about the nature of the law for the Jewish people.[110] The book, which was written with this purpose in mind, is entitled the *Mishneh Torah.* As one writer says, in the *Mishneh Torah,* Maimonides presents both the Talmudic and "the Oral law in what was meant to be definitive form, without proof texts, disagreements, and alternative views that marked the Talmud itself and all the commentaries and compilations that followed upon it."[111] Maimonides said that those who wanted to know the law could discern its nature by reading the *Mishneh Torah,* alone.[112]

For Maimonides only a few people could understand the Talmud, and those who can understand this work require "a capacious mind, a wise spirit, and a long time."[113] The *Mishneh Torah* would thus help ordinary people comprehend what only a few can know intimately. Moreover, the effort to craft a work that enables ordinary people to live in keeping with God's law manifests the view that learned rabbis have great responsibility in society. Indeed, Maimonides is like Avicenna in suggesting that whereas ordinary people need political community, only superior leaders could provide it.[114] Why is this the case for Maimonides?

For him, there are many differences among people with respect to their moral commitments and character. There are cruel people and there are those who would not even hurt an insect. Many other differences are in evidence as well. Given these differences, it will be difficult to find a way to achieve a community in which each person is willing to submit him- or herself to the same law.[115] Nonetheless, this objective must be achieved if a decent society is to be at all possible. And as Pines says, Maimonides thinks this task can only be handled well by learned men with special abilities, as opposed to ordinary people.[116]

Still, Maimonides says that at times learned men—and I say men, since women had no social or political parity with men—may not be available in particular towns, and in this case Maimonides would concede decision making to townspeople and tradesmen.[117] Here, as Amy Gutmann says, for Maimonides, the rule of ordinary men, though not as good as rule by experts, is acceptable as a matter of necessity and not as a matter of morality.[118] However, in the best of circumstances, as just stated, for Maimonides, excellence in determining the law arises not from ordinary men, but only from those sages and rabbis who spend a lifetime dedicated to developing expert knowledge of the law.[119]

I wish now to turn to another of Maimondes' concerns. As we have just seen, for Maimonides, biblical texts are important for understanding God's law. But in addition, these texts, for Maimonides, contain understandings with respect to some of life's enduring questions—such as the fundamental nature of people (are people born good or evil?), the implications for human life of reason's limitations, and the nature of justice. In addressing matters of this sort, Maimondes demonstrates the importance of reason and thus of the philosopher to society.[120] How Maimonides approaches this objective occupies the remaining part of this chapter, as I discuss the way Maimonides treats matters such as the nature of people, the limitations of reason, and justice.

As Leo Strauss points out, for Maimonides, the Torah has a literal meaning and a hidden meaning, and the worst errors with respect to understanding the complexities found in the Torah arise from approaching the Bible merely from the standpoint of its literal meaning.[121] So, to rectify this problem, in *The Guide of the Perplexed* Maimonides sought to explain the "secrets of the Law" in the Bible.[122] In doing so, Maimonides moves from what, on a surface reading, the Bible appears to be saying to what, on a deeper reading, it actually says. Yet, as he undertook this task in *The Guide,* he had to determine how to confront an ancient legal prohibition arising from Talmudic sages who forbade the explanation of these secrets to the public at large. The secrets of the Bible could be explained only in private to those with political and scientific wisdom.[123] Leo Strauss points out that in *The Guide of the Perplexed* where Maimonides "embarked upon the explanation of the secrets of the Torah, he was confronted with the apparently overwhelming difficulty created by the 'legal prohibition' against explaining those secrets."[124]

How does Maimonides confront this prohibition? He makes his explanation of the biblical secrets very difficult for the average reader to grasp. In this way, the secrets would remain hidden from most people. Indeed, Maimonides' intention was that only a few astute and shrewd readers would ever be able to fathom Maimonides' words.[125] For instance, Maimonides contradicts himself at various points throughout *The Guide* in order to force the reader to stop constantly and reflect on what meaning should be attributed to these contradictions. Readers would devote a great deal of time to addressing these matters, making the experience of reading *The Guide* too tedious for most people.[126] Moreover, *The Guide* is written to provide many hints of the truth, and the reader must make use of each clue to reveal the secrets.[127]

Perhaps one of the most important discoveries of the Bible that is articulated by Maimonides in this arcane manner is that reason has significant limitations. Indeed, Maimonides, while having great reverence for reason, still for the sake of maintaining a moral vision of life, which we describe below, hopes to note its limitations. Thus, for Maimonides it is important to understand that reason or the "intellects of human beings have a limit at which they stop."[128]

Building upon this point, Marvin Fox says Maimonides understood that "reason has its limits and an intelligent man should recognize these limits."[129] Often in facing important issues we rely upon our reason to help provide knowledge and critical judgments. Just as often, we discover that reason can provide neither. Still, the issues in question do not disappear. They remain important to others and to us, and thus we are forced by virtue of this fact to take positions on these matters, using grounds other than reason to do so. For instance, in many public debates about controversial moral issues, we realize that with the employment of reason we cannot achieve consensus on the nature of the best course. The lack of consensus does not eliminate these issues from public concern, however. Still, we must decide our stances on them. We have to do so as citizens, as parents, and as professionals. And often when we decide, we discover that reason cannot provide an adequate explanation, and then we may resort to arguments that emanate from religion.[130]

And this approach is what Maimonides took with respect to many issues of his own day. As Fox says, Maimonides' method would be to see first if reasoned inquiry could resolve a matter, and if not then he would resort to explanations based in religion. And he would be honest about what he was doing. He would not try to mask a religious argument as emanating from reason. And when he resorted to religious views to support a position, he would make clear the nature of the religious grounds he was using as well as why he chose them. Moreover, he would not reject a better argument, in this case one that did arise from reason, if such an argument emerged at a subsequent time. In particular, he would not allow himself to be limited to Scripture if a good argument from reason could be found in the discussion of an issue.[131] Thus, he would not permit religious belief to sabotage reason and the knowledge derivative from it. But if reason were incapable of helping to discern truth, he would not allow reason to mask or to subvert this fact, especially in the face of religion's possible helpful contributions.

To provide an example of this approach, I now comment on Maimonides' view of the nature of humankind; in particular, I address the question from Maimonides' perspective as to whether human beings are by nature good or evil. For this purpose, I start with the position found in Augustine, in Chapter 4, that human beings are driven by sin, and I demonstrate the possible critique Maimonides would make of Augustine's view. Maimonides would have demonstrated the frailty of Augustine's position by first resorting to reason, and then, when the limits of reason became obvious with respect to concluding his critique, he would turn to religious tradition. First, I establish the argument from reason that Maimonides would use against Augustine.

In Augustine's doctrine, it was said that as a result of the fall of man in the Garden of Eden, the stigma of sin follows humankind for all time. Maimonides would have rejected this view because he believed that each human being is born with a potential for perfection that can and should be actualized. Maimonides says that "man is not granted his ultimate perfection at the outset; for perfection exists in him only potentially."[132] Achieving perfection is a possibility because, in Maimonides' view, human beings have a "noble form," or an overall disposition, which has been created in *"the image of God and His likeness."*[133]

But how should we characterize the "ultimate perfection" that is enshrined in our noble form and that defines our possibilities? Maimonides describes human potential in terms of the rational ends that we can and must pursue if we are to realize the true possibilities inherent in our noble form. Rational ends are those universal purposes that should be sought by all human beings, regardless of their place in the world. Maimonides clarifies these ends when he says, "for example, man's apprehension of his Creator, his mental representation of every intelligible [aspect of the world], his control of his desire and anger, his thought on what ought to be preferred and what avoided, are all consequent upon his form."[134] Owing to our noble form, then, we should seek, through the proper use of reason, knowledge of the human and natural worlds. In addition, we also realize that we must as human beings with reason, or as people created in God's "likeness," seek to live in accordance with moral virtue, or what constitutes a morally right way to live.[135]

For the moment, I wish only to focus on the moral virtue dimension promoted by our human, noble form. I do so in order to address an important problem: namely, that the fact that our noble form orients us to pursue moral virtue does not mean that we in fact do live in keeping with what is morally right. For, it is also true that individuals have a capacity for sin and this fact might contradict as well as stifle the possibilities embodied in our virtuous disposition. The possibility of sin follows from the desires that emanate from the human body, or what he refers to as human "matter." Maimonides says "his [man's] eating and drinking and copulation and his passionate desire for these things, as well as his anger and all bad habits found in him, are all of them consequent upon his matter [body]."[136]

Nonetheless, sin need not be our destiny. Rather, we can live in accordance with moral virtue. And this is because, as just indicated, our lives are overshadowed by a higher capacity in life—a disposition to moral virtue located in our human form. Maimonides says, "He [God] granted it—I mean the human form—power, dominion, rule, and control over matter [the body], in order that it [form] subjugate it [the passions of the body], quell its [the body's] impulses, and bring it back to the best and most harmonious state that is possible."[137] Thus, whereas individuals, owing to their bodies, have a capacity for sin, people, owing to their form, have a fundamental need, as well as potential, to live in accordance with moral virtue.[138]

Here, Maimonides' position against an Augustinian darkness at the center of each human being is built upon a rational argument. Given the assumption that God has given humankind a form that orients people to rational ends, including the need to live a morally virtuous life, then it follows logically that individuals are not forever driven to sin. Rather, individuals can in fact live in keeping with God's hope that people will find themselves in a "harmonious state."

To achieve this possibility, God's law for Maimonides promotes the welfare of the soul and of the body. The welfare of the soul "consists in the multitude's acquiring correct opinions corresponding to their [the multitude's] respective capacity."[139] How should we understand this statement? The term *soul* is merely another word for what Maimonides referred to as our noble form. As such, the soul, like the noble form, contains two rational ends: the necessary quest for knowledge and the need to live in keeping with moral right. It is in light of these rational ends that we can understand what Maimonides means by the term, *correct opinions*. Here, it seems that the term, *correct opinions*, refers to each person understanding a requirement to pursue the rational ends embodied in our noble form, or soul.

Now, from Maimonides' discussion of the welfare of the soul, what is clear is that not all people can be taught "correct opinions" in the same way. People have different abilities when it comes to learning, and for this reason, some must be taught differently than others. This view is suggested by the statement that people acquire "correct opinions corresponding to their respective capacity." Thus, Maimonides says that some people, presumably because of their higher capacity for understanding, can be provided with "correct opinions" through explicit explanations, or explanations that are reasoned. Other people, however, with less capacity for understanding—what Maimonides refers to as the "common multitude"—must be taught through "parables" or stories that provide down to earth examples as the basis for acquiring an understanding of the rational ends of the soul.[140]

What does Maimonides mean when he discusses the welfare of the body? The welfare of the body is an idea signifying that people should not act wrongfully to each other. To accomplish this objective, people must not put the pursuit of their own capacities and objectives above the need to do what is "useful to the whole." Indeed, Maimonides argues that each person must be "forced" to do his or her part to maintain the community as an environment that serves the shared needs of all members of society. To accomplish this end, Maimonides says that each person must acquire the "*moral qualities* that are useful for life in society so that the affairs of the city may be ordered."[141] As a result of these moral qualities, or what can be called moral virtues, people limit their desires and by doing so help to make possible a community that provides for the common needs of all people.

Why is meeting this objective so important? Only if the goods of a community are made available will people be able to pursue the perfection of the soul, or the fullest development possible of their reason.[142] If people are hungry and without shelter or if they are in pain and filled with suffering, they are not likely to be reflective people able to engage in rational inquiry. Indeed, without the acceptance of basic moral qualities, the welfare of the body is not possible, and without the welfare of the body, there is no basis for securing the advancement of the rational ends of the soul.[143] Thus, the welfare of the body, which symbolizes the possibility of a moral community, contributes to the welfare of the soul or humankind's "ultimate perfection"—what is "indubitably more noble [than the welfare of the body] and is the only cause of permanent preservation."[144]

But a problem with profound consequences emerges at this point in Maimonides' discussion. His view of the soul points to serious shortcomings in human ability that we must address and in some way compensate for, if we are to achieve the rational ends postulated by the ultimate perfection made possible by our noble form. To illustrate this point, I first explain the dilemma in Maimonides' own words, and then I follow his statement with my own description and elaboration of the ideas contained in his words.

For Maimonides, human beings seek to realize their full rational potential by knowing all that can be known "within the capacity of man to know in accordance with his ultimate perfection."[145] This statement suggests that through our reason we cannot know all that we might have a longing to understand because reason is limited in its capacity to know all things. Indeed, Maimonides says that "it is clear that to this ultimate perfection [of the soul] there do not belong either actions or moral qualities and that it consists only of opinions toward which speculation has led and that investigation has rendered compulsory."[146] Thus, from intellectual activity—that is, from the use of our reason to explore the world—we do not obtain definitive answers to many of the questions that our quest for knowledge obligates us to ask. We neither solve all controversies with respect to attaining a perfect understanding of the way the human and natural world works, nor do we acquire a precise and definitive understanding as to what "moral qualities" we should embody in our actions so that we act in morally correct ways.

This outcome has important consequences for each of our attempts to live a moral life. For Maimonides, even as reason, as the manifestation of our noble form or soul, tells us to do right and to live virtuously it cannot clearly delineate right from wrong. As Fox says, "Maimonides teaches explicitly that morality is not derived from reason and that moral statements are neither true nor false."[147] To use a contemporary issue to provide an example of this point, when discussing the death penalty I will be for this punishment if I think that it is a deterrent to people committing murder. But I will be against the death penalty if I think that killing others is always wrong, no matter who does it. One perspective emphasizes the social good of the death penalty and the other manifests the public harm caused by it. The perspective one takes and the assumptions one employs to address this question will determine one's position on the issue. Can rational inquiry help to transcend these two competing perspectives and allow us to find a resolution to this conflict that can be accepted by all sides in the debate? Or is this example an instance, like many others, of Maimonides' claim that reason, while urging us to find the morally correct path in deciding the best approach to critical issues, is unable to demonstrate in a definitive way the nature of that path?

If Maimonides is correct and reason cannot determine the morally right course of action from the wrong one, how can we understand the nature of moral virtue, and, moreover, how can we live virtuous lives? Maimonides' answer is to turn to another source for determining moral right. And that alternative source is religious tradition. How does Maimonides support his position?

Following Aristotle, Maimonides says that human beings are social animals, and thus seek community and friendship. Indeed, Maimonides says, "it is well known that friends are something that is necessary for man throughout his whole life. Aristotle has already set this forth in the ninth book of the 'Ethics.' For in a state of health and happiness, a man takes pleasure in their [friend's] familiar relations with him; [and] in adversity he has recourse to them [friends]."[148]

Why are community and friendship so important? As we have seen already, the notion of the welfare of the body suggests the importance of those moral virtues that help to make possible a community in which individuals are able to secure the welfare of the soul. And clearly, for Maimonides, religious traditions—as a continuing foundation for securing moral virtue in society—have a great role in maintaining friendship and community. Thus, religious traditions in helping to secure community and friendship make possible an environment in which people can realize the rational ends of the soul.

Maimonides would thus suggest that individuals be taught many of the moral virtues embodied in these traditions. For instance, people should avoid bad habits such as gambling, but be taught good ones such as loving one's fellow Jews as well as strangers, and helping those who commit sins to understand the best way to live. In helping people who commit moral mistakes, we should not shame them publicly, but only talk to them in private, using a "gentle language," which communicates an interest in the other's good.[149] In addition, religious traditions contain a host of lessons with respect to sexuality, all in the name of protecting people against the temptation to stray from a morally virtuous course in life, thus making it difficult to create and to maintain community.[150]

Other illustrations of the way in which religious traditions teach moral virtues to limit excessive desire are given in *The Guide*.[151] In this regard, one last example is in order. The concern to maintain justice is a natural expression of the rational end to pursue moral right; or in other terms, as we saw earlier in discussing the welfare of the body, to not wrong others and to do what is useful for the community. Indeed, justice requires "granting to everyone who has a right to something, that which he has a right to and giving to every being that which corresponds to his merits."[152] But how do we carry out this principle in the different circumstances that we face? Or to use other terms, how should we practice justice—which means not harming others and doing what is useful to the community by granting everyone that which he or she has a right to expect—in the context of particular issues and cases? Rational inquiry by itself may not always be able to answer this question. In the face of this fact, Maimonides turns to the moral virtues found in religious practice. He takes this path in order to provide the rational soul with what it has a right to expect. And thus Maimonides says "for when you walk in the way of the moral virtues, you do justice unto your rational soul, giving her the due that is her right."[153]

Finally, how do we know that particular religious practices best serve the interests of justice? For instance, take the issue of the death penalty mentioned earlier. Suppose a religious practice justifies its use for those who murder. How can we be sure that we are acting justly by invoking the death penalty, even when its use is sanctioned by a religious tradition? Maimonides would say that this question highlights the importance of knowledge. For only as we acquire knowledge about the death penalty, in all of its many facets, can we be in a position to make compelling judgments about the justness or unjustness of its use. Of course, as we saw earlier, individuals are limited in their ability to acquire knowledge. Perfect knowledge is beyond our reach. Still, despite this fact, it is possible to obtain sufficient knowledge to render good judgments about how best to achieve justice in the death penalty question, as well as in many other issues of morality and politics.

Thus, communities that seek to serve the rational end obligating us to moral conduct cannot do so unless they permit the relentless pursuit of knowledge—the other rational end of the soul. Here, just communities, which enable us to unite knowledge with moral right, make possible the greatest achievement of human flourishing—wisdom.

V. Conclusion: The Implications for Civil Society

Where would Maimonides, and the Islamic thinkers discussed here, stand on the need for a civil society? Certainly, these writers would not have created a separate sphere, independent of the state. Nonetheless, I think Maimonides, like the Islamic thinkers we have discussed, can be seen as creating, in the medieval non-Christian world, an opening to civil society.

After all, in providing a place for reason alongside a respect for religious tradition, Maimonides as well as the Islamic philosophers discussed here make clear the limits of both. Reason can't by itself achieve the moral right it demands, and religious tradition may at times fall short of the expectations for moral right commanded by reason. In this circumstance, we have no choice but to search for the knowledge that helps us to ensure that religious traditions truly work for realizing justice. And, in the face of the need for knowledge that can help establish the proper relationship between faith and reason, it becomes clear that social and political settings that frustrate or deny this pursuit become viewed as archaic and as lacking legitimacy. Such becomes the fate of the medieval world.

And, what advances to the forefront is the need for a social and political setting that gives centrality of place to knowledge and to moral right, the two rational ends of Maimonides' view of the soul—thus making clear the need for civil society.

Endnotes

1. Miriam Galston, *Politics and Excellence: The Political Philosophy of Alfarabi,* (Princeton: Princeton University Press, 1990), pp. 15–16.

2. Oliver Leaman, *Averroes and His Philosophy,* (Oxford: Clarendon Press, 1988), p. 5.

3. Ibid., p. 6.

4. Ibid., p. 6.

5. Ibid., pp. 7–8.

6. Miriam Galston, *Politics and Excellence: The Political Philosophy of Alfarabi,* p. 14.

7. Charles E. Butterworth, "Introduction," in *The Political Aspects of Islamic Philosophy,* edited by Charles E. Butterworth, (Cambridge: Harvard University Press, 1992), pp. 3–4.

8. Miriam Galston, *Politics and Excellence: The Political Philosophy of Alfarabi,* p. 14.

9. Ibid., pp. 14–19.

10. Ibid., p. 43.

11. Ibid., p. 43.

12. Ibid., pp. 43–44.

13. Peter Heath, *Allegory and Philosophy in Avicenna,* (Ibn Sina), (Philadelphia: University of Pennsylvania Press, 1992), pp. 21–24.

14. Ibid., p. 19.

15. Ibid., pp. 21–24.

16. Ibid., p. 25.

17. Oliver Leaman, *Averroes and His Philosophy,* p. 52.

18. Shlomo Pines, "Introduction" to Moses Maimonides, *The Guide of the Perplexed,* translated with an introduction and notes by Shlomo Pines, with introductory essay by Leo Strauss, (Chicago: University of Chicago Press, 1963), p. xciv.

19. Peter Heath, *Allegory and Philosophy in Avicenna,* pp. 37–41.

20. Shlomo Pines, "Introduction" to Moses Maimonides, *The Guide of the Perplexed,* p. xcix.

21. Ibid., p. xcix.

22. Ibid., p. xcix.

23. Ibid., p. xcix.

24. James W. Morris, "The Philosopher-Prophet in Avicenna's Political Philosophy," in *The Political Aspects of Islamic Philosophy,* edited by Charles E. Butterworth, pp. 183–87.

25. Ibid., p. 192.

26. Oliver Leaman, *Averroes and His Philosophy,* p. 4. Also see, Fred Gladstone Bratton, *Maimonides: Medieval Modernist,* (Boston: Beacon Press, 1967), pp. 4–8.

27. Oliver Leaman, *Averroes and His Philosophy,* pp. 1–3.

28. Fred Gladstone Bratton, *Maimonides: Medieval Modernist,* p. 8.

29. Oliver Leaman, *Averroes and His Philosophy,* p. 1.

30. Ibid., pp. 8–9.

31. Ibid., pp. 127–28.

32. Fred Gladstone Bratton, *Maimonides: Medieval Modernist,* p. 7.

33. Oliver Leaman, *Averroes and His Philosophy,* p. 144.

34. Ibid., p. 120.

35. Averroes, *Averroes' Commentary on Plato's Republic,* edited with an introduction, translation, and notes by E. I. J. Rosenthal, (Cambridge: Cambridge University Press), p. 111.

36. Oliver Leaman, *Averroes and His Philosophy,* p. 120. Averroes, *Averroes' Commentary on Plato's Republic,* pp. 115, 156–63.

37. Averroes, *Averroes' Commentary on Plato's Republic,* p. 178.

38. Ibid., p. 178.

39. Oliver Leaman, *Averroes and His Philosophy,* p. 121, and Averroes, *Averroes' Commentary on Plato's Republic,* pp. 178–79.

40. Averroes, *Averroes' Commentary on Plato's Republic,* pp 209–49. Also, see Oliver Leaman, *Averroes and His Philosophy,* p. 121. In support of my view that Averroes defends democracy, see Rosenthal's comment in the *Averroes' Commentary on Plato's Republic* volume, p. 294, where Rosenthal suggests that it is possible that Averroes' favorable view of democracy arises from Aristotle, who saw democracy as the least bad of the unjust regimes. This aspect of Aristotle's thought is discussed in Chapter 3, section X, of this book.

41. Oliver Leaman, *Averroes and His Philosophy,* p. 127.

42. Averroes, *Averroes' Commentary on Plato's Republic,* p. 164.

43. Ibid., pp. 164–65.

44. Ibid., p. 165.

45. Ibid., p. 165.

46. Ibid., p. 166.

47. Ibid., p. 166.

48. Ibid., pp. 165–66.

49. Ibid., p. 166. Italics are placed in text by me.

50. Ibid., p. 214.

51. Ibid., p. 232.

52. Ibid., p. 235.

53. Ibid., pp. 212–13.

54. Ibid., p. 213.

55. Ibid., p. 213.

56. Ibid., p. 213.

57. Ibid., pp. 229–30.

58. Ibid., p. 230.

59. Ibid., pp. 213, 230.

60. Ibid., p. 232.

61. Ibid., p. 214.

62. Ibid., p. 214.

63. Ibid., p. 232.

64. Ibid., p. 230.

65. Ibid., p. 160.

66. Ibid., p. 160.

67. Ibid., p. 160.

68. Ibid., p. 213

69. Ibid., p. 213.

70. Ibid., p. 213.

71. Ibid., pp. 214, 230.

72. Ibid., pp. 214, 230. See note by Rosenthal in the *Averroes' Commentary on Plato's Republic* volume, p. 286, describing states of necessity, which provide for the necessities of life.

73. Ibid., p. 214. See note by Rosenthal in the *Averroes' Commentary on Plato's Republic* volume, p. 287, suggesting that the use of the term *association* refers to a political community, which seems to bind people to morality.

74. Ibid., p. 214.

75. Ibid., pp. 214–15.

76. Ibid., p. 215.

77. Ibid., p. 214.

78. Ibid., p. 215

79. Ibid., p. 205.

80. Ibid., pp. 216–17.

81. Oliver Leaman, *Averroes and His Philosophy,* pp. 127–28.

82. For background see the following: Fred Gladstone Bratton, *Maimonides: Medieval Modernist,* pp. 28–59; Abraham J. Heschel, *Maimonides: A Biography,* (New York: Image Books, 1982), pp. 3–24; and The Rev. A. Cohen, "Introduction," in *The Teachings of Maimonides,* with a prolegomenon by Marvin Fox, (New York: Ktav Publishing House, 1968), pp. 7–29.

83. Cohen, "Introduction," *The Teachings of Maimonides,* pp. 7–11.

84. Bratton, *Maimonides: Medieval Modernist,* p. 51.

85. Ibid., p. 52.

86. *The Random House College Dictionary,* (New York: Random House, 1988), pp. 98, 367.

87. Ibid., p. 957.

88. Ibid., p. 710.

89. *The Jewish Political Tradition, Volume One: Authority,* edited by Michael Walzer, Menachem Lorberbaum, and Noam J. Zohar, (New Haven: Yale University Press, 2000), pp. 553–54. Note that the Torah consists of the Pentateuch, or the first five books of the Old Testament, as well as the whole body of Jewish law, including the Talmud, which we discuss later.

90. Maimonides, "Introduction to the *Mishneh Torah,*" in Walzer et al., *The Jewish Political Tradition,* p. 255. Italics in text.

91. Ibid., p. 255.

92. *The Random House College Dictionary,* (New York: Random House, 1988), p. 1167.

93. From a section of a Talmudic discussion entitled "Defining the Elder's Rebellion," in Walzer, et al., *The Jewish Political Tradition,* p. 326.

94. Maimonides, "MT Laws of Rebels," in Walzer, et al., *The Jewish Political Tradition,* p. 285.

95. "Introduction" to Chapter 6, Rabbis and Sages, in Walzer, et al., *The Jewish Political Tradition,* p. 247.

96. Ibid., p. 247.

97. David Hartman, "Commentary. Expanding the Covenant," in Walzer, et al., *The Jewish Political Tradition,* pp. 266–68.

98. "Introduction" to Chapter 6, Rabbis and Sages, in Walzer, et al., *The Jewish Political Tradition,* pp. 249–50.

99. Ibid., p. 250.

100. Ibid., p. 250.

101. Noam J. Zohar, "Commentary. The Oral Law: Celebrating Radical Reinterpretation," in Walzer, et al., *The Jewish Political Tradition,* pp. 278–79.

102. "Introduction" to Chapter 6, Rabbis and Sages, in Walzer, et al., *The Jewish Political Tradition,* p. 250.

103. David Shatz, "Commentary. Interpretive Pluralism," in Walzer, et al., *The Jewish Political Tradition,* p. 340.

104. Ibid., 341. Also see Walzer, et al., *The Jewish Political Tradition,* p. 533.

105. Walzer, et al., *The Jewish Political Tradition,* pp. 547, 550, 553.

106. Maimonides, "Introduction to the *Mishneh Torah,*" in Walzer, et al., *The Jewish Political Tradition,* p. 256.

107. "Introduction" to Chapter 7, Controversy and Dissent, in Walzer, et al., *The Jewish Political Tradition,* p. 314. Also, David Shatz, "Commentary. Interpretive Pluralism," in Walzer, et al., *The Jewish Political Tradition,* p. 340.

108. "Introduction" to Chapter 7, Controversy and Dissent, in Walzer, et al., *The Jewish Political Tradition,* p. 314.

109. Ibid., p. 315.

110. Ibid., p. 315.

111. Ibid., p. 315. Also see p. 254, author's introduction to Maimonides, "Introduction to the *Mishneh Torah,*" in Walzer, et al., *The Jewish Political Tradition.*

112. "Introduction" to Chapter 7, Controversy and Dissent, in Walzer, et al., *The Jewish Political Tradition,* p. 315.

113. Maimonides, "Introduction to the *Mishneh Torah,*" in Walzer, et al., *The Jewish Political Tradition,* p. 355.

114. Pines, "Introduction," Moses Maimonides, *The Guide of the Perplexed,* p. xcix.

115. Ibid., p. xcix.

116. Ibid., p. xcix.

117. Maimonides, "MT Laws of Sales," in Walzer, et al., *The Jewish Political Tradition,* p. 419.

118. Amy Gutmann, "Commentary. Who Should Rule?" in Walzer, et al., *The Jewish Political Tradition,* p. 422.

119. Ibid., p. 422. Maimonides, "MT Laws of Sales," in Walzer, et al., *The Jewish Political Tradition,* p. 419.

120. Pines, "Introduction," Moses Maimonides, *The Guide of the Perplexed,* p. cxvii.

121. Leo Strauss, "How to Begin to Study *The Guide of the Perplexed,*" in Pines, "Introduction," Maimonides, *The Guide of the Perplexed,* p. xiv.

122. Ibid., p. xiv. The quotation marks are found in the text.

123. Ibid., p. xiv. Also Leo Strauss, *Persecution and the Art of Writing,* (Glencoe, Illinois: The Free Press, 1952), p. 46.

124. Leo Strauss, *Persecution and the Art of Writing,* p. 46.

125. Leo Strauss, "How to Begin to Study *The Guide of the Perplexed,*" translated in Pines, "Introduction," Maimonides, *The Guide of the Perplexed,* pp. xiv–xv.

126. Ibid., p. xv.

127. Strauss, *Persecution and the Art of Writing,* pp. 53–55.

128. Maimonides, Pines edition, *The Guide of the Perplexed,* I.32, p. 70.

129. Marvin Fox, "Prolegomenon," in Rev. A. Cohen, *The Teachings of Maimonides,* p. xl.

130. Ibid., pp. xl–xli.

131. Ibid., pp. xl–xli.

132. Maimonides, Pines edition, *The Guide of the Perplexed,* I, 34, p. 73.

133. Ibid., III.8, p. 431. Italics in text.

134. Ibid., III.8, p. 431.

135. I realize that Maimonides, in addition to the two rational ends cited, notes a third—"apprehension of the Creator." But I emphasize the two mentioned in this paragraph because it seems that in seeking knowledge of the natural and human worlds, and in doing as moral right requires, humankind would in Maimonides' view receive an understanding of the Creator. This means that to understand the Creator is to comprehend the nature of the Creator's world, including the way the Creator wants people to live in that world.

136. Maimonides, Pines edition, *The Guide of the Perplexed*, III.8, p. 431.

137. Ibid., III.8, p. 432.

138. Ibid., III.8, p. 431.

139. Ibid., III.27, p. 510.

140. Ibid., III.27, p. 510.

141. Ibid., III.27, p. 510. Italics are added.

142. Ibid., III.27, p. 510.

143. Ibid., III.27, p. 511.

144. Ibid., III.27, p. 511, also, p. 510.

145. Ibid., III.27, p. 511.

146. Ibid., III.27, p. 511.

147. Marvin Fox, in Rev. A. Cohen, "Prolegomenon," in *The Teachings of Maimonides,* p. xli.

148. Maimonides, Pines edition, *The Guide of the Perplexed*, III.49, p. 601.

149. Maimonides, *Commentary on the Mishnah,* and *Mishneh Torah,* in Rev. A. Cohen, *The Teachings of Maimonides,* pp. 296–97.

150. Maimonides, Pines edition, *The Guide of the Perplexed*, III.49, pp. 602–12. Also, I.34, p. 77.

151. Ibid., III.8, pp. 433–36. Maimonides advocates shaming people for their anger; promoting drinking and eating only for nourishment, not for pleasure; and avoiding obscene language, as well as discussions about copulation. There is no space available here to discuss the implications and wisdom of Maimonides' views on subjects of this sort for the modern world.

152. Ibid., III.55, p. 631.

153. Ibid., III.55, p. 631.

Partial Bibliography and Further Reading

Averroes. *Averroes' Commentary on Plato's Republic,* ed. E. I. J. Rosenthal. Cambridge: Cambridge University Press, 1969.

Bratton, Fred Gladstone. *Maimonides: Medieval Modernist.* Boston: Beacon Press, 1967.

Butterworth, Charles E. "Introduction," in *The Political Aspects of Islamic Philosophy,* ed. Charles E. Butterworth. Cambridge: Harvard University Press, 1992.

Cohen, The Rev. A., "Introduction," in *The Teachings of Maimonides,* with a prolegomenon by Marvin Fox. New York: Ktav Publishing House, 1968.

Fox, Marvin, in Rev. A. Cohen, "Introduction," *The Teachings of Maimonides.* New York: Ktav Publishing House, 1968.

Galston, Miriam. *Politics and Excellence: The Political Philosophy of Alfarabi.* Princeton: Princeton University Press, 1990.

Heath, Peter. *Allegory and Philosophy in Avicenna,* (Ibn Sina). Philadelphia: University of Pennsylvania Press, 1992.

Heschel, Abraham J. *Maimonides: A Biography.* New York: Doubleday, 1982.

Leaman, Oliver. *Averroes and His Philosophy.* Oxford: Clarendon Press, 1988.

Lerner, Ralph. *Maimonides' Empire of Light: Popular Enlightenment in an Age of Belief.* Chicago: University of Chicago Press, 2000.

Maimonides, Moses, *The Guide of the Perplexed,* translated with an introduction by Shlomo Pines, and with an introductory essay by Leo Strauss. Chicago: University of Chicago Press, 1963.

Pines, Shlomo, "Introduction," Moses Maimonides, *The Guide of the Perplexed,* and with an introductory essay by Leo Strauss. Chicago: University of Chicago Press, 1963.

Strauss, Leo. *Persecution and the Art of Writing.* Glencoe, Illinois: The Free Press, 1952.

———. Introductory essay by Leo Strauss, in *The Guide of the Perplexed,* Chicago: University of Chicago Press, 1963.

Walzer, Michael, Lorberbaum, Menachem, and Zohar J. Noam. *The Jewish Political Tradition, Volume One: Authority.* New Haven: Yale University Press, 2000.

7

THOMAS HOBBES AND MODERN CIVIL SOCIETY

I. HISTORICAL CONTEXT

Thomas Hobbes (1588–1679) designed a new relationship between citizens and their state in the face of the intense conflicts that permeated his society. Before explaining the particular dimensions of these conflicts and of the new citizen/state relationship, it is well worth discussing why Hobbes can be properly called a major architect of modern liberalism.

Hobbes's political thinking emanates from the demands of some people for the opportunity to chart a course in life previously denied expression. Traditional medieval order was predicated upon a way of life that gave prominence to certain classes, including the nobility, the landed, church officials, and of course the king. Those left without power were people who worked the land as peasants and serfs, as well as people drafted into the king's and noblemen-led army. Also left without power was a new bourgeoisie or middle class of tradesmen, merchants, and small farmers who owned their own land. The middle class made demands on the political system for inclusion. In effect, this new middle class sought opportunities for a space in which a person could pursue activities, previously denied in the old order.

In practical political terms, opportunities for the new middle class to express as well as to pursue its own interests would be provided by the provision of rights. What did these rights guarantee? Rights in Hobbes provided people with the chance to make decisions about what they wanted to do with their own lives, within certain limits established by the culture of the times. This means that people would be permitted more leeway than in the past, but not so much leeway that they would violate all the norms of the society. Thus, whereas individuals should be given the freedom to become merchants if that is what they want to be, they could not expect to be admitted to the nobility if that is what they hoped for.

The political system fashioned from this vision is the basis for liberalism. Liberalism makes possible individual freedom by enabling people to have rights, which provide both opportunities and protections, but at the same time liberalism requires individuals to ob-serve those obligations linked with the new opportunities and protections. There are sev-eral important implications of this view. In the first place, the history of liberalism will al-ways be associated in public memory with the need for critiquing in the name of freedom existing traditional ways of life, as was the case in Hobbes's time, while accepting the need for certain culturally established limits on that freedom. And this questioning will al-ways create conflict in society, which will often be resolved in the name of freedom, and less so in the name of retaining restrictions on freedom for the sake of protecting tradition.

For conservatives, as we will see in the chapter on that subject, liberalism is criticized for always seeking to make people justify tradition in the name of freedom. And doing so for conservatives can lead to the betrayal of important values—such as religious or long-standing cultural ones—needed to maintain social order and community. For liberals, how-ever, freedom is not corrosive of society because for liberals freedom is always associated with necessary and reasonable constraints needed to secure freedom. Hobbes discusses the constraints of natural law, and John Locke describes what I refer to as the constrained ma-jority. Each writer understands these constraints as necessary for securing freedom. As we shall see, John Stuart Mill argues that people should be free to do what they wish so long as they do not harm others. Immanuel Kant maintains the presence of coercive laws that are formed in keeping with universal moral standards that secure individual freedom. G. W. F. Hegel will give the state the job of enforcing the law for the sake of freedom. John Rawls will discuss the place of an overlapping consensus as the basis for necessary constraints on freedom. In short, what liberals suggest is that if tradition denies the freedom that takes place within reasonable constraints, then tradition should be reformed, as for example was the case with traditions of segregation that denied freedom to African-Americans.

Thus, the view of liberalism provided here explains why liberalism is both a history of the expansion of the number of rights made available to protect people's freedom as well as a history of the need to extend the coverage of rights to those heretofore not protected by them. In Hobbes, there is to be a basic right to personal freedom, and this right is to permit one to choose one's own occupation and core beliefs. To these ends, the right to own property will be a central concern. Later, as we move beyond Hobbes, we shall see that the number of rights will be expanded to include political rights, such as freedom of conscience, speech, as-sociation, thought, and so on. Further, those covered under those rights will be expanded to include more and more groups not previously accorded rights. Indeed, the history of our own society follows the pattern of liberalism. We have seen the list of rights grow to include, in addition to basic rights in the First Ten Amendments of the United States Constitution and the Supreme Court endorsed right to privacy, the evolving presumption of a right to health care and to an education. And we have seen the scope of rights expand to include previously excluded groups, such as women, African-Americans, Native-Americans, gays, and so on.

Another important implication of liberalism is the liberty interest that is central to the liberal project, bequeathed no doubt by Hobbes. By this, I mean that in demanding a space for persons to pursue conduct or to hold beliefs previously denied to them, individuals are said to have a prime interest in liberty. This means that other values—such as autonomy, privacy, equality, and community—are important insofar as they aid that interest. Let me briefly discuss each in turn.

Autonomy suggests that individuals should have the freedom to make major decisions about their lives, including such matters as choice of career, religion, or friendships. Without liberty there can be no autonomy of choice with respect to major issues such as these. Privacy refers to a sphere outside the reach of others or the state, a sphere in which individuals can live as they choose. Privacy in the context used here suggests that individuals must be allowed to think their own thoughts, have their own feelings, and partake in relationships of their own choice, without interference from the state or others. Equality is a value of high importance in this setting, too. Equality is seen as providing all citizens with like rights and, in consequence thereof, with equal liberty.

Finally, what liberalism emphasizes is that freedom for the individual is more important than community. This does not mean that community is incompatible with liberalism. It means only that the common good of community must be defined so as not to smother liberty. Indeed, communities are acceptable to the extent they practice norms conducive to a broader liberty.

In taking this view, Hobbes, as one of the founders of liberalism, is advocating on the whole the interests of a new class, the bourgeoisie, or what is the new middle class. This class has been both celebrated and scorned. Those who celebrate it are writers such as Hobbes, Locke, and Kant, each of whom sees it as the phalanx of freedom. Those who attack the bourgeoisie see the new middle class as mostly interested in material self-gratification and greed, rejecting in the process respect for all that is sacred. The bourgeoisie will be viewed in Jean-Jacques Rousseau as the source of the undermining of community. In Karl Marx, it is the basis for a cruel form of capitalism, and in Friedrich Nietzsche it is the foundation of herd-like, conformist thinking.

All in all, Hobbes, Locke, and Kant as leading forerunners of liberalism represent the quest of the Enlightenment to further the interests of a society based on the teachings of reason. Reason is the means by which individuals can best determine the basis for a good life. And in taking this position, reason emphasizes the importance of liberty as it defends the latter against all that may stand in its way, including well-worn traditions.

In this chapter, I wish to emphasize the liberty interest dimension and ask how well Hobbes would make this interest compatible with civil society in the separate sphere sense of the term. To that end, I will describe now the historical context of liberalism in Hobbes.

On the one hand, there were those who believed that the monarch should remain the pivotal political force, not subject to challenge. But on the other hand, there were those arguing for greater autonomy and independence from the king's power. The English civil wars, which took place during Hobbes's lifetime, were in part fought over the issue of who should have greater authority, the king or the parliament. Hobbes definitely supported the idea of an absolute monarchy.[1] In doing so, however, he predicated the king's power upon the idea of a social contract that the people in society consented to. A chief condition of this contract was that the government exists to protect the freedom of individuals. This freedom would be used ultimately by the evolving merchant or new commercial class seeking independence to pursue its own interests in a society historically dominated by a medieval structure.

In Hobbes's new social contract, then, people would consent to being ruled by a powerful monarch, in exchange for the personal freedom that the monarch would guarantee and protect. This new social contract symbolized that the medieval order in society was no longer the basis for establishing social obligations. Instead, obligations grew out of the desire for individual freedom. Central to this objective is the need to maintain a respect for civic virtue. What role does civic virtue play in the setting that Hobbes described in his writings? When people have the freedom to determine the way of life that is best for them, they are bound to face conflicts and disagreements. Still, different people holding conflicting interests can live in peace if there are common ground rules or civic virtues all can accept and abide by during the course of promoting their interests. Hobbes's effort to provide rules that secure rights and freedom is the basis for the *liberal* view of civil society discussed throughout this part of the book.

II. HOBBES'S METHOD

The method Hobbes used to find those rules that provide a common basis for politics among disparate groups derives from his fascination with geometry. Geometry was the "only Science that it hath pleased God hitherto to bestow on mankind."[2] In geometry one starts with simple, but self-evident propositions, definitions, and axioms and uses deduction to build complex systems from these simpler starting points. This approach was used to explain relationships in the physical world, and Hobbes thought that the political world could be studied in the same manner. The only hindrance to doing so was in determining the correct or valid, simple, but self-evident propositions that were the basis for explaining the general characteristics of human conduct. Once one found these, one could use them as the starting points for analysis and for building a logical system for the political world similar in nature to the one that geometry constructs for the physical world.

Hobbes approached this objective by making use of the method employed by Galileo, the resolutive-compositive approach, and applying it to the political world.[3] Galileo used this approach to understand complex motions. He did so by first, in the resolutive part, hypothesizing there to be simple forces. These simple forces could not be directly observed, but their existence was merely a creation of the imagination. He postulated these simple forces as a necessary ground for the more complex motions he wanted to explain. When these simple forces, with the use of logical reasoning, were combined into a composite, he was able to demonstrate why the complex motions he studied took place.

To take this method into the study of humankind, we can start with the whole arena of human conduct as we know it and ask what are the basic elements from which the whole is built. Hobbes starts his discussion of politics by first saying that the whole, or society when viewed as a composite, is characterized by a state of war. He will then ask what the basic elements of this system are and how they are interrelated to create a world characterized by war. Moreover, with the understanding he gains about how the whole is constituted, he can ask how the whole system of interrelations in society might be reconstituted in a new way to avoid war and to make peace possible.

So Hobbes's questions are clear. What forces in the human world contribute to war, and how might they be rearranged to achieve a peaceful world? Now, no one can know the mind of humankind for certain, but we can imagine or hypothesize what the forces are that motivate humankind, given what we know of human conduct already. Thus, if reality in general is such that individuals are prone to engage in war with others, we have a basis for explaining our general situation in terms of what can be hypothesized as self-evident and basic truths that explain these circumstances. Further, once we know why human relationships lead to a general condition of war, it should be possible to define those common rules and norms that all should uphold in order to make possible a society committed to peace.

In our discussion of the state of nature in the next section, we will describe the basic forces that suggest the potential for war and under what conditions it is possible to achieve peace. Before turning to this endeavor it is important to note the practical, political implications of Hobbes's method. In discussing society, Hobbes had to confront some very difficult conflicts. We have already referred to the one pertaining to the role of the king in relation to parliament. But as we will elaborate upon more fully in Section VI, there are grave differences in Hobbes's society pertaining to the role of religious institutions in their relationship to both society and the state. It would appear, given the nature and the depth of the differences permeating Hobbes's society, that there is no common basis upon which to establish the state's role in society.

Seen from the perspective of the particular parties in any of these conflicts, this conclusion would be understandable and inevitable. Hobbes, of course, could not accept this outcome. He believed that it was possible to find a basis for avoiding war in his society. And to do so it would be necessary to discover a common viewpoint that stood above the partisanship found in his society and that could be used to establish the common rules all could accept for securing peace. To this end, Hobbes suggested that the reasons for conflict are quite simple in nature. As a consequence, because the real basis for conflict is uncomplicated, the differences that separate people are not that large at all, and peaceful solutions to resolve people's differences are likely to be easier to identify. In effect, when people understand that the basis for their conflicts is no longer actually located in particular religious or philosophical differences, but in simpler explanations about human nature, then it is more likely that individuals will be able to find a common set of rules for organizing political and social life in a way all can accept.

As people comprehend the real roots of conflict, they can attain a basis for overcoming once and for all the conflict everyone loathes. In place of a society filled with war and strife, there can emerge a new civil society that is committed to protect, in the name of the rule of law, the individual freedom of each person. Here, a new doctrine of civic virtue emerges, one that is seen as the basis for supporting notions of individual private freedom, or the freedom to make choices about the way of life that seems best for one's self. In the new civic virtue, the rules that all must accept are rules that are used to avoid destructive forms of conflict during the course of protecting each person's private freedom. In this case, civic virtue is no longer defined in terms of a need to support a particular conception of the common good, a conception that defines for each person his or her fixed and permanent place in society, as in Plato's republic, Aristotle's polis, or Aquinas's form of medieval society. Instead, civic virtue permits each person to have the freedom to determine which way of life is best for him- or herself and, in demanding that all should have this freedom, civic virtue becomes a doctrine that embraces a moral order based upon providing each individual the same basic rights.

Still, the main problem with Hobbes's argument is that Hobbes's concept of civil society embraces a very powerful state that threatens the freedom that his view of civil society defends. Explaining the reasons for this situation is one of the main objectives of this chapter.

III. HOBBES AND THE STATE OF NATURE

What, then, is the enduring source of conflict? To explain the reasons for human conflict, Hobbes described his view of the state of nature. Hobbes's view of the state of nature represents what he thought human interactions were like before there was organized society, before there was government, and before there were any formal laws. Hobbes's views were his own imagined description of human life, and his picture of this condition demonstrated why conflict was inevitable. Moreover, given the view he provided, it is also possible to understand why it is likely that individuals will find an acceptable resolution.

In the state of nature, Hobbes argued that people are continually motivated to realize the objects of their desires. People not only want to achieve their present desires, but they have a strong need to be in a position that allows them to achieve whatever future desires they may have as well.[4] It is only when people are successful in these regards that they can attain a "contented life." People differ only in the sense that they may have different passions, but because all want to realize them, all people share a common hope of achieving contentment in their lives.[5] To obtain one's desires, however, one must have sufficient "power," or the necessary means, to acquire whatever one may need to satisfy a particular passion. Thus, given the constancy of the urge to realize one's desires the search for power is a continual enterprise that "ceaseth onely in Death."[6]

Why, one might ask, is the search for power continual? After all, once one has acquired sufficient power to attain one's objectives, why would one want to seek more power? In the state of nature, people find themselves in a situation in which they never can truly relax and enjoy whatever they are able to acquire with the power they have. People are always looking over their shoulders, wondering when and if the person next to them will cause them harm. To avert this possibility, people always feel the need to find ways to acquire more and more power. As they do, their purpose in acquiring power changes somewhat. They still need power to acquire the goods that enable them to enjoy life, of course. But in addition, they discover that it is necessary to secure power for its own sake, so that they can free themselves from the constant fear that others will cause them harm. Man, said Hobbes, "cannot assure the power and means to live well, which he hath present, without the acquisition of more."[7]

Moreover, the fear that others will take from us what we currently possess creates a condition of mutual violence on the part of each person toward the other. If each person thinks that everything one has may be taken from him by another, each person can never trust the other person, and each person thinks that the other person is always scheming to do harm. Naturally, this condition of mutual distrust leads to the development of some very destructive tendencies among people. Here, "the way of one Competitor, to the attaining of his desire, is to kill, subdue, supplant or repell the other."[8] In the state of nature, competition among people leads to the need to gain at the expense of others, to employ violence against others, and thus people seek "to make themselves Master of other men's persons, wives, children and cattell."[9] It is not surprising that life in the state of nature is "solitary, poore, nasty, brutish, and short."[10]

Hobbes's account of the state of nature seems to describe the ramifications for civil society of the market mentality in its most destructive form. Here, people compete for the financial resources that enable them to obtain the power, or the material means, to acquire the things that give them happiness and contentment in life. Thus, Hobbes had the influence of the market context in mind when he argued that our power as individuals is associated with our "worth," that is, the "price" that others would pay for our services.

We can acquire more power, or the means to achieve our ends, if we can enhance our worth, or the price we can charge others who want to make use of our services. Our worth, however, always depends upon the judgments and needs of others.[11] If others find that what we offer no longer has any value, then we would lose our ability to acquire what brings us contentment and happiness. Hobbesian persons, not unlike many today, live in constant dread and fear that, in the eyes of the market, they will have nothing of value to contribute to the society.

Given this composite picture of humankind in the state of nature, it is understandable why society becomes a dog-eat-dog world, where each is engaged in trying to dominate and subjugate the other before the other dominates and subjugates him. If this picture is accurate, then it would appear impossible for humankind to avoid war and to establish a civil society. But Hobbes suggested otherwise. For if one looks closely at the nature of human relationships one can understand how the basis for conflict among persons, the constant need to obtain more and more power, can be turned into a direction favorable to peace, instead of war. How is this possible?

Hobbes said that, in the main, despite the fact that most people think they are superior to others and are thus characterized by a "vain conceit,"[12] the fact of the matter is that most of us are equal in ability and capacity. "Nature hath made men so equall, in the faculties of body, and mind; as that though there bee found one man sometimes manifestly stronger in body, or of quicker mind than another; yet when all is reckoned together, the difference between man, and man, is not so considerable."[13] How does this fact explain the basis for transcending destructive behavior and creating the basis for a new social contract, where cooperation replaces war? In the rest of this section, I want to address this question.

Our equality of ability suggests an equality of hope that we will be able to attain the ends that bring about contentment.[14] And when, as a result of this equality of ability and now hope, two people seek the same thing, they naturally become enemies, because it is impossible for both of them to have that thing. Hobbes said, "from this equality of ability, ariseth equality of hope in the attaining of Ends. And therefore if any two men desire the thing, which neverthelesse they cannot both enjoy, they become enemies; and in the way to their End . . . endeavour to destroy, or subdue one an other."[15]

Here, in a world where people are equal in ability and where there are not enough of the things we all desire to go around to everyone, it is highly likely that each of us will seek to control and dominate others. The reason for this state of affairs is that we realize the thin line between success and failure. What differentiates me, the successful person, from you the unsuccessful person may just be luck. I got to the cherished job opportunity we both sought before you did, and so I got the job. If you had arrived before me, you would have had the job, not me. The problem here is that there is only one job and two people competing for it. And, because each of us is equal in ability, the prospective employer does not have to wait for the more talented person to show up, but instead, he will take the first person in line. Knowing this to be the factual context of life makes those who lose out very jealous and hateful to those who succeed. The loser feels that the winner wins only because of luck, not because of ability. And because each of us thinks of ourselves, with all our "vain conceits," as better than the other, we think that we should have gotten the job, instead of the other who is "less deserving." So we are very bitter, and our bitterness propels us to treat others with contempt and violence.

Furthermore, the successful person is really no better off, either. He knows that others are jealous and harbor violent feelings toward him, and so he worries that everything he has gained will be taken from him at some point in the future. He may have won the job, but, if he ever lets his guard down, even for a minute, he will find himself on the street. He can never rest easy at night because he is always insecure about losing everything to another. Moreover, in this setting, there are no standards of justice that could be appealed to as the basis for assuaging one's fear.[16]

In this situation, then, people are driven by a need to gain permanent advantage over each other, and we are prone, as well, to use violence to make ourselves the masters of others. But Hobbes argued that we are not destined to live like this, and again the primary reason seems to be the essential equality of our basic capacities. We are all commonly in possession of central passions—the fear of death, and a desire to live comfortably. "The Passions that encline men to Peace, are Fear of Death [and the] Desire of such things as are necessary to commodious living."[17] These passions become center stage for us when we realize that the constant quest for power by each of us threatens to destroy all hope for social peace, for comforts, and for release from the fear of death.

At this point, people discover that the ongoing warfare they are engaged in with each other is harmful, on the whole, to creating the conditions that make prosperity possible. Where war is ever-present, there is little industrial development, there is no art or advances in knowledge, there is no trade among nations, and so on.[18] Again, then, as part of the common equality in ability of humankind, it would appear that a cause of peace is the realization that individuals generally share a common set of expectations for life. Were people's expectations to be wildly different, there would be no basis upon which to establish a peaceful social and political order, but for Hobbes this is not the case because people want what secures their prosperity and insures their happiness.

Thus, our common fear of death, as well as a shared commitment to have what makes possible a prosperous life, moves us to seek a new basis for society, and our reason aids in this endeavor by defining the "Articles of Peace, upon which men may be drawn to agreement." The articles of peace that all can accept and make the basis of the new civil society are referred to as the laws of nature.[19]

IV. HOBBES'S CIVIL SOCIETY: THE LAWS OF NATURE AND CIVIC VIRTUE

What is the nature of the new social contract or civil society, embodying the "articles of peace" that Hobbes's citizens accept? The answer to this question revolves around what people understand to be the common element that each would accept as the basis for society. The key element is liberty or the right, ordained by nature or reason, of each person to use his "power," "for the preservation of his own Nature; that is to say, of his own Life; and consequently, of doing any thing, which in his own Judgment, and Reason, hee shall conceive to be the aptest means thereunto."[20] Here, each person is to have the personal freedom to chart his own course in life, in accordance with what his goals and desires are.

Furthermore, this kind of liberty for Hobbes is made possible only when we observe certain limits and constraints on conduct. By observing these limits on our liberty, we move from the state of nature to the state of civil society. The limits on conduct suggest for us the need to follow rules that facilitate the individually defined objectives that individuals may choose. In the state of nature, of course, liberty was defined as the right to all things, and people would never accept the kinds of limits prescribed for civil society. But the right-to-all-things doctrine of the state of nature, that is, freedom without limits, signifies only continual war.[21]

This condition cannot continue if human beings are to create a society committed to peace, a goal made necessary by the constant fear as well as the continual threat of death. In consequence, individuals are led to embrace certain laws of nature, or what can be called *civic virtues,* and to make them the basis for establishing the rules of conduct for all citizens in the society. The first and most fundamental law of nature is that all persons ought to seek peace. At the same time, it is also a law of nature that individuals may use any means, including violence, to defend themselves from harm.[22] In following a peaceful course of conduct, however, people do not have to resort to force. As a result, they move from the state of nature, where the only constant was the tendency to harm others, to a civil society.[23] In a civil society, the new constant is the second law of nature that says that no one should seek any more freedom for himself than he would accord to others. This law of nature is summed up in the Bible as the golden rule or the idea that *"Whatsoever you require that others should do to you, that do ye to them."*[24]

Here, Hobbes had in mind a cooperative framework for society, the essence of which is acceptance by each person of the need to mutually accommodate one another's liberty for the sake of securing each person's freedom. Hobbes said that only "in consideration of some Right reciprocally transferred to himselfe; or for some other good he hopeth for thereby"[25] will individuals ever accept the constraints associated with recognizing the liberty of others. No person will abide by a need to respect the liberty of others unless in doing so one's own rights and basic security are assured. To get people to respect one another's liberty, then, conditions must be created that enable people to feel that when they do so, their basic interests, including the need for self-preservation and contentment, are in no sense placed in danger.[26] When these conditions can be met, then each individual is in a position to respect the liberty of others. Hobbes's new social contract, and the view of civil society that flows from it, suggests the notion of mutual respect, or the idea that each person will act to promote the liberty of others when all people attempt to make a place for all other people's interests.

In the cooperative setting that Hobbes's social contract makes available, avenues are created that permit individuals to be engaged in relationships of mutual exchange. Here, people make contracts with other people whenever they exchange one thing for another, such as when they buy or sell with money.[27] A covenant is another form of contract. In a covenant, two people make an agreement, the provisions of which will be carried out in the future.[28] The idea of the covenant, however, brings up a serious problem that a civil society must address. What is to prevent one party to an agreement, say X, from getting what X contracted for, and then not performing, at some future date, as the contract requires with respect to the other party, Y? This question suggests that the urge to subdue others is never quite removed from individuals even in the context of a society governed by natural law. This problem can be averted only if there is a common power that can enforce the covenants and punish those who do not comply with them. Hobbes said that

> *If a Covenant be made, wherein neither of the parties perform presently, but trust one another; in the condition of meer Nature (which is a condition of Warre of every man against every man,) upon any reasonable suspition, it is Voyd: But if there be a common Power set over them both, with right and force sufficient to compell performance; it is not Voyd. For he that performeth first, has no assurance that the other will performe after; because the bonds of words are too weak to bridle mens ambition, avarice, anger, and other Passions, without the fear of some coercive power.*[29]

Based on this position, then, another very important law of nature is justice. Justice is the idea that "*men* [must] *performe their Covenants made: without which, Covenants are in vain, and but Empty words, and the Right of all men to all things remaining, wee are still in the condition of Warre.*"[30] A just society is one in which individuals uphold their agreements with others; when people do not, then there is no basis for anyone to obtain from others the cooperation they need in order to achieve their personal goals and objectives. Moreover, justice is possible only when there is a common power, that is, a commonwealth, or what can be called a state, with coercive power to compel people to uphold their agreements.[31] In the absence of a state that can enforce agreements, society returns to the state of nature, or a condition of continual warfare.

Further, Hobbes's discussion of natural law suggested that, in addition to a common power that each person is to respect, there are other forms of civic virtue (or additional laws of nature) that are useful in protecting the freedom of each person. For instance, people must display gratitude when others give them something, without expecting anything in return.[32] Hobbes hoped to create a civic culture in which people no longer perceive each other as potential enemies. Gratitude helps to achieve this end because it requires people to see the bearers of gifts as acting from a sense of goodwill.[33] If we always refused to attribute goodwill to those people who bestow gifts upon us, there would be no basis for initiating trust or benevolence among people. In this regard, we should manifest toward others the virtue of "compleasance" or the idea that an individual should *"strive to accommodate himselfe to the rest."*[34] This virtue will enable people to understand and to accept the vast diversity of interests and needs that make up society. Moreover, individuals must learn to pardon others for past offenses and to overcome the temptation to extract revenge for past wrongs. Otherwise, there would be no peace.[35] Further, people can secure peace in society only when everyone agrees to treat everyone else as equals. A violation of this principle is the vice of pride.[36] To secure the conditions of equality, individuals must avoid "arrogance" or the tendency to attribute rights to themselves that are not accorded to all others.[37] Instead, all must recognize the basic rights that belong to everyone, like the "right to governe their owne bodies; enjoy aire, water, motion, waies to go from place to place; and all things else without which a man cannot live, or not live well."[38]

These laws suggest that people must learn to deal fairly with each other. When people are not treated fairly, they will resort to violence to resolve disputes. But when people are treated fairly, disputes are resolved through peaceful means such as by impartial judges and arbitrators. In observing this commitment, individuals maintain respect for the natural law or civic virtue called "equity."[39] To achieve equity, which includes fairness in the distribution of basic goods such as property, additional natural laws or civic virtues are needed, and these pertain to the way that property is divided and disputes among citizens are settled.

Regarding property, Hobbes argued that there are natural laws pertaining to the distinction between private and public property. With respect to public property, goods that cannot be divided must be shared in common, and no one can be denied access to them. Hobbes had in mind basic goods needed for survival such as the air we breathe, the water we drink, and so on. But for things that can neither be divided nor enjoyed in common, it is necessary to find a fair procedure for distribution. In this case, Hobbes had in mind private property. He suggested that the latter be distributed by lot so that each person, presumably, believes that there is a fair chance of acquiring his share. The principle of distribution by lot is nothing more than the notion that goods that cannot be enjoyed by all in common be distributed on the basis of according entitlement of something to the person who possesses it first.[40]

Further, in situations in which individuals have differences of opinion and fall into controversy about whether certain actions are permitted under the law, it is a law of nature that a citizen must accept that he cannot properly be an arbitrator in cases involving himself. And thus each must put his faith in a neutral third party, certainly the state, which can act fairly and justly toward each individual.[41]

If the laws of nature were naturally a part of each citizen's outlook, then each citizen would respect the rights of others by his or her own volition. But the fact is that people will not embrace even these virtues unless there is the "terrour of some Power, to cause them to be observed." For Hobbes believed that the laws of nature were "contrary to our naturall Passions, that carry us to Partiality, Pride, Revenge, and the like."[42] Hobbes hoped to neutralize these powerful passions and to create a society based on the fair rules of the laws of nature by establishing a powerful state whose sole function was to use its power to promote these laws. As Hobbes said, "covenants without the sword, are but words,"[43] and so the state in a civil society must have a sword. Nonetheless, as we demonstrate in the next section, the power of the state is allowed to grow to the point at which it is quite likely that it ends up threatening the freedom a civil society seeks to preserve.

V. THE ROLE AND STRUCTURE OF THE STATE

How is what Hobbes called the *commonwealth* or the Leviathan, which is the predominant governing authority with the power to provide for the peace and defense in a civil society, created?[44] Hobbes said the commonwealth or what also could be referred to as the *state* is created when all the members of the community agree to place authority for governing the community in either one man or one assembly of men. In doing so, all agree to submit themselves to the will of a single authority. The act of consent that makes possible a state with great powers to secure peace and to protect the society from external enemies signifies for Hobbes a basis for societal unity, predicated upon each person's entering into an agreement with all others to permit only one governmental authority in society. In doing so, Hobbes indicated that it were as though each individual had said to all others the following: *"I Authorise and give my Right of Governing my selfe, to this Man, or to this Assembly of men, on this condition, that thou give thy Right to him, and Authorise all his Actions in like manner."*[45] The state or commonwealth, also called the sovereign, is vested with sovereign power over the citizens who are called the *subjects*. I will use the words *state* and *sovereign* interchangeably.[46]

Does this act of consent give the state or the sovereign unlimited authority over citizens? Hobbes would certainly claim not. Indeed, Hobbes seemed to suggest that the state's objectives are defined in a manner to limit the state's authority. What are the state's objectives? Given Hobbes's views of natural law, the state would have to follow a path that promoted justice and equity, and in doing so the state would make as its priority the protection of citizens' rights. Thus, the act of consent to create a sovereign authority, if it means anything, clearly would mean that the citizens in consenting to the state's authority do so only on the condition that the state protects their rights.[47] To this end, the state, as it arbitrated conflicts between citizens, or as it sought to maintain and uphold agreements between citizens, would have to stand above politics and attempt to render fair and impartial, publicly binding decisions. In all cases, the state would have to uphold the law with equal force for all. To achieve these objectives, the state could not allow its actions to be extensions of one private interest over another, for then public power would be used to promote specific private interests, and, in this case, the rights of all could not be protected.

But the actual state Hobbes described appears to compromise the state's main objective of protecting basic rights. For Hobbes, the state is defined as an authority with sovereign power over citizens, and that authority is vested either in a single monarch or an assembly of citizen representatives. Here, once citizens give their consent to be subject to a monarch (or to an assembly), citizens cannot, without the permission of the monarch (or the assembly), return the power to themselves for the purpose of transferring it to another.[48] Nor is there a right to revolution. Hobbes said that "protestation against any of their Decrees [of the state], he does contrary to his Covenant, and therefore unjustly."[49] In this regard, a citizen who is killed by the sovereign for trying to depose the sovereign is really the "author of his own punishment."[50] For after all, in agreeing to be governed by the sovereign, each person agrees to abide by his authority.

But how far are we obligated to the sovereign by our agreement to be governed by him? For Hobbes, we are given extreme obligations that limit our conduct quite severely. Indeed, subjects cannot even accuse the sovereign of wrongdoing. For once the state has been created, the state acts with the full authority of those who have authorized it, that is, the people. And if the state, now that all the members of society have authorized it, does wrong, the people need blame only themselves, not the state.[51] Further, the sovereign has a right to determine which doctrines and opinions citizens will be permitted to hold, and no doctrine that is a threat to the general peace of the society can be allowed.[52]

This account suggests that the state's powers are likely to be so great that the state could act with unlimited authority and in doing so threaten the rights of citizens. Further, there are no institutional constraints that would prevent the state from taking this path. For instance, Hobbes argued that all law making, all judicial powers, and all executive powers pertaining to making war and peace are to reside in a single sovereign authority.[53] These powers, as we have seen, may be located in a single person such as a monarch, or in an assembly of citizens.[54] In either case, Hobbes argued for a unitary form of government, in which the governing power is either an assembly or a monarch, but not both. This view suggests that it would be wrong for the two governing types to share power, and based on this view it is unlikely that Hobbes would have supported a separation of powers concept of government that is typical in our times. The only result of separated government is divided government, and what divided government eventuates is a return to the state of war.

> *For that were to erect two Soveraigns; and every man to have his person repre-sented by two Actors, that by opposing one another, must needs divide that Power, which (if men will live in Peace) is indivisible; and thereby reduce the Multitude into the condition of Warre, contrary to the end for which all Soveraignty is instituted.*[55]

In all cases, the government is considered a representative of the people. When the representative is one man, the government is a monarchy; when it is an assembly of all, then the government is a democracy; and when the assembly is only a part of the people, then the government is called an aristocracy.[56] Hobbes favored monarchy for several reasons. First, he argued that the monarch is more likely to understand, to articulate, and to work to realize the public interest. The monarch has no interest in harming the citizens because his authority rests with their success and prosperity.[57] Second, the monarch has only to listen to those who are experts and who as a result are most likely to make significant contributions in solving public problems. The assembly, on the other hand, is filled with those whose main concern is their own wealth rather than actions based on knowledge of the public interest.[58] These comparisons suggest that the monarch, unlike the assembly, does not have to try to please this group or that group; all he has to do is to make the best decision possible, using the best information available. As a result, the monarch can maintain consistency of policy directions over time.[59]

The assembly, on the other hand, must try to please many different interests, each of whom has a different conception of the public good. And because it cannot always succeed in doing so, the assembly opens itself and society up to the prospect of civil war.[60] Hobbes dismissed the main problem he identified with monarchy, namely, that at times flatterers may inveigle their way into the king's counsel. But for Hobbes this was a mere inconvenience that is experienced in all governments,[61] and, when this problem is weighed against the advantages of the monarchy, it is clear to Hobbes that the monarchy remains the best form of government.

To those who fear the state's power, Hobbes would argue that the sovereign cannot command a man to kill or maim himself. Further, if the sovereign interrogates a person, the latter is under no obligation to incriminate himself.[62] Still, one might today ask, once the state has been allowed as much power as Hobbes grants it, what real basis exists to protect citizens from the state's own abuse of its power? But this was not a question that Hobbes was interested in addressing. But we, of course, are. It would seem in this regard that a benefit of the separation of powers concept is that it suggests various points of access for citizens. The latter may use their access to help define the political agenda or to help influence government decisions about particular issues on that agenda. Hobbes, in denying a place to the separation of powers approach, took a step in the direction of creating a state that would deny citizens a chance to challenge its policies. How ironical a position for citizens to be in, given that the state itself emanates from their consent!

Important implications for the concept of a civil society arise from Hobbes's view of the state's role. As we saw, his civil society protects freedom by maintaining regard for civic virtues such as justice, gratitude, and the provision of rights for all. The state will have a central role in promoting these virtues. The state's necessary role arises from the fact that Hobbes did not trust people to uphold a commitment to civic virtue on their own, and he believed that individuals would only do so when the state compelled people to uphold common civic standards through fear.

But, given this view, could there be a separate sphere of voluntary groups that exists to provide a buffer against the prospect of governmental encroachment upon individuals? There is no question that values such as gratitude, justice, and respect for rights could make possible a separate sphere. Why is this the case? These values would contribute to a society in which individuals manifested toward others mutual respect, or the commitment to find ways to make room for each other, no matter how different each person might be. And one such important way to attain this objective would be to make possible a separate sphere that protected individual freedom against government encroachment. Still, even if for Hobbes a separate sphere is feasible, it would exist in tension with a state whose powers could become so vast that individuals would not be able to challenge its decisions. Certainly, this tension would not necessarily deny the possibility of a separate sphere, but it would make such a sphere difficult to achieve. Hobbes's treatment of religion demonstrates this problem of his view of civil society very well.

VI. THE CHRISTIAN COMMONWEALTH

The establishment of an English Christian church, in the aftermath of the secession from Rome, mandated that the king should be the head of the church. The church and state should not be two distinct realms, but they should form one common union.[63] Those who supported this view believed that religious life should be promoted, not as Aquinas had argued by an all-embracing Catholic Church, but by a national government in charge of a national church. In this case, the king and, where the king permitted parliamentary participation in these matters, the parliament would be in a position to determine religious doctrines and beliefs.[64]

Some groups met this perspective with opposition, of course. The Anglican or English Christian church faced demands from religious groups—Catholics, Calvinists (also called Presbyterians), and Independents—each of whom wanted autonomy from state interference for their own churches. The Catholics advocated spiritual autonomy from the state so that they could acknowledge papal jurisdiction in religious matters.[65] The Calvinists did not accept a secular head of their church, either. The Calvinists advocated a separation between the church and the state, but not in the present-day sense that makes the state a secular institution that must avoid promoting a particular religion. Instead, the Calvinists believed that they should be free from state interference to determine the doctrines for a moral and religious life, and they expected the state to make these doctrines mandatory.[66]

The Independents argued for noninterference in religious affairs by the state and by the national church so that they could establish their own religious communities. As Sabine says, the Independents wanted to ordain their own clergy and establish themselves as a "voluntary association of like-minded believers," and they did not want the civil authority to promote, as the Presbyterians had wanted, religious doctrines to people of a different religious persuasion. The Independents adopted a doctrine of religious toleration that would have to apply to both themselves and to others who did not believe as they did, although in practice the Independents were more likely to support toleration for themselves than for others.[67]

Hobbes argued that there should be one national church and that the civil sovereign, which as indicated above can mean either the king or an assembly, should have authority over the religious life of society. Indeed, the church should be subordinate to the power and the authority of the civil sovereign. The latter can make laws that pertain to both the realm of government and the realm of religion. Thus, the civil sovereign can determine the kind of church organization and arrangement that will be put in charge of the religious life of society, and whatever organization is chosen for leading the religious life of society must realize that the civil sovereign has supreme authority over its affairs. For instance, the civil sovereign may commit the state to Catholicism, but, if it does so, the pope must still be subordinate to the civil sovereign. Or, when the civil sovereign establishes a central church under a "supreme pastor or assembly of pastors," the civil sovereign maintains overall control of the church. The civil sovereign maintains control by designating interpreters of the scripture, defining the offices and powers of church officials, and determining how people will be taxed to support the church.[68] The civil sovereign may even define religious doctrine, with the intent especially of providing doctrines that help secure peace in society. And further, the civil sovereign may appoint the pastors.[69]

Justification for this view derives from the "Laws of God." For Hobbes, the latter are nothing more than the laws of nature. And one of the key laws of nature that the "Laws of God" sanction is that individuals must not violate a "commandment to obey the civil sovereign" that citizens through their own consent have created. This suggests that the "Laws of God" have permitted the civil sovereign to be the primary authority not only for civil law but for religious doctrines and for the management of the church. And thus, by the "Laws of God," citizens are to obey the precepts of the Bible in those places where the civil sovereign mandates such conduct.[70]

Given this view, it is clear that only the civil sovereign can define the basis for excommunication and for salvation. What doctrines would Hobbes's civil sovereign have established in these regards? First, Hobbes refused to accept that a believing Christian who obeys the laws of his commonwealth can in any way be harmed by being made subject to excommunication. To paraphrase Hobbes, the person who believes in Christ is free from all the dangers threatened to persons by excommunication.[71] This suggests that the civil authority has the right to minimize any church's effort to excommunicate a person who is a Christian believer. And to receive salvation, all one need do is to maintain two very important civic virtues: namely, faith in Christ and the need to uphold the civil law during one's daily conduct in society. Upholding the civil law would have been basis enough for salvation were it not for the fact of original sin and of the likelihood that, owing to a lack of perfection, we will at times transgress the law. Given human frailty and given the hope for eternal salvation, we do best for ourselves, then, when we seek "remission" for our sins, and this we can attain when we maintain faith in Christ.[72]

Hobbes, in arguing for the supremacy of the civil state over religious matters, does not deny the importance of religious life but suggests that, in his newly constructed civil society, religion must be made subject to civil control. In this setting, all Christian believers were to share a common commitment to maintaining the civil law and the natural law principles of a civil society, principles that secure respect for individual freedom. When placed in its proper relationship to the state, the religious life can help sustain the new civil society and the individual freedom it promises.

But at the same time, because Hobbes's civil authority will determine the content of religious life, his state would always live in tension with any religious organizations seeking independence from state control. Owing to this kind of state/society relationship, creating a separate sphere for groups to exist independently of the state so that they could act from their own self-determined doctrines would be discouraged at some points and perhaps disallowed at other points. And thus, Hobbes would not be a strong supporter of a civil society that contained a separate sphere of groups that would act as buffers and restraints on the state's power.

VII. RESPONSE AND REJOINDER

In suggesting that a separate sphere would have difficulty being constituted in Hobbes's civil society, it should be understood that Hobbes was not diminishing the importance of individual freedom. Indeed, Hobbes would certainly contend that one of the objectives of his thought was to protect individual freedom with the kind of state he advocated. Hobbes would claim that his system would provide individuals all the private freedom they would want and need. Here, individuals are given the ability to make their own choices about the life they want to lead. The laws are designed to remove impediments to freedom and not, themselves, to be impediments to freedom. It is for this reason, for instance, that individuals can act as they want when the laws are silent.[73] And because the laws are designed to maximize personal freedom, the laws will not dictate to people how they should live their lives in many areas of life. This approach is absolutely necessary if diverse people with different values are to be able to pursue those values in peace.

But problems with Hobbes's view remain. Some might claim that a terrible trade-off is taking place in which individuals gain freedom only if they permit a state with absolute power. Hobbes might respond by saying that, after all, government, in particular his form of government, is based upon the consent of the governed to be ruled by a particular regime. In this case, the state operates within some important limits, since the state can do only that which the citizens prescribe for it to do. Now, it is true that Hobbes does have a doctrine of citizen consent to government. But once the act of consent to be ruled by a government whose main objective is to protect private freedom and rights has occurred, it appears that people are forced to forfeit a right to challenge state policies that the citizens do not agree with. In this case, how are citizens going to protect those rights that the state is empowered to secure but which it may decide not to safeguard in the name of shoring up its own authority?

The question, then, is whether Hobbes can maintain security for the freedom he promised when the state is as powerful as Hobbes made it. Hobbes's answer might be that all he is attempting to do is to provide a fair and objective state that can enforce the law for all and prevent the reemergence of a state of war. If he is successful, equality of rights and liberty would be provided to all. Hobbes would claim that the modern state, as it is presently constituted, is often perceived as failing to be a fair and impartial force in society, working to protect the rights of each individual. Hobbes might argue, then, that very often the modern government, built upon the separation of powers model and the provision of access to all interests, falls into paralysis, unable to achieve even basic objectives for its citizens. In the modern state, government invites many private interests, each with its own view of the good, to enter government and to lobby for their own objectives. With so many different interests pushing for their own respective ends, the state is unable to achieve general, broad policies that are in the interest of all. Of central concern in this regard is that the state is unable to realize even those policies that protect the individual, private freedom of each person.

What would fuel this tendency for Hobbes is an attitude on the part of ordinary citizens to think that he or she can be the sole determiner of what is right and just.

> *From this false doctrine, men are disposed to debate with themselves, and dispute the commands of the Commonwealth; and afterwards to obey, or disobey them, as in their private judgments they shall think fit.*[74]

Hobbes argued that, whereas this doctrine might be acceptable in the state of nature, it is not acceptable in a civil society. Indeed, Hobbes considers this view to be a poisonous doctrine that weakens civil society.[75] How is the commonwealth weakened by this kind of activity? In the first place, the only measure of right and wrong should be the laws sanctioned by the commonwealth. But where people think they can determine good from bad themselves, they are encouraged to debate with each other the decisions of the state and to decide whether they want to obey them. Hobbes would no doubt contend that when people enter debates of this sort, they seek to promote their own interests with the intention of getting the state to support them. But in this case, the state would no longer be the fair, neutral arbitrator among interests that Hobbes hoped for. When the sovereign is a strong, independent, and powerful voice for equity and fairness, however, private interests cannot capture public power and use it for their own designs.

But is Hobbes right? Would individuals be so willing to allow an unlimited form of power to the state in order to have the personal freedom and the protections from the intrusions from others that Hobbes offers? We turn now to John Locke, who provides an answer to Hobbes's claims about civil society and the role of the state. Locke's answer challenges Hobbes's views in significant ways.

Endnotes

1. George H. Sabine, *A History of Political Theory,* (New York: Holt, Rinehart and Winston, 1961), pp. 455–56.

2. Thomas Hobbes, *Leviathan,* edited by C. B. Macpherson, (New York: Penguin Books, 1981), p. 105, I:4. For ease in finding sources, I include the roman numeral that signifies the part and the next number, the chapter.

3. C. B. Macpherson, "Introduction," in Thomas Hobbes, *Leviathan,* pp. 25–30.

4. Hobbes, *Leviathan,* pp. 160–61, I:11.

5. Ibid., p. 161, I:11.

6. Ibid., p. 161, I:11; p. 150, I:10.

7. Ibid., p. 161, I:11.

8. Ibid., p. 161, I:11.

9. Ibid., p. 185, I:13.

10. Ibid., p. 186, I:13.

11. Ibid., pp. 151–52, I:10.

12. Ibid., p. 183, I:13.

13. Ibid., p. 183, I:13.

14. Ibid., p. 184, I:13.

15. Ibid., p. 184, I:13.

16. Ibid., p. 184, I:13.

17. Ibid., p. 188, I:13.

18. Ibid., p. 186, I:13.

19. Ibid., p. 188, I:13.

20. Ibid., p. 189, I:14.

21. Ibid., p. 190, I:14.

22. Ibid., p. 190, I:14.

23. Ibid., p. 190, I:14; also see p. 214, I:15. Hobbes states that the laws of nature that dictate peace are the basis of a "Civil States Society."

24. Ibid., p. 190, I:14. Italics are Hobbes's.

25. Ibid., p. 192, I:14.

26. Ibid., p. 192, I:14.

27. Ibid., p. 193, I:14.

28. Ibid., p. 193, I:14.

29. Ibid., p. 196, I:14.

30. Ibid., p. 201, I:15.

31. Ibid., pp. 201–2, I:15.

32. Ibid., p. 209, I:15.

33. Ibid., p. 209, I:15.

34. Ibid., p. 209, I:15. Italics are Hobbes's.

35. Ibid., p. 210, I:15.

36. Ibid., p. 211, I:15.

37. Ibid., p. 211, I:15.

38. Ibid., p. 212, I:15.

39. Ibid., p. 212, I:15.

40. Ibid., pp. 212–13, I:15.

41. Ibid., p. 213, I:15.

42. Ibid., p. 223, II:17.

43. Ibid., p. 223, II:17.

44. Ibid., pp. 227–28, II:17.

45. Ibid., p. 227, II:17.

46. Ibid., p. 228, II:17.

47. On this point, see Frank M. Coleman, *Hobbes and America: Exploring the Constitutional Foundation,* (Toronto: University of Toronto Press, 1977), p. 91.

48. Hobbes, *Leviathan,* pp. 228–29, II:18.

49. Ibid., pp. 231–32, II:18.

50. Ibid., p. 229, II:18.

51. Ibid., p. 232, II:18.

52. Ibid., p. 233, II:18.

53. Ibid., pp. 234–35, II:18.

54. Ibid., p. 237, II:18.

55. Ibid., p. 240, II:19.

56. Ibid., p. 239, II:19.

57. Ibid., pp. 241–42, II:19.

58. Ibid., p. 242, II:19.

59. Ibid., p. 242, II:19.

60. Ibid., p. 243, II:19.

61. Ibid., p. 243, II:19.

62. Ibid., p. 269, II:21.

63. Sabine, *A History of Political Theory,* pp. 438, 441–42.

64. Ibid., pp. 441–43.

65. Ibid., p. 443.

66. Ibid., pp. 443–44.

67. Ibid., pp. 445–46.

68. Hobbes, *The Leviathan,* pp. 575–76, III:42.

69. Ibid., pp. 567–68, III:42.

70. Ibid., p. 612, III:43.

71. Ibid., p. 540, III:42.

72. Ibid., pp. 610–11, III:43.

73. Ibid., p. 271, II:21.

74. Ibid., p. 365, II:29.

75. Ibid., p. 365, II:29.

Partial Bibliography and Further Reading

Baumgold, Deborah. *Hobbes's Political Theory.* Cambridge: Cambridge University Press, 1988.

Coleman, Frank M. *Hobbes and America: Exploring the Constitutional Foundation.* Toronto: University of Toronto Press, 1977.

Condren, Conal. *Thomas Hobbes.* New York: Twayne Publishers, 2000.

Flathman, Richard E. *Thomas Hobbes: Skepticism, Individuality, and Chastened Politics.* Newbury Park, Calif.: Sage, 1993.

Kavka, Gregory S. *Hobbesian Moral and Political Theory.* Princeton: Princeton University Press, 1986.

MacPherson, C. B. "Introduction," *Leviathan,* edited by C. B. MacPherson. London: Penguin Books, 1981.

———. *The Political Theory of Possessive Individualism: Hobbes to Locke.* Oxford: Clarendon Press, 1962.

Mitchell, Joshua. *Not by Reason Alone: Religion, History, and Identity in Early Modern Political Thought.* Chicago: University of Chicago Press, 1993.

Shelton, George. *Morality and Sovereignty in the Philosophy of Hobbes.* New York: St. Martin's Press, 1992.

Skinner, Quentin. *Reason and Rhetoric in the Philosophy of Hobbes.* Cambridge; New York: Cambridge University Press, 1996.

Spragens, Thomas A. *The Politics of Motion: The World of Thomas Hobbes.* Lexington: University Press of Kentucky, 1973.

Strauss, Leo. *The Political Philosophy of Hobbes: Its Basis and Its Genesis.* Chicago: University of Chicago Press, 1966.

Warrender, Howard. *The Political Philosophy of Hobbes, His Theory of Obligation.* Oxford: Clarendon Press, 1957.

Wolin, Sheldon S. *Hobbes and the Epic Tradition of Political Theory.* Berkeley: University of California Press, 1970.

8

JOHN LOCKE, CIVIL SOCIETY, AND THE CONSTRAINED MAJORITY

I. INTRODUCTION

John Locke's (1632–1704) *The Second Treatise of Government,* published in 1690, can be construed, as Thomas Peardon claims, as an argument against Hobbes's call for an absolute monarchy based upon citizen consent. Locke supported the "Glorious Revolution" of 1688, which symbolized that the King of England should exercise his powers in keeping with the dictates of the parliament. Indeed, Locke's own political thought accepted the view that follows from the experience of this revolution; namely, that the parliament is the main source of authority in government. However, as we will demonstrate, Locke did provide a role for an executive branch, but in a setting in which the power of both the legislative and the executive branches are limited by virtue of the precise functions each is given.[1] Locke thus rejected Hobbes's view that would place absolute power in either the legislative or executive branches of government. Furthermore, Locke's concept of government in a civil society was undergirded by the view, as Richard Ashcraft argues, that productive labor, the development of land, and commercial activities all benefited society. In taking this position, Locke favored the new bourgeoisie or middle class. This class consisted of small farmers, who owned their own land, merchants, tradesmen, and artisans. Locke saw this group as the most productive members of society, and Locke thought that their interests should supersede the interests of the traditional, and for Locke, unproductive landed aristocracy.[2]

Before proceeding, it is well to point out that Locke no less than Hobbes held the view that in a civil society individuals have rights contingent upon acceptance of necessary constraints or what we have referred to as civic virtues. How did Locke approach the definition of such constraints? For Locke, as Charles Taylor says, we are to follow "the law laid down by God, which he [Locke] also calls at times the Natural Law."[3] Moreover, this law, which suggests a rational order to our existence and which therefore can be known by rational individuals, represents God's intention to secure to each of us certain basic, natural rights. With these rights, we are able, as individuals, to determine our own intentions and courses of conduct. But it must always be clear that the presence of basic rights, supported by natural law, places limits on what we can choose and how we can act.[4] Indeed, in discussing the state of nature, as we will see in Section IV, Locke outlines the constraints on freedom, or those rules that individuals must observe during the course of pursuing their own self-defined interests. These constraints secure the rights of all citizens. In upholding these constraints, individuals can be said to be maintaining regard for the civic virtues that protect the rights and the basic liberty of each person.

In the remainder of this chapter, my intention is to discuss Locke's view of civil society by pointing out the basic natural law constraints that help to govern and to shape it. Locke's central concern is to contest Hobbes by arguing that the state in a civil society must have limited powers so that it does not threaten the very basic rights the state is supposed to protect for each member of the society. In seeking a state with limited powers, Locke sought to locate the state's power in what can be called a *constrained majority.* Locke's conception of the *social contract,* or basic agreement upon which to predicate the authority of government, highlights the rule of the majority. But the majority's will must always be grounded in the natural law principles, or notions of civic virtue, that require that the majority never acts to undermine the natural rights provided to all citizens.

II. THE CONCEPT OF POLITICAL AUTHORITY

Political authority is unlike any other kind of authority. For Locke, political authority is not the same as the authority that husbands hold in the family, the master holds over the servant, or the lord holds over the slave.[5] The scope of political power is far wider and its coercive abilities to ensure compliance far more extensive. Political authority enables the state to make laws that bind the whole of society. Governments even can punish those who violate the law with death. And most important, governments may use their power only for the public good.[6] Thus, political power is the "right of making laws with penalties of death and, consequently, all less penalties for regulating and preserving of property, and of employing the force of the community in the execution of such laws and in the defense of the commonwealth from foreign injury; and all this only for the public good."[7]

The use of power to promote the public good is the most distinguishing feature of political authority. But what is the public good? Or in others terms, what is the just basis for political authority?

Before answering this question, we need to describe the definition of the public good that Locke rejected. For Locke, the public good has not one thing to do with maintaining monarchical absolutism. Advocates of absolute monarchy argue that the monarch does in fact promote the public good. On behalf of this claim, proponents of monarchy point out that monarchies provide a legal system as well as opportunities to appeal to judges to decide cases of controversy. Locke would grant that these uses of authority are good. But Locke argued that it is never in the interest of the public for a government to claim absolute power to achieve even good purposes such as these. Indeed, sensible people would never support permitting a ruler to have unlimited amounts of power, while everyone else is made subject to the rule of law. Locke said that the supporters of monarchy "think that men are so foolish that they take care to avoid what mischiefs may be done them by pole-cats or foxes, but are content, nay, think it safety, to be devoured by lions."[8] Rulers must be made subject to limits, too. And this means that there must be good reasons to justify their authority. But what are these good reasons? That answer is provided in Locke's conception of the state of nature. In discussing Locke's state of nature, we will discuss his view of the common good that is the basis for defining the legitimate grounds of political authority.

III. The State of Nature I: Justification for Political Authority

The rational grounds for political authority are located in the original intentions and understandings of people in the state of nature. The latter is a hypothetical situation that describes for Locke the natural condition of humankind prior to the entrance of individuals into formal society. Locke thought that people in the state of nature were in large part rational individuals who were able to determine the reasonable constraints that should govern each person's conduct. Locke thus described in his discussion of the state of nature a perspective that can help us understand the true purpose and basis for political authority.

For Locke, the state of nature is a state of "perfect freedom" in which individuals are entitled "to order their actions and dispose of their possessions and persons as they think fit, within the bounds of the laws of nature, without asking leave or depending upon the will of any other man."[9] In this context, people treat each other as equals because "power and jurisdiction is reciprocal, no one having more than other."[10] Further, Locke's state of nature is not a "state of license"[11] as in Hobbes's version of the state of nature as a state war, and so Locke's state of nature is not governed by Hobbes's view of people seeking to dominate and to control the lives of others. Instead, the state of nature is a place in which each knows that one is not permitted to "destroy himself, or so much as any creature in his possession."[12]

On this view, then, the state of nature is a place where people treat each other in a civil way, in keeping with norms all regard as reasonable. Locke said,

> *The state of nature has a law of nature to govern it, which obligates every one; and reason, which is that law, teaches all mankind who will but consult it that, being all equal and independent, no one ought to harm another in his life, health, liberty, or possessions; for men being all the workmanship of one omnipotent and infinitely wise Maker—all the servants of one sovereign master, sent into the world by his order, and about his business—they are his property whose workmanship they are, made to last during, his, not one another's pleasure; and being furnished with like faculties, sharing all in one community of nature, there cannot be supposed any such subordination among us that may authorize us to destroy another, as if we were made for one another's uses as the inferior ranks of creatures are for ours. Everyone, as he is bound to preserve himself and not quit*

his station wilfully, so by the like reason, when his own preservation comes not in competition, ought he, as much as he can, to preserve the rest of mankind, and may not . . . take way or impair the life, or what tends to be the preservation of life, the liberty, health, limb, or goods of another.[13]

It is well to concentrate for a brief time on this important paragraph. Several critical dimensions are revealed concerning the justification for political authority. First, Locke argued that from the rational perspective of men in the state of nature, there is a clear understanding of a law of nature, taught by reason and sanctioned by God, which all are obligated to uphold. And the principal teaching of the law of nature is that no one is to harm another. In particular, we are to act positively to protect and to preserve the lives of others by maintaining, when one's own preservation is not at issue, the "life, the liberty, health, limb, or goods of another." This idea suggests that it is reasonable to assume that individuals have *natural* rights, or rights provided to all individuals by virtue of being human beings, and no one may take them from another.

Support for this position ultimately derives from the fact that God, the "Maker" of all people, sanctions natural rights. For Locke, God created individuals as equals and furnished all people with "like faculties." By "faculties," I take Locke to mean the capacities for reason, understanding, and freedom. Had God intended that some should have more rights than others, he would have created individuals with "unlike faculties" and made them unequal to each other. But this was not God's intention.

It is now possible to answer the question asked at the conclusion of the last section, namely, what are the proper or rational grounds of political authority? The main lesson of the state of nature is that no one is to be under the arbitrary will of another, for, otherwise, individuals would lose their freedom and their rights. Political authority is legitimate when it encompasses this lesson, and it does so when individuals are under a form of authority that has been established by their own consent. And the only government that citizens will consent to is one whose laws are made by a legislative power that protects people's freedom and rights or a regime that allows "a liberty to follow my own will in all things where the rule prescribes not."[14] Here, no person is to "be subject to the inconstant, uncertain, unknown, arbitrary will of another man." A political regime that embodies these values permits individuals to live as if they were in the state of nature, governed by "no other restraint but the law of nature."[15]

IV. STATE OF NATURE II: CONSTRAINTS FOR FREEDOM

Regarding Locke's view of political authority, it is important to understand the various constraints that individuals must accept if they are to maintain the basic rights that secure the freedom of each person. Locke, in arguing for individual liberty, realized that essential to securing liberty in his natural law framework is the need for citizens to accept the presence in their lives of certain moral restraints or what we have otherwise referred to as civic virtues. Thus, further discussion of the state of nature is needed in order to help outline these constraints. Moreover, in doing so, we demonstrate at the conclusion of this section the problems that Locke's conception of life in the state of nature faces, when as it appears he embraced, as part of the state of nature, certain assumptions of market life.

To discuss this subject, it must first be clear that possessing freedom is contingent upon being able to own property. Thus, any discussion of the constraints on freedom arises from Locke's conception of property in the state of nature and the constraints that are associated with owning property. So it is first necessary to explain the basic dimensions of Locke's concept of property, and then move from there to a discussion of the constraints he associated with both holding property and having freedom.

Locke argued that God, and here he quoted King David in Psalm 115, "has given the earth to the children of men."[16] But if God has given the earth to men in common, how is private property ever justified? Locke's answer was that "though the earth and all inferior creatures be common to all men, yet every man has a property in his own person; this nobody has a right to but himself. The labor of his body and the work of his hands, we may say are properly his."[17] Here, what I am able to acquire through my own work is mine, subject to the limitation that enough is left for others as well, or as Locke said, "where there is enough and as good left in common for others."[18]

There seems to follow from the preceding argument two major justifications for property rights. The first justification for property rights is fairness. Fairness suggests that people have a right to what they produce through their own labor. People who do not work, and who expect to receive the benefit of others' work, are violating the freedom of others. Thus, Locke argued that God gave the world to those who are "industrious and rational," or individuals who through labor and work contribute something of use to the society.[19]

Second, Locke, in saying that each of us has property in our own person and that nobody has a right to this property but oneself, attaches to the idea of private property a right to make choices about the direction and purposes of one's life. Locke's conception of private property suggests that the property in the person, one's personality, one's choices and decisions about the course one determines for life, are not subject to the arbitrary power of others. "This freedom from absolute, arbitrary power is so necessary to, and closely joined with, a man's preservation that he cannot part with it but by what forfeits his preservation and life together."[20] Certainly there will be some who cannot or will not act in ways respectful of the rights of others, and these individuals use "force without right," and in doing so fail to observe the natural right to life, liberty, and property of all people. Such individuals enter into a Hobbesian state of war with others. But unlike Hobbes, Locke refused to characterize the state of nature as a state of war, since the state of nature is a condition in which people act "according to reason" and thus the constraints that protect the freedom of each person are respected.[21] Thus, those who violate the freedom of others in the state of nature represent aberrations from the general tendency to act in ways that are respectful of others' freedom.

What prevents private property from becoming a source of social instability and discord? For, clearly, some will, as a result of their efforts, end up with more property than others. When this occurs, will not private property itself be seen as a threat to freedom? Locke argued that there are common, rational constraints that legitimize differences in wealth across the society. First of all, Locke said that even though God gave the world to all people to enjoy and to achieve satisfaction and pleasure with, God did not want individuals to take any portion of the earth that people could not "make use of to any advantage of life before it spoils."[22] Here, whereas we have every right to utilize the external world in ways that bring us happiness, we do not have a right to take more than we can make good use of. For in that case, much of what we accumulate would spoil, and then we would render large portions of the world of no use to anyone. Locke made reference to the following example. If in enclosing land and calling it our own we can use the grass on that land to feed the cattle we own, we can keep the land. But, if the grass on the land rots, then we have violated a basic natural law constraint of the state of nature and that land can become "the possession of any other."[23]

But even in taking only enough so that one does not cause precious materials or resources to spoil, certain individuals may still become wealthier than others. Locke's response to this likelihood is to justify the types of wealth accumulation that are highly beneficial to society. This means that there are certain categories of individuals who in accumulating wealth are not causing important resources to spoil, but in fact they are adding to the stock of resources that others enjoy. What aids this prospect is commercial trade and finance, which permit owners of land and materials to organize the laboring efforts of people to create products that others need, and through this effort to expand the material wealth of society. This activity is symbolized by money.

Locke said that with the invention of money, it is possible for individuals to exchange perishable goods for durable and nonperishable metals, such as gold. And if an individual were able to exchange consumable items such as "nuts" or "wool" for durable goods that do not spoil, such as diamonds, then there is no limit to the amount of wealth that one could in fact accumulate.[24] Here, a person can exchange his wool for diamonds, and "he might heap as much of these durable things as he pleased."[25] The possession of durable goods such as diamonds or gold symbolizes activity that is useful to the entire society. Locke had in mind the development of productive labor that increases the total wealth of society. It is for this reason then that, for Locke, individuals accept, by a form of "tacit and voluntary consent," the fact of the "disproportionate and unequal possession of the earth."[26] This view suggests that in the state of nature people who succeed will have more wealth than others, and this fact provides an incentive for people to work hard to provide the goods that all need.[27]

Based on these constraints, it would seem that from the standpoint of natural law in the state of nature, individuals are given freedom on the condition that they do not use it in ways that harm the freedom of others. On this view, then, Locke can be interpreted as making the claim that the standard of a civil society is fairness. However, other writers, in particular C. B. Macpherson, have argued that Locke's treatment of property in the state of nature places his commitment to fairness in doubt.[28] As part of the evidence in support of this claim, Macpherson points to the place in *The Second Treatise of Government* where Locke contradicts his own principle that the fruits of each person's labor belong to the person performing that labor. Locke indicated that an owner of property who employs servants or workers has a right to the wealth produced by these servants or workers. "Thus the grass my horse has bit, the turfs my servant has cut . . . become my property without the assignment of consent to anybody. The labor that was mine, removing them, out of that common state they were in, has fixed my property in them."[29]

For C. B. Macpherson this statement indicates that Locke had incorporated into his view of property in the state of nature a market setting in which a few would end up controlling both land and labor for the purpose of obtaining ever-larger amounts of land and labor. The land and labor so acquired would be used in both the agricultural and manufacturing sectors of the economy to produce goods that could be sold for a profit by the owner class. As a result, for Macpherson, Locke accepted as natural and rational the idea that owners could control as well as own the labor of others. The effect of accepting this view is that, over time, large numbers of workers would end up transferring authority over their lives to those who claimed a right to own their labor. In this situation, the owners could pay the workers only the necessary amount to maintain the workers' self-sufficiency, and the rest of what the workers produced could be transferred to the owner for his, the owner's, own use. Not only would this situation create great social divisions in society between the workers and owners, but it would also lead to a politics of class rule in which the owner class dominated the workers, denying to them their liberty.[30]

V. THE NATURE OF CIVIL SOCIETY AND CONSTRAINED MAJORITY RULE

Putting aside for the moment Macpherson's arguments, if we take the standards of Locke's view of the state of nature as he enumerated them and make them the basis for a civil society, as Locke did, then a civil society would be a setting in which individuals have rights, conditioned upon the need to uphold the various constraints Locke outlined. Given this view of civil society, then, the purpose of government in a civil society is clear. Locke argued that people unite into a commonwealth and form a government to protect their property, which signifies citizens' basic rights and freedom.[31] Moreover, to support this objective, the state or government in a civil society, as we demonstrate in the next section, is one with limited powers.

This view of the role and powers of government suggests that Locke believed that the level of conflict in society would not be severe. Were it the case that the disputes were extreme, then, the state would have to become as powerful and as absolute as Hobbes suggested the state must be in order to protect the rights of all citizens and not just the most powerful ones. In point of fact, as we indicate at the conclusion of this section, it is likely that the conflicts will be intense and deep in Locke's state of nature. Locke actually accepted this fact himself when he described in a "second" view of the state of nature a picture at variance with the view just discussed. Unlike the "first" view that indicated, owing to the rational character of people, a commitment to fairness, the "second" view suggests something more like a Hobbesian state of war. Perhaps, the reason for this deviation from the first view is that Locke himself accepted, without saying so, some of the implications of market life that Macpherson ascribed to Locke. Before moving to a discussion of this point, however, I first want to describe Locke's conception of the state in a civil society as well as his understanding of the state's origins in consent.

Again, the purpose of a state in a civil society is clear: "the great and chief end . . . of men's uniting into commonwealths and putting themselves under government is the preservation of their property."[32] The state protects everyone's property by providing a system of "settled" and "known law" that becomes the basis for resolving "all controversies between [people]." Further, the state must act as an "indifferent judge" in deciding controversies. Finally, the state has the power to back up its decisions and to ensure their "due execution."[33]

How does the state in a civil society arise? Or in other terms what is the nature of the *social contract* or agreement people strike with each other and make the basis for the state's authority? Locke argued the state arises from the unanimous consent of the people to be ruled by the majority. In this regard, then, Locke said that the political society, or the government of a civil society, is created "when any number of men have, *by the consent of every individual,* made a community, they have thereby made that community one body, with a power to act as one body, which is only by the will and determination of the majority."[34]

Further, there is a major proviso that needs to made clear here, and this proviso indicates that the rule of the majority is really the rule of a *constrained majority,* or a majority that must respect the rights of all. Although people, in entering civil society, leave behind the state of nature, and thus give up complete and full autonomy over themselves, they do not authorize the state that they constitute in a civil society to violate or to threaten their liberty. Locke said that "the power of the society, or legislative constituted by them [the people], can never be supposed to extend farther than the common good, but is obliged to secure every one's property."[35] Consequently, the majority and those who speak for it, in this case either the executive or legislative arms of government, cannot violate the terms of the original agreement people make when they enter civil society, namely, the requirement to protect "the peace, safety, and public good of the people."[36]

Any majority opinion formed in response to a public issue must make policies that are respectful of the need to treat citizens as equals, that is, as individuals entitled to the basic protections that secure their liberty. Thus, for instance, in discussing taxation, Locke made clear that the legislative branch of society cannot tax people without their consent, that is, without the consent of the majority, who either give consent "by themselves or [through] their representatives chosen by them."[37] But the majority must be constrained by always recognizing the commitment to protect the rights of all. To take a contemporary example, the losing side in a Senate debate might not prevail on an issue pertaining to taxation. But just the fact that it loses on the issue does not mean that it must lose all its basic rights as well, including rights guaranteeing participation in government, due process of law, and so on. The state complies with this objective by maintaining a commitment to the rule of law, which means that the state governs by "laws, promulgated and known to people, and not by extemporary decrees."[38]

In the next several paragraphs, I would like to discuss the implications of this view for practical politics and for citizenship obligations. With respect to the former, Locke suggested as we argued that, in having property, people have sufficient autonomy to pursue their interests. But it must be presumed that at times, owing to the fact that society will be composed of people with different interests, it is likely that people will have disagreements as to what the law means and how it should be applied in their own cases. The state in a civil society, in operating by known laws, assumes the role of an "indifferent judge" and thus acts as an umpire. As an umpire, the state does not dictate to any individuals what way of life is best for them, as would be the case in classical or medieval thought, where the good for each person was defined by virtue of the role a person is given. Instead, Locke's state, in its indifferent judge role, would resolve differences with an intention to protect the basic rights of each person to define his or her own way of life.

Regarding citizen obligations, it was Locke's view that citizens living in a state that protected their liberties were expected to uphold the laws of that state. Citizens give their tacit consent to this arrangement. Locke said,

> *every man that has any possessions or enjoyment of any part of the dominions of any government does thereby give his tacit consent and is as far forth obliged to*

obedience to the laws of that government, during such enjoyment, as anyone under it; whether this his possession be of land to him and his heirs for ever, or a lodging only for a week, or whether it be barely traveling freely the highway; and, in effect, it reaches as far as the very being of anyone with the territories of that government.[39]

In developing the notion of tacit consent, Locke hoped to overcome a problem central to all consent theory such as the one Locke provides. Where there is no way to demonstrate explicit consent by the people to a regime, how can one maintain that the people have consented to the regime? Locke's answer to this problem was quite simple. The notion of tacit consent suggests the conditions under which rational people *would* consent, were they given a chance to give their explicit consent to the regime.[40] What are the conditions that must be obtained for citizens to give their consent? Rational individuals would say that they would consent to any regime that provided them with essential benefits. Thus, Locke, in saying that we are obligated to the state's authority simply for using a highway, is really using the highway for a metaphor. And the metaphor suggests that when we live in a society that provides us with essential goods such as protection of our basic liberty, then, we are clearly obligated to obey the laws of that state.

Finally, Locke's doctrine of tacit consent indicates, as well, that citizens are aware of a responsibility on their part to uphold, faithfully, the rights of others who, like themselves, own property. Without this sense of obligation to support constraints on freedom, the state would have to become as powerful as Hobbes's state, entering society in ways that threaten the commitment to protect the rights of all citizens. But, given the rights-respecting mentality of citizens, the state can have a more limited role in Locke's society than it would have in Hobbes's society. Here, the idea of civic virtue would have a powerful place in Locke's civil society. For there to be freedom and rights, individuals must identify as the common good the need to defend both rights and the constraints needed to preserve them, even when doing so at times requires one to accept limits on the extent to which one is able to pursue one's interests. Locke's concept of a constrained majority would seem to assume that this understanding is a necessary part of people's outlook.

Given this view of a constrained majority, then, a civil society would not experience great conflict and the state could avoid the absolutist state of Hobbes. But this view presumes that the basic peace Locke described in the state of nature would find its way into civil society. And there is some question as to whether this view is realistic, given Locke's "second" view of the state of nature. Thus, there is another more Hobbesian view of the state of nature to appear in Locke. The "second" view casts doubt on the prospects of a constrained majority perspective, along with the hope of limited government, and, in place of both, the second view suggests a Hobbesian form of absolute government. It is now my intention to explain this point.

Locke's "second" description of the state of nature seemed to suggest that the differences between people are not as low level and as harmless as Locke might otherwise suggest. To support this point, I quote now from the second part of *The Second Treatise*. It would seem that when Locke wrote the words I cite in the next sentence he was not aware of what he had written in the first part where he said the state of nature is a place of "perfect freedom" and mutual respect for rights. But in contrast, in the second part of *The Second Treatise* here is what Locke said in reference to why individuals leave the state of nature: "the enjoyment of it [freedom] is very uncertain and constantly exposed to the invasion of others; for all being kings as much as he, every man his equal, and the greater part no strict observers of equity and justice, the enjoyment of the property he has in this state is very unsafe, very insecure."[41] Locke also said that there are many "privileges" found in the state of nature, but there are many "inconveniences," too, and these inconveniences stem from the "uncertain exercise of the power every man has of punishing the transgressions of others."[42] These words indicate a Hobbesian state of nature as the backdrop of society. If this is so, the potential for intense conflict in society would be strong, and to protect the rights of all people, even Locke would need a Hobbesian absolutist state.

How can we account for this "second," more Hobbesian view of the state of nature? There is no doubt that Macpherson would explain this second view by pointing out that it emerges from Locke's acceptance of market life, which permits a few to dominate and to control both the land in society and the labor of others for their, the owner's, own economic advantage. Further, if the "second" view of the state of nature, as defined in Macpherson's terms, were the basis for developing both society and government, what kind of experience would typify social life? Society would be characterized by class conflict, between those who own most of the wealth and those who do not. In this case, the majority rule process would really only be a majority of a small minority of people. Here, the likelihood of social discord and instability would be ever present, because those outside the policy process, the nonpropertied, would demand the same rights accorded to others. Still, Locke's notion of the state of nature, as we saw in his first account of this concept, said that no one is to take away the "life, liberty, health, limb, or goods of another." This suggests that Locke was committed to extending liberty to more than just property owners. But his view of a constrained majority would have little relevance to this project were it merely oriented to protecting the property of a few against the great majority of the nonpropertied people.

What would Locke's response be to this problem? I can only provide several conjectures. One response might be a demand for the government to suppress the nonpropertied. But in this case, the state would have to assume unlimited powers for itself, a consequence that Locke rejected. On the other hand, it is possible that Locke envisioned that more and more people, as a result of advances in the economy, would acquire property so that eventually the majority would include all of the citizens in the society. Here, where all people own property, any decision by the majority must be designed to protect the rights of all citizens. In that case, the potential for intense conflict would be minimized, making possible both a constrained majority, which sought to extend to all basic liberties, as well as the need for and the possibility of the limited form of government Locke advocated. Were this view to prevail, the main question then would pertain to how to maintain a government with limited powers, a government that did not become so powerful that it threatened the rights it is supposed to protect. In the next several sections we discuss the approaches to this problem that Locke recommended.

VI. LOCKE'S LIMITED GOVERNMENT

In this section, we discuss the concept of limited government proposed by Locke. Locke rejected Hobbes's refusal to entertain a government based upon a separation of powers. Locke did so in large part because he believed that a government based upon the concept of separated powers can institute limitations on the authority and actions of government so that, in the long run, the people's liberty will be protected.

There were three functions in Locke's government: the legislative, the executive, and the federative. Federative functions have to do with making foreign policy and using the power of war and peace to this end. Federative powers are ensconced in the executive branch, so in effect the power to enforce the law with respect to domestic matters and the power to make foreign policy are placed in the same office.[43]

At the heart of his view of government was the legislative branch that for Locke is "the supreme power of the commonwealth."[44] He said, in this regard, that the "first and fundamental natural law which is to govern even the legislative itself is the preservation of the society and, as far as will consist with the public good, and every person in it."[45] The legislature, which makes the laws, is the supreme authority, but, even so, it must not abuse its authority. The legislature cannot act in an arbitrary fashion "over the lives and fortunes of the people," nor can it do anything other than "decide the rights of the subject [citizens] by promulgated, standing laws, and known authorized judges."[46]

To prevent legislative misuse of power, several remedies are provided. First, since the legislators hold authority only on the basis of the continuing trust of the citizens who elect them, the people have the right "to remove or alter" the legislature if it violates the trust the citizens place in it.[47] A second way to prevent legislative misuse of power is to establish a "separate" executive branch that is to carry out the laws the legislature passes.[48] If the legislature were to have executive functions as well as legislative or law-making ones, then it might be the case that legislators would be more likely to make laws that serve their own interests and less likely to make laws that serve the needs of the whole society.[49]

Now, it should be clear that, in discussing the executive, Locke indicated that the legislative and executive are separated only when it comes to enforcing laws that the legislative branch makes. But on other occasions, when matters of law enforcement are not at issue, Locke argued that the executive is a part of the legislative branch. Thus, Locke said that the executive should be viewed as having "a share in the legislative." This arrangement permits the legislature to make the executive subordinate to its, the legislature's, power because the latter can change the executive at its, the legislature's, "pleasure."[50]

The executive, however, has special responsibilities that the legislature does not have. In particular, the executive must, as the constitution requires, call the legislature into session to deliberate about the laws and make sure, again in keeping with the constitution, that regular elections are held for the legislature. At other times, it is left to the executive's "prudence" to call for new elections and establish a new legislature when it appears that old laws no longer are relevant to meeting current challenges that threaten the public interest.[51] Regarding the issue of elections, Locke said that, over time, population shifts may occur, and thus some districts may need more representatives and others less. The executive must examine matters of this sort and distribute representatives proportionately. "For it being the interest as well as intention of the people to have a fair and equal representative, whoever brings it nearest to that is an undoubted friend to and establisher of the government and cannot miss the consent and approbation of the community."[52]

Still, Locke was well aware that the executive may abuse its power, and this problem grows out of the practical necessities of governing. Often, when political problems confront a nation, either the legislature is not in power, or it is too slow to act. In these situations, the executive assumes the power of "prerogative" and makes decisions on behalf of the public interest.[53] Hobbes of course also saw this power as inevitable. The difference between Hobbes and Locke on this issue is that the latter did not see this power as placed, without limits, into the hands of the executive (or king as in Hobbes), and, further, Locke believed that the executive should be held accountable for misusing it. Hobbes places no such limits on the monarch. But Locke presumed that people, acting through their legislators, would allow the executive the use of its prerogative so long as good judgments are made, and, when poor judgments result, the public will seek to limit the executive use of its power of prerogative.[54]

Now, the hope of this view of separated government is that each branch will balance the other, so that in the long run government will continue to make and to enforce fair laws that protect the liberty of the citizens. However, as in our times, we have come to realize that a practical consequence of a separation of powers view of government is intense competition between the branches. Moreover, when this happens, one branch or the other of government may grow in power to such an extent that the government as a whole threatens, rather than protects, the rights of its citizens. What is the remedy in this case? Locke said that all people can do is to "appeal to heaven; for the rulers, in such attempts, exercising a power the people never put into their hands [and] do that which they have not a right to do."[55]

VII. THE RIGHT OF REVOLUTION

The right to revolt against the central government arises from the fact that in cases in which there is abuse of power and no remedy from within constituted authority, citizens always reserve for themselves the option of deciding to revolt against the rulers. Indeed, this option can never be given up by citizens, since it is not within a citizen's "power" to "submit himself to another as to give him a liberty to destroy him, God and nature never allowing a man so to abandon himself as to neglect his own preservation."[56] God ordains, on this view, that each of us has a duty to ensure that our freedom is not taken from us. In the face of errant executive or legislative power, then, Locke reaffirmed not just a natural right to liberty, but both a right to revolution as well as a duty, mandated by God, to recreate the conditions of liberty.

The right to revolt for Locke would not be a recipe to encourage continual disorder and social instability. The reason for this view is that Locke saw this right as principally exercised by the majority, and thus, for a revolution to take place, there would have to be a wholesale denial of people's basic rights. Locke said when the majority is "persuaded in their consciences that their laws, and with them their estates, liberties, and lives are in danger, and perhaps religion, too, how they will be hindered from resisting illegal forces used against them I cannot tell."[57]

The power of the majority in this case seems to be manifested more in the threat of revolution than in the act of revolution itself. What would most keep public officials from engaging in corrupt activities would be the fear that if they did, and if as a result the majority felt that their liberty was threatened, there would be a revolution which would sweep all public officials from power. Not wanting this situation to arise, public officials must maintain among themselves a modicum of honesty in their dealings with themselves and with the citizens.

VIII. TOLERATION AND CIVIL SOCIETY

Locke's view of civil society, as we have seen, provides a concept of limited government to protect the general societal principle that the rights of each person should be protected. This principle was built into his conception of the constrained majority, as well. But there is another approach to rights protection in Locke. His view of civil society included a space, outside the formal structure of government, where individuals would be protected from infringements of their rights either from others or from the government. An important element that helps to create this dimension of civil society is the civic virtue of toleration.

In discussing the civic virtue of religious toleration, Locke understood that people hold their religious beliefs with extreme conviction, and, when they do, others who do not believe as they do are inevitably perceived as less deserving of respect. How in the face of this problem will it be possible for individuals to extend rights protection to all, including those whose religion is different from their own?

Locke's solution is found in his *Letter on Toleration.* Locke argued that the state is to preserve "civil interests," such as "life, liberty, health . . . and the possession of outward things, such as money, lands, houses, furniture, and the like."[58] The state's powers extend only to matters such as these, but they do not extend to matters pertaining to religious belief. Thus, the state cannot use its powers to advocate certain religious beliefs. Indeed, the power of the state cannot be used to promote the "salvation of souls."[59]

In this view, a church is a private association that can determine its own doctrines without interference from the state. Individuals who join these associations agree to accept the doctrines that these associations teach. Moreover, whereas these associations may declare their belief of what constitutes proper religious doctrines, they cannot in the name of religion invade and thereby threaten or take away the "rights and worldly goods" of others.[60] Locke also said that moral attitudes contrary to certain religious doctrines such as idolatry, covetousness, idleness, and uncharitableness cannot be punished by the state. This is the case so long as these modes of conduct are not harmful to the rights of another or so long as such forms of conduct do not threaten the "public peace."[61]

Locke's doctrine of toleration suggests a live-and-let-live attitude. Locke said that people, who in their practice of religion cause no harm to others, should be tolerated. "This caution and temper they ought certainly to use toward those who mind only their own business, and are solicitous for nothing but (whatever men think of them) they may worship God in that manner which they are persuaded is acceptable to Him, and in which they have the strongest hopes of eternal salvation."[62] All individuals are free to believe as they wish, just so long as they do not deny the basic civil rights to others.

What are the implications of the live-and-let-live mentality for extending rights protection to all citizens? Possibly, members of the same church may want to maintain respect for the rights of other church members. Possibly, members of a church may maintain respect for the rights of nonmembers. But their doing so may not be because they believe in the priority of rights when it comes to matters of religious truth but because they want to avoid the social instability that might arise were various people to try to impose their respective religious views onto others.

The consequence of the attitude of toleration, which exists as a civic virtue of the highest importance, is to secure indirectly the rights of others, including strangers who believe differently from ourselves. Here, people support the rights of others for a reason other than a clear commitment to make the protection of rights the main priority. People may still harbor the view that the others whom they tolerate really do not deserve the same rights accorded their co-religionists. The live-and-let-live attitude helps to prevent one from acting on these views for the sake of peace and stability. Still, a deep, underlying sense of difference may remain with each side thinking the other side lacks a grasp of the truth and because of this fact ultimately poses a long-term threat to each person's religious choice.

A dimension of this attitude is manifested in Locke's views toward Catholics, atheists, and agnostics. Locke said that no "opinions," which are contrary "to the preservation of civil society, are to be tolerated by the magistrate."[63] On this view, Locke barely tolerated Catholics, claiming that there is no requirement to tolerate those (presumably Catholics) who say that "kings excommunicated forfeit their crowns and kingdoms."[64] Could Locke, then, extend rights to Catholics who believed in papal infallibility? Maybe he could, so long as he was assured that the Catholics in question were not subversive of civil society. But it is not clear that he would. For atheists, a more categorical denial of rights is provided. Locke said, "lastly those are not at all to be tolerated who deny the being of God. Promises, convents, and oaths, which are bonds of human society, can have no hold upon an atheist."[65] Finally, it is not clear that even an agnostic would find a full plate of rights in Locke's civil society. Locke said that all men are to believe in God and, in consequence, all should "enter into some religious society."[66]

Locke's doctrine of toleration, then, suggested that people who in all respects uphold the civil laws may still fall outside their protection and thus be denied the same rights guaranteed to all. Because a live-and-let-live view allows people to live side by side without interacting with each other for the purpose of creating common bonds of understanding, bonds that help them to appreciate others' beliefs, individuals may live side by side, but with a growing sense of distrust and suspicion. As a result, real barriers to communication would exist between people, and these barriers might lead individuals to form majorities that work to deny basic rights to others for no other reason than that others have different religious beliefs.

However, the civic virtue of toleration suggests a space in society where individuals can meet together and form associations and enter into relations of their choice. In these spaces, freedom of conscience would be afforded protection. But the problems we have just enumerated with respect to Locke's view of toleration suggest that this space in a civil society, what we have in Chapter 1 referred to as the separate sphere of voluntary associations, might have difficulty enduring where the civic virtue of toleration is not buttressed by the civic virtue of mutual respect. The latter symbolizes a willingness on the part of individuals to manifest goodwill to others, even to those with whom they do not agree, so that persons at least learn to understand views different from their own. As a result of this way of understanding, people create conditions that afford others a place in society where they can be protected as they go about their lives, pursuing particular religious or moral views that in no sense threaten the rights of others. But when mutual respect does not exist in a strong sense, then individuals who do not threaten others' rights may still be denied a secure place in society to practice their own views. This problem can be overcome, and the separate sphere of voluntary groups in civil society secured, only when mutual respect is made a preeminent part of the practice of the civic virtue of toleration.

Mutual respect would have particular importance for Locke, whereas, we have seen, class conflict arising from market relations could be an obstacle to securing the rights of all. Still, the existence of the civic virtue of toleration, when coupled with the commitment to constrained majority rule and limited government, goes a long way to maintaining both the possibility of mutual respect and a separate sphere. Thus, the prospect of mutual respect is not to be ruled out for Locke. Indeed, it would seem that owing to this fact the potential for avoiding destructive class conflict might well be conceivable.

IX. RESPONSE AND REJOINDER

Hobbes might argue that Locke's second view of the state of nature really is close to Hobbes's own view, the doctrine of toleration notwithstanding. Thus, for Hobbes, Locke would need the same kind of state Hobbes advocated, in order to secure the freedom that his philosophy promises. Locke might respond, however, that the doctrine of toleration is a civic virtue that would minimize conflict over religion, thus making the need for a Hobbesian form of government unnecessary. Moreover, perhaps over time, the intensity of feeling for religion would diminish. In Locke's society, after all, what would take center stage would be the pursuit of material goals, such as wealth and property, and in this context religious issues might lose their fervor. Indeed, perhaps religious issues would be less important and less divisive as freedom became more and more associated with material acquisition.

Also, even if interest in material matters did not diminish the strength of religious concerns, practicing the doctrine of toleration might make people more prone to establish, as the basis for interacting with others, a sincere commitment to understanding the viewpoints and arguments of those who differ from theirs. Were this situation to arise, then, individuals would be able to engage each other in discussions that reached for and even achieved at times a common ground. For instance, the religious fundamentalist in discussing public issues might realize that it is best not to broach in such a discussion elements of fundamentalist religious views that tend to threaten and to turn away those who reject fundamentalist religious doctrines. Thus, in addressing abortion, it is best not to argue that those who do not believe as the fundamentalists believe will end up in hell. Rather, the fundamentalist would need to frame the issue as a moral question that can be approached from common moral assumptions, assumptions that are shared across society. In this context, the issue of abortion should turn on questions of what constitutes the rights of all parties involved and how these rights can be best balanced so that, in the end, all are treated fairly. It is possible that as a result of practicing the doctrine of toleration and of learning to live-and-let-live, then, that people are able to find a basis for mutual understanding and mutual respect.

Of course, Hobbes might have the same hope that fundamentalists and nonfundamentalists would become more conciliatory to each other over time, but he probably would not believe that this outcome was realistic. Given this fact, the only way to protect the rights of all citizens is with the state he contemplates. In this case, Hobbes would argue that the doctrine of toleration would not be sufficient to protect citizens' rights. This is the case because in a situation in which people are strongly committed to a particular view, the only way they will be stopped from interfering with others is when the state uses its considerable power to compel compliance with the laws. Locke, on the other hand, would maintain that Hobbes's approach would end up threatening people's basic rights. Hobbes would no doubt argue in response that threatening rights is not the same thing as denying them. Hobbes would further add that in order to protect rights, it may well be necessary to create an atmosphere of fear so that those likely to attack the rights of others would be less prone to do so.

In contrast, Locke would argue that his view of the state that limits the powers of the various branches, in this case, the legislative and the executive branches, is more inclined to achieve a political setting that can protect the rights of individuals. Hobbes's refusal to consider a state that divides power works to hand the state so much power that the state itself becomes an enemy of rights. Locke, on the other hand, recognized that to offset this problem, it is necessary to secure conditions within the society and the state that limit the powers of the various branches of government, lest the government become the main enemy of the rights it is supposed to protect. Hobbes would have responded that it is impossible to achieve the goals of a fair and just state when the state is constantly made the target for various political opportunists who attempt to take it over and use the state's power for their own purposes. And that is just what Locke's form of state invites when he allows the power of the state to be subdivided into different branches of authority.

Finally, others might claim that Locke's main problem in maintaining a civil society that can secure the rights of citizens has to do with the difficulties of securing a constrained majority. Those who make this argument might claim that Locke has failed to address adequately the impact of market realities in his view of the state of nature. This lapse places in jeopardy a majority rule conception, which at the same time is committed to not infringe the rights of any citizen. In particular, it could be argued that Locke's citizens become so concerned, as they pursue their rights, with their own private interests, that they reject any concern for a larger, more embracing common good. Rousseau will discuss these problems as we see in the next chapter.

Endnotes

1. For some historical background, see Sabine, *A History of Political Theory,* pp. 517, 534; Mulford Q. Sibley, *Political Ideas and Ideologies: A History of Political Thought,* (New York: Harper and Row, 1970), pp. 373–74; and Thomas P. Peardon, "Introduction," *The Second Treatise of Government,* (Indianapolis: Bobbs-Merrill, 1952), pp. x–xi.

2. Richard Ashcraft, *Revolutionary Politics and Locke's Two Treatises of Government,* (Princeton: Princeton University Press, 1986), pp. 280–81.

3. Charles Taylor, *Sources of the Self,* (Cambridge: Harvard University Press, 1989), p. 171.

4. Ian Shapiro, "Gross Concepts in Political Argument," *Political Theory,* 17:1, February, 1989, pp. 56–59.

5. John Locke, *The Second Treatise of Government,* edited by Thomas P. Peardon, (New York: Bobbs-Merrill, 1952), pp. 3–4, para. 2–3.

6. Ibid., p. 4, para. 3.

7. Ibid., p. 4, para. 3.

8. Ibid., pp. 52–53, para. 93.

9. Ibid., p. 4, para. 4.

10. Ibid., p. 4, para. 4.

11. Ibid., p. 5, para. 6.

12. Ibid., p. 5, para. 6.

13. Ibid., pp. 5–6, para. 6.

14. Ibid., p. 15, para. 22.

15. Ibid., p. 15, para. 22.

16. Ibid., p. 16, para. 25.

17. Ibid., p. 17, para. 27.

18. Ibid., p. 17, para. 27.

19. Ibid., p. 20, para. 34. See also pp. 98–99, para. 173, where Locke says that "by property I must be understood here, as in other places to mean that property which men have in their persons as well as goods."

20. Ibid., p. 15, para. 23.

21. Ibid., pp. 12–13, para. 19.

22. Ibid., p. 19, para. 31; also p. 22, para. 36.

23. Ibid., p. 23, para. 38.

24. Ibid., p. 28, para. 46.

25. Ibid., p. 28, para. 46.

26. Ibid., p. 29, para. 50.

27. Ibid., p. 29, para. 48. Locke saw the profit motive as a main incentive for people to engage in work that would benefit the society. He said in relation to commerce in agriculture for instance, "what would a man value ten thousand acres or a hundred thousand acres of excellent land, ready and cultivated and well stocked, too, with cattle, in the middle of the inland parts of America where he had no hopes of commerce with other parts of the world to draw money to him for the sale of the product?"

28. For a good discussion of this aspect of Locke, see C. B. Macpherson, *The Political Theory of Possessive Individualism,* (Oxford: The Clarendon Press, 1962), pp. 204–17.

29. Locke, *Second Treatise of Government,* p. 18, para. 28.

30. Macpherson, *The Political Theory of Possessive Individualism,* pp. 215, 216, 220.

31. Locke, *Second Treatise of Government,* p. 71, para. 124–25.

32. Ibid., p. 71, para. 124.

33. Ibid., p. 71, para. 124–26.

34. Ibid., p. 55, para. 96. Italics added.

35. Ibid., p. 73, para. 131.

36. Ibid., p. 73, para. 131.

37. Ibid., pp. 80–81, para. 140.

38. Ibid., p. 73, para. 131.

39. Ibid., p. 68, para. 119.

40. My view is based upon that of Hanna Pitkin, "Obligation and Consent," in *Philosophy, Politics and Society,* ed. Peter Laslett, et al., (New York: Barnes and Noble, 1972), p. 62. She says that legitimate authority is "precisely that which *ought* to be obeyed, to which one ought to consent, which deserves obedience and consent, to which rational men considering all relevant facts and issues would consent, to which consent can be justified."

41. Locke, *Second Treatise of Government,* p. 70, para. 123.

42. Ibid., p. 71, para. 127.

43. Ibid., p. 83, para. 145–47.

44. Ibid., p. 75, para. 134.

45. Ibid., p. 75, para. 134.

46. Ibid., p. 77, para. 136; also, p. 76, para. 135.

47. Ibid., p. 84, para. 149.

48. Ibid., pp. 82–83, para. 144.

49. Ibid., p. 82, para. 143; p. 86, para. 153.

50. Ibid., p. 86, para. 152.

51. Ibid., p. 87, para. 154.

52. Ibid., p. 90, para. 158.

53. Ibid., p. 92, para. 160.

54. Ibid., p. 92, para. 161.

55. Ibid., p. 95, para. 168.

56. Ibid., p. 96, para. 168.

57. Ibid., pp. 117–18, para. 209; also, p. 96, para. 168.

58. John Locke, *A Letter on Toleration,* (Indianapolis: Bobbs-Merrill, 1955), p. 17.

59. Ibid., p. 17.

60. Ibid., p. 27.

61. Ibid., pp. 42, 26.

62. Ibid., p. 28.

63. Ibid., p. 50.

64. Ibid., pp. 50–51.

65. Ibid., p. 52.

66. Ibid., p. 35.

Partial Bibliography and Further Reading

Ashcraft, Richard. *Revolutionary Politics and Locke's Two Treatises of Government.* Princeton: Princeton University Press, 1986.

Dunn, John. *The Political Thought of John Locke: An Historical Account of the Argument of the "Two Treatises of Government."* London: Cambridge University Press, 1969.

Grant, Ruth Weissbourd. *John Locke's Liberalism.* Chicago: University of Chicago Press, 1987.

Kramer, Matthew H. *John Locke and the Origins of Private Property: Philosophical Explorations of Individualism. Community, and Equality.* Cambridge, Cambridge University Press, 1997.

Macpherson, C. B. *The Political Theory of Possessive*

Individualism. Oxford: The Clarendon Press, 1962.

Pangle, Thomas L. *The Spirit of Modern Republicanism: The Moral Vision of the American Founders and the Philosophy of Locke.* Chicago: University of Chicago Press, 1988.

Pocock, J. G. A., and Richard Ashcraft. *John Locke: Papers Read at a Clark Library Seminar.* William Andrews Clark Memorial Library, Los Angeles: University of California, 1980.

Rapaczynski, Andrzej. *Nature and Politics: Liberalism in the Philosophies of Hobbes, Locke, and Rousseau.* Ithaca: Cornell University Press, 1987.

Shapiro, Ian. "Gross Concepts in Political Argument." *Political Theory,* 17:1, February, 1989.

Simmons, A. John. *The Lockean Theory of Rights.* Princeton: Princeton University Press, 1992.

Taylor, Charles. *Sources of The Self: The Making of the Modern Identity.* Cambridge: Harvard University Press, 1989.

Tully, James. *A Discourse on Property: John Locke and His Adversaries.* Cambridge: Cambridge University Press, 1979.

9

JEAN-JACQUES ROUSSEAU:
COMMUNITY AND CIVIL SOCIETY

I. INTRODUCTION

Jean-Jacques Rousseau (1712–1778) can be read as a critique of the arguments found in Hobbes and Locke, as well as the doctrines found in the period referred to during Rousseau's times as the French Enlightenment. The French Enlightenment tracts heavily the thought of Hobbes and Locke. Both writers sought to use reason to explore ways to advance liberty. This quest often meant revising and when necessary discarding traditions that impeded liberty. Indeed, liberalism as a comprehensive political vision advances from the view that a rational life must be predicated upon expanding both the number of rights and the scope of their coverage in society. As we saw, in promoting this position, liberalism can be viewed as the philosophy of the bourgeoisie. The latter is the new class of merchants and traders and individuals who make money from banking and finance. This class clamored for changes in society so that its members could carve out for themselves opportunities to engage in new ways of life not permitted in medieval settings.

Liberalism's commitment to reason, over and against the traditions of the past, was designed to advance the cause of liberty. But in doing so, Rousseau viewed liberalism and the bourgeoisie supporting it as attacking both community and equality. Community is built upon sacred values such as respect for the common good and religious traditions. Equality suggests the opportunity for each person to participate in helping to define the common good. But liberals advanced the cause not of the community and the common good for Rousseau, but that of individual self-interest and selfishness. Further, liberals supported equality only insofar as equality before the law meant the enhancement of individual freedom, as opposed to the fostering of community life through full citizen participation by each member of the society.

In Rousseau's thinking, the Enlightenment fostered a civil society setting that equated the rule of law with the rule of materialism and greed, as well as the undermining of respect for the norms of civility and the common good. In what follows, I provide a more detailed introduction to Rousseau's rejection of the Enlightenment as developed by Hobbes and Locke.

For Hobbes and Locke, the main objective was a civil society that could advance the liberty and thus the rights of each citizen. Of course, as we showed in previous chapters, the quest for rights did not mean that individuals were to shed all regard for constraints. Indeed, for Hobbes and Locke, civil society was a place where the pursuit of individual freedom could be made consonant with certain rational constraints that secured the freedom of all persons. This viewpoint suggested that individuals did not have to accept traditional medieval roles as the sole basis for determining their identities. Here, it would appear that the effect of Hobbes and Locke was liberatory, for it fostered the need to free people from traditional, medieval structures. But for Rousseau, the contribution of either writer was extremely destructive. Rousseau believed that both Hobbes and Locke put in the forefront of all social experience the desire for rights, and this approach gave people license to seek their own personal happiness, often at great cost to those canons of civic virtue associated with the common good.[1]

The philosophers of the French Enlightenment, whom Rousseau despised, believed that the ruling powers were wedded to archaic religious, moral, and political traditions, and thus France was under the domination of powerful people who were driven by both prejudice and small-mindedness. Still, these philosophers believed that the great bulk of the people could be freed from this mentality. Through education, people could be "enlightened" or provided with a capacity for good reasoning, which would allow them to rise above existing prejudice and establish a progressive and more just and happy society. Rousseau, however, believed that this attitude had damaged the prospect for civic virtue on the part of citizens. The result of the Enlightenment was to make the pursuit of wealth and luxury more important than respect for those virtues that secure the common good of the whole community.[2]

In taking this view of the Enlightenment's impact, Rousseau harked back to the previous era of classical philosophy and looked with fondness on that period's commitment to teach the canons of civic virtue, which both the traditions of Hobbes and Locke and the new Enlightenment were destroying. As Rousseau said in his famous essay on the contributions of the sciences and arts, an essay that emphasizes the failures of the Enlightenment, "ancient politicians incessantly talked about morals and virtue, those of our time talk only of business and money."[3]

For Rousseau, then, Enlightenment-inspired education, or education in the sciences and arts, emphasized a belief in progress through science and reason. Rousseau believed that, whereas progress in knowledge had increased luxury and material comforts, at the same time this so-called "progress" has produced a demise of the moral quality of life.[4] This fact is best seen in the system of education that accompanies the Enlightenment spirit. For Rousseau, education in his times, which embodies the highest regard for material progress, "adorns our minds and corrupts our judgment" by de-emphasizing respect for the great civic virtues such as courage and love of country. Rousseau said,

> *I see everywhere immense institutions where young people are brought up at great expense, learning everything except their duties. Your children will not know their own language, but they will speak others that are nowhere in use; they will know how to write verses that they can barely understand; without*

knowing how to distinguish error from truth, they will possess the art of making them both unrecognizable to others by specious arguments. But they will not know what the words magnanimity, equity, temperance, humanity, courage are; that sweet name fatherland will never strike their ear; and if they hear of God, it will be less to be awed by him than to be afraid of him.[5]

Reversing the Enlightenment mentality became a main part of Rousseau's political agenda. Politics must help restore citizenship and all that citizenship thrives on; in particular, a common respect for the needs of the community and for the corresponding traditions of civic virtue. Attaining this outcome for Rousseau requires a certain kind of political association, one that permits individuals to feel as well as to believe themselves to be part of a community with others. In this setting, each member serves the needs and interests of the common good and, as a result, each individual subordinates private interests to the larger needs of one's community.

Thus, Rousseau would not have accepted either Locke's or Hobbes's view of government, including the latter's Leviathan or the former's conception of limited government. In both cases, these forms of government serve only to support a civil society experience in which the primary objective is to facilitate the priority of private interest over respect for the common good. For Rousseau, Locke's and Hobbes's civil society, while arguing that it supports a common good, in this case a commitment to secure the equal liberty and rights of all persons, really promotes a society that is only designed to facilitate each person's pursuit of his own private interest. Rousseau would reverse this tendency by creating a civil society that is predicated upon the experience of direct citizen participation in shaping the law by which all live.

II. Selfishness and Self-Love

As a prelude to discussing Rousseau's view of the state of nature in the next section, it is necessary to explain Rousseau's notion of self-love and how the latter differs from selfishness. In *Émile,* Rousseau's major work on education, Rousseau said that selfishness is the state of mind in which we constantly compare ourselves to others in the hopes that others will look upon us and want to be like ourselves. "Selfishness, which is always comparing [one's] self with others, is never satisfied and never can be; for this feeling, which prefers ourselves to others, requires that they [others] prefer us to themselves, which is impossible."[6] Still, despite the impossibility of the enterprise, selfish people try to make others want to be like themselves anyway. To do so, selfish people will often have to resort to various forms of deceit and trickery. So it is understandable that such individuals will become puffed up with self-importance as they manifest toward others "grand ostentation, deceptive cunning, and all the vices that follow in their wake."[7] Here, we try to convince others how important we are by showing them all our wealth, luxuries, and status, in the hopes that if they see these things others will want to become like us.

But the more genuine condition Rousseau called self-love, which is "always good, always in accordance with the order of nature. The preservation of our own life is specially entrusted to each one of us, and our first care is, and must be, to watch over our own life;

and how can we continually watch over it, if we do not take the greatest interest in it."[8] By eschewing a life in which we try to be other than whom we are in order to make others be like us, we focus upon the development of our native feelings and natural tendencies. As the latter emerge, we understand fully our real natures. Here, we would understand that "the tender and gentle passions spring from self-love," whereas the "hateful and angry passions spring from selfishness."[9] We receive from Rousseau a clear understanding of the intent of people's natural feelings when Rousseau described male adolescence prior to its becoming corrupted by the temptations of a form of wanton sexuality. An uncorrupted young man exhibits "tender and affectionate passions" and a "warm heart . . . touched by the sufferings of . . . fellow creatures." The natural self is moved by "pity, mercy, and generosity."[10]

Rousseau's argument is that these natural sentiments, which give important moral guidance, are denied full expression in a corrupted, modern society. In developing an explanation for why this tragedy occurs, Rousseau, like Hobbes and Locke, used a method that starts from what is presumed to be an accurate depiction of pre-social man. But Rousseau's view of pre-social man in the state of nature differs radically, as we show in the next section, from the views of Hobbes and Locke.

III. THE SECOND DISCOURSE ON THE ORIGIN OF INEQUALITY AMONG MEN

Rousseau's depiction of the source of the betrayal of our natural self revolves around his discussion of political inequality. So what is political inequality? Political inequality, unlike natural inequality that refers to differences in ability and capacity, emanates from the consent of people. Political inequality "consists in the different privileges enjoyed by some at the expense of others, such as being richer, more honored, more powerful than they, or even causing themselves to be obeyed by them."[11] In discussing political inequality, Rousseau wanted to demonstrate how it came to pass that the bulk of people in society end up ceding a right to a few to predominate over the rest, even though the few use their power for promoting their own interests at a cost to the common good. Not only is a politics of the common good impossible in this context, but also impossible is a society based upon respect for those natural instincts and feelings that enable people to have a continuing sense of compassion for others.

To understand how this situation evolves, it is necessary to retrace the steps of humankind, starting with people as they are in the state of nature, and then demonstrating their progress from the state of nature to modern society. Along the way, we will demonstrate what causes people to turn away from pursuing the truths of their inner selves and what helps launch a regime of political inequality that Rousseau despises. Thus, Rousseau's quest in the *Second Discourse* is to explain "the sequence of wonders by which . . . the people . . . buy imaginary repose at the price of real felicity."[12]

In Rousseau's state of nature, primitive people are not motivated by an urge for power as was the case in Hobbes, nor are they rational, subject to rules created by reason, as was the case in Locke. They live only for the present, and they do not possess a rational plan for their future. They have no social entanglements or dependencies upon others. Their natural instincts dictate their feelings and their needs. Rousseau said that people are driven by two basic natural urges, a natural drive for self-preservation (the need for food, shelter, clothing, and sex) and "a natural repugnance to seeing any sentient being, especially our fellow man, perish or suffer," or an urge not to harm another.[13] People then must pursue their basic needs without causing harm to others. Why would people be disposed not to harm others? People are moved by the sentiment of pity, and thus the compassion that people display to others arises not from any sort of "subtle arguments" on the nature of right and wrong, but from people consulting their own hearts. Here, there is no need for laws against murder, theft, and rape because there is no motivation to do such things. Owing to this natural disposition, we are to "Do what is good for you with as little harm as possible to others."[14]

To make this maxim a part of day-to-day activities requires no complex moral inquiry into proposed courses of action. Primitive people do what seems most natural for them. When they are hungry they eat, when they need shelter they find some, and when they have sexual urges, they satisfy them. But in all cases, they approach the satisfaction of their urges from a sensibility that exhorts them not to harm others. Here, personal conduct, then, is merely a consequence of one's true and most basic needs.[15] Rousseau said, "each man peacefully awaits the impetus of nature, gives himself over to it without choice, and with more pleasure than frenzy; and once the need is satisfied, all desire is snuffed out."[16] In contrast, the modern person achieves one desire only to find himself wanting to satisfy another. Each life is a never-ending series of desires no one of which, were they to be fulfilled, would make a person happy. Primitive man, however, reflects the peace of his simplicity. "His soul, agitated by nothing, is given over to the single feeling of his own present existence, without any idea of the future, however near it may be, and his projects, as limited as his views, hardly extend to the end of the day."[17]

As already indicated, primitive people are free from any kind of social dependency. Initially, primitive people live alone, independent of lasting relationships. They form associations with each other only to satisfy mutually desirable ends. Sexual liaisons take place on the basis of an urge for mutual sexual gratification. Once the latter is achieved, people separate and go in different directions, perhaps never to see each other again. Mothers nourish their children until the children can care for themselves and, once they can, mother and child each go their own ways, and after a while neither recognizes the other.[18]

Transient relationships end and permanent ones begin when primitive people discover that it is in their interests to work with each other to secure common survival needs.[19] During this phase, people work together without the need for formal language, and they learn to communicate with "inarticulate cries, many gestures, and some imitative voices."[20] In addition, primitive people invent tools such as hatchets and sharp stones that allow them to provide for their basic needs. At this stage, as well, families are formed for the first time and private ownership of property is introduced, also. Owning property at this point does not create conditions hostile to primitive people's overall happiness because each person is forced to respect the property of others, or face a fierce struggle with those they might take it from.[21] Furthermore, there is no need to engage in such a struggle, since there is enough property for everyone anyway. In effect, because everyone has as much property as they can use, no one has any need for the property of others, and thus no one desires to take another's property.

Thus, the first permanent relationships founded by primitive people, while part of the road to modern life, are not the sources of moral decay and political inequality. Rousseau described this condition in idyllic terms. The family setting represents a "habit of living together," which gives "rise to the sweetest sentiments known to men: conjugal and paternal love."[22] Moreover, this condition is associated with sufficient leisure time and conveniences. These new dimensions make people less self-sufficient and sturdy mentally and physically than they had been in the past and more prone to believe that when or if they are deprived of these advantages, they will think life cruel to them.[23]

Still, this experience was not a major factor in revolutionizing the life of humankind. More fundamental causes were at work. Rousseau envisioned people initially living on one continuous piece of land, but after floods and earthquakes had occurred, the main living area was broken up into many different islands. Now, people were forced to live together in these diverse areas and develop separate languages and distinct and diverse communities. In these new settings, people united into permanent communities and formed nations, which were united by shared traditions and customs.[24]

These new forms of permanent living arrangements had important impacts on the lives of people. People developed "ideas of merit and beauty" and because people began to compare themselves and each other with these public standards valued by the whole nation, those who came out the best aroused envy in others.[25] But even this situation did not usher political inequality into existence. For, it is still the case that individuals lived in accordance with the common moral standards of the community. No one, not even those who were the highest in ability and achievement, were exempted from them. Rousseau said that "it was necessary for punishments to become more severe in proportion as the occasions for giving offense become more frequent."[26] Primitive community life symbolized the existence of a strong sense of civic virtue that demanded that each person serve the larger good of the society. One was not allowed to claim that, because one had superior ability, one could avoid this obligation. Rousseau said that "this period of the development of human faculties, maintaining a middle position between the indolence of our primitive state and the petulant activity of our egocentrism, must have been the happiest and the most durable epoch."[27]

The structure of work in the primitive community did not represent the fatal step that plunged the community into political inequality, either. In the primitive setting each person was engaged in all phases of the production of any good. There was not, as yet, a division of labor that segmented work into simple tasks and that forced the worker to discard whatever skills he might have in order to fit into a production line. Work remained an endeavor by which one could demonstrate one's skills and contributions to the society, and from these acts, be recognized and respected by others. "As long as they applied themselves exclusively to tasks that a single individual could do and to the arts that did not require the cooperation of several hands, they lived as free, healthy, good and happy as they could in accordance with their nature, and they continued to enjoy among themselves the sweet reward of independent intercourse."[28]

The fatal step for humankind emerged with the invention of metallurgy and agriculture, "the two arts," Rousseau said, which turned society in the direction of political inequality by changing the nature of work and introducing destructive forms of private property. Rousseau in describing these events depicted the evils of a commercial, market society.

With the invention of metal, new industries were built. These industries could be maintained only if populations were shifted to manufacturing centers in cities. But as the number of workers increased there were fewer people left to perform agricultural functions to feed the rest of the society. To meet this problem, metals were used to create tools to help people farm more efficiently. Now, fewer men could produce larger amounts of food, enough to feed the growing population of the cities.[29] Private property rights emerged from this experience, too. Farmers, who worked their land to produce food, were said to create value from their labor, and thus they had a right not only to the products of their work, but also to the property on which the farmer toils. Similar to Locke, then, Rousseau said that society was required to protect the property rights of all persons.[30]

These circumstances suggest that accompanying the economic advances made possible by progress in metallurgy and agriculture were growing disparities in power and influence among people. Cities grew in size as factories were built in and around them. And those who owned the factories and controlled the labor of those who worked in them became wealthy. The farming areas lost population, but those remaining in this activity became prosperous property owners. In short, "the strongest did the most work; the most adroit turned theirs to better advantage: the most ingenious found ways to shorten their labor."[31] What of the rest? The latter, because they lacked the skills or the luck to qualify them as either factory owners or successful farmers, lost their importance and dignity in society. In this setting it is easy to understand that natural differences will be translated into political ones. Rousseau said that "if talents had been equal, and if the use of iron and the consumption of foodstuffs had always been in precise balance,"[32] society would have remained in balance and no political or social inequality would have emerged. Rousseau is moved to say,

> *thus it is that natural inequality imperceptibly manifests itself together with inequality occasioned by the socialization process. Thus it is that the differences among men, developed by those circumstances, make themselves more noticeable, more permanent in their effects, and begin to influence the fate of private individuals in the same proportion.*[33]

A powerful class emerged to dominate the rest of the society, with the result that civil war broke out between the rich and the poor.[34] But the rich could not enjoy their gains when they were always placed in jeopardy by war, and the lot of the poor could never be improved so long as class war was a constant reality. The rich schemed to create a new peace, which diffused the anger of the poor, without requiring any sacrifice on the part of themselves. The poor were tricked into believing that, as a result of peace, there would be justice and a new social order that would protect their interests and provide them with rights and justice. So the rich talked about achieving justice through the introduction of a civil society that would provide freedom to all individuals. Of course, the rich had no intention to provide for the needs of the poor. The rich only intended to make it appear as if they did. Still the poor, without sophistication and filled with greed themselves, lacked an ability to create their own solutions, and so they consented to "chain themselves [to the rich], in the belief that they secured their liberty." As a result, the poor ended up agreeing to a social contract that continued the injustice of the past, except that now the poor had given their consent to it. The rich could then rule through institutions that the poor were tricked into supporting, and it appeared that the rich no longer had to resort to naked force to justify their authority.[35]

Rousseau said in summarizing this experience: "such was . . . the origin of society and laws, which gave new fetters to the weak and new forces to the rich . . . established forever the law of property and of inequality, changed adroit usurpation into an irrevocable right, and for the profit of a few ambitious men henceforth subjected the entire human race to labor, servitude and misery."[36] Political inequality consented to by ordinary people is nothing more than ordinary people consenting to their enslavement to the rich.

IV. THE LOSS OF CIVIC VIRTUE

The picture Rousseau painted in the *Discourse on the Origin of Inequality* suggests that the economic context of modern society allows those with superior skill to acquire control over others and to use that control to continue to enhance wealth and political power in the society. A new form of class rule emerged, one no longer based on traditional class hierarchy found in the medieval world, but one based on one's ability to manipulate the processes of production to one's own advantage.

Private property in this setting came to symbolize for Rousseau not only this new type of class rule, but also a way of life that trampled the traditions of civic virtue. More to the point, the new systems of production made money the most important good. For without money, it is impossible to purchase the machines and other materials necessary for gaining an advantageous position in the new industrial-based market contexts. So systems of finance were established to create avenues that permitted investors access to money that could be used to expand the industrial base of a society. All attention is then riveted to the profit and loss sheet. Indeed, nothing else matters except profit.

But Rousseau believed that the "systems of finance are a modern invention; they have produced nothing."[37] The preoccupation with money has turned ordinary people into luxury-seeking, "scheming," "violent," and "knavish" individuals.[38] People with these attitudes have no love for the larger good of the community, nor do they wish to be acknowledged for their contributions to the needs of the community. Indeed, the quest for money has all but destroyed the prospect of civic virtue in the society.

When this happens, the politics of society becomes corrupted, too. Political leaders are more concerned to promote this or that version of the private interest, and they have no ability to conceptualize the public good. All who enter politics do so with the intention to loot and steal from the ordinary people.[39] Votes are bought, elections are rigged, and the government is unable to advance the public interest as a whole. In contrast, in a society wedded to the idea of civic virtue, the leaders are forced to show respect and regard for the larger common good. Indeed, the leaders in this setting become true servants of the people.

How, it might be asked, can a corrupted politics be turned into a new politics of civic virtue? Rousseau believed that the new economic system's worst tendencies could be countered. The key to doing so was through a form of civic education that taught individuals their duties, and taught them to make love for their country primary.[40] Rousseau believed that this objective, when properly taught, had tremendous power to reverse the ill effects of the money mentality. Once people possess a love for their country, they will be able to put the needs of the country ahead of self-interest. And, then, civic virtue will finally "reign."[41] Thus, if the objective of a corruption-free politics is to make people virtuous, then the best avenue for doing so is to teach people to maintain the canons of civic virtue, and this objective will be a major idea of the new social contract.

V. THE NEW SOCIAL CONTRACT AND THE NEW CIVIL SOCIETY

How did Rousseau expect to accomplish this goal? In his discussion of his new social contract in *On the Social Contract,* he hoped that human beings would be transformed by becoming a part of a community that was predicated upon common goals and values. Once in this community, individuals would no longer make their own private interests primary, but they would make the pursuit of the common good the most important dimension in their lives. What is the nature of this new community Rousseau had in mind? In this section, I would like to describe its central aspects in some detail.

That Rousseau is discussing a fundamental transformation of individuals from self-seeking individuals to community-minded citizens is made clear when Rousseau raises the following question. He asked how to

> *find a form of association which defends and protects with all common forces the person and goods of each associate, and by means of which each one, while uniting with all, nevertheless obeys only himself and remains as free as before?*[42]

Rousseau's answer was a new social contract that suggests that each individual must be willing to "alienate" (or turn over) all of one's rights to the community. And "since this condition is equal for everyone, no one has an interest in making it burdensome for the others."[43] Why would individuals embrace this kind of social arrangement? It is because they wish to define themselves as part of a collective organization and as such they are willing to submit, like all others, to the organization's common rules and objectives. What advantage would individuals have in doing this? Rousseau said that each person, "in giving himself to all, gives himself to no one"; that is, each person becomes governed by the same idea of the common good that is seen as benefiting all people, including, of course, one's self. No longer is any individual subordinated to the arbitrary power of another, but instead each person falls "under the supreme direction of the general will."[44]

Here, in making the general will the ground of one's life, individuals act toward each other as the natural moral feelings of primitive society had originally dictated they should. The general will symbolizes the commitment of individuals to give priority to the "general interest" or to the common good, as opposed to private interest.[45] Indeed, to maintain a community that is concerned for the needs of each person, each person must make his or her own private interests subservient to the general interest. What is required for this enterprise to work, however, is acceptance of certain understandings about society and politics, outlined in the rest of this section.

First, the general will is associated with the rights that people are to be provided. For Rousseau, rights emanate from the community's own definition of its needs. Locke had argued that each person had basic rights to life, liberty, and property. These rights are attached to each person by virtue of a person being a human being. For Rousseau, this view of rights tends to encourage individuals to think of themselves as empowered to do whatever they please. But when one realizes that one's rights emanate from the community one lives in, one understands not only that the community defines the nature of the rights one has, but associated with each right are the obligations, duties, and limits one must observe as a condition for having these rights. Rights signify not just individual freedom, but individual freedom in the context of civic virtue. Awareness of this fact is the basis for our being able to accord to others protection for their rights.

Also important is what the general will suggests for the nature of the political realm, and the approach people should take to issues there. It is in this realm that the common needs are defined with respect to those issues that broadly affect the lives of all persons. Rousseau's argument was that, because certain issues impact the lives of all citizens in major and significant ways, it is best to find a common approach to those issues, thus providing individuals with the same moral direction. Not all issues are general will issues, to be sure. Whether to put a stoplight on a certain street is not an issue that the whole society should consider because this issue affects only a small part of society. On the other hand, general will issues touch upon those things that all individuals understand to involve a common good. For instance, general will issues include matters such as how we define education policy, what should constitute our approach as a society to agriculture, what is the role to be given the police, what kind of national health care should we have, if any, and so on.

Citizens determine the nature of the common good by deliberating together in a legislative setting. Here, the citizens can make the laws that define what rights citizens will have and what corresponding duties citizens must uphold. The function of the executive is to carry out the will of the legislature and to make decisions pertaining to the application of legislative policies and principles to particular circumstances. This means, then, that the legislative power, "which belongs to the people and can belong to it alone,"[46] while it establishes the general policies and defines the common good in each issue area, leaves questions of implementation to the discretion of the executive.[47] Of course, the people acting as the legislative body can always respond to executive decisions it disagrees with. Thus, if the executive determines that a general right established by the legislative power should be applied in a certain way that the legislative power does not accept, the latter can rescind the actions of the executive.

Determining the stance on the major and most important issues rests with the people acting in their legislative function. For Rousseau, then, the "laws are merely the condition of the civil association. The populace that is subjected to the laws ought to be their author."[48] As people make their own laws, they become transformed from people who are exclusively and only accumulators of property and wealth, into people who as property holders are citizens, also. It is this transformation that creates a civil society. Rousseau said that the "passage from a state of nature to the civil state," or a *civil society,* "produces quite a remarkable change in man, for it substitutes justice for instinct in his behavior and gives his actions a moral quality they previously lacked."[49] In a civil society, each person learns to subordinate his own interests to the interests of the larger society, and this conduct is the basis for treating individuals as equals, with full respect and dignity. Real freedom is what Rousseau called "civil liberty," which emerges when individuals are equally willing to accommodate all aspects of life touched by the general will, to the general will.[50]

Unless people are able to make their own laws, Rousseau's transformation of property-holding individuals into citizens who respect the norms of the common good during the course of pursuing their own interests cannot occur, nor can civil society truly exist. For this reason, then, Rousseau did not accept the laws being made by the people's deputies or representatives as did Locke, and thus, for Rousseau, "any law that the populace has not ratified in person is null; it is not a law at all." For Rousseau, in a well-run society, "everyone flies to the assemblies."[51]

Still, Rousseau was aware that public deliberation might not, on all occasions, produce a consensus on the nature of the common good with respect to a particular area of concern. For instance, where people radically disagree with each other, as was the case when, as we saw, society became divided between the rich and the poor in Rousseau's account of inequality, it is possible that no matter how long people deliberated, they could not produce an agreement that served the needs of all members of the community. Where this kind of experience is pervasive, the deliberation might cause people to manifest destructive and hurtful passions toward each other, destroying any hope for a sustained general will.

Rousseau avoided this outcome because he envisioned deliberation as occurring in a much simpler context in which the variations in opinion are reduced in number and in degree of difference. People who approach matters from the common-sense perspective of ordinary persons, for Rousseau, do not hold widely divergent points of view, and thus they are never far from agreement. This is what Rousseau meant when he said that "peace, union, equality are enemies of political subtleties. Upright and simple men are difficult to deceive on account of their simplicity. Traps and clever pretexts do not fool them."[52] Rousseau had in mind peasants and simple, or ordinary, people making the law. "When, among the happiest people in the world, bands of peasants are seen regulating their affairs of state under an oak tree, and always acting wisely, can one help scorning the refinement of other nations, which make themselves illustrious and miserable with so much art and mystery?"[53]

But why is agreement likely among the people Rousseau described? Rousseau's society, as Charles Taylor says, is "bound together by a sentiment which is an extension of the joy that humans feels in each others' company."[54] In such a society, people share certain fundamental values, which create a unity of understanding and a basis for community. Owing to this fact, people do not approach life from widely diverse and contradictory moral perspectives. Society is not a setting in which some advocate a strong commitment to religion and others do not; where some promote a rural view of life and others an urban one; where some advocate an education in classical literature for all with the intention of making people into critical thinkers who question every tradition and where others prefer to remain uncritically obedient to existing traditions. These differences in viewpoint would shape the way people make judgments about public questions, and in consequence as people approached such questions from these different and radically opposed perspectives, their deliberations would likely always end in either stalemate or unhappy compromises.

We experience this problem quite often in contemporary society. There are many issues in today's world that cannot be resolved in a way that is satisfactory to all sides, and individuals on either side of these issues must tolerate outcomes that they do not morally accept. This situation often leads to social and political discord that is destructive of community feeling. Examples of issues that produce discord of this type include, for instance, gun control, abortion, affirmative action, and prayer in schools. But in Rousseau's society, because citizens have shared sentiments and values, they hold in common moral positions that are not far apart or contradictory; therefore, when these people discuss public questions agreement is more likely. Thus, Taylor is correct when he says that Rousseau's citizens are not destined to engage in "elaborate debate and deliberation."[55]

But Taylor's view should not be construed to suggest that Rousseau denied importance to *all* forms of deliberation among citizens as they engaged in the practices of self-government. That deliberation would not be elaborate does not mean it would not occur at all. Deliberation is the basis for citizens' making their own laws, and in the process of doing so, manifesting and maintaining the necessary civic virtue that allows individuals to uphold the commitment to the public good. But, still, as Taylor's argument seems to require, for the kind of deliberation to take place that Rousseau described, it is necessary to continue to maintain a basis for community among people by removing from society whatever prevents them from sharing common values and sentiments. Direct citizen involvement in determining the laws, the experience of democratic participation, could only succeed, then, if what causes a demise of a sense of solidarity among people could be eliminated. To this end, Rousseau discussed the conditions that are essential for the creation of the general will and continued citizen self-government.

Under what conditions are people ready for law making, Rousseau asked? Rousseau described conditions that encouraged the prospect of a strong sense of community among the members of the society, so that the members would be able to make laws that all could support. Conditions that contribute to such a setting would include, for instance, a situation in which each member of the society is known to other members; where existing customs and superstitions are not so deeply rooted that they cannot be modified to support a common basis for community; where no person is asked to shoulder a burden larger than he can handle; and where the society is free from foreign attack.[56]

Further, it would seem that among the most important conditions that contribute to creating among citizens a sense of community sufficient to ground law-making activity would be the need to prevent divisions arising from differences in wealth and property. Otherwise, the trust, so necessary to reaching agreement in a deliberation, would not be possible. To this end, individuals must learn to approach property acquisition from a standpoint of the need to use it to contribute to the interests of the whole community. Rousseau said that "in whatever way this acquisition is accomplished, each private individual's right to his very own store [of property] is always subordinate to the community's right to all, without which there could be neither solidity in the social fabric nor real force in the exercise of sovereignty."[57]

Were people to hold the view that their property entitles them to an amount of political influence proportionate to their property holdings, then a regime based on political inequality would once again become a primary factor in social life, citizens would lack trust in each other, and there would be no basis upon which to sustain public deliberations to determine the common good. Private interest would become the paramount concern, and it would deny any place of importance to the general will. And this perspective would promote policies that would no doubt maintain political inequality. "For by its nature the private will tends toward having preferences, and the general will tends toward equality."[58]

To make possible an attitude toward private property that permits individuals to act, not only as property holders, but also as citizens, it is necessary that property or wealth holdings among people be moderate in amount. Here, Rousseau took a cue from Aristotle who, as we saw earlier, in his conception of the polity advocated moderation in wealth. Rousseau said that no one should be so wealthy that he can buy another, nor so poor that he can be bought by another.[59] Moderation in wealth will limit the extent to which individuals will always focus upon achieving material success in the market. Rousseau's views of accumulation of wealth would be in direct contrast to the Lockean position that permitted wide and disproportionate distributions of wealth. For Rousseau, in the Lockean context, people become preoccupied with acquiring ever-larger amounts of wealth. Such a mentality would destroy all chances to establish the general will.

The context for the kind of community that made possible a deliberation to define the common good depends upon a society's ability to maintain the possibility of political equality. This is a situation in which all citizens, regardless of their social and economic backgrounds, would have an important say in determining the laws. But political equality depends upon more than the attitudes toward property or its distribution as just described. In addition, there is a need for leadership in the society, a leadership that helps citizens understand the essential issues at stake and to ponder them from the perspective of the need to find solutions that promote the common good or the general will.

For Rousseau, the general will is always right and tends to the "public utility." The problem, however, is that "the deliberations" among the people to make the laws do not always have "the same rectitude."[60] The average citizen is often tricked into taking actions that are harmful to the collective needs of the society. To avert this prospect, there is a need for leadership, in this case from the seasoned political veteran, the wise legislator. The legislator is an extraordinary individual who, with his powers of persuasion as opposed to compulsion, tries to frame the law-making deliberation in such a way as to convince people to embody into the laws that govern a community the idea of the common good. In undertaking this role, the legislator has the task of "changing human nature" and transforming "each individual (who by himself is a perfect and solitary whole) into a part of a larger whole from which this individual receives, in a sense, his life and his being; to alter man's constitution in order to strengthen it; to substitute a partial and moral existence for the physical and independent existence we have all received from nature."[61]

Maintaining the political equality that is so essential to citizen participation in government depends upon the possibility of a society in which citizens are capable of searching for the public interest as they discuss the issues before them. Where people do not have this capacity, then politics is turned into private-interest conflicts, with the winners' using public power to promote their own goals at a cost to the rest. Avoiding this outcome depends upon many things as we have seen, but clearly the leadership of the legislator is among the most important.

VI. ROUSSEAU'S THREAT TO CIVIL SOCIETY

As just indicated, democratic participation requires that the various factors causing divisiveness be eliminated. To this end, Rousseau instituted practices designed to maintain a strong sense of civic virtue and respect for the common good. But in doing so, does Rousseau provide sufficient protection for people from falling into a situation in which the demand to support the common good would become so strong that individuals would find themselves subject to a tyrannous community that defied the demands of individual liberty? Or in other terms, does Rousseau's approach to civil society eliminate any prospect of it? In this section, I would like to describe some of the factors that make attaining a civil society difficult for Rousseau.

Regarding voting, individuals may exercise their vote in determining the law, and the majority determines the outcome. Rousseau recognized, however, that people may not all agree before or during the voting process. Still, after the vote has been taken, each individual who disagrees with the outcome must change his view so that it supports the winning side.

> *Each man in giving his vote, states his opinion on this matter, and the declaration of the general will is drawn from counting the votes. When, therefore, the opinion contrary to mine prevails, this proves merely that I was in error, and that what I took to be the general will was not so. If my private opinion had prevailed, I would have done something other than what I had wanted. In that case, I would not have been free.*[62]

In a society filled with diverse associations, many groups, owing to their independent status, might disagree publicly with the result of the vote. In fact, groups that did disagree might want to challenge the results by fostering further discussion of the issues in question in the hope that, at a subsequent time, after further argument and after the introduction of more facts, the opinion of the citizens might be changed. But Rousseau would find this destructive of the general will. And in taking this position, Rousseau was arguing against private associations having an independently powerful political role in the society. But more important, his argument would seem to prevent individuals from demanding a reconsideration of a question, in the light of new facts or arguments. By taking this position, Rousseau's view would allow a majority to crush minority expression of opposing views.

Censorship is an important practice in Rousseau's civil society. In this case, censorship has to do with maintaining citizens' support for the appropriate public moral conceptions that support the philosophy of the general will. Rousseau said that the "opinions of a people arise from its constitution."[63] But where citizens become fascinated with ideas that take them away from the grounding moral conceptions of their society, the result is lack of commitment to citizen duties. Thus, Rousseau would have no trouble supporting the censorship of those kinds of materials that turn people into highly subjectivist, self-serving, and private individuals, no longer concerned with maintaining the common requirements of citizenship. For Rousseau, censorship is a necessary task, and those who lack the will to establish it certainly lack the toughness needed to maintain a sense of civic virtue and a concomitant dedication to the common good of the community. Moreover, once a sense of citizenship is lost, it is difficult, if not impossible, to restore. "It follows from this that the censorship can be useful for preserving mores, but never for reestablishing them."[64]

This does not mean that Rousseau outlawed, entirely, the private realm and the individual liberty associated with it; he merely hoped that the private realm would not kill in people a civic sensibility. Thus, individuals may think as they want to think, and they do not have to account for their views, but when their lives are touched by the requirements of the common good, they must accommodate their personal views to public needs. This point of view had a particularly important place for Rousseau in his discussion of religion. Rousseau said that "the dogmas of . . . religion are of no interest either to the state or its members, except to the extent that these dogmas relate to morality and to the duties which the one who professes them is bound to fill toward others. Each man can have in addition such opinions as he pleases, without it being any of the sovereign's business to know what they are."[65]

This viewpoint is part of what Rousseau referred to as the doctrines of a "civil religion," which all people, no matter what their particular religious affiliation might be, would be asked to support. The civil religion defines common values that help to maintain a sense of community and cohesion among the members of the society. What are the articles of a civil religion? Rousseau would have permitted certain basic religious doctrines such as the possibility of an afterlife, happiness for those who are just, and a benevolent deity. There is to be respect for the laws and the need to maintain the social contract. Also, Rousseau would exclude religious intolerance. As Rousseau said, "those who distinguish between civil and theological intolerance are mistaken . . . . These two types of intolerance are inseparable. It is impossible to live in peace with those one believes to be damned."[66] Individuals should be accorded freedom of religious belief, subject to the proviso that no one should treat another with intolerance based on differences in religious views.

Rousseau's conception of the values associated with a civil religion would on the surface appear acceptable, in part, to Locke. But Rousseau's approach to religious differences was not designed to support the live-and-let-live view of Locke as it was to make possible a basis for common values that could sustain a community's quest to define and to maintain the general good. Rousseau did not want religious differences to get in the way of this objective, so he hoped to take religious quarreling off the public agenda.

Now, this concern would certainly inform the way Rousseau would treat people who would continue to define the general good in ways different from the way the society as a whole defines it. People who persist in this regard would be violating the shared beliefs that help to create social unity, and such people can and should be banished. Here, for Rousseau, a society in creating a "civil religion" takes the view that the society "can banish him [a person who violates citizen norms] not for being impious but for being unsociable, for being incapable of sincerely loving the laws and justice, and of sacrificing his life, if necessary, for his duty."[67] This viewpoint would make it acceptable to excoriate those who for matters of conscience did not accept the concept of the general good. Instead of making a place for such persons, a place that would allow them to continue to question society's policies, it appears that Rousseau would remove them from society.

Given the foregoing, a separate sphere of associations, typical of civil societies (as discussed in Chapter 1), would not seem to be secured in Rousseau's society. Of course, it is possible that the common good of the whole society might be defined in such a way as to make such a sphere a reality. But what makes this arrangement unlikely is that Rousseau did not see a need for individuals to come together for the purpose of understanding radically different points of view on important moral questions. In a civil society people from diverse backgrounds join groups and work together within them for common purposes. Here, individuals come to appreciate difference. But this outcome of civil society would not be acceptable to Rousseau. He seeks a society where difference is minimized in the name of creating a context that would support the common good and the general will that flows from it. A civil society, in promoting difference, would undermine the new social contract. Indeed, when people come together in Rousseau's society, they do so to define common policies all can and should adhere to, and, if they are not willing to make this activity the main priority of their lives, they can then be called bad citizens and subject to banishment.

Making room for wide differences of life style and ideas would get in the way of this project for Rousseau. But respect for difference is fundamental to the freedom Hobbes and Locke sought, and respect for difference is pivotal to civil society. As we saw, under the civic virtue of mutual respect (as discussed in Chapter 1), people who hold quite different, but nonetheless reasonable, moral viewpoints must create ways for these different views to flourish side by side. In this setting, a shared approach to policy that all can uphold on the issues in question, say, abortion, prayer in the school, and so on, is not likely to emerge. Still, it is possible for people with different values and understandings to live together in peace when there is a sense of mutual respect among them strong enough to permit each to work with others to make an atmosphere that is respectful of all views possible.

But, whereas Rousseau had a strong commitment to maintain the elements of civic virtue that could help sustain among people a willingness to maintain support for the common good, he did not include in his view of civic virtue the notion of mutual respect as defined here. The reason he did not is that he did not need to. As we have seen, deliberation for Rousseau is based on shared beliefs that would eliminate radical differences in moral outlooks among people. And because such differences would not be present, mutual respect as a civic virtue would never be necessary. Further, if people manifested values widely different from those generally held by the society, these people would be excluded from the society. Rousseau's view of civil society would not support a liberal version (as discussed in Chapter 1), which tolerates wide diversity.

VII. RESPONSE AND REJOINDER

For Rousseau, the main problem of modern life is that society has been so corrupted by a conniving mentality, designed to obtain status and wealth that the basis for fairness, located in a natural, moral sensibility for the welfare of others, has been lost. Rousseau thus wanted to recreate the ground of society in a general will, or a conception of the common good that each individual in the society agrees to uphold. In maintaining the common good, individuals in the new social setting act by a commitment not to harm others, just as they did in the state of nature. The difference between the state of nature and the new society Rousseau hoped to create is now clear. Unlike in the state of nature where individuals show concern for each other from a natural, moral sensibility, in the new society of Rousseau's social contract such concern is a by-product of citizenship activity on behalf of the common good.

But if society has destroyed the natural, moral sensibility in individuals, how is respect for the new social contract and for the general moral will upon which it rests ever to be regained? In other terms, Locke might ask Rousseau to explain the basis for supporting the general will in a society in which a natural, moral sensibility is lacking. Rousseau could argue in response that support for the general will emanates from realistic, practical reasoning. Individuals recognize that, in the absence of supporting a society based on the general will, it is clear that society would be torn to shreds by civil war and strife. But individuals need society to supply them with the myriad goods that satisfy basic and fundamental needs. Given both these understandings, individuals realize that there is no alternative but to support the general will and to make it the mainstay of their common lives. Here, it would seem that Rousseau echoed Hobbes, who argued that the basis for civil society, based on the rule of law, is the need to achieve peace so that society is able to function in ways that serve the needs of individuals.

But this argument suggests a motivation that stands at the center of Locke's thought, also: namely the desire for happiness. Given that this is the case, how, Locke might ask, does Rousseau differ from himself? In response, Rousseau would argue that happiness is never achieved except in a society governed by the strong commitment to civic virtue, a commitment represented best in the general will. Here, a happy life is one in which individuals learn to constrain their self-interested pursuits so that their lives conform to the needs of the community. Rousseau would argue, then, that happiness is not denied a place in his society, but that he had in mind a different sort of happiness than that found in Locke. The latter's happiness, for Rousseau, derives solely from self-interested pursuits. Rousseau celebrated, on the other hand, the type of happiness that evolves from participation in and a sense of contribution to upholding the common good of a community. And the importance of the idea of the general will is that it symbolizes this distinction, and thus the general will is a powerful statement for it.

Locke might respond by arguing that the idea of the general will is really not as commanding as Rousseau thinks. In fact, many people will not trust it. Locke would argue that what he tried to do was to give people the freedom to choose their own course in life, within the context of rational norms and rules that we have referred to as civic virtues. This type of freedom leaves with each individual the question as to what one wishes to do with one's life. But Rousseau in contrast, by making people subscribe to the norms of the common good, must dictate to each person what one's life is to be about. The type of liberty advocated by the general will is, for Locke, prescriptive of what people should do, and it suggests the need for an authoritarian state that can force people to be "good."

Rousseau would counter that Locke's attitude only continues to show why Locke's individuals will never be citizens; they will remain only property holders who make the protection of their own property the only issue in politics. A society such as Locke's, where people live by rules that permit them to gain as much wealth as possible, can never be a society free from political inequality. Locke's civil society, as a result, will consist of people trying to obtain wealth in order to gain as much political influence as they can. This kind of society, however, will cause the erosion of the natural moral sensibilities, thus bringing to existence for Rousseau the individual as the beast that Rousseau loathed.

The differences between Locke and Rousseau recall the current debate between those advocating a strong conception of democracy, such as Rousseau's, and those advocating a doctrine of liberal civil society, with a strong commitment to individual rights, such as Locke's. For Locke, Rousseau's position suggests a view of democratic participation that represents a continuing threat to protecting individual rights. Rights, as Locke saw them, enable people to pursue ways of life that individuals choose for themselves. But these ways of life are always pursued within a setting of a common commitment to basic rules and laws that limit conduct so that the rights of all people can be protected. But where the democratically determined common good is made the predominant objective in society, as in the argument of Rousseau, anyone who stands in the way of its realization must for the sake of common good be banished. Obviously, in this situation, individual rights, such as freedom of conscience and thought, might be placed in jeopardy, all in the name of a very strong commitment to a far-reaching view of democracy.

What counts as good citizenship for those who uphold the liberal view of civil society, as first discussed in Chapter 1, is a willingness to endorse the civic virtues of toleration and mutual respect during the course of pursuing one's goals in life. These virtues secure individual rights. Obviously, Locke, a great advocate of toleration, would embrace at least partially this liberal view of civil society. However, those who support Rousseau's position interpret the reliance on individual rights as, at times, promoting individual self-interest, and this doctrine denies the prospect of a form of citizenship in which individuals are able to sacrifice their own particular interests for the sake of realizing the common good.

Hobbes might seek the last word by contending that neither Locke nor Rousseau can secure citizens' happiness. And the reason is simple. Locke's government, which requires a separation of powers format, is too weak and divided to protect people's basic rights. For Hobbes, Rousseau's government, which is based upon the deliberation of citizens, would be either too weak to protect people's rights or so strong and committed to the canons of the common good that it would threaten rights in general.

Rousseau would have rejected Hobbes's view with great force, pointing out that the best route to citizenship and to respect for civic virtue lies not with Hobbes's Leviathan but with the sense of responsibility gained from participating in making the laws by which one lives. Rousseau would argue that both Hobbes and Locke promote, in their individualism, the fragmentation of society by urging people to associate freedom with the right to deny the importance of those values that undergird a sense of belonging to a society that promotes the common good. For Rousseau, the tragedy of modern life, embellished by Locke and Hobbes, is that our natural moral sentiments are silenced in favor of the values that urge us to deny any importance to community and to civic virtue, as we extol wealth and self-interest.

Endnotes

1. On this point, see Sabine, *A History of Political Theory,* p. 580.

2. Roger D. Masters, "Introduction" to Jean-Jacques Rousseau, *Discourse On the Question Proposed by the Academy of Dijon: Has the Restoration of the Sciences and Arts Tended to Purify Morals?* in *The First and Second Discourses,* edited by Roger D. Masters (New York: St. Martin's Press, 1964), pp. 4–5, 9.

3. Jean-Jacques Rousseau, *Discourse On the Question Proposed by the Academy of Dijon: Has the Restoration of the Sciences and Arts Tended to Purify Morals?,* p. 51.

4. Ibid., p. 54.

5. Ibid., p. 56.

6. Jean-Jacques Rousseau, *Émile,* translated by Barbara Foxly, (New York: Dutton, 1969), p. 174.

7. Jean-Jacques Rousseau, *Discourse on the Origin and Foundations of Inequality Among Men in On the Social Contract,* translated by Donald A. Cress, (Indianapolis: Hackett Publishing Company, 1983), p.

147. All references to *On the Social Contract* and *Discourse on Political Economy* will be in this book, too.

8. Rousseau, *Émile,* p. 174. Elsewhere Rousseau says, "the first impulses of nature are always right; there is no original sin in the human heart . . . the only natural passion is self-love or selfishness taken in the wider sense," p. 56.

9. Ibid., pp. 174–75.

10. Ibid., pp. 181–82.

11. Rousseau, *Discourse on the Origin and Foundations of Inequality Among Men,* p. 118.

12. Ibid., p. 118.

13. Ibid., p. 115.

14. Ibid., p. 135. Italics are in the text.

15. Ibid., p. 137.

16. Ibid., p. 136.

17. Ibid., p. 126.

18. Ibid., pp. 128–29.

19. Ibid., pp. 141–42.

20. Ibid., p. 142.
21. Ibid., p. 142.
22. Ibid., pp. 142–43.
23. Ibid., p. 143.
24. Ibid., p. 143.
25. Ibid., pp. 143–44.
26. Ibid., pp. 144–45.
27. Ibid., p. 145.
28. Ibid., p. 145.
29. Ibid., p. 146.
30. Ibid., pp. 146–47.
31. Ibid., p. 147.
32. Ibid., p. 147.
33. Ibid., p. 147.
34. Ibid., pp. 148–49.
35. Ibid., pp. 149–50.
36. Ibid., p. 150.
37. J.-J. Rousseau, *The Government of Poland,* translated. Willmoore Kendall, (New York: Bobbs-Merrill, 1972), p. 69.
38. Ibid., p. 67.
39. Rousseau, *Discourse on Political Economy,* p. 172.
40. Ibid., p. 173.
41. Ibid., p. 171.
42. Rousseau, *On the Social Contract,* p. 24, I:6.
43. Ibid., p. 24, I:6.
44. Ibid., p. 24, I:6. Italics are in text.
45. Ibid., p. 31, II:3.
46. Ibid., p. 49, III:1.
47. Ibid., pp. 49–50, III:1.
48. Ibid., p. 38, II:6.
49. Ibid., p. 26, I:8.
50. Ibid., p. 27, I:8.
51. Ibid., p. 74, III:15.
52. Ibid., p. 79, IV:1.
53. Ibid., p. 79, IV:1.
54. Charles Taylor, *Sources of the Self,* (Cambridge: Harvard University Press, 1989), p. 360.
55. Ibid., p. 360.
56. Rousseau, *On the Social Contract,* pp. 45–46, II:10.
57. Ibid., p. 29, I:9.
58. Ibid., p. 30, II:1.
59. Ibid., p. 46, II:11.
60. Ibid., p. 31, II:3.
61. Ibid., p. 39, II:7; also p. 40, II:7.
62. Ibid., p. 82, IV:2.
63. Ibid., p. 95, IV:7.
64. Ibid., p. 95, IV:7.
65. Ibid., p. 102, IV:8.
66. Ibid., p. 102, IV:8.
67. Ibid., p. 102, IV:8.

Partial Bibliography and Further Reading

Bloom, Harold. Edited. *Jean-Jacques Rousseau.* New York: Chelsea House, 1988.

Blum, Carol. *Rousseau and The Republic of Virtue: The Language of Politics in the French Revolution.* Ithaca: Cornell University Press, 1986.

Cooper, Laurence D. *Rousseau, Nature, and the Problem of the Good Life.* University Park, Pa.: Pennsylvania State University Press, 1999.

Crocker, Lester G. *Rousseau's Social Contract: An Interpretive Essay.* Cleveland: Press of Case Western Reserve University, 1968.

Fralin, Richard. *Rousseau and Representation: A Study of the Development of His Concept of Political Institutions.* New York: Columbia University Press, 1978.

Kelly, Christopher. *Rousseau's Exemplary Life: The Confessions as Political Philosophy.* Ithaca: Cornell University Press, 1987.

Levine, Andrew. *The Politics of Autonomy: A Kantian Reading of Rousseau's Social Contract.* Amherst: University of Massachusetts Press, 1976.

Masters, Roger D. "Introduction" to Jean-Jacques Rousseau, *Discourse On the Question Proposed by the Academy of Dijon: Has the Restoration of the Sciences and Arts Tended to Purify Morals?* in *The First and Second Discourses,* New York: St. Martin's Press, 1964.

Melzer, Arthur, M. *The Natural Goodness of Man: On the System of Rousseau's Thought.* Chicago: University of Chicago Press, 1990.

Miller, Jim. *Rousseau: Dreamer of Democracy.* New Haven: Yale University Press, 1984.

O'Hagan, Timothy. *Rousseau.* London. New York: Routledge, 1999.

Shklar, Judith N. *Men and Citizens: A Study of Rousseau's Social Theory.* Cambridge: Cambridge University Press, 1969.

Taylor, Charles. *Sources of the Self.* Cambridge: Harvard University Press, 1989.

Weiss, Penny A. *Gendered Community: Rousseau, Sex, and Politics.* New York: New York University Press, 1993.

10

KANT: CIVIL SOCIETY
AND INTERNATIONAL ORDER

I. PUBLIC REASON

Immanuel Kant (1724–1804) had, unlike Rousseau, great admiration for the Enlightenment. Why is this experience so important to Kant? An answer to this question can be gleaned from Kant's demand for protecting intellectual freedom against those whose values threaten such freedom. Kant would complement the work of Hobbes and Locke, who each sought to predicate human life on the basis of the truth made possible by reason. And the central truth upon which to base life for each of these writers is the need to secure freedom for each individual. Indeed, a civil society for Kant as well as for Hobbes and Locke is a rule of law setting designed to achieve equal freedom for each individual. Necessarily, for Kant as for Hobbes and Locke, then, traditions need to be assessed both in terms of how well they promote the progress of reason, of truth, and of freedom.

For instance, Kant criticized those members of the clergy who mandate religious doctrines in order to exercise "guardianship" over the minds of others. By doing so, the religious authorities restrict or deny the "public use of one's reason." By the use of this phrase, Kant sought the kind of public reasoning that could be used to discuss openly and critically policies and laws that affect many areas of social and political life. The public use of reason, or what will also be called *public reason,* allows people to discuss important questions, and it is through this activity that people are able to expand their knowledge and "progress in general enlightenment."[1] In effect, then, Kant was making a plea for what we today refer to as critical thinking, or the need to learn how to use one's reasoning skills to examine propositions and evidence, with the overall intention of expanding the knowledge base of society.

So given the interest in public reasoning, what is involved for people engaged in the activities associated with the public use of reason? For Kant public reasoning is bound by certain rules of communication. What is the nature of these rules? Or, in other terms, what rules or authoritative standards should we follow as we engage in public reason and communicate with each other and think critically about public matters? It is necessary to make these rules of communication clear so that the Enlightenment Kant lauds can be clarified.

In the first place, to engage in public reason, a person must liberate oneself from one's "self-incurred tutelage," or one's reliance upon others who are allowed to shape their own views.[2] The first rule one should follow, then, is that each person should "think for oneself," and this rule, or what Kant called "enlightenment," suggests the need for an individual's "deliverance from superstition." The latter only places us under the control of others, who impose their thoughts on us and force us to accept their beliefs without question. The importance of this rule is that it establishes the legitimacy of comparative thinking. In particular, in order for persons to formulate their views, they must test them against, and compare them with, the views held by others. But where all views are the same, as is the case when people do not think for themselves and accept whatever way of thinking is imposed onto them, this objective cannot be met.[3]

The second important rule of public reason is what Kant referred to as the maxim of "enlarged thought." This rule is the basis for establishing with others a common and universal viewpoint that one may use for assessing one's own opinions and judgments and for searching with others for public approaches to shared concerns. What is the universal standpoint and how is it attained? Take the last question first. The basis for such a standpoint is not a point of view that transcends human discourse, say in some imagined and unreal perspective found outside the experience of society, but, instead, a common standpoint arises as people try to understand each other's views in as full a way as possible. As we communicate with others with this intention, we expand our range of understanding so that we are able to gain a comprehensive perspective on the matters under discussion.[4] Thus, the common standpoint is as full and as educated an understanding as is possible of an issue or question at hand, and obviously this standpoint transcends the boundaries of ordinary prejudice. All people have to do to achieve this expanded, or what Kant calls "enlarged," understanding, is to open themselves to the views of others. People accomplish this objective by not allowing their own "subjective private conditions" to dictate their own thoughts. The result of this enterprise is that each person is able to place himself "at the standpoint of others."[5]

The third rule to follow in making possible the public use of reason is to "think consistently."[6] Here, individuals must constantly be governed, as a matter of habit, by the first two rules. In particular, individuals must not allow prejudice to determine their thinking, and individuals must constantly seek to understand the views of others during the course of achieving a common standpoint from which to make judgments about issues. Presumably, when people follow these rules and deliberate with others in a way that maintains them, it will be possible to uphold the *civic virtue of mutual respect,* discussed in Chapter 1.

But why should people adopt these rules and make them a primary basis for their communication with each other and thus for securing the public use of reason? Kant's moral philosophy is designed to address this question. Kant's moral philosophy argued that each of us should live by a *categorical imperative,* which requires that each person in society be treated as an end, and not solely as a means. In treating people as ends, we are to respect their freedom, and we are not to make people serve as a means to the various projects of others or of ourselves. By communicating with others in the way required by the rules just elaborated we thus accommodate ourselves to the imperative to treat others as ends during the course of public reasoning. Indeed, it would appear that the categorical imperative, in obligating us to treat others as ends and not as means, would require us to conduct our interactions with others in such a way as to uphold the standards of communication that Kant defined for securing the public use of reason.[7]

Now, in order to make possible the kind of communication among people that allows them to treat others as ends and to consider fully their views, there are certain institutions and ways of life that must be established. The most obvious public institution in this regard is a commitment to permit people an "unlimited freedom to use [their] own reason to speak in [their] own person."[8] A truly free person seeks full liberation from all elements that blunt or destroy his ability to cast off the hindrances to thinking, in order to define with others those common, reasonable standards that all can respect. Clearly, given the need for freedom, it would follow that the public use of reason can take place only in a society that guarantees this freedom. And the only kind of society that does is a civil society, because only a civil society assures each person the basic rights needed to engage in an enlightened discourse.

In the next several sections, my discussion of Kant's political theory is designed to demonstrate how the principle of the need to treat others as ends can be given concrete expression. Here, I demonstrate the way the expression of this principle is manifested in both the domestic institutions of a civil society and in international relations among states that maintain the atmosphere of peace necessary to secure a civil society. In doing so, I demonstrate the institutions that support a society committed to maintain the public use of reason. The first step in addressing this objective is to discuss further Kant's notion of the categorical imperative by demonstrating how Kant derives this basic moral duty from reason and makes this principle primary to his own system of politics. To this end, it is necessary to describe Kant's understanding of *practical reason*.

II. The Process of Practical Reason

For Kant, the term *practical reason* is used to signify the employment of reason to determine the moral concepts and principles by which individuals should conduct their affairs in public, including political and social settings. Thinking or reasoning in keeping with this commitment really is designed to address a particular question. What is that question? Kant said,

> *ask yourself whether, if the action which you propose should take place by a law of nature of which you yourself were a part, you could regard it as possible through your will. Everyone does, in fact, decide by this rule whether actions are morally good or bad. Thus people ask: if one belonged to such an order of things that anyone would allow himself to deceive when he thought it to his advantage, or felt justified in shortening his life as soon as he were thoroughly weary of it, or looked with complete indifference on the needs of others, would he assent of his own will to be a member of such an order of things?*[9]

Kant believed that the way to determine universally valid moral concepts was to ask which norms all rational individuals would consider to be universally binding. Here, in determining the moral bases for conduct, one is to ask oneself what is the moral course not only for oneself but also for all rational people. When one takes this approach to determining the basis for action, one can determine moral norms that all rational persons would agree should ground actions. Thus, for Kant, no one who is rational would accept deception as a proper course in life, nor would such a person opt for suicide when times were difficult. Further, a rational individual would not accept that one should allow one's talents and abilities to go undeveloped, nor would such an individual manifest a complete absence of concern for the needs of others.[10]

These examples of moral duties derived from practical reason suggest a larger, more encompassing truth; in particular, for Kant there is a universal duty to uphold a fundamental moral principle, called the *categorical imperative.* The categorical imperative says that we are to act *"only on that maxim through which you can at the same time will that it should become a universal law."*[11]

Kant thought that his conception of the categorical imperative provided a precise statement pertaining to the way individuals should conduct themselves as they interact with each other. How is this possible? Principally, the categorical imperative is based on the principle of noncontradiction. This means that a moral norm specifies a way of life that never contradicts itself. Alternatively, some proposed moral norms would be contradictory were one to follow them, and, therefore, they should not be used. For instance, the norm of promising to repay money does not suggest a way of life that contains serious contradictions. But the notion of refusing to repay promised money does. This distinction, for Kant, is clear on its face. If the notion of promising permitted me to not repay money I promised to another, then "no one would believe that anything was promised him, but would ridicule all such statements as vain pretenses."[12]

Further, the categorical imperative, in requiring that we live by norms that are not contradictory, provides a basis for defining the specific, concrete duties we each should adhere to. And these duties indicate a clear outline of the kinds of conduct with which we are to treat each other. Thus, Kant said that the universal moral law requires that any moral norm we adopt as the basis for our action be designed so as to *treat others as ends in themselves, and not as a means to the ends of others.*[13]

In specifying the need to treat others as ends as a universal duty, Kant's intention was to define a principle that all are to follow throughout the course of their lives. To do so, the various ways by which this principle is to be manifested must be clearly outlined. Kant hoped to give this principle concrete expression not only in the definition of our duties, but in the various social and political institutions that enable each of us as well as the society as a whole to treat people as ends and not as means.

In the first place, then, Kant sought to demonstrate the actual duties individuals must uphold in order to accord others the dignity they deserve. To this end, he distinguished ethical from juridical duties. Ethical duties, which embody the requirement to treat others as ends, include duties such as not lying, developing our capacities to the fullest extent, and showing benevolence to others as we relate to them. In our day-to-day conduct, we are to demonstrate "dispositions" that include "self-constraint" or "virtue" by making these duties the basis of our actions. The rules for communication with others, which we elaborated upon earlier, would seem to fall under the category of ethical duties, since they describe how we should communicate with each other during the course of attempting to make possible the public use of our reason. Juridical duties, on the other hand, are legally binding rules imposed from the outside by legitimate political authority.[14] These duties, too, embody the commitment to treat others as ends, and, as we will see in the discussion of civil society, juridical duties are adhered to through externally imposed constraints, as opposed to, in the case of ethical duties, moral dispositions that are self-maintained and self-enforced restraints. In particular, juridical duties refer to those rules that must be followed in order to protect the same rights and freedom for each person.

We more fully demonstrate Kant's effort to embody his key moral principle of treating people as ends into the main institutions of civil society in the next section. Before proceeding, it is well to point out, as a way to anticipate our discussion of Hegel in the next chapter, that Hegel did not think that Kant had done an adequate job demonstrating the nature of actual institutions and practices that embodied Kant's central, governing moral principle. Indeed, Hegel's hope was to achieve what he thought Kant failed to attain: namely, a description of the institutions and practices that properly carry into practice Kant's hope to make genuine freedom possible.

III. KANT'S CIVIL SOCIETY

Kant's civil society is designed to achieve freedom for each person through the rule of law. A civil society is based upon the existence of laws, established and maintained by a constitution, to secure the rights of all citizens. The state in a civil society is to uphold the laws that protect the rights of people.[15] In accepting the authority of the state, then, individuals maintain a basis for securing their rights, and it is principally for this reason that they enter civil society. Affording people basic rights is in keeping with the key Kantian principle that states that individuals are to treat each other as ends. This is the case because Kant believed that in a civil society individuals are treated as ends only when they have equal liberty, but clearly the latter is not possible so long as individuals do not have equal basic rights. Thus, for Kant the "universal principle of right" is that "every action which by itself or by its maxim enables the freedom of each individual's will to coexist with the freedom of everyone else in accordance with a universal law is *right.*"[16]

Moreover, in a civil society, the principle of equal liberty is achieved with the proper use of coercion. This means that individuals have equal liberty to others only when there are juridical constraints in place; that is, legally binding laws that use coercion to ensure that people do not act as a "hindrance to freedom" or as an obstacle to others' having the rights they deserve.[17] The laws must be designed to maintain a form of "reciprocal coercion," by which Kant meant that each person is to be equally governed by rules and made subject to constraints, whose only purpose is to protect the freedom of all persons, equally. Of course, some people might do as the law requires because of an awareness of obligations they owe to others under the law, or what might be referred to as a sense of duty. Still, Kant did not want to predicate the protection of equal liberty upon a sense of duty but only upon the possibility of external coercion, which ensures that all uphold the laws that extend rights to all people.[18]

But why is coercion necessary at all? Why would not rational people accept that they have ethical duties and adapt themselves, voluntarily, to the norms that uphold the rights of others? Kant believed that, even though a civil society is founded on the central idea to protect the liberty of each person in an equal way, still, it is likely that individuals will be motivated in their day-to-day activities by nonmoral factors, such as the pushes and pulls of interest and desire. Kant is more like Hobbes than like Locke on this point. Locke's state of nature demonstrates that individuals are rational, and they accept constraints needed to secure rights. But Hobbes did not harbor a similar optimism, and *his* state of nature is a state of *war.* For Kant, then, like Hobbes, the actual motive for acting as one should is fear of punishment. People do as morality requires, then, but not always from moral motivations. Thus, a civil society is an important device that furthers the purposes of practical reason or morality, even among individuals who for the most part may not themselves be motivated to act as reason demands. In this context, Kant said "each individual can be free so long as I do not interfere with his freedom by my *external actions,* even although his freedom may be a matter of total indifference to me or although I may wish in my heart to deprive him of it."[19]

Moreover, coercion is not the only way by which to ensure compliance with the norms of moral law; in particular, respect for the rights of others. In addition, Kant suggested that in a "civic society," the various interests come to be arranged in such a way that each interest is able to check and limit the influence of others. In this way, a context arises in which no single individual or group of individuals has so much power that the rights of others might be threatened. This situation is "one in which there is mutual opposition among the members, together with the most exact definition of freedom and fixing of its limits so that it may be consistent with the freedom of others."[20] In this arrangement, individuals are able to preserve a "civic union" in which each realizes the importance of others in making possible a society in which all benefit.[21] Kant said that even a race of "intelligent devils" should be able to achieve this social organization.

> *Given a multitude of rational beings requiring universal laws for their preservation, but each of whom is secretly inclined to exempt himself from them, [the hope is] to establish a constitution in such a way that although their private intentions conflict, they check each other, with the result that their public conduct is the same as if they had no such intentions.*[22]

Despite Kant's rather Hobbesian view of human nature, it is important to note that Kant did not accept Hobbes's unitary form of state in which the major powers were located together in one branch of government. Instead, Kant accepted a state that includes Locke's separation-of-powers view.[23] By dividing up the tasks of a government in a civil society into separate branches—the executive, the legislative, and the judicial—no single element of government can become so powerful that it is able to threaten the liberty of any single citizen. As for Locke, the legislative power would be the supreme power, for it is referred to as the *ruling power,* whereas the executive is the individual who is to govern in keeping with the law. The legislative power is to make laws that are just for all people, and thus the legislature would no doubt have the responsibility for protecting the basic rights of all citizens.[24] Indeed, Kant said that, in any true republic, it is the *"representative system* of the people whereby the people's rights are looked after on their behalf by deputies who represent the united will of the citizens."[25] Here, it would seem that, like Locke, Kant did not want a state whose powers would be as potentially unchecked as was the case in Hobbes's view of the state in civil society.

For Kant, then, mechanisms are in place in a civil society that enable individuals to subordinate their interests to the larger requirement to protect the same rights for all people.

Individuals are willing to support the practices and institutions of a state that maintains this objective, even as they are more personally committed to make certain that their own interests are given priority. Why and on what basis would individuals, who are so motivated to realize their material interests, embrace this idea of civil society?

IV. NATURE'S SECRET PLAN

Kant's answer to this question arises from his approach to interpreting the meaning of history. History, when viewed only from the standpoint of individuals (each of whom lives according to his own inclinations) would suggest a world that was incapable of achieving a civil society. Each person would be content only with pursuing his or her own interests, without concern for establishing a society committed to the provision of equal freedom. But Kant believed that moral progress was inescapable and that, on this view, each human life can be seen as contributing to the rational end of equal freedom. Given this perspective on society, then, even the experience of self-interest was somehow a contributing part to the larger progress that made possible the equal freedom and rights that a civil society secures. The natural course of human development does not unfold by mere chance, for Kant, but by the "guiding thread" of reason, and, in consequence, all individuals work to help realize the larger goals of reason, even if they are unaware of doing so. Thus, when we view history from Kant's progressive perspective, it is possible to write a scenario that demonstrates the likely development of humankind from the earliest beginnings in a state of nature in which humankind is dependent upon pure instinct and desire, to the later development of culture, where rational laws and civil society frame human encounters.[26]

Kant's interpretation of the course of history resembles Hobbes's view of the evolution of civil society from the state of nature. Kant assumed that human beings in the state of nature manifest toward each other a kind of mutual antagonism that threatens to destroy society. Kant called this experience the condition of "unsocial sociability." The natural desire of humankind is for each person to "have everything go according to his own wish."[27] Instead of threatening life, however, this natural yearning helps to make people more resilient and creative. The experience of others posing a danger to one's existence awakens in persons all the basic powers that might otherwise have lain hidden. Here, individuals, in the face of the many dangers confronting them, learn to harness all the energies needed to ensure their survival.[28]

With this new-found awareness, individuals gradually become enlightened enough to begin to appreciate the importance of creating a society that is a "moral whole" or a society in which each is no longer threatened by others.[29] People then move from a condition in which they live at the mercy of one another, to a situation in which they live in social settings that facilitate the attainment of higher purposes. The "higher purposes" of life are in keeping with the dictates of morality, or respect for the constraints that protect other people's freedom. In this new situation, individuals discover that "civic freedom can hardly be infringed without evil consequences being felt in all walks of life."[30] The condition of "unsocial sociability" is really, then, a gift of nature, for, in reacting to the negative features of this condition in order to survive, people create higher forms of life that not only provide security, but civility as well. Kant said, "thanks be to Nature, then, for the incompatibility, for heartless competitive vanity, for the insatiable desire to possess and to rule! Without them, all the excellent natural capacities of humanity would forever sleep, undeveloped."[31]

On this reading of history, however, people never completely overcome their selfishness. Thus, it is the case that people discover the need to be under a "master," because even though people realize the need for laws that limit freedom as a way to protect it, it is the case that selfishness tempts people to find ways to "exempt" themselves from such laws. To counter this tendency, people need laws that will "force" them to uphold a commitment to protect the rights of all people. Thus, for Kant, each person will "always abuse his freedom if he has none above him to exercise force in accord with the laws."[32] A civil society is needed, then, to provide the laws that regulate the lives of each person in such a way that one's selfish nature does not interfere with the requirements of maintaining a civil order, a way of life based on the need to respect the freedom of others. Respecting others' freedom, a major and great *civic virtue,* becomes embodied in society when there is a "correct constitution," which supports a civil society, as well as a "good will ready to accept such a constitution."[33]

Presumably, then, history unfolds in a way that allows individuals to recognize the fundamental importance of a need to live under the constitution of a civil society. Given this evolution of culture, people who are "crooked wood" from which "nothing perfectly straight can be built,"[34] realize that, all along, nature was seeking to realize its "secret plan," that of making people subordinate to the truths of morality and reason.[35] Here, individuals become enlightened enough to understand the importance to their lives of a civil society, and in consequence are quite willing to give their allegiance to institutions that protect the rights of all persons equally. A civil society is seen as an environment in which individuals, who are prone to act from self-interest, will, owing to the coercive force of public laws that protect the rights of all, act toward each other in ways *as if* they were committed to maintaining throughout their lives the moral law.

There is another realization that accompanies the idea of civil society as well. Civil societies represent a moral order that cannot be sustained so long as nations are continually committed to preparing for or engaging in war. States that seek to expand their power through war divert resources from the kind of education that improves the minds of citizens and that makes possible respect for morality.[36] As a result of war's actual or potential devastation, then, individuals conclude that it is best to enter into a "league of nations," committed to peace and to an international environment that ends war.[37]

V. THE NEW WORLD ORDER:
A FEDERATION OF CIVIL SOCIETIES

Kant's intention, then, was to help advance the cause of civil societies by demonstrating a way to make peaceful relationships possible among states. There are two steps in the process. The first step is to accept certain basic or what he called "preliminary articles for perpetual peace among states." They include the following: "no treaty of peace shall be held valid in which there is tacitly reserved matter for a future war, . . . no independent states, large or small, shall come under the dominion of another state by inheritance, exchange, purchase, or donation, . . . standing armies . . . shall in time be totally abolished,

. . . national debts shall not be contracted with a view to the external friction of states, . . . no state shall by force interfere with the constitution or government of another state," and "no state shall, during war, permit such acts of hostility which would make mutual confidence in the subsequent peace impossible."[38]

These basic articles are not in themselves sufficient to secure a lasting and enduring peace among nations. In addition, there are the "definitive articles for perpetual peace among states." Taken together, both the preliminary and definitive articles of peace suggest that even if the natural condition among states is war, this condition can be defeated if an environment is created that encourages civil societies to flourish on a worldwide basis.[39] We turn now to the definitive articles of peace.

The first definitive article is that the "civil constitution of every state should be republican."[40] As seen earlier, the legislative branch was the most important branch of government. Kant believed that, in a republican regime, citizens make the laws through their representatives, and, since citizens are desirous of securing their rights, they instruct their representatives to make laws that protect their rights. Moreover, because citizens have such an important place in the law-making process, no republican regime can engage in war without the consent of the citizens. And, since average citizens are most affected by war and it is they who have to pay for it or fight in it, it will be less likely that in a republican regime there will be a war tendency. Kant said "if the consent of the citizens is required in order to decide that war should be declared . . . nothing is more natural than that they would be very cautious in commencing such a poor game, decreeing for themselves all the calamities of war."[41]

The second definitive article for perpetual peace is that "the law of nations shall be founded on a federation of free states."[42] Of critical importance to making this framework of peace possible is the absolute commitment on the part of nations to end war. In effect, nations must take an oath that says that "there ought to be no war among us . . . [and instead of war] we want to establish a supreme legislative, executive, and judiciary power which will reconcile our differences peaceably."[43] Why would a state join such a federation? Kant believed that, as societies became republics, there would be an inherent interest in avoiding war, and this interest would help to propel such states into alliance with other states who similarly wanted to avoid war. Kant said, "for if fortune directs that a powerful and enlightened people can make itself a republic, which by its nature must be inclined to perpetual peace, this gives a fulcrum to the federation with other states so that they may adhere to it and thus secure freedom under the idea of the law of nations. By more and more such associations, the federation may be gradually extended."[44] The federation or "league of peace" would end all wars among member states. Moreover, member states would achieve this objective without threatening their sovereignty. Thus, "this league does not tend to any domination over the power of the state but only to the maintenance and security of the freedom of the state itself and of other states in league with it, without there being any need for them to submit to civil laws and their compulsion, as men in a state of nature must submit."[45]

The third definitive article states: "the law of world citizens shall be limited to conditions of universal hospitality."[46] Citizens from one state will be able to move freely into other states and exchange ideas and engage in business opportunities. Whereas states will not extend citizenship status to visitors from other states, each state will extend to foreign visitors full respect and dignity. For Kant, hospitality would no doubt cultivate a "spirit of commerce" that is "incompatible with war," and that "sooner or later gains the upper hand in every state."[47]

These articles of peace suggest that individuals look at the world from two standpoints: namely, as members of their particular home state, possessing legal citizenship status, and as citizens of the world, possessing a moral responsibility to maintain an international order that can sustain civil societies everywhere. As citizens of particular states, they are to uphold the laws and interests of their own nations. But, at the same time, these individuals are also citizens of the world, and, as such, they must see to it that their own state maintains its commitment to the principles of a peaceful international order, lest it find itself outside the family of nations, subject to censure. It is this sense of being part of the audience of world citizens that provides the basis for a sustaining pressure, emanating from an international culture, to enable different parts of the world to be at peace with each other. Kant hoped that "the human race can gradually be brought closer and closer to a constitution establishing world citizenship."[48]

VI. PUBLIC REASON AND CIVIL SOCIETY

As we said at the beginning of this chapter, practical reason established the basis for a civil society by justifying the key moral principle to treat others as ends. Further, Kant's view of civil society, including its domestic institutions and its need for a federation of peaceful nations, helps to explain the way this principle is given a concrete form of embodiment. In this setting, there is a chance for the public use of reason to become an integral part of the lives of citizens. Here, individuals, despite the presence of self-interest concerns in their lives, can still learn to conform their public deliberations to the rules, described at the beginning of this chapter, that allow people of different views and understandings to search with each other for acceptable and reasonable solutions to shared public problems.

Now, it might be the case that individuals, who engage in a deliberation on the basis of Kant's conception of the public reason, may end up disagreeing with the results. For instance, people who debate the best policy with respect to school prayer may, as a result of following Kant's rules for public reasoning, each be able to understand fully the points of views of all others in the debate. Thus, each will be in a position to think about the question from a broad and encompassing, or common, perspective that includes respect for all points of view. Here, those who want prayer understand the reasons behind the view of those who do not, and vice versa. Still, after the deliberation has concluded and a result has been reached, as for instance by a vote of the chief legislative institution of the society, it still may be the case that, because people feel so strongly about their respective, differing views, there is no basis for reaching an agreement on a policy all can fully support.

But even in this situation, people may find themselves able to tolerate the policy outcomes they do not accept personally. Why is this the case? The public use of reason suggests an ability on the part of each person to consider carefully the views of others one does not agree with. In doing so, space would be created in society that would include a wide variety and diversity of people. As a result of the public use of reason, individuals manifest to each other the civic virtue of mutual respect. And, because they do, people who disagree with the outcome of a deliberation could still tolerate the results because they each realize that every effort has been made, and will continue to be made, to preserve the basic freedom and rights of each person.

From this account, it is clear that Kant's conception of society could accommodate a civil society understood as a separate sphere of associations, standing independently of the state. Indeed, as we saw, Kant envisioned a society with a diversity of interests, each of which would be checked and limited by the others, thus creating an environment that works to prevent any single group or interest from becoming dominant over the rest. Clearly, this environment of diverse interests would not only permit individuals opportunities to pursue self-defined life choices, but it would provide a setting suitable to a government based on the idea of separation of powers.

Finally, in Kant's view of civil society, a principal concern of those using public reason would be to find ways to create approaches to rights that made them secure and available to all throughout the society. In doing so, the key principle of Kant's moral philosophy, the need to treat others as ends and not as means, would be given concrete expression. What kinds of questions would be addressed? Using today's experience as examples let me provide some illustrations. For instance, in discussing the principle of the right to speak one's views, there would be questions pertaining to what kinds of limits are acceptable on speech and what kinds are not. Or in discussing the right of persons to determine their religious preferences, there would be much debate and disagreement pertaining to how far the state may go in limiting access to public schools by religious organizations. During the process of public reason, individuals in the society would have to make such determinations. A civil society should be hospitable to encouraging public deliberations on matters of this sort, deliberations that involve the widest possible range of views in the society and that aim to make clear the meaning and application of basic rights that all are to enjoy in society.

Whereas this kind of political agenda follows from Kant's view of the public use of reason, it is not at all clear that Kant would take a democratic approach to who is and who is not to be included in the deliberative processes that are grounded in the public use of reason. I hold this view of Kant because Kant excluded a long list of people from citizenship based on the criterion that for a person "to be fit to vote, a person must have an independent position among the people."[49] Here, Kant's view on exclusion is based on his position that some people in society will not have sufficient independence to engage in the public use of reason with others. Excluded from participation and voting are people engaged in apprenticeships, domestic servants, minors, and women in general because they must depend for livelihood on others. Even though these people can and should be accorded the same basic rights provided all other citizens, these people "do not have a right to influence or organise the state itself as *active* members, or to co-operate in introducing particular laws."[50] Kant argued that the public use of reason was the preserve of those who approach matters from the standpoint of the scholar, or those people who were willing and able to "submit for public testing their judgments and views which here and there diverge from the established symbol [or sets of opinions]."[51] Presumably these people had sufficient independence, so that they would be able to approach questions from the standpoint of enlightened, public reason.

Now, to be sure, Kant's conception of civil society, as we know, will later be used by proponents of a liberal civil society to justify access to the public realm to previously excluded groups. Indeed, it is possible that Kant left open the door to this possibility by suggesting that the basis for exclusion was social position, or the idea of being dependent upon another for one's livelihood. As individuals are provided social independence over time, then more people would be included in the citizen category. That Kant did not advocate such a policy himself should not deflect attention from the fact that, in promoting the idea of the public use of reason, he sought to maintain civil society upon the great civic virtue of mutual respect. It would seem then that, given his commitment to this civic virtue, Kant's civil society would grow to the point that all of those previously excluded would over time become a main part of society.

A theme that will be apparent in the chapters on Hegel, Mill, and Rawls that follow is that each of these writers in developing further the idea of public reason will attempt to provide a more democratic approach to the practice of public reason. In taking this view, Hegel, Mill, and, Rawls seek to expand both the number of rights as well as the number of people covered by them in a given society. The person providing the most comprehensive account of this activity, an account that embellished Kant's view of public reason while accepting most facets of it, is John Rawls, whom we discuss in a subsequent chapter.

VII. RESPONSE AND REJOINDER

There are several problems that Locke and Rousseau would find with Kant's arguments. First, I comment on Locke. As we saw, Locke tied the existence of rights to his concept of private property. Locke said that individuals who work and who add value to the world through their labor have a right to enjoy the benefits of their endeavors. Indeed, for Locke, God has given us property for the sake of our enjoyment. It is in relation to the right of private property that individuals must accept restraints on their conduct with respect to accumulating wealth, including, for instance, that it is acceptable to accumulate wealth on the condition that one's activities in this regard benefit society as a whole.

But Kant would question this approach to ensuring support for rights because it would predicate such activity on a commitment to securing material happiness, and thus not predicate rights on an authentic dimension. What is the authentic dimension of rights? If we return to Kant's approach to defining the moral foundations of life, then the basis for guiding concepts such as rights should be moral reasons as mandated in his view of the categorical imperative. But when rights are based on the material pleasures associated with them, then rights are used to support almost any kind of behavior, including behaviors that are a threat to Kant's key moral principle, that is, the need to treat individuals as ends and not as means.

Indeed, a case could be made to support Kant's position. Originally, we associated in our culture the doctrine of rights with political liberties, with due process of law, and with private freedom of choice. These rights are justified by the argument that it is morally acceptable to grant rights if the latter permit citizens sufficient independence in thinking and action so that they can make judgments free from the arbitrary control of others. But today, we hear people talking about a right to see pornography, even though it depicts women made subject to death and rape. We hear people demanding a right to own a machine gun, even though these guns have no other use but to kill people. Over time, where rights are linked merely to what brings pleasure to individuals, rights become nothing more than licenses to promote individual interests at the expense of many others. And in the process, the notion that having rights includes respect for those limits and constraints that secure each person's liberty is lost.

What would Locke have said in response? Locke would argue that in the end governments are predicated upon the consent of the great majority of citizens. And the majority does after all have some political wisdom. Because, for Locke, majorities are constrained by the need to protect the general rights of all citizens, they will discover that, at times, they may permit too much freedom in certain areas. When the majority recognizes this reality, they will realize the need to limit and narrow the content of rights, as reason and experience dictate. Here, the majority will recognize that, in extending rights to own machine guns and to see violent pornography, the majority actually invades the rights of those who are harmed by these experiences. Given that the majority must provide rights to all in an equal manner, it will realize the need to pull back and to place some limits and constraints on people so that the rights of all can be protected.

But Kant would have questioned Locke's majority, wondering whether, in its quest to achieve material satisfaction, it could exercise the public use of reason. If it could not, then it would not be in a position to establish a common, universal point of view from which to overcome the impact of prejudice and self-interest on thought. But Locke would wonder how the public use of reason could be sustained if people in their ordinary lives are motivated by self-interest. Kant's answer would be that the public use of reason is a natural by-product of civil society and the Enlightenment. Because of these cultural realities, individuals are more and more likely, as the Enlightenment continues, to make public reasoning a part of their outlooks, even if in their private lives they remain as always, dedicated to self-interest. To Locke's critique, Kant would argue that in an enlightened age it would not be uncommon for individuals with various prejudices of one sort or another to avoid relying upon them when discussing public issues.

Who is right here, Kant or Locke? Ordinary experience indicates elements of truth in both views. For instance, in defense of Kant, in our society today, no one publicly utters racist or anti-Semitic views on behalf of supporting one's positions without being classed as a person whose arguments lack worth. If people want to be heard and to be seriously considered by others, they will avoid certain kinds of utterances, even though they might maintain them in their private lives. Thus, on college campuses today, many administrations discourage racist speech and so students and faculty avoid it in order to appear enlightened. However, when alone with friends and close associates, the language of the gutter may well reappear. On the other hand, Locke might point out that the public and private worlds easily become entangled, and the result is a situation in which individuals really have no desire to defend the rights of those whom they think are inferior because of race, religion, and so on. That is why Locke suggested the live-and-let-live option of his doctrine of toleration. Knowing that people would not be able to remove bigotry from their understanding, it is best to expect only that people will learn to tolerate those who are different from them. Hopefully, then, the rights of all will be protected, even if individuals have no respect for each other.

Now, Kant would have accepted Locke's notion of toleration, but he would have argued that toleration must be predicated on a firmer ground than just a live-and-let-live attitude. In particular, toleration can only survive as a principle of conduct when individuals are competent in the art of the public use of reason. For in this case, individuals learn to understand the views of others, and in the process of doing so people make room for them, thus displaying the civic virtue of mutual respect.

Rousseau, like Locke, would criticize Kant for inconsistency. Kant, like Rousseau, started off hoping for a general moral will. Indeed, all Kant was really doing in arguing that individuals should live by a law that all rational persons would accept, was giving greater specificity to Rousseau's notion of the general will. Here, in treating others as ends, we live, as for Rousseau, by a general moral will that all rational human beings would support. But owing to the inability of people to adhere to it, Kant constructed a system that allowed people to live by nonmoral motives and still achieve moral ends. Rousseau would find this approach destructive to the general will. Rousseau hoped that individuals would learn to put to the side the impact of self-interested concerns in their lives and instead promote the interests of the community as the primary objective in their lives. To this end, Rousseau's social contract sought to transform people from self-seekers into citizens, who make the commitment to the common good the most prominent dimension of their lives.

Kant and Rousseau would probably disagree on the possibilities of public reasoning as well. Indeed, Kant and Rousseau would be likely to hold different expectations as to what could be achieved by public reason. For Rousseau, public reason cannot always resolve wide differences between people over major issues. As we saw in Rousseau, the kind of public reasoning that makes possible a definition of the common good can materialize only when people hold views on major issues that are for the most part already close to each other in substance.

Now, based upon my interpretation discussed in the last section of the implications of public reason for Kant, Kant would not want to restrict public reason as much as Rousseau did. My view of Kant's conception of public reason suggests that Kant's position would require him to accept that public reason might not lead to agreement on every issue. However, a virtue (which Rousseau does not see) can be gleaned from public reason for society, even in this circumstance. Kant might argue that, when public reason does not resolve differences among people, still, because people respect the process of public reason and because public reason allows people to understand fully the views of others, people are able to live together in peace, in a setting of mutual respect.

Rousseau would question this presumption and likely say that, were Kant to hold this view, it would be acceptable to charge Kant with being overly naïve. Rousseau would argue, in support of this position, that, where wide differences exist over major issues, there is likely to be internal hostility in society and an absence of a shared commitment to uphold the common good. Rousseau hoped to avoid this outcome by advocating a situation in which differences in views and opinions, both as to quantity and intensity, could be reduced as a result of people's sharing common perspectives and values. Remember that Rousseau had hoped that peasants, a metaphor for ordinary people, would make the law, unencumbered by complex and competing ideas and ideologies.

But Kant would certainly claim in response that this picture of life does not describe modern society well, where people will no doubt come into contact with many diverse views on many different issues. To impose a Rousseau-inspired homogeneity of outlook on this kind of pluralism, for the sake of eliminating many contesting views, would be destructive of freedom in a civil society, and this approach would deny any need for the public use of reason, promised in the new enlightened world.

Endnotes

1. Immanuel Kant, "What Is Enlightenment?" in *On History,* edited by Lewis White Beck, (Indianapolis: Bobbs-Merrill, 1957), p. 7 and pp. 6–8. Also, see, Onora O'Neill, "The Public Use of Reason," *Political Theory,* Vol. 14: 4, November, 1986, pp. 533–34.

2. Immanuel Kant, "What Is Enlightenment?" p. 3.

3. Immanuel Kant, *Critique of Judgement,* trans. J. H. Bernard, (New York: Hafner, 1951), pp. 136–37. See also Onora O'Neill, "The Public Use of Reason," pp. 543–44.

4. Kant, *Critique of Judgement,* p. 136.

5. Ibid., p. 137. Also, O'Neill, "Public Use of Reason," p. 544.

6. Kant, *Critique of Judgement,* pp. 136–37. Also, O'Neill, "Public Use of Reason," pp. 544–45.

7. O'Neill, "Public Use of Reason," p. 541.

8. Kant, "What is Enlightenment?" p. 6.

9. Immanuel Kant, *Critique of Practical Reason,* trans. Lewis White Beck (Indianapolis: Bobbs-Merrill: 1956), p. 72.

10. Immanuel Kant, *Groundwork of the Metaphysic of Morals,* translated by H. J. Paton (New York: Harper Torchbook, 1956), pp. 89–91.

11. Ibid., p. 88. Italics are in the text.

12. Kant, "Metaphysical Foundations of Morals," in *The Philosophy of Kant,* edited by Carl Friedrich, (New York: Modern Library, 1949), p. 171.

13. Immanuel Kant, *Groundwork of the Metaphysic of Morals,* p. 95. Also, "Metaphysical Foundations of Morals," in *The Philosophy of Kant,* p. 178. Here, Kant says that the main practical imperative is: *"Act so as to treat man, in your own person as well as in that of anyone else, always as an end, never merely as a means."* Italics in text.

14. Immanuel Kant, *Ethical Philosophy, Part II. Metaphysical Principles of Virtue,* translated by James W. Ellington, (Indianapolis: Hackett, 1983), pp. 53, 82–141.

15. Immanuel Kant, *The Metaphysical Elements of the Theory of Right,* in *Kant's Political Writings,* ed. by Hans Reiss, (Cambridge: Cambridge University Press, 1970), p. 136.

16. Ibid., p. 133. Italics in text.

17. Ibid., p. 134.

18. Ibid., pp. 134–35.

19. Ibid., p. 133. Italics in text. See on this point,

Patrick Riley, *Kant's Political Philosophy,* (Totowa, New Jersey: Rowan and Littlefield, 1983), pp. 9–17.

20. Kant, "Idea for Universal History," in *On History,* p. 16.

21. Kant, "Idea for Universal History," pp. 16–17; "Perpetual Peace," *On History,* p. 113.

22. Kant, "Perpetual Peace," *On History,* p. 112.

23. Kant, *The Metaphysical Elements of the Theory of Right,* p. 139.

24. Ibid., pp. 138–39. Italics in text.

25. Ibid., p. 163. Italics in text.

26. Kant, "Idea for a Universal History," pp. 11–13.

27. Ibid., p. 15.

28. Ibid., p. 15.

29. Ibid., p. 15.

30. Ibid., p. 22.

31. Ibid., p. 16.

32. Ibid., p. 17.

33. Ibid., p. 18.

34. Ibid., pp. 17–18, 21.

35. Ibid., pp. 21–22.

36. Ibid., p. 21.

37. Ibid., pp. 18–19.

38. Kant, "Perpetual Peace," pp. 85–89.

39. Ibid., p. 92.

40. Ibid., p. 93.

41. Ibid., pp. 94–95.

42. Ibid., p. 98.

43. Ibid., p. 101.

44. Ibid., pp. 100–101.

45. Ibid., p. 100.

46. Ibid., p. 102.

47. Ibid., pp. 103, 114.

48. Ibid., p. 103.

49. Kant, *The Metaphysical Elements of the Theory of Right,* p. 139.

50. Ibid., p. 139–40. Italics in text.

51. Kant, "What Is Enlightenment?" p. 9; also, pp. 5, 6, 7. Here, Kant had in mind "venerable ecclesiastics," who would submit their opinions to public testing, but his view of public reason would suggest that others engaged in public offices, as well as active citizens, should also adhere to the standards of public reason, too.

Partial Bibliography and Further Reading

Arendt, Hannah. *Lectures on Kant's Political Philosophy.* Edited and with an interpretive essay by Ronald Beiner. Chicago: University of Chicago Press, 1982.

Beiner, Ronald, and Booth, William James. Edited. *Kant and Political Philosophy: The Contemporary Legacy.* New Haven: Yale University Press, 1993.

————. *Political Judgment*. London: Methuen, 1983.

Howard, Dick. *The Politics of Critique*. Minneapolis: University of Minnesota Press, 1988.

Hutchings, Kimberly. *Kant, Critique and Politics*. London; New York: Routledge, 1996.

Kant, Immanuel. *Kant's Political Writings*. Edited by Hans Reiss. Cambridge: Cambridge University Press, 1970.

Lingis, Alphonso. *The Imperative*. Bloomington: Indiana University Press, 1998.

Morgan, Diane. *Kant Trouble: The Obscurities of the Enlightened*. London; New York: Routledge, 2000.

Riley, Patrick. *Kant's Political Philosophy*. Totowa, N.J.: Rowan and Littlefield, 1983.

Rosen, Allen D. *Kant's Theory of Justice*. Ithaca: Cornell University Press, 1993.

Saner, Hans. *Kant's Political Thought*. Chicago: University of Chicago Press, 1973.

Schell, Susan M. *The Rights of Reason: A Study of Kant's Philosophy and Politics*. Toronto: University of Toronto Press, 1980.

Schott, Robin May. Editor, *Feminist Interpretations of Immanuel Kant*. University Park: Pennsylvania State University Press, 1997.

Williams, Howard Lloyd. Edited. *Essays on Kant's Political Philosophy*. Chicago: University of Chicago Press, 1992.

11

HEGEL: CIVIL SOCIETY
AND THE STATE

I. INTRODUCTION

In this chapter we discuss G. W. F. Hegel (1770–1831), whose *Philosophy of Right* presents an important statement on civil society. The starting point for this discussion is Hegel's critique of Kant. Hegel believed that Kant's approach to morality represented a kind of "empty formalism." What this claim means is that Kant's depiction of his basic moral principles merely says that individuals are to act in keeping with what constitutes necessary moral duties, but, at the same time, Kant's approach to defining these duties does not clearly specify their actual content.[1] Kant's moral philosophy is an empty formalism for Hegel, then, because although Kant tells us that we are always obligated to do our duty, we are never told what precisely that duty is. Kant, of course, would have objected to Hegel's characterization of his views, and Kant would have argued that in fact he did demonstrate the concrete character of people's duties when he developed his views of civil society. The latter represents those institutions that can best realize equal liberty and by doing so carry into practice the requirement to treat each other as ends and not as means. In my view, Kant would seem to have a good case against Hegel. However, Hegel thought otherwise.

Thus, Hegel, in his discussion of what he called the *ethical life,* sought to demonstrate the precise content of the modes of conduct and required obligations that individuals are to uphold. His chief concern was to argue not only that individuals have an obligation to respect the rights of others but that, in addition, there must be institutions in place that describe the nature of the conduct that individuals must uphold in order to meet this objective. For Hegel, then, each person possesses a "capacity for rights," and it is the obligation of each person to respect these rights and thus to live by the imperative that says we are to "be a person and respect others as persons."[2]

II. PHENOMENOLOGY OF SPIRIT

The institutions for realizing this purpose are discussed in Hegel's views of both the state and civil society. Before proceeding to discuss Hegel's view of civil society, however, we stress Hegel's view that the state and society of his time represent a triumph of the highest forms of these institutions over less desirable ones. He approaches an argument to this effect initially in his *Phenomenology of Spirit,* published in 1807. This work provides a basic justification for the concepts of both civil society and the state, which we discuss in subsequent sections of this chapter.[3] His general argument is designed to demonstrate that history has followed a course that clearly shows that the highest and best form of society and state is one that upholds the rights of each citizen in a regime characterized by a representative government with strong leadership in the executive branch.

In the *Phenomenology of Spirit,* Hegel illustrated the different levels of human understanding, starting at the level of experience, as nothing more than raw sense perceptions and moving from there to attain full knowledge of the rational and moral content of human experience. Moreover, for Hegel, moral awareness evolves across history, starting with notions of society that lack moral completeness and concluding, at the "end of history," with a comprehensive understanding of both the nature of morality and of the material structures necessary to realize it. For Hegel, history had ended in 1806, when humankind reached a point beyond which further moral progress was not possible. At the end of history, the ideals of liberty and equality have been spread throughout the world, and these ideas have been embodied in the modern state and, in particular, the modern civil society that Hegel described.[4]

Space permits only a brief summary of Hegel's pathway to knowledge of Spirit (or the attainment of complete moral awareness) in the *Phenomenology of Spirit.* In the first stages of awareness, called *sense-certainty,* a person's self-understanding is merely that of raw sense perception of the world, or a "knowledge of the immediate or of what simply *is.*"[5] In this phase, one points out the characteristics of objects of perception, as a "this Now" or a "this Here." But one is unable to integrate the perceived features into a unified form, and by doing so constitute the whole object of which each of the perceived features is an essential part. I may see "this branch" and "this leaf," but I lack the conceptual ability, at this point, to derive from these experiences the statement that says, "this tree."[6]

The next level of awareness is that of self-consciousness. Here, we understand ourselves to be independent, particular persons, possessing an identity that makes ourselves distinguishable from other people. At the earliest phases of self-consciousness, we do not possess a full knowledge of Spirit or of the moral concepts that should govern life, but still the existence of self-awareness signals that such knowledge "lies ahead."[7] In this stage, then, we leave behind a life defined in terms of an experience charted as the here and now, and we begin to move to the higher level of self-conscious moral understanding. "It is in self-consciousness, in the Notion of Spirit, that consciousness first finds its turning point, where it leaves behind it the colourful show of the sensuous here-and-now . . . and steps out into the spiritual daylight of the present."[8]

Self-consciousness begins to manifest its full moral character in what Hegel depicted as the "first man." The discussion of the latter is akin to the description of the state of nature, as provided earlier in chapters on Hobbes, Locke, and Rousseau. As the reader will remember from previous chapters, the state of nature is a description of what is presumed to be the condition of people prior to formal society, and thus the conception of the "first man" provides a picture of human character in its earliest phases. For Hegel, individuals in this category need to be "recognized" by others and to receive from others acceptance of themselves as human beings.[9] In seeking recognition from others, people are shown to want more than just satisfaction of essential desires, such as the need for food, shelter, or sustained life. In addition, for Hegel, people want others to accord worth and significance to their lives, what Hegel refers to as recognition. Individuals could not become aware of themselves as particular persons, unless others accord them recognition or worth as particular people.[10] But at this point in history, when the main experience is that of the "first man," destructive relationships ensue. Why is this the case? For Hegel, whereas each person seeks recognition from the others, it is natural for a person to try to get recognition from others without returning it to others. This situation culminates in strife, reminiscent of Hobbes's state of nature, in which each person seeks to force others to accord himself the worth he seeks from others, while not according similar respect for the worth of others.[11]

Hegel's account of this experience embodies his view of his often-cited conflict between master and slave. For Hegel, in a setting such as a Hobbesian state of nature in which each person seeks to gain from others recognition without returning it, those who are the victors, the masters, subordinate the others and make them into slaves. Here, the masters permit the slaves to live, but only in order to serve the masters as slaves. Indeed, this situation creates the relationship of master and slave, where the slave is reduced to a frightened animal, without dignity or humanity. But this experience is self-defeating, and it leaves both the master and the slave unhappy.[12] For the master finds himself receiving recognition from a slave for whom the master has no respect. In consequence of this fact, the master is recognized by someone that cannot really accord him the regard he demands. Similarly, in this relationship the slave cannot be happy either, for he is never recognized as a real human being, but only as a device the master uses for his own ends.[13]

The slave's experience ultimately becomes the basis for his freedom and for the creation of a civil society based on the commitment to full rights for all. How does this event take place? Initially, the slave finds himself working for the master, and through this work providing for the master's satisfaction. Here, the slave's motive for working is fear of the master. Later in history, however, the slave develops a capacity to perform work from motives that give work value, motives such as a sense of responsibility. In developing these motives, the slave realizes that he is not just a tool of the master, but a real human being. His evolution as a human being proceeds further when he realizes that he is capable of creative work, which leads to his inventing technologies that allow him to alter the external world. This experience enables him to envision a society in which he overcomes his fear of the master and claims his freedom. Still, since the slave is bound to his master, he is not yet free. The slave is at a stage at which he can only yearn for freedom and envision what life would be like were he to have it.[14]

The slave develops a philosophy that speaks to his desire for freedom, and the most important of these is Christianity. The latter is for Hegel a way of thinking that ultimately leads to building a civil society based on the idea of providing liberty to all. How does this event take place? Christianity is based on the view that all people have a capacity to make moral choices. Thus, to be free is to be in a position to choose morality over evil. With their freedom, then, individuals can make morality the basis for their lives. But this objective for the Christian cannot be realized fully in life on earth, but only in the life beyond this world, or in God's Paradise. Thus, whereas Christianity has the correct understanding of freedom, it told people not to expect it in this life. For Hegel, with the progress of humankind in history, a civil society emerges that permits people to realize the Christian moral vision in *this* life. Civil society is a setting in which the quest for freedom materializes in the possibility of *mutual recognition,* or shared respect for the rights of all people.[15] This experience is discussed in the *Philosophy of Right,* in which Hegel described the relationship of the state to civil society.

III. CIVIL SOCIETY

But what is a civil society and how does it achieve mutual recognition? For Hegel, a civil society is viewed as a separate sphere of interests existing outside the state, and thus a civil society is conceived as a "battlefield where everyone's individual private interest meets everyone else's." Owing to this viewpoint, a civil society represents a sphere of life that is hostile to the state and its commitment to promote a "higher outlook," or conception of the common good.[16] In this view, the civil society experience suggests a setting in which individuals pursue their self-interests, often without regard for obligations and duties that are considered essential for protecting the rights that all members are to be accorded. The state must work to overcome the destructive features of these tendencies toward self-interest in order to make possible an atmosphere of civic virtue and a concomitant support for the common good, including respect for the rights of others.

What are the features of modern life that make civil society into a "battlefield" of competing interests, and how is civil society to rise above this situation to create a community in which mutual respect for rights is possible? We will discuss the first part of this question in the next several paragraphs, and the discussion of both the roles of corporations and the state will address the second part of this question.

In the first place, people are both workers and consumers of the products of others' work. Take the latter dimension first. For Hegel, unlike for Marx as we will see later, the main characteristic of individuals in civil society is not that they are commodities. As commodities, people are bought and sold by more powerful people who seek to exploit the labor power of the less powerful. But for Hegel, individuals are driven by desires to create a variety of new needs, each of which they hope to satisfy in the marketplace through the purchase of goods.

Why do needs proliferate? People, said Hegel, hold to a "demand for equality of satisfaction with others." In emulating each other as consumers, individuals create a sense of equality among themselves. Furthermore, in this context where everyone manifests similar desires to consume goods, there is always a need to be different from the rest, and this need to be distinctive is expressed when individuals demand to own distinctive goods. Thus, in this setting, there is an ongoing and continual expansion of needs, as individuals develop appetites that must be satisfied with the development of new products.[17] Hegel, in discussing the proliferation of needs, certainly had in mind the modern market setting, where people hope to make enough money to satisfy their desires, and where people hope to find ways to satisfy the many desires others may be engendered to have, as a means of making money. The American shopping center, filled with diverse brand names and styles, is emblematic of what Hegel means.

We provide for our needs through *work*. It is work that produces the goods that people consume and, in the process, use to satisfy basic needs.[18] The work each person performs is part of a larger work process or division of labor. This system allows the work of each worker to be made "less complex," and thus each worker's tasks are easier to perform. By virtue of this fact, each worker's overall output is increased. Here, individuals find themselves in mutually dependent relationships, contributing to the larger task of producing as efficiently as possible the various goods that will satisfy the various needs that members of the society have. For Hegel, the division of labor symbolizes "everywhere the dependence of men on one another and their reciprocal relation in the satisfaction of their other needs."[19] Moreover, as time goes on and as work becomes more and more defined in terms of a division of labor, the work becomes so mechanical and routine that machines can replace individuals.[20]

Undergirding the entire market environment of consumption and work is a civil society built upon class divisions. There is an agricultural class, a business class, and a class of civil servants. The agricultural class consists of the landowners whose income derives from farming activities. Their cohesion as a class is located in that which secures their independence in society; in particular, the social importance and prominence society accords certain families and their property holdings. The business class constructs the system of work that produces the goods that make the attainment of needs possible. Included in this group are the mass production workers and the craftsmen, who work in the system set up by the businessmen to produce goods, and those types of businessmen who are engaged in the art of exchange and trade of manufactured goods. Naturally, this group is interested in finding ways to make financial gains or profits a primary objective of their endeavors. The class of educated, middle-class civil servants make up the executive bureaucracy, whose main task is to implement the law in a fair and objective way, and thus these individuals are called the "universal class" because they are presumed capable of rising above self-interest.[21]

Civil society in this setting is characterized by many factors. Included among them is the need of individuals to make a living, the hope of gaining ownership of the resources with which to fulfill desires, the efficient organization of work, and the class structure of society. These factors when taken together turn civil society into a setting characterized by competing interests, without regard for the common good. How are these competing interests to be transcended, so that the interests of one class alone, say the business class, is not made predominant, thus denying any importance to the needs of other groups in society? To achieve this end, Hegel turned to a discussion of *corporations*.[22]

Corporations are associations of workers and businessmen, and they are designed to achieve some productive end in society. In this regard, then, each corporation performs an important type of work, which is necessary to the well-being of society. Moreover, each corporation would, as Hegel said, "look after its own interests within its own sphere."[23] Thus, there could be corporations for various types of manufacturing activities, say (to use modern examples), making steel or electrical equipment, and each of these corporations would have a monopoly of control over the production of the products associated with its own sphere of activity. Further, these corporations as they operate in their own spheres might become competitors with each other. For instance, the interests of the electrical corporation might conflict with those of steel, as the former hoped for a reduced steel price so that electrical equipment would become less costly. But because Hegel said the corporations are subject to the "surveillance of the public authority," it is the case that their activities would be regulated by the state.[24] Conflicts could be mediated in the name of the general welfare of the whole society. Given this possibility, the state would have as one of its main tasks that of coordinating the activities of the corporations, so that each could, as it contributed to its own good, contribute to the common good as well.

Part of that larger good would be to provide people with useful and productive employment. In the corporation, which becomes a "second family" to an individual, a person is given the training needed to learn the skill he is to perform, and, in addition, he is monitored so that he continues to maintain a high level of competence. Moreover, in exchange for his work, a person is guaranteed a suitable livelihood. Also, as a member of a corporation, in good standing, a person is provided in the eyes of the world with public recognition, or, as Hegel says, with the evidence "that he is a somebody," and that he "belongs to a whole which is itself an organ of the entire society."[25]

Further, the pursuit of recognition seems to indicate that unless one is able to perform work well and thus be a member in good standing of a corporation, one might not even be permitted to enjoy, to their fullness, the same rights guaranteed to all persons. "Unless he is a member of an authorized Corporation, . . . an individual is without rank or dignity, his isolation reduces his business to mere self-seeking, and his livelihood and satisfaction become insecure."[26] Although not arguing here that a person without membership in a corporation should have his rights taken from him, Hegel did seem to indicate that whatever rights such a person might have would have much less value than the rights of a person enjoying full membership in a corporation.

Given this view, then, a person in a profession that is highly esteemed would certainly have more respectability than would a person without a job or what Hegel and we would call a "day laborer"—a person who engages in casual as opposed to long-term career employment.[27] The day laborer would have the same rights as others, but owing to his lowly position in society these rights would give him much less leverage in society to get for himself what those rights are said to guarantee. Thus, the day laborer might be able to exercise the right of free speech, but who would listen to him? He might have access to health care, but would it be as good as that provided the more respectable members of society, and so on?

The likely failure to provide full worth to the rights of all those who fall outside the sphere of the corporations appears as well in Hegel's treatment of the poor. For Hegel, a prosperous economy will emphasize jobs for those with the skills most needed by the society. But, at the same time, there will not be jobs for those who do not have the requisite skills.[28] Consequently, there will be a "large mass of people [who] falls below a certain subsistence level." What should be done for them? Hegel did not advocate that the poor be provided direct cash payments either from the wealthy or from charities. He took this position because he believed that if the poor were given direct welfare assistance they would not be encouraged to work. And in the absence of work they could not gain for themselves what for Hegel is a main principle of a civil society: namely, a sense of self-respect and independence.[29]

Finally, Hegel did not think the state should create work for the unemployed because this action would inflate the "volume of production," producing more goods than society actually can afford to pay for. And this situation would only cause growing unemployment as many were laid off in the face of a weakening of demand for goods. It follows for Hegel that a free-market-oriented civil society is often not able to keep people from falling into poverty and becoming part of the "rabble," or those individuals who, owing to their poverty, have no regard for basic moral values such as right, wrong, and self-respect.[30] Hegel's state is to enter civil society and regulate conflicts with regard to work, class, production, and consumption. But it is never clear that the state should be concerned to protect the interests and needs of the poor.

IV. THE STATE AND CIVIC VIRTUE

For Hegel, the state thus stands above the particular interests that make up a civil society and provides a basis for moving society toward a concept of the common welfare. Once again, it is worth reminding readers that, for Hegel, the state must not be confused with "civil society." In the latter, individuals manifest particular interests, each of which expresses a person's conception of personal freedom. Were individuals to identify themselves exclusively with the interests they hold as members of civil society, then they would think that their membership in the state was "optional" and largely predicated upon whether the state would support their particular interests. But for Hegel, each person, as part of what it means to live a fully civilized life, is destined to live his life in keeping with universally valid and binding notions of obligation. The state that embodies these obligations is thus not optional, but a necessary fact of any fully flourishing human life.[31]

Thus, Hegel did not predicate the authority of the state upon a notion of the consent of various interests in society to accept the state's authority. The state's authority rests upon the understanding that there is a rational truth that exists independently of the various interests in society and that the state exists as an autonomous agency in relation to these interests, with the sole purpose of promoting this truth.[32]

Hegel's view of the state differs significantly from those we have studied thus far. Locke's state, because it emanates from the consent of the citizens, is conceived as representing the different interests in society. For Locke, it would not be possible to create a state separate and distinct from the society, since the state, as a representative of the majority, is an embodiment of the various interests that constitute society. Kant's state is closer to Locke's state, and thus it is predicated upon the need to support the basic interests of society as well, even as it expects these interests to approach issues from the standpoint of public reason.

Hobbes would seem to define a state as that which contained both Lockean and Hegelian aspects. Like Locke, Hobbes's state evolves from consent, and thus it too would have to advance the common good of society. But for Hobbes, one of the expectations that people in society want to advance through their consent is the need for a strong unitary or non-separation-of-powers state. Such a state is needed to stand above competing interests in order to resolve conflicts and to uphold rights. As a result, Hobbes described a state that can stand outside and be independent of competing interests for the purpose of achieving stability. Hobbes's state, then, would take on a Hegelian character. In consequence, Hobbes would be more likely than Locke and Kant to accept Hegel's separation of the state from "civil society."

Finally, Rousseau probably would not accept Hegel's separation of the state and society. The state, its purposes and goals, is always associated with the citizen's conception of the general good. On the other hand, Rousseau is with Hegel in not wanting society filled merely with a variety of self-interest-oriented groups who have little or no concern for the common good. Were it not possible to achieve a general will in society among the different interests, Rousseau might find Hegel's separation of the state and civil society appealing, as a way to define and then impose the general will onto an otherwise unruly and interest-contentious society.

Who is right in these matters, Hegel or the others? In general, it would seem that a state in a civil society contains elements of both views, each of which coexists with the other. In this case, the state in a civil society is neither defined in exclusively Hegelian terms, nor in exclusively Lockean terms. For in the first place, there is no question that the state is in some sense a product of the different interests that constitute the society over which it has authority. Thus, it is not possible to separate the state completely from the sphere of civil society as Hegel tried to do. But on the other hand, the state must exercise independent powers of judgment on behalf of those critical and fundamentally important principles that rational people uphold. In this role, the state must at times stand apart from society, as depicted by Hobbes and Hegel. Even for Locke the state is to be a neutral umpire between competing interests, all in the name of protecting the rights of each citizen.

Returning to Hegel's view of the state, when the state is able to provide the concept of the common welfare, then civil society becomes transformed from a milieu of conflicting interests into a setting in which the diverse groups are able to cooperate for the achievement of long-term, shared interests. In this context, Hegel expected that all members of society would contribute to the common welfare; and, if they would, then instead of remaining as competing interests, they would become integrated into a community, working toward the same goals. For Hegel, even as individuals have private interests, they are still able to consider themselves as contributing members of a community.

How is Hegel's state arranged to achieve this objective? The modern state is predicated upon its *constitution,* which consists of both the basic, universally rational principles that define the state's nature and the institutions that carry these principles into practice.[33] This means that the principles that guide the state are not so much the product of social consensus among different groups, but they manifest the universal truths of reason, which should always be followed. First, we will discuss the main principles upon which the state rests.

In general, the modern state is committed to securing the basic rights of each individual. A right helps to secure a person's freedom to make fundamental choices about the way he or she wishes to live. But at the same time, rights are seen as existing in a context in which individuals also must recognize basic duties. These duties must be upheld by all as a condition for securing the rights of all citizens. Duties and rights are bound together, and both are "united in one and the same relation."[34] Individuals have particular interests, and they use their rights to pursue them, but, in doing so, they should uphold all the norms associated with the duties considered to be universally binding on all citizens. Indeed, an individual realizes that it is in upholding his duties during the course of pursuing his interests that he becomes a member in good standing of community with his rights fully protected. Hegel said that "the *isolated* individual, so far as his duties are concerned, is in subjection; but as a member of *civil society* he finds in fulfilling his duties to it protection of his person and property, regard for his private welfare, the satisfaction of the depths of his being, the consciousness and feeling of himself as a member of the whole; and, in so far as he completely fulfills his duties by performing tasks and services for the *state,* he is upheld and preserved."[35]

The institutions of the state that carry into practice the protection of both rights and duties are organized into three divisions: the crown, the executive, and the legislature.[36] At the apex of Hegel's state is the *monarch.* Hegel believed that constitutional monarchy was "the achievement of the modern world."[37] The monarch symbolizes the state's commitment to both its general principles and to the institutions that can best put them into practice. Now, the idea of monarchy as developed here is not an absolutist one, and indeed it is clear that the monarch is viewed as sharing responsibility for ruling with others. Hegel's discussion of the relationship between the monarch and the other elements of government helps show how the sharing of responsibility takes place. How Hegel avoids falling into monarchical absolutism is an important topic for a state committed, as Hegel's state is, to securing basic rights for all. This topic is doubly significant given the fact that the monarch is not an elective office but an hereditary one.[38]

The monarch, for Hegel, is responsible for initiating a political deliberation, or what we have already referred to in discussing Kant as a form of *public reason.* What is the objective of public reason for Hegel? Public reason includes consideration of all points of view with respect to various issues. The hope in taking this approach is to achieve an agreement on those issues that preserves a societal commitment to the universal principles of the constitution, in particular, the need to protect the rights of all, while making clear the duties associated with this endeavor.

Thus, the monarch as the person to whom "ultimate decisions belong"[39] demands that any particular policy be one that carries forward and in no way violates the basic principles of the constitution. Here, the crown determines that the particular policies always be subsumed under the "universal." This means that the monarch and his council can initiate discussions about policy, making suggestions about "the current affairs of state or the legal provisions required to meet existing needs."[40] The monarch will consider the needs of the society, the state of existing law as it pertains to these needs, and suggest certain policy initiatives that the society should consider. Throughout, the monarch's intention is to remind members of society to guide their thoughts about an issue so that particular conceptions of interest do not supersede the importance of solutions that carry forth and embody the universal principles of the constitution.

Further, the monarch's decisions are carried out by the executive agency of government, which includes the judiciary and the police, as well as the civil servant class. The latter, as members of the middle class, as we see below, oversee the activities of the corporations to ensure that the latter carry out their objectives in keeping with the general principles established by the constitution and maintained by the monarch. The function of the executive is to "make the universal interest [the notion of the common good] authoritative over its [civil society's] particular aims."[41] The executive always has the task of insuring that the main purpose of the monarch, the commitment to promoting the same basic rights and duties, is always upheld. The way Hegel describes the executive agency of government suggests that it is a wing or branch of the crown, always obligated to uphold in its activities the basic principles that the crown embodies and symbolizes to the nation. Indeed, Hegel said that key elements of the executive branch report to top executive officials who are in "direct contact with the monarch."[42] These "key elements" are the civil servants who oversee the corporations and the advisory officials who give advice to the executive on how to implement or interpret policies so that they embody the commitment to securing basic rights and duties.

In the remaining part of this section, I would like to discuss Hegel's view of public reason, which largely occurs between the monarch and the legislature. As an illustration of how public reasoning to achieve a rational consensus takes place, I will use the example of health care. The monarch might suggest, after reviewing with his council the needs of the society and its existing laws with respect to them, that the country needs a policy on health care. In discussing health care, the monarch would provide a version of the commitment to equal rights for all that would be relevant to the health care arena. He might, for instance, suggest that, whatever policy is adopted, it should be one that makes possible universal coverage for all citizens. Then the monarch would, upon reviewing existing laws and traditions on the subject, suggest certain limits that should not be abridged. For instance, if protecting private choice of doctors seems to be essential, he would point out the need for doing so in any plan that was finally accepted. The monarch might even suggest possible plans that would work to achieve the universal coverage.

The actual decision, however, about how best to attain the principle of universal coverage would rest with the legislature. In doing so, the legislature seeks to realize the basic "well-being and happiness" of the citizens by defining the specific rights each is to have with respect to the policies in question, as in this case, health care. At the same time, the legislature defines for citizens the basic duties they must uphold as a condition of achieving these rights. Hegel refers to these duties as the "services to be extracted from people," or, using other terms, he refers to what people must contribute financially to receive the rights accorded them. Thus, in our example, included in the list of citizen duties is a requirement to pay the necessary costs of the health care rights that are provided to people.[43] The legislature would pursue the cost issue by allowing the different views of the society on the matter to be articulated, and the hope would be that a consensus would be reached on what tax policy would best be able to realize the principle of universal coverage.

To accomplish this task, the legislature, also called the *Estates,* has two houses, each representing a different class found in civil society.[44] The upper house consists of the agricultural class, and the lower, the corporations. Hegel believed that the "Estates are a guarantee of the general welfare and public freedom."[45] The classes in the legislature, over time, gain experience in government, and they understand the needs of the ordinary people and the problems of the executive in governing corporations. Indeed, the classes in the legislature are most likely to anticipate "public criticism," from the "Many" before it occurs, and thus they are able to suggest policies that avert unnecessary conflict.[46]

The upper house contains members of agriculture who are able to maintain their detachment and independence because their wealth is not affected by the ups and downs of the business cycle or by the "quest for profit," so near and dear to the businessman. Another reason for this class's independence is that it is not tied to the state's financial base. Indeed, its inheritance rights guarantee the agricultural class's place in society, and thus they do not have to predicate their political views on the need to seek favor either from the public or from the executive class.[47] Further, Hegel envisioned members of this class being able to represent themselves in person in the legislature.[48] Since this class never has to run for office, they will be free from having to engage in political gamesmanship. Owing to their detachment, then, they would be able to carry out one of the chief functions of the legislature by acting as mediators between the monarch and the other interests of civil society.[49] With respect to health care, then, this class might be able to work out compromises between the crown, for instance, who wished to move toward a form of state-sponsored medical care and those interests in civil society who wanted to establish a system of private care. As a result of the agricultural class's effort, there would be "less chance" that the other classes of civil society would be in "direct opposition" to the monarch or to the executive, thus avoiding government stalemate or societal warfare.[50]

The lower house is composed of deputies, or representatives, from the various communities, in particular, the corporations. Hegel saw this part of the government as the "fluctuating" element because corporations are more affected by changes in the external or economic circumstances than are people engaged in agriculture. The deputies in the lower house, then, are to represent "the special needs, difficulties, and particular interests" of the corporations.[51] The members of this branch would be more in tune with the day-to-day problems corporations face as they perform their functions in society. In fashioning legislation, in this case a health care plan, the lower house would hope to make certain that the general principle, universal coverage, could be construed in such a way as to respect the needs of corporations. Indeed, this understanding might lead to the creation of a plan neither proposed by the monarch nor initially acceptable to the other house. But owing to the discussion that would occur about the proposed plan, over time, both the other house and the monarch might, in the end, make needed concessions.

The crown can "summon" a corporation to send a representative to the lower house, and when this happens the corporation in question elects a deputy for this purpose.[52] Each corporation, then, elects its own members to represent it. Hegel emphasized that each of the "essential spheres" in a civil society should have a representative to represent its respective interests. Hegel presumed that each person's political commitments and concerns would be tied directly to the particular communities in which he works. To think of himself as isolated from those communities during political deliberation would be to deny a reality central to his identity.[53]

Hegel hoped that permitting the different spheres of civil society to be represented in this way would not lead to social fragmentation, however. How is this state of affairs possible? As we saw, the corporations manage the day-to-day work needs of the society and operate within the context of the "higher outlook" defined by the state. This objective is achieved because the heads of the corporations are chosen by a combination of popular elections and certification by those in executive authority. Moreover, those who run the corporations do so under the guidance of the civil servants in the executive branch. Presumably, then, the civil servants, who make up the executive branch as educated, professional bureaucrats, would oversee the corporations and make certain that, during the course of achieving particular commercial and business objectives, the corporations adhered to the policies established by the state.[54] In consequence, the officials and members of corporations, aware of the presence and watchful eye of the state officials, become oriented to uphold the policies of the state as they carried out the work of the corporation. Any tendency, then, for the corporation to move off in its own direction, defying public directives, is thus severely limited. Indeed, Hegel said that "the corporation mind . . . is . . . inwardly converted into the mind of the state," and this experience is the "secret of patriotism."[55]

Thus, when corporations enter the legislature, they do so not just to promote a narrow conception of the public good, but to promote a conception of the public good that embodies the full commitment to realize the policies and initiatives of the monarch. Here, even if the experience of corporate life is more directed to particular interests, because the corporation is part of the larger community governed by the policies of the state, individuals in espousing corporate interests are more likely to be cognizant of the need to define them in ways that promote the interests of the community, also. Clearly, corporations would then practice as well as teach civic virtue or the need to promote the common welfare.

In this context, each class in the legislature must contribute "something peculiarly its own to the work of deliberation,"[56] and the hope of this enterprise is the creation of a consensus that embodies the state's main principle to secure the rights for all, within a setting of respect for the associated duties. Here, the policy that is developed on health care would carry into practice the main rational principle, the need for universal coverage, articulated by the monarch at the beginning of the policy discussion.

The great tragedy of modern politics for Hegel is that it often takes place outside the type of public reasoning just described. Public opinion for Hegel suggests a tendency of people too often to promote their own private and personal views, devoid of a concern for the rational principles that should ground public decisions about public matters. Hegel said that "to be independent of public opinion is the first formal condition of achieving anything great or rational whether in life or in science."[57]

Hegel's view of public opinion brings to the forefront his commitment to secure the civic virtue of mutual respect in a civil society by making possible the prospect of mutual recognition. Mutual recognition could be achieved in a variety of ways. In the first place, recognition arises from an effort to protect the rights of each person. Also, recognition arises from a public deliberation in which major public issues would be decided in a setting committed both to shared rational principles and to a willingness to listen to diverse views in determining how best to put these principles into practice.

V. RESPONSE AND REJOINDER

Hobbes and Locke would probably claim that Hegel's approach to protecting individual freedom fails because Hegel's view of corporations places individuals into groups that shape and define the identity of each individual. To the extent that individuals become dependent upon corporations, they would lose the independence they must have if they are to define a way of life separate from the path prescribed by the norms of group life. Hegel would no doubt answer that his view of the state and corporations, designed as it is to limit and to constrain the private interest orientation of civil society, intends to restore civic virtue to civil society. Without compliance with the norms of civic virtue taught by the corporations and the state, civil society would be overrun by the self-serving, selfish conduct of those who seek, within the market setting of civil society, their own private interests. A civil society, for Hegel, is not just a setting for individuals to accumulate as much as they can, but it is a context that locates each individual in a community that is grounded in the norms of civic virtue.

Moreover, Hegel could maintain that, in this setting, the great civic virtue of mutual respect, or what Hegel called *mutual recognition,* would become a mainstay of life. Indeed, in the context of public reason that Hegel devised, individuals of different viewpoints would come to understand and to make room for one another. Self-interest considerations would not become an obstacle to achieving respect for diversity. If this is the case, then Hegel could argue that, by promoting the civic virtue of mutual respect, his view of civil society avoids the tyrannous implications that others might associate with it.

Rousseau would have accepted the importance of civic virtue to achieving freedom, but he would have questioned Hegel's approach to achieving civic virtue. For Rousseau, Hegel would have failed to define civic virtue in terms of a general will that all members of the society would be able to uphold. And the reason that this is the case for Rousseau is that Hegel did not have a view of citizenship that would ensure full participation to all members in determining the common good. Hegel's system of representation from the various classes would for Rousseau permit only a few to make the decisions for all, and instead of a general will emerging from this activity, only a particular will would emerge, and this particular will would be imposed on the rest. Hegel would respond to this criticism by arguing that the general will and Rousseau's concept of participation are abstractions. To give real substance to either of these terms, it is necessary to define the institutional setting in which both emerge. And that is what he, Hegel, tried to do.

It must be remembered, as pointed out at the beginning of this chapter, that Hegel was convinced that, over time and across history, human progress followed a path that made possible a rational social and political order. This order embodied in the concrete institutions and practices the key moral and ethical norms that secured the conditions of real freedom. As he stated in the *Philosophy of Right,* "what is rational is actual and what is actual is rational."[58] This means that, at the advanced stages of history, and in particular during the period that encompassed Hegel's life, the material circumstances of day-to-day life embody the concepts and practices necessary for a rational social order that secures the rights of each individual.

Now, there are those who, like Alexandre Kojève, claim that Hegel was in the main correct when he argued that, in 1806, history had come to an end, with the emergence of the modern state and civil society. This setting makes possible mutual recognition, or the shared and reciprocal provision of basic rights. A person becomes for Kojève "truly human—that is, [an] individual" only to the extent that he or she is "recognized" as a citizen of a modern state dedicated to securing the liberty of each person. For Kojève, then, the reason history is completed at this point is that the fully developed state, which makes possible full liberty and equality for all, presents a condition that all humankind would accept. Indeed, no reasonable individual would "be tempted to negate" this condition and thus attempt "to create something new in its place."[59]

But others would question Kojève's view. In the first place, Kant would wonder whether Hegel had properly conceptualized the end of history because Hegel did not embrace Kant's view of a peaceful federation of civil societies. Hegel, ever the realist in international matters, scoffed at this idea because he believed that Kant's idea presupposed an underlying basis for accord among states. But attaining such accord is fraught with many difficulties for Hegel. Indeed, nations follow their own interests, and they are often prone to settle their differences by war and not by resorting to Kant's league of nations.[60] Kant would respond by saying that Hegel's view of history, in that it makes continued war necessary and likely among civil societies, demonstrates an underdeveloped view of what a civil society is. For Kant, a civil society cannot achieve freedom and rights in a setting characterized by a constant commitment to war-related activities. In this contest, there would be insufficient attention to education, and the state would become so committed to war that it would lose interest in securing the rights citizens demand.

Francis Fukuyama also takes issue with Kojève's support for Hegel's end-of-history view. For in the first place, inequality remains in today's civil society. A major source of continuing inequality today arises from differences in cultural circumstances. Those who are part of an underclass culture, which includes the absence of suitable home environments to prepare people to perform well in society, must inevitably suffer from having to live in social conditions that make them unable to take advantage of educational opportunities. And in a society in which status depends largely upon educational attainment, an underclass culture works only to continue to maintain the underclass in a situation of perpetual inequality. In consequence, achieving the end of history and by doing so providing full legal equality as well as economic opportunity to the underclass will make little difference in the lives of underclass people if they cannot overcome the cultural obstacles that prevent them from using these opportunities fully. But for Fukuyama, "no one has solved the problem of 'creating culture'—that is, of regenerating internalized moral values, as a matter of public policy." Thus, while the principle of equality of opportunity has been established in the United States, it has yet to be fully implemented throughout the society, and the prospect of its happening remains problematic.[61]

Whereas those who argue for mutual recognition of each other's rights are disappointed by its lack of attainment and thus use this fact to demonstrate that we have not reached the end of history, others will question whether mutual recognition is a good thing to have in the first place. For instance, Fukuyama argues, following Nietzsche (whom we discuss in a subsequent chapter), that the ethos of mutual recognition ends in making everyone content with equality of conditions. But what of those who do not see themselves as equal to others and who, in consequence, demand special privileges from the rest of society? Here, there are always some people who strive to be superior to others and who create things of lasting value and importance to society, things such as "great symphonies, paintings, novels, ethical codes, or political systems."[62]

But in a democratic civil society, where equality is the norm, the actions of the few who seek to leave a lasting impact on society are always stifled. Why is this? A main value of a democratic civil society is toleration, which suggests that we should learn to live-and-let-live and to see all ways of life as basically equal in worth, with no way of life better than any other. The best way to achieve this objective is to diminish the importance of those with superior talent, ability, or vision and to concentrate only upon common, everyday needs, such as those having to do with insuring our material and physical comforts. Here, the focus is to make everyone as materially satisfied as possible and eliminate as much physical suffering as is feasible. This attitude means that there is a preoccupation in civil societies with achieving material happiness and with allowing people to be successful in the market setting, where they compete for the variety of goods provided there.

Such an environment leaves little room for the individual who is unique and different and through whose efforts important contributions to culture are made.[63]

Thus, in this environment, how can there be the contributions of greatness, such as are found in new philosophies, new forms of politics, or new styles of art?[64] For writers such as Nietzsche, Hegel's "end of history" is associated, then, not with a great roar of approval, but with a yawn, as many find themselves bored by the absence of anything majestic and enduring.

Endnotes

1. G. W. F. Hegel, *Hegel's Philosophy of Right,* translated by T. M. Knox, (Oxford: Oxford University Press, 1952), pp. 89–90, para. 135. Also see Peter J. Steinberger, *Logic and Politics: Hegel's Philosophy of Right,* (New Haven: Yale University Press, 1988), pp. 149–50.

2. G. W. F. Hegel, *Hegel's Philosophy of Right,* p. 37, para. 36.

3. G. W. F. Hegel, *Phenomenology of Spirit,* trans. by A. V. Miller with analysis of text by J. N. Findlay, (Oxford: Clarendon Press, 1977). My discussion follows, in part, the excellent synopsis of the argument provided by Findlay, "Foreword," pp. v–xxx.

4. In discussing this aspect of Hegel, I rely upon Francis Fukuyama's discussion of Alexandre Kojève's view of Hegel in Fukuyama's *The End of History and the Last Man,* (New York: The Free Press, 1992), pp. 66–67.

5. G. W. F. Hegel, *Phenomenology of Spirit,* p. 58, para. 90. Italics in text.

6. Findlay, "Foreword," p. xvi. Hegel, *Phenomenology of Spirit,* p. 62, para. 102–3.

7. Hegel, *Phenomenology of Spirit,* p. 110, para. 177.

8. Ibid., pp. 110–11, para. 177.

9. Fukuyama, *The End of History,* p. 146. The latter uses the term "first man." See also Charles Taylor, *Hegel,* (Cambridge: Cambridge University Press, 1975), pp. 152–53.

10. Fukuyama, *The End of History,* pp. 146–47.

11. Ibid., p. 147. Also, Taylor, *Hegel,* p. 153.

12. Fukuyama, *The End of History,* pp. 192–93. Also, Taylor, *Hegel,* p. 154.

13. Fukuyama, *The End of History,* pp. 193–94. Also, Taylor, *Hegel,* p. 154.

14. Fukuyama, *The End of History,* pp. 194–95.

15. Ibid., pp. 196–98.

16. Hegel, *Hegel's Philosophy of Right,* p. 189, para. 289.

17. Ibid., pp. 127–28, para. 193.

18. Ibid., pp. 128–29, para. 196.

19. Ibid., p. 129, para. 198.

20. Ibid., p. 129, para. 198.

21. Ibid., pp. 131–32, para. 203–5.

22. Ibid., pp. 152–55, para. 250–56.

23. Ibid., p. 152, para. 252. Also, p. 152, para. 250–51.

24. Ibid., p. 152, para. 252, 251.

25. Ibid., p. 153, para. 253, 252.

26. Ibid., p. 153, para. 253.

27. Ibid., p. 153, para. 252.

28. Ibid., pp. 149–50, para. 243. Also, p. 153, para. 253, and p. 153, para. 252.

29. Ibid., p. 150, para. 244–45.

30. Ibid., p. 150, para. 244–45.

31. Ibid., p. 156, para. 258.

32. Ibid., p. 157, para. 258.

33. Ibid., p. 174, para. 272.

34. Ibid., p. 161, para. 261.

35. Ibid., p. 162, para. 261. Italics are in text.

36. Ibid., p. 176, para. 273.

37. Ibid., p. 176, para. 272.

38. Ibid., p. 185, para. 281.

39. Ibid., p. 195, para. 300.

40. Ibid., p. 187, para. 283.

41. Ibid., pp. 188–89, para. 287. Also p. 189, para. 289, p. 193, para. 297.

42. Ibid., p. 189, para. 289.

43. Ibid., p. 194, para. 299.

44. Ibid., p. 203, para. 312–13.

45. Ibid., p. 196, para. 301. Also p. 198, para. 303.

46. Ibid., p. 196, para. 301 and p. 197, para. 302.

47. Ibid., p. 199, para. 306.

48. Ibid., p. 199, para. 307 and p. 200, para. 308.

49. Ibid., p. 197, para. 302. See also Knox's note p. 373, section 312.

50. Ibid., p. 203, para. 312–13.

51. Ibid., p. 202, para. 311. Also p. 200, para. 308.

52. Ibid., p. 200, para. 308; p. 201, para. 309; p. 202, para. 311.

53. Ibid., p. 202, para. 311 and p. 198, para. 303.

54. Ibid., p. 189, para. 288–89.

55. Ibid., p. 189, para. 289.

56. Ibid., p. 203, para. 312. Also p. 201, para. 309.

57. Ibid., p. 205, para. 318. Also, p. 204, para. 316–17.

58. Ibid., preface, p. 10.

59. Alexandre Kojève, *Introduction to the Reading of Hegel,* (New York: Basic Books, 1969), pp. 236–37. See as well Fukuyama, *The End of History and the Last Man,* p. 66.

60. Hegel, *Philosophy of Right,* pp. 213–14, para. 333–34.

61. Fukuyama, *The End of History,* pp. 291–92.

62. Ibid., p. 304.

63. Ibid., pp. 304–5.

64. Ibid., pp. 305–6.

Partial Bibliography and Further Reading

Avineri, Shlomo. *Hegel's Theory of the Modern State.* Cambridge: Cambridge University Press, 1982.

Cullen, Bernard. *Hegel's Social and Political Thought: An Introduction.* New York: Gill and MacMillan, 1979.

Kelly, George Armstrong. *Hegel's Retreat from Eleusis: Studies in Political Thought.* Princeton: Princeton University Press, 1978.

Kojève, Alexandre. *Introduction to the Reading of Hegel,* ed. Allan Bloom. New York: Basic Books, 1969.

Lakeland, Paul. *The Politics of Salvation: The Hegelian Idea of the State.* Albany: State University of New York Press, 1984.

Mills, Patricia Jagentowicz. Editor. *Feminist Interpretations of G. W. F. Hegel.* University Park, Pa.: Pennsylvania State University Press, 1996.

Pelczynski, Z. A. Edited. *The State and Civil Society: Studies in Hegel's Political Philosophy.* Cambridge: Cambridge University Press, 1984.

Pinkard, Terry P. Hegel. *A Biography.* Cambridge: Cambridge University Press, 2000.

Plant, Raymond. *Hegel.* Bloomington: Indiana University Press, 1973.

Priest, Stephen. *Hegel's Critique of Kant.* Oxford: Oxford University Press, 1986.

Steinberger, Peter J. *Logic and Politics: Hegel's Philosophy of Right.* New Haven: Yale University Press, 1988.

Taylor, Charles. *Hegel.* Cambridge: Cambridge University Press, 1975.

Wood, Allen W. *Hegel's Ethical Thought.* Cambridge: Cambridge University Press, 1990.

12

JOHN STUART MILL:
CIVIL SOCIETY AS A HIGHER CALLING

I. MILL'S PERFECTED CIVIL SOCIETY

John Stuart Mill (1806–1873) is a strong proponent of a liberal civil society whose rule of law commitment is dedicated to securing as broad a liberty as possible for people. In taking this view, he not only supports equal liberty in the tradition of Kant, but in addition he seeks a liberty that is as inclusive as possible of all the choices individuals may wish to make in life. But Mill is interested not just in expanding the choices individuals have, but he also wishes to make it possible for people to use their freedom to enhance what is best in humankind, in particular, their intellectual and moral qualities. In promoting this view, Mill is equally a stern critic of civil society, suggesting that civil society may be a way of life that in the end destroys what is best in us. For this reason, it might be possible to place Mill into the last section of the book, as one of civil society's major critics. But I have resisted the temptation to do so, because in the long run I believe that Mill believed that civil society was the best approach to achieving a humane existence.

In this chapter, starting with Mill's revision of Jeremy Bentham's utility principle, I explain how Mill's view of civil society is designed to facilitate what Mill most treasured, the development of the higher mental and moral capacities. Here, Mill argued for a conception of civil society that lessened the impact of the worst features of the market economy on the lives of individuals. As players in the market setting, individuals often engage in destructive relationships. Often in the market setting, individuals, as they pursue their self-interest, only seek to enhance their power and position against others. Indeed, Mill said that economic life is "the parent of envy, hatred, and all uncharitableness; it makes everyone the natural enemy of all others who cross his path, and every one's path is constantly liable to be crossed."[1] Mill's discussion of the utility principle points the way to the cultural context that can promote, despite the experience of economic life, the higher capacities of persons.

In this reformed and revamped culture, which a civil-society is to embody, restraints can be placed on the economic arrangements, posed by the market setting, to avoid the threats to Mill's fuller freedom.

II. MILL AND BENTHAM AND THE PRINCIPLE OF UTILITY

Mill's starting point was Jeremy Bentham's principle of utility, which Mill both adopted and revised in his essay, *Utilitarianism.*[2] The utility principle, also called the greatest happiness principle, as found in Bentham, says that "actions are right in proportion as they tend to promote happiness, wrong as they tend to produce the reverse of happiness. By happiness is intended pleasure and the absence of pain; by unhappiness, pain and the privation of pleasure."[3] Mill argued that this principle was the "ultimate appeal on all ethical questions, grounded on the permanent interests of man as a progressive being."[4] Bentham's main concern in discussing utility was to demonstrate how it would be useful in making judgments pertaining to the development of laws and public policy.[5]

A. Bentham's Pleasure Calculus

In Bentham's view of the utility principle, before putting into law a proposed measure, a legislator must determine the sum total of pain or pleasure that the proposed measure suggests. He said that "pleasures then, and the avoidance of pains, are the *ends* which the legislator has in view: it behoves him therefore to understand their *value*. Pleasures and pains are the *instruments* he has to work with; it behoves therefore to understand their force, which is again, in other words, their value."[6] The objective of this enterprise is to compare the total quantity of pleasure of a proposed action to the total quantity of pain. Those policies that, on balance, provide greater pleasure describe a "*good* tendency" for the community and those policies that, on balance, suggest more pain than pleasure suggest an "*evil tendency.*"[7] To make this calculation, it is presumed that all pleasures are quantifiable in terms of the following indicators of pleasure or pain: the amount or degree of a pleasure's or pain's "intensity," "duration," "certainty," "remoteness," "fecundity," "purity," or "extent" (the number of people it affects).[8] Bentham's calculus is followed by a long list of possible pleasures, including things such as making money, achieving good reputation, gaining power, realizing goodwill, having hope for the future, and being a part of associations with others.[9]

Clearly, the pleasures listed by Bentham represent the objectives that individuals, as competitive businesspeople in a market setting, always have. Thus, Bentham's political program embraces an ethics that derives directly from the market experience in a commercially based capitalist society. And Mill, by seeking to revise Bentham's philosophy does not reject the modern market context so much as he seeks to reform it, making it capable of embracing the possibilities of enhanced intellectual and moral life. How does Mill go about achieving this objective?

Mill rejected Bentham's approach to measuring the value of a given pleasure, and, in doing so, Mill provided an alternative basis for grounding his ethics and his politics. Mill believed that measuring a particular way of life's worth should not depend solely upon the quantity of pleasure associated with that way of life but should include an assessment of the quality of pleasure connected to the way of life in question, also.[10] Thus, let's say I enjoy reading philosophy as well as watching television. Still, when faced with the choice of being able to read more or watch television more, let's assume I choose reading philosophy even though reading is associated with a greater amount of work and concentration than watching television. On what basis would I make this choice? The reason for my choice would be that reading represents a higher quality pleasure, and consequently no additional amount of television watching would be sufficient to warrant my choosing television over reading.

For Mill, pleasures that are qualitatively rich are those associated with the use of the "higher faculties" of the mind. Now it is true that those people who set their sights very low in life will have a greater likelihood of realizing their objectives than those people whose objectives aim to realize the fullness of the "higher faculties." After all, a life dedicated to achieving the "higher faculties" may always be associated with various forms of unpleasantness, such as hard work and a risk of failure. But still, despite these difficulties, people, who understand both the "higher faculties" of mind as well as those pleasures that Mill referred to as those of "lower animals," will pursue the life of the "higher faculties" of mind over all animal pleasures. People who appreciate the "higher faculties" will take this course despite the fact that they may be convinced that the lower pleasures bring more satisfaction and less discomfort. Mill said that it is better to be a dissatisfied Socrates than a satisfied fool.[11]

Why are the "higher faculties" of mind so important? Mill said that

> *[A] cultivated mind—I do not mean that of a philosopher, but any mind to which the fountains of knowledge have been opened, and which has been taught, in any tolerable degree, to exercise its faculties—finds sources of inexhaustible interest in all that surrounds it; in the objects of nature, the achievements of art, the imaginations of poetry, the incidents of history, the ways of mankind past and present, and their prospects in the future. It is possible, indeed, to become indifferent to all this, and that, too, without having exhausted a thousandth part of it; but only when one has had from the beginning no moral or human interest in these things, and has sought in them only the gratification of curiosity.[12]*

Several important points seem to follow from this view of intellectual life. Mill was contending that only when we make satisfactory use of the "higher faculties" of mind do we find unlimited interest in life. Through experience we can know that there is a vast world out there, of course, but unless we really engage that world with our mental faculties, we can never know the joy and the happiness of learning about, as well as confronting, the world's mystery and allure. As a consequence of this engagement, the world is always a place that fascinates and that presents new avenues of discovery and delight.

In this view, then, what would seem to disturb Mill so much about the ways of life that have quantifiable pleasures as their objectives is that, in pursuing those pleasures exclusively, one makes only a limited and incomplete use of one's mental faculties. Thus, if the one thing one most wants to do is to make money, one can go into business and use only that part of one's mental abilities that is useful in the business world. If one wants to lead a life dedicated to acquiring power, then one must engage only that capacity of mind concerned with this objective. In all these cases, real and enduring happiness cannot be attained because the "higher faculties" of mind are not properly employed. On the other hand, a businessman might have a fully cultivated mind, too, thus enabling him to engage and to find wonderment and interest in all aspects of life, especially those beyond the business world. The same could be true for those involved in the pursuit of power.

A truly satisfactory life, or a life dedicated to the pleasures that are high quality in nature, is also associated with an ability on the part of individuals to be concerned for others. Mill argued that people who think only of their own needs become disconnected from "the collective interests of mankind." It is only when we retain an intimate association and concern for the needs of others that we are more likely to have "as lively an interest in life on the eve of death as in the vigor of youth and health."[13]

Some might argue that Mill's view is elitist, since not all people have the *capacity* for engaging in the cultivation of the higher quality pleasures just mentioned. But Mill would deny this claim. "There is absolutely no reason in the nature of things why an amount of mental culture sufficient to give an intelligent interest in these objects of contemplation [such as history, poetry, etc.] should not be the inheritance of every one born in a civilized country."[14] As a matter of fact, the utilitarian project suggests the need to eradicate whatever stands in the way of all people's enjoying what is their birthright, namely, their full mental and moral life. Poverty and disease as well as other factors that are obstacles to the full enjoyment of the mental life can be eliminated. "All the grand sources, in short, of human suffering, are in great degree, many of them almost entirely, conquerable by human care and effort," and people who enter the field to fight for the full development of persons in this way "will draw a noble enjoyment from the contest itself."[15]

B. Utility, Justice, and Rights

The utility principle, defined broadly to include not only the provision of quantitative pleasures, but qualitative ones as well, is conceived by Mill as contributing to and supported by what he understood to be a "natural sentiment" or desire to "be in unity with our fellow-creatures."[16] For Mill, as for Aristotle, we are social animals by nature, and because we are we seek ways to create cooperative settings that facilitate the happiness of each individual. But for Mill, unlike for Aristotle, this project cannot be achieved unless we all regard each other as equals. In Mill's view, a "society between equals can only exist on the understanding that the interests of all are to be regarded equally."[17] And this means that, in pondering actions, individuals must always consider the interests of others, and, in particular, individuals must see themselves as part of an association in which each of the members accepts the obligation to be a cooperative citizen promoting a collective objective.[18] Indeed, the utility principle requires that each person be concerned with his own happiness as well as with the happiness of others. Here, the Golden Rule propounded in the spirit of Jesus is "the ideal perfection of utilitarian morality." The utilitarian is committed, then, to "laws and social arrangements," as well as to a system of education that enables each person to live in harmony with the whole of the society, while advancing the quest for freedom defined in both quantitative and qualitative terms.[19]

As an embodiment of the Golden Rule, the utilitarian ethic presumes a "sentiment of justice" or the feeling of a need to be rightly outraged and to seek punishment for those who harm us or those with whom we sympathize. This "sentiment of justice" is widened to include all persons in society by virtue of "the human capacity of enlarged sympathy" and "intelligent self-interest." As a result, we find ourselves experiencing the harm caused to others as though it were caused to us, and, in light of this experience, we are driven to demand protection by society for the rights of all people.[20] Here, to have a right is to have something that, for Mill, society must defend "either by the force of law, or by that of education and opinion."[21] Only then can individuals have "*security,*" for Mill, "the most vital of all interests."[22]

From this account, it is clear that Mill wanted a broader and richer happiness than Bentham had ever contemplated. Moreover, Mill predicated this broader happiness on the civic virtue commitment to mutual respect, which he saw as central to the utilitarian ethic. But what kind of culture, political and social, will be needed to secure the setting that makes possible the happiness that Mill's utilitarianism seeks? This question will be addressed in the rest of this chapter, first with a discussion of Mill's *On Liberty,* and then later with discussions of Mill's views of political economy and government.

III. ON LIBERTY: *THE CULTURE OF CIVIL SOCIETY*

A. Well-Developed Persons

On Liberty was written to suggest the kind of culture a civil society must have if individuals are to become "well-developed human beings."[23] What is sought is a social and political environment that enables individuals to develop to the fullest extent possible their mental faculties. Key to their doing so is that individuals be permitted every opportunity to make their own choices as to which paths in life to take. Mill argued that the basic faculties, those "of perception, judgment, discriminative feeling, mental activity, and even moral preference, are exercised only in making a choice."[24] In making choices, people learn to rely on their own faculties of mind as they evaluate the various options before them. As they do so, they further develop these mental capacities, leading, then, to a fuller, happier life. "The mental and moral, like the muscular powers, are improved only by being used."[25]

Thus, human capacities are stunted to the extent that a person allows customs and traditions to dictate his or her way of life. Mill's point is not that customs are always necessarily wrong, but that, in living as they require us to, without questioning them, we desist from making choices about what is best for ourselves. And when we follow this course, we do not develop the kinds of qualities that enable us to reach our higher capacities. "He who lets the world, or his own portion of it, choose his plan of life for him, has no need of any other faculty than the ape-like one of imitation."[26] Blind following of custom makes all people uniform and thus incapable of becoming what for Mill are the "noble and beautiful objects of contemplation."[27]

Human liberty, and the self-development that evolves from it, is best nurtured when society permits individuals to be free to pursue their own choices, within settings they design either by themselves or with others.[28] In these contexts, individuals are not to be interfered with by the state or by other individuals. What secures this prospect is the assurance of certain basic liberties, including, for instance, the liberty of conscience, of expression, of determining one's own life plans, and of being able to join together in groups and associations.[29] Here, a civil society is not just a place for people to act upon market imperatives and seek to own property, gain riches, or perform necessary work, but, in addition, a civil society is a place in which people further enhance their higher qualities.

Mill's view of civil society suggests a recurrent danger for Mill's approach to individual development. Society, with its basic social and political institutions, cannot provide the rights or the protective space Mill hoped for without exercising power over individuals. But the power society possesses might itself make impossible the kind of liberty Mill expected. Therefore, the quest for individual development always in the end becomes a question of how to define "civil liberty," or "the nature and limits of power which can be legitimately exercised by society over the individual."[30]

In addressing this question, Mill started from what he considered to be a basic truth about government in modern society. Governments are no longer conceived of as entities with interests separate from the people, but as institutions that are responsible to the interests of the citizens.[31] Still, a new threat to freedom emanates from the idea that governments, as democratic republics, should be ruled by the "will of the people." Instead of signifying a form of government in which each citizen governs himself, the idea of the "will of the people" has come to mean "the will of the most numerous or the most active *part* of the people; the majority, or those who succeed in making themselves accepted as the majority; the people, consequently, *may* desire to oppress a part of their number: and precautions are as much needed against this, as against any other abuse of power."[32] A politically active class may consist of a small number of people, but owing to its skills and its endurance, it may be able to dominate the policy-making process. These groups achieve their objectives by having great influence on government, as well as by imposing their orthodoxy onto all members of the society. The result of this strategy is "to fetter the development, and, if possible, prevent the formation, of any individuality not in harmony with its [prevailing opinion] ways, and compel all characters to fashion themselves upon the model of its own."[33]

Mill's political solution to this problem involved his drawing a distinction between opinions and the actions that might follow from opinions. Whereas people should not be hindered in their expression of opinions, it may be necessary at times to place limits on the actions that various opinions suggest. For instance, Mill said that the view that corn dealers are corrupt and negligent ought to be able to be communicated in the press without restraint. The same idea, issued before a mob standing in front of the house of a corn dealer, may have to be limited, owing to the potential harm that might result from an emotionalized group.[34] Mill suggests that freedom of speech is not unlimited. We cannot use speech to cause a riot that results in injuries, just as we cannot give state secrets to another nation.

The freedom of speech of those seeking through their speech to dominate others represents a special problem for Mill. Mill knew that in a society dedicated to open speech, those seeking to dominate the political process through public position taking cannot have their right to speech or association limited. This situation for many describes the current problem with the demand for more thorough campaign finance reform. For some, extensive reforms of campaign funding might deny full freedom of political speech to those who are placed under these limitations. Yet, with the freedom candidates have to garner large amounts of money, it is possible for special interests to dominate vital policy areas in society. So what is the solution in a situation where outright bans on speech are not possible?

Mill was insistent, as we demonstrate throughout the rest of this chapter, that a civil society be a place where public policy decisions be made in the context of a full, open, and rational public discourse, as opposed to the shoving-match tactics of powerful interest groups. No doubt, Mill would have rejected the appeals to emotion found in many political advertisements today, because these techniques deny the proper place to reason in political discourse. By emphasizing in the public culture the role of fair, rational, and open public deliberation the hope was that the tactics of oppressive, single-issue groups would be avoided.

B. Opinion Advocacy and Civic Virtue

Mill, like all civil society thinkers discussed to this point, including Hobbes, Locke, and Kant, argued that a civil society must secure liberty. Further, Mill followed other civil society thinkers in arguing that people who receive benefits from society are obligated to "observe a certain line of conduct toward the rest."[35] Thus, with freedom goes the need to observe certain basic social obligations or what we have referred to as civic virtues. In particular, we are not to harm the interests of others by denying others their legally provided or tacitly-understood-to-exist rights, and, further, each person is to share the burdens of defending the society "or its members from injury or molestation."[36]

Mill's *On Liberty* would seem to provide two approaches to defining the precise limits or the particular content of the civic virtues that individuals must observe if the harms just described are to be avoided. The first approach, discussed in this subsection, pertains to Mill's view of the culture of open discourse and the discovery of truth. The second approach, discussed in the next subsection, has to do with what can be referred to as self-regarding conduct, or the denial to the society or to individuals the authority to interfere with those individually chosen ways of life that do not cause harm to others or to society. The institutional settings that seem most able to promote a respect for the limits that maintain Mill's civil society are embodied in Mill's views of a stationary economy and representative government, both of which are discussed in subsequent sections of this chapter.

First, we need to discuss Mill's view of open discourse. For Mill, the basis for discovering truth in a society with diverse opinions on the many issues before society is that we must not deny a hearing to any opinion, lest, in doing so, the truth may be suppressed. Where opinions are suppressed, there is in place a presumption of infallibility on the part of those who are able to avert discussion.[37] Mill's view was that we do not learn what is best for us simply from experience alone, but also, in addition, "there must be discussion, to show how experience is to be interpreted." In this context, "wrong opinions and practices gradually yield to fact and argument."[38] No one can marshal by himself all the facts pertaining to a question, or generate all possible arguments against which to test his view. We have an obligation, therefore, to listen to all the views that can be given against our positions and to consider them carefully during the course of deriving our positions. Mill advocated the benefits of an enlarged discourse, or what has been called *public reason*, when he said,

> The steady habit of correcting and completing his own opinion by collating it with those of others, so far from causing doubt and hesitation in carrying it into practice, is the only stable foundation for a just reliance on it: for, being cognizant of all that can, at least obviously, be said against him, and having taken up his position against all gainsayers—knowing that he has sought for objections

and difficulties, instead of avoiding them, and has shut out no light which can be thrown upon the subject from any quarter—he has a right to think his judgment better than that of any person, or any multitude, who has not gone through a similar process.[39]

In promoting this view of opinion advocacy, Plato's Socrates lurks in many passages of *On Liberty*.[40] Like Socrates, Mill exhorted holders of any opinion to provide the grounds for their judgments. Mill rejected the kind of argument for an opinion that starts out with the statement "the reason I believe in X is that I feel that X is correct." What are the reasons, Mill would ask, for your holding to X? And can you defend those reasons in the face of the following counterarguments I can give to them? This approach is not only the source of truth, but it is the basis for a culture in which individuals maximize the development of their highest-order mental capacities. In contrast, "where there is a tacit convention that principles are not to be disputed, where the discussion of the greatest questions which can occupy humanity is considered to be closed, we cannot hope to find that generally high scale of mental activity which has made some periods of history so remarkable."[41]

Further, when we have to justify our positions with good arguments, we not only develop our mental capacities, but, in addition, we demonstrate both to others and to ourselves why we feel justified in believing as we do. In effect, we acquire throughout this process a publicly defensible ground for our opinions, and consequently we are less likely to be timid or hesitant to act on their behalf.[42] There is in the modern world a tendency to associate firm commitments with dangerous fanaticism. But Mill would no doubt argue that fanaticism arises from a need to flee from subjecting beliefs to the give and take of argument and debate. The latter relies upon the participation of others, particularly those holding views different from our own. Fanaticism would close us off from a discourse of this type. For this reason, unreflective acceptance of beliefs, a mental state associated with fanaticism, would have no place in Mill's discourse setting.

C. Self-Regarding Conduct

Mill distinguished self-regarding conduct, or individual actions that do not harm others by denying them their rights, from other-regarding conduct that harms others by taking their rights from them. In general, Mill thought that society should permit each person to live his or her own life as that person chooses. Thus, even though it is best for individuals to pursue ways of life that enhance their "higher faculties," still, all individuals, in their "ripe years" or as mature, experienced adults, should have the freedom to determine that way of life that they consider best for themselves. When society interferes with a person's choices, perhaps in order to promote what it considers to be the best interest of a person, it unnecessarily limits that person's freedom and quite often makes mistakes about what is best for another.[43] Moreover, actions that demonstrate deficiencies in our character and that are harmful to us, such as a tendency to deny importance to the higher faculties, what Mill referred to as "self-regarding faults," should not be made subject to legal sanction. Mill argued that behaviors that cause harm only to the individual engaging in them are "inconveniences" that society "can afford to bear, for the sake of the greater good of human freedom."[44] However, this view does not mean that we are obligated to show respect for people who commit self-regarding faults. Such individuals will neces-sarily be viewed with less favorable opinion by most people.[45] Still, only acts that injure others, such as those that violate another's rights, are acts that can be punished. To use Mill's example, although it is permissible for a person to become drunk, it is not permis-sible for a policeman or soldier to become drunk on duty.[46]

For Mill, then, the state may regulate the lives of people only to prevent serious harm to others or to society. An example of particular importance to justify state inter-ference into others' lives is when one person's conduct denies rights to others. Men of-ten act toward women with precisely this intention and effect, and Mill condemns this kind of other-regarding conduct. Mill was adamant that men should not be able to con-trol the lives of their wives, with the result that women suffer loss of opportunities, and to remedy this situation, he believed it necessary to give to women the same rights that men have.[47]

Furthermore, Mill argued that there is a duty incumbent upon parents to educate their children. And those parents who do not perform this duty have, for Mill, committed a "moral crime." To prevent such crimes, both against children and society, the state has the right to force parents to educate their children. Still, Mill feared placing the task of educat-ing people exclusively into the hands of the state because he believed that a state educa-tion would end up molding people to be copies of each other. Thus, he argued that, if the state must sponsor schools, these schools should be designed to provide a standard that other systems of education in society, including presumably private ones, should try to match or to exceed. State-sponsored schools should try "to keep the others up to a certain standard of excellence."[48] Ultimately, however, the state's right to ensure an education for everyone is justified by the fact that education is the best way to teach people to avoid ac-tions that exceed the proper limits of conduct. For Mill, "if society lets any considerable number of its members grow up mere children, incapable of being acted on by rational consideration of distant motives, society has itself to blame for the consequences."[49]

In conclusion, it is well to make clear the nature of the civic virtues that the notions of open discourse and the need to avoid interfering with the lives of others both suggest. By not interfering in the lives of those who harm only themselves, individuals manifest the virtue of toleration found in Locke. By manifesting understanding of views different from one's own, as is required in Mill's form of enlarged discourse, individuals manifest the civic virtue of mutual respect. Each of these ideas, as argued in Chapter 1, can mutually support the other, and taken together they are fundamental to securing rights for all in a civil society.

IV. THE STATIONARY ECONOMY AND PRIVATE PROPERTY

From the preceding account of self-regarding freedom, it is clear that Mill believed that civil society must be designed to protect people from intrusions that threaten their personal liberty. Mill argued that, whereas civil societies understand this need, they are often blind to the factors that threaten it. Indeed, civil societies, ironically, end up promoting certain ways of life that actually make the protection of the full development of persons extremely difficult. Here, Mill had in mind the concept of a free market economy that is associated in Mill's time with furthering industrial growth and individual freedom, but that, in fact, often jeopardizes the general happiness. In this section, we explain Mill's position by discussing his advocacy of both a stationary economy and of the concept of private property.

The conventional wisdom held by many people even today and the view that Mill was attacking is the idea set forth by Adam Smith, discussed in Chapter 1, that says that the total amount of wealth and capital in society must always be expanding and growing. But Mill believed that a fixation on growing "as rich as possible," what Mill also referred to as "one of the phases of industrial progress," makes the "normal [or Smithian growth] state" a competitive jungle filled with "trampling, crushing, elbowing, and treading on each other's heals [sic]."[50] Although the quest for economic growth may be a "necessary stage in the progress of civilization," it is not for Mill the kind of social setting he would want to encourage. A better condition is one in which there is a "stationary state of capital and wealth," a situation in which "no one is poor, [and] no one desires to be richer."[51] Mill's position is clearly offered as a challenge to Smith's views.[52]

Now, in supporting the idea of a stationary economy, it should be clear that Mill did not deny the principle of private property. For Mill, private property suggests that individuals should be permitted to keep both the fruits of their own labor and of the various sacrifices they accept as a consequence of their work.[53] However, this principle is violated in a society in which the actual distribution of property, as embodied in the law, has worked to heap "impediments upon some, to give advantage to others."[54] Still, Mill believed that the principle of private property was not the cause of this imbalance as socialists in Mill's time claimed. The source of this imbalance was the government's failure to diffuse wealth, and, by failing to do so, to permit large concentrations of wealth to remain in the hands of a few.[55] Indeed, Mill believed that "the principle of private property [which has been attacked as the source of imbalances in wealth] has never yet had a fair trial in any country."[56] Thus, Mill hoped for legislation that, while "favoring equality of fortunes," does so in a way consistent with respect for "the just claim of the individuals to the fruits, whether great or small, of his or her own industry."[57]

The idea of a stationary economy is associated with several important ideas. For Mill, there should be efforts to limit the growth of the population so that the quest for ever-larger amounts of wealth will not be necessary in order to feed ever-larger numbers of people. Indeed, Mill's support of equal rights for women evolves not just from his commitment to equal rights for all. His commitment to equal rights for women arises from his view that when women are kept in the household and denied the same opportunity for employment as men, it is likely that women will produce larger numbers of children than the world needs, thus contributing to overpopulation.[58]

Moreover, in a stationary economy there would be an ethos of ecology and conservation, both of which would humanize society and make it more into a place hospitable to the full development of people's "higher faculties." In contrast, an ever-expanding economy is bent upon turning every scrap of land into an instrument to aid further production. Forests and beautiful fields filled with flowers and clean rivers are turned into trash dumps for factories. In laying waste to the environment in this way, there are fewer places on the earth left where a person can stand apart from others, in "solitude," and reflect on the course and direction of his or her life. "Solitude in the presence of natural beauty and grandeur is the cradle of thoughts and aspirations which are not only good for the individual, but which society could ill do without."[59]

Finally, within the stationary economy, it would be possible to advance methods of manufacturing that reduce the total amount of time spent in laboring, so that individuals would have the free time needed to develop their "higher faculties." Mill wanted a work setting in which the workers would be able to pursue the "art of living," or a life in which the enhancement of "mental culture" and "moral and social progress" is made possible. But he lamented that, in the circumstances of his day, the laboring class had grown without any decrease in the drudgery associated with work. In contrast, the expanding economy has been a great boon to the manufacturers or the owner classes that have made great amounts of money. The comforts of the middle class have been greatly increased, too. For Mill, this circumstance was a great injustice that needed to be corrected, and it could be if the economy were put on a stationary as opposed to an ever-expanding basis.[60]

Correcting the imbalances between workers and owners was a primary consideration of his argument, then. To this end, Mill also hoped for a fairer distribution of influence in the workplace. But this goal is hindered by the demand for an expanding economy. Indeed, in a setting in which growth is constantly demanded, the owner stands toward the workers as a superior, demanding more and more sacrifice, and turning worker sacrifices into profits to fund more growth. But this kind of relationship creates hostility between owners and workers, and it freezes the worker out of important decisions affecting what is produced and how production occurs. When the worker has no chance to participate in major decisions in the workplace, the worker does not develop the "higher faculties" of mind that allow him to contribute to critically important decisions affecting society. Mill wanted to correct the imbalance between the owners and workers by giving the workers a larger stake in the production process. Thus, Mill hoped that the relationship between workers and owners would be transformed to permit partnerships either between owners and workers or among the workers themselves.[61] In the first instance, workers would share profits with the owners, and, in the second instance, workers would own the entire production setting and help choose their own managers.[62] These new economic arrangements would permit the workers to take part in the decisions concerning the productive process, and in consequence workers' intellectual and moral capacities, as well as their sense of responsibility to society, would be enhanced.

It would appear that Mill's commitment to a stationary economy, as well as to cooperative work arrangements, is designed to reform, but not to eliminate, a private-property-based market economy. Socialism, the collective ownership of property, remains an alternative if it becomes the case that the reforms he advocated did not come to pass. At the time he wrote, however, Mill believed that the most desirable form of economy was yet to be decided. Indeed, the form of economy that is considered best for society still remains to be determined by the future course of events. "We are too ignorant either of what individual agency [private property forms of society] in its best form, or Socialism in its best form, can accomplish, to be qualified to decide which of the two will be the ultimate form of human society."[63]

V. ON REPRESENTATIVE GOVERNMENT

The kind of civil society most likely to produce the reforms just discussed is one that engenders in citizens an active participatory role in politics and society. Citizens would develop the capacity to consult the views of others as well as the guiding principles that secure the greater good, during the course of devising their own opinions. Mill believed that this experience was already a part of contemporary English lower-middle-class life. Mill said that the English citizen who sits on juries, who participates in parish offices, and who participates in public functions

> *is called upon, . . . to weigh interests not his own, to be guided, in case of conflicting claims, by another rule than his private partialities, to apply, at every turn, principles and maxims which have for their reason of existence the general good: and he usually finds associated with him in the same work minds more familiarized than his own with these ideas and operations, whose study it will be to supply reasons to his understanding, and simulation to his feeling for the general good.*[64]

Furthermore, Mill, in keeping with his commitment to active citizen participation in the affairs of society, believed, for several reasons, that many social functions should be performed by citizens themselves rather than by the government. In the first place, citizens are likely to do a better job than government in performing such functions. And in the second place, even in those situations in which citizens may not perform certain functions as well as the officers of government, society is better off overall when citizens take an active role in their society. Here, Mill believed that citizen participation in government and society is a means to people's "mental education—a mode of strengthening their active faculties, exercising their judgment, and giving them familiar knowledge of the subjects with which they are thus left to deal."[65] Mill feared government by bureaucracy because these agencies, in putting the most capable men into government positions as Hegel had wanted to do, would ensure that "all the enlarged culture and practised intelligence in the country . . . would be concentrated in a numerous bureaucracy."[66] This situation would exclude the rest of the citizenry from taking part in broad discussions of key public issues. As a consequence, the public would not be encouraged to participate in the shaping of policy themselves.

Mill thus advocated a view of civil society that, in addition to having a culture that emphasized the importance of protecting rights and enhancing the intellectual faculties of citizens, also emphasized, as part of this culture, the importance of direct citizen involvement in government functions. Citizens would engage in these functions either in the context of local governments and juries, or through a separate sphere of voluntary groups, which undertook, for instance, philanthropic activities.[67] Clearly, Mill supported and indeed made room for what we have called the separate sphere of a civil society, in which individuals can participate in a variety of groups and associations, learn the skills of citizenship and deliberation, and build a strong buffer to central government power.

Moreover, as an additional way to promote broad public participation in the governmental processes, Mill supported representative forms of government, because he believed that these forms of government would encourage a wide-scale public discourse of public policy. He took this position in spite of the fact that he did not envision the representative body itself as the sole arena for making laws. Mill said that the representative assembly is too unwieldy and cumbersome to be in a position to make good laws through its own deliberations. Thus, Mill advocated a "Commission of Legislation" whose task it would be to craft laws. The crown would appoint the Commissioners for a fixed term, unless removed by the Houses of the Parliament. The Commissioners would be above politics, acting with expertise as they addressed the issues before them and acting with a full understanding of the whole structure of law. The proposals of the Commission would be presented to the representative bodies who would ultimately have to approve them.[68]

The representative branch, while the "ultimate controlling power" in government,[69] must not take upon itself administrative duties.[70] The representative branch cannot administer the laws and lead the nation, but it can perform a useful watchdog role. Thus, the representative agency should always be in a position to "throw the light of publicity" on the actions of the administration, demanding explanations of the administration for any acts considered questionable.[71]

But how, in this case, does a representative government contribute to a participatory, self-educating form of politics? A great danger of representative government is that it could make individuals passive citizens, willing to turn over the affairs of state to others. Mill said that the main function of the representative body is to provide a forum for public discussion of the issues before society. Mill said that "I know not how a representative assembly can more usefully employ itself than in talk, when the subject of talk is the great public interests of the country, and every sentence of it represents the opinion either of some important body of persons in the nation, or of an individual in whom some such body have reposed their confidence."[72] The representative body must be a place where all the diverse opinions can be shared and debated. Each representative must form his or her own opinion by first consulting the opinions of all the others. Mill believed, apparently, that representatives engage in deliberation in a fishbowl setting, with the great bulk of the society watching. Indeed, citizens themselves, as they watch and listen to the debates taking place in front of them, necessarily form their own opinions by carefully and fully considering the positions of others. And in this atmosphere, individuals are able to enlarge their own understandings of issues and predicate their judgments on a careful consideration of others' views. Clearly, this experience would support a form of public reason in which people formed their opinions by carefully considering and testing the views of others, in as broad-based and as societal-wide discussion of the issues as is possible.

Representative government is threatened by two major dangers: class conflict and ignorance. Regarding the former problem, it is always desirable that no single class is allowed to be in a position to dominate the politics of society. This situation would divide society into hostile camps and destroy the chances for open deliberation, based on mutual respect for political differences. Mill had in mind, when he talked about the dominant interests, the "employers of labour," those who control industry, and the laboring class. To prevent one class from dominating the other Mill argued for balancing these giant interests off against each other in the legislative setting by allowing each to have the same number of votes in the representative body.[73] Presumably this approach would require that the two classes learn to compromise with each other as a precondition for achieving public-policy objectives.

The second problem, ignorance, can best be addressed by limiting, not eliminating, public participation. Mill argued that those less capable in the society develop enhanced capacities, including a respect for the needs of the community, a respect that helps to overcome the forces of divisiveness by engaging in public discussion about the issues of the day with their fellow citizens. "It is from political discussion, and collective political action, that one whose daily occupations concentrate his interest in a small circle round himself, learns to feel for and with his fellow citizens, and becomes consciously a member of the great community."[74] But when people are denied the franchise, they are precluded from taking part in the public deliberation. They are forced into isolation from the rest of the society; they engender feelings of resentment on the one hand or, on the other hand, they may just become indifferent to public concerns. The best remedy to defeat ignorance then, and at the same time to promote political community, is participation.[75]

But Mill argued that, although all should participate, not all should be allowed to do so equally. In this regard, everyone who pays taxes and who can "read, write and do arithmetic" should have a voice. This includes women who should have political rights equal to men.[76] But not everyone should have an equal voice.[77] Mill advocated a system of weighted voting by which those individuals with greater ability than others would be provided with more votes. The actual procedure to be followed in determining who gets more or less votes is not extensively developed. Mill did provide some examples of his position, however. For instance, an employer of labor, because he uses his mind, is more competent than a common laborer, whereas a foreman is more qualified than an ordinary worker, and a banker or merchant more qualified than a tradesman, and so on.[78] Furthermore, Mill did not support the idea of the secret ballot. If the vote is a public trust, why should not others know how we vote? Part of voting entails responsibility to the public interest. Should we be able to say one thing in public, but vote the opposite way in the privacy of the voting booth?[79] Mill thought not.

Even though these remedies may seem a bit farfetched to some, it is important to keep in mind Mill's central objective. Mill felt that civil society, one that protected the liberty of each person under the rule of law, could survive only in a setting that encouraged widescale public discussion of the major issues before the society. Such discussion would prevent the likelihood of powerful classes or groups from dominating politics and acting against the interests of the whole society. Moreover, this discussion would help ground civil society in a context that protected the full development of each individual as well as respect for protecting political community.

VI. RESPONSE AND REJOINDER

Mill's commitment to the full development of the "higher faculties" for all citizens gives civil society a mission that previous writers on civil society might seriously question. It is not that previous writers would refuse Mill's objectives. The other thinkers we have studied might question Mill's strong emphasis on them. For instance, individuals in Mill's views are to be free to make choices, as we saw in Hobbes and Locke, about which ways of life people think best for themselves. If individuals want to be exclusively businesspeople, fine. If they want to be farmers, fine. If they want to make money the main interest of their lives, fine. Just so long as people, as for Kant, uphold for others the same freedom they each want for themselves; the choices people make should not be questioned. But, in addition, Mill would urge that each person must assess the likelihood that a given way of life would open the doors to the full development of his or her higher mental faculties. If the ordinary day-to-day opportunities for people do not facilitate such development, Mill could not say that people in this situation would be truly free. However, from the standpoint of Hobbes, Locke, and Kant, Mill placed too high an expectation for most individuals to achieve; indeed, most individuals are happy with ordinary endeavors, and thus most do not wish to pursue Mill's concept of self-development. To press them in this direction in spite of themselves would be a great threat to their freedom.

Mill would respond by saying that the views of his critics manifest too low an expectation of people, and it is because of this fact that people are assumed unable to carry important burdens for the sake of a higher freedom. But if it is important for individuals to experience the richness associated with the "higher faculties," then individuals will have to accept the various burdens associated with these experiences. After all, developing one's higher capacities is not always easy. This kind of conduct takes hard work, persistence, and sacrifice. It is for this reason alone that society has to encourage people in this activity.

Rousseau would argue that Mill was reaching for a level of life that would be well beyond the general will. People form into associations to provide those things that all acknowledge are of common benefit. The things in question here are the goods that most understand will contribute to an ordinary life. Once again, it is necessary to remember that the people who make Rousseau's laws are the peasants who sing and dance under a tree. This view of political participation is a metaphor for Rousseau to describe a society in which the differences in viewpoint among people are not very great or intense. For Rousseau, without this possibility, there would be no basis upon which to build a community founded upon a commitment to the common good. But in emphasizing the "higher faculties," Rousseau would say that Mill has made the same mistake that the philosophers of Rousseau's age had made. For Rousseau, Mill would teach people to criticize existing ways of life and traditions. And, in the process of doing so, Mill, in Rousseau's view, would engender in people a general disrespect for the traditions of civic virtue that help to create consensus among the people of the society and that help to make possible respect for the common good.

Mill would have countered this view by pointing out that his conception of deliberation in a representative democracy, or of what we have called *public reason,* is designed to include as wide a participation as possible by all. Indeed, participation for Mill, just as for Rousseau, enhances a sense of the importance of civic life, and it builds the ties of community. No doubt Kant would have embraced Mill's commitment to a type of public reason that encompasses as broad a spectrum of views as is possible. Like Mill, Kant would have supported the freedom of intellectual opinion and speech that supported this process. But unlike Mill, Kant did not strive to make his discourse of public reason as inclusive of everyone as did Mill. Kant would not have accepted Mill's compromise position, which, in allowing all to participate, sought to limit the participation of those whose capacities made them less capable than others.

Hegel would have argued that a commitment to uphold the public good, within a setting that secures basic individual rights, cannot be attained by Mill, because Mill does not establish a proper relationship between the state and the civil society, defined as a separate sphere from the state. The state must stand above civil society, ready to control and regulate it as necessary. Hegel saw civil society as filled with competing groups and interests, which taken together might not promote the common good. To overcome this problem Hegel would allow the state the power to intervene in civil society and institute the common good.

Mill would no doubt argue that Hegel's view of civil society is harmed by Hegel's emphasis on those institutions that carry out his plan, in particular, the corporations. These entities would constantly intrude into people's lives and dictate to them the terms of their existence. How could real freedom ever be achieved in this setting? Mill would ask. Moreover, the corporations provide a basis for a bureaucratic life that over time places a group of experts in charge of society. And these people would monopolize information and decision making to such large degrees that the rest of society would no longer have an interest in participating in making decisions. When this event occurs, people's ability to fully take part in government would be diminished, along with the mental faculties needed for this enterprise. In consequence, Mill advocated, as part of his conception of civil society, the notion of a separate sphere of groups that would be able to perform, without the interference of government or of bureaucracy, many of the functions of both. This setting would encourage the development of public reason among all members of the society, in contrast to Hegel, whose corporations, from Mill's point of view, would severely limit the extension of public reason to all citizens.

Endnotes

1. John Stuart Mill, "Chapters on Socialism," in *Collected Works,* vol. 5 (Toronto and Buffalo: University of Toronto Press, 1967), p. 715, quoted in Richard J. Arneson, "Prospects for Community in a Market Economy," *Political Theory,* 9:2, May, 1981, p. 207.

2. John Stuart Mill, "Utilitarianism" in *The Philosophy of John Stuart Mill,* edited by Marshall Cohen, (New York: The Modern Library, 1961). *On Liberty,* which I will refer to, is in this volume, too.

3. "Utilitarianism," p. 330. Also see, Jeremy Bentham, in *Introduction to the Principles of Morals and Legislation, John Stuart Mill and Jeremy Bentham: Utilitarianism and Other Essays,* ed. Alan Ryan, (London: Penguin Books, 1987), pp. 65–66.

4. Mill, *On Liberty,* p. 198.

5. Jeremy Bentham, in *Introduction to the Principles of Morals and Legislation,* pp. 86, 97–111.

6. Ibid., p. 86. Italics are in text.

7. Ibid., p. 88. Italics in text.

8. Ibid., p. 87.

9. Ibid., pp. 89–97.

10. Mill, "Utilitarianism," pp. 331–32; 336–37.

11. Ibid., p. 332–33.

12. Ibid., pp. 338–39

13. Ibid., p. 338.

14. Ibid., p. 339.

15. Ibid., p. 340.

16. Ibid., p. 358.

17. Ibid., p. 359.

18. Ibid., p. 359.

19. Ibid., p. 342.

20. Ibid., p. 384.

21. Ibid., p. 384.

22. Ibid., p. 385.

23. Mill, *On Liberty,* p. 258.

24. Ibid., p. 252.

25. Ibid., p. 252.

26. Ibid., p. 252.

27. Ibid., p. 257.

28. Ibid., p. 199.

29. Ibid., p. 200.

30. Ibid., p. 187.

31. Ibid., p. 189.

32. Ibid., pp. 190–91. Italics in text.

33. Ibid., pp. 191.

34. Ibid., p. 249.

35. Ibid., p. 271, also, p. 275.

36. Ibid., p. 271.

37. Ibid., p. 205.

38. Ibid., p. 208.

39. Ibid., p. 209.

40. Ibid., p. 213.

41. Ibid., p. 224.

42. Ibid., p. 231.

43. Ibid., pp. 273, 282.

44. Ibid., pp. 280, 274–76.

45. Ibid., pp. 274–75, 79.

46. Ibid., pp. 279, 275.

47. Ibid., pp. 306–7. Additional discussion of this position will be provided in Chapter 16 where I discuss his essay on *The Subjection of Women.*

48. Mill, *On Liberty,* p. 308, also pp. 306–8.

49. Ibid., pp. 280.

50. John Stuart Mill, *Principles of Political Economy,* ed. by W.S. Ashley, (New York: Longmans, Green, and Co., 1929), p. 748.

51. Ibid., pp. 748–49.

52. Ibid., p. 747–48. Here, Mill said that Smith believed that a stationary economy "pinched and stinted people," unlike a growth economy. But Mill said that he cannot accept the "political economists of the old school" such as Smith who hold this view.

53. Ibid., pp. 208–9 and 749.

54. Ibid., p. 209.

55. Ibid., p. 209.

56. Ibid., p. 208.

57. Ibid., pp. 749, 209.

58. Ibid., pp. 759–60.

59. Ibid., p. 750.

60. Ibid., p. 751.

61. Ibid., pp. 763–64.

62. Ibid., pp. 768, 773.

63. Ibid., p. 209.

64. John Stuart Mill, *Considerations on Representative Government,* introduction by F.A. Hayek, (Chicago: Henry Regnery Co., 1962), pp. 72–73.

65. Mill, *On Liberty,* p. 312.

66. Ibid., p. 314.

67. Ibid., p. 312.

68. Mill, *Consideration on Representative Government,* pp. 104–9.

69. Ibid., p. 92.

70. Ibid., p. 98.

71. Ibid., p. 111.

72. Ibid., p. 112.

73. Ibid., pp. 136–37.

74. Ibid., p. 168.

75. Ibid., p. 169.

76. Ibid., pp. 187–89, 170, 172.

77. Ibid., pp. 178–79.

78. Ibid., pp. 178–81.

79. Ibid., pp. 204, 206–7.

Partial Bibliography and Further Reading

Barros, Carolyn A. *Autobiography: Narrative of Transformation.* Ann Arbor: University of Michigan Press, 1998.

Berger, Fred R. *Happiness, Justice, and Freedom: The Moral and Political Philosophy of John Stuart Mill.* Berkeley: University of California Press, 1984.

Cowling, Maurice. *Mill and Liberalism.* Cambridge: Cambridge University Press, 1990.

Gray, John. *Mill On Liberty: A Defense.* London: Routledge & K. Paul, 1983.

Hollander, Samuel. *John Stuart Mill On Economic Theory and Method.* London; New York: Routledge, 2000.

Ryan, Alan. *John Stuart Mill.* New York: Pantheon Books, 1970.

Semmel, Bernard. *John Stuart Mill and the Pursuit of Virtue.* New Haven: Yale University Press, 1984.

Stephen, Sir James Fitzjames. Edited. *Liberty, Equality, Fraternity.* Indianapolis: Liberty Fund, 1993.

Ten, C. L. *Mill on Liberty.* Oxford: Oxford University Press, 1980.

Ten, C. L. *Mill's Moral, Political, and Legal Philosophy.* Aldershot, England; Brookfield, Vt.: Ashgate, 1999.

Thompson, Dennis F. *John Stuart Mill and Representative Government.* Princeton: Princeton University Press, 1976.

Thornton, Neil. *The Problem of Liberalism in the Thought of John Stuart Mill.* New York: Garland, 1987.

13

John Rawls: The Just and Fair Civil Society

I. Introduction

John Rawls is among the most influential political theorists in the twentieth century, and his concept of justice as fairness is of central importance to contemporary discussions of civil society. Rawls's conception of justice responds, in part, to two different political concerns. In the 1960s the problem of American society was how to make a part of the mainstream life of society those people, in particular African-Americans, who for so long had been excluded by both custom and law from jobs, rights, and political participation. Today, in addition to continuing the quest for equality of opportunity for minorities and women, we face the problem of how to maintain the stability of a democratic regime in the face of competing views of religion, of gender, of sexuality, and of culture. Rawls's work tracks both concerns. In *A Theory of Justice,* published in 1971,[1] Rawls's concept of justice as fairness was designed to secure basic liberties and opportunities for all citizens, including those who have been subject to forms of iniquitous discrimination. His book, *Political Liberalism,*[2] published in 1993, revamps his concept of justice in a way that makes possible a civil society that contains a broad diversity of equally rational, even if contradictory, ways of life. In both works, Rawls wants to show how his theory of justice defends continued and long-term support for the basic institutions and principles of a constitutional democracy.

As we examine Rawls's doctrines, I not only hope to provide a lucid picture of modern liberal civil society, but I also hope to provide a discussion of some of the problems that this kind of society must address.

II. RAWLS'S PRINCIPLES OF JUSTICE
IN A THEORY OF JUSTICE

To begin, it must be made clear why it is vital to determine the principles of justice upon which a liberal civil society rests. Justice is a value of central importance to a civil society because the concept of justice is the basis for determining how basic goods, including rights and opportunities, should be distributed among citizens. Now, a civil society is composed of individuals, each of whom has his or her interests to pursue, and often enough, there will be conflicts over how these goods should be distributed. For instance, every civil society guarantees individuals equal access to basic rights, but at the same time, there always emerges differences in wealth and social and political influence. Reconciling the provision of equal rights with differences in wealth and social power becomes an important issue in a civil society. Central to resolving this conflict are clearly established and generally accepted principles of justice. Once these principles are determined, then, all public institutions, such as the government and the economy, must distribute basic goods in accordance with them. Rawls's concept of justice as fairness regulates the institutions of a just civil society in keeping with a clear statement as to how rights and basic goods must be distributed to ensure equal freedom in a setting characterized by differences in wealth and status.[3]

The major question for a civil society to address pertains to which principles of distribution are most fair. There are many possible conceptions of justice from which to choose. For instance, one might argue that goods should be distributed in such a way as to ensure the greatest benefit for the greatest number of people, even if this means accepting certain injustices for the rest. Still others, as Locke had argued, might claim that each person should be allowed to pursue his or her own interests in keeping with rules that encourage those with the most talent and ability to keep the gains of their work. The only restriction on this principle is that the work individuals perform must contribute to the general welfare of society. Or some might argue for a purely egalitarian form of distribution in which each person is entitled to the same amount of basic goods.

Rawls realizes that there are many possible principles that persons could choose to make the basis for distributing basic goods such as rights and opportunities. Given the diversity of possibilities, how does a society determine the set of principles that all would consider fair? Owing to Rawls's intention to find a single set of principles that all members of the society would accept as fair, it is necessary to start from a perspective that is common to all rational persons. This approach would exclude from the deliberation about justice all forms of bias. For if people were to discuss the question of justice from the standpoint of their particular interests, then each person would define a conception of justice that best suits his own needs, and in consequence, no common, shared view of justice would emerge.

To find a common standard, Rawls starts from what he considers an imaginary, but nonetheless, universal standpoint. His viewpoint, called the "original position," is presumed to be a point of view that all rational persons would find as an acceptable starting point for deliberating about justice. The original position is built upon what Rawls calls the "veil of ignorance." Each individual in the original position wears this veil when considering which principles of justice to choose. This veil would prevent him from knowing anything about his or her particular life circumstances, including his or her place in society, his or her abilities, his or her fortunes, and so on.[4] What kinds of knowledge would people have behind the veil? All persons in this situation would have general knowledge about the way society is structured and how it works in carrying out its basic functions. Rawls says that people in the original position "understand political affairs and the principles of economic theory; they know the basis of social organization and the laws of human psychology."[5] Of particular importance is that individuals will know that society has a top and bottom rung, as well as stages in between. Some people, owing to greater abilities than others, will occupy more important positions than will others. Moreover, each individual realizes that every person in society will want as many as possible of the goods that facilitate the enjoyment of life.[6] Thus, all people would like to end up in the most important positions, but at the same time, each knows that there are not enough of these "top" positions to go around.

But, and this is the most critical point, no one from behind the veil of ignorance knows for certain in which level of society he or she will end up. In the original position, then, uncertainty pervades people's minds. Responding to the uncertainty is a major factor determining one's choice of principles. Indeed, given the uncertainty, each person is prone to pursue a strategy that makes it possible for him or her to have a reasonable life, should he or she end up at the bottom. Each person does so by choosing a view of justice that guarantees those in the worst-off position a decent life, thus assuring their self-respect. In taking this view, each one assumes that the worst outcome could befall him, and, given that this outcome is possible, he or she hopes to make the worst situation as much a harbinger of a decent life as is feasible. Here, persons are not prone to gamble on the hope that, when they leave the veil of ignorance behind and enter society, they will be in the best position. Were they to take this gamble, they, of course, would want to fill the best situation with as many benefits as possible, and they would care little about securing the fortunes of worst situation. However, Rawls's original position is predicated upon the premise that people would be far more cautious and "conservative" and much less prone to taking a risk of this sort.[7]

So what are the principles of justice individuals would derive in the original position? That is, which principles will be the basis for distributing what Rawls calls fundamental "social primary goods,"[8] such as rights, liberties, opportunities, income, wealth, and self-respect? His principles are the following:

> *First: each person is to have an equal right to the most extensive total system of equal basic liberties compatible with a similar system of liberty for all. Second: social and economic inequalities are to be arranged so that they are both: (a) to the greatest benefit of the least advantaged . . . , and (b) attached to offices and positions open to all under conditions of fair equality of opportunity.*[9]

Rawls's principles of justice distinguish between two parts of the social system, with the first principle applying to the first part and the second principle applying to the second part. The first of his principles of justice protects equal basic liberties, and the second of his principles is concerned with the social and economic inequalities that arise even in just societies. Included under the first principle, the principle of equal liberty, is the need to provide to each person, regardless of his or her social position, basic political liberties such as the right to vote and hold public office, as well as the freedoms of speech, conscience, thought, and association. The list of basic liberties also includes what Rawls calls "freedom of the person." The latter protects people from physical assault as well as "psychological oppression." Also, there is a right to own personal property. Finally, Rawls's list of basic liberties includes "freedom from arbitrary arrest and seizure as defined by the concept of the rule of law."[10] The second principle, which addresses social and economic inequalities arising from the distribution of wealth, in particular the second part of the second principle, what Rawls calls the "liberal principle of fair equality of opportunity," requires that all people should be accorded equal opportunity to compete for all positions.[11]

Now, Rawls realizes that as a result of open and fully fair competition some people will end up with more important positions as well as more wealth and status than others. Inevitably, then, there will be inequalities emerging from a situation in which a firm commitment to equal opportunity exists. The question for Rawls is how to permit inequalities without at the same time creating a society that denies full rights and basic opportunities for all. To achieve this objective, Rawls approaches the concept of justice from the standpoint of what he calls "democratic equality." Here, by adding to the fair equality of opportunity principle the *difference principle,* which is part *a* of the second principle, he argues that "the social order is not to establish and secure the more attractive prospects of those better off unless doing so is to the advantage of those less fortunate."[12]

Two important commitments are embodied in the principles of justice. First, the basic structure of the society's political institutions must be designed to protect the same basic rights for all persons. To this end, the equal liberty principle is given priority. This means that in order to secure wider economic and social opportunities for people it is not acceptable to deny to others their basic liberties. Still, at times, liberty can be limited for the sake of securing a greater overall liberty for each person in society. For instance, liberties can be limited when they conflict with each other. In this circumstance, what is sought is an overall system of liberty in which competing liberties, such as speech and freedom from personal harassment, are placed in a reasonable, balanced relationship so as to better approximate the ideal of equal freedom for each person.[13] Second, Rawls recognizes that owing to the differentials in status and wealth, it is possible for a deep sense of unfairness to emerge in society. Those who lack similar status or whose status provides them with little or no opportunity whatsoever will be deprived of what Rawls calls the most important primary good of self-respect, without which "nothing may seem worth doing."[14] To avert the loss of self-respect and the social instability such a situation causes, it is necessary, according to the difference principle, that the better-off classes transfer some of their gains to the least well-off members. This transfer is undertaken in the hope of ensuring for these individuals not just a basic minimum, what we call a safety net today, but a fair chance to achieve success at a variety of opportunities pertinent to their needs and specific abilities. For Stephen Holmes, it is the quest for equality of opportunity for everyone that makes Rawls a "radical among liberals." Rawls does not just settle for the safety net or a basic social minimum, but, in addition, he wants the better off to help make possible full equality of opportunity for all people.[15] Inequalities are seen as acceptable by all, including of course the worst-off members, because these inequalities are shown to be to the advantage of everyone. This state of affairs manifests the intention of what Rawls calls the "general conception of justice":

> *All social values—liberty and opportunity, income and wealth, and the bases of self-respect—are to be distributed equally unless an unequal distribution of any, or all, of these values is to everyone's advantage.*[16]

Why would people choose Rawls's principles of justice over others? In the first place, his concept of justice ensures all people that, if misfortune should befall them and they end up in the lowest position in society, their lives will be decent, and they will be afforded an opportunity for self-respect. Here, whatever else happens, individuals will have their basic rights secured, and in addition all people will have a full plate of opportunities. In addition, Rawls's concept of justice incorporates merit as opposed to inherited social position as the basis for distributing opportunities. Yet, society as a whole must benefit from meritorious acts. Certainly individuals who are meritorious would benefit personally, but their actions are to contribute to the welfare of society as a whole, too. Finally, Rawls argues that individuals realize that there is more to gain from cooperation than from conflict. Indeed, cooperation is the basis for achieving the highly prized primary good of self-respect, which has a "central place" in his scheme.[17] As a first step toward realizing a cooperative society, it is necessary to remove the potentially destabilizing consequences arising from differences in power and ability by allowing them only on the condition that these differences benefit everyone. Only in this kind of social setting, governed by Rawls's view of justice, will there be sufficient peace and stability to ensure the basic rights and opportunities that make possible the attainment of self-respect for all people.

III. THE WELL-ORDERED SOCIETY

Given this view of justice, Rawls believes, in *A Theory of Justice,* that it would be possible to construct what he referred to as a *well-ordered society.* A well-ordered society is one in which all citizens accept the principles of justice and each person in the society has a "strong and normally effective desire to act as the principles of justice require."[18] What kind of social experience emerges for people in this setting? Rawls describes a society in which purely private interests do not motivate individuals. In a "private society" people have their own ends, each has little or no concern for the "good of others," and each "prefers the most efficient scheme that gives him the largest share of assets."[19] A private society is a place in which each person acts by his own calculations to both define and to pursue his personal ends without regard for a larger conception of justice that should regulate everyone's life. Presumably, in a private society, or what we have also at times referred to as the market setting, individuals remain in an antagonistic and competitive relationship with others and each is concerned to find ways to accumulate and to acquire as much for himself as possible. But in a well-ordered society, where each person shares the conception of justice just described, people understand that they need each other as "partners," each realizing that "the successes and enjoyments of others are necessary for and complementary to our own good."[20]

Here, each understands that people have various capacities and that the latter are best realized in a cooperative society in which different people help each other to realize their potential. Moreover, because people are seen as cooperating with each other to realize diverse capacities, there is no destructive competition, and thus individuals "appreciate the perfections of others."[21] The result of this experience is a social cohesiveness in which "we are led to the notion of a community of humankind the members of which enjoy one another's excellences and individuality elicited by free institutions, and they recognize the good of each as an element in the complete activity the whole scheme of which is consented to and gives pleasure to all."[22]

IV. POLITICAL LIBERALISM AND VALUE PLURALISM

Rawls's depiction of a well-ordered society illustrates a fear common to some civil society theorists such as Mill and Hegel. The fear is that the market orientation and the private freedom it encourages could create a society filled with self-serving individuals, no longer committed to maintaining mutual respect or regard for the needs and rights of others. But a well-ordered society would not suffer this fate. Instead, a well-ordered society offers a picture of cohesiveness based on the fact that individuals, of whatever type, can all agree to maintain a commitment to the same principles of justice and to see to it that these principles are embodied into the main institutions of the society.[23]

Rawls's view of a well-ordered society suggests, then, that individuals are to make his principles of justice the basis for all relationships. Here, a single doctrine of justice would govern all phases of life for all people. This doctrine, for instance, would ensure each person equal political liberty throughout their lives, either as members of any particular group and as members of society in general. For instance, as a member of a labor union, I must agree to accord others who are not members of my union the same basic rights guaranteed by the first principle of justice. In this case, then, during a strike, I would grant those people who do not want to abide by the picket line a chance to cross it, enter the company I am striking against, and if need be even take the job I had. The same right to freedom of expression that guarantees me the right to strike guarantees my opponent the right to cross the picket line. Moreover, internally within the union, I would have to abide by the principle of equal political liberty for how decisions within the group should be made. For instance, each member should have the same right to run for positions of union leadership. Thus, where there has been a tradition of preventing certain members, say minorities or women, from holding union office, this tradition must be changed and union life made to be in accord with the principle of equal freedom.

Rawls even provides a view of moral development that indicates how people are socialized to make the principles of justice the main dimensions of their lives.[24] For instance, children must experience a family setting that nurtures a sense of self-respect by providing them with unconditional love. Once one leaves the family, respect for the principles of justice is further enhanced, as individuals become part of cooperative associations with others. In these settings, individuals must learn to understand the way people contribute differently to achieve the common ends of an association, and, further, they must develop a basis for cooperation through building ties of friendship and maintaining virtues such as fidelity and trust.

These views suggest that in a well-ordered society individuals accept that the principles of justice should be the key governing factors throughout all major phases of their lives, including their associations in groups, or with families, or with friends. In this case, there is a single, comprehensive political doctrine that should be the basis for regulating all relationships and for thus achieving a just and stable society. Rawls, now, in *Political Liberalism,* finds this depiction of the route to a just society "unrealistic."[25] What is unrealistic about suggesting that one comprehensive political doctrine for all of life should be made the basis for society?

Rawls realizes that his argument for a single comprehensive political doctrine to guide all the affairs of life will not be practical where there are, as in today's society, so many people holding different moral, religious, and philosophical doctrines. For instance, a deeply religious person may argue for a way of life encompassing prayer throughout the day and a less religious person will find such a life onerous in the extreme. Some people may demand a chance to promote certain moral doctrines that conflict with the moral views of others, on such matters as abortion, prayer in the school, and so on. Further, Rawls realizes that many of these doctrines are reasonable, even if they conflict with each other. Consequently, there is no single doctrine, including the doctrine that undergirds his view of a well-ordered society, that can be given a priority, without denying some space to the different moral doctrines in society. For Rawls, a modern democratic society "is characterized not simply by a pluralism of comprehensive religious, philosophical, and moral doctrines but by a pluralism of incompatible yet reasonable comprehensive doctrines."[26] The new problem Rawls addresses in his discussion of political liberalism, then, is how it is possible to have a *"stable and just society"* or a society in which citizens "live together and . . . affirm" the principles of a constitutional democracy, even when it is the case that citizens are "divided by reasonable though incompatible religious, philosophical, and moral doctrines."[27]

Given this new problem Rawls identifies, the approach to achieving stability must be "recast" from the strategy developed in his view of a well-ordered society.[28] Because of so many different ways of life, no single political doctrine, as was the case with his conception of the well-ordered society, can be made primary. This means that Rawls's principles of justice cannot be pushed down to cover all phases of life of each person in each domain of society. The principles of justice should only extend to the relationships individuals have with each other as citizens, but not to relationships they have to each other in the family or in private clubs. As citizens, individuals are to have to equal rights, but in the setting of family, the parents do not accord to children equal say. And in many private organizations, such as religious ones, the congregation members do not have the same input as do those who are in authority, such as elders or priests.

In place of an approach to achieving justice that would extend his principles of justice deeply into all phases of life in society, in his book *Political Liberalism* Rawls now argues for a *political conception of justice* as the basis for society. In this view, there are certain fundamental political ideas that are said to be "implicit" in a democratic society, and, furthermore, these ideas would permit a wide range of diverse moral doctrines to flourish.[29]

As we now explain, Rawls's concept of *political liberalism* embodies and defines the nature of these understandings.

In developing his doctrine of political liberalism, Rawls first refers to what he calls the "basic structure" of modern constitutional democracy. This structure pertains to the basic political, social, and economic institutions, which, together, constitute a system that makes possible social unity and continuing cooperation among citizens with diverse beliefs and views, from "one generation to the next."[30] For instance, Rawls has in mind the various government institutions on which a society depends, the type of economic life that a society upholds, and the general and basic institutions that a society seeks to maintain, such as a system of education, forms of socialization, and so on.

Now, these institutions, or the basic structure of a constitutional democracy, are directed by certain shared public values, defined in what Rawls calls a *political conception of justice.* These values orient society and arrange the basic institutions to achieve certain shared purposes or what Rawls calls the "public political culture of a democratic society." If this is the case, to what ends and purposes would the major institutions of the basic structure be arranged?[31] In general, the main public political principles that a constitutional democracy is designed to achieve are a commitment to secure basic rights to all citizens, and to ensure that these rights are given priority.[32] To this end, Rawls will discuss, as we describe below, elements of the political culture such as an overlapping consensus and public reason, both of which are designed to make certain that the chief objective of the public, political culture—to protect the basic rights of all citizens—is secured. On this view, then, the main institutions that make up the basic structure of a society are to be arranged in keeping with a commitment to the major values of the public political culture, thus securing basic rights for all citizens.[33]

Outside of the public political culture is a social or what Rawls also calls the nonpublic domain, or "the culture of daily life." Rawls refers to this realm as the "background culture of a civil society," or a setting in which exist the diverse associations of daily life, including "churches and universities, learned and scientific societies, and clubs and teams."[34] Here, individuals are to guide their lives by the particular values found in the group setting that they elect to be a part of.

Rawls, in referring to the nonpublic dimensions, is careful to point out that he is talking about a social sphere in which individuals guide their lives by certain moral conceptions, pertinent to the associations they are members of.[35] Moreover, in the nonpublic setting, there will be many different values, and these values will be attached to the different nonpublic associations. Further, these values are freely accepted by people, whose choices are based on their experiences with a host of commitments and attachments to nonpublic groups that they develop over a lifetime.[36]

Each of the nonpublic groups or associations has what Rawls refers to as a *comprehensive doctrine.* A doctrine is comprehensive "when it includes conceptions of what is of value in human life, as well as ideals of personal virtue and character that are to inform much of our nonpolitical conduct." Thus, a comprehensive doctrine defines the general values and virtues that are found in various associations in the nonpublic settings and that govern the outlooks of people who choose to live in those settings.[37] Moreover, there are many conflicting and competing moral doctrines. Some groups will advocate strong religious upbringings; others will advocate atheism; some groups who are religious advocate this religion and not that one; others who reject religion may make a particular philosophical view of life a dominant element, and so on.

Given the presence of many diverse comprehensive doctrines, it is clear now how Rawls's doctrine of political liberalism differs from the concept of a well-ordered society found in *A Theory of Justice*. Rawls's political liberalism suggests a political conception of justice that refers only to the "main institutions of political and social life, not for the whole of life."[38] Rawls no longer sees his conception of justice as designed to present a single set of principles that would be applicable to all dimensions of life, from activities related to interacting with government, to associations with friends and family. Our lives take place in two cultures, and, when we enter the public political culture, we live by values that are not necessarily operative for us in the nonpublic setting. Still, the values of the public culture are considered reasonable and thus worthy of our support because they contribute to the maintenance of a constitutional order that people in a democratic culture generally support. Indeed, these values are taken for granted and are considered "latent in the public political culture of a democratic society."[39]

In developing the distinction between nonpublic and public cultures, Rawls has conceived of a civil society in the two senses that have permeated this book. First, a civil society consists of public principles and laws that sustain a commitment to basic rights and a constitutional democracy. Second, a civil society also includes a separate sphere of groups, independent from the state or large economic organizations, whose particular moral conceptions guide association life. Indeed, the political conception of a constitutional democracy is defined in such a way as not to interfere with the ways of life of the various nonpublic settings, each of which is driven by different moral, religious, or philosophical conceptions. But at the same time, the political conception of society also suggests that no single comprehensive doctrine, which might emanate from a nonpublic setting, is to become the preeminent basis for determining the nature of justice in society. Were this to happen, the state would be turned into an oppressive regime, losing thereby its constitutional democratic character.[40]

V. THE OVERLAPPING CONSENSUS AND CIVIC VIRTUE

In line with the preceding point, then, for Rawls the values of the political conception of a constitutional democracy are fundamental ones. Thus, when other values come into conflict with the main values of the political conception of a constitutional democracy, in particular the importance and priority of basic rights, the latter always must "outweigh" in importance other values.[41] Unless this commitment is possible, then society would not retain its character as a constitutional democracy.

Rawls's willingness to make the values of a constitutional democracy have priority evolves from his concern to find a basis for maintaining the unity and stability of this kind of society. It is in keeping with this view that Rawls emphasizes the importance of an overlapping consensus. What is an overlapping consensus and why is it important?

In his discussion of political liberalism Rawls argues that a constitutional democracy can only survive when support for its basic institutions is shared universally by all citizens.

This means that all citizens, regardless of the particular comprehensive doctrines they adhere to, must make as the primary basis for their citizen role a commitment to an overlapping consensus that enshrines support for constitutional democracy throughout society. The central idea of an overlapping consensus is that supporters of different, but reasonable comprehensive doctrines find it possible to "endorse the political conception [of a democracy], each from its own point of view."[42] For Rawls, support for the overlapping consensus involves people being able to uphold, regardless of their nonpublic commitments and values, a general commitment to the "liberty of conscience and freedom of thought, as well as fair equal opportunity and principles covering certain essential needs."[43]

In addition to a commitment to these principles, the overlapping consensus includes support for three important dimensions. The first is to clearly fix "once and for all" the nature of the basic rights and liberties that all citizens are to secure as a "special priority." This principle removes the definition of basic rights from the "calculus of social interests, thereby establishing clearly and firmly the rules of political contest." The second idea is that, in discussing public matters, citizens must rely upon the processes of what Rawls calls *public reason*.[44] I will discuss the nature of public reason below. For now, suffice it say that public reason represents a shared approach to deliberating and developing judgments about public matters, an approach that will be helpful in achieving a principled consensus or a consensus that protects basic liberties for all. The final element of the overlapping consensus is a willingness of people to meet each other "halfway," and to "cooperate with others on political terms that everyone can publicly accept."[45]

Before proceeding further, it is well to enumerate the important implications for civic virtue of the notion of an overlapping consensus. In particular, the overlapping consensus embodies the civic virtue dimensions of Lockean toleration and of a Kantian view of mutual respect. Rawls's overlapping consensus includes Lockean toleration when he says we should learn to meet others halfway. By doing so, we practice the art of learning how to live-and-let-live. The first two dimensions of the overlapping consensus, on the other hand, are versions of the mutual respect principle. In according to others the same rights as we expect for our close associates and ourselves we ensure that each person is treated with dignity and is accorded self-respect. Moreover, the doctrine of public reason, like Kant's view of the public use of reason discussed earlier, asks individuals to engage one another in a deliberation about common issues. And this enterprise requires us, as we will see below, to consider the points of view of others with whom we disagree. In doing so, we manifest toward others respect once again, but this time, respect is associated with the effort of each of us to include others in forging agreements on important public issues.

Further, it should be clear that Rawls incorporates Locke's notion of toleration, but in a manner that recasts the idea considerably. As we saw, Locke did not include toleration for Catholics and atheists, in large part because his view of toleration suggested that, even when people of differing views agree to live-and-let-live, a deep sense of difference might remain between people. And this sense of difference might contribute to a tendency to deny to those who differ widely from accepted social norms the same rights guaranteed to all. Thus, Locke's notion of toleration would be used to impose certain comprehensive conceptions of justice, appropriate for the nonpublic setting only, onto all people. Rawls avoids this problem for himself by grafting the practice of mutual respect onto toleration.

VI. PUBLIC REASON AND CONSTITUTIONAL ESSENTIALS

The concept of public reason is based upon the view that individuals, in discussing and in resolving their differences with respect to public matters, should explain the basis for their views in terms that all could "reasonably expect that others might endorse as consistent with their freedom and equality."[46] To this end, Rawls adopts Kant's approach to the public use of reason, discussed earlier. In particular, Rawls hopes to find a common, public standpoint from which to discuss the reasons used by people to support their views and to determine the reasons all should support.[47] So what is the nature or the precise content of the common standpoint that Rawls employs to make possible his view of Kant's conception of the public use of reason?

For Rawls, public reason requires that citizens "conduct their fundamental discussions within the framework of what each regards as a political conception of justice based on the values that the others can reasonably be expected to endorse."[48] The acceptable political conception of justice Rawls has in mind is a liberal one, in keeping with the view of what grounds a constitutional democracy. In this regard, public reason supports a political conception of justice that "specifies" certain basic rights, liberties, and opportunities, it is to "assign a special priority to these rights, liberties, and opportunities," and it is to provide individuals with the means to make use of their basic rights, liberties, and opportunities.[49] Generally, Rawls's basic rights include the right to vote, the right of participation in politics, freedom of conscience, thought, and association, and coverage by the rule of law.[50] In my discussion below, of how to use public reason in addressing the abortion question, I will add both the rights of privacy and of equal treatment to Rawl's list.

Moreover, public reason must adhere to certain guidelines that specify the way that reasoning should take place.[51] What are these guidelines? First, in discussing matters of public importance, we are to use both the beliefs and approaches to reasoning found in common sense as well as the methods and conclusions of science.[52] Second, people must uphold political values that make possible open public discussion of political questions. In particular, there must be a commitment to civility, as well as a refusal to define the nature of the most just approach to a public issue, or "basic justice," in terms of particular non-public, comprehensive religious or philosophical doctrines.[53]

To demonstrate how public reason goes about addressing issues, I will use the example of abortion, and thus I will refer to those conditions under which women should be free to terminate their pregnancies. To discuss this issue, we first need to know which right, among those that might be relevant in this case, should have jurisdiction. There are several candidates. First, there is the right of privacy or freedom of choice, and next there is the right to equal treatment. Take the right of choice first. Here, the question pertains to whether the idea of individual private freedom, which protects freedom of choice with respect to one's religion, covers a woman's choice to carry a pregnancy to term. Is there a right of choice that allows the state to prevent interference with one's private beliefs in one area but not in another? If the state can prevent placing restrictions on women in the area of religious beliefs but allow restrictions in matters of abortion, how can this inconsistency be justified in the name of choice? Regarding equal treatment, the question is whether it is fair for women to be denied a right to have an abortion when men are not similarly burdened, even though men's responsibilities in conceiving children are equal to those of women.

On what basis does one determine which right—privacy or equal treatment—has jurisdiction in the matter at hand? One must use accepted standards of reasoning and argument commonly employed in society. Not only does this mean avoiding particular comprehensive doctrines, such as religious arguments as the basis for judgment, but it also means providing good evidence backed by sound reasoning. For instance, let us say that I want to argue for the right of privacy as the basis for abortion rights. I might argue that this right is necessary to prevent terrible harms to women. I can point out that when women did not have the right to choose an abortion, as the right of privacy would permit, control over their bodies was ceded to others, and this led to terrible consequences. Women who needed abortions had to go to "back alley" clinics run by unscrupulous people. Often abortions in these settings were performed without regard for the safety of women.

Alternatively, the proponent of the equal treatment principle might argue that there is a grave injustice committed against women when women's lives have been disproportionately and unfairly affected by having to carry the lion's share of the responsibility for children. Pointing to empirical studies, the advocate of the equal treatment standard would say that it is because of the lack of equal treatment that women do not have as good a chance as men in achieving success in various careers. The equal treatment standard should have priority over the privacy standard on this view because equality is a value of higher importance, over all, than privacy. Of course, the proponent of the privacy standard would argue otherwise.

The advocate of either position would go on to demonstrate how, practically speaking, the law should be designed to allow public policies that achieve the objectives of the respective views. The privacy advocates would seek policies that protect women's unrestricted access to abortion clinics. Those wanting to interfere with women in this regard should be restrained and made subject to severe penalties. The equal treatment advocate would hope to place into public policy funds to allow women of whatever economic background an opportunity to choose an abortion. This possibility would allow women to have the same flexibility as men to choose career paths.

Obviously, those who are against abortion will argue that neither the right of privacy nor the right of equal treatment can be used to justify abortions, at least as abortion proponents apply these concepts. Those denying abortion rights will argue that abortion proponents, in using either the right of privacy or the right of equal treatment to justify abortions, do not include a concern for the interests of either the fetus or the father. Here, if one is to accord privacy or equal treatment to either the fetus or the father, then it could be argued that under these conceptions of rights, abortion must be denied. For what privacy rights does an aborted fetus or a father who is against an abortion of his prospective child have, or in the same way what chances for equal treatment can an aborted fetus or a father who loses his child to an abortion expect?

Eventually the discussion must come to an end, and based on the discussion a decision must be rendered by a legal body, such as a court or a legislature, which determines the policy on the issue. Given Rawls's view of public reason, we presume that the various points of view just discussed were a part of the deliberation process. Still, after the decision has been rendered, it is both possible and likely that people will disagree with the policy outcome. This may be the case even among people who agree with the basic principles of public reason and the need for the common standpoint it suggests. At this point, what will ensure that those who disagree with the result will nonetheless tolerate it, as well as the society that produces it?

Generally, as long as the overlapping consensus is maintained, then individuals could tolerate not only outcomes they do not agree with, but also they could continue to tolerate the social and political setting of society that produced these outcomes. And the reason for this view is that this consensus suggests support for what Rawls calls *constitutional essentials,* or the main elements of a constitutional democracy.[54] The constitutional essentials refer first to a shared understanding of what constitutes basic rights and freedoms, including, for instance, as mentioned earlier, the right to vote, to participate in politics, freedom of conscience and of thought and association, and the protection of the rule of law. Moreover, constitutional essentials include those principles that define the general structure of government, including the different powers of the various branches and the rules of the political process all are to follow.[55]

Thus, when people disagree with the results of public reason, all can tolerate them and the political process that produces them, because they accept the constitutional essentials that provided the context for their determination. The stability of the regime in the face of continuing disagreements on policy can thus be preserved.

VII. CIVIL SOCIETY AND POLITICAL LIBERALISM

In general, Rawls's society, which embodies his view of political liberalism, can survive only if people uphold the values of the overlapping consensus. Were people to hold as well as to act upon beliefs that violated the principles of this consensus, then it would not be possible to maintain a constitutional democracy. Thus, Rawls expects that in a society incorporating the values of political liberalism, comprehensive moral doctrines that reject the principles of the overlapping consensus would never gain such importance that they would be able to undermine the "essential justice" of society.[56] For instance, in a society holding Rawls's overlapping consensus, any religious group seeking to use the instruments of the state to deny religious rights to members of other religions would "cease to exist."[57] Moreover, certain issues would never even be considered in the society Rawls describes. Thus, any effort to legislate serfdom and slavery would be considered a violation of basic principles of justice, and so would be "off the [political] agenda."[58]

What are the ways to maintain support among people for the values of the overlapping consensus? Rawls's view of political liberalism points to several suggestions, and I will list three of them in the following paragraphs. It should be clear before proceeding, however, that the suggestions that follow would be compelling only to those who found Rawls's brand of political liberalism acceptable and who in consequence wanted to maintain the form of constitutional democracy he advocates. For those who do not support his view of political liberalism, the suggestions I discuss below would not appear to be compelling justifications for upholding the overlapping consensus.

First, Rawls argues for minimum forms of civic education for all. For instance, children who are members of different religious sects, including those who oppose modern culture and who in consequence want to have their members live apart from the modern world, should be taught the constitutional essentials of a liberal regime. This is necessary so that "they [the children] know that liberty of conscience exists in their society and that apostasy is not a legal crime, all this to ensure that their continued membership in a religious sect when they come of age is not based simply on ignorance of their basic rights or fear of punishment for offenses that do not exist."[59] Moreover, education in the religious setting should prepare children to be self-sufficient individuals who are able to cooperate with other members of the society on fair terms, or terms that maintain the basic rights of each person.[60]

Second, Rawls is aware that people who support the values of the overlapping consensus do so because they expect the state not to interfere in the lives of the diverse groups, which hold different, even if reasonable, moral doctrines. To this end, the state must be neutral to the various values and ways of life apparent in society, subject to the provision that the values in question fall within the "public political conception of justice." Thus, it is clearly the case that Rawls's view of neutrality, or the idea that the state should provide room for a diversity of competing values without giving favor to any one of them, does not mean that people have a right to pursue a way of life that threatens the basic rights of other citizens. Indeed, Rawls says that his view of neutrality, what he refers to as the "priority of right" or the idea of securing basic rights for all, "allows [that] only permissible conceptions (those that respect the principles of justice) can be pursued."[61]

In this case, then, it would not seem appropriate for a religious group to teach that gay people are inferior. Now, some might argue that Rawls's neutral state should allow religious groups to at least teach that gays act in defiance of God's commandments if that is what such groups believe, so long as at the same time they teach that gays must be accorded the same rights as others. But how could one teach that a person is inferior in the eyes of God and then turn around and teach that "inferior" people should have the same rights as others? It would seem, then, that Rawls's doctrine would require groups professing an anti-gay sentiment to change their teachings. A similar point can be made for religious groups who hold anti-Semitic views. These groups might argue that it is perfectly all right for them to teach anti-Semitism as part of a religious orthodoxy and not violate Rawls's norm because at the same time that they preach intolerance, they are urging members to maintain the rights of all people, including Jews.

Third, people will support the overlapping consensus when as citizens they are permitted to promote their particular comprehensive moral doctrines during the process of public reasoning about public issues. Now, Rawls would agree that it is acceptable for individuals to enter the public realm and present particular reasons derived from their religious experience as the basis for their position on a public issue. They may do so, that is, subject to one important limitation. In particular, as they present their comprehensive moral values, they must act "to strengthen the ideal of public reason itself."[62] Here, one could argue that the society needs to be made more respectful of religious values for a whole host of reasons, including that religious beliefs contribute to moral stability or that they help people to find contentment and happiness not otherwise available in the highly competitive setting of modern society. These values in the public realm could be presented in a way that demonstrated how religious traditions strengthen the values of public reason. For instance, during the process of discussing how to handle out-of-control children, I, who am not wedded to promoting religious ideas for this purpose, may be shown the virtue of such a practice. I would have to be shown that religious practices help sustain an environment that secures what is a major value of public reason, the basic rights for all people.

Clearly, the effect of Rawls's political liberalism on the members of a society would be to demand that, throughout the variety of nonpublic associations such as the church and family as well as all the other groups of civil society, it would be necessary to teach the values of the overlapping consensus and to expect that nonpublic groups conform to them. This outcome contradicts his hope that the principles of justice not reach down into all phases of life of all people in society. There is no question, then, that Rawls's political conception of justice promotes a single comprehensive moral doctrine not unlike the concept of a well-ordered society in *A Theory of Justice.* And his political conception does reach deeply into many phases of life in society. This means that Rawls's views require that individuals throughout their engagements in the nonpublic spaces of civil society— including families and religious institutions—should make certain that the major doctrines of Rawls's political conception of justice, in particular respect for basic rights and for public reason, should always be maintained. As Susan Okin indicates, Rawls seems with his concept of political liberalism to be arguing that "persons in the just society should order their whole lives—not just the political aspects of them—in accordance with justice."[63]

It is the comprehensive nature of Rawls's political liberalism, however, that makes it very appealing to advocates of a liberal civil society. In the first place, Rawls's political liberalism would make possible the separate sphere of various nonpublic groups, and these groups would certainly permit not only diverse life possibilities, but they would act as buffers against the power of government. Further, Rawls's separate sphere exists within and upholds a larger moral environment that includes respect for the civic virtues of toleration and mutual respect. The former virtue asks that we live-and-let-live with people holding values different from our own, and the virtue of mutual respect requires us to consider carefully the views of others when we discuss public issues and make use of the process of public reason.

VIII. RESPONSE AND REJOINDER

Rawls could contend that his view of civil society goes beyond the live-and-let-live toleration found in Locke. Individuals because they engage in public reason with each other are dedicated to considering the different points of view pertinent to public issues. Locke might respond that he could accept Rawls's approach, but he might wonder how Rawls will be able to convince people to embrace the doctrines of public reason in the midst of a society in which people are heavily committed to the values found in nonpublic life. Locke would probably argue that for individuals to accept public reason even as the basis for discussing public issues, the hold that nonpublic values have over individuals would have to be reduced significantly. And this objective could be achieved only if individuals could approach nonpublic values with a certain degree of skepticism. But is this outlook likely, especially in a society in which so much of one's sense of identity is associated with a belief in the truth of one's nonpublic values?

Rawls would argue in response that skepticism is not the issue here. More important is understanding the priority of a civil society in the lives of people. Where individuals do not understand the overall importance of a civil society, then, there is no strong will to maintain a liberal civil society. Rawls would claim that his arguments for civil society demonstrate its importance for securing rights in a society with highly diverse moral points of view. The implication of his argument is that the alternative, a society dominated by a state that imposes one moral perspective to the exclusion of others, is a setting that only a civil society could rescue us from.[64]

To Rousseau, Rawls would say that Rousseau had hoped to make possible a general will that, to be sure, would not eliminate the nonpublic realm, but would, in all likelihood, reduce its significance. Rousseau had no choice but to diminish the nonpublic realm, given his commitment to the norms of the public realm. Now, Rawls would argue that modern civil society would reject Rousseau for devaluing the nonpublic setting. Most people in the contemporary world want to make the nonpublic realm ever larger and more prominent, and they resist public encroachment into the private life by a democratic experience. Further, for Rawls, Rousseau's view of public participation, while laudable to some extent, lacks the kind of structure provided by Rawls's view of public reason. Rawls would argue that the great virtue of public reason is that it permits individuals to achieve a form of principled consensus, in this case, a majority view that does not deny equal protection of rights to all. But Rousseau's general will, for Rawls, might encourage people to meet together to decide issues without regard for the rights of individuals who did not agree with the concept of the general good defined by the collective will of the people. Although Rousseau would hope this would not happen, what is to prevent this situation from occurring? Rawls's public reason would ensure, as Hegel had hoped to do, that the consensus that emerges is a principled one that carries forward the commitment to shared rational principles.

No doubt Rousseau would respond to Rawls by declaring that Rawls no less than himself has diminished the nonpublic realm by making it subservient to the norms of public reason. Further, Rousseau would say that Rawls has not fully developed a basis for public reason and deliberation among the citizens, because Rawls permits many diverse and often contradictory views of life to remain a part of the common life of the members of civil society. After all, Rawls argues that there is a multitude of reasonable if not contradictory moral doctrines existing in the nonpublic sphere of civil society. Rousseau would argue that, if this be the case, then deliberation on issues will always be suffused with diverse and contradictory moral viewpoints, making agreement on the nature of the common good difficult, if not impossible, to realize. Rousseau would argue, then, for the need for a civil religion that would reduce the presence and impact of such doctrines on public debate, so that a conception of the common good could be reached. Rawls would view this move as a threat to basic rights.

Mill's liberalism, for Rawls, would seek to impose a single comprehensive moral doctrine onto the whole of society.[65] As we saw, Mill emphasized the importance of the higher faculties of mind and associated them with a fuller and more wholesome freedom. Rawls would argue that for some, indeed for many, there are more important values, such as living within religious traditions, building friendships, or enjoying leisure. None of these values can be denied without undermining the full freedom of each individual. Mill would respond to Rawls by claiming that Rawls in promoting public reason is in fact fostering Mill's own outlook without admitting it. If people are to make public reason the basis for decisions about public issues, people must diminish in importance attitudes that hinder the development of Mill's higher faculties, for it is the latter that make possible the full attainment of public reason. Rawls would, of course, not accept this critique of his view of public reason. He would claim that, as he discussed the notion, public reason and certainly his view of political liberalism are designed to provide a wide array of diverse ways of life. But Mill would argue that Rawls cannot have it both ways. He cannot promote a conception of public reason that requires making the higher faculties a priority in life, while, at the same time, denying that these faculties should have priority.

Kant would argue that, to ensure that just institutions are protected, it would be necessary to establish a system in which the various interests in society are arrayed in such a way as to limit and to check each other. Unless this approach is taken, even just institutions, or those intending to uphold fair principles, would be overrun by whatever interest or coalition of interests dominated society. But Rawls would reject what he refers to as a "modus vivendi" basis for supporting just institutions. He alludes to the example of religious toleration to make his point. In this situation, various groups learn to put up with each other. But their doing so depends upon a power equivalence between them. When that equivalence no longer exists, as for instance happens when one group gains superior power to others, then the modus vivendi breaks down and the inferior group, powerwise, is no longer tolerated.[66] For Rawls, there needs, then, to be a stronger basis for securing just institutions. And so he argues that, to maintain a civil society committed to securing the rights of all, the citizens must have a strong commitment to the values associated with his view of political liberalism, including support for what he calls the overlapping consensus.

Hegel would respond to Rawls by arguing that the latter's view of the relationship between the state and society is not well conceived. Hegel, it will be remembered, described civil society as composed of competing interests, none of which by themselves would maintain respect for the needs of the larger society. To achieve the prospect of the common good, the state entered civil society and defined the norms that the various social interests should adapt themselves to. The state achieved this objective through the maintenance of what Hegel called corporations. Now, Rawls would respond to this view of the state's relationship to society with a great degree of skepticism. Of fundamental importance to Rawls is that the various groups that make up the separate sphere of a civil society are free to pursue their own self-determined moral doctrines and ways of life. Were the state to enter into the activities of these groups and determine their outlooks, then the state would be imposing on these groups a particular comprehensive moral doctrine, and, by this act, the state would be undermining the autonomy these groups deserve. This approach might threaten the rights that Rawls's political liberalism guarantees.

To Hegel's view that the common good could never be well served in a civil society without his conception of the state, Rawls would respond that the state operates in terms of respect for those constitutional essentials that secure basic rights for each person in society. Further, there is to be a process of public reason by which the members of the society share views and search together for the common reasons that all can accept and make the basis for policy. This approach will be able to help individuals overcome self-serving attitudes, so that they can work with others to learn the needs of the society as a whole, without the presence of either of Hegel's corporations or of what for Rawls might be Hegel's too-intrusive form of state.

IX. TRANSITION TO CONSERVATIVES:
THE COMMUNITARIAN CRITIQUE OF RAWLS

To complete my view of Rawls, I would like to provide a communitarian critique of his work. This critique provides a transition to conservative views of civil society that we discuss in the next chapter. Like conservatives, communitarians view individual identity as evolving from the attachments that people have to each other and to collective values in communal settings. Do liberal views of civil society destroy these attachments in the name of promoting liberty and rights? This question is central to both communitarian and conservative thinking. To develop an important communitarian critique of Rawls, as a bridge to the conservative argument, I refer to Michael Sandel's *Liberalism and the Limits of Justice.*[67]

Michael Sandel argues that Rawls's conception of community, what Sandel calls a "sentimental concept" of community, is far too weak to achieve the objectives of Rawls's concept of justice.[68] Sandel claims that to make the sacrifices to achieve Rawls's theory of justice, including, for instance, that those better-off members of society distribute benefits to those least well-off members, it would be necessary for people to have very strong bonds to the community for which they were asked to make sacrifices. And to develop a strong enough bond that makes it likely that the better off would share their advantages with others, it would be necessary for individuals to define their own identities and their chief goals in ways that are in keeping with the conception of the community's norms and common objectives. When people's identities are, in part, seen as arising from the shared experience with others who, like themselves, are committed to maintaining similar standards and norms, people not only develop a strong bond with those norms, but with the people upholding them. And this fact makes it more likely that people would be willing to sacrifice some of their benefits for the larger good of the community. This view does not mean that people cannot, upon reflection, break these ties to community. But it does mean that if people are going to make sacrifices for others, they must think of themselves in some sense as tied very closely to those whom they help and for whom they make sacrifices. Thus for Sandel, "on this strong view, to say that the members of a society are bound by a sense of community is not simply to say that a great many of them profess communitarian sentiments and pursue communitarian aims, but rather that they conceive of their identity . . . as defined to some extent by the community of which they are a part."[69]

Rawls's society would, for Sandel, never be strong enough to ensure the kind of sacrifices that people will in fact have to make for it, if they are to achieve Rawls's goals. This is the case because Rawls rejects a strong sense of community as the basis for establishing individual identity. Why would Rawls's political society be so weak? For Sandel, Rawls's persons define their personal objectives and plans of life not *within* a given community setting, but *outside* of it.[70] Rawls's self, of course, emerges within the context of circumstances that include certain common values and viewpoints. But this self acts as if these values have no necessary impact upon the self that one becomes. Sandel says, in Rawls, "the subject [person] . . . is always, irreducibly, prior to his values and ends, and never fully constituted by them."[71] Because the self stands always at a distance from the values of the settings he or she is in, Rawls's self is by virtue of this fact always living at a distance from these values. Moreover, since the basis for common attachments to others resides in people's predicating their identities on shared, common values, and because Rawls's persons would not in fact do so, Rawls's persons do not develop a strong basis for common attachments to others. In consequence, for Sandel, Rawls's view suggests that, "no commitment could grip me so deeply that I could not understand myself without it. No transformation of life purposes and plans could be so unsettling as to disrupt the contours of my identity. No project could be so essential that turning away from it would call into question the person I am."[72]

None of this is to say, of course, that Rawls denies a place to a common setting in terms of which individuals live out their lives. Rawls establishes the framework of rules that secure to each person those rights that permit each individual to pursue the life plans and ways of life that he or she chooses. Each person should be in a position to determine whatever particular good he or she wishes to pursue. There is not to be in place a particular conception of the good that each would have to be subordinate to and in the process be denied the freedom to determine the conception of the life that each one wants to pursue. Rawls always gives to rights priority over any conception of a larger good to which each individual would have to subordinate himself.[73]

Now, for Sandel, Rawls's rights-oriented framework suggests a shallow self, or a self that "seems little more than an awareness of our immediate wants and desires."[74] This type of self acts only on behalf of those desires and wants that are present to him or her throughout life. But Sandel argues that there is a deeper, more reflective self. This reflective self allows one to understand one's connection to the type of community that Rawls discards but that, as just indicated (for Sandel) Rawls really needs. The deeper self is a product of "its various attachments and acknowledges their respective claims . . . ."[75] Sandel's self realizes that it relies heavily upon a particular community, and the self shares with that community common moral values and purposes. In reflecting on oneself from this standpoint, one understands the way one's inner identity is formed by the various attachments one has with others who, together, share many things and values in common. The deeper self is not simply in pursuit of desires and wants, but, rather, this deeper self is capable of postponing the pursuit of these factors while it determines whether the larger, more long-standing claims of the community should be given priority.

Sandel's self would seem to be fashioned by the prevalent values of one's community and by the need to uphold those values throughout the course of one's life.[76] In this regard, Sandel's self would manifest the earmarks of an individual dedicated to upholding the canons of a community's civic virtue commitment to the common good. In doing so, this self would put the structure of rules that guarantee rights to each person in a context that made certain that the communal dimensions of life are in no way threatened by these rights. Whereas individuals have rights, they would have them in a context in which the aims and objectives of life, or the ends that we pursue with our rights, are defined in terms of the leading values and norms of community. Only when we define rights in this manner is it possible for people to continue their sense of mutual attachment to shared conceptions of the common good.

Rawls would of course respond that his liberal civil society is predicated upon the leading values of the community, in particular, the norms of his overlapping consensus. Here, individuals could identify with the norms of particular communities and make them the basis for their identities. If one wants to be a religious individual, one would identify with religious norms and become a member of a religious community, if one wants to be associated with the goods of an aesthetic life, then one could become a member of an art community, and so on. All that Rawls demands is that during the course of joining any association one not be put into a position in which one's basic rights are taken away. The community commitment cannot be so strong that these rights are threatened. Thus, Rawls would wonder whether the communitarian critique does not, in the name of promoting a communal basis for identity, threaten basic rights.

Endnotes

1. John Rawls, *A Theory of Justice,* (Cambridge: Harvard University Press, 1999). The first edition was written in 1971, but I have used the new edition here.

2. John Rawls, *Political Liberalism,* (New York: Columbia University Press, 1993).

3. Rawls, *A Theory of Justice,* pp. 10–15.

4. Ibid., pp. 118–19.

5. Ibid., p. 119.

6. Ibid., p. 123.

7. Ibid., pp. 132–33.

8. Ibid., p. 54.

9. Ibid., pp. 266, also p. 53.

10. Ibid., p. 53.

11. Ibid., pp. 73, 53.

12. Ibid., p. 65.

13. Ibid., pp. 53–54, 266.

14. Ibid., p. 54. Also, Rawls, *Political Liberalism,* p. 318.

15. Stephen Holmes "The Gatekeeper," review of Rawls's *Political Liberalism, The New Republic,* October 11, 1993, p. 42.

16. Rawls, *A Theory of Justice,* p. 54.

17. Rawls, *Political Liberalism,* pp. 318. Also Rawls, *A Theory of Justice,* p. 54.

18. Rawls, *A Theory of Justice,* p. 398.

19. Ibid., p. 457.

20. Ibid., p. 458.

21. Ibid., p. 459.

22. Ibid., p. 459.

23. Ibid., pp. 400–401.

24. Ibid., pp. 403–4, 406–13, 414–19.

25. Rawls, *Political Liberalism* p. xvii. Also see, Susan Moller Okin's review of Rawls's *Political Liberalism* in *American Political Science Review,* 87:4, December, 1993, p. 1010.

26. Rawls, *Political Liberalism,* p. xvi.

27. Ibid., p. xviii. Emphasis is added.

28. Ibid., p. xvii.

29. Ibid., p. 13.

30. Ibid., pp. 11–13.

31. Ibid., pp. 13–14.

32. Ibid., pp. 175, 156–57.

33. Ibid., p. 175.

34. Ibid., p. 14. Also, p. 220.

35. Ibid., p. 220.

36. Ibid., pp. 221–22.

37. Ibid., pp. 175, 14.

38. Ibid., p. 175.

39. Ibid., p. 175.

40. Ibid., p. 37, also p. 175.

41. Ibid., pp. 156–57.

42. Ibid., p. 134.

43. Ibid., p. 164.

44. Ibid., pp. 161–62.

45. Rawls refers to these three dimensions as central to describing the basis of a "stable constitutional consensus," but in his account these dimensions are also integral to and incorporated into the idea of an overlapping consensus. See Rawls, *Political Liberalism,* pp. 144, 156–57, 161, and 164–65.

46. Ibid., p. 218.

47. On this point see, James Bohman, "Public Reason and Cultural Pluralism," *Political Theory,* 23:2, May, 1995, pp. 258–60.

48. Rawls, *Political Liberalism,* p. 226.

49. Ibid., p. 223.

50. Ibid., p. 227.

51. Ibid., p. 223.

52. Ibid., p. 224.

53. Ibid., pp. 224–25.

54. Ibid., pp. 227–28.

55. Ibid., pp. 227, 230, 232.

56. Ibid., p. 39.

57. Ibid., pp. 196–97.

58. Ibid., p. 151.

59. John Rawls, "The Priority of Right over Idea of the Good," *Philosophy and Public Affairs,* 17:4, Fall, 1988, p. 267.

60. Ibid., p. 267.

61. Rawls, *Political Liberalism,* pp. 192–93.

62. Ibid., p. 247.

63. Susan Moller Okin's review of Rawls's *Political Liberalism* in *American Political Science Review,* 87:4, December, 1993, p. 1011.

64. Rawls, *Political Liberalism,* p. 37.

65. Ibid., p. 199.

66. Ibid., pp. 147–49.

67. Michael J. Sandel, *Liberalism and the Limits of Justice,* (Cambridge: Cambridge University Press, 1983).

68. Ibid., pp. 147–51. Also see Michael Sandel, "The Unencumbered Self," *Political Theory,* 12:1, Feb. 1984, p. 90.

69. Michael J. Sandel, *Liberalism and the Limits of Justice,* p. 150.

70. Ibid., 19–22.

71. Ibid., p. 22.

72. Ibid., p. 62.

73. Michael J. Sandel, "The Unencumbered Self," p. 86, and *Liberalism and the Limits of Justice,* p. 154.

74. Michael J. Sandel, *Liberalism and the Limits of Justice,* p. 160.

75. Ibid., p. 153.

76. Ibid., p. 173.

Partial Bibliography and Further Reading

Alejandro, Roberto. *The Limits of Rawlsian Justice.* Baltimore: Johns Hopkins University Press, 1999.

Barry, Brian M. *The Liberal Theory of Justice: A Critical Examination of the Principal Doctrines in* A Theory of Justice *by John Rawls.* Oxford: Clarendon Press, 1973.

Booth, James W. "Communities of Memory: On Identity, Memory, and Debt." *American Political Science Review.* 93: 2, June, 1999.

Charney, Evan. "Political Liberalism, Deliberative Democracy, and the Public Sphere," *American Political Science Review,* 92:1, March, 1998.

Daniels, Norman. *Reading Rawls: Critical Studies on Rawls'* A Theory of Justice. New York: Basic Books, 1985.

DeLue, Steven M. *Political Obligation in Liberal State.* Albany: State University of New York Press, 1989.

Elshtain, Jean Bethke. *Democracy on Trial.* New York: Basic Books, 1995.

Frohock, Fred M. "The Boundaries of Public Reason," *American Political Science Review,* 91:4, December, 1997.

Klosko, George. "Political Constructivism in Rawls's *Political Liberalism.*" *American Political Science Review,* 91:3, September, 1997.

Macedo, Stephen. *Diversity and Distrust: Civic Education in a Multicultural Democracy.* Cambridge: Harvard University Press, 2000.

Nozick, Robert. *Anarchy, State and Utopia.* New York: Basic Books, 1974.

Okin, Susan Moller. *Justice, Gender and the Family.* New York: Basic Books, 1989.

———. Review of Rawls's *Political Liberalism* in *American Political Science Review,* 87:4, December, 1993.

Rawls, John. *A Theory of Justice.* Cambridge: Harvard University Press, 1999, first edition, 1971.

———. "The Idea of an Overlapping Consensus." *Oxford Journal of Legal Studies,* 7:1, Spring, 1987.

———. *Political Liberalism.* New York: Columbia University Press, 1993.

Sandel, Michael J. *Liberalism and the Limits of Justice.* Cambridge: Cambridge University Press, 1982.

———. "The Unencumbered Self." *Political Theory,* 12:1, Feb. 1984.

———. *Democracy's Discontent: America in Search of a Public Philosophy.* Cambridge, Mass.: Belknap Press of Harvard University Press, 1996.

Walzer, Michael. *Spheres of Justice: A Defense of Pluralism and Equality.* New York: Basic Books, 1983.

Wolff, Robert Paul. *Understanding Rawls: A Reconstruction and Critique of* A Theory of Justice. Princeton: Princeton University Press, 1977.

14

THE CONSERVATIVE VIEW: BURKE, TOCQUEVILLE, AND OAKESHOTT

I. INTRODUCTION

In this chapter, I examine the ideas of Edmund Burke (1729–1797), Alexis de Tocqueville (1805–1859), and Michael Oakeshott (1901–1990). For these writers, society is a repository of the wisdom contained in cumulative experience. Each writer discussed society in terms of those values, traditions, and institutions that have stood the test of time during the course of confronting recurring and enduring challenges and problems. The conservative tends to view these traditional dimensions of society as the critical bases for establishing a civil society, which can provide rights and liberties as well as an atmosphere of civic virtue.

There are several reasons for this approach. First, conservatives will seek to learn from these traditions the practical and enduring truths that, when properly upheld, help to maintain the long-term commitment to a civil society. Moreover, these traditions will be the ground for each person's identity. A similar point was argued by Sandel's communitarian critique of Rawls, as we just saw in the last chapter. Individuals receive a clear sense of their identities, including knowledge of the core values that give substance to their lives, when they share common traditions and values with others. For conservatives, no matter how free we are, without the presence of shared traditions, our lives would lack meaning. And the reason for this is that while freedom permits us to have many choices, it does not provide, by itself, those core values, as for instance are found in religious or particular cultural settings, that enable our lives to have enduring meaning.

In the cases of the three conservative writers discussed in this chapter, existing traditions and customs are seen as major contributing sources for securing among citizens a sense of personal identity, the protection of basic rights, and a commitment to civic virtue.[1] Each of the writers discussed in this chapter will advocate different kinds of social values that are considered responsible for both social cohesion and individual identity, and thus there will be different conceptions of society and of the role civic virtue plays in society. For Burke, in addition to religion and regard for the traditions associated with both a natural aristocracy and a natural order to society, society is characterized by respect for the importance of local affiliations and of moderation. For Tocqueville, who, like Burke, also demonstrates the importance of religion and moderation, there is a supreme importance placed upon the separate sphere of voluntary associations as well as a form of individualism that is receptive to and is formed by the democratic experience. Also, for Tocqueville, a spirit of equality replaces Burke's natural aristocracy. Oakeshott seeks to define those traditions that make possible a wide array of life possibilities while freeing people from the tyranny and the regimen of large organizations that impose their will on people, thus denying their freedom. In choosing these three representative thinkers, then, my intention is to demonstrate that conservatism, no less than the different liberal views of civil society, has diverse voices, too.

II. EDMUND BURKE: THE PURPOSE OF CIVIL SOCIETY

Edmund Burke had a long political career as a member of the British parliament during the eighteenth century, and he was among those who attacked the French Revolution.[2] It should be clear, however, that Burke was not unalterably opposed to revolution, because he supported the American Revolution. Why support one revolution and not the other? He supported the American cause because he disagreed with British policies that threatened prosperous commercial enterprises in America. Burke believed that the American commercial setting followed a free market approach that was associated with a form of self-regulating economic life that both acted as a restraint upon government interference in people's lives and that contributed to societal stability by securing property rights. But in France, the revolutionaries sought to tear asunder the guiding traditions of society, including those having to do with property and commerce, and the only institution that was attempting to preserve them was the monarchy that Burke supported.[3] So in the American case, the revolutionaries protected useful social traditions, but in France they threatened them. Burke supported the former and not the latter as a consequence.

Most of Burke's political writings appeared as speeches or arguments provided in response to particular political issues. His reaction to the French Revolution was an occasion for writing a statement of the political principles upon which he acted.[4] In discussing his *Reflections on the Revolution in France,* I develop some of these principles and provide a review of Burke's account of civil society. In this section, I discuss Burke's views of the bases of civil society, including the importance of rights, as well as the role of government in a civil society.

So what is Burke's view of civil society? A civil society must protect the rights of individuals. In emphasizing rights, for Burke there is no question that a civil society is prized because it is a way of life that is best able to meet basic human needs. Burke said that "if civil society be made for the advantage of man, all the advantages for which it is made become his right. It is an institution of beneficence; and law itself is only beneficence acting by a rule."[5] Thus, by virtue of having basic needs individuals have a right to a variety of goods, including, for instance, a right to justice both with respect to the way the state treats them and with respect to their relationships with other people, a right to benefit from their own labor and to be able to make a decent living, a right to have their children educated, a right to inherit the property of one's parents, and a right to obtain "consolation in death," or, in other terms, people have a right to partake in religion.

Moreover, a civil society is to allow citizens to "have a right to a fair portion of all which society, with all its combinations of skill and force, can do in his favor."[6] On this view, however, even though all have the same right to be treated justly, it is not the case that each will end up with the same advantages and material benefits. For Burke, "men have equal rights; but not to equal things."[7] Burke's view of civil society would permit those with greater ability to gain larger shares of the society's wealth, when their efforts are productive and useful to society. This characteristic of civil society signals Burke's intention to place heavy emphasis on protecting a natural aristocracy, a feature of Burke's thought that we will discuss below.

Burke's account of civil society helps to explain why he did not ground government in a natural rights argument. A natural rights doctrine, such as Locke had used to justify the obligations of government to protect property rights, for instance, suggests that individuals have certain freedoms by virtue of being human beings. No government can abridge natural rights. Although not denying that there are certain basic natural rights for all, Burke argued that natural rights doctrines couldn't be used as the basis for establishing a government.[8] Burke rejected this approach because, as we have seen, Burke believed that rights arise from a society's commitment to secure human needs. Burke said that "government is a contrivance of human wisdom to provide for human *wants.* Men have a right that these wants should be provided for by this wisdom."[9]

In refusing to accept a natural rights foundation for government, Burke rejected the view that a government exists to promote an abstract and perfected view of society. A perfected view of society suggests a vision of a future society that would replace the existing order in a complete way. Why is this approach such a problem for Burke? There are several reasons. First, when individuals are told that they can live in keeping with an abstract idea of the perfect society, they necessarily take the view that anything they have a desire for they can have. And the justification for this view is that they have a natural right to all things made possible in the perfected vision of society. Thus, "by having a right to every thing they want every thing."[10] Were this attitude to prevail, there would be anarchy, and society would not be governable. Burke rejected this position because he believed that "society requires not only that the passions of individuals should be subjected, but that even in the mass and body as well as in the individuals, the inclinations of men should be frequently thwarted."[11]

Citizens need to recognize their obligation to uphold the norms of civic virtue because these norms check and restrain unruly passions. Possessing rights, then, means more than just having a license to act in ways that attain basic needs. In addition, rights signify the constraints on life that we are to abide by. "In this sense the restraints on men, as well as their liberties, are to be reckoned among their rights."[12] A central doctrine of civil society that Burke shares with other civil society thinkers is that rights can be sustained only in a setting where there is a commitment to those civic virtues that define the restraints that all must obey.

The second problem for Burke of a natural rights argument and with the abstract conception of a perfected society that the natural rights argument symbolized is that this approach fails to recognize that rights are not written in stone but that they may change as the circumstances of society change. Burke said that the nature of liberties as well as restraints varies with circumstances, and "they cannot be settled upon any abstract rule; and nothing is so foolish as to discuss them upon that principle."[13] As circumstances change, controversies develop pertaining to what should count as a right or a proper limitation on human conduct. For instance, today we have seen great controversy around the issue of what due process of law means in the area of police conduct. Can police stop and "frisk" people who look suspicious or must they have more stringent guidelines, lest they violate the privacy rights of individuals? Where controversies exist with respect to what is best in matters of this sort, we cannot rely upon an abstract principle to determine the best course. This means, for instance, that, instead of making an abstract principle, such as the right of privacy, the basis for judgment, we should ask ourselves in determining the nature of proper police practice, what the overall effects of changes in existing practices will be. If we determine that the consequence of giving the police more authority is to limit criminal activity, then the community may support giving the police enhanced powers, even if it means that the right of privacy is in some sense violated. This outcome may be acceptable because sometimes it will be necessary to expand police powers at the cost of privacy rights so that individuals can go about their daily business without fear.

Burke's approach is conservative because his starting point for thinking about issues such as police practices is to ask what the effect will be to society of changing an existing practice. If we deem that effect to be in the interest of people, then the existing practice can be changed. But, in discussing changes to society, if we start from an abstract picture of an ideal society, we seek a society that can embody an ideal. In this case, we do not ask nor do we care whether the proposed changes to existing ways of life cause serious harms to the people in the society.

Burke would thus reject the rationalist view of civil society, a view typical in the thinking of many of the liberals discussed earlier. In general, liberal views often started with basic assumptions about political life, such as those found in Hobbes's or Locke's view of the state of nature, Hegel's expectations for and understandings of a civil society, or Rawls's conception of the original position. From these assumptions a perfected vision of politics and society was sketched. But this approach misses the mark entirely, for it fails to take into consideration how the disruption of existing practices might harm a civil society's ability to secure basic needs. It is necessary always to understand clearly what Waldron, quoting Burke, referred to as the "mysterious wisdom" that undergirded and explained society.[14] It is this wisdom that rationalist approaches disregard, but that individuals must understand and work with if a society that can preserve human freedom is to be maintained.

Given Burke's views of the bases for civil society, including the place of rights, the final question to ask is what role government has in Burke's civil society. For Burke, government, as Frohnen says, "does very little and . . . acts according to rather utilitarian rules."[15] Governments must promote equity and utility. Equity means that the government is to treat individuals equally in conjunction with the law, and, in promoting utility, the government must ensure that the laws are in the interest of all citizens and thus secure basic needs.[16] But government in undertaking these activities must move carefully and cautiously, refusing to make as the basis for its conduct an abstract, perfected vision of society. Further, government is not to be the main social force for instilling virtue. The real instructors of virtue are the traditions and customs of society that the government should protect from those who would undermine these traditions, such as atheists, and, as Frohnen says, "those men who do not recognize the need for the maintenance, and supremacy, of existing traditions, manners, and prejudices."[17]

III. THE NATURAL ARISTOCRACY

As we have indicated, a society based on tradition is a society that has worked out, over a long period of time, the best way to achieve and to maintain basic needs. Individuals must respect the resulting arrangements. Thus, citizens have distinct obligations that are given in their traditions and customs. What is the nature of these obligations? It is absolutely essential that individuals accept the fact that society is divided into various, hierarchically organized roles and those individuals serve society through the roles they find themselves in. Frohnen argues that for Burke there is a "Great Chain of Being" in which each person has a particular place in the overall organization of society. Some, owing to their superior talent and virtue, can make a larger contribution to public life, including the political, social, and economic structures, than others.[18] In this regard, Burke accepted the existence of an hereditary aristocracy. He said, "some decent regulated preeminence, some preference . . . given to birth, is neither unnatural, nor unjust, nor impolitic."[19]

But at the same time, he also accepted a "natural aristocracy." Burke said "woe to the country which would madly and impiously reject the service of the talents and virtues, civil, military, or religious, that are given to grace and to serve it [society]."[20] Burke expected that positions should be filled on the basis of talent. The different needs of society can best be met when those most capable of performing them are given the opportunity to do so. Hereditary class background in this case must not stand in the way of the evolution of a natural aristocracy. In his *Reflections on the Revolution in France,* Burke said in response to a critic, "You do not imagine, that I wish to confine power, authority, and distinction to blood, names, and titles? No, sir. There is no qualification for government, but virtue and wisdom, actual or presumptive. Wherever they are actually found, they have, in whatever state, condition, profession or trade, the passport of Heaven to human place and honour."[21]

In supporting a natural aristocracy, then, Burke defended a society predicated upon a qualified elite as the best way to maintain stability and the overall justice of society. How would a natural elite be selected for purposes of managing government? Elections would be an acceptable basis for determining the natural aristocracy.[22] As Hanna Pitkin says, Burke's concept of representation presumed an elected "aristocracy of virtue and wisdom governing for the good of the entire nation." But since the actual people who voted were limited in England to a small minority, a few citizens would elect an elite to represent the entire nation. Here, persons are "virtually represented" even if they do not participate directly in electing those who represent them and even if those who represent them are an elite who do not come from the same class of people they represent.[23]

Still, as Pitkin argues, this version of virtual representation is not the only version Burke held. For Burke, each locality was usually associated with a particular interest such as agriculture, mercantile, or professional. Also, it can be the case that some localities have a representative and others will not. In those instances in which people of a particular locality do not directly elect a representative, instead of "actual" representation there can be "virtual" representation. Here, the elected members in representing the interest of a locality represent the interests of that locality, say agriculture, wherever agricultural interests exist in the country. In Burke's words, there is "a communion of interest and sympathy in feelings and desires between those who act in the name of any description of people and the people in whose name they act, though the trustees are not actually chosen by them."[24] Moreover, Burke believed that the best representatives of any constituency should be a qualified elite. Only an educated and well-informed elite, skilled in deliberation about the needs of a constituency, can determine its real interests.[25]

IV. THE ROLE OF VIRTUE: THE IMPORTANCE OF MODERATION

Regarding who was qualified to be a part of the political elite, at least with respect to parliament, it was clear that owning property was the key consideration. Indeed, Burke attacked the French National Assembly because it was virtually without men of property.[26] Singled out for criticism were lawyers whose litigiousness encouraged disregard for the traditions that accorded protection to private property. Referring to lawyers, Burke asked, "was it to be expected that they [lawyers] would attend to the stability of property, [when their, the lawyer's] existence had always depended upon whatever rendered property questionable, ambiguous, and insecure?"[27]

No doubt, a major reason for Burke's support of men of property was that he viewed them as being capable of practicing the virtue of moderation. Learning to avoid extremes in outlook and deeds during the course of pursuing life goals or considering public issues is a civic virtue of utmost importance. When extreme positions are the order of the day, the social fabric is severely strained, threatening the sustaining traditions and customs. Thus, the legislative assembly must be a place where individuals are able to manifest what Burke called "steady and moderate conduct." And the best way to achieve this condition is when the legislative body of society is composed of people who have the following traits: property, a good education, and "such habits as enlarge and liberalize the understanding."[28] Burke had in mind, then, individuals who as property owners were still subject to the constraints that a good education and an enlarged view of events helped to secure. People so educated have been schooled in the main qualities of good conduct. In particular, they have been exposed to science and the arts, they are able to have a broad view of a large range of issues that society addresses, they have been trained to be diligent and respectful of the standards of justice, and they have learned how to reconcile the ways of man to that of God.[29]

Moreover, in order to maintain the civic virtue of moderation, Burke advocated a political environment composed of different interests, each of which could check and balance the others. In a society where no one group has all the power, but where each realizes the necessity of sharing power, people are more able to compromise, thus avoiding extremist forms of thinking. This setting is the basis, then, for rendering "deliberation a matter not of choice, but of necessity." And the benefit of this approach is that decisions made by deliberation and principled compromise ensure moderate policies and politics. This view of politics prevents "the sore evil of harsh, crude, unqualified reformation; and rendering all the headlong exertions of arbitrary power, in the few or in the many."[30]

V. LOCAL AFFILIATIONS AND RELIGION

The natural aristocrat must perform well the tasks allied with public service, just as the person with other talents must perform well the various duties connected with his role in life. In doing so, people manifest a commitment to a life of civic virtue. Maintaining this orientation is fundamental to the good order of society. Burke supported this objective by arguing that a love for virtue grows from the local affinities associated with family, neighborhood, and shared beliefs, including religion. For Burke, the affections that people develop for those people and those ways of life closest to them become the basis for a sustained and continuing commitment to uphold the norms of civic life.[31] How is this possible?

When we view society from the perspective of our local affinities, such as family, society becomes for us not a large and impersonal world, a world toward which each member feels a sense of estrangement and distance. Rather, society is a friendly and pleasing setting; it is the neighborhood we grow up in, the friends we have for a lifetime, the religious institutions that provide solace, and the local government with which we interact on a day-to-day basis. In viewing society in this way, people develop strong affections for those civic responsibilities that preserve the way of life in society and the traditions of the common life that all love. Instead of a society consisting of competing interests always at war, it is a unity based on shared affinities.

Of special importance to maintaining respect for civic virtue and for society is religion. Each person is by nature a "religious animal." In consequence, atheism is against not only reason, but people's basic instincts, and thus "it cannot prevail long."[32] Indeed, religion is the "basis of civil society, and the source of all good and all comfort."[33] Burke had nothing but distaste for the French revolutionaries who would sabotage religious life by attacking the Catholic Church and threatening its property holdings. Individuals need to understand their relationship to the divine, and thus all social institutions must aid "the rational and natural ties that connect the human understanding and affections to the divine."[34] Religion is the foundation of a civil society because it teaches that all that is good comes from God, including virtue, good manners, and of course the state itself. Burke said that people "conceive that He who gave our nature to be perfected by our virtue, willed also the necessary means of its perfection—He willed therefore the state."[35]

The enemies of civil society for Burke, then, are those who would destroy the great traditions of civility and religion in the name of equality, which is what Burke believed the advocates of the French Revolution were doing. And in sweeping away the traditions of good order, what is lost in the process are the conditions to secure the rights upon which a good civil society is built. Tocqueville, as we will see, demonstrates a way to maintain Burke's commitment to civic virtue while embracing equality, as well. Before turning to Tocqueville, it is necessary to make a few additional comments on Burke.

VI. IDENTITY AND CIVIC VIRTUE IN BURKE

How would individual identity be constituted in Burke's society? For Burke, one's basic needs could be secured only by a society that protected the rights of each and that expected each individual to maintain those civic virtues associated with having rights. Part of what is included in this understanding is that society is predicated upon a natural order of abilities in which each person has a role to play. What helps to maintain a commitment to fulfill these roles is that individuals view themselves as linked in close and intimate ways to others who are friends and neighbors. Moreover, a strong sense of religious commitment further cements one's sense of community with the others who form an integral part of one's life. In this setting, people would feel themselves a part of society's natural order, and they would thus not be prone to question it.

Now, people's identities would reflect these values, and, in the civil society Burke described, it is not likely that individuals would question the moral order that all are expected to accept. There would not be competing conceptions of society, as is the case in our own society, in which some argue for a natural order and others argue against it, or in which some support religious practices and others condemn them. It is the contemporary diversity of moral views that caused Rawls to argue that there are many different moral conceptions, and each of them pertains to the particular self-identity that individuals carve out for themselves. Rawls sought to provide a way to ensure that people who hold different moral conceptions have a way to live in peace with mutual respect for one another's rights. The moral complexity of life addressed by Rawls would not be a major item of concern on Burke's agenda. Indeed, had Burke had to confront the issue of moral pluralism, he might have argued that the fact that it exists at all represents the triumph of destructive individualism urged on by a perfectionist view of government and society.

VII. ALEXIS DE TOCQUEVILLE AND THE COMMITMENT TO EQUALITY

Tocqueville published the first two volumes of *Democracy in America* in 1835 and the last two volumes in 1840.[36] He was a sociologist as well as an active politician in France.[37] Tocqueville provided an analysis of American mores, based on his visit to America—what he called the "habits of the heart" or the basic ideas and opinions held by Americans as well as an understanding of the ideas that shape the general outlook and "mental habits" of Americans.[38] Like Burke, for Tocqueville, liberty was not a license to do whatever one wanted, but the right to engage in those activities that the existing beliefs and traditions permitted and encouraged. In abiding by the norms of that order, one manifested, during the course of promoting one's liberty, virtue.

But each had a very different concept of the existing order that gave shape and pattern to liberty. For Burke, an aristocratic order, either natural or hereditary, was the predominant shaping force in society, but, for Tocqueville, American life had replaced the aristocratic order with a new commitment to individualism and equality. Tocqueville sought to demonstrate the nature of liberty within a society committed to these new values. There is no question that in doing so he believed that a society promoting individualism could at the same time maintain a civil order. This means that in an individualist-oriented society there could still be a commitment to virtue, if self-interest, as he put it, were "properly understood." Self-interest, properly understood, is a condition in which individuals, in pursuing their own particular needs, do so in ways that at the same time promote a larger good than just their own interest. Tocqueville said that "Americans . . . enjoy explaining almost every act of their lives on the principle of self-interest properly understood."[39]

Tocqueville thought that in America there was a good chance for self-interest to be understood in precisely these terms, but there was also a chance that it would not be. In the event of the latter, civil society would give way to despotism. So what is a civil society when self-interest is properly understood? And what are the threats that American society must confront in order to secure a civil society and avoid despotism?

VIII. The Passion for Equality

There is a passion for equality in America, and this passion, common to democracy, is so strong that it "seeps into every corner of the human heart, expands, and fills the whole."[40] Individualism is the way of life that democracy and its commitment to equality bring into existence, and individualism will grow "as conditions become more equal."[41] Individualism suggests a way of life in which people think it best to "isolate" themselves from the great multitude of society by placing themselves into small groups of people, such as families or friends. In this setting, an individual "gladly leaves the greater society to look after itself."[42] Individualism is an attitude that, for Tocqueville, "dams the spring of public virtues," and in the end may destroy regard for all other virtues, too, as it becomes the basis for a form of highly self-centered egoism. Individualism, then, is viewed as a threat to a form of self-interest properly understood, or a life that embraces regard for civic virtue.

Tocqueville, nonetheless, saw the possibility that this unfortunate state of affairs could be avoided and that individualism could be constrained and made to conform to the norms of good citizenship. At the heart of his argument is the view that American society provides an experience, located in a society based on equality that teaches to all people the traditions of civic virtue. Central to this experience is the place in society of voluntary associations and local government.

IX. Voluntary Associations and Local Government

The irony of democracy and the individualism it helps to spawn is that it makes people both "independent and weak." "They [people] can hardly do anything for themselves, and none of them is in a position to force his fellows to help him."[43] In contrast to an aristocratic society in which the privileged join together around the common class objective of protecting their place, in American society people are weak because, as equals to everyone else, each stands alone and no one is obligated to help another. The only way that individuals can muster the strength to achieve particular self-defined ends is to form themselves into groups.

"As soon as several Americans have conceived a sentiment or an idea that they want to pro-duce before the world, they seek each other out, and when found, they unite."[44] Participation with others is designed to achieve a variety of purposes. Indeed, for Tocqueville, there are associations for all activities and occasions, "to give fetes, found seminaries, build churches, distribute books," and so on.[45] By grouping together, people gain the collective power to achieve their objectives. In a democratic society, "associations must take the place of pow-erful private persons [typical of aristocracies] whom equality of condition has eliminated."[46]

The purposes pursued inside groups affect fewer people in comparison with societal wide activities that might affect everyone in society. But the experience of participation in smaller groups, such as those involving business endeavors, can teach people the required virtue needed to pursue interests that encompass not just the members of one's own group, but the interests of many others in society, including people beyond one's own group. "The more there are of these little business concerns in common, the more do men, with-out conscious effort, acquire a capacity to pursue great aims in common. Thus civil associ-ations pave the way for political ones."[47]

Civil society groups consist of people from different social outlooks and with diverse values. In civil society groups, then, individuals learn to work with people from diverse walks of life to achieve shared ends and purposes. To do so, individuals must learn the art of communicating across the many differences that make up society. As people engage in this activity, each learns about the needs of others, and each becomes more capable of making space for those who are different. People in this context practice the art of give and take with each other, and from this experience realize that in order to achieve common objectives, individuals must subordinate at times their interests to the needs of the whole. As a result, individuals learn the importance of thinking in terms of the many interests that make up society and that must be accommodated to achieve a definition of the common good. This is the essence of civic virtue, or self-interest properly understood.

Individuals who gain these skills in civil society are prepared to make good use of them in their participation in government. Individuals participate in government at many levels. People may have direct input into matters involving local concerns at the village or state government levels. As the governing unit becomes larger in scope and power, indi-viduals have less access and less chance to have direct influence on government policies. At the federal level, individuals may have impact indirectly through the election of legisla-tors or the executive. But because of their ability to understand diverse interests, individu-als can conceptualize politics as containing a broad arena of needs, each of which must be considered during the course of determining the common good. And in this way individu-als advance to thinking in public terms, and not solely private ones, and this public point of view once again is another manifestation of self-interest rightly understood.

Thus, the lessons of civil society help to create active, educated citizens whose impact is conducive to democracy. These lessons, owing to the reality of political liberty, can be used by all and not just, as for Burke, the aristocratic few. Indeed, when people enter the po-litical arena they are able to converse with many different people who otherwise might have remained strangers.[48] Moreover, during this experience, people redefine their own interests to include the needs of others, for, unless they do, people realize they will get nothing for themselves. Here, one defines as one's self-interest "forgetting about" oneself so that one can think about others.[49] For Tocqueville, Americans have used political liberty "to combat the individualism born of equality, and they have won"[50] because they have forged linkages to achieve shared ends.[51] The experience of civil society prepares individuals to pursue their own interests, but in ways that are always cognizant of the needs of others. As a consequence, politics remains democratic and political liberty is protected for all citizens.

As just indicated, an important political setting in which this experience is nurtured is the environment of local government. Because of the absence of a centralized administrative authority over all society, local governments must manage the towns and counties. Through them, people manifest a robustness of initiative as they build schools, churches, and roads, each of which reflects the needs of the local areas. In this context, people maintain a firm commitment to the idea that they should not rely upon national government to take care of them, and by virtue of this attitude they protect their freedom.[52] Moreover, the experience of citizen involvement in local government helps to sustain a citizen's respect for the nation as a whole. Indeed, for Tocqueville an understanding of the needs of the whole society is woven into the fabric of local government life. One cares for one's country in much the same way that one would care for one's family.[53]

Experiences such as those just mentioned in this section would help make possible Tocqueville's doctrine of "self-interest properly understood." Now, it must be clear that this doctrine "does not inspire great sacrifices, but every day it prompts some small ones."[54] Thus, self-interest when properly understood is associated with "orderly, temperate, moderate, careful, and self-controlled citizens."[55] These habits of civic virtue contribute to people's being able to be good citizens who make the needs of the larger community important reference points in their daily lives. For with these habits, people can be citizens who approach large public concerns not simply from a one-dimensional desire to achieve their own ends, but from a willingness to consider other needs, including those of the society in general.

X. MATERIALISM AND RELIGION

The religious life buttresses the idea of self-interest properly understood. In order to see how religion is important in this regard, it is first necessary to discuss a major consequence of equality for Tocqueville, namely, materialism. Equality reduces all people to a common denominator of belief, just as it reduces all to the same social status. In democracies, "all men are alike and do roughly the same things."[56] To say that all are equal is to say that all for the most part hold the same beliefs about what is important in life and that all are committed to pursue whatever everyone considers important. What is the one thing all wish to pursue? In America what is good is the acquisition of material things, the goods that bring immediate pleasure and happiness to the person who possesses them. "Americans cleave to the things of this world as if assured that they will never die, and yet are in such a rush to snatch any that come within their reach, as if expecting to stop living before they have relished them."[57] Here, the experience of market life, where each seeks to realize his material desires, becomes a major focus of concern for Tocqueville, as it did for others we have studied, such as Mill. As Tocqueville says, people in democratic settings, governed by the ethos of equality and market life, have many different passions, but each of them redounds to the same thing: a quest for wealth.

But at the same time each realizes that owing to differences in intelligence some will end up with greater advantage in the market setting. This fact creates an understanding among individuals that society will never achieve the "equality they long for," an equality in which each is content with what he has and where no one has an unfair advantage over others. Given this understanding, each looks warily at the other, worried that the other may have an unfair advantage over him in the pursuit of wealth. After all, in the age of equality no one should have more advantage than another, but equality of conditions, including intelligence, is not perfectly realized, and all individuals, knowing this, live with the constant anxiety that another will succeed where they have failed. This is the reason for "strange melancholy" in democracies, including, of course, America.[58]

But the requirements of group life are such that individuals must learn to temper their quests for immediate material pleasure. Indeed, individuals must practice a degree of self-discipline, so that they are able to postpone immediate pleasure and satisfaction for the sake of achieving long-term goals. A person must be able to avoid yielding to the "first onrush of his passions," so that he is able to "effortlessly sacrifice the pleasure of the moment for the lasting interests of his whole life."[59] But where material prosperity has such a prominent place, achieving self-discipline is difficult. Religion helps to counter the negative effects of materialism by giving us a wider and broader vision of life. The religious experience encourages people to focus upon a life beyond this one. And in the context of the life beyond this world, the quest for material things becomes much less important and pressing.[60] Thus, when individuals have no concept of a future broader than the present moment, they easily fall into a pattern of behavior in which their main objective is to "satisfy their least desires at once; and it would seem that as soon as they despair of living forever, they are inclined to act as if they could not live for more than a day."[61]

Given the quest for equality and material self-enhancement, the pressure to live for today is very strong. Indeed, this outlook may even diminish the ability of religion to install a sense of the future in the minds of people. Tocqueville said that the interest in the future is something "which neither religion nor social conditions any longer inspire[s]."[62] Tocqueville hoped that government might re-instill a concern for the future in people so that, with a broader horizon, they will not be so wedded to material self-enhancement. He believed that, if governments succeeded in this regard, people would be brought back to religious belief. And this moment will help restore the importance of moral values and civic concern.[63]

XI. THREATS TO CIVIL SOCIETY

Still, there were forces afoot in American society that threatened to destroy the sense of a civic virtue commitment to uphold the common good. In this case, neither the experience of voluntary associations nor religion could secure a society with civic virtue. What reasons did Tocqueville provide to justify his fears? There were two main ones. The first had to do with the possibility that citizens would forfeit their political liberty, and the second had to do with the failure of America to realize its commitment to equality for *all* citizens. In the next two paragraphs, I will discuss the threats to equality, and in the paragraphs after these, I will discuss Tocqueville's reason for suggesting that individuals would be willing to give up their political liberty.

African-Americans, owing to the experience of slavery, were not permitted to become a part of normal community life that was dominated by white people. An African-American did not even own his own body, and he could not sell his own labor without committing what for society was a crime.[64] These practices were in direct contradiction to the tradition in society that emphasized equality. Tocqueville saw the treatment of African-Americans as cause for a "great revolution."[65] Here, in a society in which equality is the norm, inequality is certain to create the conditions that would lead African-Americans to engage in an upheaval that would win for themselves what the whites already had.

Another harmful way of life, again one which ran contrary to equality, was the experience of industrialization.[66] The workplace Tocqueville described pitted the owner class against the working class, and in doing so, created a "new aristocracy" whose main concern was to organize the work of others for the sake of enhancing the wealth of the owner class. Opportunities for success in the manufacturing arena abounded, Tocqueville argued, because as the conditions in society become more and more equal, the need for acquiring manufactured products becomes more widespread. Everyone who is an equal to everyone else has a right to own what every other person owns. To make this possible, goods must be produced more cheaply so that everyone can have them. But efficiency in production could not be attained unless the new manufacturing aristocracy could find ways to harness properly the labor of the workforce. To this end, the owner classes introduced a division of labor into society, and workers who wanted to make a living had to enter the factory and produce goods in keeping with the labor patterns that the new, more efficient process mandated. In consequence, the worker, who might have been a skilled craftsman before the industrial system was established, now had to give up his craft to become a factory worker. The worker has no choice but to sell his labor, as Marx will point out, to the owner class, and this class used the worker's labor to enhance the owner's position and wealth at great cost to the working class. The worker was no longer able to nurture his skills as an individual craftsman, and he belonged entirely to the industrial production process owned by the new aristocracy. Inequality between the two, owners and workers, grew. In this context, as in the slavery problem, it is difficult to understand how, given the animosity likely to be generated, a civic virtue commitment to the common good could have been sustained.

A final threat to civic virtue was the loss of political liberty. As already indicated, Tocqueville feared that over time it might be the case that the quest for material goods, so central to the new life of an industrial nation, might overwhelm religion and its positive effect on accommodating individuals to virtue. Tocqueville worried about American society's turning itself into a milieu of "men, alike and equal, constantly circling around in pursuit of the petty and banal pleasures with which they glut their souls."[67] These types of people exist only for themselves, and they have no concern for others, including their country. Having no interest in public affairs, and no time for it either, they look to someone else to take care of their interests. Here, individuals forfeit entirely their political liberty, turn the state into a father figure, and ask it to take care of them. The state "gladly works for their happiness but wants to be the sole agent and judge thereof. It provides for their security, foresees and supplies their necessities, facilitates their pleasure, manages their principal concerns, directs their industry, makes rules for their testaments and divides their inheritances."[68] In this context, "the exercise of free choice" becomes "less useful and rarer." Indeed, to maintain this "fatherlike" form of government, individuals must be made subject to more and more control by those in authority, and ultimately each citizen, over time, is robbed of the "proper use of his own faculties."[69]

Tocqueville might have been describing the plight of many people today under what many conservatives attack as the welfare state. In this view, people become dependent upon a state who rules as a benevolent dictatorship. The old ways of tyranny, in particular, resort to torture and brutality, are no longer needed to maintain control in the modern world. In the new form of despotism, a state resorts to gentler means of subduing citizens. The despot Tocqueville worried about would use more "mild" forms of control than those used by the old-fashioned tyrannies. The new despotism "would degrade men rather than torment them."[70]

XII. TOCQUEVILLE, IDENTITY, AND CIVIC VIRTUE

The individual in Tocqueville's society locates him- or herself in traditions or habits that sustain equality, the equality that is necessary to maintain for people their personal freedom and rights. Unlike Burke, the Tocquevillean individual would be suspicious of natural forms of social order that place people into various roles and that permit an elite to rule, owing to their enhanced place in the social hierarchy. But for Tocqueville, equality is best manifested in settings that permit individuals to take part in the ongoing activities of group and local government life and in the forming of group and local government objectives and goals. Moreover, individuals in Tocqueville's society must manifest those civic virtues, such as self-control and moderation, as a basis for maintaining an atmosphere suitable for democratic participation. But just as important, these individuals, by virtue of being able to help formulate solutions to common problems in local government settings, would be fiercely independent people, who do not look for government to take care of them. Further, Tocquevillean individuals would be people who would try to avoid becoming seduced by the lure of materialism. To this end, individuals, while seeking the goods associated with a life of material self-aggrandizement, would be suspicious of allowing the latter to dominate society. For, in this case, some would end up far better off than others, and the state would reduce the rest to a status of social dependency.

XIII. INTRODUCTION: MICHAEL OAKESHOTT AND CIVIL SOCIETY[71]

Michael Oakeshott, a twentieth-century British conservative philosopher, attacks the rationalist perspective in politics. He does so because for him a rationalist outlook reduces knowledge about the world to a system of principles and maxims or to a perfectionist vision that denies regard for variety and that has no appreciation for the "cumulative effect" of experience.[72] For the rationalist, experience is counted as important only as it fits into a systematic scheme, such as the one provided by Hegel, to demonstrate that scheme's overall intent and purpose, which for Hegel was the revealing, over time, of the moral and ethical purposes in history. But in order to understand the actual context of our lives, we must for Oakeshott, like Burke and Tocqueville, set aside rationalist schemes of a perfected form of social order, and instead concentrate upon the "customary or traditional ways of doing things."[73] In other terms, we must understand the day-to-day context of life in which people make decisions and undertake actions. In taking this approach, we can best understand how our lives are "qualified by a genuine, concrete knowledge of the permanent interest and direction of movement of a society."[74] Providing an understanding of the actual context of life, as well as discussing the view of politics that emerges in this setting, is the objective of his *On Human Conduct*.

XIV. Oakeshott's Free Agent

Oakeshott's understanding of European civilization is predicated upon a conception of the individual as a "free agent." Oakeshott's free agent is a person with "intelligence." And the latter permits one to recognize the nature of the situation in which one lives. What does Oakeshott mean by one's "situation"? He suggests that each of us shares a setting that is governed by various "moral and prudential procedures and practices."[75] Now, a practice refers to a particular "way of life" that individuals can engage in during the course of pursuing their objectives. As such, practices denote basic rules, customs, standards, or canons that people engaged in a particular practice are to follow. And there are many different types of practices and thus many different rules by which to be governed. For example, to name only a few practices, there is the practice of teaching, of doctoring, of lawyering, of parenting, and so on.[76] An intelligent person understands the nature of the rules that govern a practice and adapts to them. To fail to recognize the common rules of conduct that are used to regulate, limit, and constrain interactions is to condemn one's self to failure. For instance, were I to try to practice my craft of teaching outside the norms of the teaching profession, I would be a failure as a teacher. These norms require that I prepare my lectures, that I respect the views of students, and so on. Were I to teach a class without preparation and without respect for students, I would not be able to pursue my career choice, nor would I be able to engage in the common activities referred to as teaching and learning.

A person is a free agent when one is not driven solely by "biological or other urges." In this mode, one is unable to understand the basic practices to which one is to adapt oneself during the course of engaging in activities of one's choice, such as teaching, or parenting, and so on.[77] Here, it would seem that an unfree person, owing to the presence of uncontrolled passions, would be unable to understand the practices one must learn in order to engage in self-chosen activities in society. People are free because they are intelligent individuals who are capable of understanding the different practices of society, and such individuals are able to use them to participate in the activities that are most important to them. What kind of social setting best secures the life of the free agent? And what kind of social setting most upsets it?

XV. Civitas Versus Universitas

Oakeshott compares the *civitas* or civil society to the *universitas*. Each of these forms of life exists in modern Europe in tension with the other. Now, to be sure, the *civitas* represents an ideal character of society, which in no sense can be found in completed form. Nonetheless, the possibility of a *civitas* is suggested by the patterns of ongoing ways of life or practices.[78] As just indicated, there are many different practices pertaining to a variety of different activities that individuals may choose, from doctoring to parenting, to buying and selling, and so on. In a *civitas* these practices are defined in terms of "rules of conduct" that people who take part in the practice together must follow. By following the rules of the practice, each party in a relationship, governed by a particular practice, understands what to expect from the other and how to interpret the other's actions.[79] Here, we "acknowledge the authority of certain conditions in acting."[80] For instance, owing to the practice of buying and selling, as a buyer I understand what to expect from the seller when I relate to him, and, in a similar fashion, the seller understands the buyer's behaviors in terms of the practice of buying and selling. In contrast, a *universitas* is a form of society in which all members acknowledge shared objectives, and each member of society accommodates to them. This kind of association suggests "some identified common purpose, in the pursuit of some acknowledged substantive end."[81] In abiding by the norms associated with achieving the common purpose, our ability to engage in the wide variety of activities linked to free agency is very much limited for the sake of achieving the common purpose or substantive end.

Now, had the *civitas* become the main mode of life in modern Europe, then "the disposition to cultivate the 'freedom' inherent in agency" would have become the principal undertaking of society. Here, the main virtue of society would be personal autonomy, gained through the fullest possible understanding of the rules that govern the activities a person wants to engage in. While the idea of the *civitas* remains strong in Europe, it has not been fully realized, nor has it been made the main mode of life. Instead, the *universitas* or what Oakeshott also called a "compulsory enterprise association" emerged as the dominant mode of life.[82] The latter, when it defines the "character of a state," in addition to mandating a common, substantive good, establishes the reign of a managerial class, or a government that imposes an order on all in the hope of achieving the postulated ends. In this context, individuals have to tailor their lives to include only those activities that the dominant purpose and the managerial class implementing that purpose sanction. Indeed, the government as a compulsory enterprise association makes "substantive choices" for people about how they should live, and often these people are unable or unwilling to make such choices for themselves.[83]

XVI. Civitas, Politics, and Government

Political life in a *civitas* suggests the right of citizens to inspect and to assess the rules that govern various kinds of practices and determine whether these rules should be changed and modified. In a *civitas,* there are "known procedures" by which this conversation and inquiry take place, and here Oakeshott has in mind the rules of the political process that govern rule making and rule modification.[84] In our political system, discussions and decisions pertaining to the rules governing various domains of activity must be made in keeping with the law-making process established by the Constitution of the United States. For instance, let us say that we accept, after a deliberation in the United States Congress, a need for changing the rules pertaining to the way public parks are used for recreational purposes. At present, the rules do not permit as wide a variety of activities as people are calling for. The parks permit hiking and fishing, but they do not allow dirt biking. The problem that may emerge is that hikers do not want to extend much additional space to bikers, because in doing so the bikers may enter areas normally reserved for hikers. And when bikers ride their bikes on the hiking trails, hikers may believe both that they will be subject to possible injury by bikers who run over them and that the trails will be eroded. The challenge of the political discussion is to determine rules that permit all the various activities that different individuals may choose to engage in while they are in the wilderness.

The role of government in the setting of the politics of the *civitas* is to find ways to re-duce the "collisions" between competing views, so that rules of conduct can be defined that allow individuals to take part in those activities that they themselves choose. Here, government does not insist that all citizens, in the manner of a *universitas,* accept the way of life posed by a grand vision of a better society to come. But government provides a way to reconcile divergent needs, so that, to refer to our previous example, hikers and bikers can utilize, without conflict, the great forests of a society.[85] In this setting, governments provide rules of conduct not to impose collective goals onto people, but to enable people "to pursue the activities of their own choice with the minimum [of] frustration."[86]

What the politics of a *civitas* is not about, however, is equally clear. Oakeshott would not use the word *politics* to refer to the exclusive pursuit of the things that facilitate want satisfaction alone. "We do not need the word 'politics' to distinguish the engagement of satisfying wants whatever they may be."[87] For in a politics of want satisfaction, all that matters is to design a system for distributing those goods that satisfy basic wants. Rawls, as we saw, discussed principles of justice to distribute basic goods that all people need, and Rawls's expectation was that the political and economic system would distribute goods in keeping with these principles. Indeed, people in his original position defined these goods as necessary to secure basic wants.

But in emphasizing want satisfaction, for Oakeshott, we de-emphasize something that is just as important if not more so. In particular, Oakeshott sees the *civitas* as making pos-sible a variety of practices in which individuals can choose to participate. And the purpose people have in utilizing these practices is to provide a context in which individuals are able to engage in activities the performance of which by themselves brings enjoyment. This viewpoint is the essence of what Oakeshott calls "conservatism." For Oakeshott, "there are relationships . . . in which no result is sought and which are engaged in for their own sake and enjoyed for what they are and not for what they provide."[88]

For instance, the enjoyment a baseball player should receive from the game of baseball derives from the activity of the game itself. Thus, for baseball players what should be enjoy-able about baseball are the activities associated with playing the game: hitting, fielding, run-ning the bases, and so on. The player should love the game for itself, including all elements associated with it, such as the grass, the fans, and the excitement. These things symbolize a place where the player can engage in activities that by themselves are enjoyable. In addition to sports, there are many activities that Oakeshott might accept as enjoyable for their own sakes. He might point to friendship,[89] to intellectual undertakings, to listening to music or seeing fine art, to aiding others in need, to loving another, and so on. For Oakeshott, a con-servative disposition includes "all activities . . . where what is sought is enjoyment spring-ing, not from the success of an enterprise but from the familiarity of the engagement."[90]

Now, to be sure, not all relationships can be the type that Oakeshott's conservatism celebrates. Clearly, some relationships in a *civitas* are entered into not simply because of the pleasures associated with the activities themselves, but because these activities provide something we want. For instance, a consumer seeks from the seller a product, a worker seeks from his employer a wage, and so on. It would be a mistake to argue that what makes these kinds of relationships pleasurable is solely the performance of the activities associated with them. People enjoy the activity of work for the most part when they re-ceive adequate pay, they enjoy consuming when they can purchase the products they seek at prices they think are favorable, they enjoy selling when they receive an adequate profit, and so on. But few enjoy these activities simply for the fact that they perform them.[91]

Given the foregoing, it is clear that sometimes relationships pertain to activities that are pursued for their own sakes, and at other times activities are pursued on behalf of the ends associated with them. What fascinates Oakeshott are the rules that must be followed in either case. This concern with understanding the rules for relationships and practices of all kinds carries over into politics. Oakeshott thinks that discussions of basic relationships between actors in the public realm should be concerned with describing rules that enable actors in a relationship to work through their differences. The politics of *civitas* does not prescribe outcomes, but it creates rules that allow the actors to determine outcomes based on judgments emerging from the adjustments each makes to accommodate the other.

For instance, in discussing the relationship between owners and workers, the concern should be to define the rules that govern the activities of each party in their relationship to each other. The state is not to determine both the amount and the types of specific benefits that should be provided to each party, such as certain profit levels for owners or certain wages and benefits for workers. Within the context of the rules that govern the relationship of owner and worker, each party is free to pursue ends such as wages or profits with each other, with the agreement reached between the parties being determinative. Here, each side must find ways to accommodate the wishes of the other, and the rules that govern their relationship insure this possibility. Or in the health care debate, the state should create a rule-governed environment that permits the relevant actors to determine what is best on this issue. To do otherwise is to put the state into the position of a commander, making decisions for each of the actors.

Modern political economy and modern politics are designed to make the state the commander, however. The reason for this situation is the powerful influence of an economy that emphasizes satisfying the many desires that people have, along with a state that is committed to sustaining this kind of economic enterprise. In this context, people are to be permitted to purchase whatever they may desire to have in life. Here, each seeks to acquire as many goods as possible. But a market setting of this type is subject to various problems, including, says Oakeshott, "external enemies and internal corruptions." The state is asked to intervene and to protect the market setting from its enemies, and the state achieves this objective only when it is able to establish itself as a powerful, compulsory enterprise association. In this role, the state manages the economy by instituting bureaucratic organizations that organize the work of the society. Here, work is organized in as efficient a way as possible and the benefits from that work are distributed to the members of the society. The cost to people of this approach to government is clear, however. Individuals are given a role in society that defines their tasks even as it ensures them basic benefits. From this point on, individuals accept a life that is orchestrated by powerful actors who control the bureaucratic organizations that all people find themselves in. In effect, individuals are no longer capable of making their own choices, and, instead, the organization they are part of determines the entire course of their lives.[92]

Why do people forfeit their freedom in this way? Sometimes in searching for activities in which we can place our mark on the world, we find ourselves in domains that do not work well for us. We may try the intellectual life, but we may find this activity just too onerous. Or we may embark upon a life of helping others and discover we are not happy in it. Not wanting to face defeat, many people opt for a safer route. In doing so, they enter into those domains where they can attain the goods that secure them a niche in life, a life in which the price of success is forfeiture of one's judgment to others who make decisions for them.[93] Of course people who put themselves in this situation deny both their autonomy and jettison having responsibility for their own lives. This situation, while demeaning to many, is offset by the many goods they receive in return. Here, the enterprise association triumphs, but people lose a prime basis for meaning when they shed autonomy and responsibility in exchange for material benefits that provide both security and comfort.

When we fully embrace the life of want satisfaction, we pave the way for the *universitas,* which seeks to provide for our wants, but this way of life causes the destruction of the *civitas* that is the ground for freedom and agency.[94] Here, Oakeshott may have in mind the modern welfare state, which some think caters to those who want to be taken care of by the state. The rest of society, who want to take responsibility for their own lives and embark on individually defined missions in life, find their efforts interrupted constantly by the need to serve the state's larger goals of providing basic goods that satisfy the different material wants of citizens.

Civitas is always threatened, then, by the abandonment of freedom. The fear of the voluntary dismissal of freedom remains as strong in Oakeshott as in Tocqueville. As Hanna Pitkin said, Oakeshott like Tocqueville feared in politics the "short-sightedly utilitarian, narrowly selfish, crassly competitive orientation"[95] that the modern market setting helped to spawn. Individuals would not have civic virtue in Oakeshott's society unless they manifested the capacity for self-direction and respect for those rules that facilitate individually defined life objectives.

Oakeshott's view of politics has many troubling aspects, however. In emphasizing the priority of rules that define the practices that regulate conduct, Oakeshott denies a place in politics for the pursuit of ends. But Oakeshott, as Benjamin Barber has argued, by "proscribing ends" in favor of the rules that are to govern conduct, excludes from politics concerns for matters such as "distribution [of basic goods, such as rights], allocation, equality, and justice."[96] How, one can ask, can the rules that regulate conduct ever be fair if concerns about the distribution of basic rights, a central objective in modern life, cannot be considered a necessary dimension of political life? Oakeshott's conservative account of politics sweeps these concerns aside because he is worried that any distribution system, even one that is designed to achieve good ends, will only undermine the chances for autonomy and freedom that a politics dedicated to defining the procedures and rules of a *civitas* can provide.

XVII. RESPONSE AND REJOINDER

How does Oakeshott's view of identity differ from the other conservatives? In the cases of Burke and Tocqueville, the bases for identity are substantive values. And these values suggest a way of life to which people are to accommodate their lives. For Burke, one is to orient one's life to "fit" the natural order of occupations and status in society, and for Tocqueville identity is shaped by equality and its concomitant values, in particular, the importance of individuals helping to forge common purposes with others. When confronted with choosing between group participation or totally private pursuits, the norms of Tocqueville's society push one to the former over the latter. Similarly, Burke gives a priority to people following ways of life associated with a natural order.

But for Oakeshott, substantive values, which define a general way of life for each person, are a danger to personal freedom in a civil society. Oakeshott saw the community as grounded in practices and rules that, while not dictating to each individual what each one should do with his or her life, nonetheless gave to each person the opportunity to determine that life. The role of government is merely to help these practices along and to prevent their diminishment by a welfare state that, if it were to exist, would assign people their identity, taking from them the freedom to determine their own ways of life. In this way, the Oakshottian individual understands civic virtue to mean having respect for the collective processes of the society, including an understanding of the need to abide by fair rules. Further, in a way similar to Tocqueville, the Oakshottian individual would understand civic virtue to suggest a desire to not become dependent upon government. But the difference for Oakeshott is that a person's sense of responsibility would be nurtured not by communities that focus an individual's attention on the democratic obligation of helping to shape the common ends, but by rules that put into place practices that permit a wide range of individual choices. Of the three people discussed in this chapter, Oakeshott comes closest to moving into the liberal column.

Putting aside the differences among the four conservatives, what in general would each share with respect to a possible critique of liberal views, discussed earlier, including those of Hobbes, Locke, Mill, Kant, Hegel, and Rawls? The likely critique of liberal views of civil society that conservatives would provide is the fear that liberal individualism would orient people away from regard for traditional civic virtue. For Burke this outcome would mean a diminished concern for the traditions associated with each person's contributing to the well-being of society as his abilities allowed him to do. For Tocqueville liberal individualism means that equality would become the basis for a form of egoism wherein people have no regard for the needs of the larger community. For Oakeshott liberal individualism means that individuals, because they have turned over the authority for their lives to a state that provides basic benefits, have no capacity for individual agency.

Liberal proponents of civil society would all agree that individualism can erode a sense of civic virtue and undermine the overall commitment to secure basic freedoms for each person. To offset this outcome, each of these writers hoped to maintain a kind of civic virtue that could constrain individualism in ways that avoided the unleashing of its harmful effects. For instance, Locke spoke of the virtues of toleration and the live-and-let-live mentality that toleration suggested. Other writers, in particular Rawls, Mill, and Hegel, held not just to the ethic of toleration, but each of these writers wrote about various forms of mutual respect. Rawls's commitment to public reason sought to create a deliberation in which each person not only recognized the rights of others, but listened to and took into consideration the views of others during the course of making public judgments. Mill maintained the importance of individuals according to each other the respect that permits each person to develop his higher faculties. Hegel hoped to place individuals into corporations overseen by an ethical state, and he expected this institutional setting to accord each person not only his basic rights, but a respect for the larger good of the community as well.

Liberals, in trying to avoid the negative ramifications of their own forms of individualism, also suggested the need for establishing governmental structures that protect the rights of citizens against intrusions by others. Thus, Hobbes's unitary state is provided with all the power it must have to protect the rights guaranteed to individuals. Locke,

Kant, Mill, and Rawls hoped to avert the absolutism suggested by Hobbes's unitary state by creating a state based on the idea of separation of powers.

Still, the conservative fear is always that the liberal state may, in the name of meeting its objectives, grow in power to such an extent that the state ends up ultimately opposed to its commitment to secure the rights of each person. We saw the tendency to manifest a concern of this type in Burke's fear of a French revolutionary government that would destroy all pre-existing traditions involving religion and private property rights. Similarly, fear of the liberal state was manifested in Tocqueville's concern that the central government would become a father figure that controls the lives of each citizen. And Oakeshott's paean to individual agency and his condemnation of the state as a compulsory enterprise association would fit well with those who advocate a minimalist state. The argument concerning how powerful government must be to protect our rights rages today between conservatives and liberals, along similar lines.

But with respect to this question, liberals and conservatives do share a common concern. Both advocate sources of power outside of government to balance government and to prevent its becoming too powerful. Tocqueville's voluntary associations, Burke's local affinities to neighborhood, and Oakeshott's shared practices would achieve this end. Liberals take the same course when they advocate institutions such as Locke's constrained majority, Kant's competing-interest view of society, Mill's commitment to workplace participation in determining job requirements, and Rawls's respect for and protection of groups in the nonpublic realm. In both instances, then, conservatives and liberals see a civil society as a place with a separate sphere in which people can join together in associations that act as buffers and restraints on the state's authority.

For the conservatives, the separate sphere is buttressed by traditions found to exist in various forms of associations, which the members of the society consider to be essential to the development of their own identities. Thus, there are strong commitments to uphold a separate sphere owing to the long-standing respect for a host of traditions found in religious organizations, families, neighborhoods, or other voluntary associations. For liberals, these traditions are acceptable only insofar as they maintain the norms found in the moral environment of a civil society, in particular, the commitment to secure basic rights, within a setting where there is a strong commitment to both the civic virtues of toleration and mutual respect. Where the traditions supporting a separate sphere threaten these civic virtues by teaching people to act intolerantly to those who are different from them or where these traditions deny any importance to mutual respect, then the traditions the conservatives extol actually harm, rather than aid, a civil society. The question liberals always pose to conservatives, then, is whether the latter are willing to take a similar questioning stance toward traditions that are considered harmful to the moral environment of a civil society.

Liberals might argue that they are just as much concerned to maintain healthy traditions as conservatives are. Indeed, each of the liberals might argue that he hoped for traditions that would sustain the central features of the society he proposed. Locke would hope for traditions that secured toleration; Hegel, for traditions that maintained corporation life; Mill, for traditions that secured open inquiry and toleration; and Rawls, for traditions that embodied in more complete forms the overlapping consensus. The traditions liberals support in each case make rights and liberties a primary objective. Here, for liberals, to use an example, whereas religious traditions are important, they are only acceptable when associated with toleration and hopefully mutual respect.

Conservatives, without denying the importance of toleration and mutual respect, might wonder, however, whether liberals miss the fact that many core values people need for giving their lives worth and meaning are contained in traditions. Not only is freedom associated with certain traditions, but so too is religious life, as well as many other significant values found in society. And for conservatives the mark of traditions is their contribution to helping people experience life's significance. Here I have in mind the happiness associated with participating in voluntary groups (as in Tocqueville), the life setting conditioned by religion and a natural order (as in Burke), or the happiness found in engaging in activities that are enjoyable for their own sakes (as in Oakeshott). It is important not to neglect these (other than freedom) dimensions of tradition. What good is freedom, a conservative might ask, if in the process of gaining freedom all other important and critical ideas—ideas that give value and meaning to life—are lost sight of or destroyed? This issue raises important questions that will be addressed in the next part, especially when we discuss Nietzsche.

Endnotes

1. In developing my view of Burke, I rely upon Bruce Frohnen, *Virtue and the Promise of Conservatism: The Legacy of Burke and Tocqueville,* (Lawrence Kansas: University Press of Kansas, 1993) and Jeremy Waldron, ed., with introductory and concluding essays, *Nonsense Upon Stilts,* (New York: Methuen, 1987), pp. 77–96.

2. Sibley, *Political Ideas and Political Ideologies,* pp. 503–4.

3. Waldron, *Nonsense Upon Stilts,* pp. 79–80.

4. George Sabine, *A History of Political Theory,* p. 611. For good background sources, see as well Bruce Frohnen, cited in note 1, and Frank O'Gorman, *Edmund Burke: His Political Philosophy,* (London: George Allen and Unwin Ltd., 1973). Finally, the main source on Burke is his *Reflections on the Revolution in France,* ed. by Conor Cruise O'Brien, (London: Penguin Books, 1982).

5. Burke, *Reflections on the Revolution in France,* p. 149.

6. Ibid., p. 149.

7. Ibid., pp. 149–50.

8. Ibid., p. 150.

9. Ibid., p. 151. Italics in text.

10. Ibid., p. 151.

11. Ibid., p. 151.

12. Ibid., p. 151.

13. Ibid., p. 151.

14. Waldron, *Nonsense on Stilts,* p. 91.

15. Frohnen, *Virtue and the Promise of Conservatism: The Legacy of Burke and Tocqueville,* p. 60.

16. Ibid., p. 60.

17. Ibid., pp. 60–61.

18. Ibid., pp. 73, 71.

19. Burke, *Reflections on the Revolution in France,* p. 141.

20. Ibid., p. 139.

21. Ibid., p. 139.

22. Hanna Fenichel Pitkin, *The Concept of Representation,* (Berkeley: University of California Press, 1967), p. 171.

23. Ibid., p. 172.

24. Burke quoted in Pitkin, *The Concept of Representation,* p. 173; also, pp. 172, 174.

25. Pitkin, *The Concept of Representation,* p. 176.

26. Waldron, *Nonsense on Stilts,* pp. 88–89.

27. Burke, *Reflections on the Revolution in France,* p. 131, also pp. 130. Also, see Waldron, *Nonsense on Stilts,* p. 89.

28. Burke, *Reflections on the Revolution in France,* p. 129.

29. Burke cited in Frank O'Gorman, *Edmund Burke: His Political Philosophy,* p. 121.

30. Burke, *Reflections on the Revolution in France,* p. 122.

31. Frohnen, *Virtue and the Promise of Conservatism: The Legacy of Burke and Tocqueville,* p. 84; also p. 85.

32. Burke, *Reflections on the Revolution in France,* p. 187.

33. Ibid., p. 186.

34. Ibid., p. 189.

35. Ibid., p. 196.

36. Alexis de Tocqueville, *Democracy in America,* ed. J. P. Mayer and Max Lerner, (New York: Harper and Row, 1966). See J. P. Mayer's essay in this volume, "Tocqueville's Democracy in America," pp. xi–xii.

37. Mayer, pp. xiii–xvii.
38. Tocqueville, *Democracy in America,* p. 264.
39. Ibid., p. 498.
40. Ibid., p. 475.
41. Ibid., p. 477.
42. Ibid., p. 477.
43. Ibid., p. 486; also, p. 648.
44. Ibid., p. 488.
45. Ibid., p. 485.
46. Ibid., p. 488.
47. Ibid., p. 492.
48. Ibid., p. 482.
49. Ibid., p. 482.
50. Ibid., p. 482.
51. Ibid., p. 482.
52. Ibid., pp. 83–85.
53. Ibid., p. 85.
54. Ibid., p. 499.
55. Ibid., p. 499.
56. Ibid., p. 590.
57. Ibid., p. 508.
58. Ibid., pp. 510, 590.
59. Ibid., p. 501.
60. Ibid., p. 519.
61. Ibid., p. 519.
62. Ibid., p. 521.
63. Ibid., p. 521.
64. Ibid., pp. 292–94.
65. Ibid., p. 614.
66. Ibid., pp. 528–29.
67. Ibid., p. 666.
68. Ibid., p. 667.
69. Ibid., p. 667.
70. Ibid., p. 666.
71. I will refer to Oakeshott in two major works,
Rationalism in Politics and Other Essays, (London: Methuen, 1962) and *On Human Conduct,* (Oxford: Clarendon Press, 1975).
72. Oakeshott, *Rationalism in Politics and Other Essays,* pp. 10–11, 5–7, 1–2.
73. Ibid., p. 10.
74. Ibid., p. 22.
75. Oakeshott, *On Human Conduct,* pp. 234–35.
76. Ibid., pp. 55–57.
77. Ibid., pp. 234–35.
78. Ibid., p. 108, 180–81, 203.
79. Ibid., pp. 112–13.
80. Ibid., p. 201.
81. Ibid., p. 203.
82. Ibid., p. 274.
83. Ibid., pp. 157–58, 205–6, 264, 274.
84. Ibid., p. 161.
85. Oakeshott, "On Being Conservative," in *Rationalism in Politics,* pp. 188–92.
86. Ibid., p. 184.
87. Oakeshott, *On Human Conduct,* p. 162.
88. Oakeshott, "On Being Conservative," pp. 176–77.
89. Ibid., p. 177.
90. Ibid., p. 178.
91. Ibid., p. 176.
92. Oakeshott, *On Human Conduct,* pp. 294–95.
93. Ibid., pp. 277–78. See his discussion of the "individual *manqué*" who is unable to accept the responsibility which accompanies freedom.
94. Ibid., p. 294–95.
95. Hanna Fenichel Pitkin, "The Roots of Conservatism, Michael Oakeshott and the Denial of Politics," *Dissent,* Fall, 1973, p. 513.
96. Benjamin R. Barber, "Conserving Politics," *Government and Opposition,* 10:3, Oct. 1977, p. 459.

Partial Bibliography and Further Reading

Burke

Ayling, Stanley Edward. *Edmund Burke: His Life and Opinions.* New York: St. Martin's Press, 1989.

Canavan, Francis. *The Political Reason of Edmund Burke.* Durham, N.C.: Duke University Press, 1960.

Chapman, Gerald W. *Edmund Burke: The Practical Imagination.* Cambridge: Harvard University Press, 1967.

Cone, Carl B. *Burke and the Nature of Politics.* Lexington: University of Kentucky Press, 1957.

Frohnen, Bruce. *Virtue and the Promise of Conservatism: The Legacy of Burke and Tocqueville.* Lawrence, Kansas: University Press of Kansas, 1993.

Furniss, Tom. *Edmund Burke's Aesthetic Ideology: Language, Gender, and Political Economy in Revolution.* Cambridge: Cambridge University Press, 1993.

Kramnick, Isaac. *The Rage of Edmund Burke: Portrait of an Ambivalent Conservative.* New York: Basic Books, 1977.

Morley, John. *Edmund Burke: A Historical Study.* New York: Knopf, 1924.

O'Brien, Conor Cruise. *The Great Melody: A Thematic Biography of Edmund Burke.* Chicago: University of Chicago Press, 1992.

O'Gorman, Frank. *Edmund Burke: His Political Philosophy.* Bloomington: Indiana University Press, 1973.

Tocqueville

Commager, Henry Steele. *Commager on Tocqueville.* Columbia: University of Missouri Press, 1993.

Hadari, Saguiv A. *Theory in Practice: Tocqueville's New Science of Politics.* Stanford: Stanford University Press, 1989.

Kahan, Alan S. *Aristocratic Liberalism: The Social and Political Thought of Jacob Burckhardt, John Stuart Mill, and Alexis de Tocqueville.* Oxford: Oxford University Press, 1992.

Siedentop, Larry. *Tocqueville.* Oxford: Oxford University Press, 1994.

Tocqueville, Alexis de. *Democracy in America.* Edited by J. P. Mayer and Max Lerner. New York: Harper & Row [1966].

Zetterbaum, Marvin. *Tocqueville and The Problem of Democracy.* Stanford: Stanford University Press, 1967.

Oakeshott

Barber, Benjamin. "Conserving Politics," *Government and Opposition,* 10:3, Oct. 1977.

Devigne, Robert. *Recasting Conservatism: Oakeshott, Strauss, and the Response to Postmodernism.* New Haven: Yale University Press, 1994.

Franco, Paul. *The Political Philosophy of Michael Oakeshott.* New Haven: Yale University Press, 1990.

Fuller, Timothy, (ed.) and Oakeshott, Michael Joseph. *Religion, Politics, and the Moral Life.* New Haven: Yale University Press, 1993.

Greenleaf, W. H. *Oakeshott's Philosophical Politics.* New York: Barnes & Noble, 1966.

King, Preston, and Parekh, B. C. (ed.). *Politics and Experience: Essays Presented to Professor Michael Oakeshott on the Occasion of His Retirement.* Cambridge: Cambridge University Press, 1968.

Oakeshott, Michael. *On Human Conduct.* Clarendon Press, 1975.

———. *Rationalism in Politics and Other Essays.* New York: Methuen, 1967.

Pitkin, Hanna F. "The Roots of Conservatism, Michael Oakeshott and the Denial of Politics," *Dissent,* Fall, 1973.

15

THE MARXIST CRITIQUE
OF CIVIL SOCIETY

I. INTRODUCTION

This chapter provides the general outlines of a Marxist critique of civil society. To this end, the centerpiece of this chapter is Karl Marx's (1818–1883) views of a liberal civil society. This is a setting that has a separate sphere of groups and associations as part of the overall commitment to securing the rule of law dedicated to providing equal rights for all persons. In addition, I will supplement these views with those of Herbert Marcuse (1898–1979), an important recent Marxist. My intention in doing so is to address an obvious problem Marx's ideas must confront: namely, how is it possible to remain a Marxist and continue to attack civil society as a setting that denies human freedom, even in the face of the continuing endurance of capitalism? But first, we discuss Marx's views in some detail.

II. MARX'S REACTION TO HEGEL

To understand Marx's starting point, it is necessary to discuss, briefly, his reaction to Hegel.[1] As we demonstrated in Chapter 11, Hegel, in the *Phenomenology of Spirit,* had argued that history can be understood as driven by a central idea Hegel called *Spirit.* The latter signifies the moral directions that should be embodied into the social, political, and economic institutions that govern human life. This knowledge evolves incrementally over time, and, as understanding of Spirit, or our moral possibilities, emerges, individuals gain a more precise picture of what morality consists of and how it is made manifest. Ultimately, at the "end of history," Spirit is fully revealed, and thus as full an understanding as possible of both the moral concepts that govern life and of their corresponding institutional forms is made known to humankind. The Hegelian state is the most essential embodiment of Spirit, because it, the state, stands over civil society, which is a setting of competing interests, and gives to civil society necessary moral parameters. Thanks to the moral direction provided by the state, there can be many diverse interests in civil society, but at the same time there will be no social fragmentation or destructive competition.

Hegel's vision suggested that Spirit constructs a way of life and an identity for humankind, in keeping with the objectives of Spirit. Marx, however, turned that argument around and argued that Spirit is a function of the projections and thoughts of human beings. Moreover, the thoughts and projections of human beings that create a concept of Spirit, and thus moral order, reflect the real course of events that occurs in history. This means that history is said to unfold according to a certain logic and pattern. The main feature of this pattern is that human beings initially find themselves in circumstances that deny their authentic possibilities, and this fact is overcome later when capitalism is replaced with socialism. Marx, then, in arguing that human self-understanding is a function of the evolving pattern of historical events, sought to turn Hegel "right side up." Marx did so by demonstrating that Spirit is not an independent force existing outside the lives of people and having the power to determine how we come to see and to understand ourselves.

Rather, for Marx what Hegel calls Spirit is really our conscious understanding of our needs and how well our environment either serves our needs or hinders them. For Marx, people find themselves in circumstances that deny the full expression of their capacities. Marx was in many ways starting from the same point of view as Mill. Marx believed that real freedom involved the fullest development possible of our highest capacities. But Marx understood that the material settings in which we live often thwart that development. As we recognize this fact, we become alienated from our world, believing that it does not support our real interests and needs. In responding to this situation by demanding constructive changes, we hope to create a better world, one that will facilitate our potential to the fullest. So when Marx sought to revise Hegel, his intention was to demonstrate how the structures of material existence create estrangement for humankind by denying humankind fulfillment of people's real needs and potentials.[2] Only when these structures were both understood and then changed would humankind finally be capable of realizing its most authentic needs and desires.

In this vein, Marx argued in his critique of Hegel's *Philosophy of Right* that Hegel misunderstood the proper relationship between the state and society. Hegel's state as a manifestation of the idea of Spirit reverses the relationship between the state and society.[3] For Hegel, the highest hope is a state that embodies his ideal of moral life. This state then would create the conditions that define the bases for human life. But for Marx, democracy is the highest ideal that a state can embody. In a democracy the citizens acting together create their own constitution and determine the conditions under which they will live and at the same time prescribe the conditions under which the state will relate to its citizens. "Hegel starts from the state and makes man the subjectified state; democracy starts from man and makes the state objectified man."[4] In fact, Marx believed that democracy, as a form of government, was the only true expression of the universal interests of people. "Only democracy . . . is the true unity of the general and the particular."[5]

Further, Marx rejected categorically Hegel's suggestion that the bureaucracy stands for a class of high-minded and well-educated civil servants who carry forth the idea of Spirit and form civil society in a manner that is able to attain this ideal in practice. Hegel, as will be remembered, saw civil society as a battleground of private interests, and he expected the state, working through its bureaucracy, to turn civil society into a community with shared interests. But for Marx, bureaucrats tend to represent a "crass materialism."

The highest concern of each member of the bureaucracy is his own separate ambition and need for advancement within the organization. Further, bureaucrats are people who accept their subordination and obedience to the state as a condition for securing their future. Instead of being independent thinkers and actors, they do what is needed to maintain the state's power, all in order to promote their own material ambitions. In doing so, the bureaucracy sets itself up, under the guise of promoting the general interest, as a very powerful private interest that competes with other private interests.[6]

A theme that runs throughout Marx and that helps to explain the views just stated is Marx's critical view of Hegel's notion of civil society. For Hegel, as we saw, a civil society is located in a market setting that permits individuals to pursue their own interests, subject to the rules and constraints placed on the market by the state. Indeed, Hegel's view of the state/civil society relationship suggested that the state could bring community and a sense of the common welfare to a market-oriented society. But Marx, as the views just described indicated, did not believe that a civil society that is predicated on the free pursuit of self-interest, even if subject to a conception of the common good ordained by the state, could produce community and a sense of the shared welfare. All such a setting could produce are individuals who each had their own self-interests to pursue and who each had little or no concern for a larger good.

Finally, Marx believed that Hegel's view of the state tended to mystify it or, in other terms, to try to convince people that the existing state actually manifested notions of freedom and rights for all when in fact it did not. To demystify the state and thus to expose the fact that Hegel's ideas are not actually realized in the state Hegel described, it is necessary to cast off Hegelian misconceptions. To this end, Marx sought to point out that Hegel's liberalism really places blinders on people. People who wear these blinders think that society is becoming progressively more free over time, with more and more people enjoying the benefits of a rights-based state, including the opportunity to realize and to be recognized for the fulfillment of their highest capacities. This depiction of society by liberalism prevents people from understanding the alienation and exploitation produced by capitalism. Liberalism works to shield capitalism from criticism by suggesting that the latter is the basis for the rights provided by the former. Marx hopes to strip away these misunderstandings so that he can expose the real tragedies of capitalism and what for him is the untruth of liberalism. Marx's early writings, including *Economic and Philosophical Manuscripts* and his essay *On the Jewish Question,* were written with this objective in mind. We now turn to these essays.

III. POLITICAL EMANCIPATION: RIGHTS IN CIVIL SOCIETY

Marx's discussion of modern civil society is multi-layered. At the core of a civil society is a capitalist economic system. Wrapped around that core are various layers, or ways of life, each of which I propose to discuss here and each of which contains a description of how life in a civil society denies priority to the full development of persons. In discussing the different layers of life, I will start from the outside and work inward. My first concern is Marx's discussion of a liberal civil society and what significance, in his view, the idea of equal rights has for people's lives. Once we have completed this discussion we will discuss the next layer of reality, alienation. After that, we will address the sources of alienation and its corresponding experience, exploitation. In discussing these matters, we examine Marx's historical and economic critiques of capitalism. As we do, we return to the core problem, a discussion of the dynamics of a capitalist economy.

To begin, in *On the Jewish Question,* which includes Marx's view of the significance of rights in a civil society, Marx said that the modern, secular state suggests a "double existence." On the one hand, individuals, as members of civil society, view themselves as private persons pursuing their own interests and seeking their own welfare. But, on the other hand, individuals see themselves as citizens committed to the common good. In discussing the individual element of civil society, Marx had in mind the view that life in a civil society takes place in a capitalist-dominated market setting. Here the members of this environment compete with each other as individuals to gain as much for themselves as they can, subject of course to the rules that govern the competitive process. Each person thus "acts simply as a *private individual,* treats other men as means, degrades himself to the role of a mere means, and becomes the plaything of alien [market] powers."[7]

But with regard to the communal element, individuals think of themselves as citizens in a *political community,* and in this role believe that the state is able to create a prospect for a universal, rational order binding on all.[8] Indeed, as we saw, this was Hegel's view of the modern state/society relationship. For Hegel, the state that stands above civil society as well as the market setting would produce order and unity within both domains. Here, as a result of state actions, individuals in civil society would see themselves not as separate individuals competing with each other but as members of a community sharing a common sense of responsibility for the welfare of the society. This perspective, for Marx, substitutes for the Christian religion a new secular version of religion. Thus, Marx said that the political state "in relation to civil society, is just as spiritual as is heaven in relation to earth."[9]

For Marx, of the two faces of life in civil society, the private, individual dimension seems to dominate and dictate outcomes, making the creation of community impossible. Marx demonstrated this point by indicating that the main advance of civil society, the provision of basic rights for all people, leads to conditions antithetical to community. The *"rights of man,"* in the French *Declaration of the Rights of Man and of the Citizen* of 1793, signify for Marx "the rights of a *member of civil society,* that is, of egoistic man, of man separated from other men and from the community."[10] The rights that Marx referred to here were liberty, property, equality, and security. Liberty is the right to do whatever one wants so long as one does not harm others. The right of property is the right to "enjoy one's fortune and to dispose of it as one will; without regard for the other men and independently of society." This right signifies nothing more than a "right of self-interest."[11] Equality is equal liberty or the equal entitlement to do what one wants and on this view each person is a "self-sufficient monad." Security is the protection of all one's rights or, as Marx puts it, the *"assurance* of egoism."[12]

Having rights in a civil society, dominated by market relations, then, tends to turn individuals into people who think of themselves as separated from every other person during the course of doing whatever they want, so long as they do not harm another. Here, each person knows others only as co-participants in a quest to realize his own self-interest, but, in this setting, individuals are unable to find a basis for a mutual commitment to a shared notion of the common good and to the conditions that make community possible. As a consequence, Marx said that in a civil society "liberty as a right of man is not founded upon the relations between man and man, but rather upon the separation of man from man. It is the right of separation. The right of the *circumscribed* individual, withdrawn into himself."[13]

The problem of living in an environment such as this, where people are so separated from each other and living in antagonistic relationships to each other, is that there is no basis for "human emancipation."[14] To attain this status, another set of rights must be considered as ultimately more important than the rights of man. Here, Marx had in mind the "*rights of the citizen.*"[15] The latter pertain to the right to take part in determining the common policies, the right to have open and free communication of views, and the right to demand that public officials justify their actions. Having political rights enables individuals to establish a basis for engaging in common action with each other.[16]

Indeed, Marx said that "human emancipation will only be complete when real, individual man has absorbed into himself the abstract citizen . . . and when he has recognized and organized his own powers . . . as *social* powers, so that he no longer separates this social power from himself as *political* power."[17] Marx meant by this statement that individuals must have the capacity to forge a political community that represents the common interests and needs all share. Moreover, such a political community must be arranged in a way that permits individuals to shape and organize the economic life of society, so that the full development of people's potential is made possible. Thus, individuals must be a part of communities that are engaged in the production of goods, and, furthermore, these communities must be grounded in social relationships that the members themselves control and organize. In this setting, the workers use their rights as citizens to determine what will be produced and how the various skills and powers of people will be arranged to produce these goods.

For Marx, people obtain meaning in their lives when they are recognized for their contributions through the productive work they perform. But when others control people's work, in this case the capitalists, then individuals are never allowed to express their full capacities in their work, nor are workers allowed to be recognized by others for their contributions to society. Only when workers control the economic process will real emancipation—the kind that allows full recognition by others for the work people do—be possible. As Jeremy Waldron says, for Marx, "full-blooded emancipation, therefore, requires not just the existence of a political community, but the involvement of that community in the democratic organization and running of productive economic life."[18]

The problem, however, is that political rights, although an important, progressive step, will not permit full emancipation so long as these rights take place in a capitalist society.[19] Liberalism's great failure is that it permits people to use their freedom to promote only the individualistic, egotistical existence that Marx said characterized modern civil society. And as a result of this experience individuals will never become the citizens, taking part in shaping the economic life of society, that Marx hoped for. Continuing alienation, in a capitalist society, explains why this outcome is inevitable.

IV. MODERN ALIENATION

The fundamental fact of life for the ordinary worker in a capitalist-dominated civil society is that the worker not only produces commodities, but he becomes a commodity as well.[20] The worker is a mere commodity because his only value comes from the fact that he has only his labor to sell to those who can use it to manufacture products. In a capitalist economy, workers are not recognized for their diverse and different skills or for their particular powers and capacities. Instead, workers are understood to be a package of energy that, when employed properly like any other machine, can produce certain desired results for the owner class. And yet, what Marx most wanted was to engender the full development of people's potentials, just as Mill had desired. Marx said that the "the *real,* active orientation of man to himself as a species being, or his manifestation as a real species being (i.e., as a human being), is only possible by his really bringing out of himself all the *powers* that are his as the *species* man."[21] In consequence of capitalism, however, the worker knows himself only through what he becomes as an individual engaged in "estranged labor," or in activity that separates him from both recognizing and fulfilling his basic skills and powers. From the standpoint of this experience, *alienation* refers to a type of work that prohibits an individual from either knowing or from developing one's talents and powers.

In the *Economic and Philosophic Manuscripts of 1844,* Marx discussed four different ways in which alienation manifests itself. First, there is the estrangement from *the product the laborer produces himself.*[22] In effect, as a result of the work that workers engage in they become dependent on society needing the products that they produce, because unless society needs these products there is no work for the workers and thus no means for the worker to support himself. But at the same time, the products the worker produces do not change in any way the social conditions under which production takes place. These conditions are radically alienating in the sense that they deny the worker a basis for engaging in the kind of work that would allow the worker to realize his or her potential.[23] The goods workers produce in a capitalist society symbolize, then, the continuation of economic conditions that create alienation for workers by making it impossible for them to control their own workplace for the purpose of creating goods and arranging productive relationships that make human emancipation possible.

There is also alienation from the *"act of production"* itself.[24] Here, an individual is forced to engage in work in which he has no interest in performing and that has no relationship to the evolution of his basic potential as a human being. "He is at home when he is not working, and when he is working he is not at home. His labour is therefore not voluntary, but coerced, it is *forced labour.*"[25] The experience Marx had in mind was that of the production-line workers who labored long hours, repeating in endless fashion the same routine over and over.[26] This kind of work leads to the "emasculating" of workers' physical and mental powers.[27] Moreover, because work of this sort makes us live in a remote relationship to our basic powers and capacities, we live with a sense of permanent estrangement from ourselves. In effect, we can never know the nature of what we can be, nor how to go about a life that permits us to realize to the fullest extent all our basic capacities and powers. "Here, we have *self-estrangement,* as we had previously the estrangement of the *thing.*"[28]

Moreover, in the third form of estrangement, *we lose an ability to understand our potential as a species.* This means not only that we cannot discern our particular capacities as unique persons but also we cannot discern the whole panorama of capacities that human beings as a species have open to them. Here, Marx made a distinction between the capacities associated with human work and those related to animals. Animals can produce goods only to satisfy immediate needs associated with their survival. Humankind knows how to produce goods that are in keeping with the standards of all types of species, and not just the lives of human beings.[29] Further, as conscious beings who seek to produce the basis for all of life, human beings, unlike animals, can make judgments "in accordance with the laws of beauty."[30] Of significance here is that human beings can know their capacities and choose to pursue those ways of life that ensure human flourishing. This possibility is denied in the work setting Marx critiqued in large part because human beings are never freed from living like animals, concerned only to secure their immediate physical survival needs.

But in a culture that fails to protect this prospect, individuals naturally become, in the final form of alienation, *estranged from others.* For just as one cannot understand one's own essential nature, then it is also the case that no one can know the essential nature of another.[31] The sad aspect of this experience is that it dashes the Kantian hope of respecting others as ends and not solely as means. To treat others as ends in the Marxian context requires a person's being able to recognize and to support in others the qualities of their wholeness, including acknowledgment of their full powers. But in a capitalist society, where each person is nothing but a commodity pursuing basic survival needs, this objective cannot be realized.

V. THE NORMS OF ALIENATED LIFE

Perhaps, the greatest tragedy of alienated existence is that the norms of alienated life produce in citizens, workers and owners alike, a loss of regard for the basic virtues that make possible a society dedicated to the fullest possible development of each person. The major values that replace virtues of this sort are those associated with avarice. Two key factors in this tragedy are the introduction of machines and the overwhelming urge for money.

As we have seen, the organization of work makes each worker a machine tender. "He [the worker] becomes an appendage of the machine, and it is only the most simple, most monotonous, and most easily acquired knack, that is required of him."[32] By requiring each person to perform a simple task for a machine, each person is kept as an "immature human being" or as a "child."[33] Moreover, in order to serve machines, workers must adapt to the doctrines associated with wealth production. This means that workers must accept a subsistence-level existence so that the major portion of the earnings of their work will go to a fund, controlled by the owners, that can be used to purchase new machines. To accomplish this objective, workers are taught to lead a life of self-denial. Indeed, the worker is changed into "an insensible being lacking all needs."[34] Here, the worker is made into a compliant person who has no needs beyond a subsistence-level life so that the owner can use the wealth the worker generates, not to enable the worker to realize his full powers, but to acquire more machines or capital for the owner. Marx said, "the less you [the workers] think, love, theorize, sing, paint, fence, etc., the more you [the capitalists] *save, the greater* becomes your [the capitalist's] treasure . . . your *capital.*"[35]

Moreover, in this setting, there is one goal that motivates the owner class—the quest for money.[36] Indeed, money must be given pride of place. But at the same time, owing to the preoccupation with money, another value becomes fundamental, namely, avarice. "*Excess* and *intemperance* come to be . . . [the] true norm."[37] This tendency is associated with the effort to create within the minds of people a sense of the need for specific kinds of goods that people are told they should learn to desire. The goods in question are promoted by those who know that, if they can get enough people to buy them, then they, the sellers, will acquire wealth and social power over the consumers as well as over the workers who produce them. The objective of the seller, then, is to create in the mind of the consumer a "*new* need" for the things that the seller is producing. Here, the seller must convince the buyer to want something for which he presently has no need. When the seller is successful, the consumer now must make the necessary sacrifices to accumulate the money the seller demands for the good, and in making these sacrifices a new form of dependency is born, one that makes the consumer subordinate to the producer class. In this way, the seller has "seduced" the consumer into a "new mode of *gratification* and therefore economic ruin."[38]

Finally, money is the basis for determining what each person can be and who each person is. This means that who I am always is a function of the money I have as well as what I have to do to acquire money. If in order to obtain money, it is necessary for me to forgo my native powers, then I will. Perhaps, owing to my native powers, I could be a great doctor, but because my father has no money to help me become one I cannot pursue that career. Instead, I turn myself into a businessman whose sole interest in life is to acquire money. But on the other hand, let us say that I have no acumen to be a doctor, but nonetheless I have the desire and the money to become one. In this case, I will become a doctor despite the fact that I should not be one. Marx said, "that which I am unable to do as a *man,* and of which therefore all my individual essential powers are incapable, I am able to do by means of *money.*"[39] It is easy to understand how in this setting many traditional virtues lose their place of importance. People still talk about virtues such as fidelity and love, but these virtues are easily displaced with their opposites, vices such as hatred and infidelity, when for the sake of making money it is necessary to do so.[40] Thus, if today in order to be successful in achieving wealth I must be loving, then I will be, but, if tomorrow I must be nasty and mean-spirited for the sake of getting ahead and making money, then I will be as nasty as I have to be. Here, no permanent, fixed, and traditional virtues can ever become the mainstays of my life. Instead, my values will be modified with the changes in my circumstances.

How in this setting can people have relationships based upon mutual regard for the development in each person of his best, most important powers? For Marx the exchanges we have with each other should be designed not so much to make people materially wealthy, but these exchanges should make possible a community based upon virtues that help sustain mutual respect and love for the basic powers and abilities of human life. In particular, our relationships should be designed to be honest efforts to enable others to share their hopes and powers with us and to enable us to share our hopes and powers with others.[41]

VI. HISTORICAL CONTEXT OF ALIENATION

Understanding the source of alienation is critical to ridding ourselves of it. The purpose of Marx's philosophy is, after all, not just to understand existing reality but to change it. "The philosophers have only *interpreted* the world, in various ways; the point, however, is to *change* it."[42] Marx believed that history must be used to change the circumstances of human beings for the better. In effect, it is possible to learn from history and in doing so, use the lessons of the past to change the course of the future. History demonstrates the way in which individuals are part of processes designed to produce for human needs.[43] These forces often shape human lives in ways that are against their best interests, as in a capitalist society, but at the same time, individuals can and do react to the forces shaping them, with the intention of creating productive relations that are no longer alienating. Marx said that "circumstances make men just as much as men make circumstances."[44] In this section, we set forth a reading of history from Marx's standpoint to demonstrate the opening history provides to change human circumstances and free humankind from alienation.

For Marx, after the medieval society had already passed from the scene, civil society emerged in the eighteenth century, with a system of production and commerce dominated by the bourgeoisie. Further, it is this class that is associated with the "superstructure" or social and political values that grounded the idea of civil society and that provided cultural support for maintaining the system of production found in a capitalist society.[45] But at the same time, the new system of production created tensions between itself and the workers, and ultimately these tensions would be resolved in a revolution that brings about communism. Before discussing the economic argument that explains this contention, a few paragraphs are in order that describe the character of the society that the bourgeoisie built and that explain why a civil society for Marx will have to be transformed into a communist one.

Civil society emerged from the transition from a productive process based on guilds in the Middle Ages to large-scale factory manufacturing. This change brought about a new relationship between worker and owner. In the guilds, which were home for many craftsmen producing needed goods, a "patriarchal relationship" characterized the association between the "master" and the skilled, so-called "journeyman," worker.[46] The patriarchal relationship gave the master power over the worker, but the master's power did not lead to intense worker-versus-owner antagonism. The reason was that the worker, himself, wanted to become a master, and he hoped that by working in a guild he could gain the experience and means to become one. Given this desire, the worker had no interest in overthrowing the guild system, even if the master had complete power over him.[47]

But with the emergence of the "big bourgeoisie" or new owner class who promoted factory manufacturing, the seeds were planted to create worker-versus-owner conflict, and this conflict ultimately for Marx would lead to the overthrow of the owners by the workers. Why is this? The new owner class, unlike the guilds, wanted to be part of a trading system that included not just the local economies but the world economy, also. To compete on this basis, it was necessary to accumulate large amounts of "movable" capital, or resources that could be shifted from region to region as business and production needs might dictate. The guilds were always locally based, and the guild owners, the "petty bourgeoisie," did not envision investing their resources in a distant endeavor. But the new "big bourgeoisie" seized on the opportunity to invest resources wherever they thought it would be helpful in augmenting their share of the world market.[48]

Naturally wanting to provide security for their investments, the "big bourgeoisie" sought ways to secure their positions against any would-be competitors. To this end, for instance, they received from home governments protective tariffs and customs legislation.[49] Still, despite these protective policies, competition among large industries in the seventeenth and eighteenth centuries became the main mode of interaction among producers. The competition compelled individuals to channel their energies to achieve success in the market, and in doing so the only objective that mattered was to increase industrial growth. In this context, all investment money was used to support the development of industry and of what supports industry, such as modern means of communication and the development of a supporting financial system. Moreover, the ownership of industrial capital became concentrated into the hands of a few. Large industrial cities emerged, and, as they did, all traditional crafts found in guild life were destroyed, and the countryside lost importance in the political and social affairs of capitalist countries. In the face of these changes, "ideology, religion, and morality," all factors that might threaten the new way of life, were diminished as important sources of public belief. Moreover, while the "big bourgeoisie" in each country saw themselves as each holding separate national interests, this class had the same interest, and, because of this fact, all the nations they dominated made that interest primary, even to the point of denying any place to nationality. In each case, each industrial nation made the promotion of the needs of "big industry" its main goal, with the result that the life of the working class was made "unbearable."[50]

In this context, the state itself, then, could only become a protector of the interests of the bourgeoisie. Now, as we saw, for Hegel, the state was conceptualized as a separate, independent force, standing above particular interests engaged in competition and defining the common good that each separate interest in the civil society was to uphold. But for Marx, this conception of the state was a fiction. The state is "nothing more than the form of organization which the bourgeois necessarily adopt both for internal and external purposes, for the mutual guarantee of property and interests."[51] Indeed, the state is the vehicle by which the "ruling class" promotes its interests by forming and shaping other institutions, in particular the law, to meet the needs of manufacturing.

In this environment, a system of production is established that maintains a division of labor among the various parties who are part of the process of production. The owners provide the tools and organize the work, and the workers, who have no other means by which to make a living, must enter the workplace on terms assigned to them by the owners. The owners demand control of the process of production because without it they cannot continue to accumulate the capital they must have in order to retain competitive advantage over other manufacturers. Private property comes to symbolize for the worker a division of labor that gives the capitalist complete control over the nature of work. In this setting the worker has no hope that he at some point will, as the journeymen in the guilds had expected, acquire some control of the process of the work, himself.[52]

The spiraling demands for greater profit lead to the owners' seeking to acquire more and more power over the workers, but this situation culminates in the evolution among the workers of the need to overthrow the domination of the owner class. The workers have no choice because they are the ones continuing to bear more and more burdens without gaining any advantages, even as they are the majority of the society. The workers cannot appeal to the state for reforms because the bourgeoisie controls the state. Thus, the objective of the workers is to overthrow the bourgeoisie and the capitalist system that protects their interests. The hope is to create a society in which for the first time class rule is completely abolished.[53] For this kind of action to take place, "the alteration of men on a mass scale is necessary, an alteration which can only take place in a practical movement, a *revolution*."[54] The result of this revolution will be as Marx described the outcome in the *Communist Manifesto*. "In place of the old bourgeoisie society, with its classes and class antagonisms, we shall have an association, in which the free development of each is the condition of the free development of all."[55]

VII. THE ECONOMIC ARGUMENT: THE SOURCES OF EXPLOITATION

Coinciding with this historical analysis is an economic critique of capitalism that explains the inevitability of the downfall of the capitalist class and the transition to communism. In this section, my intention is to explain the rudiments of Marx's analysis of the emergence of exploitation as well as to show how the tendencies that produce exploitation also contribute, in the end, to the overthrow of capitalism.

In a capitalist society, the worker becomes a wage laborer when he is forced to exchange his labor for the means of survival. The worker, then, is not in a position to demand parity with the capitalist, suggesting, for instance, that both should share in the profits of work.[56] The capitalist's power over the worker stems from the fact that the capitalist owns the conditions of work or *capital*. The latter includes (but is not limited to) the raw materials and the tools and machines used to produce "new raw materials, new instruments of labour [such as machines], and new means of subsistence [that are used to make possible the workers' survival]."[57] Further, the capitalist is in a position to control all the social relationships that surround production.[58] This means that the capitalist controls the conditions that advantage him against the workers, and the capitalist promotes norms that benefit him by diminishing workers' status. Moreover, the capitalist has the power to introduce new technologies or machines into the workplace in the hopes of reducing the cost of production.[59] When the capitalist does this, he creates more capital which enables the capitalist to strengthen his power over workers.

Maintaining this favorable (to the capitalist) relationship is crucial to his ability to accumulate capital or the resources, including machines and raw materials, that are the bases of the capitalist's control of the economic system and ultimately of the capitalist's *exploitation* of the workers.[60] To understand what exploitation is and how it arises, it is necessary to comprehend the relationship between "constant capital," "variable capital," and "surplus value." The "constant capital," which includes machinery and raw materials, is tied to the value of the labor power or what Marx referred to as the "sum total of wages" or "variable capital." The work force, of course, is used to run the machines that turn raw materials into finished products sold for a profit in the marketplace. Now, the owners seek to make the labor process as efficient and inexpensive as possible. It is only in this way that the owners can increase their profits. To this end, the owners have every interest in taking as much value as they can from the worker and using it to purchase machines to make the work process more profitable. And this owner interest takes us to a consideration of surplus value.

Surplus value originates from a situation in which the worker produces enough wealth to support himself as well as additional amounts of wealth, or a surplus, which the capitalist controls.[61] Here, it must be clear that surplus value for Marx derives only from the labor of workers, who produce the basis for their survival in many fewer hours than they actually work.[62] This fact and this fact alone is what makes capitalism for Marx an enterprise of exploitation. The workers always end up, as one commentator says, performing "more labor than is necessary to produce the goods he consumes."[63] And the surplus value of their labor, or that amount above what is necessary to maintain them in the work place, is returned not to the workers but to the owners. The latter use this added value to purchase more machines to make the work process more profitable.

The evils of capitalism and of exploitation are associated with the capitalist's drive for higher rates of surplus value, a drive that initially requires the capitalist to increase the length of the workday. How does this situation come about? As just indicated, the capitalist is constantly seeking to take the surplus value from the worker and, with this wealth, purchase more machines with which to replace the worker. But as the workers are replaced with machines, there will be fewer workers and since surplus value comes from making the workers produce more than is needed to maintain themselves, there will be less surplus value for the capitalists to control. So to overcome this problem, it is necessary to lengthen the workday of those workers who remain. Marx used the example of a workforce shrinking from 24 to 2 workers, where, before the contraction of the workforce, each person contributed 1 hour of surplus value in a 12-hour day or a total of 24 hours for the whole workforce. With 2 workers, the owner wants to have just as much surplus value, if not more, than in the past. So 2 workers will have to produce 24 hours of surplus value or 12 hours each. It is unlikely that the two workers can provide such a large output of surplus value even if they work longer hours. Still, the capitalist will try anyway, for his quest is to increase the amount of surplus value he controls. The capitalist, said Marx, without even being "conscious of the fact" must move to "excessive lengthening of the working day in order that he may compensate [for] the decrease in the relative number of labourers exploited."[64] In other terms, capitalism requires that the capitalist must constantly exploit the worker, making his life more and more miserable.

In addition to lengthening the workday, other methods of exploitation are used. First, because machinery requires workers who need not be overly strong, women and children can be employed in the productive process. Indeed, "machinery by throwing every member of that family on to the labour-market, spreads the value of the man's labour-power over his whole family. It thus depreciates his labour-power."[65] Further, work becomes more and more regimented and beyond the control of the worker. The workplace is organized like an army unit with officers and overseers constantly making sure that workers walk in lockstep compliance with the productive order the owners lay down.[66] Here, the work itself becomes overly simplified so that the "special skill of the worker becomes worthless."[67] As a consequence, in the factory, the worker's mind and body are crippled.[68] Moreover, by making work as simplified as possible, the pool of workers is dramatically increased. In the guild system, the journeyman was a skilled worker who could not be easily replaced. Now, there is no obstacle to replacing any worker with any other worker, and this explains the existence of a large pool of workers competing for work, thus driving down the cost of wages. An "industrial reserve army" of unemployed workers is inevitable, and the owners keep these individuals, ever ready to step in and take the job of any worker who will not accept the discipline of the workplace, in misery.[69]

VIII. CRISIS OF CAPITALISM: DECLINING PROFITS

The most serious crisis for capitalism is explained in Marx's falling-rate-of-profits theory. As we explained, the capitalist is seeking constantly to replace workers with machines. When capitalists replace workers with machines, capitalists act in a manner that is contrary to their own interests. Because the main source of all value is the surplus value produced by the workers, the rate of the capitalist's profit declines as the workforce engaged in production declines. Thus, said Marx, as the production process is characterized by ever-larger amounts of constant capital and ever-smaller amounts of labor time, or variable capital, the "rate of profit" for the capitalist falls.[70]

Capitalists respond to this problem by repeating the process of replacing workers with machines in the hope of introducing efficiencies that can enhance the capitalists' profit picture. To this end, capitalists will further reduce as much as possible the number of workers engaged in production by introducing new machines to take the workers' place. This strategy increases the amount of surplus labor or, in other terms, drives many workers into the unemployment line.[71] But this strategy cannot be repeated forever before the whole system breaks down. Marx said that "the highest development of productive power together with the greatest expansion of existing wealth will coincide with depreciation of capital, degradation of the laborer, and a most straitened exhaustion of his vital powers."[72] This situation will only result in "recurring catastrophes," repeated on higher scales and "finally to violent overthrow."[73]

As many would argue today, however, worker rebellion actually leads in the end, not to a Marxist revolution in which the workers own the capital and shape the work setting, but to a society in which there is a balance between the power of both groups. That balance of power is manifested in liberal forms of government, which seek to secure the rights of each individual. Mill's approach to achieving the full development of persons was to equalize the power of both classes in the government. He would have seen Marx's route as futile just as Marx would have seen Mill's approach as more liberal masking of the evils of capitalism.

IX. THE NEW ORDER

What is the ethos of the communist society that will follow the capitalist society? It is easier to understand Marx's views on this issue by first being clear about what he did *not* support. Marx rejected "the application of an equal standard" as the basis for distributing basic goods in society. Here, each person is considered to be a worker only, and as such each person is paid for the work he performs in accordance with a common standard. Thus, if the common standard requires that each person be paid ten dollars an hour, then each person is to be paid that much so long as each person meets his obligations under this standard. Marx referred to this view of the treatment of people as an "equal rights" approach. But this approach does not take into consideration that each person is more than just a worker. Each person has different needs. One worker "is married, another not; one has more children than another, and so on and so forth."[74]

Now Marx believed that, in a "higher phase" of communism, the forces of production in society would evolve to enable "the all-around development of the individual." In this new setting, workers will no longer be commodities owned by the capitalist, but they will be regarded as full human beings with diverse powers in need of development. Here, workers will not be regarded as just machines that tend machines, but as people who, in addition to having basic physical needs, have intellectual and moral ones, too. In consequence, the focus of society will be how to secure the fullest possible development of each person. Some people, because they have larger families, will need more income. Others, because their musical talents require special training, will require from society help to make possible the development of their musical skills. In advanced communism, the ethos is: "From each according to his ability, to each according to his needs!"[75]

Thus, Marx hoped to make possible a community in which each person could develop as fully as possible all of his many and varied skills and capacities. Marx said that in a capitalist society a person is confined to a single sphere of activity and "is a hunter, a fisherman, a shepherd, or a critical critic and must remain so if he does not want to lose his means of livelihood." But in a communist society, "where nobody has one exclusive sphere of activity but each can become accomplished in any branch he wishes, society regulates the general production and thus makes it possible for me to do one thing today and another tomorrow, to hunt in the morning, fish in the afternoon, rear cattle in the evening, criticise (*sic*) after dinner, just as I have a mind, without ever becoming hunter, fisherman, shepherd or critic."[76]

X. RESPONSE AND REJOINDER

The proponent of civil society might respond to Marx by pointing out that the commitment to political rights makes possible the creation of many groups and associations, each of which can enter the public sphere with the intention of making changes and modifications in the public policy of society. Indeed, the civil society proponent would argue that a civil society secures a separate sphere, where worker groups (or labor unions) can develop themselves as independent forces that challenge government and large economic actors such as capitalists. It is this kind of activity that in fact has led to major reforms of the capitalist system in the United States. Worker movements throughout this century have had impact not only at the collective bargaining table, but in the legislative arena of Congress as well.

Marx would not so much reject this possibility as reject its importance. After all, if the main variable that affects the way we live is the dominant economic class, then voluntary associations that seek redress will never be in a position to do anything more than to make cosmetic changes. Thus, the separate sphere of a civil society will always be overridden by the power of the dominant class, and the larger environment of rights that is to protect this separate sphere will never be strong enough to resist the power of the dominant economic class. In this case, a civil society is largely irrelevant in providing a basis for worker liberation from capitalist structures. Marx would insist that the latter must be removed, before workers regain any dimension of freedom.

The proponent of civil society might see some truth in this response. After all, there is no reason why civil society advocates would not recognize some of the dangers of capitalism. Certainly the society Marx described represents tendencies that, if left unchecked, can seriously damage a civil society by making large numbers of individuals feel that civil society does not treat them fairly and therefore does not deserve their support. Any society, for instance, that is predicated on maintaining an exploitative relationship between the worker and owner classes would create a sentiment of unfairness among many people. If most of what I work for is taken from me and used by others for their benefit, leaving me with nothing, then why should I feel good about a civil society that protects this kind of undertaking?

Indeed, Locke would have agreed with Marx on this very point. People deserve to receive the benefits of their work and, when they see those benefits taken from them, they become justifiably angry. And Mill would accept Locke's definition of property, too. That is, individuals should be rewarded for their work and their sacrifice, and private property symbolized this commitment. Marx would have argued, however, that Locke settled for too little. Locke accepted property rights as the protection against the loss of rewards for one's efforts. But, for Marx, Locke failed to see the way that the owner class uses private property to maintain an exploitative relationship to workers.

Still, Marx might have been more sympathetic to Mill's argument or even, for that matter, Rawls's position. Mill demanded that society not shortchange the mental and intellectual capacities of people in the name of property rights, for, in doing so, individuals never develop as fully as possible their completeness as persons. And Rawls established a distributive principle that made sure that the better-off classes contribute to the enhancement of the less well off. The major difference, however, between Marx and other civil society proponents, including Mill and Rawls, would be that for Marx there is an ever-constant quest for surplus value among capitalists. And this fact would seem to supersede, if not destroy, any effort to make reforms that sought to diminish the worst effects of the market on civil society relationships. Mill might talk about reforms that secure a chance for the development of the higher faculties, and Rawls would ask that his principles of justice be given a chance, but in each case, for Marx, these hopes would be dashed on the mantle of capitalist greed. Certainly, Mill and Rawls both recognized the harm done to civil society by the failure to control the power of the better-off, capitalist classes. But for Marx, recognizing a danger and being able to overcome that danger require a clearer picture of the evils of the capitalists, which neither Mill nor Rawls possesses.

Mill and Rawls would no doubt respond to Marx by arguing that, as the members of the society become aware of the political, cultural, and social needs all people have, civil society can place limits on any and every dimension that threatens the shared needs of society. In a civil society, capitalists can be placed under restraints just as any other member of society can. And accomplishing this objective does not require a revolution in which the entire society is transformed from a civil society into a communist one. Mill and Rawls would maintain that a civil society with its emphasis on the political restraints of a constitutional democracy is absolutely necessary. In taking this position, Mill and Rawls would have defended Hegel against Marx.

For Mill and Rawls and most liberals, Hegel's view that a constitutional republic limits and constrains the worst aspects of private interest in a civil society must be taken seriously. Hegel's state is designed to provide individuals with settings that secure opportunities for useful work, work in which individuals can fully manifest their powers. Further, Hegel's state requires that the diverse interests that make up the state learn to share power with each other. Hegel, as Rawls and Mill, would ask Marx whether the communist society Marx wanted would create a state that, because it had so much power, would end up threatening the full freedom Marx wanted.

Of course, Marx would have said in response that he was not completely unmindful of some of the good effects of some of the reforms that a civil society might provide. Evidence for this view exists in the fact that Marx did advocate proposals that today are taken as standard reforms of modern civil society. Indeed, the Marx of the *Communist Manifesto* advocated reforms such as a free education for all, a progressive system of taxation, a central bank not unlike our Federal Reserve system, a work requirement for all (now advocated by many reformers of the welfare system), and public ownership of factories (which modern society has adopted in some areas of the economy such as those having to do with power generation, for instance).[77] All of these advances were possible and continue to be possible in a rights-based civil society.

Moreover, as we saw earlier in Section II, Marx would say that he was not opposed to democracy nor opposed to some of the reforms that have been made a mainstay of civil society. But in taking this position, Marx's point would be that it is not enough to establish, in the manner of Hegel, a constitutional form of state that seeks to limit and to constrain the market features of a civil society. Hegel had advocated this position in order to make possible respect for communal needs. For Marx, the latter objective would be attained only by transforming society into a setting hospitable to a form of democracy that permitted workers to structure the economic life of society. The challenge to civil society from Marx is his demand that workers be in a position to determine through democratic institutions the objectives of production as well as the ways the economy would be structured to reach those goals. Civil societies, which promise rights for all citizens to permit influence over the political realm and over the private life choices of individuals, would have to include, in the conception of rights, the notion of worker determination and direction of the economy.

Marx would no doubt argue, then, that modern liberal civil societies that provide rights to individuals do not encourage individuals to use these rights to shape the political community and to forge the direction of the economy. The major economic decisions are left to an elite few, those who are the owners or managers of capital. Yet, these decisions impact the lives of most people in the most significant ways imaginable.

This democratic approach to the economy would surely be seen as a way to overcome the bureaucratic state that Hegel had argued for. For Hegel, as will be remembered, the state stood above civil society, in charge of managing the economy for the common good. But this objective could not be met unless there was a class of experts in charge of carrying out the state's directives, especially in the settings of the various corporations. Here, a powerful bureaucratic caste, composed of experts in policy management, would manage the economic life of society. But in doing so, average individuals would be told that they were to do whatever their function in the work environment might be and not to expect to participate in the decision-making process that determined the overall objectives of the economy. Clearly, Hegel would have had no sympathy for a democratization of the economy, in contrast, of course, to Marx who would.

Notwithstanding this fact, however, Marx would have difficulty demonstrating the success of his theory, and it is on this basis that Marx's critics might rest their case. Of principal concern here is that the communist revolution Marx prophesied and the demise of capitalism it was supposed to bring about have not occurred. Indeed, in the wake of the extinction of the former Soviet Empire it would appear that both capitalism and civil society are more popular and powerful forces than ever before. How might Marx have responded to this contention? Or in other terms, is it still possible to defend Marxism in our times?

To address this issue, I would like to discuss the critique of civil society made by Herbert Marcuse, an American political philosopher and political radical during the 1960s. Marcuse provided a critique of modern capitalism, suggesting as Marx did its ultimate demise, but Marcuse's approach made the factors responsible for capitalism's extinction the very same ones that have secured its survival: in particular, the evolution of an ever more efficient, rationalized process of production. To discuss Marcuse's views, it will first be necessary to describe, briefly, the German sociologist Max Weber's (1864–1920) critique of modern industrial society, because Weber's critique anticipates and is incorporated into Marcuse's views.

XI. MAX WEBER AND HERBERT MARCUSE: THE BUREAUCRATIC STATE

Herbert Marcuse's critique of technology, as Morton Schoolman points out, is heavily indebted to Max Weber's argument that the types of bureaucratic techniques used to organize modern society are a source of domination that deny the individual freedom promised by a civil society.[78] For Weber, the ability to determine one's own life plans and to develop a rational plan to pursue them was critical to a liberal civil society, and so too was the emerging structure of an increasingly powerful organizational bureaucracy, which was the foundation of the production system. But Weber believed that the latter tendency threatened the former one.[79]

What is the basis for this contention? First, it must be clear that, in the modern era Weber knew, capitalism was no longer predicated upon small companies competing with each other in the free market setting. Instead, large monopolistic, industrial organizations became the main source of the production and distribution of goods. These organizations embodied the techniques of modern science, including methods to standardize production. The impact on individual initiative of these methods was telling. Indeed, individuals, in order to conform to the mechanisms of production, had to learn to subordinate their autonomy to the needs of the production process. Further, in this context, individuals became more dependent upon the state, which undertook toward citizens a welfare orientation by providing them with goods to satisfy basic needs. As Richard Bellamy argues, "the new factories regimented workers along hierarchical lines, reducing them to a mass and sapping their capacity for self-help with paternalistic welfare measures which rendered them docile."[80]

Moreover, for Weber the growing bureaucratic presence limited the capacity of individuals to use their reason to determine important and enduring life values. For instance, the kind of rationality used to define the substantive goals of life, "a value oriented rationality," was driven to the sideline in favor of a form of an "instrumental rationality" designed to achieve efficiency.[81] A value-oriented reasoning process seeks to identify the major values and objectives that individuals should pursue in order to have meaningful and fulfilling lives. On the other hand, an instrumental-reasoning process has as its main concern the use of science to determine the most efficient means to the attainment of goals. And when this form of reasoning becomes primary, then there emerges what Weber referred to as the "disenchantment of the world," or the idea, as Bellamy says, that there is "no single objective meaning [that] could be ascribed to the nature of things."[82] The problem with the methods of science is that they cannot provide a basis for determining the substantive ends that should be made the foundation for life.[83]

Weber further elaborates this view in his discussion of the Calvinist, Protestant religious outlook in creating the Protestant ethic. Weber, in his famous *The Protestant Ethic and the Spirit of Capitalism,* had argued that the origin of capitalism, and the rationally efficient society it requires, resided not in Marx's argument about the exploitation of one class by another, but in the Protestant view of predestination. This doctrine stated that some are destined "to everlasting life, and others foreordained to everlasting death."[84] In this view, the basis for grace, that is redemption in the life to come, is not mere observance of the sacraments. Even if one observed all religious rituals, if one were predestined to hell, one would still find oneself in hell. Obviously, this belief caused great anxiety or "inner loneliness" in people.[85] Not knowing which path one was fated to, but wanting to be on the path to everlasting life, each individual sought to think of himself as chosen for eternal life. To do so, one had to "combat all doubts [about one's being chosen for heaven] as temptations of the devil."[86] Individuals were to resist the fear of hell by engaging in "worldly activities," that is, performing well and with dedication those activities associated with one's basic calling in life: "the fulfillment of the obligations imposed upon the individual by his position in the world."[87] The Calvinist creates, through hard, dedicated work a "conviction" that he will be saved. As Weber says, conceiving work and labor as a calling was "often in the last analysis the only means of attaining certainty of grace."[88]

Creating and strengthening that conviction required individuals to adopt those civic virtues that demonstrated one's worthiness. The virtues in question taught individuals to lead a highly ascetic life in which one accepted the need to sacrifice present pleasures for future, eternal happiness. For instance, individuals must avoid all the sins associated with wasting time, such as indulging in luxuries, in sleeping more than is necessary, in socializing too much, and in engaging in talk that is unrelated to one's work.[89] Sports were acceptable only if they contributed to rational conduct within the division of labor in society. Any activity that produced spontaneous forms of emotion or passion and the need to pursue such passions for the sake of enjoying life were to be banned from one's frame of reference.[90] Finally, it is acceptable to acquire goods only if they are used for rational or utilitarian ends, or ends that allow one to function in one's role in society.[91]

Despite this regimen's denial of so much that gives life pleasure, ironically, the Protestant ethic demonstrates for the modern person how life can acquire, as well as lose, its meaning. Why is this the case? The Protestant ethic for Weber is a set of values that human beings internalized and made their own through choice. The ascetic morality of this way of life was an acceptable response to the pressures on their lives in the world they knew. Thus, as Bellamy says, the Protestant ethic demonstrates for Weber that it is only through freely self-determined actions that we define the basis for giving meaning and purpose to our lives.[92]

Why is this approach to attaining meaning to life valid? Weber's answer emanates from his view of what instrumental rationality, the dominant way of thinking, contributes to self-understanding. Instrumental rationality helps us to understand the consequences of particular value systems as well as enables us to determine the means to achieve our chosen goals. Nonetheless, instrumental rationality also makes clear that we live in a world filled with many competing value systems and that no single system can be said to provide a basis for a rational consensus among all people. We are thus faced with various value systems, each of which has different implications for how we arrange our lives. And like those who embraced the Protestant ethic through choice, we must make choices with respect to which values to make the foundation of our lives, given a realistic assessment of our circumstances. Here, values provide meaning to life not because they are rationally valid for all people, but because we, through our choices, have made them the basis for how we wish to arrange our lives.[93]

However, in the modern world, the capacities which enable us to choose the values that govern our lives have been eroded. This circumstance arises from the imposition on our lives of a rational, efficient work setting typical of modern capitalism, which itself derives from the successes of the asceticism bequeathed by the Protestant ethic.[94] In this context, as central to wealth creation and accumulation, instrumental rationality is used to determine the role each person should have in an economic setting dominated by machine production. And in consequence people lose their ability to make their own choices about which ways of life and values to pursue. Here, since we no longer choose the values that guide our lives, our lives are emptied of meaning.[95]

Living in the "iron cage" of modern rational, bureaucratic life, people are, as Bellamy says, "egoistic, rational, utility maximizers," and they no longer look toward ends larger than those contained in the value of efficiency.[96] The only values, indeed the only virtues, that matter are ones such as those that contribute to efficiency, such as "precision, speed, unambiguity, knowledge of files, continuity, discretion, unity, strict subordination."[97] These values facilitate adaptation to the processes of an efficient organizational structure. But these values do not provide life with a larger, substantive purpose, which gives meaning and significance to life. And thus individuals are condemned in modern society to the "inner loneliness" that, as we demonstrate in the next chapter, Nietzsche will try to overcome through the efforts of those like himself who create new values to give substance and meaning to life.

The world Weber described would not be changed by Marx's revolutionary prophecies. Weber argued that Marx's view of the impending demise of capitalism, including the rate-of-falling-profits theory, was disproved by circumstances. Capitalist firms manifested an ability for overcoming threats to their existence by their capacity for technological innovation. As a consequence, production was increased along with basic living standards and the conditions for revolution evaporated.[98] Moreover, for Weber, the same professional bureaucracy that preserves capitalism would be central to coordinating the modern industrial economy found in socialism. And thus workers in socialist states—where all property is held in common so workers can control the uses of their own labor—also would find themselves confined to a bureaucratic hierarchy, thus ensuring that worker alienation continues.[99]

Can the political leaders of society reintroduce into society substantive political directives that resist the forces of bureaucratic rationalization? At times it appeared that Weber wrote as if such an outcome were possible. Weber said that political leaders should be people with sufficient understanding of the consequences of proposed actions. He hoped for politicians with a keen sense of responsibility for their actions. These are people who at the same time manifested convictions for moving society in a direction that provided individuals with a chance to embrace substantive values. Weber said that "an ethic of ultimate ends and an ethic of responsibility are not absolute contrasts but rather supplements, which only in unison constitute a genuine man—a man who *can* have the 'calling for politics.'"[100]

Now, Morton Schoolman suggests that, in the end, Weber was ambivalent on the question as to whether a politics and political leadership committed to substantive values could triumph over bureaucratic rationality.[101] As we turn to Marcuse, however, it is clear that Marcuse believed that political action could ultimately achieve mastery over the dulling character of modern bureaucracy and restore substantive values.

Herbert Marcuse can be viewed as embarking from Weber's view of capitalism. Marcuse argued that, in the technological society of modern capitalism, a technical mentality prevails. This technical rationality destroys critical reasoning, the reasoning process by which we become able to unmask the repressive character of society and establish in its place a basis for a fully developed life as Marx had advocated in his attack on alienation.

In his discussion of one-dimensional thinking in his book, *One Dimensional Man,* Marcuse explained the context of the loss of critical thinking. In later writings, he developed an argument that explained the basis for a revolution that is able to restore critical thinking and, once and for all, overthrow the one-dimensional society. We will discuss both elements of Marcuse's thought in the following pages.

So what is one-dimensional thinking and who is the one-dimensional man? For Marcuse, technological rationality, which pertains to the processes of material production, pervades all areas of thinking and life in modern, capitalist society. Like Weber, Marcuse's view was that not only is the life of production organized in keeping with the canons of efficiency, but, in order to support this approach to the organization of production, the life of the mind was forced to mimic this process during the course of thought. In effect, we must learn to think in terms that always support a technically efficient production process. Marcuse said "mass production and mass distribution claim the *entire* individual. . . . [T]he result is . . . *mimesis:* an immediate identification of the individual with *his* society, and through it, with the society as a whole."[102] Of great significance here is that, as a result of this experience, the "power of negative thinking" or the critical power of reason to assert a different, more liberatory approach to life is denied any place.[103] As Morton Schoolman says, for Marcuse, this situation means "losing all independence from the rationality of society's basic production relations, cultural and political discourse ceases to be critical of the relations and goals of a technologically organized society."[104]

On this view, technical reason is a form of repression, because individuals find themselves constantly reproducing in their thoughts and in their actions all the ways of life that are conducive to a rational production process. And there is no ability in this setting to criticize the existing course of life. The social relationships that individuals find themselves in are ones that represent forms of domination from which individuals have no way to escape.[105] This view does not mean that individuals are held in bondage as, for instance, in an analogy with a slave labor camp. Enslavement in the rationalized world of technical reason is much subtler than this. Indeed, the society Marcuse attacked allows people many opportunities to experience pleasure, but only on terms acceptable to the maintenance of the rational/technical structure of society. For this reason, then, pleasure "generates submission."[106] In a society dominated by technocratic reason, sex is allowed and encouraged just so long as it is experienced in the context of relationships acceptable to the larger production system. "Sex is integrated into work and public relations and is thus made more susceptible to (controlled) satisfaction."[107] Individuals need not deny their basic drives to partake in the societal processes of production, as long as they manifest those drives in ways that are conducive to maintaining the system of production itself.

For Marcuse, individuals in contemporary capitalist society think they are happy, when in fact they can never really tap the real sources of life that would allow them to be truly free and happy. This view suggests that we are forced by the existing order to suppress many abilities and capacities that if realized would provide us with great pleasure. However, although we might sense that something is missing in our lives, we cannot really define what that "something" is, and, indeed, we are socialized by the system of oppression to think of ourselves as happy. Here, individuals are made to accept the system of domination without ever actually feeling that they are dominated!

In the context of this view, liberation means creating a new system of needs, a system that deviates from the needs that the prevailing exploitative order tells us we should want.[108] Marcuse embraced the radical politics of the 1960s period, and, in taking this position, he discarded, as Schoolman points out, the notion that all people even in a one-dimensional society are locked into one-dimensional thinking. Instead, some individuals, those who will become Marcuse's radical leaders for social change, are able to identify a new vision that can be the basis for a liberated, moral way of life.[109]

How will the transformation to a new order occur? In Marx, the basis for revolution was crisis, emanating from the falling-rate-of-profits theory. Marx argued that, as a result of the growing misery, this theory predicted that a working-class revolution would be inevitable. But for Marcuse, it is not crises of this sort that will spur a revolution, nor will the revolution be spurred along by the strictly working-class movement that Marx predicted. Instead of crisis and a single-class movement, Marcuse believed that, in the midst of modern prosperity that continues to oppress people in the way just outlined, there could still emerge a coalition of people, led by a new left movement. And this coalition would include traditional blue-collar workers, as well as many students, intellectuals, and civil rights activists. Also included would be professional and technical workers, who, along with factory workers, constitute the foundation of the entire production process.[110] Eventually the hope is that the left and the entire working class will form a revolutionary element to take collective action on behalf of transforming capitalism.[111]

But in forging this alliance and in making it the counterforce to the one-dimensional perspective, Marcuse emphasized the central importance of the "new sensibility." The latter suggests a way of seeing and understanding that is oriented by biologically based impulses, or impulses that have been denied or repressed in a one-dimensional society. Marcuse views these impulses as representing the best, moral possibilities of human life. For instance, they all emphasize a need for a nonrepressive society built on nonviolence, an appreciation of beauty, and a rejection of poverty, aggression, and forms of repressive work. The new sensibility as Schoolman says "celebrates the playful, the calm, [and] the beautiful."[112] In effect, the new sensibility suggests that individuals will seek a basis for relationships to each other that permits them to explore freely and cooperatively all of their untapped abilities and capacities, those elements of their lives now bottled up and suppressed by the regimen of one-dimensional life. A socialist society would be a setting that incorporated this promise and that was carried forth by a new type of individual who fully realizes and appreciates the importance and reality of the new sensibility.[113]

Thus, a radical or new sensibility suggests that our senses are not merely passive receptors of stimuli from the external world, a world that tells us to accept the order we experience. But our senses, in addition, shape what we experience and give our experience a moral form.[114] This means that, in experiencing the world, we do so from a perspective that orients us to look upon the world from the standpoint of whether it fulfills the need to realize the inherent demands of a new sensibility. Or are their obstacles to our doing so? When the latter is the case, the new sensibility moves people to act to remove these obstacles. Here, Marcuse's new sensibility would seem to augur a way of seeing and experiencing that was in tune with a Kantian need for people to treat others as ends, in a setting in which all the impediments to that prospect were eliminated. To this end, Marcuse hoped for a radical change in consciousness as the first step to changing the world.

If successful, then, a new day will dawn, and it will be symbolized for Marcuse in the way of seeing and understanding found in art. Here, the hope is to discover human nature, defined here as our basic "impulses and senses," as our real ally in creating a world that allows us the liberation we seek.[115] Indeed, art helps us to depict a view of our nature by which we help to define our real possibilities; most especially those that the current order of technical reason will not permit us to express. What is presumed here is that art allows us to look at ourselves not only from particular historical contexts that are the settings of our lives, but also from the unique experience that art suggests. This experience is one that demonstrates the need to give expression to the many dimensions of ourselves, including, as Schoolman says, our wishes, hopes, and desires, all of which current circumstances may deny expression. Thus, when we liberate our "impulses and senses" so that they are no longer determined by the demands of technical reason, we can depict universally shared and existing possibilities for our lives that would have otherwise remained hidden from us. In doing so, we have a basis for acting to make the external world into a place that is helpful to our quest to realize our full potential.[116]

How does art enable us to see our authentic possibilities in settings that seem hostile to their realization? The answer to this question resides in the fact that art is a construct of the aesthetic imagination. Indeed, art suggests an aesthetic imagination that operates by rules that differ from the rules of a world dominated by technical reason. The aesthetic imagination deviates from the formal course set by the latter experience and follows its own free and spontaneous path. In the process of doing so, individuals recognize dimensions of their lives that if developed would help them to realize as Schoolman says "an alternative truth, the truth of fulfillment."[117] By seeing the world from the standpoint of art, then, we enable ourselves to envision our possibilities in ways not permitted by an oppressive world. As a result, we are likely to uncover new ways for living and new possibilities for ourselves that we would not otherwise see.

Marx's revolutionary perspective as found in Marcuse, then, would throw off the domination of the rationally structured world that denies our ability to feel and to experience in keeping with the true purposes of human nature as depicted in art. But is Marcuse right? Are people in a capitalist-dominated civil society oppressed without knowing it? Are the freedoms people think they have in this society without substance? Or is civil society a setting that provides a way to resist the iron cage and in its place to establish the institutions that secure the kind of freedom that Marcuse advocated?

Endnotes

1. For the sake of simplicity, unless otherwise noted, the works of Marx referred to here will come from Robert C. Tucker, editor. *The Marx-Engels Reader,* second edition, (New York: W.W. Norton and Company, 1978). The only exception is when I cite the *Grundrisse* below.

2. Ibid., Introduction by Tucker, p. xxiii.

3. Marx, *Contribution to the Critique of Hegel's Philosophy of Right,* p. 18.

4. Ibid., p. 20.

5. Ibid., p. 21.

6. Ibid., pp. 24–25.

7. Marx, *On the Jewish Question,* p. 34. Italics in text.

8. Ibid., p. 34. Italics in text.

9. Ibid., p. 34.

10. Ibid., p. 42. Italics in text.

11. Ibid., p. 42.

12. Ibid., pp. 42–43. Italics in text.

13. Ibid., p. 42. Italics in text.

14. Ibid., p. 35.

15. Ibid., pp. 42–43.

16. Ibid., p. 41, and Jeremy Waldron, editor, with introductory and concluding essays, *Nonsense Upon Stilts: Bentham, Burke and Marx on the Rights of Man,* (New York: Methuen, 1987), pp. 129–30.

17. Marx, *On the Jewish Question,* p. 46. Italics in text.

18. Jeremy Waldron, *Nonsense Upon Stilts,* p. 131.

19. Marx, *On the Jewish Question,* pp. 35, 41, 43.

20. Marx, *Economic and Philosophic Manuscripts of 1844,* p. 71.

21. Ibid., p. 112. Italics in text. On the nature of species life, see Jon Elster, *An Introduction to Karl Marx,* (Cambridge: Cambridge University Press, 1986), pp. 43–44.

22. Marx, *Economic and Philosophic Manuscripts of 1844,* p. 72. Italics in text.

23. Ibid., pp. 72–73.

24. Ibid., p. 73.

25. Ibid., p. 74. Italics in text.

26. See Marx, *Capital, Volume One,* pp. 399–403.

27. Marx, *Economic and Philosophic Manuscripts of 1844,* p. 75.

28. Ibid., p. 75. Italics are in book.

29. Ibid., p. 76.

30. Ibid., p. 76.

31. Ibid., p. 77.

32. Marx, *Manifesto of the Communist Party,* p. 479.

33. Marx, *Economic and Philosophic Manuscripts of 1844,* p. 95.

34. Ibid., p. 95.

35. Ibid., pp. 95–96. Italics in text.

36. Ibid., p. 96.

37. Ibid., p. 93. Italics in text.

38. Ibid., p. 93. Italics in text.

39. Ibid., p. 104. Italics in text.

40. Ibid., p. 105.

41. Ibid., p. 105.

42. Marx, *Theses on Feuerbach,* p. 145. Italics in text.

43. Marx, *The German Ideology,* p. 164.

44. Ibid., p. 165.

45. Ibid., p. 163.

46. Ibid., p. 182.

47. Ibid., p. 177.

48. Ibid., p. 182.

49. Ibid., pp. 183–85.

50. Ibid., pp. 185–86.

51. Ibid., p. 187.

52. Ibid., pp. 189–90.

53. Ibid., pp. 192–93.

54. Ibid., p. 193. Italics in text.

55. Marx, *Manifesto of the Communist Party,* p. 491.

56. Marx, *Wage Labour and Capital,* pp. 204–5.

57. Ibid., p. 207.

58. Ibid., p. 207.

59. Ibid., p. 210.

60. Marx, *Capital, Volume One,* pp. 419–21.

61. On this point, Elster, *An Introduction to Karl Marx,* p. 67.

62. Marx, *Capital, Volume One,* p. 405.

63. Elster, *An Introduction to Karl Marx,* p. 80.

64. Marx, *Capital, Volume One,* p. 406.

65. Ibid., p. 404.

66. Ibid., p. 386.

67. Marx, *Wage Labour and Capital,* p. 214, and Marx, *Capital, Volume One,* p. 409.

68. Marx, *Capital, Volume One,* pp. 399, 408–9.

69. Ibid., p. 413.

70. Marx, *Grundrisse,* trans. by Martin Nicolaus, (New York: Vintage Books, 1973), p. 747.

71. Ibid., p. 750.

72. Ibid., p. 750.

73. Ibid., p. 750.

74. Marx, *Critique of the Gotha Program,* pp. 530–31.

75. Ibid., p. 531.

76. Marx, *The German Ideology,* p. 160.

77. Marx, *Manifesto of the Communist Party,* p. 490.

78. Morton Schoolman, *The Imaginary Witness: The Critique Theory of Herbert Marcuse,* (New York: The Free Press, 1980), p. 137. My account of Marcuse is heavily influenced by Schoolman's very fine book.

79. Richard Bellamy, *Liberalism and Modern Society,* (University Park, Pennsylvania: Penn State Press, 1992), p. 179. My view of Weber follows closely Bellamy's fine account.

80. Ibid., p. 180.

81. Ibid., p. 184.

82. Ibid., p. 184.

83. Ibid., p. 184.

84. Max Weber, *The Protestant Ethic and the Spirit of Capitalism,* trans. Talcott Parsons, (New York: Charles Scribner's Sons, 1958), p. 100.

85. Ibid., p. 104.

86. Ibid., p. 111.

87. Ibid., pp. 112, 80.

88. Ibid., pp. 115, 178.

89 Ibid., pp. 157–58.

90. Ibid., pp. 167–68.

91. Ibid., p. 171.

92. Bellamy, *Liberalism and Modern Society,* p. 185.

93. Ibid., pp. 184–85.

94. Ibid., pp. 185–86.

95. Ibid., pp. 185–86.

96. Ibid., p. 186; also p. 185.

97. Ibid., p. 187.

98. Ibid., p. 191.

99. Ibid., pp. 191–92.

100. Max Weber, *Politics as a Vocation,* trans. by H. H. Gerth and C. Wright Mills, (Philadelphia: Facet Books, 1965), p. 54. Italics in text.

101. Schoolman, *The Imaginary Witness,* pp. 180–81. Italics in text.

102. Herbert Marcuse, *One Dimensional Man,* (Boston: Beacon Press, 1968), p. 10. Italics in text.

103. Ibid., p. 11.

104. Schoolman, *The Imaginary Witness,* p. 149.

105. Ibid., p. 177.
106. Marcuse, *One Dimensional Man*, p. 75.
107. Ibid., p. 75.
108. Marcuse, *An Essay on Liberation*, (Boston: Beacon Press, 1969), p. 4.
109. Schoolman, *The Imaginary Witness*, p. 291.
110. Ibid., pp. 296–97, 299.
111. Ibid., p. 300.

112. Ibid., p. 311.
113. Ibid., pp. 311–12. Marcuse, *An Essay on Liberation*, pp. 24–25.
114. Marcuse, *Counterrevolution and Revolt*, (Boston: Beacon Press, 1972), pp. 62–63.
115. Ibid., p. 59.
116. Schoolman, *The Imaginary Witness*, pp. 330–31.
117. Ibid., p. 330.

Partial Bibliography and Further Reading

Bellamy, Richard. *Liberalism and Modern Society.* University Park, Penn.: Penn State Press, 1992.

Berlin, Isaiah. *Karl Marx, His Life and Environment.* Oxford: Oxford University Press, 1959.

Cohen, Gerald Allan. *Karl Marx's Theory of History: A Defense.* Princeton: Princeton University Press, 1978.

Cohen, Jean L. *Class and Civil Society: The Limits of Marxian Critical Theory.* Amherst: University of Massachusetts Press, 1982.

Elster, Jon. *An Introduction to Karl Marx.* Cambridge: Cambridge University Press, 1986.

Giddens, Anthony. *Capitalism and Modern Social Theory: An Analysis of the Writings of Marx, Durkheim and Max Weber.* Cambridge: Cambridge University Press, 1971.

Hook, Sidney. *From Hegel to Marx.* New York: Humanities Press, 1950.

McLellan, David. *Karl Marx: His Life and Thought.* New York: Harper & Row, 1974.

Marcuse, Herbert. *An Essay on Liberation.* Boston: Beacon Press, 1969.

———. *Counterrevolution and Revolt.* Boston: Beacon Press, 1972.

———. *One Dimensional Man.* Boston: Beacon Press, 1968.

Martin, Joseph. *A Guide to Marxism.* New York: St. Martin's Press, 1980.

Miller, Richard W. *Analyzing Marx: Morality, Power, and History.* Princeton: Princeton University Press, 1984.

Ollman, Bertell. *Alienation: Marx's Conception of Man in Capitalist Society.* Cambridge: Cambridge University Press, 1976.

Plamenatz, John Petrov. *Karl Marx's Philosophy of Man.* Oxford: Clarendon Press, 1975.

Schoolman, Morton. *The Imaginary Witness: The Critique Theory of Herbert Marcuse.* New York: The Free Press, 1980.

Tucker, Robert C. *Philosophy and Myth in Karl Marx.* Cambridge: Cambridge University Press, 1972.

———. *The Marxian Revolutionary Idea.* New York: Norton, 1969.

Waldron, Jeremy, editor, with introductory and concluding essays. *Nonsense Upon Stilts: Bentham, Burke and Marx on the Rights of Man.* New York: Methuen, 1987.

Weber, Max. *The Protestant Ethic and the Spirit of Capitalism,* trans. Talcott Parsons. New York: Charles Scribner's Sons, l958.

———. *Politics as a Vocation,* trans. by H. H. Gerth and C. Wright Mills. Philadelphia: Facet Books, 1965.

Zeitlin, Irving M. *Marxism: A Re-examination.* Princeton: Van Nostrand, 1967.

16

FRIEDRICH NIETZSCHE'S CRITIQUE OF CIVIL SOCIETY

I. INTRODUCTION

Friedrich Nietzsche (1844–1900) is perhaps best known for his view that Christianity, once the dominant value system of the Western world, had lost its force in modern society. This event is of singular importance, for, with the demise of Christianity, human experience has suffered what E. E. Sleinis says, in referring to Nietzsche's views, "a belittlement, a vilification, a devaluation of this world." The present setting suggests that there is not a sufficient basis to justify human existence. To those who ask why is life worth living, then, the circumstances of the times do not suggest a good answer, and new, substantive values must be found to replace the Christian ones to demonstrate why life has significance and *is* thus worth living. The problem, however, is that to create new values individuals must have what Nietzsche often referred to as a "will to power." Such individuals marshal the power, as a result of making proper use of their abilities and energy, to embed new substantive values into the day-to-day reality of society. These values are the basis for instituting new ways of understanding and seeing that enhance life and that create the conditions, as Sleinis says, for "the thriving and flourishing of life." In augmenting life-enhancing values, a person with a will to power would embark upon actions that lead to the many products of human flourishing, such as those found in art or in new forms of social organization.[1]

For Nietzsche, however, a civil society possesses an atmosphere that can often frustrate and discourage the willfulness that Nietzsche demands. In a civil society, we find ourselves unable to call forth our full powers, and we lack, in short, the focused intensity we need to create new values. Nietzsche's arguments in this regard would agree with some of the views about modern civil society found in Weber, who, as we just saw, demonstrated that modern, rationally organized, technocratic life denies to individuals a chance to maintain substantive values that secure significance to life. For Nietzsche, a civil society, then, suggests a kind of pervasive sickness of the spirit. And it is this sickness for which Nietzsche hoped to provide a remedy in his discussion of an aristocratic culture of creative people, those who do have the "will to power" that makes possible the full freedom that civil society extols but that it seems unable to deliver.

In this chapter, I discuss both Nietzsche's influential critique of civil society as well as the vision that he hoped to create and make the basis for his new philosophy and politics. As I undertake this enterprise, I will describe the characteristics of the moral system that Nietzsche rejects. Throughout, the person who manifests the will to power is the unique individual Nietzsche extols as the creator of the new values that civil society must have to enhance life, his "free spirit."

II. DIONYSUS VERSUS APOLLO AND THE QUEST FOR A NEW CULTURE

The first question we must ask pertains to where we should turn to find a justification for life, a justification that is "life-preserving, species-preserving, perhaps even species-breeding."[2] Nietzsche argued that we cannot rely upon modern Enlightenment philosophers of reason, especially Kant and Hegel. These writers hope to use reason, or a "cold, pure, divinely unperturbed dialectic," to determine those objective truths that can be made the basis for justifying life. But a major theme in Nietzsche's thinking is that what modern philosophers label as *truth* merely represents the philosophers' particular values or prejudices that they "baptize as truth." Nietzsche believed that this was certainly the case with regard to Kant's categorical imperative, the idea that there exist universally valid moral propositions. Nietzsche characterized Kant's efforts to make us believe in universal moral truths as nothing more than the "subtle tricks of old moralists and moral-preachers."[3]

On what basis did Nietzsche assert this view? He argued that prevalent internal impulses or drives dominate philosophers, like anyone else. In the case of philosophers, the "ultimate goal of existence" and "the legitimate *master* of all other drives" is not, for Nietzsche, a "drive to knowledge," but another impulse that may take hold of the philosopher and use knowledge as a means to achieve the impulse driving him.[4] To understand a philosopher, we need to comprehend the nature of his various "innermost drives," and in addition, we need to know how they have been ordered, and which one has been made dominant. Ultimately, then, one impulse captures a philosopher's attention and focus, and it becomes the basis for his point of view and approach to understanding. When we understand this dimension, we can know the nature of the philosopher's values and perspective. Thus, the philosopher's "morality bears decided and decisive testimony to *who he is*— that is to say, to the order of rank the innermost drives of his nature stand in relation to one another."[5]

What a philosopher says about the world is highly dependent upon the philosopher's own values and perspective. To clarify this point, we need to provide more details that pertain to the way values and perspectives are shaped. Human values are developed from a combination of realities, including our instincts and passions as well as by customs and traditions that are part of our lives. Thus, in the first place, as we just saw, there are the impulses that lie at the core of one's life. Nietzsche, following the ancient Greeks, referred to this dimension as Dionysian, after the Greek god, Dionysus. For Nietzsche, human beings are a combination, as Bruce Detwiler puts it, of "conflicting tendencies and impulses."[6] There is no inherent, natural order among our passions and feelings, as there was for Plato and Aristotle. For them, even the appetite was susceptible to rational constraint. But as Detwiler says, for Nietzsche, the Dionysian element suggests that a person "is at bottom a chaos, he needs guiding principles in which he can believe to order his life so that he can function in the world."[7]

Civilization and culture are invented in order to provide life with structure and continuity. Again, following the ancient Greeks, Nietzsche called this need for order Apollonian, after the Greek god, Apollo. Here, our identities and thus our values are also fashioned by the existing cultural realities such as customs and traditions. Often, however, over time these norms come to emphasize order above all else, and, in doing so, throw up roadblocks to people in the course of developing their lives according to their deeply rooted passions. The Apollonian dimension seeks to squelch the inner passions of the Dionysian dimension. But for Nietzsche, Dionysus often comes to the rescue with, to use Detwiler's words, "orgies of creative annihilation and awakened passions that had fallen asleep under the orderly governance of his [Dionysus's] counterpart, Apollo."[8] Thus, the source of willfulness is clearly the Dionysian element, which defies Apollo's quest for order and which, for Nietzsche, in the modern world is largely denied its proper voice.[9] The Dionysian dimension is the basis for resisting a life setting that is overly constraining and confining, if not numbing. Indeed, the Dionysian dimension seems to save us from a world in which the traditions and customs, rules and methods for securing order, deny any chance for forms of creative expression that can transform the structure of human living.

There is great emphasis, then, upon our Dionysian-based drives by Nietzsche, for it is his view that in the modern world this dimension is not given its full due. But in taking this position, it is not correct to conclude that Nietzsche advocated only the Dionysian dimension. Indeed, he wanted a culture in which Apollo's dictates for order could facilitate the richness of Dionysus, and thus he called for a society that was not dominated by either tendency.[10] The Apollonian quest for order should be redesigned to house properly and to permit the fullest possible expression of Dionysian demands to manifest one's drives, passions, and creative powers.

As we demonstrate in the next section, there is a place for morality in Nietzsche's scheme, as long as the order it provides makes possible a setting that allows for the creative expression of Dionysus. In this regard, politics is not so much concerned with achieving a liberal civil society, one that emphasizes equal rights, as it is with establishing those forms of order that permit the flourishing of our creative instincts. Nietzsche's politics would encourage an aristocratic class of willful persons, or what he would call "free spirits," to create new values that replace the discredited Christian ones.[11]

III. THE PLACE OF MORALITY

From Nietzsche's position that the morality espoused by philosophers manifests more than anything else the particular values of the philosophers in question, it is clear that Nietzsche embraced the view that moral notions emanate from many important factors, including culture, tradition, drives, and impulses. Nietzsche's view of morality indicates that what we understand as truth, in this case moral truth, is a function of the particular perspective we hold, and thus we are not capable, intellectually, of establishing moral absolutes.[12]

This view does not mean that, for Nietzsche, it is impossible to demonstrate that some perspectives have more value than others. After all, Nietzsche spent much time attempting to diminish the importance of Christian arguments and Western philosophy since Socrates.[13] Further, Nietzsche suggests that there is much to praise in those perspectives that make morality a preeminent part of existence. Such contexts can provide a kind of Apollonian order that makes room for Dionysian creativity. Moral systems suggest constraints that are used to create substantive values.

In discussing morality, then, in the first place for Nietzsche, "the essential and invaluable element in every morality is that it is a protracted constraint."[14] This view suggests the possibility of a focused intensity during the course of pursuing one's basic insights or impulses, and this capacity is critical to creating substantive values that enhance life. Whatever a person's dominant drives or passions, a person must focus on them and overlook those distractions that might deny one's ability to pursue them. Here, acts of creation, which take place when one pursues an insight, such as an artist might experience during the course of attempting to render a particular feeling for nature in a painting, can only be carried to fruition when the artist maintains a disciplined commitment to see his or her project to completion.

Indeed, Nietzsche said that individuals are often moved to act in keeping with a flash of inspiration. "Anyone who looks at the basic drives of mankind [realizes that they] . . . come into play as *inspirational* spirits."[15] That inspiration prescribes the path one is to follow, and that path is raised almost to the level of a moral law that one is commanded to obey. "Every artist knows how far from the feeling of letting himself go his 'natural' condition is, the free ordering, placing, disposing, forming in the moment of 'inspiration'— and how strictly and subtlely he then obeys thousandfold laws which precisely on accord of their severity and definitiveness mock all formulation of concepts."[16] From this experience, of "protracted *obedience* in *one* direction," we derive everything that makes life "worthwhile to live on earth" including "virtue, art, music, dance, reason, spirituality" and these experiences are "transfiguring, refined, mad and divine."[17]

All the great value systems, including Aristotelian and Christian perspectives, symbolize a disciplined commitment to embody into an age particular values arising from strongly held passions. Indeed, "all these violent, arbitrary, severe, gruesome and antirational things [or passions] have shown themselves to be the means by which the European spirit was disciplined in its strength, ruthless curiosity, and subtle flexibility."[18]

Because disciplined actions create values that enrich life, it is clear that another important element of morality is that it is the basis for changing the world, and not merely for maintaining the world as it is.[19] Thus, in discussing morality, Nietzsche was not interested in using morality as the basis for explaining and for maintaining the current order of society. That is what Hegel did when he said philosophers can only explain the "truths" embodied in the existing ways of life, which in Hegel's case meant his view of what he said was the arrival, at the end of history, of the ethical state. Nietzsche rejected those "philosophical laborers" who follow Hegel and who have taken "everything that has hitherto happened and been valued, and make it clear, distinct, intelligible and manageable."[20] The new "philosophers of the future," Nietzsche's *true free spirits,* will seek to embody the values that are uniquely theirs into the world.[21] Indeed, Nietzsche's new philosophers will become commanders and leaders. "*Actual philosophers . . . are commanders and law-givers.*" The new philosopher's willfulness manifests a "*will to power.*" And Nietzsche asks "are there such philosophers today? Have there been such philosophers? *Must* there not be such philosophers?"[22] For Nietzsche, the answer to this question must be yes, because the new philosophers or free spirits will lead the way in demonstrating the need to transform culture so that it is once again hospitable to the Dionysian dimension and thus to a new manifestation of a will to power.

IV. THE MASTER AND SLAVE MORALITIES

Nietzsche's discussion of civil society is designed to demonstrate the differences between the values of the free spirits, who are his practitioners of the new philosophy and who are Nietzsche's new aristocratic class, and the slave mind. In pointing out these differences, Nietzsche demonstrated the wide gulf between two different systems of morality. Nietzsche gave a greater importance to the master morality because it is the basis for creating values that enhance life and give it meaning, in contrast to the slave morality that is seen as central to modern civil society.

The noble type of man, also referred to as the "free spirit," "feels *himself* to be the determiner of values, he does not need to be approved of, he judges 'what harms me is harmful in itself,' he knows himself to be that which in general first accords honour to things, he *creates values.*"[23] This man embodies the master or aristocratic morality, and he has an iron will that makes it impossible for anyone to make him doubt either himself or his values. Nietzsche said of this individual that "he shall be the greatest who can be the most solitary, the most concealed, the most divergent, the man beyond good and evil, the master of his virtues, *the superabundant of will;* this shall be called greatness: the ability to be as manifold as whole, as vast as full."[24] Nietzsche told these people to "remain *hard,* we last of the Stoics!"[25] And thus the noble type will persist toward his goals despite the presence of the many obstacles, including the temptation to just give up the fight and return to a less difficult life. But this persistence hardens him and makes him capable of waging continuing struggle. Nietzsche said that "continual struggle against ever-constant *unfavourable* conditions is . . . that which fixes and hardens a type."[26]

Moreover, this individual "counts intolerance itself among the virtues under the name justice."[27] For the master class mainly seeks to create conditions that are favorable to himself and that enhance the lives of the noble type only.[28] He cannot afford to tolerate anything that might impede his efforts. In this regard, unlike the slave class who as we see below establishes universal values designed to stop suffering, the master class is mostly concerned to embellish his own life through the values he creates. Still, Nietzsche argued that what the noble type creates is valuable in general, because the noble type's willfulness is the basis for life-enhancing, substantive values, such as are found in art, philosophy, and in many areas of life. Indeed, through his activity, the aristocratic personality seeks to make his own values the dominant ones in a culture.

In contrast to the master morality, there is the slave point of view, which is the moral orientation of modern society. The slave point of view represents the understandings of the "abused, oppressed, suffering, unfree, [and] those uncertain of themselves." Were these people to create a moral system, what would it contain?, asked Nietzsche.[29]

The slave mentality distrusts the values and way of life of the aristocratic class, and in consequence sees little in it that is good. After all, the slave sees the master class as the oppressor class, and, given this fact, it is likely that the slave would always count the master class's values as contrary to the needs and interests of the slave. Perhaps the latter's attitude can be better understood if we associate the word *slave* with ordinary persons. The latter distrust the values of a self-appointed cultural elite that attempt through their art or philosophy to shape the way a whole society should interpret experience.

The slave typifies in modern society the individual who lacks the self-confidence to free himself from the misery of uncertainty, emanating perhaps from a need to find the significance to existence. The slave seeks to overcome the unhappiness that emerges from his uncertainty by promoting universal values that would end the suffering of all people. Thus, unlike the master class, the slave class supports values such as pity, charity, patience, industriousness, humility, and friendliness. The slave emphasizes these values because they are "useful" and because they are the only "means of enduring the burden of existence."[30]

In saying the values just mentioned are useful, Nietzsche suggested that, for the slave, the best way to give meaning and purpose to life is to pursue a course that embodies the value of utility. In doing so, each person finds a way to make contributions to society that are considered necessary to maintaining an ordinary life. One does not aspire to the values of the master class in this case, but one seeks to absorb oneself in activities that, if performed well, will, it is hoped, give significance and importance to life. This view of dealing with the demise of substantive values or "inner loneliness," to use Weber's terms, is similar to the way Weber described the way people handled the concept of predestination. Where people do not know for sure whether they are heaven or hell bound, they can convince themselves that they are likely to land in heaven if they engage feverishly in useful activities. For Nietzsche, then, utility "is the source of the famous antithesis [between] 'good' and '*evil*.'"[31] One does "good" by giving oneself over to the norms of good order, or as in the case of Weber, by finding a niche in society where one can perform an acceptable function.

But in keeping with the norms of good order, and thus in doing what is good or useful in life, the slave is likely to prompt a kind of nagging doubt about slave values. For in adhering to the requirements of a useful life, one does not necessarily make primary to one's life those substantive values that give one's life a sense of significance. Instead, one may just become a cog in a routine and mechanical work environment or one may become oriented to attaining material and financial improvement. But these experiences, which tell one how to get along on a day-to-day basis, do not necessarily speak to the nature of those enduring values that give overall importance and significance to life.

In fact, after a fashion, it is likely that many in society will question the slave's way of life. Nietzsche said that there comes a time when a kind of "benevolent disdain" is attached to the slave morality, and those holding this mentality are viewed as basically "good-natured" and "*harmless*" people, who are "easy to deceive, perhaps a bit stupid." This view of the slave suggests that the slave mind, in order to gain his happiness and his undying hope for freedom, buys into a way of life that is far short of what he needs to live a substantive and meaningful life.[32]

Nonetheless, one might contend that the slave's values at least bring into existence a humanistic orientation that suggests that society should be designed to secure the same rights for all. Thus despite their shortcomings, slave values might be considered important additions to society. Indeed, it is the case that, because the ordinary man of civil society, or Nietzsche's slave, hopes to refrain from "mutual injury, mutual violence, mutual exploitation, [and instead] to equate one's own will with that of another,"[33] the slave would extol the Kantian ethic of treating others as ends. Now, Nietzsche said that the slave's commitment to these principles is acceptable only when understood as the basis for "good manners" between individuals. But when these principles are made the fundamental basis for society, there emerges a "will to the *denial* of life," and the principle of good manners is then turned into the basis for "dissolution and decay."[34]

For Nietzsche, the Kantian ethic is unrealistic, especially from the standpoint of the master class who creates values. Nietzsche said that "life itself is *essentially* appropriation, injury, overpowering of the strange and weaker, suppression, severity . . . exploitation."[35] The concept of the will to power suggests that Nietzsche's noble man can survive only by conquering. Exploitation is at the center of the noble individual's experience. Exploitation "pertains to the *essence* of the living thing as a fundamental organic function, it is a consequence of the intrinsic will to power which is precisely the will of life."[36]

It is only through this activity that the foundation of a "higher culture" is made possible, a culture that includes morality, religion, art, and philosophy. But these achievements cannot take place without the strong, in this case, the free spirit, dominating the weak. Nietzsche said,

> *Let us admit to ourselves unflinchingly how every higher culture on earth has hitherto* begun! *Men of a still natural nature, barbarians in every fearful sense of the word, men of prey still in possession of an unbroken strength of will and lust for power, threw themselves upon weaker, more civilized, more peaceful, perhaps trading or cattle raising races.*[37]

For a "healthy aristocracy," society is merely a "scaffolding upon which a select species of being is able to raise itself to its higher task and in general to a higher *existence*."[38] The master class or free spirit is a man who must order society to serve his need to create new values, and the weak must be made servants to this effort, totally subordinated to the demands of the strong. Obviously, then, a tendency toward equality of rights, which is a doctrine that would emerge from the Kantian dimension of slave thinking, is a proclivity to make slave values predominant, and, were this to happen, the way of life of the superior person would be diminished, if not denied entirely. It is this frame of mind, which prepares the ground for the herd mentality, that we discuss in the next section.

V. ORIGIN OF SLAVE AND HERD MORALITIES

For Nietzsche, there is a ranking of moralities. Clearly, the master morality is superior to the slave morality. In this section, I want to discuss the origin of the slave morality in order to demonstrate a basis for another inferior morality, the herd morality.

To begin, it must be clear that, in demonstrating the origin of the slave thinking, we can also demonstrate the basis for the herd morality as well. Now, at first it might appear that the two ways of thinking are quite different in nature. The slave seeks to change the world in keeping with universal values that end suffering and the domination of the master class. The herd mind hopes to keep things the way they are and to avoid change. So how is it possible for the slave mentality to have an affinity with and even to contribute to the herd mentality?

As just indicated the morality of the slave represents universal values whose ultimate purpose is to end suffering. But when people make these universal values their own, what is good is what is useful, and from this view there follows the commitment to conform one's conduct to the regimen of an ordinary life. The herd mind has a similar view. Thus, the herd mentality condemns anyone who challenges the ordinary in the name of pursuing strong Dionysian passions, such as the master class of course does. Such people are seen as evil and dangerous by the herd mentality. Indeed, the herd mentality preaches values such as obedience, modesty, fairness, and the lasting importance of a mediocre life in keeping with "mean and average" desires.[39] These values fit in with the need to lead an easy life, a life that is free from suffering. As in the case of the slave mind, then, there is a desire that all suffering be abolished, and, to this end, there must be equality of rights and sympathy for all who suffer.[40] However, the doctrine of equality of rights, played out in the midst of society dominated by the herd mind, is easily abused and transformed into a doctrine of the "equality of wrong doing," in which there is a "general war on everything rare, strange, privileged, the higher man, the higher soul, the higher duty . . . creative fullness of power and mastery."[41]

It would seem, then, that the slave mind, insofar as it is a basis for commonality of outlook and universality of values, creates the foundation for the herd mind. In discussing the origin of the former, we discuss as well the basis for the latter. Thus, for Nietzsche, we live in an age in which the values of the slave class predominate, and, in consequence, have led to the herd mentality. But how and why has this occurred? Addressing this question, which we discuss in the rest of this chapter, requires an assessment, or reevaluation, of existing values, demonstrating where and how the values of the slave class have arisen, and why and on what basis these values may begin to lose prominence.

To provide a general overview of Nietzsche's argument before discussing its details, it must be clear that for Nietzsche moral categories arise from a struggle between competing social forces. In a battle, the side that wins determines the substance of morality, including the ethos that the losers must accept. The earliest struggle of this kind took place, beginning in pre-Christian days, between an aristocratic class and the rest of society. In effect, the struggle between Apollo and Dionysus is mirrored in society as the conflict between a powerful aristocratic class attempting to impose its values onto all, and a weak, enslaved class. The slave class's rebellion against the powerful culminates in Christianity and the slave mind, which makes protection of the weak the main objective. Let us now turn to an examination of the details of this argument.

Modern morality has its roots in pre-Christian times as a result of a desire of an aristocratic class to maintain in society an order that made it the predominant source of values. Their view of morality diminished the place in society of the lower classes. The latter, however, could not accept their subordinate position. And in revolting against the master class, modern Christian morality was born. This revolt had already begun in Greece during the fifth century before Christ. But the main round of the revolt involved ancient Judea and Jewish resistance to Roman domination.[42] Here, the Jews, the weak and subordinate class, were determined to reorder the values of society, making their own values superior to that of the Romans. By doing so, the Jews sought to create a revolution in culture, one that would make themselves and what followed from their efforts, Christianity, predominant.

A brief description of this revolt is now in order. To begin, all of society was designed by the Roman aristocracy to manifest and to highlight *their* personality and values. To them, the low-born were to be used as means to serve the larger ends that the high-born determined were right for the society and, most important, themselves. This situation was the basis for a special kind of revolt by the Jews. Nietzsche said that prior to the revolt the Jews were powerless before the high-born types whom they had to serve. The Jews had no ability to resist the nobility physically because the master class simply had too much power. But the Jews did not accept a way of life that kept them in subordination. As a result, their resentment became very strong and even turned to hatred.[43] Nietzsche said that the Jews' "hatred grows to monstrous and uncanny proportions, to the most spiritual and poisonous kind of hatred."[44] Jewish hatred fueled a drive for resistance. Nietzsche said that a slave morality cannot exist without "a hostile external world; it needs, physiologically speaking, external stimuli in order to act at all—its action is fundamentally reaction."[45]

Jewish resistance was clever and successful. The Jews, unable to conquer the nobility in war, found a more resourceful way to bring down the high-born. They hoped to replace the values of the master class with new values. In effect, the Jews committed an act of "*spiritual revenge*"[46] in which they redefined and reshaped culture so that, in the new culture, they and all ordinary people were viewed as the protectors of sacred values. Here, the Jews "inverted" the values of the aristocratic class by saying that everything that is good and noble and beautiful and the source of happiness derives not from the aristocratic class, but from a "love of God." A reversal of rank follows from this reevaluation of values. Now it is said that those who love God, the low-born types, are of a higher importance than the aristocracy who, because they are godless, are condemned to eternal damnation. The Jews proclaim, then, that "the wretched alone are the good; the poor, impotent, lowly alone are the good; the suffering, deprived, sick, ugly alone are pious, alone are blessed by God, blessedness is for them alone—and you, the powerful and noble, are the contrary, the evil, the cruel, the lustful, the insatiable, the godless to all eternity; and you shall be in all eternity the unblessed, accursed and damned!"[47]

The words used by the Jews to conduct their campaign were splendid for the purposes the Jews had in mind. These words did not exhort victory on a battlefield where the Jews were outnumbered and militarily weak, but it urged the masses to triumph by being better, spiritually, than the hated aristocratic class. The masses were told: "Let us be different from the evil, namely good! And he is good who does not outrage, who harms nobody, who does not attack, who does not requite, who leaves revenge to God."[48] But this message really is another way of saying "we weak ones are, after all, weak; it would be good if we did nothing *for which we are not strong enough*."[49] As Detwiler says, this account demonstrates how it came to be that "the downtrodden and oppressed, who had no hope of attaining physical superiority over the nobler type, proclaimed their moral superiority and proceeded to conquer the world with their gospel of meekness and love."[50]

VI. DEMOCRACY AND CIVIL SOCIETY

The Jewish revolt for Nietzsche was "remarkable"; it defeated Roman rule, and it became the basis for Christianity. But for Nietzsche this revolt, remarkable as it was, created a value system that has now, even though still in force, outlived its usefulness. Nietzsche indicated this latter view when he said that Christian images, in the form of such individuals as Jesus and Mary, continue to exist, "as if" Christianity "were the epitome of all the highest values—and not only in Rome but over almost half the earth."[51] This statement suggests that Christianity is for Nietzsche no longer the major source of substantive values, even as Christian culture continues to have prominence.

Christianity, although no longer a value system that can give life significance, continues to be an important factor in the modern world for Nietzsche. Its importance is manifested in the modern effort to end suffering through democracy. In effect, the Christian idea has been given a secular form of expression. "It has got to the point where we discover even in political and social institutions an increasingly evident expression of this morality: the *democratic* movement inherits the Christian."[52] But these values merely mirror the values of ordinary slave life, values that pose a threat to the creation of a higher culture. Nietzsche said that throughout Europe are people, whom he referred to as "anarchist dogs," whose main objective is to promote the philosophy of the herd life, using in the process "the religion of pity, in sympathy with whatever feels, lives, suffers; (down as far as the animals, up as far as 'God'—the extravagance of 'pity for God' belongs in a democratic era); at one and all, in the cry and impatience of pity, in mortal hatred for suffering in general."[53] This secularized form of Christianity has no sympathy for the special man, the free spirit, and instead argues that all are to be reduced to the same common level. Everyone is to be equal, and there are not to be any "special rights and privileges" for those who are truly superior, the free spirit.[54] Unlike Hegel, who saw the master/slave conflict as a basis for a civil society that Hegel celebrated because of its securing basic rights for all, Nietzsche saw the outcome of the master/slave conflict as supporting conditions of oppression for society's most honored class, his free spirit.

Like Burke, there is a tendency in Nietzsche to yearn for a society that would create a special place for a natural aristocracy. For Nietzsche, as we have seen, it is clear that the values of the slave mind, a concern to provide respect for all, will lead only to a leveling of all to the same mediocre standard. The result is that there is no effort to provide a special place for the free spirit, but instead all people are made into passive and unwillful individuals of the herd. Nietzsche condemned this condition, and he hoped that this situation would lead to its own undoing. For, in point of fact, as people become more and more oriented to a civil society, people become very passive and soft. Indeed, Nietzsche said that Europe is marked by a "paralysis of the will," a situation in which people "no longer have any conception of independence of decision, of the valiant feeling of pleasure in willing."[55]

When individuals and society lack a sense of energy, arising from a belief in values that give significance to life, society, as well as individuals, begin to feel vulnerable and weak before anything and anyone who challenges society. Indeed, the herd mind readily succumbs to those with the stronger will. Ironically, this circumstance may create an opening for the master class. For as the weak become less capable of taking care of themselves, others who are stronger, in this case those of the master morality, may then ascend to a position of authority in society.[56]

In asserting this position, Nietzsche saw in the imminent collapse of democracy the basis for a new and positive form of tyranny. He said,

> *The democratization of Europe will lead to the production of a type prepared for* slavery *in the subtlest sense: in individual and exceptional cases the* strong *man will be found to turn out stronger and richer than has perhaps ever happened before . . . . What I mean to say is that the democratization of Europe is at the same time an involuntary arrangement for the breeding of* tyrants—*in every sense of that word, including the most spiritual.*[57]

The new, "spiritual tyrant" will not engage in the "petty" politics of our times. Nietzsche did not accept politics as an activity reduced to determining what rights people should have and how they were to be distributed. Instead, he hoped for the emergence of a strong class of people who had the will to end the morass of civil society and who, in doing so, would make themselves the pinnacle of the new culture. The new politics would be what Nietzsche referred to as "grand politics." Nietzsche said, "the time for petty politics is past: the very next century will bring with it the struggle for mastery over the whole earth—the *compulsion* to grand politics."[58]

Who is this tyrant Nietzsche had in mind? He is the artist. For Nietzsche, as Sleinis says, "the potential of art to enhance life is ranked above that of morality and religion."[59] Thus, Nietzsche believed that the artist is the source of the values that would enhance life. And for Nietzsche a politics fueled by the artistic imagination would seek to define a basis for celebrating the joyfulness of life in a way that, as Sleinis says, makes possible "the thriving of the human spirit" and a "love of life."[60] This way of life suggests a new, yet-to-be-fully-experienced freedom, within a new, yet-to-be-fully-created social and political world. But the aesthetic vision such individuals create can nonetheless give us a good taste of what a life-affirming, life-enriching way of life would provide us. That taste would be the basis for building a politics that could make possible a significant and meaningful life, one that would restore to people a sense of self-importance and purpose.

VII. POLITICS OF BAD CONSCIENCE

During the course of creating the new society, what enemies would Nietzsche's new aristocracy hope to slay? It would seem that Nietzsche's politics would be dedicated to resisting the oppressive reality associated with attitudes of guilt and bad conscience, for these attitudes are at the heart of what helps to conquer and deny a reality to willful conduct. To understand the enemy that Nietzsche's politics has in mind, it is necessary to explain the nature and impact of bad conscience on society. And this can best be accomplished by comparing good conscience with bad.

Good conscience is associated with the fact that the individual defines himself as a *"sovereign individual,"* the man "who has his own independent, protracted will and the *right to make promises*—and in him a proud consciousness, . . . a consciousness of his own power and freedom, a sensation of mankind come to completion."[61] This individual experiences the "privilege of *responsibility*." Now the sense of responsibility communicated by good conscience suggests that an individual has "power over oneself and over fate."[62] Here, a person realizes that he is accountable for the consequences of his actions and choices, and thus he must accept the need to restrain his passions when restraints become the best way to organize one's life as a way to create values. The experience of good conscience, typical of the master morality, demonstrates real mastery over oneself and, insofar as a man possesses this quality, he is able to have both an intense sense of self-affirmation as well as a sense, as Detwiler says, of "mastery over others."[63]

But it must be clear, given the model of good conscience, that in restraining one's impulses, one should not relinquish or terminate them, for to do that would be to cut oneself off from the real energy that motivates life and that is the foundation of one's willfulness. It is here where the difference between good and bad conscience becomes apparent. The difference between the two states of mind arises from the fact that society does not want individuals thinking that their instincts are a proper basis for conduct, lest individuals lose respect for society's norms and rules. Once again, then, Dionysus's demand for spontaneity in keeping with one's passions and drives confronts Apollo's hope to maintain order. How does society historically approach the concern to maintain order? In addressing this question, we can see the importance society places on bad conscience.

Initially society established respect for its rules through severe punishment. Here, society's approach to morality was to associate a failure to observe rules with excruciating pain. This experience taught people not to allow their instincts full play, and instead people were to learn to repress them. In discussing the ways society used to achieve conformity to rules, Nietzsche pointed out that, at first, methods of torture were used to burn forever into our collective memory a fear of doing wrong. Indeed, the first techniques of punishment were extraordinarily severe, including stoning, piercing people with stakes, tearing flesh off the body, and "smearing the wrongdoer with honey and leaving him in the blazing sun for the flies."[64] These harsh forms of punishment became a public spectacle or a kind of shared entertainment. People were drawn to watch others suffer, and the occasion was cause for celebration, even. Here, all watched what might happen to them, happy that it was happening to another, so joyful in fact that all were willing to celebrate the other's pain. Indeed, cruelty, as a way to mold people to uphold their obligations under custom and law, was even spiritualized and deified.[65] In this setting, "to see others suffer does one good, to make others suffer even more [good]."[66] The lesson, however, was not lost on anyone. Do what the norms require, or risk being made the object of public celebration yourself!

This experience, no doubt, began to create the outlook of the herd mentality by teaching people to suppress their instincts because the latter could get them into trouble and make them liable for punishment. Moreover, the herd mind's aversion to instinct was further shaped by cruelty when society linked instinct life with all that brings shame.[67] Here, Nietzsche discussed the efforts of society to make man become "ashamed of all his instincts."[68] Christianity is a primary source of this lesson. Nietzsche quoted with sarcasm how the medieval Pope Innocent III carried out this project by listing as "repellant" many of our basic instinctual functions, such as gestation, procreation, salivation, and excretion of our natural wastes.[69]

In modern civil society, a new way is invented to teach people the rules of society and to carry on the Christian tradition of maintaining a basic distrust for one's instincts.

The principal difference between the premodern and the modern approach is that in the latter setting, conformity is taught not through torture, but by forging within the consciousness of individuals a sense of guilt for contemplating or for engaging in actions that violate the norms of society. People must learn to control their "unconscious and infallible drives." Society attempts to "tame" us by substituting for our native drives and instincts, a life dictated by "the oppressive narrowness . . . of custom."[70] In society, we are turned into people who fashion our lives so that they are in keeping with what society says is best for us, and not with what we know is best for us, given the deep-seated drives and impulses we feel.

But when people are forced to suppress their inner Dionysian drives in the name of social order, they end up at war with themselves. Here, because people are in a society that requires them to hold back and to not let their instincts have full play, they must learn to contain and to keep within themselves some of their sharpest feelings. And when instincts are suppressed, they acquire "depth, breadth, and height," and as they do they become aggressive emotions "of wild, free, prowling man turned backward *against man himself.*"[71] Indeed, Nietzsche described these emotions as "cruelty, joy in persecuting, in attacking, in change, in destruction" and these emotions have as their target those who hold them, and thus they are "turned against the possessors of such instincts." Owing to the need to control the Dionysian side of our personality, we develop toward our own selves hostile emotions. Another way to refer to the hostility people have toward themselves is to say that people with such self-loathing manifest a sense of guilt and a *bad conscience.* Both of these states of mind symbolize the modern tendency to teach people to control their instincts by thinking of themselves as unworthy whenever they experience them.[72] And people are taught to experience guilt and bad conscience whenever they violate social norms.

Bad conscience is a "serious illness" because, while it teaches people to suppress the Dionysian side of their personalities, it necessarily creates for people a sense that they are prisoners within their own minds, without any hope of achieving freedom.[73] It is no wonder, then, that in a society that generates bad conscience each person is a "desperate prisoner," "rubbing himself raw against the bars of his cage." It is understandable as well that for such individuals, their willfulness is completely vanquished. For Nietzsche, this condition is the "gravest and uncanniest illness, from which humanity has not yet recovered."[74]

Clearly, the master class is the group in possession of good conscience, and the herd man is the group in thrall to bad conscience. The former is able to "stand security for [him]self and to do so with pride, thus to possess also the right *to affirm [him]self.*"[75] The noble man is not afraid of his passions and basic drives, he has sufficient self-constraint to pursue a life that embodies them in ways that manifest his full powers, and thus he is in complete control of his life, taking complete responsibility for it. Such a person would not be tricked by society into repressing his emotions and restraining the aggression that results from this repression by embracing the mentality of bad conscience. But the herd man who must suppress all his impulses experiences only unrelenting self-contempt and the continuing presence of bad conscience.

The politics of the new aristocracy would be a form of resistance against all the social and cultural institutions that are used to maintain the hegemony of bad conscience and guilt. Nietzsche's politics would suggest that we can imagine a life in which the forces of

Dionysus fully triumph, in a setting that at the same time maintains some dimensions of Apollo intact, so that there remains a necessary degree of order and self-restraint for the flourishing of Dionysus. The person who best embodies this approach to politics in the modern times is Michel Foucault, whose politics we will discuss after first touching upon how modern civil society thinkers might have responded to Nietzsche.

VIII. RESPONSE AND REJOINDER

How would modern proponents of civil society respond to Nietzsche? For the most part, they would argue that Nietzsche's noble soul can really live only in the setting of civil society. It is true that the free spirit will not be allowed to dominate. He will not be permitted to reestablish the reign of aristocracy, but he will be allowed a place, even if it is an isolated and remote place. It is true that few will probably listen to him or even care what he is doing. But there will always be some who will care, and they will listen to his teachings about conscience and guilt and wonder whether these realities do not tyrannize just as Nietzsche said they did. Still, because a civil society can find a place for free spirits just as it finds a place for all the ways of life that the free spirit hates, civil society provides an even stronger defense of itself.

Now the free spirit might say that such an argument as this is really backhanded to the extreme. For what choice does the free spirit have? He cannot entirely free himself from his context, and thus he must do the best with what his context offers him. He will try to become an example of a willful life, demonstrating to others the importance of creating values that enrich life. Moreover, the willful individual will seek ways to circumvent, to evade, or, when necessary, to resist the norms and circumstances that stand in the way of realizing this objective. Such a life will be difficult, often lonely, and at times dangerous. Civil society then cannot be exonerated from the hard times it will give its most creative people.

In response, the proponent of civil society would argue that the dangers of an unconventional life are exaggerated. The proponent of civil society will remind the free spirit that a civil society gives the free spirit precisely what he needs, a set of rules and constraints against which to rebel. No creative person can create anything unless there is a current pattern of life in place that the free spirit hopes to change by resisting. In effect, the free spirit needs the order he condemns, for without it, there would be no basis for creation. Further, what better target than a civil society whose weapons are the ideals of rights and private freedom, instead of the instruments of torture? In this setting, the free spirit always lives to fight another day, and he always stands a chance to create a new culture that completely revolutionizes society. The proponents of civil society accept this challenge, for, in refusing it, they would be forced to bring down the civil society itself by denying the basic commitment to equal rights.

Moreover, there is greater likelihood that the free spirit will meet with success in a civil society than in other settings. People with an aesthetic vision of a better way of life have had great impact on civil societies in the past, and they may have even greater impact in the future. For instance, during the counterculture movement of the 1960s the so-called "flower children," the free spirits of that time, demanded a freer, more unrestrained life even as they were told by society to clean up, get a haircut, and find a job. This version of the free spirit's aesthetic vision of a life liberated from the technocratic structures Weber described has impacted greatly contemporary experience for most people. Many more opportunities for expression of individually defined viewpoints exist today than for instance in the 1950s. Discussion of abortion, of sexual freedom, of women leaving behind conventional family settings, and so on, were rare during the 1950s. These ways of life have been given sanction today, at least in part, from the visions of a liberated world initially provided in the great counterculture movements of the 1960s. Obviously, these ways of life and the values they embody have truly enhanced the lives of many.

This response brings us to another, equally important concern. What kind of society would the free spirit bring into existence? We know that the new society would have an aristocratic ruling class, but what kinds of values and ways of life would the new ruling class put into place? Indeed, is it not fair to ask whether there would be respect for basic rights, if there would be programs that educate all people, if there would be efforts to provide people with interesting and useful work, and so on? The free spirit might say that question is unfair, since we cannot know ahead of the effort to overthrow an existing order what the processes of creation will bring into existence. If we worry about the consequences of a rebellion, then we would never rebel. And without rebellion society would remain a place of conformity to norms no one ever questioned.

But the proponent of civil society might respond by asking whether all the free spirit is advocating is one group's emergence to power at the expense of others. Here, the basis for justification is nothing more than power, the sheer might of some to dominate others, without the benefit of good reasons to justify a change in power. The free spirit, of course, would scoff at having to present good reasons for the new regime he contemplates, for that smacks of the kind of Kantian rationalism he discarded. But can we not ask for assurance that the new regime might be based on something other than the will to power of some who are desirous of evening the score with those who have been their detractors?

On the issue of the justified use of power, proponents of civil society would certainly take seriously Nietzsche's argument that the commitments to democracy and civil society make persons so weak that in the end they are prone to welcome a tyrant to power. But a civil society proponent would view the problems of democracy in different terms. What citizens look for from democracy is fairness, and when they do not receive it they have a tendency to manifest a weaker commitment to a civil society. Indeed, a theme of this book is that when society is seen as lacking fairness individuals lose a sense of strong commitment to society, hastening the demise of civil society's institutions. Rawls's response to this problem was to find ways to make society fairer, including ways to create toleration among people with diverse views and interests. Nietzsche would respond to Rawls's framework by saying that Rawls's overlapping consensus is nothing more than the slave mentality, rationalized to justify people's holding different variations of the same overriding commitment to civil society and to accepting its spiritual tyranny.

Finally, Nietzsche, were he alive, would point out how right he was about the dangers to modern society of the lack of the master morality among many people today. For the free spirit, the lives of people in civil society are too directed and controlled, and people tend to cede too much of what they are and can be to others. The result of this kind of existence is a pervasive sense of boredom, bordering on despair. In consequence, people are constantly looking for ways to engender excitement in life, and the ways they choose are often destructive. For instance, we see people indulging in harmful drugs, in dangerous forms of sexuality, and in quests for other bizarre forms of diversion, such as watching unusually high levels of graphic violence on television and in the movies.

But does civil society require this outcome? Or is this outcome merely a function of a civil society gone lame and in need of the breath of fresh air that a Nietzschean critique can provide? And the fresh air in this case might be more readily defined in terms of a Rawlsian commitment to a more just society as opposed to placing our fate into the hands of the Nietzschean master class. Why would not the hope of achieving a more just society enliven people to their possibilities and to the need to become their own masters, denying society's chokehold over their lives?

Or should we see in Nietzsche another, more dire possibility, one symbolized by the Holocaust? In this case, Nietzsche might have added to his three moral systems of master, slave, and herd, a fourth, that he might have called a *beast morality*. Here, as people give up any hope of finding significance to life, they may be led to a form of extreme resentment and hatred, which culminates in a nihilist way of life and which destroys any chance for creating and maintaining a civil society. Is the beast morality not afoot today in our society? Is Nietzsche's medicine, then, the right approach to ridding ourselves of the beast, and thus preserving, after a fashion, a civil society?

IX. Michel Foucault's Nietzschean Critique

Michel Foucault (1926–1984) has made an attempt to develop a political and social vision for the present times based upon some of Nietzsche's insights, with important echoes of Weber. In following Nietzsche, a major theme of Foucault's critique of modern society is the conflict between the Apollonian and the Dionysian elements of personality. Individuals experience dual pressures. On the one hand there is the pressure of culture, which imposes order-creating norms. On the other hand are internally located instincts, which seek a more spontaneous life, apart from the patterning force of everyday life. Often Apollo gets the best of Dionysus, and those who resist being made into cogs in a larger machine of social order are perceived by society as dangers to good order.[76]

Foucault thus focused upon the way society often responds to marginalized individuals, people whose lives are unconventional from the standpoint of society's norms, such as the insane or those in prison. In undertaking to describe the way society responds to such unconventional individuals, Foucault's interest was the implication of the Enlightenment to society. The Enlightenment, as we saw in Kant, promoted the kind of inquiry that sought to replace superstition as the basis for discussions of public matters with doctrines, supported by reason, which could secure the widest possible human freedom. Foucault's concern, however, was that, to a large extent, existing social and political attitudes in the modern world are fashioned by the Enlightenment. In accepting these attitudes without analyzing them, we may also accept political, economic, social, institutional, and cultural contexts that shape our experience, often to the detriment of the freedom that the Enlightenment promises. Thus, Foucault argued that we should neither be "for" nor "against" the

Enlightenment, but instead we should try to keep an open mind about its contributions, so that we are able to distinguish between its useful and its detrimental legacies.[77]

Foucault will point out both dimensions. In his early work, he describes some of its harmful effects, and we will discuss these elements as a prelude to discussing its more lasting and important contributions. Here, we need to be clear that reason, which the Kantian Enlightenment praised, is not necessarily always our enemy, but it is not always our friend, either. In consequence of this fact, we should not fear that critiquing the contributions of reason "risks sending us into irrationality."[78]

Of great concern to Foucault's critique of the Enlightenment was that he believed that it helped to institute and to validate structures of power that were actually hostile to freedom. To understand how this development arose, it is necessary to understand the way power is used in the modern world.

Those who dominate others in society achieve conformity to norms by the use of power. What is Foucault's view of power? For Foucault, person "A" has power over "B" when "A" can "determine" "B's" conduct, without the use of brute force. In the modern age, an age that celebrates human freedom, brute force as a device for achieving conformity to patterning norms would be a violation of the commitment to freedom. Instead, power is exercised when individuals become "induced" by various behavior-managing techniques to do as patterning norms require. In this case, a person presumably always retains the possibility of doing other than what is being impressed upon him or her. Thus, "A's" power over "B," where "A" gets "B" to do as "A" wants, is always accompanied by the notion that "B's" behavior is not coerced. Foucault said that there is no exercise of power "without potential refusal or revolt."[79]

The main approach, then, to achieving power over others is through means that induce people to do as those in power want, without resort to brute force. In *Discipline and Punish,* following the path of Nietzsche in *The Genealogy of Morals,*[80] Foucault, through the analysis of punishment, hoped to demonstrate the techniques that have replaced brute force as the basis for domination, not only in penal institutions but in many domains of day-to-day life. In this case, then, punishment is not only a way to deter crime, but to shape the way people act and think.[81]

Following Nietzsche, Foucault points out that in the premodern setting, punishment involved terrible forms of torture inflicted upon the wrongdoer in a public ceremony. People's limbs were pulled out and their skin was burned with hot lead and boiling oil. The purpose of this enterprise was to make an example of the individual in the presence of the public that was brought to watch, in the hopes that others, after seeing the agony of the prisoner, would become frightened of committing a similar crime. Others must see the punishment because "they must be made to be afraid."[82]

But in the enlightened world this kind of punishment is rejected because it denies respect for a person's humanity and for the legal limits that must be observed if a person's humanity is to be left intact. In consequence, different forms of punishment, which no longer include infliction of pain upon the body, are used.[83] The new form of punishment did not need to resort to physical torture to control people. How was this objective achieved?

Foucault discussed Jeremy Bentham's model prison, the Panopticon, to address this question. The Panopticon was arranged as a circle of prison cells. The lighting allowed an observer to look into the cell from the outside to watch each prisoner. In the middle of the circle was a watchtower where the guards could observe each person in his cell. At all times, then, the prisoners could know that the guards watched them. However, each individual was in a cell that did not open to any other cells, thus denying each prisoner all contact with other prisoners. In this context, the guards can view each prisoner, but the prisoner is never in a position to communicate with anyone else. As Foucault said, the prisoner "is the object of information, never the subject of communication."[84]

The guard's gaze communicates to the prisoner that the prisoner is always being watched, monitored, and supervised. This setting is the basis for the guard's power over the inmate to make the latter conform to the regimen of prison life. But how does the guard communicate this message through a gaze alone? Remember, the prisoner has no human contact with any other person. In the absence of such contact, the sole source of external "support" for a prisoner is the guard in the watchtower who is always staring and monitoring the prisoner's behavior. In this setting, so transfixed does the prisoner become with the guard's gaze that it is as if the guard is always watching him, even when the guard is not physically present. In effect, the guard is always there, in the prisoner's imagination, acting as a control on the prisoner's thoughts, and the prisoner can never escape the guard's presence. It is in this way that power is exercised over the prisoner's life, and the latter does as he is told, as if voluntarily, without the use of brute force to ensure compliance.

Furthermore, for Foucault, the Panopticon is not to be "understood as a dream building; it is the diagram of a mechanism of power reduced to its ideal form."[85] Moreover, this new "political technology" is used throughout modern society to impose discipline and order onto people in all walks of life. "It [the political technology] serves to reform prisoners, but also to treat patients, to instruct school children, to confine the insane, to supervise workers, to put beggars and idlers to work . . . . Whenever one is dealing with a multiplicity of individuals on whom a task or a particular form of behavior must be imposed, the panopticon schema may be used."[86] Indeed, this approach to power is a form of "subtle coercion" that governs modern social relationships.[87] The gaze of others, in this case those in positions of supervisory power over people in the institutions of society where people work, attend religious services, or go to school, defines the norms all are to uphold. And this gaze, which represents a continual effort to manage and to supervise people, exercises power over people as it is internalized and made a part of each person's consciousness. Thus, whereas a person knows that he could violate the norms of society, he will not do so, because he does not want to live with a sense of condemnation. Foucault in referring to this experience said, "what developed, then, was a whole technique of human dressage by location, confinement, surveillance, the perpetual supervision of behavior and task, in short, a whole technique of management of which the prison was merely one manifestation."[88]

Foucault's discussion of prisons embodies the view that societies are governed by various techniques, each of which is designed to achieve particular ends. There are techniques that allow people to produce goods, those that define how to use language, and finally those that enable some to determine the way others should live. The latter type of techniques, which Foucault referred to as the *techniques of domination,* speak not just to the experience of prison but to the way in which that experience is exported to many domains of society beyond the prison. And the purpose is the same: to maintain the control needed to mold the lives of people.[89]

The picture Foucault drew of modern civil society, while critical of the circumstances that threaten freedom, does not rule out another more salutary approach to identity formation. In this alternative view individuals may indeed carve out for themselves an identity that manifests a self that is different from and in contrast to the one society requires. Foucault believed that such an endeavor could be achieved by a technology "oriented toward the discovery and the formulation of the truth concerning oneself."[90] To suggest such a possibility indicates that Foucault was able to demonstrate the positive contributions of the Enlightenment, especially in his later work. In this work, as Alexander Nehamas said, Foucault provided the Enlightenment with a kind of "serious, if qualified, respect," arguing that the whole quest of the Enlightenment, as celebrated by Kant, to realize the full liberation of human beings was still in process.[91] Indeed, Foucault said that "I do not know whether it must be said today that the critical task still entails faith in Enlightenment; I continue to think that this task requires work on our limits, that is, a patient labor giving form to our impatience for liberty."[92]

What are the implications for politics of Foucault's technology for self-development? To address this question, we first have to define clearly what he meant by the technology that enables us to capture the truth about ourselves.

To provide an example of what Foucault intends in his discussion of the techniques of self-development, it is necessary to turn to his *The Care of the Self*. In this work, Foucault used the example of the Stoic philosopher Seneca, who recounts the style of self-reflection that was the hallmark of his life.[93] In the morning, he prepared himself for the tasks of the day by examining these tasks and by asking himself what was necessary for him to achieve them. In the evening, he reviewed the events of the day. He asked himself about the bad habits that he had faced that day, of the personal weaknesses he had resisted, and how, as a result of this reflection, he is or is not a better person.

As he reflects upon himself, he is desirous of finding not only the legitimate purposes of his life, but the "rules of conduct" that would enable him to achieve his ends. But a life of reflection does more for us than just provide us with rules of conduct that enable us to achieve particular ends. Presumably, reflections on the self are concerned as well with enabling us to preserve our freedom.[94]

How is this possible? As we reflect upon our lives and consider the various possible courses of life, including the different desires and passions that move us, we should accept only those over which we have control. Astute reflection makes a clear distinction, then, between passions and desires over which we have control and those that we do not. For instance, suppose we know that to be successful in a particular type of work, we will have to work very hard. Let us also suppose that we know we want to retain time for the development of other aspects of our life, such as are provided by friends and family. But as we reflect on our lives, we realize that in allowing work to dominate our lives it is possible that we will become so obsessed with work that we will not be able to feel good about time spent with friends or family. In this case, we would begin to resist time with friends and family, even as we longed for that experience. As a result of this reaction, we would lose our freedom to do what provides us with enjoyment.

To secure our freedom, we must plan ahead as we develop our preparation for the work we want to do by building into our lives habits that insure we will never feel bad about making time for friends and family. Moreover, we must constantly monitor our lives to make certain we have not allowed ourselves to depart from a course that continues to be open to all our legitimate desires. Foucault refers to the activity of self-reflection as a kind of "administrative review" by which we continually evaluate our conduct with the intention of making certain that we do not lose the essential control necessary to maintain a course that keeps alive the possibilities we so want to pursue.[95] By carefully inspecting ourselves and admitting in an honest way the negative consequences to our freedom of taking certain approaches to life or of not pursuing others, we make certain we do not fall into situations in which we lose our freedom to direct our lives. Foucault says that "this inspection is a test of power and a guarantee of freedom: a way of always making sure that one will not become attached to that which does not come under our control." We are to accept as motivations in life only "that which can depend on the subject's free and rational choice."[96] Or in another place, in speaking of the lessons of the Stoics with respect to the self, Foucault says that, for the Stoics, "the experience of the self is not a discovering of a truth hidden inside the self, but an attempt to determine what one can and cannot do with one's available freedom."[97]

It would seem, moreover, that an essential element of following this course of conduct is that we would be concerned constantly to distinguish situations in which circumstances prevent the pursuit of certain possibilities from those situations in which circumstances merely offer roadblocks to possibilities of our liking. In taking care of ourselves, we would preserve our freedom by not seeking to overturn those circumstances that could not be affected by us. Resisting circumstances that permit no chance for success draws all our energy and attention, and, in consequence, we would lose the freedom to pursue other elements of life that we want just as much. Alternately, settings which offer us merely roadblocks, we would try to surmount creatively.

For Foucault, as for Nietzsche, to care for the self is to follow the model of the artist. For the artist, creative projects take place in time and history. In consequence, the artist's reach is limited by circumstances, and not everything the artist imagines or wants to realize will be possible, given the reality that constrains the artist's life.[98] But the artist, in framing projects, pushes his or her circumstances to their outermost limit by pointing to those possibilities seemingly not permitted by current circumstances and by showing the way these possibilities could be realized, even within these circumstances. That is what makes the artist's painting or music so unique and liberating. Similarly, a person committed to the ethos associated with the care of the self would be an individual who recognized how arrangements in society might deny one certain hoped-for opportunity. But in reflecting on oneself and rearranging the relationships among the various dimensions of one's life, one may find a way to achieve these possibilities anyway, thus liberating oneself from the conditions that otherwise oppress one's life.

Foucault argued in *The Care of the Self* that his approach permits individuals to locate a basis for the "art of existence" in an ethos of "self-control."[99] To think in these terms is to be cognizant that in defining strategies for achieving goals more than just the goals in question are involved. In addition, we are to find ways, as we pursue our goals, to preserve our freedom to make our lives encompass many possibilities of our choice, by not falling into a situation in which our conduct is determined by circumstances or feelings over which we have no control. Here, the "art of existence" "revolves around the question of the self, of its dependence and independence, of its universal form and of the connection it can and should establish with others, of the procedures by which it exerts its control over itself, and of the way it can establish complete supremacy over itself."[100] When an individual masters the technology of the care of the self, one is no longer dependent, but one is completely free to depict one's life in ways that enable a person to have a rich and dignified existence, a life that includes many of the possibilities that one hopes to realize.

The kind of self-mastery that Foucault suggests is essential and that he associates with Stoic practices can be viewed as having been made a part of sixteenth- and seventeenth-century Christian moral life. Here, Christianity, in embracing Stoic approaches, advocates that people engage in self-reflection or "administrative reviews," with the intention of discovering the limits of their freedom. Foucault points out, however, that whereas seventeenth-century Christianity wants to use these practices to build an increasing sense of "dependence upon God," the Stoic and Foucault (who supports the Stoic view) want to use the tactics of self-mastery to achieve "sovereignty over himself" so that a person is "dependent upon nothing."[101]

The political ramifications for society of Foucault's Stoic personality are clear. Such a person stands above others, like Nietzsche's free spirit, making a statement to all of the need to forge one's own life, despite the iron cage that seeks to place us under the throes of domination. Further, on this view of the care of the self, the essential activity that politics must protect is the ability of individuals to speak and to manifest the truth about themselves. Would this view of politics be receptive to supporting a civil society, as Kant claimed was necessary to sustain his view of Enlightenment?

Foucault would question whether the notion of a civil society can contribute to the care of the self. Foucault points out that, starting in the late eighteenth century, a civil society was conceived as a separate sphere that opposed the power of the state and thereby permitted individuals, often in the name of economic freedom, a degree of independence from state intrusions in their lives. This view suggests that the separate sphere of civil society symbolizes freedom and initiative, whereas the state in a civil society symbolizes authoritarian control. Consequently, the separate sphere of a civil society is a force for good, and the state is a force for evil.[102]

But for Foucault this depiction is too simplistic, and it may hide the fact that power pervades the separate sphere of a civil society in ways that might be detrimental to people. Foucault suggests that even a separate sphere in a civil society would establish a power relationship between individuals and itself. And the question one would have to ask pertains to how to limit the effects of power, because for Foucault "every power relation is not bad in itself, but it is a fact that always involves danger."[103] It is thus necessary to examine carefully the power relationships that might appear in the separate sphere of a civil society to determine whether in fact they are harmful and how they should be rearranged if they are. This is precisely what Foucault has sought to do throughout all his work. For Foucault, power pervades society by imposing on individuals certain ways of seeing, acting, and living, as Foucault discussed in his references to Bentham's model prison. In doing so, society denies people their freedom by requiring people to experience constant or continual supervision, manifested in the gaze of a powerful few who stand over and manage their lives.

Now, the proponents of civil society discussed in this book made, as a central theme, the importance of civil society for securing basic rights. To this end, our point has been not only that a civil society suggests a separate sphere that stands as a buffer against the state.

But, just as important, a civil society is a moral environment that seeks to secure individual liberty while at the same time providing respect for the necessary constraints, or civic virtues, that make such liberty possible. Hence, it must be clear that there are several ways by which liberty is promoted in a civil society. Not only is the state in a civil society required to protect the rights of individuals, but, in addition, there must be respect for civic virtues such as toleration and mutual respect that help to carry on a commitment to liberty, as well.

It would seem that, since liberty is essential to engaging in the techniques of the care of the self, a civil society, which preserves such liberty, is a necessary basis for Foucault's self. But it may well be the case that what is central to a civil society, the civic virtue necessary to maintain it, Foucault would find as one more expression of the kind of power that denies one a chance to manifest care for the self. The question then is whether Foucault would accord a place to the civic virtues of a civil society as a means for protecting the rights of all individuals. A civil society depends on this possibility. In effect, will there be a general commitment to toleration and mutual respect, for instance, or will these values be condemned as they were by Nietzsche, who associated them with slave values and thus with an order destructive of the will to power? Or to put the question in another way, can Foucault tolerate civil society any more than Nietzsche, even though it is quite clear that, like Kant, Foucault would need a civil society to ensure the care of the self?

Endnotes

1. E. E. Sleinis, *Nietzsche's Revaluation of Values: A Study in Strategies,* (Urbana: University of Illinois Press, 1994), pp. 152–54, 13, 17.

2. Friedrich Nietzsche, *Beyond Good and Evil,* (New York: Penguin Books, 1973), p. 35, sec. 4.

3. Ibid., p. 36, sec. 5.

4. Ibid., p. 37, sec. 6. Italics in text.

5. Ibid., p. 38, sec. 6. Italics in text.

6. Bruce Detwiler, *Nietzsche and the Politics of Aristocratic Radicalism,* (Chicago: University of Chicago Press, 1990), pp. 64–65.

7. Ibid., p. 64.

8. Ibid., p. 65.

9. Ibid., pp. 65–66.

10. Ibid., p. 66.

11. Ibid., p. 66. My use of the word *willful* in relation to Nietzsche is influenced by Richard Flathman, *Willful Liberalism: Voluntarism and Individuality in Political Theory and Practice,* (Ithaca: Cornell University Press, 1991), p. 185. Flathman says that willful conduct "presupposes considerable command [by the agent] over the agent's deliberations, decisions and choices."

12. E.E. Sleinis, *Nietzsche's Revaluation of Values: A study in Strategies,* pp. 30, 58. See also Detwiler, *Nietzsche and the Politics of Aristocratic Radicalism,* p. 21. He cites Nietzsche as saying, "there is *only* a perspec-tive seeing, *only* a perspective knowing." Italics in text.

13. Detwiler, *Nietzsche and the Politics of Aristocratic Radicalism,* p. 25.

14. Nietzsche, *Beyond Good and Evil,* p. 110, sec. 188.

15. Ibid., p. 37, sec. 6. Italics in text.

16. Ibid., p. 111, sec. 188.

17. Ibid., p. 111, sec. 188. Italics in text.

18. Ibid., p. 111, sec. 188.

19. E.E. Sleinis, *Nietzsche's Revaluation of Values: A Study in Strategies,* p. 58.

20. Nietzsche, *Beyond Good and Evil,* p. 142, sec. 211.

21. Ibid., p. 71, sec. 44.

22. Ibid., pp. 142–43, sec 211. Italics in text.

23. Ibid., p. 195, sec. 260. Italics in text.

24. Ibid., p. 144, sec. 212. Emphasis is mine.

25. Ibid., p. 156, sec. 227. Italics in text.

26. Ibid., p. 200. sec. 262. Italics in text.

27. Ibid., p. 200, sec. 200.

28. E.E. Sleinis, *Nietzsche's Revaluation of Values: A Study in Strategies,* p. 61.

29. Nietzsche, *Beyond Good and Evil,* p. 197, sec. 260.

30. Ibid., p. 197, sec. 260. Also on the issue of universal values, see E.E. Sleinis, *Nietzsche's Revaluation of Values: A Study in Strategies,* pp. 61–62.

31. Nietzsche, *Beyond Good and Evil,* p. 197, sec. 260. Italics in text.

32. Ibid., p. 197, sec. 260. Italics in text.

33. Ibid., p. 193, sec. 259.

34. Ibid., pp. 193–94, sec 259. Italics in text.

35. Ibid., p. 194, sec. 259. Italics in text.

36. Ibid., p. 194, sec. 259. Italics in text.

37. Ibid., p. 192, sec. 257.

38. Ibid., p. 193, sec. 258. Italics in text.

39. Ibid., p. 123, sec. 201; and Sleinis, *Nietzsche's Revaluation of Values: A Study in Strategies,* p. 87.

40. Nietzsche, *Beyond Good and Evil,* p. 72, sec. 43.

41. Ibid., p. 144, sec. 212.

42. For a good account of Nietzsche's history of slave morality, see Bruce Detwiler, *Nietzsche and the Politics of Aristocratic Radicalism,* pp. 119–25.

43. Friedrich Nietzsche, *On the Genealogy of Morals,* in *The Classics of Moral and Political Theory,* edited by Michael L. Morgan, (Indianapolis: Hackett Publishing Co., 1992), pp. 1245, 1243.

44. Ibid., p. 1243.

45. Ibid., p. 1245.

46. Ibid., p. 1243. Italics in text.

47. Ibid., p. 1243.

48. Ibid., p. 1250.

49. Ibid., p. 1250. Italics in text.

50. Bruce Detwiler, *Nietzsche and the Politics of Aristocratic Radicalism,* p. 122.

51. Nietzsche, *On the Genealogy of Morals,* p. 1254.

52. Nietzsche, *Beyond Good and Evil,* p. 125, sec. 202. Italics in text.

53. Ibid., pp. 125–26, sec. 202.

54. Ibid., p. 125, sec. 202.

55. Ibid., p. 137, sec. 208.

56. Bruce Detwiler, *Nietzsche and the Politics of Aristocratic Radicalism,* pp. 174–75.

57. Nietzsche, *Beyond Good and Evil,* p. 173, sec. 242. Italics in text.

58. Ibid., p. 138, sec. 208. Italics in text.

59. E. E. Sleinis, *Nietzsche's Revaluation of Values: A Study in Strategies,* p. 123.

60. Ibid., p. 146–47, also, pp. 128–31.

61. Nietzsche, *On the Genealogy of Morals,* p. 1257. Italics in text.

62. Ibid., p. 1257. Italics in text.

63. Bruce Detwiler, *Nietzsche and the Politics of Aristocratic Radicalism,* p. 124.

64. Nietzsche, *On the Genealogy of Morals,* p. 1258.

65. Ibid., pp. 1260–61.

66. Ibid., p. 1261.

67. Ibid., p. 1261.

68. Ibid., p. 1261.

69. Ibid., p. 1261.

70. Ibid., pp. 1271–72.

71. Ibid., p. 1271. Italics in text.

72. Ibid., p. 1271.

73. Ibid., p. 1271.

74. Ibid., p. 1272.

75. Ibid., p. 1257. Italics in text. Also, see Detwiler, *Nietzsche and the Politics of Aristrocratic Radicalism,* p. 124.

76. James Miller, *The Passion of Michel Foucault,* (London: Simon & Schuster, 1993), pp. 69–70.

77. Michel Foucault, "What Is Enlightenment?" in *Foucault Reader,* edited by Paul Rabinow, (New York: Pantheon Books, 1984), pp. 42–43, 50.

78. Michel Foucault, "Space, Knowledge, Power," in *Foucault Reader,* p. 249.

79. Michel Foucault, "Politics and Reason," in *Michel Foucault, Politics, Power, Culture,* ed. Lawrence D. Kritzman, (New York: Routledge, 1988), pp. 83–84.

80. Miller, *The Passion of Michel Foucault,* pp. 219–23.

81. Michel Foucault, *Discipline and Punish,* trans. Alan Sheridan, (New York: Pantheon Books, 1977), pp. 23–24.

82. Ibid., pp. 3, 58.

83. Ibid., pp. 73–74.

84. Ibid., pp. 200–201.

85. Ibid., p. 205.

86. Ibid., p. 205.

87. Ibid., p. 209.

88. Michel Foucault, "On Power," in *Michel Foucault, Politics, Power, Culture,* p. 105.

89. Michel Foucault, edited by Mark Blasius, "About the Beginning of the Hermeneutics of the Self," *Political Theory,* 21:2, May, 1993, pp. 203–4.

90. Ibid., p. 204.

91. Alexander Nehamas, "Subject and Abject," *New Republic,* Feb. 15, 1993, p. 33.

92. Foucault, "What Is Enlightenment?" p. 50.

93. Michel Foucault, *The Care of The Self: The History of Sexuality,* Volume 3, (New York: Vintage Books, 1988), pp. 60–62.

94. Ibid., pp. 62–64.

95. Ibid., p. 61.

96. Ibid., p. 64.

97. Michel Foucault, "On Genealogy of Ethics," in *Foucault Reader,* p. 368.

98. Nehamas, "Subject and Abject," p. 34.

99. Foucault, *The Care of The Self: The History of Sexuality,* p. 238.

100. Ibid., pp. 238–39.

101. Foucault, "On Genealogy of Ethics," in *Foucault Reader,* p. 368.

102. Michel Foucault, "Social Security," in *Michel Foucault, Politics, Power, Culture,* pp. 167–68.

103. Ibid., p. 168.

Partial Bibliography and Further Reading

Detwiler, Bruce. *Nietzsche and the Politics of Aristocratic Radicalism.* Chicago: University of Chicago Press, 1990.

Foucault, Michel. "About the Beginning of the Hermeneutics of the Self," edited by Mark Blasius. *Political Theory,* 21:2, May, 1993.

———. *The Care of The Self: The History of Sexuality,* Volume 3. New York: Vintage Books, 1988.

———. *Discipline and Punish,* trans. Alan Sheridan. New York: Pantheon Books, 1977.

———. *Michel Foucault, Politics, Power, Culture,* ed. Lawrence D. Kritzman. New York: Routledge, 1988.

———. *Foucault Reader,* edited by Paul Rabinow. New York: Pantheon Books, 1984.

Hayman, Ronald. *Nietzsche.* New York: Routledge, 1999.

Hunt, Lester H. *Nietzsche and the Origin of Virtue.* London: Routledge, 1990.

Kariel, Henry S. *In Search of Authority: Twentieth-Century Political Thought.* New York: Free Press, 1972.

Love, Nancy Sue. *Marx, Nietzsche, and Modernity.* New York: Columbia University Press, 1986.

Magnus, Kathleen M. et. al. Edited. *The Cambridge Companion to Nietzsche.* Cambridge: Cambridge University Press, 1996.

Mahon, Michael. *Foucault's Nietzschean Genealogy: Truth, Power, and the Subject.* Albany: State University of New York Press, 1992.

Miller, James. *The Passion of Michel Foucault.* London: Simon & Schuster, 1993.

Nehamas, Alexander. "Subject and Object," *New Republic,* Feb. 15, 1993.

Racevskis, Karlis. *Critical Essays on Michel Foucault.* New York: G. K. Hall, 1999.

Sleinis, E. E. *Nietzsche's Revaluation of Values: A Study in Strategies.* Urbana: University of Illinois Press, 1994.

Strong, Tracy B. *Friedrich Nietzsche and the Politics of Transfiguration.* Berkeley: University of California Press, 1988.

Thiele, Leslie Paul. *Friedrich Nietzsche and the Politics of the Soul: A Study of Heroic Individualism.* Princeton: Princeton University Press, 1990.

Warren, Mark. *Nietzsche and Political Thought.* Cambridge: MIT Press, 1988.

———. "Nietzsche and Political Philosophy." *Political Theory,* 13 (May 1985).

17

FEMINIST RESPONSES
TO CIVIL SOCIETY

I. THE PUBLIC AND THE PRIVATE

Discussions of civil society in the last part of this book showed a continuing tension between the individual as rights holder who has the freedom to determine his or her own way of life and the individual as citizen who must accept the guidance of the norms of civic virtue. Further, this tension suggests two important realms in which individuals carry out their lives. First, there is the public realm, a common world, whether that of the market or of the workplace or of the political setting. In the public realm, individuals interact with each other to purchase or to sell goods, to make a living, or to help make public policy. The private realm is the setting of friends, family, religion, sexual relations, and voluntary associations.

When individuals enter the public realm to pursue their own self-determined ends, they may carry with them the values of the private realm and promote them, in some sense, in the public setting. Thus, at work, people may request days off for religious holidays. Or when they participate in addressing political questions, they may take positions that manifest the moral orientations taught them in their religion. For instance, those whose religious traditions require them to disavow abortion may take this point of view into the political setting when discussing abortion policy. To be sure, the nature of the public/private dichotomy is such that individuals must be governed, no matter what their private values may be, by common public norms that are applicable to all citizens. In a civil society, accepting common norms means that all must respect the rights of all other citizens. Owing to this commitment, then, persons must accept limits on how far they can press their private values in the public realm. For instance, a civil society could not protect the rights of all if one religion were imposed onto all members of the society. Thus, although it may be possible for a person to promote in the public realm a particular religious orientation on the abortion question, it would not be acceptable as part of this effort to demand that the state make *one* religion the predominant religion for all citizens. Finally, in a civil society, the public/private-realm relationship presumes that the private realm must teach people to respect the norms of public life. Respect for the rights of others must be stressed within the private settings of church, family, and other groups or associations that are entered into voluntarily.

The public/private dichotomy becomes associated with injustice and unfairness when it is conceived as a relationship that prevents individuals from participating fully in society. Our discussion of feminism in this chapter like our discussion of Marxism in Chapter 15 will examine the claim that the private realm in a civil society is designed to exclude from the public realm whole groups of people. In the case of feminism, the people excluded are women, and the reason for this outcome is gender, and in the case of Marxism, the people excluded are workers, and the reason is class.

II. THE SILENCING OF WOMEN

Major examinations of the history of political theory have been written in recent years demonstrating the way in which the relationships between the public and the private realms in the history of political theory have been designed to deny women a chance for full participation in the public realm. Jean Bethke Elshtain says in *Public Man, Private Woman* that, in large part, the history of political thinking demonstrates a commitment on the part of political thinkers to refuse to recognize that women have a legitimate place in the public realm.[1] Elshtain's analysis of the history of political theory shows how, in political theory, women are located in the private realm, where they are connected to "sexuality, natality, the human body (images of uncleanness and taboo, visions of dependency, helplessness, vulnerability)."[2] Alternatively, the public realm affords women no ability to participate fully as equals with men. Indeed, the public realm exhibits a tendency to define and to limit the private realm in such a way that women's voices go unheard in the political world. "Politics is in part an elaborate defense against the tug of the private, against the lure of the familial, against evocations of female power."[3]

The political implications of this view for women are unmistakable. A civil society is supposed to be a contract that provides the same rights to all citizens. But on Carole Pateman's reading of the social contract formulated for civil society by modern thinkers, in actuality, civil society is designed as a contract among men, a fraternal contract, which excludes women from any significant role in the public realm and which defines their lives as occupying a subordinate relationship to men politically, socially, and economically.[4] The fraternal social contract, in essence, maintains a patriarchy, details of which we outline in Section IV when we discuss another of Pateman's influential books, *The Sexual Contract*.[5]

Before moving to this task, it is well to provide some further details about the way feminist authors understand how the tradition of political theory has conceptualized the public realm. For this purpose, I want to discuss two thinkers of fundamental importance to the idea of a civil society, Hegel and John Stuart Mill. The feminist critiques of these two writers we describe here are important because they demonstrate how even thinkers committed to the idea of providing equal rights to all, as civil society proponents must of course do, can end up with a conception of women's role in the society that denies to women an adequate stake in the public realm where they can take full advantage of these rights.

III. POLITICAL THEORY AND THE FEMINIST CRITIQUE: HEGEL AND MILL

Hegel, in the *Philosophy of Right,* said that a woman's "destiny" is in the family, and that "family piety is her ethical frame of mind."[6] For Elshtain, this means that in Hegel, as between husband and wife, only the man is capable of being fully integrated into the rational setting of the state, including the public structures such as the economy and corporations. This fact enables men to enter the public world as workers, as political actors, and as private persons to achieve self-defined ends. On the other hand, women lack a similar opportunity because their identities are located in and largely based upon the role requirements they assume as wives and mothers.[7] Women have an ethical significance only insofar as they are wives and mothers, contributing to their husbands' and their sons' participation in the public world of civil society. A woman's value is derived from her being connected to a man who allows her to perform the role of wife and mother. In consequence, women are not capable of or even interested in articulating their own interests as particular individuals who seek access to the public world of work and politics in order to fulfill these interests.

On this view, women exist to help support men as the latter enter the public realm and engage in the many activities offered there. But it would seem less appropriate for women to have roles similar to men. The question of whether women should have the same role as men does not arise in a setting in which it is taken for granted that women do not need or demand such a role. And indeed, by defining society in the way Hegel does, the question of how to extend the public realm to women does not become a question of fundamental importance or interest.

John Stuart Mill took the position that women should be given the chance to participate in the public realm in the same manner as men. Mill in his essay, *The Subjection of Women,* argued that the principle of equality, "admitting no power or privilege on the one side, nor disability on the other," ought to be the primary basis for regulating relationships between the sexes.[8] For Mill, however, women are treated much like slaves, with men acting as their masters. While slavery of the male sex has been abolished, slavery of the female sex "has gradually changed into a milder form of dependence."[9] Female subordination is maintained through a system of socialization and control whose focal point is the family, which, to maintain male control, is designed as a "school of despotism," "in which the virtues of despotism, but also its vices, are largely nourished."[10] This situation, by not teaching democratic values to children, not only hinders the progress toward democracy in the larger society,[11] but it imperils the prospects of women's full intellectual development, making women into people who manifest "feebleness and childishness of character."[12] Moreover, this condition is also harmful for men, because, when a man is married to a woman of "inferior intelligence," the husband "finds her a perpetual dead weight, or, worse than a dead weight, a drag, upon every aspiration of his to be better than public opinion requires him to be."[13] A good marriage, a marriage between equals, allows mutual respect because each sees the other as contributing to the development of their higher faculties.[14]

For Mill, as we saw in his discussions of *On Liberty,* society's main objective should be securing freedom for each person because it is only as a free person that an individual can be elevated as a "moral, spiritual, and social being." If this objective is to be realized for women and men both, then women must be treated equally with men.[15] Mill suggested that women should be able to take part in public life, engaging in public affairs and the professions.[16] But at the same time that Mill advocated this position, he also contended that women should have the right to stay at home and to uphold the traditional roles of wife and mother. Indeed, for Mill, choosing marriage suggests that a woman "makes a choice of the management of a household, and the bringing up of a family, as the first call upon her exertions, during as many years of her life as may be required for that purpose; and that she renounces, not all other objectives and occupations, but all which are not consistent with the requirement of this."[17]

Susan Moller Okin criticizes Mill in voicing this view because this position assumes the "immutability of the family structure." Okin argues that Mill failed to "discuss its [the family structure's] repercussions for the lives of women," and this failure "constitutes a gap in this feminist thought which the current feminist movement is attempting to remedy."[18] Of concern to Okin is that, even though Mill accepts the idea that women should be able to support themselves financially, he nonetheless rejected in *The Subjection of Women* the "idea that they should do so," because he felt that this practice would harm women's ability to perform their roles as wives and mothers. Moreover, even though Mill realized that the family is a barrier to women's having professional success, he "condones the continuance of this barrier for most women." He does not discuss, for instance, the sharing of household duties as a way to enable women to enter the public realm.[19] Although Mill suggested full participation in public life by women, Okin claims that Mill's acceptance of traditional family settings "places serious limitation on the extent to which he can apply the principles of freedom and equality to married women."[20] In a similar fashion, Elshtain points out that the equality that Mill hoped to reproduce in the family cannot be achieved when he embraced a "traditional division of labor *within* the family based on males' being actively employed *outside* the home."[21]

Even for a thinker such as Mill, who wanted to usher women into the public realm as equals with men, the main problem Mill leaves unattended is the need to reconfigure the private realm in a way that permits women full participation in society. A similar lack of attention to the family in today's society may have the same result for women. In particular, the family setting, instead of being a place that is based on a sharing of duties so that each adult partner can partake in the public realm, becomes a barrier to women's access to the public realm. Unfortunately the perspectives of writers such as Mill and Hegel cannot help modern readers adequately understand and critique such situations. And this is precisely why feminist critiques of writers such as Mill and Hegel are important. With the feminist perspective in hand, it is possible to point out how modern civil society fails to live up to its commitment to promote equality for women, and, as a result, we are in a better position to propose remedies. Using the feminist perspective in the next section, we discuss Pateman's sexual contract, and in the sections that follow we discuss, again using this perspective, various approaches to making possible a public realm that welcomes women as equals and a private realm that supports this endeavor.

IV. PATEMAN AND OKIN ON PATRIARCHY

Both Hegel's and Mill's arguments suggest an inability to come to grips with what Pateman called the *sexual contract,* the condition symbolized by men's patriarchal power over women. Here, men, in establishing civil society, do so from a perspective that suggests that women do not have the same "attributes and capacities" as men. Men use this argument to establish a society that guarantees them civil freedom or basic rights. At the same time, women are made subject to men's patriarchal authority.[22] The result of this endeavor is that women are denied the same rights that men have. In this section, I will demonstrate some of the details of the sexual contract, first by referring to elements of Pateman's view of it and then turning to discuss Okin's statement of the problem.

For Pateman, there is sexual division of labor in a civil society governed by an ethos of patriarchy. In discussing the nature of work, for instance, Pateman argues that women, in the modern patriarchal system, become dependents of men. The first sign of this appears when women obtain their means of support from their husbands. "She is dependent on the benevolence of her husband and can only endeavour to obtain a 'good master.'"[23] This relationship is manifested throughout society. Indeed, in the modern setting of civil society, where women have a juridical standing that is equal to that of men, women, nonetheless, do not enjoy the same status or opportunity as male workers. Free workers, that is most men, can enter the labor market and sell their labor to the highest bidder. But the unfree worker, in this case the housewife, lacks "jurisdiction over the property in her person, which includes [her] labour power."[24] A wife cannot contract out her labor power to her husband and earn a wage from him, and so the labor of the women becomes a form of "domestic service."[25]

One reason given for providing males the status of free workers, who can sell their labor on the market, is to ensure that they will be able to make enough money to support their families. However, increasingly in the modern civil society, it is the case that men cannot support their families by themselves and in consequence women must enter the public world of work, also.[26] But when women enter the marketplace to work, what they discover is an "aristocracy" of male laborers. This fraternity not only determines when and whether a wife will work, but, when wives work, the best and highest paying jobs are reserved for men. Moreover, the working wife finds herself in a position where, in addition to receiving lower wages than her male counterpart, when she returns home at the end of the day most of the household and child-rearing duties remain her responsibility.[27]

Patriarchy is a pervasive fact of modern civil society, not only for Pateman, but for other writers as well. For instance, for Susan Okin male domination manifests itself in open violence against women within the family, a reality now taking place in epidemic proportions. Civil society no longer legally tolerates violence against women, unlike in the past when husbands were permitted by law to "chastise" their wives, but male violence against women continues unabated anyway.[28] Moreover, it is a myth to claim that the public/private dichotomy requires that the state not interfere in the family life. In point of fact, the state interferes in the family setting on behalf of maintaining unjust male power structures when it refuses to create laws banning marital rape and when it has not, until recently, accorded women the independence they need by permitting them the same rights in the workplace, in the marketplace, and in politics that are provided to men.[29] Further, a male-dominated public sphere, which affords greatly reduced life options (in comparison with men) for women, is replicated time and again through a socialization process that continually teaches young girls to identify with the nurturing role of the mother. In this context girls, unlike boys, are not taught to hold aspirations that orient them to demand full participation in the public realm. Finally, in the public sphere women's claims are not given the same legitimacy accorded to the claims men make. One example of this reality is gender bias in the courts where women, particularly in matters involving their vital interests, such as in domestic violence, alimony, or child-support issues, are not taken seriously.[30]

The question I want to address for the rest of this chapter pertains to how both the public and the private realms should be reconfigured so that the goals of a civil society can be met for all, permitting women to participate fully in public life. In the following sections of this chapter, my intention is to demonstrate several different approaches articulated by different feminists to reconceptualizing both the public and the private. Here, it must be clear that feminist critiques of civil society contain different voices. The views that we will discuss include a liberal conception found in Okin, a view of female empowerment found in Catharine MacKinnon, a humanist discourse view found in Elshtain, a Marxist view found in Nancy Hartsock, and a Nietzschean perspective advocated by Camille Paglia.

V. OKIN AND THE NON-GENDERED VIEWPOINT: THE LIBERAL CONCEPTION

Okin's approach to reconceptualizing the public and the private realms steps off from Rawls's conception of the original position. As was demonstrated in Chapter 13, Rawls created a hypothetical perspective, called the *original position,* from which to determine principles of justice that all members of the society would support. In the original position, the parties are rational, and although no one knows one's particular circumstances, including the nature of one's talents, skills, and potential in actual society, all know the general facts about the way society works and is structured. From this point of view, the members of the original position must determine the principles of justice that should guide how the basic goods of society, including rights and liberties, are to be distributed. Okin's problem with Rawls's view is that he does not include in his discussion of the general facts the issue of gender and how gender structures society in ways to constrict women's opportunities.[31] Thus, for Okin, the original position is a powerful tool that allows one to consider "traditions, customs and institutions from all points of view, and [that] ensures that the principles of justice will be acceptable to everyone."[32] The problem, however, is that Rawls does not use the original position to examine "the justice of the gender system," which has "its roots in the sex roles of the family and its branches extending into virtually every corner of our lives, [and which] is one of the fundamental structures of society."[33]

In formulating and applying principles of justice, the parties in the original position should have knowledge of the way in which the gender structure of society disadvantages women.[34] This understanding is called by Okin the "standpoint of women." Okin's intention in including the standpoint of women is to ask that it be fully considered by all parties in the original position, men and women alike. When deliberation takes place on these terms, a fair set of principles can then be derived. As Okin says, "the notion of the standpoint of women, while not without its problems, suggests that a fully human moral and political theory can be developed only with the full participation of both sexes. At the very least, this will require that women take their place with men in the dialogue in approximately equal numbers and in positions of comparable influence."[35]

The revised original position, which included consideration of the "standpoint of women," would make it clear that Rawls's principles of justice "are inconsistent with a gender-structured society and with traditional family roles."[36] This suggests for Okin that Rawls's principles of justice would stipulate that gender could no longer be made the basis for apportioning positions and opportunities either inside the family or outside of it. Women should not have to bear the lion's share of the responsibility for household and child-care duties, but these responsibilities should be shared, permitting women to have as many unrestricted choices for public sphere activity as men have. Included in this concern are not just fair opportunities for careers, but opportunities for full political participation, as well. Finally, the commitment to self-respect, so central to Rawls's conception of justice, is not made possible in a society where, owing to gender-caused social and economic inequalities, girls are forced to play servile roles to males.[37]

Okin's position is typical of liberal conceptions of civil society. Each person is to be given the same rights, and any and every obstacle to individuals utilizing them, such as gender or race, must be eliminated. Thus, in formulating public policies so that they are in keeping with the principles of justice in Rawls's thought, or the provision of equal liberties for all, it would be necessary that "public policies and laws should generally assume no social differentiation of the sexes."[38] This means then that Okin's addition of the female point of view leads here to promote a *gender-neutral* perspective. The central idea of this perspective is that individuals are not to be accorded rights by virtue of their gender status. Or to use other terms, to say that individuals are to be accorded the same rights is to say that no rights should be accorded to any one individual that are not accorded to all individuals.

A few examples of the impact of a gender-neutral approach to the provision of rights are in order. First, the private realm would be reconstituted to include shared responsibility for child care. To support this objective, there would have to be high-quality, subsidized day care, as well as workplace policies that support equal responsibility for child rearing.[39] In this context, women as well as men would be able to enter the public realm of work without fear that their chances for success at work would be harmed by the fact of their having children and a family. In particular, women's chances for advancement in a company or profession would not be impeded by their taking a childbirth leave. Moreover, women and men, both, should be given chances for parental leave during post-birth months.[40] This policy would permit men as well as women to take full part in child rearing without harm to their career development. Further, the educational system must be designed to teach children about the difficulties that present inequalities pose for women throughout the society. Unless children are educated to the problems women face, reforming the public and private realms so that women and men will be treated equally in both will be difficult to achieve. Further, the problem of the missing father, now rampant throughout society, must be resolved so that all children have a fair chance in society. This means identifying missing fathers and ensuring they pay support, and when they are unable to pay support, the government must provide backup aid. After a divorce, the family standard of living of either spouse should not suffer serious loss. Only then will all children have a fair chance in life.[41]

Also, Okin wants to ensure equal legal entitlement of both spouses in a marriage to all family earnings. To this end, employers should divide paychecks so that half of the money goes to the wife (or husband if the husband is staying at home while the wife works) and the other half to the husband (or to the wife, if the wife is the main wage earner). This plan would provide money to women, directly, for their labor in the house, and thus women would no longer remain as unpaid laborers in a male-dominated household.[42] Direct payment to women of part of their husbands' earnings would enable women to have greater independence from their husbands, an independence that would permit them freer access to the public realm of work and politics.

In conclusion, the objective of a gender-neutral, equal-rights-for-all approach to the family would secure full access for women to the public realm while at the same time expecting men and women, both, to share equally in the burdens of child rearing and housework.

VI. MacKinnon: Female Empowerment

Catharine MacKinnon rejects the gender-neutral approach advocated by Okin and argues that it is necessary, before rights can be made equal for both sexes, to correct those underlying power relationships in society that define women as subordinate to men. Until this transformation can occur, merely providing equal rights to women will never work to overcome the subordination they experience on a daily basis.[43] She argues that "abstract equality of liberalism permits most women little more than does the substantive inequality of conservatism."[44] The solution MacKinnon urges is one that overcomes the reality of social and political relationships that deny women equal status to men. Then women will "participate in defining the terms that create the standards [and they will have a] voice in drawing the lines."[45]

For MacKinnon, then, a liberal conception of individual rights is blind to the fact that in order to have the full legal rights the state grants, persons must be free socially from any kind of impediment that would make it impossible for them to make full use of these rights. For instance, what good are the rights of speech, opportunity, and private property, to say nothing of due process of law, if the person granted these rights lacks the characteristics that enable a person to make full use of them? Here, a familiar contrast can be made between the plight of poor and rich people who are accused of murder and who seek to clear themselves in a court of law. Many think that a poor person accused of murder cannot get just as good an opportunity to defend him- or herself in a court of law as a millionaire can. And the reason is lack of money. Money buys lawyers skilled in manipulating the judicial system in ways that give their clients an advantage. By analogy, this fact of life extends to women's rights. One can argue that even with laws that provide women equality of opportunity, how can women make good use of these laws when men are ever present throughout a woman's career finding ways to legally deny her her due? To overcome these barriers, women need the kind of social and political power that enables them to remove men from their paths, so that they can make full use of the opportunities they are entitled to. MacKinnon says, "no one who does not already have them [rights] socially is granted them legally."[46]

But as long as men can structure social relationships so that women are always subordinate—that is, have the worst jobs, have to perform the lion's share of the housework, and so on—the social reality women experience will be one that makes them unequal in power and stature to men. How can women be liberated from this situation? This question is particularly difficult to answer in view of the fact that, for MacKinnon, the power relationships that suppress women in civil society are not only pervasive, but they are in fact "invisible." Here, social relationships, specifically designed to place women in bondage to men, are considered by most members of society to be "just the way things are."[47] Women's lives, as subordinate to men, are viewed as a reality that cannot be changed. In this case, women are bound by chains that, unlike the chains of traditional slaves, are invisible. If one cannot see the chains that must be broken in order to free the enslaved person, how can one be freed? More to the point, if there are no visible chains holding one down, how can one even say one is unfree?

This terrible situation for women emerges from the way men have chosen to see and to experience women, and what best symbolizes men's oppressive view of women is pornography. MacKinnon says that "men's power over women means that the way men see women defines who women can be. Pornography is this way."[48] The most important objective on the male agenda as they go about defining women is to put women in a situation in which they are objects of male sexual satisfaction. Indeed, pornography carries out this objective when it "defines women by how we look according to how we can be sexually used. Pornography codes how to look at women, so you know what you can do with one when you see one."[49]

Here, a woman's identity stems from men's making women into an "under-class," who "become objects for male sexual use."[50] Gender, as it is defined for women by men, refers to men's need to control women's bodies for men's pleasures, and for this reason men maintain a dominant position toward women.[51] In keeping with this view of gender, "pornography turns a woman into a thing to be acquired and used."[52] But ironically, the abuse of women in the setting of pornography does not suggest a state of affairs that women are said to reject. Indeed, women are depicted in hard-core pornographic situations as wanting to be bound and as enjoying being viciously assaulted and even murdered. Soft-core pornography depicts women as desirous of being made the objects of male sexual pleasure.[53] In either case, pornography depicts women as never having enough abuse thrown their way because they can never have enough of the sexual "pleasure" that comes from such an experience. Men, by sexualizing the subjugation of women, then, create the illusion that women enjoy their inferior status. In consequence, women are really not like slaves in the old South, many of whom hoped to flee their masters, but women willingly accept their inequality without a hint of frustration with it. Not only are women kept in bondage to men through these means, but the fact that they are in bondage is no cause for concern for society as a whole, and thus there is no need to discuss how to create equality of power between men and women in society. Pornography suggests that women's natural role is bondage, a role that women accept, and thus the call for liberation makes no sense.

For MacKinnon, as for all reasonable people, this viewpoint represents an absolute outrage and a tragedy of great proportions. After all, we live in a society dedicated to the freedom for all, but even as we say this we accept terrible forms of terror aimed at over half the people in society. To change this situation, it is necessary to unmask and to expose the harm that pornography inflicts on women. MacKinnon thinks that any work of pornography is designed to define the way men see women as powerless individuals to be used for men's needs.[54] Thus, an analysis of the impact of pornography is important because it is a form of activity by which men legitimize real harm to women, harm that prevents women as a class from full participation in the public realm. Indeed, the list of the kinds of harm that pornography is associated with is very long. For instance, in MacKinnon's view, pornography harms women who make the pornographic films. These women are nothing more than sexual slaves, often forced against their will to perform a variety of harmful and crude acts.[55] Pornography is associated with physical assaults on women, including rapes.[56] Pornography harms men's ability to relate to women as human beings with authentic needs and emotions. Instead, when women are looked at through the lens of pornography they are merely playthings in vicious and barbaric male fantasies.[57]

Overall, for MacKinnon, pornography is a practice that maintains the continued subordination of women to men in the most brutal ways possible. We must liberate women from this terrible, oppressive institution. But how? This will be a difficult question to answer because presently pornography is not viewed as a civil rights violation in the same way racial discrimination is a violation of the rights of African-Americans. Yet, for MacKinnon in order for women to make political and human progress, it is necessary to "define pornography as a practice of sex discrimination, a violation of women's civil rights, the opposite of sexual equality."[58]

But in a modern, liberal civil society, the protection of free speech is always used to counter the claim that pornography is a civil rights violation. To counter this view, MacKinnon, with Andrea Dworkin, wrote an anti-pornography law that was passed by the Indianapolis City government. The law would have allowed a person who proved harm from pornography to seek civil damages from its distributor or its producer. The U.S. Court of Appeals overturned this law on the basis of the First Amendment protection of speech.[59]

This example manifests a general tendency of the courts to view pornography as "only words," which may defame women but do not discriminate against them.[60] Words bespeak ideas that can offend, but offensive words do not necessarily harm. But in MacKinnon's view these words are not just ideas; they represent harmful social practices that deny women their full entitlements as citizens, and, moreover, these words allow activities that brutalize and terrorize women. In short, pornographic language symbolizes a system of power, just like the system of segregation in the old South, which renders women unequal and powerless to men.[61] For this reason, these words are not just words that defame, but they are words that discriminate, and thus women should be protected from them by laws that guarantee women their civil rights.

Now the question might be asked whether we do not protect women from pornography already with obscenity laws. After all, these laws are at times used to ban what MacKinnon would consider pornography. But MacKinnon argues that obscenity laws are premised on prevailing moral standards, but prevailing moral standards tend to favor the male's continued subordination of women. In consequence, obscenity laws would only reinforce existing pornographic activities.[62] But some would argue in response to MacKinnon that the problem with obscenity laws is not that they represent male standards solely, but that they reflect the quandary of determining what is pornographic from what is not. Is *Playboy* or *Playgirl* magazine pornographic? What about a television show that shows sexual activity? Is this pornographic and should it be banned? Answers to these questions split along many lines, including disagreements among women as well as disagreements among men.

At any rate, for MacKinnon, because pornography is a form of unjust discrimination against women, free-speech provisions should not protect pornography, for, in doing so, what the state does is to permit discrimination based on gender.[63] MacKinnon's approach to empowerment of women, then, is to win the society over to the need to accept that certain words define a social reality for people, including women, that continues to subordinate and to repress them. She would ban, then, child pornography not as the courts have done, on the basis that "if the harm of speech outweighs its value, it can be restricted by properly targeted means," but on the basis that child pornography perpetuates the inequality in power between children and adults.[64] Thus, MacKinnon advocates a new way of discussing the idea of freedom of expression. For her various groups—such as Nazis, Klansmen, and pornographers—would not be accorded absolute freedom of speech, but their speech would be limited for the reason that they seek to harm people who, in the context of the particular circumstances of our history, have been kept in subordinated positions.[65] In this view, then, certain rights, in this case the right to produce pornography, would no longer be protected under the freedom of speech provision.

But a major problem with her view remains. To understand this problem, for the moment put aside the difficulties that MacKinnon's liberal opponents would no doubt raise, such as the issue of defining the nature of pornography, especially when dealing with works of art. Also put aside for the moment the claim some opponents of MacKinnon might make that, to follow MacKinnon, one may end up placing political speech in jeopardy, as well. But even after these issues are put to the side, another critical one remains: namely, will making pornography a civil rights violation be enough to change the power relationships that humiliate women and favor men? This is a question that MacKinnon seems to leave untouched. The next three sections will approach this matter in three radically different ways: one from the standpoint of creating a humanist public discourse, another from the standpoint of a need for a political revolution built along the lines of Marx, and another based upon Nietzschean assumptions.

VII. ELSHTAIN: THE DISCOURSE OF JUSTICE

Elshtain's approach to reconstructing the public/private relationship is to start with the female person's understanding of what is important and meaningful about life. To know women's minds in this way, we must not make them into a product of so-called external social forces, grounded in some abstract theory, but we must move beyond that to learn what constitutes for them, from their own testimony, the fundamental goods that make their lives significant.[66] Knowledge of this sort, itself, comes from discussion and dialogue with women about their lives and about the way the existing circumstances in society are viewed as either helping or hindering their pursuit of what is important to them.

The dialogue that Elshtain has in mind involves women discussing issues, such as abortion rights, over which there is significant disagreement. And this discussion would not be coerced or manipulated, but it would be marked by openness to views some people may not share initially with others in the dialogue. Central to this undertaking is the assumption that many views people have on matters of controversy need "probing and exploratory re-examination." This undertaking is designed to encourage people, through discussion, to examine "unreflectively" held positions.[67]

If this discussion took place, what would it tell us about the nature of the way women see life and what would the consequences be for a reformulating of the public and the private? A main objective of this dialogue would be to realize and to make a part of public life the different point of view, from men, that women bring to issues of morality and politics. On this point, Elshtain embraces the views of Carol Gilligan who, in Elshtain's words, said that the moral lives of women are grounded in a "concern for others, responsibility, care, and obligation, and hence, a moral language profoundly at odds with formal, abstract models of morality defined in terms of absolute principles."[68] Elshtain's support of Gilligan suggests an ethics of care and of responsibility, which we need to discuss more fully.

It is Gilligan's view that women approach moral issues from the standpoint of an ethics of care or responsibility, and this orientation to social problems suggests that women form their identities through activities that seek to maintain affiliations to others.[69] Men, by contrast, approach others from the standpoint of a quest to realize equality, or a situation in which everyone is treated the same, in accordance with a shared conception of rights and basic moral principles. In doing so, men must approach others from the standpoint of intellectual objectivity and detachment, for without these qualities the system of rights and principles men seek to realize would be jeopardized by emotional bias. But to achieve detachment, it is necessary to deny centrality of place to values that women emphasize, such as caring for others. In consequence, men place less importance on retaining attachments to others, and thus male identity is more associated with separation and the absence of the deep connections to others that women seek.[70]

Thus, men and women speak in different voices; women speak in a language of care and responsibility, and men use a language of abstract rules and rights. Elshtain, in following Gilligan, would like to make certain that the discourse she, Elshtain, establishes, includes the female voice, thereby encompassing men in the ethic of care and responsibility, too.

This viewpoint would be central to understanding why the family for women and men is so important for society. The family is critical to maintaining in children a sense of their humanness. Indeed, by providing loving care and nurturing, the family setting develops and furthers the best human capacities in us. A childhood based upon love develops in children a sense of empathy, pity, and compassion. Without these qualities, individuals, when they become adults, lose their "capacity for human identification." But these important qualities, which are critical to a society seeking to uphold the dignity and freedom of others, can be developed only within the context of the special relationships of family life.[71]

So the feminist argument Elshtain provides demands that women and men work to strengthen the family. To do so, it is necessary to support the importance of parenting throughout society by resisting the various forces in society that "erode, impoverish, or preclude the flourishing of our most basic human ties."[72] Once we recognize the importance of the family, which is the epitome of the private realm, we can then turn to the public realm.

For Elshtain the public realm consists of the wide diversity of people who make up society and who shape its politics by engaging in a discourse with each other about what is best for the society. "Where any number of citizens is gathered in the name of acting together in common toward ends they debate and articulate in public, there is citizenship."[73] Rights have an important role here. Rights do not emanate so much from a (male) abstract conception of equality as from the need to protect people from the abuses of public authority, so that each can share his or her views with others, during the course of defining common needs.[74]

Moreover, this experience of citizenship is associated with the transformative potential made possible by civic life. When men and women are engaged together in a deliberation to reconfigure the relationship between the public and private realms so that all can be treated with dignity, it is quite likely that men and women will both undergo changes that make full participation in public life for women possible, while enhancing the circumstances of men as well. A feminist outlook that is not open to "the possibility of transformation of men as well as women is deeply nihilistic," and the reason is that such a politics does not "believe in . . . the ideal of genuine mutuality."[75]

Why would the discourse Elshtain urges achieve the transformations she hopes for? Clearly, she presumes that real discourse rests upon a possibility of an ethic of caring, in which individuals willingly listen to each other and attempt to find ways to accommodate legitimate interests. In taking this approach, Elshtain maps out a "politics of compassion" that makes clear that "no good can come from the widespread dehumanization and destruction of others."[76] Indeed, she hopes for a politics that incorporates an ethic of caring and responsibility, in order to create a public realm that rests upon ethical conceptions conducive to citizenship, or a desire on the part of people to support each other in maintaining those conditions that ensure fairness for all. From the standpoint of an ethic of caring, all enduring political issues would be addressed.

> *A clear notion of what ideals and obligations are required to animate an authentic public, an ethical polity, must be adumbrated: authority, freedom, public law, civic virtue, the ideal of the citizen—all those beliefs, habits, and qualities which are integral to a political order.*[77]

Here, following Gilligan, the basis for restoring a civil society that is fair to all, men and women alike, is a context in which people have genuine concern for each other.

An interesting problem naturally emerges from Elshtain's position. She nicely depicts the kind of dialogue, along with the consequences, of a politics that incorporates Gilligan's ethic of care. Such a politics would transform people so that, in a setting of mutual care and compassion, people would build spaces for citizenship, in which there was a common concern to protect the rights and to recognize the needs of others. But a major problem of this approach pertains to what comes first, the institutionalized acceptance of rights or an ethics of care and concern? Can we depend upon the latter to provide a setting that is capable of sustaining rights in a civil society? Or do we need first to have a well-established and well-maintained rights orientation, as manifested in Gilligan's depiction of the male voice? What if the ethics of care is not strong enough to sustain the transformation Elshtain hopes for in people? Then, isn't it best to rely less on a dialogue of compassion and more on the (male, for Gilligan) machinery that abstractly and fairly, in a Hobbesian (male) way, upholds rights? Or are we doomed from the start if we take this approach? Does the failure to allow the female voice its full hearing deny a chance to build spaces for compassion, so necessary for maintaining in people a sense of responsibility for each other?

Or perhaps the two dimensions, rights and caring, are intertwined and mutually reinforcing. As argued in Chapter 1, a civil society is built upon a foundation of respect for both rights, which secure individual choices, and basic civic virtues such as toleration and mutual respect, which maintain a basis for community and the sense of caring that Elshtain advocates.

VIII. HARTSOCK AND THE MARXIST, FEMINIST VIEWPOINT

In the next view, we examine the work of Nancy Hartsock, who, in *Money, Sex and Power*,[78] provides an analysis of the situation women find themselves in from a "feminist standpoint." In developing this standpoint she takes what she considers to be a Marxist approach to analyzing society. In particular, she believes that, by looking at the society from the standpoint of women in the same way that Marx viewed society from the standpoint of the working class, there emerges a "privileged vantage point on male supremacy, a vantage point that can ground a powerful critique of the phallocratic institutions and ideology that constitute the capitalist form of patriarchy."[79] What will this critique demonstrate? Hartsock believes that, as women analyze their experience, they will understand the way in which men structure their relationship of dominance toward women. In this context, not only will women understand these relationships as detrimental and inhuman, but women will realize as a result of this understanding the possibilities for liberation from their oppressive setting. In consequence of this understanding, all ideological arguments used to justify this oppression can no longer be tolerated. In fact, the objects of the oppression, in this case, women as for Hartsock or workers as for Marx, will turn against those who use these justifications to continue the status quo.[80]

So what are the basic components of the class outlook that can be the basis for women as a group forming a powerful political alliance that will radically change the existing structure of society so that women can be liberated fully from their subordinate status?

Her construction of the feminist standpoint takes place within the context of a capitalist society. Here, workers find themselves forced to be producers of commodities for an owner class who monopolizes the profits from the worker's labor and uses these profits to enhance his, the owner's, own status and power in society. A woman not unlike a male is a commodity producer in the society, but, in addition, unlike the male, the woman is also a producer of various services in the family setting, such as housework, nurturing, and so on.[81] In consequence, women not only work more than men, but a large proportion of their work is devoted to tedious labor in the household.[82]

The differentiation of work roles is the basis for extreme conflict between men and women, and this conflict manifests itself in the fact that women, unlike men, are able to develop close communal connections to others. The fact that men are so closely tied to commodity production and women to providing services in the family symbolizes the reality that women are more prone to see themselves as relationally linked to others who depend on them. And the reason for why this happens is simple. Women's work in the home is essential to maintaining the lives of each of the members of the family. Women cook, keep house, take care of children, and so on. These are activities that men, who are engaged in work producing goods in places outside the house, are less familiar with.[83] Women, on the other hand, are tied directly to their families because of the work they must perform in the house. In this role women help others to evolve into mature human beings, and to do so, they must maintain an attitude of nurture and concern.[84]

These relational ties women have to their families are strongly reinforced in girls, but not in boys. Girls learn their role from their mothers who are always present. Boys do not learn their role from their fathers because the father is for the most part absent, and this fact has importance for the way males come to see the world. Boys as a consequence of their socialization are less likely than girls to define the world in terms of direct relational ties. In consequence, boys, unlike girls, tend to separate themselves from others.[85] This experience coincides with a young male's development of his sexual identity. Initially, the young male identifies closely with his mother, but society reminds him through the various institutions of socialization that maleness requires that he separate from his mother. He does so by constructing "barriers to femininity" as for instance when he sees his mother as an "evil creature."[86] Here, the boy constructs his sense of self by establishing a kind of hostile relationship to his mother, but this relationship becomes the prototype for the masculine relationship in general. A male's "construction of self in opposition to unity with the mother . . . sets a hostile and combative dualism at the heart of both the community men construct and the masculinist world view by means of which they understand their lives."[87] This experience is the basis for Hartsock's contention that the developmental paths of boys follow a course in which a boy's identity is a function of the need to define his self in opposition to others. Hartsock argues that this tendency "reverberates throughout the construction of both class society and the masculine world view and results in a deep-going and hierarchical dualism" in which there is a "we versus them" relationship.[88]

The masculine perspective of "we versus them" sets the terms for the way the dominant male voice organizes society. Men define their identities in terms of what they conceive to be a hostile world. "Masculinity must be attained by means of opposition to the concrete world of daily life, by escaping from contact with the female world of the household into the masculine world of politics or public life."[89] By the same token, the relational ties that women engender orient them to seek to break down the "we versus them" mentality and instead move to a situation in which there is a sense of connection and community among people. Indeed, this orientation is the basis for women's exposing the masculine perspective as perverse and in need of transformation.[90] The masculine response to the female aspiration for community is to reject this hope completely. The male has been socialized to separate himself from his mother and from any dimensions of community associated with family life, and this experience is the basis for a "profound lack of empathy and refusal to recognize the very being of another."[91] To prevent women from achieving their communal agenda, men try to isolate women from each other in the hopes of stopping them from building natural communities. To this end, the male structures society so that women are left alone with their children, isolated from the rest of the society. Here, without the connection to and interaction with other women, women work alone in the house, serving others and denying themselves their connection to community. Ultimately, then, the male viewpoint becomes the dominant one, and the activities of women in the family as mothers "mark the transformation of life into death, the distortion of what could have been creative and community activity into oppressive toil, and the destruction of the possibility of community present in women's relational self-definition."[92]

From the feminist standpoint, then, men and women owing to their different work roles have different life experiences, and these experiences are the basis for a radical conflict that leads to the denial of freedom and humanity to women.[93] Given these painful consequences for women, there is a need for "a vast and far-reaching social transformation."[94] What would be the essence of this change? Since the source of the conflict is a ruinous division of labor between men and women, in the new society this division would have to be eliminated. Presumably, then, the entire makeup of the economy would have to be modified to end the division of labor that produces the conflict that is so harmful to women. To accomplish this objective, private property, or the ownership of the industrial context by capitalists, should be abolished, and there will be a need for "seizing the state's power" and for a "lengthy post-revolutionary class struggle."[95]

Hartsock does not describe in rich detail the nature of the new society she hopes for. But she makes clear that she is talking about an event akin to a socialist revolution. Her new society would not accept Mill's approach to change in which the workers end up managing their own factories. For Hartsock, as indicated, private property would be eliminated and the state's power would be seized and used to promote objectives that from her feminist standpoint would be liberating for women. It is not clear how a new system of property ownership or a new "liberated" government would achieve these ends. What is clear is that the new world she hopes to realize will be one in which there are no longer any "institutionalized gender differences" between men and women. Associated with these changes would be the "transformation" of human relationships in society, in a direction that would liberate women from their subordination to men. Indeed, every human relationship will be transformed so that men as well as women would become involved in all the activities associated with maintaining human beings. Included here would be a need to institutionalize the participation of men and women in carrying out child-rearing responsibilities. In this new society, the old division of labor will be replaced with a new approach to work that will free men and women from past forms of class warfare that only harmed women.[96]

In this view, then, Hartsock would not accept Okin's liberal approach to civil society that stressed provision of equal rights for all, irrespective of gender. Okin, for Hartsock, fails to recognize that Okin's approach would not work in a society in which the relationship between men and women is always defined so as to make sure that women are subordinated to the interests of men as a class. The effort to provide rights, applied fairly and equally to all, would be seen by Hartsock as hopeful rhetoric that could never be realized in practice. Until the system that places men and women into different and conflicting work roles is removed, there will be no liberation for women, nor for that matter will there be a chance for women to have equal rights to men.

Further, Hartsock would probably accept MacKinnon's critique that requires redefining the nature of existing uses of rights, such as the freedom of speech doctrine, in the light of the need to give to women social and political power they do not yet have. But to achieve this goal, for Hartsock, it will be necessary to go further than MacKinnon suggests is necessary. Hartsock would agree that women need more power to neutralize the power men have, but she would argue that to attain this power it would be necessary to transform the economic and social relationships in society. And the only way to achieve this objective is not just through efforts to focus on pornography with the hope of unmasking its perverse realities for women, but through a revolution that entirely changes the system of production and the division of labor in society.

Finally, Hartsock would not see in the discourse presented by Elshtain an adequate solution either. Elshtain's discourse does not start from the presumption that men and women occupy different classes, each at odds with the other. Instead, Elshtain expects that discourse can be "transformative," and for this reason a discourse can allow men and women to create a common ethical universe. Elshtain presumes, then, that men and women are capable of listening to each other and working for a world that benefits all. Hartsock, who sees men and women defining themselves as class opponents, would label Elshtain's view naïve.

IX: PAGLIA'S NIETZSCHEAN PERSPECTIVE

Camille Paglia's views represent a Nietzschean approach, and in consequence, as we will see in this section, her views would conflict with the views of those writers just presented. To begin, it should be clear that there is no question that Paglia shares with her feminist colleagues a commitment to provide women the fullest range of life options possible. Equal opportunity is "a crucial ideal that all must support."[97] Indeed, a main objective of her undertaking would be to eliminate the impediments to women's advancement in society.[98] Further, like many liberals, she is committed to permit the broadest possible freedom of speech, and she takes this position in order to protect many lifestyles that otherwise might be denied full expression. In rejecting policies to police speech, then, she "respects and honors the prostitute," permits open availability of pornography, and advocates the fullest possible freedom for gays.[99]

Still, Paglia does not define patriarchy as women's collective enemy. She argues that patriarchy symbolizes the larger culture that men and women share, and this culture has provided women a great deal of freedom. Patriarchy, which is "blamed for everything," after all provided the birth control pill, "which did more to free contemporary women than feminism itself."[100] Moreover, abuses of women such as rape have always been condemned as part of an ethics that is an integral part of a patriarchal culture. Indeed, throughout history, "men have protected women. Men have given women sustenance. Men have died to defend the country for women." Paglia argues, "we must look back and acknowledge what men have done *for women*."[101]

So if patriarchy is not the real nemesis, what is? To understand her answer to this question, it is necessary to describe the general background conditions that, for Paglia, explain a central dynamic that rules and shapes the relationship between men and women. Paglia understands human life to be played out against the backdrop of a struggle between two opposing forces, each of which is integral to our personalities, Apollo and Dionysus. As we demonstrated in our discussion of Nietzsche, Apollo symbolizes a natural human disposition for order, and Dionysus symbolizes a natural counterneed to wreck Apollo's regimen. Paglia says, "Dionysus is energy unbound, mad, callous, destructive, wasteful. Apollo is law, history, tradition, the dignity and safety of custom and form. Dionysus is the *new,* exhilarating but rude sweeping all away to begin again. Apollo is tyrant, Dionysus a vandal."[102]

Paglia builds upon Nietzsche's argument when she suggests that the effort to subdue Dionysus is not always successful. The Western way of understanding views the world not only as Apollo suggests but often as Dionysus demands. Paglia refers to the latter tendency as pagan, and she argues that the Judeo-Christian tradition, which promotes Apollo, is unable to prevent the emergence of Dionysus.[103] The Dionysian impulses from within our own selves constantly seek to break away from a patterned consciousness, and in doing so shatter the structures of ordered life we are supposed to abide by.

The desire to live as our Dionysian passions require is best expressed in our sexuality. We cannot escape looking at others with sexual longing. The norms of Apollo, while trying to limit and to constrain, do not stop us from fantasizing sexual gratification with others. But we are often stopped from fulfilling these fantasies by an Apollonian-imposed regimen. Erotic torment then is inevitable because we cannot completely have what our fantasies point to, nor can we ever stop our desire for the things denied to us. This torment is depicted in various ways in both art and literature.[104] Thus, the so-called Western way of viewing the world is always motivated by a tendency to look for what will satisfy our unending sexual yearnings, irrespective of the ordering norms that orient us to do otherwise. The will to power is never choked to death, but it is always prevalent in our lives, directing, goading, and motivating us to triumph over an ordered, rational life.

For Paglia, gender differences arise not from conventions but from our biologic natures and hormones.[105] We create culture to control and to subdue these hormones, but, owing to our Dionysian desires, there is an ever-recurrent need to overturn these cultural limits. Naturally, then, instead of being Rousseau's peaceful individual in the state of nature, we are depicted by Paglia as raging and filled with anger. Paglia follows the Marquis de Sade and not Rousseau, then, in arguing that deep within all of us is a tempestuous sea, with extraordinary explosive power and force, ready to cause pain and destruction to anything that stands in its way.[106] In this context, men become the natural aggressors. Paglia argues "man is contoured for invasion, while woman remains *the hidden,* a cave of archaic darkness."[107]

Why are men aggressors? In the procreative act, women are clearly the superstars, and men, by comparison, the minor, supporting role players. Women do the greatest and the most creative work in bringing new life into the world. But men are not satisfied with such a minor role in the life process. Thus, Paglia says, "Women have it. Men want it. What is *it?* The secret of life."[108] Women who bear primary responsibility for reproduction represent a "monumental challenge to our understanding."[109] For men, then, sex is a very complicated undertaking. At first it is an act designed to achieve a unique kind of satisfaction, but later it becomes associated with a sense of impotence and loss of significance. Sex signifies to men that they will never gain, through the act of sex itself, control of nature's mysteries. The latter is a domain reserved by nature to women alone. And yet what is more important than the power of creation? Men cannot tolerate being made small players in the creation process, and as a result they demand for themselves the power women have.

It is this experience, and the frustration and the concomitant aggression, that explains why men commit violence against women. Rape must be understood not simply as a crime of violence as most feminists claim it is, but it is a symbol of "male power fighting female power," with the male wanting to appropriate for himself what only the female has: in particular, control over the mysteries of life.[110] This experience explains why men are potential rapists. Men face a continual and perpetual form of injustice that women never know. Yet, it is the protective character of Apollo, located in the laws of society, that seek to save women from the injustice of men who would commit rape.

From the foregoing, it is clear that for Paglia, women, identified with nature, represent the Dionysian instinct.[111] Men rebel against this reality and create systems of order in which to place women and to control them. It is necessary to understand this classic and all-pervasive conflict as the foundation of our culture. Only when we do, can we begin to understand the problems with finding a way for men and women to live together in a setting that secures the fullest freedom possible for each.

How would this understanding or outlook affect our political judgments? For Paglia, we must design policies that respect both Apollonian and Dionysian dimensions by not moving so far in one direction that the other bursts forth with a vengeance that is destructive and harmful to the freedom of everyone.[112] A life that is too much geared to the Dionysian impulses overindulges these impulses, producing nothing but chaos and death. A life that is strictly Apollonian interprets natural desire as wrong and perverted, and it causes the objects of such desire, in particular women, to be treated with violence and hate. Moreover, the life of Apollo is a life of complete denial of our will, a life in which we do whatever we are told, and in the process forfeit whatever freedom and creativity we may have. This way of life must be balanced by a Dionysian orientation, so that we can continue to retain some degree of spontaneity and feeling needed for creativity. For Paglia, then, the challenge is to find a proper balance between Apollo and Dionysus. She says, "we must learn how to make tiny corrections to avoid the uncontrolled swing of the pendulum [from Apollonian to Dionysian] that, over a generation, swept us from Fifties conformism to Sixties rebellion to Seventies excess and the cataclysm of AIDS. We now live with the smell of funeral pyres."[113]

This means to be sure, then, that we are not to wipe away one half of the culture, the Judeo-Christian tradition that stands for Apollo. We must not, however, allow the latter to deny completely the Dionysian dimension that she associates with pagan or pre-Christian tradition.[114] Nietzsche generally believed that we needed to create a new order that would allow the Dionysian impulses to thrive. Paglia in the main, despite her fears just expressed about AIDS, would agree with this view. Thus, her language and mode of argument are often designed to pierce through the barriers of society and of modern ideology that stand against Dionysus. But always, like Nietzsche, she is willing to recognize the need for Apollo, in order to prevent the kind of extreme despair and destruction typified for instance by the AIDS epidemic.

Paglia's view would suggest highlighting a way of life akin to one professed by Nietzsche: in this case, an ethic of extreme individualism. To break the bonds of Apollo, to allow one's instincts free expression, and to avoid destructive forms of self-imposed repression, it would be necessary to allow individuals to contemplate any life they want to engage in, and, subject to individuals not harming others (for Paglia, that is, and not necessarily for Nietzsche), pursue that way of life wherever it leads. This point of view makes pornography a necessary and natural part of life for Paglia. Unlike MacKinnon and Dworkin, who argue that pornography symbolizes rape and the male need to subordinate women, Paglia sees pornography as a need to get in touch with all the desires that nature generates. Nature, forever shrouded in mystery, allows an unruly imagination, which leads us to embrace passionately, ways of life that are clearly not conventional. Continuous and nonconforming desires, as depicted in pornography, are inherent in life. Thus, "far from poisoning the mind, pornography shows the deepest truth about sexuality, stripped of romantic veneer."[115] Indeed, pornography suggests that we have "eternal fires of desire, without fatigue, incapacity, aging or death."[116]

Given this view, for Paglia, MacKinnon is a "totalitarian" who seeks a "risk-free, state controlled world."[117] MacKinnon, by telling women how to approach their own bodies, would deny the liberated individualism that Paglia extols. MacKinnon takes this approach because she is incapable of understanding the "great god Dionysus" who symbolizes the full manifestation of the flesh, in all of its "grandeur and messiness." MacKinnon would, if she could, deny and block what in essence is "life itself."[118]

In the end, Paglia's call to Dionysus is similar to that found in Nietzsche and Foucault. To provide new values to the world, values that help to give substantive meaning and purpose to life, there needs to be the unusual, creative individual, who often stands by herself, defying existing norms, but who, in doing so, manifests the willfulness necessary to create the basis for new ways of seeing and understanding. Such individuals mainly express themselves, as does Paglia, through her art, and in this way, she stands with Nietzsche and Foucault. Barriers to this enterprise are greeted with contempt, but those people deserving special contempt are people who, as advocates of reform, create further barriers to Paglia's undertaking.

Given these views, what would Paglia likely say to the other feminist discussions of civil society touched upon in this chapter? In the first place, Paglia would argue that most feminists are victims of their own ideology. Feminists, in the name of trying to make civil society into a setting that eliminates patriarchy and restores full rights to women, end up failing to grasp the real problems threatening the freedom women seek. Elshtain's and Gilligan's ethic of care would revive civil society by requiring women and men to constrain their needs so that all can relate together in communities of shared responsibility and concern. Paglia would ask whether this point of view does not tend to drown out the unique inner voices of people and force them, for the sake of being pleasant to each other, to subdue their Dionysian instincts.

Okin's gender-neutral argument would create similar difficulties for Paglia. Whereas the idea of a gender-neutral approach as the basis for securing everyone the same rights may be laudable, it may be the case that to achieve this condition people would have to accept common standards and constraints. But in order to do so, many of the yearnings emanating from the Dionysian dimension of life would have to be suppressed. Would the truly unique individual be permitted any voice at all in this setting? Paglia would wonder then whether Okin's position would not reduce all people to the same level of mediocrity so that all can have the same rights.

Hartsock's call for a Marxist revolution to overthrow the capitalist system would be the wrong turn for Paglia. Indeed, Paglia would have to defend capitalism for its encouragement of a full-bodied egoism, which exists at the center of all activities within the market setting. How else is one to manifest a will to power? Indeed, do not Nietzsche's and Paglia's commitment to a will to power lead them both to support an extreme form of bourgeoisie individualism, the very type that Marx identified as the source of all that is wrong with civil society?

How would each of the writers Paglia might have criticized in the way just mentioned respond to Paglia? Elshtain's politics of compassion would tolerate Paglia, but Elshtain would not see Paglia as a vital part of Elshtain's political agenda. Elshtain would ask how anyone professing Paglia's individualism would ever develop relationships of caring and concern that would ground a sense of responsibility on goals and objectives larger than one's own needs. Of course, Paglia would see herself as having an ethic of responsibility, too, but it would differ from Elshtain's and Gilligan's. Paglia, unlike Gilligan and Elshtain, does not predicate her view of responsibility on a notion of empathy. Instead, Paglia wants people to take responsibility for their own lives and not expect the state to do so. This means that the education system should develop our abilities, but that it should not be in the business of trying to make people feel good about themselves. People must accept the fact that their identities are forged only in the context of struggle, just as Nietzsche had argued. When schools try to save people from having to face adversity, they perpetuate a gigantic fraud.[119] A primary mistake in education policy, for instance, is that we have to make life "easy" for people so that they can gain self-esteem.[120]

A good case in point would be Paglia's views on sexual harassment. For instance, Paglia argues that if sexual harassment rules are overdone, they will harm women.[121] Why is this? Women must learn to defend themselves from speech they think offensive. Otherwise, there is no way for women to develop the abilities they must have to succeed in the world of men. And when women are encouraged to rely on sexual harassment claims, they do not develop the hardheadedness and tactical skill that men have learned in order to survive in the world of work. The world of work, after all, is a milieu filled with "traps" of all sorts. Men dominate that world because they know how to set traps and how to overcome them. Women must learn the same tactics, but they will not if they rely only upon sexual harassment rules to protect them.[122] If women do not learn how to be as aggressive as they must be to succeed, not only will they be denying themselves opportunities, but, in addition, they will have no one but themselves to blame.

Okin would respond to Paglia by arguing that the doctrine of gender neutrality does not require constraints that reduce all to a common denominator of mediocrity so that each can have the same rights. Indeed, gender neutrality would provide opportunities for individuals to enter areas of life that were formerly denied to them. Included in this list of people with new opportunities awaiting them as a result of gender neutrality would be Paglia herself. After all, her arguments would be considered by most to be highly controversial and unconventional. In a previous era, before gender-neutral rules with regard to speech, women who had unconventional ideas and who wanted to express them in print either had to forget about the enterprise or write under a male pen name. Paglia would probably accept this dimension of Okin's argument, but say that is why she is not against patriarchy, since it has provided her with opportunities of great importance.

MacKinnon would claim that Paglia's support of pornography makes her an accomplice of those males who commit rape. In effect, Paglia is an individual who gives aid and comfort to the enemy of all women. But Paglia would respond not so much by repeating liberal commitments to the freest possible speech for all, but by arguing that individuals, men and women alike, should be left free to determine their own courses in life. If men and women both find pornography acceptable, they are merely allowing their inner dispositions to have full reign, and in telling them to repress these desires, people are denied their essential freedom. Here, ironically, for Paglia, the paternalism feminists so much loathe actually originates in feminist thinking itself, much to the detriment of human freedom.

Marxists such as Hartsock would respond to Paglia's charges by saying that Paglia, like Nietzsche, as already indicated, represents a destructive bourgeoisie individualism. Indeed, a Marxist perspective would suggest that Paglia is merely a kind of free enterprise, booty capitalist, who wants nothing to impede her pursuit of pleasure (or possibly her profits from her books). The Marxist would argue that Paglia is not interested in creating communities in which workers together determine the basis for a type of work that allows for the full development of each person's potential. Paglia would see nothing wrong with this characterization of her views. For Paglia, communities of the sort Marx discussed are merely idealistic, pie-in-the-sky hopes, which have little chance of bringing about the liberation they augur. But what is certain is that during the course of bringing such communities into existence, a fierce and repressive form of Apollonian life would be installed to deny Dionysian freedom.

X. RESPONSE AND REJOINDER

All civil society theorists would in the light of the critiques provided here have to accept that the private sphere can be used to deny women full participation in the public setting. Of chief importance in this regard is the idea that the equality promised to all people in the public realm can only be realized in full for women when the private realm is transformed and made into a setting where equality is extended to men and women alike. Here, there must be sharing of household duties, mutual respect for the needs of each of the members of the household, and a broad general commitment by the members of the household to defend the rights of each person in society to participate fully in the public realm. Of the civil society writers discussed in this book, only Rawls would seem most likely to be in a position to embrace this view fully.

Now a writer like Rawls could accept without a problem the critique made of him by Okin of his thought and move with her to provide a gender-neutral view of society. The rights of all people could be accorded protection, and, further, women and men would have equal rights that have the same relative worth. On this reading, Rawls would accept proposals that required sharing of household duties, as well as many of the other proposals discussed by Okin.

Rawls would reject any view that tended to lump together all women as a class, as MacKinnon and Hartsock do, unless of course it could be shown that all women as a class fell into the category of the worst-off members of society, from an economic and social standpoint. But Rawls would certainly point out that not all women are equally oppressed, and further, there have been advances made for some women along the lines suggested by Rawls's principles of justice. Consequently, Rawls would ask how those women who are not doing as well as other women can be provided enhanced opportunities. And in asking this question, Rawls would suggest that factors other than gender intrude upon the chances for success, and these factors must be considered, too. Indeed, one might consider race, opportunities for an education owing to family background, and so on.

Hartsock, on the other hand, would not accept this distinction. The only way to approach the plight of women is to analyze their condition as a class and to understand how gender relationships in a capitalist society threaten women's opportunities as a class. Rawls's approach looks at society as a collection of individuals and asks how each one can be liberated from any impediment that might stand in the way of individual success. Here, there are not obstacles that harm people as a class, but only barriers that harm individuals *qua* individuals. But for Hartsock in viewing society in these Rawlsian terms, not only does one forfeit full understanding of the actual causes of women's plight, but the solidarity necessary to overcome oppressive gender relationships cannot be achieved. Instead, one group of women, the successful, are contrasted to another, less successful group. People define themselves as members of either camp, incapable of identifying with the plight of women as a whole. And in this situation, there is no group solidarity based on gender to move society to make the changes Hartsock hopes for. Civil society theorists of whatever stripe (and here I include the conservatives as well) would respond to Hartsock in a similar way. Their response would be to ask whether her view is not just one more instance of just one more group attempting to claim power over others, without a clearly defined statement of justification. Okin and Elshtain might well ask the same question.

MacKinnon might argue that Rawls's failure to include the point of view of women in the original position is an oversight that evolves from the structure of male dominance, sanctioned by pornography. Therefore, unless the latter is targeted as the number one institution that must be defeated, then any discussion of rights will lead to solutions that only reinforce women's bondage. Rawls would no doubt argue that pornography, although a danger, is not so pervasive that it prevents individuals in his original position from thinking in a fair and judicious way that will lead to just principles. All that is necessary for them to do so is to hear the competing arguments, and Okin has done a great service by helping to provide them.

Paglia would find difficulty with Rawls's approach, but for reasons not discussed by the others. Paglia might question Rawls's view of what constitutes authentic individualism. Rawls's individual in the original position, for Paglia, might be conceived as overly cautious and in general hesitant to engage in high-risk activity. His individual would gravitate to the security of various social groups found in the context of a civil society. But Paglia would demand a space in society where individuals would stand by themselves, willing to take risks on behalf of their objectives and hesitant to move into the group settings of civil society for fear that such environments would erode their chances for a truly individualistic life. Rawls might respond by complaining that Paglia's view of the nature of individuals is primarily a call to give special rights and privileges to the few, the aristocratic elite of Nietzsche. In the main, then, Rawls might wonder whether her individualism is capable of supporting, in full, the need to extend the protection of the principles of a liberal civil society to everyone.

Who among those discussed here best supports the traditions of civil society as a place that provides rights for all, regardless of gender? I leave it to the readers to decide.

Endnotes

1. Jean Bethke Elshtain, *Public Man, Private Woman: Women in Social and Political Thought* (Princeton: Princeton University Press, 1981), p. 15.

2. Ibid., p. 15.

3. Ibid., pp. 15–16.

4. Carole Pateman, *The Disorder of Women* (Stanford: Stanford University Press, 1989), pp. 34–38.

5. Carole Pateman, *The Sexual Contract* (Stanford: Stanford University Press, 1988).

6. Hegel, *Philosophy of Right,* p. 114, para. 166. see Elshtain, *Public Man, Private Woman: Women in Social and Political Thought,* pp. 174–75.

7. Jean Bethke Elshtain, *Public Man, Private Woman: Women in Social and Political Thought,* pp. 175–77. She provides a close reading of *Phenomenology of Spirit* to support her position.

8. John Stuart Mill, *The Subjection of Women,* ed. by Susan M. Okin (Indianapolis: Hackett Publishing Co., 1988), p. 1.

9. Ibid., pp. 5–6.

10. Ibid., pp. 46–47.

11. Ibid., p. 47.

12. Ibid., p. 97.

13. Ibid., p. 96.

14. Ibid., pp. 102–3.

15. Ibid., p. 104.

16. Ibid., p. 90.

17. Ibid., p. 51.

18. Susan Moller Okin, *Women in Western Political Thought* (Princeton: Princeton University Press, 1979), p. 228.

19. Ibid., p. 229.

20. Ibid., p. 228.

21. Jean Bethke Elshtain, *Public Man, Private Woman: Women in Social and Political Thought,* p. 144. Italics in text.

22. Pateman, *The Sexual Contract,* p. 6.

23. Ibid., p. 129.

24. Ibid., p. 135.

25. Ibid., p. 136.

26. Ibid., pp. 137–38.

27. Ibid., pp. 138–40.

28. Susan Moller Okin, *Justice, Gender and the Family* (New York: Basic Books, 1989), pp. 128–29.

29. Ibid., pp. 129–30.

30. Ibid., pp. 131–33.

31. Ibid., pp. 90–91.

32. Ibid., p. 101.

33. Ibid., p. 101.

34. Ibid., pp. 102–3.

35. Ibid., p. 107.

36. Ibid., p. 103. To summarize, again, Rawls's principles of justice require that the basic institutions of society must be regulated, first by a commitment to equal basic liberty, and, second, by a principle of equal opportunity that says that all positions in society should be open to all persons, and that when open competition leads to a situation where some people have greater wealth, authority, or responsibility, these differences must redound to the benefit of the least-well-off members of society.

37. Ibid., pp. 103–5.

38. Ibid., p. 175.

39. Ibid., pp. 175–76.

40. Ibid., p. 176.

41. Ibid., pp. 177–79.

42. Ibid., pp. 180–81.

43. Catharine A. MacKinnon, *Feminism Unmodified* (Cambridge: Harvard University Press, 1987), pp. 8, 14, 22, 34.

44. Ibid., p. 16.

45. Ibid., p. 228.

46. Catharine A. MacKinnon, *Toward a Feminist Theory of the State* (Cambridge: Harvard University Press, 1989), p. 163.

47. MacKinnon, *Feminism Unmodified,* p. 166.

48. Ibid., p. 172.

49. Ibid., p. 173.

50. MacKinnon, *Toward a Feminist Theory of the State,* p. 140.

51. Ibid., 112–13, 128.

52. Ibid., p. 199, also 140.

53. MacKinnon, *Feminism Unmodified,* p. 172.

54. Ibid., p. 173.

55. Ibid., pp. 179–80.

56. Ibid., pp. 184–85.

57. Ibid., p. 189.

58. Ibid., p. 175.

59. Catharine A. MacKinnon, *Only Words* (Cambridge: Harvard University Press, 1993), pp. 91–92.

60. Ibid., pp. 11, 14.

61. Ibid., pp. 38–41.

62. MacKinnon, *Feminism Unmodified,* pp. 152–53.

63. MacKinnon, *Only Words,* pp. 12–17.

64. Ibid., p. 91.

65. Ibid., p. 109.

66. Jean Bethke Elshtain, *Public Man, Private Woman: Women in Social and Political Thought,* pp. 303–4.

67. Ibid., pp. 312–13.

68. Ibid., pp. 335–36.

69. Carol Gilligan, *In a Different Voice* (Cambridge: Harvard University Press, 1993; originally published in 1982), pp. 73, 171.

70. Ibid., pp. 161, 173–74.

71. Elshtain, *Public Man, Private Woman: Women in Social and Political Thought,* p. 329; also, pp. 326–30, 336–37.

72. Ibid., p. 337.

73. Ibid., p. 348.

74. Ibid., p. 343.

75. Ibid., p. 349.

76. Ibid., p. 350.

77. Ibid., p. 352.

78. Nancy C. M. Hartsock, *Money, Sex and Power: Toward a Feminist Historical Materialism* (New York: Longman, 1983), p. 232.

79. Ibid., p. 231.

80. Ibid., p. 231.

81. Ibid., p. 234.

82. Ibid., p. 235.

83. Ibid., p. 236.

84. Ibid., pp. 236–37.

85. Ibid., pp. 238–39.

86. Ibid., p. 239.

87. Ibid., p. 240.

88. Ibid., p. 241.

89. Ibid., p. 241.

90. Ibid., pp. 242–43.

91. Ibid., p. 244.

92. Ibid., p. 245.

93. Ibid., p. 246.

94. Ibid., p. 247.

95. Ibid., p. 247.

96. Ibid., p. 247.

97. Camille Paglia, "Sexual Personae: The Cancelled Preface," in *Sex, Art, and American Culture* (New York: Vintage Books, 1992), p. 109.

98. Camille Paglia, "No Law in the Arena," in *Vamps and Tramps* (New York: Vintage Books, 1994), p. 30.

99. Ibid., pp. 50, 57–58, 69.

100. Ibid., p. 38.

101. Camille Paglia, "The M.I.T. Lecture" in *Sex, Art, and American Culture,* p. 273. Italics in text.

102. Camille Paglia, *Sexual Personae: Art and Decadence from Nefertiti to Emily Dickinson* (New York: Vintage Books, 1990), pp. 96–97. Italics in text.

103. Ibid., p. 33, also pp. 8, 10, 12.

104. Ibid., p. 33.

105. Paglia, "Sexual Personae: The Cancelled Preface," p. 107.

106. Ibid., pp. 105–6.

107. Ibid., p. 108. Italics in text.

108. Paglia, "No Law in the Arena," in *Vamps and Tramps,* p. 32. Italics in text.

109. Ibid., p. 30.

110. Paglia, *Sexual Personae: Art and Decadence from Nefertiti to Emily Dickinson,* p. 23.

111. Ibid., p. 12.

112. Paglia, "No Law in the Arena," in *Vamps and Tramps,* p. 93.

113. Ibid., p. 93.

114. Ibid., p. 40.

115. Ibid., p. 66.

116. Ibid., p. 66.

117. Paglia, "The Culture Wars," *Vamps and Tramps,* p. 108.

118. Ibid., pp. 111–12.

119. Paglia, "The M.I.T. Lecture," in *Sex, Art, and American Culture,* p. 284.

120. Ibid., p. 284.

121. Paglia, "No Law in the Arena," in *Vamps and Tramps,* p. 53.

122. Ibid., pp. 53–54.

Partial Bibliography and Further Reading

Bryson, Valerie. *Feminist Political Theory: An Introduction.* New York: Paragon House, 1992.

Elshtain, Jean Bethke. *Public Man, Private Woman: Women in Social and Political Thought.* Princeton: Princeton University Press, 1981.

Gilligan, Carol. *In a Different Voice.* Cambridge: Harvard University Press, 1993.

Hartsock, Nancy C. M. *Money, Sex and Power: Toward a Feminist Historical Materialism.* New York: Longman, 1983.

Jaggar, Alison M. *Feminist Politics and Human Nature.* Totowa, N.J.: Rowman & Allanheld, 1983.

MacKinnon, Catharine A. *Feminism Unmodified.* Cambridge: Harvard University Press, 1987.

———. *Only Words.* Cambridge: Harvard University Press, 1993.

———. *Toward a Feminist Theory of the State.* Cambridge: Harvard University Press, 1989.

Mill, John Stuart, edited by Susan M. Okin, *The Subjection of Women.* Indianapolis: Hackett Publishing Co., 1988.

Okin, Susan Moller. *Justice, Gender and the Family.* New York: Basic Books, 1989.

———. *Women in Western Political Thought.* Princeton: Princeton University Press, 1979.

Paglia, Camille. *Sex, Art, and American Culture.* New York: Vintage Books, 1992.

———. *Sexual Personae: Art and Decadence from Nefertiti to Emily Dickinson.* New York: Vintage Books, 1990.

———. *Vamps and Tramps,* New York: Vintage Books, 1994.

Pateman, Carole. *The Disorder of Women.* Stanford: Stanford University Press, 1989.

———. *The Sexual Contract.* Stanford: Stanford University Press, 1988.

Sunstein, Cass R. edited. *Feminism and Political Theory.* Chicago: University of Chicago Press, 1990.

18

Civil Society and Its Challenges

I. Introduction: A Return to Civil Society

As we stated in the first chapter, the term *civil society* refers either to the character of the national political community or to a separate sphere of voluntary associations within the space existing between the individual and the national government. In the first instance, a civil society refers to national political institutions that have as their main objective a commitment to uphold the rule of law on behalf of a shared notion of the common good. The common good—in addition to referring to the need for the government to provide important items such as economic well-being, public safety, public health, and education—includes the provision of basic rights such as speech, association, freedom of conscience and religion, due process, protection of private property, and so on.

The second use of the term *civil society,* which is the predominant way used throughout this book, refers to a separate sphere of groups and associations that individuals may choose to join. Each of these groups and associations upholds values and purposes shared by the members. Individuals become members of different groups and associations to realize these values, both for themselves and for the groups in question.

Further, a civil society as a separate sphere acts as a buffer to the national government or to other powerful economic organizations, such as business corporations, that control vast areas of a particular market. In effect, a civil society limits the range and reach of the national government and of powerful economic organizations by establishing the boundaries over which each must not step. Neither the national government nor economic organizations should enter civil society and regulate the groups that exist therein. Doing so might prevent civil society groups from forming themselves in ways considered necessary by the members. This basic right of association is protected by the First Amendment.[1] Thus, if the Girl Scouts organization wants to exclude boys, they can, and if the American Legion wants to include only war veterans, they can do that. Neither the national government nor powerful economic entities are allowed to interfere with a civil society group's prerogative to determine membership or its own agenda.

There is a line that the groups and associations must not cross as well. That line emerges from the fact that a civil society as a separate sphere exists inside the larger context of a civil society as a national political community dedicated to uphold, as part of what is meant by the rule of law, the basic rights of each person. Were, for instance, the Boy Scouts to deny their members either religious freedom or the right to express political views in a public forum, then federal authorities, acting under the First Amendment, could legally compel the Boy Scouts to change their policies.

For many, however, the way the federal government draws this line may seem at times to be inconsistent with the overall commitment to secure basic rights for all. A recent Supreme Court decision—*Boy Scouts of America v. Dale* upholding the exclusion of openly gay people from the Boy Scouts—helps to underscore this point.[2] In this case, the Court permitted exclusion of gay males in the Boy Scouts by saying that voluntary associations in civil society have a right, under the freedom of association provision of the First Amendment, to determine their basic values and to decide membership consistent with these values.[3] Chief Justice Rehnquist said in his majority opinion for the Court that "it is not the role of the courts to reject a group's expressed values because they disagree with those values or find them internally inconsistent."[4]

Now, the Court's decision was formulated only on legal grounds and thus fashioned to be in accord with the Court's application of the First Amendment's freedom of association provision. The Court was silent on the issue of whether it thought that the Scouts should admit gay members as a matter of promoting toleration. The Court's silence on the moral dimension of this case leaves open the prospect of a transformative public discussion on this matter. Most Americans believe that gays should have equal rights in the workplace and in the educational setting. Given this viewpoint, it is possible that the Scouts may be moved to reexamine their own standards in light of the public's view that exclusion of gays from full participation in many parts of the society is viewed as unfair. Indeed, factors are now at work to promote public reflection on this issue. For instance, in light of the Scouts' exclusion of gays, several major corporate donors have cut back substantially their contributions to the Boy Scouts. And cities such as Chicago, San Francisco, and San Jose, California, have told local Scout leaders that they can't use parks, schools, or other municipal sites.[5] In the wake of actions of this sort, as well as the public discussion that follows from them, the Boy Scouts may reconsider its opinion and decide to admit gays.

II. WHY WE SHOULD CARE: CIVIL SOCIETY, LIBERAL DEMOCRACY, AND CIVIC LIFE

Many writers believe that a civil society as a separate sphere, with a variety of voluntary groups, is now in decline. We discuss the reasons for this view in the next section. In this section, I discuss the civic values imparted by civil society, and I suggest that we should be concerned about the decline of civil society in light of the need to maintain civic values and the liberal democracy they make possible.

The first reason to fear the decline of civil society as a separate sphere is that this setting teaches people the importance of *common deliberation.* People who deliberate together search for *shared* reasons that all members of an association can support as the basis for action and judgment. And these reasons arise only after people have considered diverse points of views and after they have employed sound reasoning and solid argument, including marshalling evidentiary support for their positions.

Common deliberation is also important because it helps people to understand and to respect the views of others. Indeed, to discover shared reasons for action, individuals must learn to think from the standpoints of others and to compare and to contrast different views. Further, individuals as they deliberate together develop the skills needed for democracy. In particular, individuals learn how to work for consensus at meetings, how to carry out shared plans, and how to speak effectively in public. Moreover, within the setting of a common deliberation, individuals engage in a give-and-take discourse that teaches moderation and accommodation, and this experience helps people avoid becoming targets for extremist groups or becoming involved in arguments that promote hatred and intolerance.[6]

Another important dimension of civil society, no doubt fueled by the experience of common deliberation, is teaching *civic virtue*—a key moral value that emphasizes respect for the common values and ways of life that empower people to search for as well as to uphold the common good. As a result of this experience, quite often, individuals acquire an appreciation for the important civic virtues discussed in Chapter 1, including, especially, toleration and mutual respect. Toleration and mutual respect, as discussed in Chapter 1 and throughout this book, are woven implicitly throughout the entire discussion in this section and chapter.

Acquiring civic virtue in the context of groups has important implications for the larger society. Indeed, people who gain an understanding of civic virtue in the group setting of civil society are likely to carry this viewpoint over into their dealings with the national community. When this happens, individuals will demand that national issues be discussed by decision makers in a manner that replicates the experience of common deliberation found in the separate sphere of voluntary groups and associations. In consequence, the national policy makers, in assessing their own positions and the positions of others, would consider a host of views, and they would seek to exercise sound reasoning, as opposed to seeking short-term political advantage, during the course of making decisions. Moreover, public discussions with respect to national issues would be designed to find *public reasons* that most or all citizens can accept as the basis for action and laws. In supporting the search for public reasons during the course of confronting national issues, a civil society experience creates the general expectation that politicians who are incapable of this approach to discussion will and indeed should be penalized where it most hurts them—at the ballot box.

The identification of the civic traits arising from civil society brings us to another important dimension taught by the civil society experience. Groups in civil society, no matter how focused they may be on a particular interest or value, impart the importance of *inclusion.* As we have seen, groups uphold certain criteria or prized characteristics. Sometimes these characteristics stem from the inherent qualities of people such as race, gender, ethnicity, or sexual orientation. Individuals may choose to form groups around these realities in order to promote the values affiliated with them, such as educating the public about gay issues or advancing the rights of women and minorities. At other times, group characteristics arise merely from particular interests and tastes. Some people join reading groups because they wish to discuss books with others, whereas others may form garden clubs because they wish to enjoy flowers with others.

Still, groups in a civil society, however they may originate and for whatever reason they are maintained, should be open to people from diverse walks of life. For instance, a charitable organization such as the Red Cross includes people committed to helping others in emergencies, and the League of Women Voters includes those dedicated to providing citizens with nonpartisan information about issues and candidates. But a civil society as a separate sphere creates the expectation that these groups permit membership from people with diverse religious, class, race, and ethnic backgrounds. Even within groups based solely upon shared ethnic or gender characteristics, there should be room for people from different economic classes or sexual orientations. Churches and synagogues in a civil society should be places for people from different social classes, with diverse histories and ideas. Indeed, a civil society as a separate sphere is an intersection where people with different interests and values meet together, learn from each other, and determine with each other how to achieve shared purposes.

Now, on occasion groups may define standards for membership that are designed primarily to reinforce the practices of exclusion that result from powerful cultural realities that intrude into civil society. Here, I have in mind broadly pervasive and powerful actualities that impose social divisions and that engender intense conflict around matters such as economic class, religion, race, sexual orientation, or ethnicity. These practices, however, violate the spirit of a civil society to ensure inclusiveness within the context of each group setting. Certainly, groups are designed, as we have already said, to promote certain fixed interests and values. As a result, groups may exclude people based on the fact that prospective members do not agree with the expressed purposes and values of the group. This right is guaranteed by the freedom of association provision of the First Amendment. Still, even in these circumstances, groups should be as inclusive as possible by including people representing diverse walks of life, religions, values, social classes, genders, and so on.

Moreover, groups in civil society should be willing to reach out to other groups who have different views on the issues at hand, with the intention of engaging these groups in honest and open discourse and from this activity finding a common ground for accommodation.[7] A great threat to a civil society as a separate sphere is the tendency at times for groups to forge such strong bonds among their members that these groups can't search for a common ground with those who disagree with them.

A civil society seeks inclusion, then, by emphasizing *bonding* among the membership, but not to the extent that bonding circumvents *bridging* to other groups in society. Mass-based, national political parties have always performed this function as have coalitions of religious organizations working together for a common cause such as peace, justice, or social welfare needs. But other types of groups have often failed to make bridging possible. Clearly, civil society is filled with what are referred to as "interest groups" or, in other terms, associations lobbying the government and the public on behalf of specific economic or social agendas. Among many such associations, there are business, agricultural, labor, and moral advocacy groups. Interest groups of these sorts often exclude consideration of the claims of competing and different groups. However, in a civil society the experience of bridging encourages as well as enables members of different interest groups to interact with each other and through this activity to find a basis for accommodating their different needs and interests.

Promoting *fairness* in the larger national community is another key civic value of a civil society, and fairness is an important outgrowth of a civil society that encourages inclusion within and among the various groups and associations that make up society. Because people in making decisions in civil society must consider the needs of others, individuals recognize the necessity of fairness as a standard for national decision making. People who promote fairness seek to ensure that each person will be accorded due regard in both the discussion about and in the actual distribution of essential benefits, such as education, opportunities to make a decent living through respectable work, and so on. Indeed, the main objective of fairness in politics is to advance the enhancement of all people's best prospects, where the prospects are understood both in terms of individual fulfillment and overall social improvement. When a fair politics does not take place, politics is reduced to nothing more than a shoving match among competing social or economic interests.[8] The voices of those who cannot push back, and who therefore are not able to hold their ground against those with greater power, are silenced.

Finally, we turn to the last important reason for sustaining civil society as a separate sphere—securing *liberal democracy*. I will also, in subsequent sections of this chapter, refer to liberal democracy as "political liberalism," which is a term used to refer to John's Rawls's conception of liberal democracy discussed in the Rawls chapter, and these terms will thus be used interchangeably. A liberal democracy consists of democratic and representative institutions and practices that together promote basic rights for each person through the rule of law.

Now, the idea of a liberal democracy suggests an enduring tension between each of its terms. The "liberal" part advocates rights and freedoms on behalf of promoting autonomy for each person. Individuals are autonomous when they are able to make major decisions about their own lives, based upon their own reflections and their own best judgments. Here, I have in mind the freedom to make determinations with respect to matters such as career, friends, lifelong partners, general lifestyle, and core values. To ensure autonomy, which permits people to develop their full potential as human beings, individuals must be given basic rights and freedoms in such areas as conscience, speech, religion, property, due process, and association.

The "democracy" part is associated with a shared commitment to uphold the common good. Thus, democracies promote basic, constitutionally protected rights for all—in areas such as speech, religion, conscience, association, and due process of law—as well as a variety of other goods such as public safety and health, education, resources that help to ensure commerce, and so on. In promoting items of this sort, the common good is inevitably associated with a second category of rights—those arising not from a national constitution as is the case with basic rights, but those whose origin is *legislative activity* occurring at the national levels of government. For example, legislatively created national laws that promote clean air and water suggest rights to breathe air free of pollution and to drink water uncontaminated by sewage.

Democracies secure the common good in its various manifestations only when democracies can produce majorities on behalf of the common good. For instance, the common good includes providing adequate education for all citizens. But if and how this objective is achieved ultimately depends upon society's ability to muster a majority on behalf of universal education. There are many ways democracies create majorities on behalf of common good issues. Principally, democracies engineer majorities through adherence to procedural rules that all citizens acknowledge as legitimate sources for defining the public's position on the common good. Specifically, well understood processes often create majorities with respect to particular issues through elections for various public offices—from the President of the United States down to the local mayor or state representative. Indeed, forming majorities on behalf of the common good requires leaders whose appeals on behalf of a view of the common good are certified one way or another at the ballot box.

Moreover, the "democracy" part of liberal democracy, in giving prominence to the majority, suggests that individuals have a duty to support the common good. This means that individuals must limit their autonomy in the name of various obligations arising from their role as citizens. For instance, to support the common good—which includes providing basic as well as legislatively created rights—I, like others, may have to accept limitations on autonomy. Thus, in affording all children an education through the public school system, it is necessary that I, like others, accept paying taxes that reduce the money others and I have for personal goals.

On the other hand, in a liberal democracy it is recognized that at times the reach of majorities will have to be limited, for the sake of protecting rights—both basic and legislatively created ones—as well as autonomy. Here, the majority has an obligation to avoid interfering with personal commitments, as when the majority is told that it cannot dictate an individual's religious beliefs. And when individuals disagree as to what constitutes the line between rights and obligations, individuals have an even greater obligation to encourage if not take part in a common deliberation that helps to achieve accommodations that are fair and inclusive.

Often, however, people may find it difficult to accept obligations, because the latter are seen as limiting rights too severely or as constraining the reach of majorities too strictly. Civil society values help to reduce the influence of this mindset. Values such as inclusion, fairness, common deliberation, and the civic virtue of mutual respect—the great *civic values* taught by a civil society—enable individuals to understand that rights cannot be secured without accompanying obligations.

In promoting a viable balance between rights and obligations, a civil society as a separate sphere is, in addition to helping to secure liberal democracy, a setting that makes possible *civic engagement.* Citizens engage in civic activity when they take an active part in public affairs, and when, as they engage in such action, they uphold the civic values taught by a civil society, including the obligations of citizenship in a liberal democracy.

III. The Decline of Civic Engagement

What is the evidence to support the contention that civil society is now in decline? Robert Putnam lists several reasons for this claim. Each of his reasons points to a lessening of commitment by ordinary citizens to civic engagement. Why is a weakened sense of civic engagement a symbol of the decline of civil society as a separate sphere? Since a civil society is central to sustaining support for civic values, where civic engagement is diminished in importance, then it is reasonable to presume that its source—a civil society—must be in decline as well.

To support the view that civic engagement has declined, Putnam shows that there have been decreased rates of voter turnout in national elections. Indeed, voter turnout in the 1990's has declined by a quarter since it reached its high point in the 1960's.[9] Other indicators of civic decline are just as telling. For instance, in his book *Bowling Alone,* we learn that since the mid-1960's Americans, despite an increase in education levels, are 10–15 percent less prone to express their views "publicly by running for office or writing Congress or the local newspaper, 15–20 percent less interested in politics and public affairs,. . . . roughly 35 percent less likely to attend public meetings, both partisan and nonpartisan, and roughly 40 percent less engaged in party politics and indeed in political and civic organizations of all sorts. We remain, in short, reasonably well-informed spectators of public affairs, but many fewer of us actually take part in the game."[10]

Indeed, Putnam says that, except for the Depression years, during the first sixty years of the last century participation rates in civic associations "rose steadily." Yet, over the last third of the twentieth century "only mailing list membership has continued to expand," thus reducing substantially "face-to-face" organizational memberships. Moreover, in the final thirty years of the twentieth century, "active involvement in clubs and other voluntary associations has collapsed at an astonishing rate."[11] Indeed, membership in civic and fraternal organizations that require extensive time and participation has declined substantially. For instance, the League of Women Voters has declined by 42 percent since 1969, the Red Cross by 61 percent since 1970, and the Boy Scouts by 26 percent since 1970.[12] Furthermore, he points out that "volunteering declined by roughly one-sixth" over a period from 1974–1989.[13]

Putnam even says, of course whimsically, that the decline in civic participation is manifested in people bowling alone. Organized bowling leagues have dropped in number by almost 40 percent during 1980–1993, even though the number of bowlers has increased by 10 percent. People are now bowling alone at record numbers he tells us, and if the present pace continues there will be no bowling leagues left within the next ten years.[14] Overall, Putnam says that "most Americans no longer spend much time in community organizations—we've stopped doing committee work, stopped serving as officers, and stopped going to meetings. And all of this despite rapid increases in education that have given more of us than ever before the skills, the resources, and the interests that once fostered civic engagement. In short, Americans have been dropping out in droves, not merely from political life, but from organized community life more generally."[15]

Americans, says Putnam, must reverse this tendency in order to create "social capital," which "refers to connections among individuals—social networks and the norms of reciprocity and trustworthiness that arise from them."[16] Social capital pertains to the trust that people must have toward each other and toward their primary social and political institutions in order to realize shared public values and purposes. Without trust, people are more likely to give priority to their personal needs, and as a result people are less likely to make the display of civic virtue a major priority in their lives. Thus, civic virtue "is most powerful when embedded in a dense network of reciprocal social relations," which are built upon trust between citizens and key political and social institutions.[17]

None of the foregoing means that Americans have sworn off civic activity entirely. It is just that the nature of what we call "civic activity" today has changed from what these terms signified in an earlier time. Robert Wuthnow describes as well as explains the changed quality of civic engagement in today's society. Wuthnow's account, not unlike Putnam's view, contains a call for increasing society's stock of social capital.

For Wuthnow, in a former time, civic involvement, in addition to voting and taking part in political rallies, meant participation in large groups like the Kiwanis or Rotary Club.[18] Service organizations like these came into existence at the end of the nineteenth century, and these groups established local chapters that were similar to branch offices in corporate hierarchies.[19] As Theda Skocpol describes them, groups comparable to these not only built local and state chapters, but these groups created national offices as well, and thus this organizational arrangement paralleled the three-tier format of the United States government. Further, these groups were characterized not only by trust and loyalty at the local level but also by strong connection to the surrounding world.[20] This multi-tiered arrangement grew to prominence from the 1880's to the 1920's and these forms of group life were the foundation of American civil society through the mid-1960's. Over the last twenty-five years, however, multi-tiered, membership organizations have witnessed serious decline.[21]

Indeed, Skocpol says that "professionally run advocacy associations" have replaced multi-tiered civic organizations.[22] Wuthnow would agree. In the current setting, then, old line, hierarchical organizations have been eclipsed in importance by advocacy coalitions, strung together and managed by professional organizers and pollsters, who bring together different constituencies on an issue by issue basis. For instance, Wuthnow points out that coalitions of groups, including clergy, teachers, law enforcement officials, and outside experts, can be brought together to fight school violence. The glue that holds these groups together is not the long-term loyalty and trust that people had to the older, hierarchical groups, but professional organizers who are capable of forging strategic connections among diverse constituencies.[23] When the prominence of an issue recedes, group solidarity erodes and only reemerges in relation to new issues and fresh efforts to forge cross-group alliances. These coalitions come and go, form and re-form, and individuals maintain only loose connections to them.

For Wuthnow, then, the present setting is characterized by "looser, more sporadic, ad hoc connections in place of the long-term memberships in hierarchical organizations of the past."[24] He argues, like Putnam, that Americans have withdrawn in large numbers from service clubs, labor unions, and churches "apparently believing it makes little difference whether they engage in civic activities or not."[25] Still, people have not cut their ties to others and to their community altogether. Indeed, people partake in activities that do not require great amounts of time and an enduring loyalty to groups. Individuals may take part in little league in order to enhance the lives of their children. They will maintain friendships through e-mail, phone calls, visits, and greeting cards. People gain a sense of belonging from these relationships, no doubt. But modern relationships like these, unlike in a previous era, are looser in the sense that they are less binding on people, and these factors for Wuthnow "allow for many acquaintances which may be more superficial and require little care to maintain."[26] This approach allows individuals to shift their commitments, leaving one relationship for others, as circumstances and needs may warrant.[27]

For Wuthnow the moral tone established by loose connections is clear. "Loose connections . . . depend more on individual deliberation. Sporadic contact is less likely to provide occasions for reflection about enduring values and identity."[28] Would this more individualist, less communal viewpoint reinforce a sense of civic engagement? Clearly, Wuthnow would conclude that it does not. "Contexts that re-enforce the language of self-interest, personal happiness, and pleasure are abundant [in modern settings]. A consumer economy encourages people to think in these languages in order to sell entertainment, therapy, fast food, expensive automobiles, vacations, and the like. Contexts that re-enforce values of service and sharing are often submerged relative to those emphasizing gratification."[29] Wuthnow would share Putnam's call to enlarge society's stock of social capital for the sake of encouraging wider and more intensive civic engagement.

IV. WHY IS CIVIL SOCIETY IN DECLINE?

What are the reasons that explain the decline of civic engagement and thus by implication the diminished status of the civil society setting that helps engender social capital? Putnam sees several.[30] The first, which in his view accounts for about 10 percent of the decline, are the many pressures experienced by two-career families. Working long hours in a job, especially by both adults in a family, diverts both time as well as money away from civic life. Another element responsible for roughly 10 percent of the decline of civic life is suburban sprawl, which often requires that people spend many hours in their cars, alone, commuting to and from work. The third factor, which accounts for about 25 percent of the decline, is the increased role of electronic entertainment, especially television, in the lives of people. Television orients people to use their leisure time almost exclusively for private matters, as opposed to participation with others in civic activities.

Finally, Putnam suggests that about 50 percent of the decline is due to the passing from the scene of the World War II generation, whose strong civic habits developed in response to the need to win the war against Nazi Germany and Japan. The children and grandchildren of this generation don't manifest a similar civic commitment, in large part because in the present setting there are no major crises—war or non-war—which incur a strong civic bond. Furthermore, in today's climate of general peace and prosperity, as well as the end to the Cold War, the likelihood of great, unifying non-war events that rekindle the need for a robust civic life—what William James called the "moral equivalent of war"—seems remote.[31]

Putnam leaves 5 percent of the explanation for the decline of civic life unspecified. Perhaps, he does so to leave room for other reasons than those he mentions. One additional reason that could be cited in this regard is the perceived disintegration of the family as a result of high divorce rates. Families have always provided opportunities for children to become acclimated to the work world, to acquire knowledge of religious and moral values, and to provide emotional support to children.[32] Many believe that these factors contribute to teaching people civic values, and thus the wearing down of family life may contribute to a decline in civil society as well.

V. THE QUEST FOR CIVIC RENEWAL

Some people respond to the diminished status of civil society by engaging in actions that renew civic life. This phenomena is particularly visible in those settings referred to in the first chapter as mediating groups, those nongovernmental associations that serve the public good by providing important services to people. No doubt activities in these groups reproduce what Putnam referred to as social capital.

Organizations such as the National Commission on Civic Renewal recount many of the activities of these public service or mediating groups.[33] Examples of such groups include some of the following:

- The Local Initiatives Support Corporation, which has raised 2.2 billion dollars to improve housing and to create jobs in the inner city areas of America;

- The Children's Aid Society, which serves the health and education needs of more than 100,000 children in New York City;

- The Hands on Atlanta Program, which organizes volunteers to help disadvantaged children, the sick, and the homeless;

- The National Fatherhood Initiative, which seeks to increase the number of children growing up with involved, caring fathers;

- Big Brothers and Big Sisters, which recruits adults to serve as role models and mentors for young people;

- The Youth in Action, San Francisco Conservation Corps, which provides job training for many young people;

- The Character Counts! Coalition, which develops school curricula to teach students good character;

- The Close Up Foundation, which seeks to develop civics programs that enhance civic engagement; and

- The Project Vote Smart program, which offers on its Web site free and detailed information on elected officials and candidates running for office.

These groups and many like them are viewed by some people as the key to civic renewal in America, and in particular to helping enhance the circumstances for the least well off members of our society and of the world.[34] Of special note in this regard are the actions of religious groups to run programs that help people in poverty to advance their prospects for successful lives. John DiIulio, Jr. writes about faith-based groups, which provide services that revitalize poor neighborhoods, help at-risk children lead successful lives, and offer substance abuse programs, as well as day care programs and food banks.[35] The importance of these groups to civic renewal must not be overlooked in large part because these groups can galvanize many resources to improve the lives of people. Indeed, DiIulio indicates that churches are the "single biggest source of volunteers, way ahead of workplaces, schools or colleges, fraternal groups, and other civil institutions."[36]

Some now think that mediating groups affiliated with religious organizations can do a better job helping people move from "welfare to work" than can governmentally managed welfare agencies. But this approach creates several questions. Many believe that the recent success of moving people from welfare rolls into jobs rests upon the unprecedented economic growth of the 1990's. If the economy begins to contract, will religious groups, which do not possess a large public purse, have the extensive resources to do what is necessary to aid people who lose their jobs? Some respond to this claim by suggesting that the federal government should help religious groups provide services to people who are now in need and who might be in need, as result of a slumping economy, later.

A related question, then, is can the national government support religious groups wishing to provide services to people in need, without violating the principle of the separation of church and state?[37] This principle says that neither is the state to establish a common religion for the nation, nor is any individual to be denied the freedom to choose his or her disposition to religion. Thus, I can choose not only to be a member of this religious organization as opposed to that one, but I can choose to be a member of no religion as well. Some might contend that religious organizations could provide welfare assistance to individuals without requiring them to accept a particular sectarian religious viewpoint. After all, religiously oriented service groups need not make acceptance of sectarian religious instruction a requirement of receiving welfare benefits. Whereas these groups can make such instruction available to individuals who elect to receive it, religious groups supported in their efforts by the national government can provide essential services without imposing religious creeds on individuals who accept these services. In contrast, others might respond by saying that people down on their luck have no choice but to accept religious instruction from the sectarian religious groups providing them with welfare benefits, and so the wall of separation may be violated when religious groups receive public money to assist others.

VI. CIVIL SOCIETY, LIBERAL DEMOCRACY, AND MULTICULTURALISM

In this section, I discuss the relationship between multiculturalism and civil society. A multicultural society such as the United States or Canada contains groups from diverse walks of life, holding many different, and often conflicting, core values and conceptions of the good life. Despite these differences, in a multicultural society, there is sufficient stability to permit each particular way of life to flourish alongside others. And the term *multiculturalism* refers to a political doctrine that is used to make possible a multicultural society, in which all groups, no matter how different, are able to survive without harm to social stability. The word *difference* in this context is often defined in terms of race, ethnicity, religion, gender, class, sexual orientation, region, and ability.

Multiculturalism, as a political doctrine, suggests how to approach conflicts arising from difference in the hopes of reducing the social instability that might otherwise emerge. These conflicts include matters such as affirmative action programs to help minorities and women who have been unjustly treated historically. I will discuss this topic further in section VIII. Another example of a conflict arising from difference is whether a minority language in a certain region of a country should be the language of instruction in the schools of that region. This matter is discussed below. Conflicts emerging from difference also involve abortion policy, discussed in the chapter on Rawls, and the place of religion in society, which is discussed in the next section. Many other conflicts arising from difference that we do not have space to discuss could be mentioned as well.

In the discussion that follows, I will emphasize two major views of multiculturalism. The first view of multiculturalism reflects Rawls's political liberalism, a term, as mentioned earlier, I use interchangeably with the idea of liberal democracy. The second view of multiculturalism is predicated on what Charles Taylor calls the "politics of difference." At the conclusion of this section, I will discuss the implications of each approach to multiculturalism for a civil society as a separate sphere of groups.

Rawls's political liberalism, as we saw in the chapter on Rawls, seeks a civil society that permits people with diverse values and ways of life to live in peace and with mutual respect for each other's basic rights. To achieve this objective, Rawls promoted an overlapping consensus that could be shared by people from diverse walks of life and with different core values. The overlapping consensus would include support by all people in society for a liberal democracy, one that guaranteed basic rights to each citizen within a setting of representative and democratic institutions. Rawls's view of multiculturalism thus suggests that societies with diverse cultures should permit a flourishing of these cultures, but always within the context of a strong commitment to a shared *national community* built upon common standards and rules that protect the basic rights of each person. And this is the case even when in doing so it would be necessary to limit the effect and hold of particular cultural traditions on the lives of individuals.

The second, "politics of difference" view of multiculturalism recognizes that society consists of a national community with common norms and rules for each citizen to follow, as well as many different sub-communities representing diverse ways of life. At times, these sub-communities seek to uphold their own shared traditions and values as part of the effort to highlight the uniqueness that distinguishes them from other groups and other traditions. Taylor's politics of difference would find ways to support sub-communities seeking to maintain their unique identities even when doing so clashed with the standards of the national community.[38]

How might Taylor argue for his position against Rawls, and how might Rawls respond to Taylor's contentions? To address these questions, it is helpful to make reference to a concrete issue arising from difference that Taylor uses in discussing his view of multiculturalism—the demands of Quebec citizens in Canada. Quebec, as a province of Canada, sought to make the French language the primary language of the province, despite the fact that English is the predominant language in the Canadian national community. Thus, there was legislation in Quebec to mandate French commercial signage as well as to forbid citizens whose first language is French and immigrants from sending their children to English-language schools. This provision only allows Canadians in Quebec whose first language is English to send their children to English-language schools.[39]

Taylor points out that this restriction was perceived by many Canadians, and most specifically by those whose predominant language is English, as running counter to the basic rights granted to all citizens under the Canadian Charter of Rights and Freedoms established in 1982. I will discuss the issue of rights violation below, but for now I wish to put this matter aside. The question that is pertinent at this point is if the Quebec laws on education, by mandating where children can go to school, violate the ability of parents to decide to which school to send their children.[40] For instance, what if parents—either as citizens or immigrants—who are French speakers in Quebec, want to send their children to an English-language school? This would be forbidden.

Alternately, would a student in Quebec whose first language is English be permitted to attend a French-language school? The Quebec law on language instruction in the schools does not seem, at least as Taylor describes this law, to bar this option, nor does the Canadian Charter of Rights and Freedom. Thus, it would seem likely that a person whose first language is English could attend a French-language school.[41] Still, as Taylor himself says, the Quebec law favors French speakers over English speakers, and this reality can foster humiliating discrimination by the first group against the second. And even if discrimination doesn't occur, Taylor acknowledges that the "collective end" embodied in the education law "will probably involve treating insiders and outsiders differently."[42] This circumstance could create a psychological hesitancy among English-speaking—or outsider—parents, and as a result these parents might not send their children to French-language school, despite wishing to do so. Thus, even if English-speaking parents are allowed to choose a French-language school for their children, this choice might not be practical.

Nonetheless, despite these limitations on parental choice, Taylor defends the Quebec laws on education as sanctioned by his politics of difference approach to multiculturalism. His argument on behalf of this position is that his politics of difference contains a view of liberalism that is more appropriate for the needs of Quebec than Rawls's brand of political liberalism.[43] To make Taylor's argument clear, I will distinguish the two types of liberalism to which Taylor refers by first explaining further the implications of Rawls's conception of political liberalism, and then I follow this discussion with a description of Taylor's view of liberalism.

In Rawls's political liberalism the state—understood here as the national government—is to protect the basic rights of each citizen as its first and foremost obligation, and the state does so when it maintains a procedure that "insists on uniform application of the rules defining these rights without exception."[44] Furthermore, the state is not to impose onto any of the citizens a shared doctrine pertaining to "what constitutes a good life which we and others should strive for."[45] The state upholds the right of the individual to choose his or her conception of the good life by treating people with equal respect through securing such basic freedoms as association, thought, religion, and conscience.

In political liberalism, then, the state remains "neutral" before the different conceptions of the good life that might be advanced by various members of the society, and thus the state does not seek to impose any particular conception of the good life on society. Given this view, Rawls's political liberalism would not have supported the notion that citizens whose first language is French or immigrants should be barred from English-language schools. Political liberals would also want the option for English-language parents to send their children to French-language schools, as the Quebec law seems to permit. On this point, for political liberals, the Quebec law is problematic, not because it legally denies English-speaking parents the choice to send their children to French-language schools. Rather, the law is troublesome for political liberals because it may promote an atmosphere of humiliating discrimination against English speakers and/or the cultural schism between insiders and outsiders discussed above. And this experience could make the full exercise of parental choice next to impossible.

Taylor's politics of difference approach to multiculturalism, which would support Quebec's desire to maintain French cultural supremacy by upholding the school policy just cited, advocates a different type of liberalism. Taylor claims that the fundamental or basic rights of any individual—such as freedom of religion, due process, rights to life and liberty, free speech, and so on—can't be taken away during the course of promoting the interests of particular groups, such as those wanting to maintain French culture in Quebec. Still, for Taylor people can be asked to forgo certain "privileges"— such as in this context allowing parents who are French or English speakers to send their children to the school of their choice—without violating basic rights. Basic rights are not the same as privileges, and it is acceptable to violate the latter for public policy reasons, which promote diverse cultural settings throughout society—provided that basic rights are secured.[46]

To put this point another way, as Susan Okin suggests for some multiculturalist doctrines—and Taylor's falls into this category—protecting the rights of individual members of a minority culture may not be sufficient to secure that culture's way of life. And in this case added protections, called "special *group* rights" not granted to members of the majority, must be extended to the minority culture in question.[47] A sharp tension between political liberalism and the politics of difference arises at this point. The tension centers around whether it is best to use rights on behalf of individuals, as Rawls seeks to do, or on behalf of groups, as Taylor wants. The fear of political liberals is that by pursuing the group rights approach, it is impossible to protect the basic rights of individuals, regardless of what Taylor may say to the contrary.

This dilemma can be made tangible through the following question. Is the ability of parents to send their children to the school of the parents' choice a "right" that must always be preserved, or a "privilege" that can be taken away for specified good public policy reasons? Taylor's answer is that since parental choice is a privilege and not a guaranteed basic right, parental choice can be severely restricted if not eliminated altogether in the name of a special group right designed to protect a minority culture. But it is quite possible that many other people would see this choice as a parental right that is as fundamental as any other basic right, and thus not as something that can be abridged in the name of a special group right. Such people would then embrace Rawls's political liberalism by saying that giving priority to a group right violates a basic right provided to each individual.

Nonetheless, political liberals who think parental choice is an individual right—no matter whether it is viewed as a basic or as a legislatively created one as described in section II—might still accept Taylor's position on according a group right to Quebec on this matter. Political liberals might accept a group right in this case, if it could be shown that doing so doesn't severely hamper the ability of some people to make fundamental choices about the good life. But Taylor would more than likely dismiss this claim. He would contend that his position is still permissible even if, by virtue of providing a group right in this instance, certain options were limited or even denied for some parents with respect to choosing the good life for themselves and their children. And the reason for Taylor's position is clear. If the French citizens of Quebec, on the whole, believe that their culture is transmitted through the French language, then they would want to maintain the approach to schooling demanded here. Indeed, Taylor would see a political liberalism that did not accept this position as "inhospitable to difference because it can't accommodate what the members of distinct societies really aspire to, which is survival."[48]

Political liberals would respond to this argument by claiming that an individual rights approach protects the survival of various cultural identities. Within political liberalism, individuals are free to choose their own way of life, and part of this choice may include associating with a particular cultural lifestyle. Thus, cultural lifestyles must be secured for the sake of individual choice, not despite it. But what individuals cannot ask the state to do is to give priority to any particular group's claims over and against any other particular group's claims. This approach is necessary to secure the basic rights and the freedom of choice of each person. For this outcome to occur, a civil society, based on the presumptions of political liberalism, is built upon the hope of finding a common ground (or what Rawls called an overlapping consensus) and maintaining that commonality across the national community. Identifying that common ground should be the highest goal of each person in the civic arena; indeed, it should trump interests arising from group identity.

What is the nature of the common ground that political liberals might reference? The common ground for political liberals certainly includes, in addition to the agenda of basic rights and the freedom of individual choice, what helps people to realize these dimensions—the hope that all people will learn about and respect difference. For instance, for political liberals the common standards of the national community should include teaching children about the different ways of life and diverse values that exist within the United States. Some orthodox religious groups, however, prefer to have their children exempted from this requirement, fearing that if their children learn about difference, they will question their own group's religious culture and as a result ultimately leave the religion.[49]

Political liberals would reject this argument. Political liberalism contains the view that people should be able to engage in common deliberation and to obtain what common deliberation makes possible—shared public reasons for resolving differences. For people to take part in common deliberation, it is necessary for them to learn how to compare and contrast a diversity of views. And how can this goal be met if people refuse to consider views different from their own? Those who support the position of political liberals and who advocate teaching an understanding of different cultures argue as Stephen Macedo that "a basic aim of civic education should be to impart to all children the ability to reflect critically on their personal and public commitments for the sake of honoring our shared principles of liberal justice and equal rights for all."[50]

How would Taylor's politics of difference respond to this issue? Taylor's politics of difference approach to multiculturalism would agree with political liberalism and reject fundamentalist religious tenets that deny teaching understanding of and respect for difference. After all, Taylor does make, in addition to his commitment to providing protection for basic individual rights, respect for diverse cultures a major public policy goal.

But there would still be a major difference between Taylor's politics of difference and the approach to multiculturalism from political liberals. The difference centers on the *intensity* of commitment to promote the norms and rules of the national political community. The political liberal would emphasize giving priority to these national norms, unlike Taylor, who would highlight a relaxing of national standards in deference to the traditions of particular cultural groups.

This distinction is certainly one that bears important consequences for civil society. Let me give a few examples by mentioning certain national norms common to our society today. Here, I have in mind not just national standards discussed already—such as respect for basic rights, a commitment to the rule of law, and support for the common good and its accompanying civic virtues. I also include the need to adapt to the national standards deemed necessary to compete successfully in the economic and social systems of the nation. Individuals must master basic curricula in school settings and become competent in the use of English and other basic skills in order to qualify for advancement in various school settings and professions.

To meet these standards, we often have to reduce time and energy spent cultivating ethnic or sub-cultural connections. As a result, we are forced to make a choice between strengthening ethnic or group ties or reducing their influence in our lives. If we take the latter route for the sake of promoting the norms of a national community, we are free to maintain our group connections in the private sphere protected by civil society. But over time, it is possible that participation in common shared values will cause us to weaken the hold that group values have in fashioning our identities. Here, as the place of national values is perpetuated across generations, decades of ethnic memory become reduced in importance and are replaced by the need to accommodate to the values of the national community.

Is this outcome desirable? Taylor would object to this result more so than would political liberals because Taylor worries more about the survival of group identities than do political liberals. The latter as we have seen are more concerned with the protection as well as the teaching of the standards of the national community. Indeed, political liberals would be concerned that unless national standards are emphasized, people will not adapt well to the demands of the economy and its requirement for highly skilled people. And in this context, individuals will fail to compete on the basis of the standards set by the national community for professions, for higher education, and for citizenship. This circumstance would lead to the denial of the background conditions that secure basic rights and a full plate of opportunities for each individual.

For instance, recent studies have shown that two years after California voted to end bilingual education and immerse Spanish-speaking students in English, school test scores have risen dramatically. These studies demonstrate that educational success is quite likely when English is the language of instruction.[51] In the face of these studies, should we protect bilingual education in the name of group survival, as Taylor might want, or abandon it in the name of national standards, as political liberals would call for?

Moreover, political liberals would worry that in emphasizing group over national community values, we will move to a more fragmented and conflict-filled society in which group counters group and in which genuine communication among people from different backgrounds is less likely. In this case, a civil society cannot be a setting in which groups maintain a prospect of common deliberation internally and in which groups in their external relations to other groups can work to build an inclusive society. Orlando Patterson manifests this concern in discussing American contexts when he says "certainly on college campuses, diversity no longer means genuine cultural exchange, but the promotion of differences; in politics, the protection of ethnic turfs is at stake. While most African-Americans and the middle classes generally still say they favor integration, some prominent black political leaders have given up on this strategy."[52]

VII. CIVIL SOCIETY AND RELIGION

What place does religious life have in a liberal democracy? Obviously, liberal democracies, in keeping with the First Amendment, protect religious expression and practice in the private realm of family, friends, and religious organizations. Individuals should be able to make their own religious preferences and pursue them, without interference, within the many different religious organizations found in a civil society. Moreover, the First Amendment protects religious speech in the public realm, which is the government or nongovernmental setting where issues affecting society in different ways are discussed and acted upon. Individuals in the public realm should be able to discuss public issues from the standpoint of their religious perspective in the search with others for establishing public reasons on behalf of these issues.

By protecting religious life in the ways just mentioned, it might be thought that liberal democratic states deserve praise from those who place an important emphasis on religious life in society. Instead, some friendly critics of political liberalism such as Michael Sandel, discussed in the chapter on Rawls, accuse political liberals of supporting policies that diminish the importance of religion in a civil society.[53] Why is this the case, and is the criticism valid?

To address these questions, it is first necessary to remind the reader that Sandel criticized Rawls's political liberalism because it defined the self as independent of those attachments and beliefs inherited from social and historical settings. For Sandel, much of our identity is shaped by what we imbibe from our unique circumstances growing up in a particular community dominated by certain core moral and cultural values. Families transmit to each of us our religion or our ethnic backgrounds, just as our birth situation provides us with our sexual orientation or skin color, and each of these dimensions is crucial in shaping core elements of our identities.

For Sandel, then, our core identities are embedded into our memories from our personal history and from nature. And we often understand who we are as we reflect on our lives and reveal to ourselves the values that lie at the heart of our self-understandings. This means that personal identity is not a function of choice, but it is a "given" to be discovered by self-reflection. If I am born gay, as I grow older and reflect on my needs and proclivities, I will discover that as a gay person my needs are different from heterosexuals. If I am born and raised Catholic, I will realize, again from self-reflection, that if I try to change I still must address the impact of my past on my desire to be other than Catholic. Here, values that are embedded into our lives through socialization or by nature are the primary bases for identity. And we have no choice as to whether we will abide by them or not. Our choices only pertain to how we are going to integrate into our lives these socially or naturally ingrained values.

Now, for Rawls's political liberalism, identity formation is not so much a process of Sandel's recovery of embedded values as it is a matter of choosing the values we want to make the basis for our identities. Yes, Rawls could certainly agree with Sandel that we have core values given to us at birth and maintained through our childhood. But these values need not dominate our identity. In effect, we can define our identity in substantially different ways than what might be the case if we just see ourselves in terms of the "givens" in our birth situations and the childhood that follows. I may be disabled and owing to this reality I may be kept in a wheelchair where I am made subject to a battery of difficulties. Still, this circumstance need not dominate my identity since I may decide to pursue a legal career and ultimately become a United States senator, known not for my disability but for my civic contributions. Here, it is not an ascribed core value that gives fundamental shape to my identity, but rather what grounds my identity are a series of fundamental choices as well as their consequences for my life.

Given the importance of individual choice in Rawls's political liberalism, it is essential for Rawls that the autonomy of each person be protected so that each can choose his or her core values and way of life. This is especially the case with respect to those decisions that mark a person's conception of the good life. For Rawls, as we have seen, to protect the personal autonomy to make these choices, basic rights must remain primary. To this end, the state—once again understood as the national government—should be neutral among the different conceptions of the good life.

The state remains neutral by not giving a higher value to, or even imposing on others, a particular view of the good life. And as Sandel points out, in political liberalism the national government should be "neutral toward religion for the same reason it should be neutral toward competing conceptions of the good life generally—to respect people's capacity to choose their own values and ends." [54] Critics of this position, such as Stephen Carter, argue that "the religions are more and more treated as just passing beliefs—almost as fads, older, stuffier, less liberal versions of so-called New Age—rather than as the fundaments upon which the devout build their lives."[55]

Sandel would affiliate himself with Carter's view of the effects of political liberalism on religion, and Sandel supports his position by showing the impact of United States Supreme Court decisions on religious life. Sandel's view is that the Court's position on the "constitutional law of religious liberty" is informed by political liberalism, and so the Court inevitably diminishes religion as a result.[56]

To give one example of Sandel's argument, Sandel cites a United States Supreme Court case in which the Court overruled a Connecticut statute that "gave all workers the right to one day off each week, [and] it gave to Sabbath observers alone the right to designate their day."[57] The Supreme Court objected to the Connecticut law because, according to Chief Justice Burger, only Sabbath observers were *guaranteed* the right to choose the day of the week they wish not to work. Religious believers who observe the Sabbath would no doubt choose a weekend day to be off work, but so too might the nonreligious people. And in the Court's view the reasons the latter might use for not working on the weekend should be treated with the same respect as those reasons used for not working on the Sabbath by the religious observers. The Court took the view that, for the sake of protecting freedom of choice, the state should remain neutral by not favoring religious over nonreligious groups on the question of who has a right to choose a weekend day off from work. And so it struck down the law.[58]

Sandel's complaint is that the Court has "confused the right to exercise a duty with the right to make a choice."[59] For the nonreligious what is involved is the right to choose a day off. For the religious people what is involved is the right to exercise a duty dictated by religious needs.[60] By giving greater emphasis to a right to choose a day of rest than to a right to uphold a religious duty, religious convictions are unnecessarily reduced in importance, as is religion. Moreover, to the extent that this circumstance typifies political liberalism, Sandel says that the latter "fails to secure the toleration it promises."[61]

How would political liberals defend themselves against Sandel? Political liberals would justify the use of the neutrality perspective in this case by pointing to the value context out of which this perspective emerges. In particular, political liberalism is grounded in the values of a civil society as a separate sphere. As such, political liberalism is bound to promote the values of civil society—including common deliberation, civic virtues such as mutual respect, inclusion, and fairness. Seen against the background of this perspective, political liberalism recognizes the continuing existence of difference in all of its manifold forms. The objective of political liberalism is to create spaces for the many differences—such as those pertaining to race, sexual orientation, religion, gender, social class, and so on—to flourish, despite the tensions that arise as a result of these differences. Here, religiously based duties would be taken very seriously during the quest to realize the values of civil society for all people. Indeed, it is likely that a political liberal would hope that the effect of the Court's decision in the Connecticut case would be that people would demonstrate a willingness to accommodate each other by trading days off on a rotational basis.

Inclusion is an important theme in recent Supreme Court decisions involving what Sandel referred to as the "constitutional law of religious liberty." Let me provide another example of a case—no doubt approached from the standpoint of political liberalism—in which protecting choice once again is associated by the Court not with disrespect for religious convictions, but with a concern to create an inclusive society.

In *Santa Fe Independent School District v. Doe,* student-led prayer before football games was ruled a violation of the United States Constitution.[62] The school policy included several steps to avoid the imposition of a particular religious view on anyone. Indeed, the students voted whether to have prayer, and the students even voted who should lead it. Moreover, the policy does not require nor exclude nonsectarian and nonproselytizing forms of prayer.[63]

So why did the Court turn down school prayer at football games? Furthermore, did the Court's use of political liberalism signify evidence of intolerance toward religion?

To address these questions, it is necessary to explain the rationale for the Court's decision. The Court said that prayer in this setting represented the viewpoint of the majority supported by the school administration. In this circumstance, the minority is left unprotected from a majority that might require viewpoint conformity. This arrangement permits the majority to intrude upon the private sphere, the place where each person is to be free to make his or her own decisions about religion without interference from external public sources, including the school administration and the student majority. Thus, from the Court's point of view, the majority of students may "impermissibly invade that private sphere" if these students are given the power through school elections to determine whether there should be prayer as well as who should lead it.[64]

The Santa Fe school policy is attacked further by the Court because this policy "constitutes prayer sponsored by the school," an agency of government.[65] And this position violates the establishment clause of the First Amendment. Under the establishment clause, "Congress shall make no law respecting an establishment of religion." This provision means that the majority speaking through the instrument of the national government—or as in this case the majority of students speaking through the public school administration—cannot violate the right of any person to determine his or her views of religion. The Court must uphold the establishment clause in this setting not just from the standpoint of a requirement to remain faithful to the United States Constitution, but because doing otherwise would encourage unhealthy social division. Indeed, the Court says that the Santa Fe policy would create "divisiveness along religious lines in a public school setting, a result at odds with the establishment clause."[66]

Furthermore, the Court rejected Santa Fe's argument that there was no harm caused to those who were uncomfortable with prayer, because no one was coerced into attending football games. If prayer were mandated in the setting of a required activity, such as a class, then Santa Fe could agree that the religious freedom of those who did not want to be exposed to prayer would be violated. But the Court rejected this argument. In the first place, the Court points out that some students—such as cheerleaders, band members, and team members—must attend the games because these people are major participants. Moreover, for other students, taking part in these activities is part of their "complete educational experience." Finally, for many students, high school football games are essential to building community among faculty and students on behalf of a common objective— winning a football game and enjoying each other's company in the process. And many people in these settings wish very much to be a part of this community. Thus, to tell students they do not have to attend the games if they are offended by the school invocation is to force students to decide if they wish to be excluded from a community they hope will embrace them. And the Court took the position that "the Constitution . . . demands that the school may not force this difficult choice upon these students."[67]

In effect, from the standpoint of political liberals, the Court's commitment to neutrality in this case is just another way of arguing for the civil society value of inclusion by saying that associations should be as open as possible to individuals from as many different ways of life as possible. To do so, the Court is asking individuals to recognize that the right to practice freedom of religion presumes an obligation on the part of each person to respect the beliefs of others, however different those beliefs may be. Indeed, political liberals might point out that the flourishing of religious diversity in this country has been aided historically by civil society values such as mutual respect and inclusion.

So much for what political liberals would say about why they think liberal democracies do much to protect religious life in its various forms. Now to a question that naturally follows this issue. What role would political liberals say religious life must play in helping to support a liberal democracy?

Religious cultures could play an important role for political liberals in helping to sustain a liberal democracy to the extent that religious activities help to preserve the values that emanate from civil society. For in endorsing these values—values such as common deliberation, inclusion, the civic virtues of tolerance and mutual respect, and fairness—religion contributes to teaching as well as to buttressing the public principles that help maintain a liberal democracy. Thus, public officials who make use of religious rhetoric on behalf of supporting particular issues in the public domain must make sure that their employment of religion ultimately is designed to support the public values that make possible liberal democracy. Political liberals would surely argue that this undertaking is not antagonistic to religious practice. After all, religious traditions at their best certainly teach civic values akin to those that emanate from civil society and that serve as the foundation of liberal democracies.

VIII. CIVILITY, PUBLIC DISCOURSE, AND CIVIL SOCIETY

In the context of a civil society, "civility" as a way to address others does not refer to a mode of conduct common to an aristocratic European society of generations past. In that setting civility signified an undemocratic deference on the part of the lower classes to their "betters," where the latter is defined in terms of social standing and rank. Nor is civility merely politeness in speech and manners. Surely, in the context of civil society civility means avoiding the slash and burn rhetoric of extreme partisanship that is common in political discourse today. But in addition, because civility is grounded in the main values of a civil society—common deliberation, the civic virtues of toleration and mutual respect, inclusion, and fairness—civility suggests a particular approach to reasoning about public issues.

What is that approach? To answer this question, it is first necessary to accept that civil society, owing to the diversity found there, is a place characterized by efforts to achieve agreement on a host of issues, despite widespread differences of view. And in consequence, a civil society must possess a public language that enables people, holding different value perspectives and manifesting diverse ways of life, to speak with each other and to communicate across their differences. Indeed, the public language helps people to stand in each other's shoes and to visit the minds of others whose views are different. And this enlarged perspective and understanding makes it possible for people to compare and to contrast their own opinions to those held by others. This experience is critical to enabling people from diverse backgrounds to identify public reasons that can stand as the bases for public policies, laws, and actions.

By contrast, using a private language—such as may be found in a particular ethnic group tradition—to discuss issues of shared concern with others would make it extremely difficult to establish public reasons for actions and judgments. A private language helps people from the same tradition to communicate in intimate ways about personal matters, or a private language reenforces shared traditions with other members of one's group for the sake of maintaining the bonds of community with them. But if while discussing public issues with others, I insisted on staying within the context of a language that solely represented a cultural minority perspective, it would be difficult for me to understand others whose cultural perspective is different from mine. In this case, I would be unable to work with others to find a way to discuss as well as to negotiate differences in perspective and from this experience achieve an accommodation that would be acceptable to all participants.

A natural question to ask is, is the public language biased in the direction of certain values, and if so, which ones? Clearly, the public language is biased. Because the public language embodies the values of a civil society, this language will orient those who use this language to support the institutions of a liberal democracy. And this means that people will be prone to frame issues in certain ways. In the first place, people will make the quest for fairness a central concern with respect to the issues before them. Here, we ask questions such as, Which health care plan is most fair, or Which reform of social security is most just to each generation of people, old and young? Or we ask, Which tax reform plan among several before the country is fair to each economic and social class?

Further, the public language casts shared issues in terms of the continuing need in a liberal democracy to balance basic constitutional as well as legislatively created rights, discussed in the second section, with accompanying obligations. A civil society teaches this lesson above all. And people who say they have rights but no obligations manifest neither civility nor any capacity to help determine the public reasons for achieving a just resolution of policy differences. Let me provide in the next several paragraphs the way in which rights and obligations are central features in civil discourse.

Sometimes, issues are discussed in terms of basic rights that must be extended to groups heretofore denied such rights, as has been the case in recent history for African-

Americans, gays, women, and others. At other times, the political discourse is concerned with creating, through the legislative process, new rights and extending them to each person in society. Thus, there is much talk today of making possible, on a national basis, portable health insurance programs so that all people are always covered even when they move from job to job. On other occasions, competing and contrasting conceptions of rights must be put into balance. For instance, a person denied admission to the Boy Scouts because of his sexual orientation might claim that his basic right to association is denied. But that same person does not lose his basic right to use speech to bring pressure to bear on the Scouts in the public setting of society, in the hopes that doing so will cause the Boy Scouts to change their policies. Here, one right is balanced by and compensated for by another, thus securing the rights of each party.

Each example just described implies the need to recognize certain obligations as a condition for securing the rights in question. For instance, in order to extend basic rights to others who have been denied these rights in the past, sometimes individuals are obligated to resist bigotry or at other times individuals have a duty to help provide opportunities heretofore denied to the people in question. In the same way, creating a new right, through legislative action, to a portable health care plan and extending this right to all people requires that individuals accept an added tax burden. And in according individuals the basic right to speak freely, as in the case of gays who object to their exclusion from the Boy Scouts, there is a corresponding obligation on the part of those who disagree to listen carefully and to consider fairly.

The public language orients a public discussion on issues not only toward describing the rights and obligations at stake, but also toward demonstrating why and on what basis these rights and obligations are justified. In accomplishing these objectives, we are providing public reasons, or reasons all can support, as the basis for demonstrating how rights and duties should be understood with respect to a given issue. But how do we construct public reasons? The first thing to understand is that public reasons are built from political concepts, and when we use them well we can make good arguments, but if we use them poorly we fail to establish public reasons for the positions we support. I wish to explain this point further by first clarifying what I mean by political concepts and then, in subsequent paragraphs, by demonstrating what it means to use them well or poorly.

Political concepts stand for various behaviors and supporting beliefs with respect to political and social phenomena. For instance, the concept of basic rights signifies certain constitutionally protected forms of conduct, such as speech, association, and so on. Concepts like basic rights initially are defined generally, and this means that the concepts describe the kinds of conduct that all people who are granted a particular right are permitted to perform. Corresponding beliefs justify the conduct that is permitted and deny acceptance to the conduct not permitted under the concept. The right of association, for instance, says generally that I can join political associations of my choice, and the belief supporting this form of conduct suggests that without this option I would have no political liberty. Further, political concepts are refined as they are applied to specific situations, and this happens often in response to particular problems. Yes, I can join any political group I choose, except I am not to join one that plans to commit treason against the United States government. The belief that supports this position is that liberty is not sustainable unless I observe certain limits, including the one that protects the national government's existence.

Now, as we have said, the political concepts employed in any discussion of issues must be arranged to produce public reasons for showing how rights and obligations should be understood and used in society. But to make arguments of this sort it is important *not* to use political concepts in a manner that bases an argument for a set of public reasons on factually weak grounds and/or on conceptual inconsistencies, or worse still, contradictions. Let me provide an example of what I mean when concepts are used well and when they are used poorly.

In discussing affirmative action policy, the main goal is to promote equality of opportunity among people—minorities and women—who, because historically they have been denied full opportunity, stand to be denied equality of opportunity today and in the future. Affirmative action also includes a commitment to the concept of merit, in which the best qualified, from the standpoint of the stated criteria for a job, receive the position. Showing how equality of opportunity is properly allied with merit is the challenge of those people who suggest that there are public reasons for supporting affirmative action policies. How might this process of reasoning work? Take the issue of an affirmative action job search.

First, in such a search there is a need, in the name of equal opportunity, to ensure fair representation of all groups in an applicant pool. Often, this means guaranteeing that all efforts are made to attract a representative pool of applicants with the intention of expanding in substantial ways participation from previously underrepresented groups. Once the applicant pool is as broad and as representative as possible, then the best individuals, in keeping with the standards used to define the position, are hired. Minority status or gender, for instance, only becomes a decisive factor in determining who gets hired when the finalists for a position are considered equally worthy. The process, as just described, embodies both the concepts of merit and fair representation in a manner that allows them to complement and to bolster each other, and in this situation neither of these concepts appears to be inconsistent with the other.

What upsets this linkage however and causes the concept of merit to be in conflict with the concept of fair representation is the introduction of the idea that the hiring process must make as its *chief* hiring criterion a particular fixed percentage of people from this or that group. Thus, at times some have said that to make possible in the workplace proportions of minorities and women equal to those in the larger population, it will be necessary to hire a fixed percentage of people from these groups. In this case, we would seek a representative pool not as the basis for merit hiring, but as the basis for achieving a precise quota of certain individuals who share the desired status characteristics. As a result, it will appear that the quest for fair representation is not necessarily in sync with the merit ideal. Indeed, at times the latter might be considered as a threat to the former, and as a result the hope of promoting equality of opportunity would be dashed.

Of course, some will say that a quota approach to hiring allows representation and merit to remain in harmony. But in the absence of evidence to demonstrate this connection, it is impossible to devise a public reason for an affirmative action program. On the other hand, there is plenty of evidence to demonstrate that the prospects of historically disadvantaged groups can be advanced while maintaining merit hiring—so long as there is broad representation in the search pool and a selection based on merit from that pool takes place. Indeed, this approach to affirmative action is fair because all are given full consideration, thus removing any stigma being attached to a person hired under an affirmative action program. Further, the public reason to support affirmative action policy rests upon demonstrating the way in which the concepts of merit and representation complement each other. And this public reason makes clear the rights and obligations that each person engaged in this policy must observe during and after the hiring process.

Reaching agreement on public reasons is not easy and often the effort ends in failure. Why is this? Because political issues are heavily contested matters, people will hold contrasting beliefs as to the best way to define key political concepts. Moreover, as a result of differences in belief, people may have radically different views of the significance of supporting factual material in a political argument. Owing to both these possibilities, people may be unable to agree on the meaning of the political concepts that people are using as an attempt is made to arrive at public reasons with respect to the issues at stake. For instance, referring back to the affirmative action discussion, some people, who view affirmative action as favoring one group over another for reasons not of equity but of political advantage, will inevitably see this policy associated with fixed hiring quotas. Whereas others, who see affirmative action as part of a needed strategy to achieve equal opportunity for groups long denied this prospect, will be prone to associate this policy with hiring based on merit, rather than fixed quotas.

Still, the public language of a liberal democracy allows people to tolerate contest and disagreement, owing to the presence of contrasting political positions. And this language does so by equipping us to find short-term agreement with respect to matters over which we can't find permanent agreement, all in the name of avoiding serious disaffection and destructive forms of interaction among the contesting parties. Where civility exists, citizens are willing to endure short-term solutions and the expectation of continuing discussion in the hope that doing so paves the way for identifying enduring public reasons in the future.

IX. CONCLUSION: GLOBALIZATION AND A LIBERAL CIVIL SOCIETY

Securing civility, which is the public language of a liberal democracy, is a daunting task in the face of many group experiences that emphasize more the private language of particular group cultures than the values of civil society as a separate sphere. Nancy Rosenblum demonstrates that some groups accentuate a particular history and identity that frame the way all members interact with society.[68] When people are so thoroughly embedded in particular group settings that the individual outlooks are completely determined by group perspectives, individuals are less likely to be able to reach toward other groups and work with them to find public reasons to resolve differences.

These kinds of *thick* ties promote a comprehensive and consuming unity. For some groups who follow this path, there is a refusal to accept the larger influence of the national community as was the case with those fundamentalist religious believers, discussed earlier, who refuse to allow their children education in religious diversity. For other groups, such as those representing major economic interests, the group culture is so thick that members can't participate in a common deliberation with the rest of the society to identify the shared good.

So if bridging among different groups and ways of life is to take place, the bonds of group life must be eased somewhat and made *thinner* so that individuals can experience other ways of life and learn to communicate with people from different backgrounds. This approach to group life would permit individuals to manifest what Nancy

Rosenblum calls a capacity for "shifting involvements," or the capacity to move freely among different associations for the purpose of learning about and experiencing many different perspectives and ways of life.[69] Here, individuals move from one group context to another, and as they do, they are able to visit other minds, and stand in others' shoes. Further, as individuals move through civil society they will in all likelihood maintain primary identifications to certain groups. I may be Catholic, for instance, and yet encounter other religious environments in order to understand and to interact with people who are different from my own religious outlook. This social context—which in the first chapter we referred to as the setting of a liberal civil society—helps individuals to learn how to communicate across their many differences in order to find the public reasons that are the basis for a common ground.

In this milieu, individuals are not completely detached from group membership, but they are detached enough so that they can build bridges to other group contexts. Groups of this sort are inclusive by nature, and each group is thus capable of welcoming people from various walks of life to the group, while at the same time maintaining a willingness to work with other groups. Such groups, which practice the civic virtues of toleration and mutual respect, permit individuals the freedom to make their own judgments on issues after consulting various group perspectives. Yet at the same time, in this circumstance groups are not so weak that people lack a sense of responsibility to support them.

But how far and wide may individuals, who have "shifting involvements" with a variety of groups, range? Are people limited to the nation, or may they move beyond it? There is no question that in the modern setting of many liberal democracies individuals who confine their range of life to the nation find themselves inevitably facing a large part of the world. This kind of experience results from the fact that countries like the United States and Canada, by virtue of being multicultural societies, are also multinational in character.

Recognition of the diversity of world cultures is fueled by the current reality of globalization, which is the linking of people across nations to engage in a variety of activities, including communication about many issues, acquiring information about diverse subjects, and engaging in commerce. And the Internet has hastened both the scope and rapidity of globalization in the present world.

But can globalization bring into existence a global civil society in which the public language of civility is propagated throughout the world? Benjamin Barber helps us to frame this question well when he discusses the competition between what he calls two leading approaches to understanding the world today, "McWorld" and "Jihad." McWorld, which is the view of the so-called modern world, shares the Enlightenment's attachment to freedom, its commitment to reason, its skepticism toward tradition, its faith in free markets, and its "disdain for parochial culture." Jihad, on the other hand, represents a still pervasive traditional worldview, built upon a fondness for communal hierarchies and for the mysteries of religion and the pull of habit. Naturally, Jihad stands in opposition to McWorld.[70]

Achieving a global civil society, which would make room for civility and democracy throughout the world, is a major challenge in a world characterized by the distrust and animosity that often arises between the holders of these two divergent value perspectives. There are other obstacles to creating a global civil society that have to be surmounted as well. In the first place, it is now the case that globalization advanced through the Internet has not yet reached those who occupy the lower economic strata of the United States as well as the world's population. In consequence, the Internet could well become a way to maintain the advantages and status for those already in relatively more privileged positions in the world as well as to perpetuate the conditions that keep others in social and economic subordination. And this situation would create, not a global civil society, but what Putnam calls "cyberapartheid."[71]

Others, like Barber, worry that globalization can be used as a tool to promote, not a global civil society, but corporate business interests the world over.[72] In this case, instead of teaching the language of common deliberation, inclusion, and the pursuit of the common good, there is only the language of the business deal. Here, often the quest for the accumulation of material wealth by major corporations—or greed—is the essence of all that is true and good in life. Thus, notions of inclusion and common deliberation—so essential to a civil society at the national or global levels—are pushed to the side in favor of those values that secure the triumph of corporate business. Further, a corporate-driven globalization is perceived often as a threat to local traditions and ways of life of Jihad cultures. These countries, however, not only worry that their own traditions will be eroded by corporate globalization, but in addition, many political leaders in Jihad settings who might embrace elements of corporate globalization will not accept the democratizing aspect of a global civil society.

Still, many think that the wealth that globalization helps to create can be distributed to numerous poor countries, thus emphasizing that wealth creation needn't be reserved only for those seeking private, personal accumulation. Indeed, in a recent economic forum of world business leaders in Davos, Switzerland, 50 percent of the business leaders said that the Internet-driven, new global economy would help close the gap between the rich and the poor nations.[73] Moreover, for others, Internet-powered globalization is viewed as extending the benefits of a civil society across the world. People in countries that have not yet built civil societies, after looking through the Internet-created window at those countries that have, may decide to make their own countries as democratic and as committed to building a civil society as possible.

Thus, there remains the hope that as individuals from different cultural contexts interact with each other through the Internet, and as economies flourish as a result, it is possible that this experience could help fuel a movement toward a global civil society. In this case, civic values such as inclusion, fairness, and common deliberation would begin to have a strong worldwide presence. As a global civil society becomes a strong force in the world the impetus for building civil societies within individual countries would become powerful as well. And countries that experience a renaissance of civil society will also strengthen their democratic institutions and practices. Moreover, a global civil society, which encourages the movement toward more democracy in particular countries, would necessarily mean an increased commitment to secure basic citizen rights in many areas of the world. Here, globalization would aid the growth of liberal democracy in many societies, and in doing so globalization would become a positive voice for human rights everywhere in the world.

So which scenario will triumph? Does the future portend a globalization that threatens civil society in the countries of the world or does the future suggest a globalization that helps to strengthen civil society across the world? I leave the reader to ponder this question, hopefully in an ever more global and inclusive setting, governed by civility.

Endnotes

1. The First Amendment of the U.S. Constitution states: Congress shall make no law respecting an establishment of religion, or prohibiting the free exercise thereof; or abridging the freedom of speech, or of the press; or the right of the people peaceably to assemble, and to petition the Government for a redress of grievances.

2. Boy Scouts of America v. Dale, *New York Times,* June 29, 2000, p. A22.

3. See note 1.

4. Boy Scouts of America v. Dale.

5. Kate Zernike, "Scouts' Successful Ban on Gays Is Followed by Loss of Support," *The New York Times,* August 29, 2000, p. 1.

6. Robert D. Putnam, *Bowling Alone: The Collapse and Revival of American Community* (New York: Simon and Schuster, 2000), pp. 338–39.

7. Richard Bellamy, *Liberalism and Pluralism: Toward A Politics of Compromise* (London: Routledge, 1999), pp. 129–30.

8. On this point, see Jean Bethke Elshtain, *Democracy on Trial* (New York: Basic Books, 1995), pp. 42–44.

9. Robert D. Putnam, "Bowling Alone: America's Declining Social Capital." *Journal of Democracy,* 6:1, 1995, p. 67.

10. Robert D. Putnam, *Bowling Alone: The Collapse and Revival of American Community,* p. 46.

11. Ibid., p. 63.

12. Putnam, "Bowling Alone, America's Declining Social Capital," pp. 69–70.

13. Ibid., p. 70.

14. Putnam, *Bowling Alone: The Collapse and Revival of American Community,* pp. 111–13.

15. Ibid., pp. 63–64.

16. Ibid., p. 19.

17. Ibid., p. 19.

18. Robert Wuthnow, *Loose Connections: Joining Together in America's Fragmented Communities* (Cambridge: Harvard University Press, 1998), p. 4.

19. Ibid., p. 208.

20. Theda Skocpol, Marshall Ganz, and Ziad Munson, "A Nation of Organizers: The Institutional Origins of Civic Voluntarism in the United States." *American Political Science Review,* 94:3, September, 2000, pp. 532, 540–41.

21. Ibid., p. 542.

22. Ibid., p. 542.

23. Wuthnow, *Loose Connections,* p. 208, also p. 4.

24. Ibid., p. 5.

25. Ibid., p. 3.

26. Ibid., p. 206.

27. Ibid., p. 206.

28. Ibid., p. 221.

29. Ibid., p. 221.

30. Putnam, *Bowling Alone,* p. 283. See also, Don Eberly, *America's Promise: Civil Society and the Renewal of American Culture* (Lanham: Rowman and Littlefield, 1998), pp. 117–18.

31. Putnam, *Bowling Alone,* pp. 272, 275–76, 283. The William James quote is found on p. 276 in Putnam's *Bowling Alone.*

32. Allen D. Hertzke, "The Theory of Moral Ecology." *The Review of Politics,* 60:4, Fall, 1998, p. 643.

33. See "A Nation of Spectators: How Civic Disengagement Weakens America and What We Can Do About It." *Final Report of the National Commission on Civic Renewal,* (College Park: University of Maryland), pp. 53–64. The Web site for the National Commission on Civic Renewal is http://www.puaf.umd.edu/civicrenewal/.

34. William A. Schambra, "Local Groups are the Key to America's Civic Renewal," in *The Brookings Review,* 15:4, Fall, 1997, pp. 20–22.

35. John J. DiIulio, Jr. "The Lord's Work." *The Brookings Review,* 15:4, Fall, 1997, pp. 27–31.

36. Ibid., p. 31.

37. See note 1 for First Amendment.

38. Charles Taylor, "The Politics of Recognition," in *Multiculturalism,* edited by Amy Gutmann (Princeton: Princeton University Press, 1994), pp. 38–39, 54–55.

39. Ibid., p. 55.

40. Ibid., pp. 54–55.

41. See Canadian Charter of Rights and Freedom, section 23, paragraph 1.

42. Taylor, "The Politics of Recognition," in *Multiculturalism,* p. 55.

43. Ibid, pp. 59–61.

44. Ibid., p. 60, also p. 56. In Rawls this approach was embodied in his notion of public reason, as discussed in the Rawls chapter.

45. Taylor, "The Politics of Recognition," in *Multiculturalism,* p. 56.

46. Ibid., pp. 52–59, especially p. 59.

47. Susan Moller Okin, (ed.) "Introduction," *Is Multiculturalism Bad for Women?* (Princeton: Princeton University Press, 1999), pp. 10–11. Italics in text. Also, see Charles Taylor, "The Politics of Recognition," in *Multiculturalism,* pp. 39–40.

48. Charles Taylor, "The Politics of Recognition," in *Multiculturalism,* p. 61.

49. Stephen Macedo, *Diversity and Distrust: Moral Plurality, Civic Education and American Liberalism,* (Bloomington, Ind.: The Poynter Center, 1997), pp. 11–12. He discusses the U.S. Supreme Court case *Mozert v. Hawkins County Board of Education* in which some families with fundamentalist religious views did not want their children involved in a public school reading program

designed to expose their children to a diversity of views, including religious diversity. The families sought to be permitted to opt out of the reading program while remaining in the public schools.

50. Stephen Macedo, *Diversity and Distrust: Civic Education in a Multicultural Democracy* (Cambridge: Harvard University Press, 2000), p. 239.

51. Jacques Steinberg. "Test Scores Rise, Surprising Critics of Bilingual Ban," *New York Times,* August 20, 2000, p.1.

52. Orlando Patterson, "The G.O.P. Isn't the Only Party to Dissemble on Race," *The New York Times,* August 6, 2000.

53. Michael J. Sandel, "Freedom of Conscience or Freedom of Choice?" in *Articles of Faith, Articles of Peace: The Religious Liberty Clauses and the American Public Policy,* edited by James Davison Hunter (Washington, D.C.: The Brookings Institution Press, 1990), p. 92.

54. Ibid., pp. 88–89.

55. Stephen L. Carter, *The Culture of Disbelief: How American Law and Politics Trivialize Religious Devotion* (New York: Basic Books, 1993), p. 14.

56. Michael J. Sandel, "Freedom of Conscience or Freedom of Choice?," p. 74.

57. Ibid., p. 89. This case is *Thorton v. Caldor, Inc.* (1985).

58. Michael J. Sandel, "Freedom of Conscience or Freedom of Choice?," p. 89.

59. Ibid., p. 89.

60. Ibid., p. 89.

61. Ibid., p. 92.

62. *Santa Fe Independent School District v. Doe,* in *New York Times,* June 20, 2000, p. A22.

63. Ibid., p. A22.

64. Ibid., p. A22.

65. Ibid., p. A22.

66. Ibid, p. A22.

67. Ibid., p. A22.

68. Nancy L. Rosenblum, *Membership and Morals: The Personal Uses of Pluralism in America,* (Princeton: Princeton University Press, 1998), pp. 323–26.

69. Ibid., p. 350.

70. Benjamin R. Barber, *Jihad vs. McWorld,* (New York: Times Books, 1995), pp. 156–57.

71. Robert D. Putnam, *Bowling Alone: The Collapse and Revival of American Community,* p. 175.

72. Benjamin R. Barber, *Jihad vs. McWorld,* pp. 280, 285.

73. Alan Cowell, " What Can The New Economy Do For Places Without An Old One?" *New York Times,* April 23, 2000, p. 7.

Partial Bibliography and Further Reading

"A Nation of Spectators: How Civic Disengagement Weakens America and What we Can Do About It," *Final Report of the National Commission on Civic Renewal.* College Park: University of Maryland.

Barber, Benjamin R. *Jihad vs. McWorld.* New York: Times Books, 1995.

Berkowitz, Peter. *Virtue and the Making of Modern Liberalism.* Princeton: Princeton University Press, 1999.

Bellamy, Richard. *Liberalism and Pluralism: Toward A Politics of Compromise.* London: Routledge, 1999.

Carter, Stephen L. *The Culture of Disbelief: How American Law and Politics Trivialize Religious Devotion.* New York: Basic Books, 1993.

DeMott, Benjamin. "Seduced by Civility." *The Nation.* 263:19, Dec. 9, 1996.

Dionne, E. J., editor, *Community Works: The Revival of Civil Society in America.* Washington, D.C.: Brookings Institution Press, 1998.

Eberly, Don E. *America's Promise: Civil Society and the Renewal of American Culture* Lanham: Rowman and Littlefield, 1998.

Ehrenberg, John. *Civil Society: The Critical History of the Idea.* New York: New York University Press, 1999.

Elshstain, Jean Bethke. *Democracy on Trial.* New York: Basic Books, 1995.

Flacks, Richard, and Thomas, Scott L. "Among Affluent Students, A Culture of Disengagement." *The Chronicle of Higher Education,* November 27, 1998.

Freidman, Thomas L. *The Lexus and the Olive Tree.* New York: Farrar Sraus Giroux, 1999.

Fukuyama, Francis. *The Great Disruption: Human Nature and the Reconstitution of Social Order.* Free Press, 1999.

Gutmann, Amy, and Thompson, Dennis. "Moral Conflict and Political Consensus." *Ethics.* 101, October, 1990.

Kymlicka, Will. *Multicultural Citizenship: A Liberal Theory of Minority Rights.* Oxford: Oxford University Press, 1995.

Levy, Jacob T. *The Multiculturalism of Fear.* Oxford: Oxford University Press, 2000.

Macedo, Stephen. Editor. *Deliberative Politics.* Cambridge: Oxford University Press, 1999.

Okin, Susan Moller. Edited. *Is Multiculturalism Bad for Women?* Princeton: Princeton University Press, 1999.

Putnam, Robert D. *Bowling Alone: The Collapse and Revival of American Community.* New York: Simon and Schuster, 2000.

Rosenblum, Nancy L. *Membership and Moral: The Personal Uses of Pluralism in America.* Princeton: Princeton University Press, 1998.

————, edited. *Obligations of Citizenship and Demands of Faith: Religious Accommodation in Pluralist Democracies.* Princeton: Princeton University Press, 2000.

Schmidt, James. "Civility, Enlightenment, and Society: Conceptual Confusions and Kantian Remedies." *American Political Science Review,* 92:2, June, 1998.

Skocpol, Theda, and Firorina, Morris, P., editors, *Civic Engagement in American Democracy.* Washington, D.C.: Brookings Institution Press, 1999.

————, Ganz Marshall, and Munson, Ziad. "A Nation of Organizers: The Institutional Origins of Civic Voluntarism in the United States." *American Political Science Review,* 94:3, September, 2000.

Seligman, Adam B. *The Problem of Trust.* Princeton: Princeton University Press, 1997.

Sinopoli, Richard C. "Thick-Skinned Liberalism: Redefining Civility." *Amercian Political Science Review.* 89:3, September, 1995.

The Nation. Articles on Civil Society. December 9, 1996. 263:19.

Young, Iris Marion. *Inclusion and Democracy.* Oxford: Oxford University Press, 2000.

CREDITS

T. Bottomore. *Karl Marx: Early Writing.*
Copyright 1963 by McGraw-Hill, Inc.
Reprinted by permission of McGraw-Hill, Inc.

Selected lines from *Democracy In America By
Alexis De Tocqueville*. Edited by J.P. Mayer
and Max Lerner. Translated by George
Lawrence. English translation copyright ©
1965 by Harper and Row, Publishers, Inc.
Copyright renewed. Reprinted by permission
of HarperCollins Publishers, Inc.

From *On The Geneaology Of Morals And Ecce
Homo* by Friedrich Nietzche, translated by
Walter Kaufman, copyright © 1967 by
Random House, Inc. Translated & edited,
with commentary by Walter Kaufmann. Used
by permission of Random House, Inc.

From *The Philosophy Of John Stuart Mill* by
Marshall Cohen, copyright © 1961 by
Marshall Cohen. Used by permission of
Random House, Inc.

From *The Prince And The Discourses* by Niccolo
Machiavelli and introduction by Max Lerner,
copyright © 1950 by Random House, Inc.
Used by permission of Modern Library, a division of Random House, Inc.

Immanuel Kant. *On History*, edited by Lewis
White Black. Copyright © 1963. Reprinted by
permission of Prentice-Hall, Inc., Upper
Saddle River, NJ.

From *Second Treatise of Government* by Locke
(trans.) Peardon, T.P., © 1952. Reprinted by
permission of Prentice-Hall, Inc., Upper
Saddle River, NJ.

Rousseau. *Basic Political Writings*, translated by
Donald A. Cress, 1987. Reprinted by permission of Hackett Publishing Company, Inc. All
rights reserved.

Plato. *Republic*, translated by G.M.A. Grube.
Revised by C.D.C. Reeve, 1992. Reprinted by
permission of Hackett Publishing Company,
Inc. All rights reserved.

From *Political Liberalism*, by John Rawls. ©
1993 Columbia University Press. Reprinted
by permission of the publisher.

From *Bowling Alone: The Collapse and Revival
of American Community* by Robert D.
Putnam. Copyright © 2002 by Robert D.
Putnam. Reprinted with the permission of
Simon & Schuster.

From *A Theory of Justice* by John Rawls,
Cambridge, Mass.: The Belknap Press of
Harvard University Press, © 1971 by the
President and Fellows of Harvard College.
Reprinted by permission of the publisher.

Moses Maimonides. *The Guide of the Perplexed*,
ed. Pines. Reprinted by permission of The
University of Chicago Press.

INDEX